The Political Status of
the Negro in the Age of FDR

THE UNIVERSITY OF CHICAGO PRESS
DOCUMENTS IN AMERICAN HISTORY
A Series Edited by Arthur Mann

RALPH J. BUNCHE

The Political Status of the Negro in the Age of FDR

Edited and with an Introduction by
DEWEY W. GRANTHAM

THE UNIVERSITY OF CHICAGO PRESS
CHICAGO AND LONDON

The Political Status of the Negro in the Age of FDR is a Carnegie-Myrdal report emphasizing the American South.

The photographs shown in this book were taken by various photographers for the Farm Security Administration during the 1930s and were supplied through the courtesy of the Library of Congress, Department of Prints and Photographs. The photographer and negative number for each picture are as follows: *Frontispiece*, Jack Delano, LC-USF 34-44616-D   *Chap. 1*, Marion Post Wolcott, LC-USF 33-30570-M3   *Chap. 3*, "Oliver" [?], LC-USZ 62-3118   *Chap. 4*, Dorothea Lange, LC-USF 34-9596-C   *Chap. 5*, Lange LC-USF 34-19848-E   *Chap. 6*, Lange, LC-USF 34-9572-C   *Chap. 7*, Lange, LC-USF 34-18220-E   *Chap. 8*, Walker Evans, LC-USF 342-8147-A   *Chap. 9*, Wolcott, LC-USF 34-52688-D   *Chap. 10*, Evans, LC-USF 342-8074-A   *Chap. 11*, Delano, LC-USF 34-46275-D   *Chap. 12*, Delano, LC-USF 33-20539-M5   *Chap. 13*, Ben Shahn, LC-USF 33-6055-M2   *Chap. 14*, Russell Lee, LC-USF 33-11692-M1   *Chap. 15*, Wolcott, LC-USF 33-30626-M3   *Chap. 16*, Lange, LC-USF 34-17335   *Chap. 17*, Wolcott, LC-USF 34-52678-D   *Chap. 18*, Delano, LC-USF 34-441970   *Chap. 19*, Arthur Rothstein, LC-USW 3-4476.

THE UNIVERSITY OF CHICAGO PRESS, CHICAGO 60637
THE UNIVERSITY OF CHICAGO PRESS, LTD., LONDON
© 1973 by The University of Chicago
All rights reserved. Published 1973
Printed in the United States of America
International Standard Book Number: 0–226–08028–5
Library of Congress Catalog Card Number: 72–96327

Contents

Author's Preface

IT must be emphasized at the outset that this memorandum is not a finished product. What is here set down is merely a first draft, designed to make available as much of the material at hand as possible, and to indicate roughly the essential approaches to the subject. For these reasons the field materials, as primary source materials, have been liberally, perhaps too liberally, employed. Had time permitted, I would have presented less of the field material itself, and more of its analysis. In the latter months of the study, the necessity for meeting deadlines has overshadowed what would seem to me to be the fundamentally important objective of sound, carefully worked out, substantive study. Some effort has been made to summarize the important points and to indicate the main trends.

It will appear, perhaps, that secondary sources have been ignored to an alarming extent. This has been in part deliberate and in part unavoidable. Except for the historical treatment, there is a paucity of worthwhile published analyses of Negro political status, especially for the South. The limits of time were such that we had to make some choices, whether these were desired or not. I chose, therefore, to lean heavily upon the fresher field materials rather than to attempt to rehash what little has been written on the subject. The Negro in politics has remained a virgin field for research, and thus assembled data of all kinds are at a premium.

We have, nevertheless, gotten what I consider to be some very useful materials. These are not, as I think they should be, the products of intensive work, since the field workers were permitted to spend only a short time in each locality, but they do give a sort of over-all view of the situation. The great task has been that of attempting, within a very short period, to put together the diverse materials at hand. The subject of Negro political status is extremely wide in scope and, if it is to be treated at all comprehensively, requires a great deal more time than I have had for the task. The result here produced is a terribly hurried, poorly integrated, and roughly written job. There has been no opportunity to check references. There has been no time for prolonged reflection on any of the points involved or the issues raised in this memorandum.

Many things that we had hoped to do have been left undone or are very superficially treated here. To mention but a few:

1. A statistical analysis of Negro voting in selected Northern cities, based upon analysis of population and election returns data.

2. An intensive analysis of the shift in Negro political preference from Republican to Democratic in selected cities.

3. Statistical estimates of the extent of Negro voting based on a careful check of all available sources. We have no careful calculations of the extent of Negro voting. This is such a huge job that it has not been possible for use to tackle it on a national scale. We have had to rely solely upon hit-and-miss estimates which were already available, tempered by whatever other information we could easily lay our hands upon. But such data could not be employed as the basis of any earnest correlations.

4. An analysis of the relationship between the collection of poll taxes and the intensity of political campaigns in selected counties.

5. A compilation of secondary data for counties in which intensive political analysis might be made—covering such matters as income, property, landholding, tenancy, literacy, education, union organization, and other relevant subjects—as a vital backdrop for the political analyses.

6. A careful appraisal of the quality of Southern representation in state legislatures and Congress.

7. A thorough investigation of the effect of the development of unionization in Southern communities upon white attitudes toward Negro political participation, and upon that participation itself.

8. A careful analysis of Southern liberalism and its effect upon Negro political status in the South.

9. An inquiry into the extent and nature of the relationship

between Negro political activity and vice in Northern urban centers.

10. A careful appraisal of Negro political leadership based upon assembled data.

I feel it necessary to include a word of acknowledgment and appreciation for the fine cooperation extended to me by the field workers—Wilhelmina Jackson, George Stoney, and James Jackson—and my assistant, William J. Bryant. Miss Jackson and Mr. Stoney did especially fine work under difficult circumstances, because of the extreme press of time and the wide scope in both subject matter and territory which their field investigations embraced. Stoney's interviews with Southern county officials have been invaluable; without these frank expressions by one Southerner to another, the picture we attempt to portray here would be woefully incomplete. Mr. Bryant was a loyal fellow-sufferer from beginning to end; he gave unstintingly of his time and energy, and at this hour of 5:45 on the morning of the last day of the project, he is steadily at work, though his vacation—a vacation that he will now never know—was to have begun two weeks ago.

Ralph J. Bunche
Howard University
31 August 1940

Editor's Introduction

I

LATE in the summer of 1938 a young social economist affiliated with the University of Stockholm sailed from his native Sweden for the United States. He had embarked upon what would prove to be a momentous enterprise: to become director of "a comprehensive study of the Negro in the United States, to be undertaken in a wholly objective and dispassionate way as a social phenomenon."[1] The project resulted in the publication of *An American Dilemma: The Negro Problem and Modern Democracy* (1944)—two large volumes, containing 1,024 pages of text in 45 chapters and 462 pages of introductions, appendixes, notes, and bibliography. Its impact was immediate and far-reaching. The eminent sociologist Robert S. Lynd described it as "the most penetrating and important book on our contemporary American civilization that has been written." Another distinguished scholar, Rupert B. Vance, has pointed out that the work represented a new trend: the impact of modern research organization developed in the United States on the tradition of the foreign observer and such famous commentaries as those of de Tocqueville and Lord Bryce.

The foreign observer in this case was Gunnar Myrdal, an internationally known scholar and successor to Gustav Cassel in the chair of social economics at the University of Stockholm. Myrdal was a close observer of the American scene. He had

1. Gunnar Myrdal, with the assistance of Richard Sterner and Arnold Rose, *An American Dilemma: The Negro Problem and Modern Democracy*, 2 vols. (New York, 1944), 1:ix.

earlier spent a year in the United States as a Fellow of the Spelman Fund, and he traveled extensively in this country during the three years which he spent working on *An American Dilemma* while on this side of the Atlantic. He wrote, and was solely responsible for, the final report. Yet the work was truly a cooperative study, authorized and financed by the Carnegie Corporation of New York, employing six top staff members to assist Myrdal, thirty-one independent workers outside of the staff, thirty-six assistants to the staff members and outside collaborators, a corps of secretaries and typists, and some fifty experts who acted as consultants. Myrdal's most important sources were forty-four monographs (comprising about 15,000 typewritten pages) which were largely prepared by authorities outside his staff. Nine of these memoranda have been published; the others are now located in the Schomburg Collection of the New York Public Library.

One of the American scholars who contributed most as a member of the Myrdal research team was a young Negro political scientist named Ralph Johnson Bunche. At the time Bunche joined the Carnegie-Myrdal project, he was a thirty-four year old professor at Howard University who had already demonstrated unusual ability and great promise as a student of race relations and international affairs. He had written a Ph.D. dissertation at Harvard on colonial administration in French West Africa. He had traveled and studied in Europe, Africa, and Southeast Asia under fellowships from the Rosenwald Fund and the Social Science Research Council. Bunche was a dynamic, knowledgeable, and fair-minded scholar, a man of great personal charm and savoir faire, with an intuitive grasp of racial complexities in America. The possibilities of the Myrdal study excited his imagination, and he joined it enthusiastically. He helped shape the research design for the work, and, as one of the half-dozen staff members, he was intimately involved in the investigation from early 1939 to the end of the summer of 1940. He was the author of four of the forty-four research monographs, the most substantial of which was "The Political Status of the Negro."[2]

Bunche's memorandum on politics was strongly influenced by his own experience as an American Negro and by his scholarly interest in such questions as Negro improvement organiza-

2. Bunche's other memoranda were "Conceptions and Ideologies of the Negro Problem," "The Programs, Ideologies, Tactics, and Achievements of Negro Betterment and Interracial Organizations," and "A Brief and Tentative Analysis of Negro Leadership."

tions and the impact of the New Deal on black people and other disadvantaged groups. But a large part of the raw material that found its way into his lengthy memorandum came from the field notes on hundreds of interviews conducted with whites and blacks. Some of these interviews were carried out by Myrdal and Bunche, who made an automobile tour of the South in the autumn of 1939. Their reception in the Deep South during that memorable trip was not always friendly. They left one Georgia town in a hurry when the local sheriff warned: "You folks are goin' around insultin' people by askin' them fool questions? You'd better get outta town before I run you in." On another occasion they were forced to flee from an irate band of Alabamians, who followed them in an automobile and fired a gun at them![3]

Most of the interviews were conducted by Bunche's assistants in the fall of 1939 and the first half of 1940. The first to begin was Wilhemina Jackson, a Howard student, who moved through the South Atlantic states from Virginia to Florida, interviewing many Negroes and some whites. Another of the interviewers was James E. Jackson, who had earlier worked in the labor movement. He traveled from Virginia to Tennessee, and then to Arkansas, Kentucky, Mississippi, Texas, Louisiana, Oklahoma, and Missouri. The third of the interviewers was George C. Stoney, a recent graduate of the University of North Carolina who had been working at the Henry Street Settlement in New York. He concentrated his field work in Alabama, Georgia, and South Carolina. Stoney, the only white member of the group, made a special point of talking with local officials. He conducted about half of all of the interviews.

The interviewers were given a rough itinerary and a list of counties to visit, but, once in the field, they were largely dependent upon their own resources in making contacts, unearthing data, and deciding whom to interview. Stoney had earlier toured the South in search of material for a series of stories he wrote for the Raleigh *News and Observer*. As an interviewer for Bunche, his technique was to visit the office of the local newspaper when he first arrived in a community, to acquaint himself with recent elections by reading extensively in the back files of the paper, and then to search out the public officials, including the members of the election commission. As a result of his

3. J. Alvin Kugelmass, *Ralph J. Bunche: Fighter for Peace* (New York, 1952), pp. 89–91.

research, he frequently found that he had more "facts" about the local situation than the people he interviewed. He made notes during his interviews and prepared a report on each person he questioned. Stoney thought of his investigations as "county and precinct studies," and he sought to gather as much demographic data, illustrative newspaper stories, and other information as possible.[4] After finishing his interviews in Putnam County, Georgia, he added a note to Bunche: "So much attention was given to the political views of the Justices of the Peace because I want to show the kind of men who are in control of precinct politics. These men, as you can tell, have absolute power over the polls."[5]

The heart of the reports prepared by Stoney and the other interviewers was their interview notes. Stoney in particular had a remarkable talent for reproducing the language he heard, for spotting the revealing comment and the vivid expression. An open, friendly, and engaging young man, he seemed to know how to approach all manner of people, to make them feel comfortable in his presence, and to get them to talk freely. Although he remembers being threatened (as was James Jackson) on two occasions, he was never harmed. He soon discovered that when he talked with Southerners individually, they had plenty of complaints about politics and government; but that they would not voice these complaints as readily or tell him the same story when he talked with them in groups. Stoney's reports were filled with interesting vignettes and the personal experiences of ordinary people. They often contained a touch of humor. In reporting on his visit to Six Mile, South Carolina, for instance, he told of his efforts to locate a Republican physician in the community. "I never found him, or any other Republican," he wrote, "though I went on a number of wild goose chases." When he entered one "dingy junk-shop of a store" in Greene County, Alabama, the young and embittered proprietor greeted him by demanding: "Who are you looking for?" When Stoney had explained his mission, the merchant exclaimed, "Hell, what's there to see around here but cows and niggers?"

Since most of the field notes on these interviews are not available, it is impossible to determine how many individuals were questioned in connection with the project. A tabulation of the references in "The Political Status of the Negro" provides a figure

4. Interview with George C. Stoney, New York City, 9 June 1971.
5. Undated field report in Stoney's possession.

of approximately 550 persons, but the total was undoubtedly much larger than that, since Bunche was selective in his use of the interview material. A breakdown of the references to interviews in the memorandum reveals that some 342 whites and 208 Negroes were questioned. The geographical distribution of persons interviewed shows Alabama with 148, Georgia with 118, South Carolina with 92, and North Carolina with 53. There were fewer interviews in Virginia, Florida, and Texas, while Mississippi, Louisiana, and Arkansas were largely ignored, as were the border states. Only a handful of interviews was carried out in Northern cities.

While the interviews were in progress, Bunche spent considerable time in Myrdal's New York headquarters working on a variety of tasks. He was concerned not only with the Negro's place in politics, but also with Negro organizations, leadership, and ideology, and he wrote reports on all of these subjects. Formulating the various memoranda was an awesome assignment, and meeting Myrdal's deadline of 1 September, 1940, for the completion of all research monographs seemed altogether impossible. "The Political Status of the Negro"—the longest of the four Bunche memoranda—was the last to be finished, and it was completed only by dint of round-the-clock labor during the late summer of 1940. Using the limited secondary material that existed at that time and relying heavily upon the copious field notes of his assistants, Bunche dictated for hour after hour during those hectic August days.

In its original form, "The Political Status of the Negro" ran to 1,660 typed pages divided into 19 chapters, 3 appendixes, and a bibliography. The first part of the memorandum contains a lengthy section on the American political tradition and the historical background for the study of the Negro's political condition in modern times. Then there are chapters on the Southern political process, registration procedures in the South, the white primary, and the poll tax; on Negro registration, the Negro at the Southern polls, Negro voting in the Agricultural Adjustment Administration's (AAA) cotton referenda, Negroes in Atlanta and in Memphis, the Negro as an issue in Southern politics, and benefits derived from Negro political activity in the South; on Republican politics in the Southern states; on liberalism in the South; on Negro political involvement in the North; and on black officeholders in the federal government.

The memorandum was not a finished product, as Bunche was careful to point out in the preface he wrote in 1940. It was rather

"a terribly hurried, poorly integrated, and roughly written job."
Frankly, the author remarked with some exasperation, the procedure he and his assistants followed had been "quite mad."
Meeting rigid deadlines had been made a fetish, and the keynote had been "pell-mell, headlong, furious production." Consequently, there had been little time for reflection and analysis.
The great task had been "that of attempting, within a very short
period, to put together the diverse materials at hand." The Howard professor noted that little scholarly work had been done on
the Negro in American politics, but he was still somewhat apolo-
getic about the inclusion of so much primary material in the
memorandum. Yet, ironically, it was his skillful use of the field
notes that made his report an extraordinary document.

II

The subtitle that Bunche added to "The Political Status of the
Negro" tells a good deal about the work's fundamental character.
It reads: "With Emphasis on the South and Comparative Treatment of the 'Poor White.' " In his comprehensive consideration
of Southern politics, Bunche singled out three salient features
of political affairs south of the Potomac: (1) the looseness and
corruption of political practices; (2) the extent of the disfranchisement of both Negroes and whites; and (3) the lack of effective reform movements at the grass-roots level. The memorandum gave only limited attention to Negroes in Northern
and Midwestern politics.

The Bunche report contains voluminous testimony concerning the inefficient, unfair, and fraudulent conduct of elections
in the Southern states. Election officers were frequently ignorant
of their duties, and they were sometimes dishonest. Registration
lists were poorly kept, usually inaccurate, and often padded.
The purging of the voting lists was a hit-or-miss process. There
was little if any state supervision of voter registration. Enrollment for primary elections, except in the case of Negroes, was
extremely informal. A member of the local enrollment committee in a South Carolina community observed that all he did was
to take the enrollment book when the chairman of the party
brought it to his drugstore, where the registration occurred,
spread it out on his counter, and keep the pencil sharp! In most
cases, the rules required that a registrant sign in person, but in
practice a person was frequently allowed to sign for other members of his family and for the sick and disabled. Nevertheless,
some registration boards took their jobs seriously. One registrar

declared that he liked to think of registration as "a kind of quality test" and that people "ought to have certain responsibilities." But there was much evidence to support the comment of a registrar in Coffee County, Alabama: "The sentiment's against refusing to register a man [white and Democratic] unless he's plumb out crazy."

The registrar in the South, Bunche concluded, was seldom an obstacle to would-be white voters. A registration officer in Lee County, Alabama, observed, in referring to the various constitutional tests in that state: "We [have] never used any of those things against a white man. I'll just be honest with you." On the other hand, the chairman of the board of registrars in Beaufort County, South Carolina, asserted that literacy and property tests were strictly enforced in his locality. "We do that to keep down the niggers," he confessed. The tax collector of Macon County, Georgia, who registered all voters in that civil division, expressed shock at the suggestion that in other Georgia counties people were registered without having to make a personal appearance. "Good Lord!" he exclaimed. "If it was that way, I could put a couple of hundred people's names down on the books myself, pay up their poll taxes, and haul them in and get elected to anything I wanted to."

The Bunche memorandum called attention to the widespread absence of a secret ballot in Southern elections. Voting booths frequently were not employed and sometimes tables were not even provided. Many voters had to have their ballots marked for them, thereby opening the door to fraud and improper interference by election officials. Such voters would often say to the clerk, after indicating their choices among a few of the candidates, "You fill in the rest." Election officers and others were able to use the numbers on ballots to check on the way people voted. In some precincts the man who wanted to sell his ballot would let one of the officials see him mark his ticket. If he marked it right, he was given a "little blue bead" (or perhaps a poker chip) which he then exchanged for the sale price. Absentee ballots were another source of election irregularities, and in some cases the candidates themselves were allowed to call for such votes.

There was a close connection between the misuse of the ballot and county (and municipal) political machines in the South. According to Bunche, "Votes are controlled and checked by registration slips, the 'chain letter' system, vote buying, poll tax payment, double voting, vote stealing, 'counting out' unfortunate candidates, employment of 'agents' to sign up voters, and many variations of these methods." When a new board of registrars assumed office in Chatham County, Georgia, in 1936, it found that the "ring" had padded the voting list with hundreds of dead and removed persons for whom it was continuing to pay poll taxes. The registrars in Jefferson County, Alabama, were said to have struck the names of two thousand deceased people in a recent purge of the voting roll. The political machines themselves were frequently beholden to powerful business interests, which also followed questionable tactics in some elections. Vote buying was so widespread as to form an integral part of the election process in much of the region. In Bibb County, Alabama, for example, the Bunche interviewer was told that between four and five hundred of the two thousand votes normally were "bought." The complaint was often heard that people had "gotten in the habit of selling their vote." Most candidates found it necessary to provide some "hauling" and "favors," and a certain amount of this kind of expenditure was considered quite proper. The really ambitious candidate, remarked one Alabama registrar, made a house-to-house canvass. He "backslaps, baby-kisses, and bites a chew off the same plug with every farmer from here to Tennessee, and, if he has enough two dollar bills, he gets elected." If there was a benign aspect to such practices, there was also an occasional note of humor in them, as the field reports showed.

Bunche and his assistants provided a great deal of evidence to support their contention that the poll tax was a serious medium for the corruption of elections. In many places the administration of the exemption clauses was very liberal, and little effort was made to apply the tax as a systematic registration and voting requirement. An officer of elections in Madison County, Alabama, stated that candidates paid the poll taxes of many voters in his area: "I seen them pay up as much as $15 for a fellow, and I say it's a good thing, too, because there's so many people just ain't got that much money—folks on the WPA and all. They wouldn't be able to vote unless somebody helped them." A clerk in the office of probate judge in the same county estimated that one-third of the votes there were "bought," many of them twice—once with poll taxes and again with the "pay-off" at the polls. The registration in Greene County, Georgia, in the spring of 1940 was the largest in the county's history. Over three thousand dollars in back poll taxes were collected, and, according to a Greensboro justice of the peace, "two-thirds of this was paid by the candidates."

Although many white Southerners were able, in one way or

another, to escape the maze of suffrage qualifications and get their names on the registration lists, low-voting percentages were among the most pronounced characteristics of the region's politics. A Charleston, South Carolina, party official explained the pervasive political apathy by saying, "The trouble is you got to give people something before they'll vote." Because of the one-party dominance, "they don't get nothing for the general election." Typical of many disadvantaged whites was the remark, "No, I don't vote. I don't care nothing about it. Whoever they elect, it's all right with me." Such indifference was sometimes feigned. Politics, some people asserted, "is the rottenest thing in this world. . . . It will make a liar out of you quicker'n anything I know of." On the other hand, the interviewers reported that they were occasionally told that "there's a class of white people that oughtn't to vote." While the poll taxes of some voters were paid for them by candidates and machines, a larger number failed to vote because of the tax requirement. As one humble white woman said, "My husband's talked about voting ever since I can remember. He was going to vote this time, but he couldn't get the money together in time. When he does, I'm going to make him save up for *me*, too."

Defenders of the poll tax made much of the point that the revenue from the levy went to the support of the schools. They were even more insistent in arguing that the poll tax held back a potential flood of black political power. Asked whether he thought the poll tax should be repealed, the clerk of the election commission of Hamilton County, Tennessee, expressed a view common among white Southerners:

> Why? And have some big, black son-of-a-bitch sitting up in the courthouse sending white men to jail? That's what would happen if the niggers started voting heavy here. They'd have a black commissioner at City Hall—some sporting black reared back like God Almighty. No, Sir! Son, I'm not for that! I'm a Southerner and a Democrat. I was born and bred in the South, and that kind of thing ain't in the blood that runs in *my* veins.

The mayor of Chattanooga was just as emphatic: "Yea! What you want to do, repeal it and have the niggers in this town bond us to death? They'd have this town in the poorhouse in two years. They don't pay taxes, so they don't care how much you spend." Nevertheless, many Southerners expressed dissatisfaction with their local officials.

If the percentage of white Southerners on the voting lists was small by national standards, it was still magnificent when compared with the percentage of enfranchised Negroes in the region. For all his knowledge of the South, George Stoney was struck by the "complete freeze-out of Negroes" in local politics. Bunche estimated that in 1940 no more than 200,000 Negroes were registered in the eleven ex-Confederate states, and that over half of those qualified were located in the three states of Virginia, North Carolina, and Tennessee. Only about 1,500 Negroes voted in the whole state of Alabama in 1936, despite the fact that some 18,000 Negro veterans were included in that state's blanket exemption of World War I veterans from the necessity of paying the poll tax. Whereas the registration of white people was often informal and slipshod, that of Negroes almost always involved "a harsh, hostile, and rigid application of the law and often something more than the law." A registrar in Lee County, Alabama, recalled: "We have had a good little bit of trouble with niggers. . . . Way back in 1920, when I was on the board before, we had a world of nigger women coming in to register. There was a dozen of them, I reckon, come in one registration period. We registered a few and then we stopped."

A Negro's ability to register in a particular locality in the South, Bunche wrote, was determined in large part by the attitude of the local registrars, which varied considerably. Many responsible whites in Southern communities were willing to permit a token registration of the more successful blacks. This was not considered "dangerous." But most registration officials seemed to consider Negro efforts to register as "trouble." The chairman of the board of registrars in Macon County, Alabama, a woman, reported that the only "trouble" the registrars had with Negroes resulted from the efforts of orderlies at the Veterans' Hospital in Tuskegee to register. "Honestly, it's awful the way they are doing," she exclaimed. "Oh! They come in and they say they have been here two years when they haven't. They are not really intelligent nigras like the ones out at Tuskegee [Institute], you know. We have to ask them a lot of questions about the Constitution and everything to keep them out." Even with a sympathetic chairman of the registration board, Negroes customarily could not get their names on the voting list the first time they tried. There were some examples of registrars who accepted Negro applicants after hours as a favor to black friends.

The chairman of the board of registrars of Dougherty County, Georgia, claimed that there was a "good nigger vote" in his

county, perhaps two or three hundred, and that they were property holders and taxpayers. Continuing in a philosophical vein,
he declared:

> You know, we've spent a fortune educating the niggers
> down here. The nigger race has come a lot farther than the
> white race in such a short time. You just look back at slavery
> times and count up. . . . It's wonderful, and it's all due to the
> credit of the Southern white man. The Yankees haven't done
> a damn thing for the niggers, and we'd be a lot better off if
> they'd leave us alone to handle things as we know how to.

There were only four or five Negroes on the voting roll in Coffee
County, Alabama, according to the chairman of the board there.
"We aren't troubled with that here," he remarked. "The people
wouldn't stand for it. Now, I recognize that some niggers are
capable of voting a lot more intelligently than a lot of white men
who do vote. They are exceptions, of course, and I believe they've
got sense enough to know why white people don't want them to
vote." The fact was that the social climate and mores of the
South created an atmosphere of essential intimidation for Negro
registrants. The tax collector of Newton County, Georgia, admitted that blacks were discouraged from voting, but he asserted
that he had never tried to keep a colored person from registering,
provided he paid his taxes. In his words, "Negroes just don't have
the nerve to come up and ask for registration. They feel that they
could not and should not register." An Alabama official was brutally forthright: "There ain't a fuckin' nigger in this end of the
county who'd so much as go near a ballot box."
    A Negro leader in Macon County, Alabama, explained some
of the difficulties his people encountered with the board of
registrars:

> First, they started making you get two witnesses to vouch
> for you—two legal voters. When we got that easy, they made
> us get two white witnesses. I started putting pressure on peo-
> ple who I trade with and they signed for them all right. Then,
> they started saying we had to get two white people who
> worked in the courthouse. Then was when we started putting
> pressure on candidates we'd supported. Now, they'll let us
> sign with about anybody. . . . They've started this year asking
> a lot about the Constitution.

This note of subterfuge recurs again and again in the Bunche
memorandum. For example, the chairman of the Negro Voters'

Club of Huntsville said that Negro teachers in that community had been trying to register for a long time. He described what happened: "You go up there and they might tell you the blanks have given out or it's closing time. Most of the time they just walk out on you. The law says, they say, that all three of the registrars must be there before they can register a person. This isn't so, because I've seen them register white people when only one is there, but just as soon as they see a Negro coming, one of them gets up and walks out, and that's the end of it." In another Alabama community a Negro applicant was told that he would have to recite the Constitution. In desperation he recited the Gettysburg Address, whereupon the registrar said, "That's right. You can go ahead and register."

A justice of the peace in Greene County, Georgia, described three Negro voters who "come in every time. They're mighty polite. . . . Always with their hats in their hands. I haven't got any kick there. . . . Naturally, they vote for the New Deal, because give a nigger a little sweetnin' and he'll vote any way." Continuing, he declared: "You can't get a nigger to chop wood or wash clothes any more. It's past history! They're working for the government." A patent medicine salesman in one Alabama community was alarmed at the thought of Negro enfranchisement. "If you don't watch out," he warned, "you're gonna have the same kind of niggers you got over in Miami. They know now, by God, they can control an election and they've got the police department scared." According to the chairman of the county board of registrars in Montgomery, "All niggers—uneducated and educated—have one idea back in their mind—that they want equality. . . . It is necessary to keep the Negro from voting, for voting would lead to social equality. The niggers are in the majority in this county and in Alabama. They would take over the power in the state. The white people are never going to give them this power."

Bunche emphasized the mood of apathy and hopelessness that characterized the Negro's political outlook in the South. He also noted the way in which white Southerners rationalized this condition. Senator Byron Patton Harrison of Mississippi gave a classic statement when he declared: "The nigra is satisfied down there from a political standpoint. In my state, the nigra has played no part in politics for forty years and has no desire to do so. We are all content to leave the situation alone as it is." Southern registration officials usually explained the absence of Negro names from the voting rolls by saying that Negroes "just don't care to register." Many of these officers contended that Negroes were free to vote in all elections except the Democratic primaries. This was a dubious privilege even in places where it was a reality, in view of the overwhelming finality of the primary results.

The "what's the use?" attitude of most Southern Negroes was evident in the interviews Wilhelmina Jackson conducted among black workers on Butler Island, near Darien, Georgia. One woman told her: "Yes, I register, but I do not vote. I just don't have time. You see, I always be working at voting time and all like that." A young woman: "I don't vote, but what I got to vote for?" A pulpwood worker: "Naw, I don't vote. Black man ain't got no right. Even Negroes serving on the juries are so old that they can't get out of their own way, and all they can do is 'yes' the white man." A fisherman: "No, I don't vote. I didn't pay my taxes. Tain't much use anyway."

The whites' fear of the Negro as a voter seemed to stem not so much from doubt about the black man's intentions as from fear of the way "white politicians" would manipulate Negro voters or apprehension that they might be used by labor unions, mill owners, or landlords. It was not fear "of black domination at all," in Bunche's opinion, "but a fear of white domination, in a political game in which the Negro voter is only a pawn." The tax collector of Putnam County, Georgia, remarked that "niggahs would be all right voting if the whites was what they ought to be. That was the trouble before [disfranchisement]. White fellows wouldn't leave them alone." There was also some evidence that Southern politicians opposed Negro enfranchisement on the practical grounds that it would enlarge the electorate, make campaigning more expensive, and result in a less predictable outcome.

Stoney encountered some old-time politicians who enjoyed the opportunity to describe their part in the "nigger vote buying" and "nigger vote stealing" of the "old days." They liked to tell of the fights that broke out over the attempts to steal the "nigger vote," of how their Negro votes were brought with liquor and women, and of how they led the black voters along with music like the Pied Piper of Hamlin. High-jacking the other man's Negro voters was a vital part of this "progress." It was rather ludicrous, observed Bunche, for Southern officials to claim that this situation made Negro disfranchisement necessary and that "clean government" in the South was the result of that disfranchisement.

The Bunche report contains some information on the way Negro votes were used by political machines in such places as San Antonio and Memphis. One informant estimated the number of "controlled Negro votes" in Hamilton County, Tennessee, at two thousand. A reporter for the Chattanooga *Times* graphically described the "system" employed by Walter Robinson, an influential Negro politician in that county. The chairman of the Democratic committee in Ware County, Georgia, said that two hundred Negroes had voted in a recent election in that county. As he put it, "Their so-called leaders lined them up and they voted like sheep. That is what always happens. I know every time we start to have a bond election, they go out and round up the nigras." Occasionally, even in the Deep South, white politicians would appeal for Negro support, but they were reluctant to do so openly.

Despite the fact that Negroes were almost completely disfranchised in the South at the time he prepared his memorandum, Bunche expressed the view that an increasing number of blacks in the region were showing a determination to exercise the ballot. Some Negroes were beginning to question the old "back door" methods that enabled a few members of the race to get their names on the registration lists, and these critics were demanding a more militant approach. Here and there one could find examples of greater Negro involvement in politics. An organizational drive in Macon, Georgia, added almost 200 Negroes to the voting list. By 1939 approximately 2,100 Negroes were registered in Atlanta, as compared with fewer than 1,000 in 1936. The number of black registrants in Duval County, Florida, increased from fewer than 1,500 in 1936 to more than 8,000 in 1938. Negroes were taking a more active political role in a number of municipalities in the South, and some were being admitted to the Democratic primaries. One Negro worker said to an interviewer: "They's talked more politics since Mistuh Roosevelt been in than ever befo'. I been here 20 years, but since WPA, the Negro sho' has started talkin' 'bout politics."

Perhaps the most promising development, certainly in the Deep South, that seemed to point toward the political activation of the Negro was his participation in the AAA cotton referenda. As Bunche wrote, "Many thousands of Negro cotton farmers each year now go to the polls, stand in line with their neighbors, and mark their ballots independently, without protest or intimidation, in order to determine government policy toward cotton production control." An Alabama county agent reported that a larger proportion of Negro than white farmers voted in these referenda. As he explained, "It's the only election they get to take part in." The county agent in Greene County, Georgia, said of the Negro voters in these elections: "They look forward to it." But, he added, "I don't think half of them know what they're voting about." In retrospect, it appears that Bunche exaggerated the significance of the black man's participation in the cotton referenda. Seldom, if ever, was a Negro allowed to serve on the local committees that supervised the elections, and Negroes do not seem to have had much part in the selection of the members of the committees.[6] Yet these referenda did permit many Negro farmers some part in public affairs.

There was an undercurrent of expectation, no doubt associated with the ferment of the New Deal, that seemed to promise the likelihood of future changes even in the Negro's role in Southern politics. A former mayor of Charleston expressed it this way: "The nigger's going to get the vote in the South one of these days. I don't like to see it coming, but it is." Some white farmers, one Alabamian noted, had come to feel that Negroes should have "a few more rights. . . . It hasn't been so long since a lot of these big farmers in Alabama thought what mattered to a nigger, didn't matter." The chairman of the Hall County, Georgia, Republican party declared: "All over the country it's the trend to give the nigger the vote. I don't see how they can keep it out of Georgia long. It does look like they ought to get a vote somewhere, but I don't know what the black counties will do when that day comes."

III

Fundamentally, Ralph Bunche's interpretation of "The Political Status of the Negro" was consistent with Gunnar Myrdal's theme in *An American Dilemma*. To Myrdal, race relations in the United States represented, not a "Negro problem," but a "white man's problem." The white man had imposed a way of life on the Negro which was at variance with the "American Creed" which the white man himself espoused, and it was the responsibility of white men to formulate and effect a more adequate and morally correct treatment of Negroes. The existence of the his-

6. Myrdal was more cautious in his evaluation, explaining that Negroes voted because "their votes are needed." He noted that they "are seldom allowed to vote for committeemen. Even when Negroes do exercise some privileges, it seldom means that they have any real influence on the decisions" (*An American Dilemma*, 1:259).

toric ideals in the United States, Myrdal contended, had set up
a great ideological conflict, in large part a psychological struggle within the individual, who recognized that racial prejudices
and discriminatory practices did not conform to the generally
accepted creed. Bunche seemed to be less optimistic than Myrdal about the potential power of American Negroes as a result
of the split in the moral personality of whites. He gave greater
weight than Myrdal to the existence of a countercreed in the
South which provided white Southerners with sanctions for their
support of traditional racial attitudes and institutions. Like Myrdal, Bunche tended to exaggerate the role that labor unions
would play in resolving the nation's racial dilemma, to explain
racial prejudice too much in terms of class divisions, and not
to foresee the extent to which impetus for future changes in the
Negro's status would come from Negroes in the South.

Although Bunche did not neglect ideological factors (he had
a sharp word for those who contended that it mattered little to
the American Negro whether the Nazis or their opponents won
the struggle in Europe), he stressed economic and class conflict. "The so-called Negro problem in America," he declared, "is
only incidentally a racial one. Many of its major roots go deeper
than race and are themselves embedded in the fundamental
problems of economic conflict and distress which afflict the entire society." Like Charles A. Beard, he saw the Civil War as essentially a clash between the growing industrial power of the
North and the agrarian landholding interests of the South. He
adopted a revisionist view of Reconstruction. The Democratic
party in the Southern states, he wrote, represented the upper
and middle classes. The political South was basically an oligarchy, effectively run by large landholders, bankers, and corporations. Yet the South had never really been solid, according
to the Howard political scientist. "Only the clever manipulation
of the threat of black dominance has kept the underprivileged
white masses and the privileged upper classes of the South from
coming to a parting of the political ways." Negro disfranchisement was the one thing on which the white South was "99 and
44/100 per cent pure," and even that, as carried out in the 1890s
and early 1900s, had been the subject of bitter controversy
among white men.

While Bunche referred to the South as a political oligarchy,
he pictured it as being decentralized, almost anarchistic. He
placed great emphasis on the limited suffrage in the region and
sought to show the depressing and stultifying influence of the

poll tax upon white Southerners. Yet, as a result of his study, he saw some signs of change, some easing of the old white attitude of "absolute hostility toward Negro voting," some inclination on the part of white Southerners to abandon "the Negro diversion." In *An American Dilemma* Myrdal wrote: "Despite all professions to the contrary, the acceptance in principle even by the conservative white Southerners of the American Creed explains why so many exceptions are made to the rule of excluding Negroes from voting." In fact, he concluded, the "Southern franchise situation" was "highly unstable" and would be *"politically untenable for any length of time."*[7] Bunche himself was not without hope for the future democratization of the South, seeming to find some modest gains in the extent of liberal sentiment, interracial cooperation, and awareness of common economic problems in the Southern states. He was cautiously optimistic about the Negro's chances of entering more fully into Southern political affairs in the coming years. He also suggested the improving possibility of a more competitive party situation in the South. "The lily-white Republican movement in the South might actually be of some ultimate advantage to the Negro," he observed. "That is, if the Republican party, as a white party, can attract to itself the large number of severe critics of the New Deal in the region, it may actually be an opening wedge for a two-party system in the South." But Bunche was not misled into believing that the Negro's status would change overnight. His memorandum reveals how limited and inchoate black protest of even the mildest sort was in the Southern states during the 1930s. There was no genuine reform movement that affected the mass of the people—white or black—and Southern liberalism was, to Bunche, a weak reed indeed.

Even at the time it was prepared, the Bunche memorandum suffered from a number of deficiencies. The narrative was rambling and repetitious. There was little that was original in the author's commentary, which was intended to summarize existing scholarship and to point up the findings of the field investigations. Bunche pointed out, in his chapter on the historical background, that he was not attempting any "original postulations." "I don't mind 'sticking my neck out' on occasion," he wryly remarked, "but I do not care to do so recklessly and without some chance of getting it back in again." More serious was Bunche's failure to make distinctions of a subregional kind. He

7. Myrdal, *An American Dilemma,* 1:461, 518.

emphasized the point that there were many Souths, but the fact that his data was drawn so largely from the Southeast (particularly Alabama, Georgia, and South Carolina) made it difficult for him to speak authoritatively about regional patterns and internal contrasts. Bunche had planned a much more elaborate treatment, including a quantitative analysis of Negro voting and the factors associated with the Negro's political status in the South, but lack of time and money made it impossible to undertake any of these studies on a thoroughgoing basis. The treatment of Negro politics in the North was even less adequate, being largely derivative and based on little empirical research. The only extensive interviewing done outside of the South and border states was Wilhelmina Jackson's investigations in Philadelphia. Bunche had hoped to carry out a statistical analysis of Negro voting in selected Northern cities and to study several other aspects of Negro politics in the North, but lack of time and resources rendered this impossible.

Many scholars, including V. O. Key and Alexander Heard, have used "The Political Status of the Negro." These writers and others made use of the memorandum's interview material, and some of them were influenced by Bunche's interpretation of such phenomena as the South's limited suffrage, the white primary, the role of the "courthouse gang," the crucial importance of the South in Congress, and, especially, the place of the Negro in Southern politics. The Negro exercised very limited suffrage, wrote Bunche, but his very presence was "a dominating influence upon Southern politics." Indeed, the "nonvoting Negro remains the greatest single political influence" in the region, the "essential vehicle of Southern politics."

Bunche's massive report on the Negro in politics is a valuable historical document. It did a great deal to shape Myrdal's treatment of the subject in *An American Dilemma*, particularly the chapter entitled "Political Practices Today." The memorandum supplies us with a backdrop against which we can measure change in the Negro's political status and interpret the origins and consequences of the Second Reconstruction. The work's most enduring value, however, lies in its wealth of personal interviews and firsthand impressions of the Negro and Southern politics.

The memorandum is important as a source of information about political practices in the Southern states—registration procedures, the application of suffrage qualifications, the extent of white and black disfranchisement, the conduct of elections, the operation of local political machines, and the limited nature of the Negro's involvement in the political process. It offers some insight into the historical, economic, sociological, and psychological factors that accounted for these practices, as well as some understanding of the myths, stereotypes, and symbols that contemporaries often used to explain and justify them. The report is also significant because of the light it throws on the characteristics of Negro political life, on the levels of black political involvement, and on the patterns of race relations, particularly in the South. It tells us something about Negro political leadership during the New Deal era—about the styles and meaning of that leadership—and the nature of Negro advancement organizations. It provides some impressions of the kinds of Negroes who participated in politics, which areas of the South they inhabited, and which factors encouraged their political involvement.

Perhaps the most interesting aspects of the Bunche report as a historical source are those that disclose the attitudes of the people interviewed. These are quite revealing and all the more fascinating because they are so frequently expressed in everyday language. They bear on all manner of things: the ballot, the community, the government, the New Deal, local concerns, class differences, and matters of race. Racial feelings and attitudes, by the very nature of the investigation, are most prominent. The reader will find it rewarding to explore any number of questions touched on in this study. For example, what does it reveal about the differences in racial attitudes between Southern whites and blacks? How wide was the range of racial attitudes in the two subcommunities? Did either whites or blacks correctly perceive the attitudes of the other race? Is there evidence of a reorientation of the Negro's thinking as a result of the economic depression and the New Deal? Is there evidence of a shift in white attitudes toward Negroes during the Roosevelt era?

One has only to compare Talcott Parsons' and Kenneth B. Clark's recent study, *The Negro American* (1966), with Myrdal's *An American Dilemma* to realize how extensive the changes have been during the last two decades, both in the Negro's place in American society and in the scholarly methods of analyzing racial and minority problems. For all its information and illumination, *An American Dilemma* has become outdated as an approach to the "Negro problem." Today it is essentially a historical document. This is preeminently true of Ralph Bunche's memorandum on Negro politics. As a historical document, "The Political Status of the Negro" can be read with much profit, not only for what it tells us about election procedures, political practices, and black proscription, particularly in the South, but also for what it reveals about the lives of ordinary Americans in the era of Franklin D. Roosevelt—their conditions, habits, prejudices, myths, and aspirations. Before the opinion survey had become a well-established technique of the social scientist, the interviews and personal observations of Bunche and his assistants provided the basic ingredients for a unique source in understanding more fully the nation's most tragic domestic failing. Thus the memorandum is an important contribution to the new literature on the historical experience of black Americans, not least because of the perspective it offers on the Negro revolution of our own time.

Dewey W. Grantham

A Note on the Editing

THE Bunche memorandum was intended to serve as a working paper for Gunnar Myrdal's use in writing *An American Dilemma*, and it naturally possesses the characteristics of a hurriedly-prepared first draft. It is disjointed, rambling, and repetitious. Its organization, apportionment of space, and internal cohesiveness leave much to be desired, as Bunche fully realized. Yet the report is impressive in spite of its shortcomings, and a reader of the original manuscript can only admire the ambitious scope of the study, the care with which it dealt with many aspects of the subject, and the seriousness of purpose and scholarly commitment that are reflected in its pages. Bunche was determined to incorporate in his work both the empirical findings of his interviewers and the results of other scholarship. In preparing the memorandum for publication, I have sought to retain the basic organization and as much of the original language as possible.

Some changes in the organization of the report have been made in the interest of greater coherence. The major modification in this respect was the separation of the commentary from the main body of field interviews and special reports. In the 1940 version, Bunche interspersed his own opinions and conclusions throughout the report. Most of these evaluations have been extracted from the body of the memorandum and combined with the author's original introduction, historical background chapter, and conclusion to form part 1 of this volume. Great care has been taken to retain the language, context, and logic of the draft report. Some rearrangement of material has been made in part 2, where a few of the original chapters have been divided or combined, but the general order that Bunche followed has been preserved. A good deal of repetitious material has been eliminated, and the three appendixes and the selective bibliography have been omitted.

I have tried to keep all, or almost all, of the interview material and to present without change the exact words of the people being quoted. Some silent changes have been made in capitalization and punctuation for the sake of consistency. Although the full report contains the names of most of the people interviewed, these individuals are ordinarily not named here, in order to avoid possible embarrassment to living people. This edition of the memorandum does identify, in the text or in footnotes, the names of the interviewers, except in those few instances where the original report fails to provide such information.

I gladly acknowledge my indebtedness to the late Ralph J. Bunche for his cooperation and support in the editing of this volume. Although his serious illness prevented me from discussing the memorandum with him, he was enthusiastic about the undertaking from the beginning and unfailing in his efforts to facilitate my work. I am also grateful to Judge William B. Bryant, who generously took time from his busy schedule to talk with me about his part as Bunche's research assistant in the preparation of "The Political Status of the Negro." My thanks go to Professor Guy B. Johnson of the University of North Carolina for telling me about his association with Bunche as a member of Myrdal's staff in 1939 and 1940. I am happy to acknowledge the help of George C. Stoney, the principal interviewer for the project, who not only described for me his role in the work but also made available some copies of the extensive field reports he made during his swing through the South in 1940. Finally, I am greatly indebted to Miss Martha H. Swain of Vanderbilt University for valuable research assistance and for preparing the index.

The photographs that appear in the text were taken between 1935 and 1941 by the Farm Security Administration in the areas covered by this study and are included as a visual reinforcement of the discussion of the period. I would like to thank the Library of Congress Department of Prints and Photographs for its assistance in making these photographs available. I am especially grateful to Dr. Alan Fern, the director of the department, and Mr. Leroy Bellamy, whose specific knowledge of the Farm Security Administration collection made the difficult task of selection somewhat easier.

Dewey W. Grantham
13 July 1971

PART ONE

The Political Status of
the Negro: A Commentary

ONE

The American
Political Scene

PERHAPS the starting point should be the influence which eighteenth-century liberalism had upon American political thought and institutions. It is sufficient to note that the influence of civil libertarianism upon American thought at the time of the American Revolution was great. From this revolt there emanated, it is true, a high regard for the rights of property, but of even greater importance for the Negro is the fact that the Revolution, though bourgeois in character, handed down to American society fundamental concepts of human equality and human rights. It is within this conceptual milieu, inherited from the American Revolution, that the Negro now carries on his struggle for political emancipation in the South.

The revolutionary tide had already begun to recede at the time of the calling of the Constitutional Convention of 1787. The struggle at the convention was between the interests that feared democracy as a "hydra-headed monster" and those that subscribed to the principles of equalitarianism. The constitution itself represented a compromise solution between these conflicting interests. It surrounded property interests with unusual protection and elevated property to a level of equality with human rights; and it afforded more than ample opportunity for undemocratic practices. But, contradictory as it may seem, the constitution did lay the basis for the broadest ideological pattern of human equality, human liberty, and human rights that the modern world has known.

It hardly needs to be pointed out that the American moneyed and landed aristocracy exerted a controlling influence over political, social, and economic life in the early days of the nation's constitutional history. For our purposes, special note should be taken of the rather severe limitations upon the exercise of the franchise in this early period, the provisions for the indirect election of the president and senators, the loose organization of political parties and their domination by the upper classes through the operation of the caucuses, the conservative decisions of the Supreme Court, and undemocratic legislation such as that represented by the Sedition Act. During these years there was a good deal of distrust of the instability and recklessness of the masses, and it was widely feared that the American ship of state would founder upon the shoals of irresponsible legislation should too much authority be placed in the hands of the unlettered.

Some reference should be made to such nineteenth-century developments as the struggle for dominance and power represented in the Civil War and the growth of industrial barons coincident with the course of the Industrial Revolution. Without presuming to dig into the history of class division in the United States, it can be pointed out that there has been a long running conflict between the landed aristocracy and the proletarian offspring of the Industrial Revolution. The reverse of the picture of the American ruling class necessarily reveals the American masses. The latter began with the indentured servants and the slaves, and formed the basis for an American working class and an American peasantry—the poor whites of the rural South and the industrial workers of the urban centers of both North and South. The significance of these great American masses—black and white, largely inert and inarticulate—to the nation's political process is abundantly clear. It is here that we encounter a historically permanent blind spot in the operation of American democracy, for these people, by and large, have enjoyed but slight participation in the processes of government. This is true of great sections of the white population of the South even today.

It is of the greatest significance that there has never been, in democratic America, a real movement embracing and representing the masses of the population. The most startling feature of the great growth of labor unionism in this country has been the lack of any political orientation and consciousness on the part of the movement. Only recently has the Congress of Industrial Organizations embarked upon this course in somewhat haphazard fashion. The American Federation of Labor traditionally pursued a policy of political individualism. The most significant of the early efforts leading toward the formation of a mass movement was that of Populism, arising out of the agrarian revolt. The history of that movement is of prime importance to the subject of Negro political status.

Sectionalism has played an extremely vital role in American politics. Most of the great political issues have had their roots in sectional interests, and certainly until recent years, if not still, these sectional differences have been the dominant feature in the nation's politics. It is, I think, still an open question whether, in American politics, sectional interests are giving way before class interests. It is not difficult to relate the interest of the Negro to these sectional divergencies in politics, especially in view of the fact that the vast majority of Negroes live in one section of the country—the South. Sectional conflicts must also be considered in terms of their effect upon the strength of political parties and the heterogeneity in party membership.

The American party system is of the greatest importance to Negro political status. On the one hand, it is through party organization that that portion of the black population which exercises the franchise has an opportunity on occasion to exert political influence far in excess of its numerical strength in the particular locality. On the other hand, the recognition of the authority of the political party to determine its own membership constitutes the basis for the most effective instrument yet employed to deny the largest part of the Negro population—that of the South—any real political participation. For it is the peculiar nature of our party setup which makes it possible for the Democratic party in the South to exclude Negroes from membership and, therefore, from participation in the only real elections held in the South—the Democratic primaries.

Many other aspects of the American party system have a direct or indirect relevance to the Negro's political status. I think that a great deal might be written upon the subject of the two-party system and its relationship to the political interests of such a minority group as the Negro. Why has it been impossible to develop a multiple-party system in America? Why have all third-party movements failed here? What would be the significance of a multiple-party system to the Negro? Would the solid South have developed in the face of a multiple-party tradition? What significance have third-party efforts had for the Negro and his political status?

Notice must also be taken of the broad importance of the

frontier for political and economic life in the United States, and especially for the peculiarly American psychology of individualism and escape, which the presence of the frontier stimulated. For black people, however, the frontier provided no important physical means of escape, since there was no substantial migration of Negroes to the West. The Negro remained anchored in the South: first, because the great masses of blacks after emancipation lacked the means to undertake the journey to the free lands of the West; secondly, because there was hostility in both South and West to Negro migration; and, thirdly, because the Negro was led to nurture high hopes concerning the land which presumably would be made available to him in the South—a hope symbolized by the "forty acres and a mule" dream, which was never realized. Nevertheless, the frontier and its psychological derivative, the "American dream," did have an important influence upon the thinking of Negroes, as it did upon the thinking of the nation as a whole. The black citizen, too, began to think in an optimistic vein and to take it for granted that his class and group status must inevitably improve here.

American politics is so typically machine politics that it would be impossible to broach the subject realistically without discussing the nature and influence of the machine. This, of course, has an important bearing upon Negro political activity, because wherever this activity is found, it quite naturally tends to follow the pattern of American politics and to lend itself to machine control. It is sufficient to note at this point that a weighty factor in the evolution of the political machines in local politics has been their ability to prey upon illiterate immigrants, other disadvantaged whites, and the Negro masses. The great ring bosses have been prone to take their votes where they found them and to take the easiest votes first. Until very recently, the Negro and immigrant votes have been among the most readily bought and the most tractable.

Mention should be made of the peculiar attraction which the demagogue seems to have for the American electorate. It is, perhaps, a tendency in the United States to make a fetish of leadership and to ascribe our troubles and our accomplishments to it. There is no question in my mind but that the American public attributes much more importance to personalities than it does to principles and issues. Thus, it is possible for an individual without principle or program, but endowed with a good radio voice and an engaging smile or an unusual ability to harangue, to win enthusiastic support from large numbers of voters. This makes it easy for the demagogue to gain power. Although the demagogue is not confined to any one section, the South has had many more than its share and has contributed its own peculiar breed. The significance of this particular characteristic of American politics to the Negro is ominously clear. Given the proper circumstances, demagogic leaders might foment movements which could easily nullify whatever progress the Negro has been able to make since emancipation and do to the Negro here what Germany has so efficiently done to the Jew there.

Negro political leadership merely simulates the broad patterns of conduct of white political leadership. One is tempted to suggest that perhaps there is a difference, in that the Negro political leader would naturally tend to make greater appeal to race and race consciousness, but it is hardly possible that any black political leader could be any more racially demagogic or any more dependent upon racial appeals than the Southern political leaders who follow closely the patterns set by the Vardamans, the Bleases, and the Heflins.

Another characteristic of American politics, closely related to the foregoing, is the cordial reception which American voters traditionally give to crackpot schemes. In recent years, we have seen large numbers of people marching enthusiastically behind banners with such slogans as "Every Man a King," "Thirty Dollars Every Thursday," and "Ham and Eggs Every Friday." The programs of organizations such as the Ku Klux Klan are in the same vein, but they are of more serious import to minority groups like the Negro. The burning of crosses, the wearing of hoods, and the mysterious rituals of secret societies have been significant factors in the American political process. There is always the possibility, particularly in crucial times like these, that real Americanism will be given a perverted interpretation, loaded with destructive possibilities for the Negro.

Since the Civil War, our two major parties have seldom been differentiated by significant ideological positions. Certainly it can be shown that, with the exception of the Negro issue and the tariff, there has been no fundamental difference in their programs. The two parties really stand for no fundamental programs. They shift positions at will and are now reversing themselves on the issue of centralization versus decentralization, which has so long been held to constitute an essential difference between them. Thus, the analysis tends to reduce itself to a statement of what the particular party stands for in the particular election rather than an analysis of a broad position, traditionally assumed by either party. The absence of opposition parties of any significance has made it possible for the two big parties to monopolize political power without producing any basic programs, and without representing anything in particular except the financial interests that subsidize them.

This explains why the Negro, in giving his traditional support to the Republican party, has had to do so on the basis of Republican legend rather than because of any constructive program which the party offered for the improvement of black status. It explains, also, why in the period of depression the Negro readily forswore his allegiance to the Republican party when the Democratic party offered him relief and relief jobs. The Republicans established the tradition of including in GOP platforms a short statement of some kind relating to their interest in Negro welfare. This has been considered good strategy in the presidential election years.

It is, perhaps, not surprising that neither of our major parties has ever considered it necessary to offer a constructive program looking toward the amelioration of the country's Negro minority problem—one of the most troublesome in our history. The recognition extended to the Negro has been in the most glittering generalities, but the fact is that neither party has ever seen fit to offer a constructive and comprehensive program looking toward the social well-being of the population as a whole. The one effort made in this direction—and that a rather feeble one— has been the desperate activity of the New Deal during the depths of the depression. Significantly, now that the depression has lifted slightly, much of the social program of the New Deal is being subjected to serious attack, and many important aspects of it may be scuttled before all the shooting is over.

The Negro population, resting at the bottom of society, is almost entirely within that low income group which has the greatest need for a broad and liberal governmental policy of social welfare. It is one of the ironies and the inconsistencies of our social system that, despite our democratic foundation, so large a part of our population is unable to express its will on those very aspects of governmental policy which most vitally affect its welfare.

The American government is responsive less to the will of the electorate than to the demands of organized pressure groups. Negroes have been forced to adopt lobbying and pressure group tactics as a measure of self-preservation, and Negro organizations have done some of their most effective work through employment of these methods. Similar tactics are pursued by black organizations toward state legislatures. No Negro lobby, however, can be altogether effective, because there is no such thing as Negro unity, the black vote is not a bloc vote, and there is neither the leadership nor the organizational control necessary to weld the Negro population into a formidable pressure group.

The study of the political status of the Negro is, in itself, a partial record of the shortcomings of American democracy. I think that we should at least raise some questions concerning the seeming inability of American democracy to "democ" and the essential reasons for this failure. This is especially important in a period in which there are already too many people who are apparently lukewarm toward democracy and who are willing to make snap judgments about it. There are too many who will say that if democracy cannot quickly correct its shortcomings in the world today, it does not deserve to survive. There are others who adopt an air of futility and defeatism, and who wail that it is impossible for democracy to compete with the highly centralized governments of the totalitarian nations. Among those who take such views are many Negroes, despite the fact that it would be racially suicidal for the black man if totalitarianism in any form should be substituted for our present democratic concepts. Yet, all who swear by the democratic system know that there are serious questions to which we must find the answers.

Why is it that, with our extremely democratic educational system, we do not produce a more politically intelligent and a less politically apathetic electorate? Why is it that American voters are so easily led away from their own political and economic interests and are so ready to enter upon ideological wild-goose chases? Why is it that there is so little independent voting and so much machine regimentation? Why is it that votes are so easily bought; that elections are so corrupt; that long ballots persist; that in many places secret ballots are unheard-of; that elections are so loosely administered; and that candidates do not need either platforms, intelligence, or honor? What possibility is there for an American brand of fascism under the guise of one-hundred-percent Americanism? Finally, what steps can we take to safeguard our democratic institutions and to move toward realization of our democratic ideals?

TWO

The Historical Background

THROUGHOUT American history, the South has been distinguish-
able as a separate region of the country with its own peculiar social, political, and economic institutions and ideologies. Though
we speak of the solid South, the region has not in any sense been
solid in the past, nor is it today, except in its traditional adherence to the doctrine of white supremacy on the one hand and to
the political derivative of that doctrine—a blind allegiance to
the one-party system—on the other. There have always been
severe class distinctions in the South. Negroes and poor whites
have always occupied the two bottom rungs of the ladder, and
the white landlords, industrialists, and bankers—the Bourbons
—have always been at the top. In between the white and black
masses at the bottom and the numerically small aristocracy at
the top, there has developed an intermediate class of small
farmers, who today are in serious danger of being pushed down
into the agricultural and industrial proletariat. Between these
upper and lower classes in the South there has been a traditional
and deep-seated hostility. Only the clever manipulation of the
threat of black dominance has kept the underprivileged white
masses and the privileged upper classes of the South from coming to a parting of the political ways.

The slave population of the South took on political significance at a very early date in American history, as is evident in
the "three-fifths" compromise at the Constitutional Convention of 1787. This provision of the Constitution gave the slave
states a disproportionate share of representation in the House
of Representatives—and in the electoral college—but it was

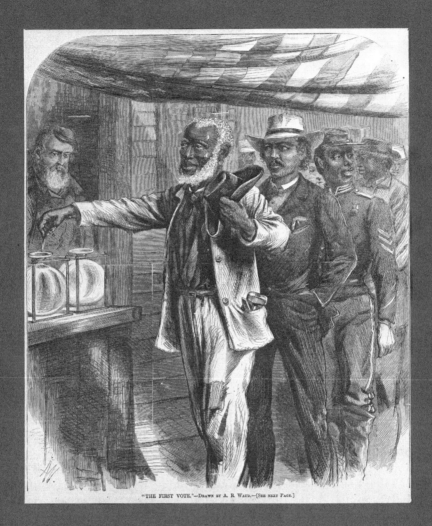

"THE FIRST VOTE."—Drawn by A. R. Waud.—[See next Page.]

the price the Northerners were compelled to pay for the Southerners' support of the great document.

The two main characteristics of the antebellum South were the institution of slavery and the problem of the Negro. Slavery created an intense rivalry between the slave-owning planters of the tidewater and "black lands" regions, on the one hand, and the non–slave-owning white farmers, artisans, and mountaineers, on the other. The very nature of the plantation system produced a wide gap between the plantation owners and the rest of the population. This gap was widened because the institution of slavery tended to degrade labor and to cause it to be looked upon as disreputable. Not only did slavery as an institution place labor in disrespect, it also discouraged the development of industry and commerce. In another sense, however, slavery provided the basis for the South's solidarity; for when Southern institutions that supported black bondage were attacked by outsiders, both classes in the South tended to make common cause in resisting the interference by designing Northerners.

The North early began a moral offensive against the South's peculiar institution, and this was soon extended into a political and economic offensive. Toward the moral offensive, the South itself was at first not altogether unsympathetic. Many people in the region harbored grave doubts as to the ultimate social and economic effects of the slave system. But after 1830 the new profitability of the slave economy to the South and the irritating abolitionist sentiment of the North tended to stiffen the Southern defense of slavery. The South quickly stopped flirting with Jeffersonian ideas and ceased doubting and apologizing for slavery. The presence of the Negro made it impossible for the South even to think in democratic terms. Southern sectionalism was also encouraged by the region's unhappiness over a variety of economic policies that were attributed to Northern influence in the national government. All of these factors helped to push Southerners into the Democratic party and to create the basis for a sectional loyalty south of the Potomac River that transcended party and factional lines.

There was no Negro political activity of any consequence in the antebellum period, for restrictions against even the free Negro were widespread. Early black political leadership was confined primarily to that expressed through scattered slave revolts and to that of the free Negroes, whose burdens were great and who feared that they would be pushed down to the level of the slaves. As free persons, these Negroes found themselves in an increasingly difficult and paradoxical position. In all of the Southern states and most of those of the North as well, these black people, though "free," were disfranchised, denied fundamental rights in the courts, and otherwise treated in a manner far different from that accorded other American citizens. Nevertheless, all of the New England states except Connecticut permitted Negroes to vote; Wisconsin gave the suffrage to free Negroes in 1849; and a few scattered court decisions upheld the black man's right to vote. There is sufficient evidence of Negro political activity in some of the Northern states to demonstrate the historical errors implicit in Chief Justice Taney's dictum, in the Dred Scott case, to the effect that the Negro had not been accorded the status of citizenship in the United States. There was certainly a fundamental recognition of the status of citizenship for the free Negro, though his political influence was practically nil. It should be noted that even Lincoln was greatly troubled by the Negro problem and that he went so far as to seek a means of escape from it through colonization.

A combination of many factors brought on the Civil War, but its central cause was the fundamental antagonism between the interests of North and South resulting from the essential differences in their economies. The war would not have been fought merely for the sake of freeing the slaves. That the Civil War freed the slaves was only an incident in the violent clash of interests between the industrial North and the agricultural South —a conflict that was resolved in favor of the industrial North. In this struggle the Negro was an innocent pawn. Although his future here depended upon the outcome, he had very little part in it until the latter stages of the war.

Two of the legends that derived from this internecine struggle must be mentioned. One holds that Lincoln was the great emancipator and that the North was engaged in a great missionary crusade. Lincoln became a great emancipator and humanitarian in the minds of Negroes because the North eventually won the war and the slaves were freed; but the basic interests that dictated Lincoln's attitudes and actions in the presidency were those related to his determination to keep the Union intact. If the conflict of interests between the two sections had not become so acute that it was no longer possible to hold the country together without destroying the institution of slavery, there is no evidence to indicate that Lincoln's humanitarian tendencies would have induced him to risk breaking up the Union in order to free the slaves. Similarly, while it must be admitted that there was strong abolitionist sentiment in many sections of the North and West, it cannot be said that all of this sentiment was prompted by sincerely humanitarian motives. William Lloyd Garrison and his followers were undoubtedly sincere in their fanatical opposition to the enslavement of human beings, but there were many abolitionists in the North whose attitudes on the question of slavery were dictated by the strategy of sectional warfare. The fact that there were potent elements in the Northern population that were not moved by the appeal of the crusade against human bondage is sufficiently testified to by the difficulty encountered by the North in raising an army and by the violent riots which broke out when the conscription law was belatedly enforced.

Yet these Civil War myths have exerted a tremendous influence on the thinking of Negroes and, at least until 1932, were the controlling factor in determining the political attitudes and activities of Negroes. The Negro voter's blind loyalty to the Republican party can be interpreted in no other terms. It is also important to note that the Civil War did not immediately stimulate any great political awakening and social consciousness among Negroes. The black masses lacked the ideological drive characteristic of any people who have fought their way through a revolutionary period.

The Civil War, in unchaining the Negro in the South, put a temporary stop to the developing antagonism between the white classes. This interjection of the racial issue checked what inevitably would have been a vigorous upsurge of the white masses in the South and a process of thorough democratization of that region. Thus, class differences and class antagonisms continued, but, for reasons of alleged self-preservation, the South became convinced that it was necessary to call a halt to political divisions through which these class differences would otherwise have found their natural expression. The white South was determined to keep the black man in a subordinate economic, political, and social status.

The vital significance of the Reconstruction period to the political status of the Negro is found in the temporary eclipse of white supremacy and the rise of the new black estate in the South. Major consideration must be given to the great hope which the Negro placed in his affiliation with and protection by the Republican party. Such black leaders as Frederick Douglass,

P. B. S. Pinchback, and John M. Langston saw in this affiliation the salvation of the Negro. They turned their backs on those spurious efforts then being made to align the black man with labor organizations and cautioned the Negro that "the Republican Party is the ship; all else is the sea." This early Negro political leadership set the pattern that was not broken until Franklin D. Roosevelt and the New Deal came along.

Classified on the basis of their motives, the advocates of Negro suffrage after the Civil War fall into two groups. In the first and smallest group were theorists like Charles Sumner who believed suffrage to be a natural right and hence favored universal suffrage in the North and the South. The larger and more influential group among the so-called Radicals was made up of politicians of the Thaddeus Stevens type. Stevens and his cohorts feared, above all else, the increased representation which the South would get by virtue of the freedmen and the probable alliance of the Southerners with the Northern "copperheads" or Democrats. Such a combination would threaten the continuance of Republican domination of the national government; and in Republican supremacy, they assumed, lay the safety and welfare of the Union. Probably a more important consideration from the politician's point of view was the safety of the political careers of the party leaders.

One might well speculate as to what would have happened in this period if a different course had been followed. What would have happened had Lincoln lived and attempted to offset the severe proposals of the Radical Republicans? What would have happened had the large plantations of the South been broken up and distributed among the poor whites and blacks? Had the owners been compensated for the slaves which were taken from them, would the South have altered its harsh attitude toward the Negro? Would it have made any great difference in the relative position of the races had the Reconstruction governments not been crammed down the throats of the brooding South? Is it likely that, without the Emancipation Proclamation, the institution of slavery would have soon broken down from its own internal weaknesses and thus left less ill feeling and hostility in the South? Is it likely that a milder policy toward the South would have led the poor whites to develop an increasingly active class consciousness instead of being engulfed by the emotional doctrine of white supremacy? What would have been the result had the North and the South assumed a joint guardianship over the emancipated slave instead of throwing him out on his own resources? Would it have been possible to invoke some sort of reservation scheme similar to that employed for the protection of the Indian, at least until the harsh feelings engendered by the conflict between the two sections had become tempered by time?

A great many attempts have been made to evaluate Negro political activity during this period, and to appraise the quality and achievements of the black legislators. This is undoubtedly one of the most controversial chapters in American history. Negro historians generally try to picture these legislators as great reformers who introduced democratic institutions to the South. White historians in general are quite critical of the activities of these black statesmen and damn them with faint praise, if they do not condemn them outright for their alleged ignorance and venality. This group consideration of the black legislators seems to me to be unfortunate. These men were all individuals, just as all elected officials are. They represented no movement, and they had no organization. Some of them were well educated and competent, and some of them were poorly trained, incompetent, and dishonestly opportunistic. They can and should be appraised as individuals, with due consideration being given to the milieu in which they had to work. What it all amounts to, it seems to me, is that in the period of Reconstruction there were some thoroughly good and some very bad Negro politicians. That is true of white politicians in all periods.

The South still inveighs vigorously against the black horror of Reconstruction and fights it as the basis for the unpleasant relationship between the races in the Southern states today. This is the catastrophe theory of the South, as opposed to the extreme claims made by Negro chauvinists concerning the great contributions to democracy offered by the black legislators. Even the Southern white liberal accepts at face value this interpretation of the terror visited upon the South when the Negro exercised political power during Reconstruction. There is enough evidence now unearthed to present a reasonable picture of what actually did transpire. In the first place, there was no "black domination." The Reconstruction governments in the South were essentially army-of-occupation governments, for the Southern region was a conquered country and was treated as such. The all-pervading influence was the victorious armed force of the North as symbolized by federal troops. The Reconstruction governments were not Negro governments; they were

Negro-carpetbagger-scalawag governments operating under the shadow of Northern dominance.

Nor was there any dictatorship of the black proletariat in the Reconstruction period, as Du Bois suggests in his *Black Reconstruction*.[1] Nor, for that matter, was there a dictatorship of the white proletariat, as he also suggests. The Reconstruction governments in the South were supported by the Northern military arm and served the interests of the industrial North. The newly freed black had no working class consciousness; in fact, no class consciousness at all. His thinking was tied to the land, to "forty acres and a mule," and he certainly had no proletarian consciousness. His psychology, even after emancipation, was that of the serf or, at best, the peasant. The poor white was beginning to develop a class consciousness but was inarticulate and played only a feeble role in the political drama of the period.

The white South, while ostensibly remaining aloof from and indifferent to the new political order created by the Radical Republican Congresses, set itself with firm determination to the task of reestablishing the old order and putting the Negro back in his place. It was during these days that the Ku Klux Klan had its inception and that the whole process of shameful intimidation and deprival of the Negro began. The Southerners were determined to block the constructive transition of the black man's status from that of slave to citizen.

Following the short political honeymoon of the Negro during the Reconstruction period, there ensued a severe time of reaction. The essential feature of this era is found in the fact that the North left the Negro to the mercy of an embittered South. It was a period of political and social flux in the South, of political jockeying, of bitterness, of class conflict and vengefulness. It was during these years that the South began to manufacture the devices which have been employed successfully to put the Negro back in his place. The Negro bore the brunt of the political attack, for the black man was the symbol of the South's humiliation.

After 1877 the Southern conservatives were able to put through the reforms they thought best. Then, too, the turn in national affairs was a further boost to the reestablishment of white supremacy. National problems, such as the agricultural

1. William E. B. Du Bois, *Black Reconstruction: An Essay toward a History of the Part which Black Folk Played in the Attempt to Reconstruct Democracy, 1860–1888* (New York, 1935).

depression, claimed the attention of Congress. Little by little the restrictions on the South disappeared. It is also important to note that the courts were handing down decisions which had the effect of pulling the teeth of the suffrage amendment and the Civil Rights Act. In general terms, the Supreme Court laid down the principle that neither the Fifteenth Amendment nor its enforcing acts implied any positive grant of suffrage.

In their efforts to insure the permanence of white supremacy and to eliminate the Negro vote as a serious factor in political affairs, the Democrats of the South adopted almost every conceivable measure that might tend to accomplish this purpose. To many white Southerners, the partisan election laws, poll tax requirements, and the irregular practices which were used at the polls were not enough assurance of maintaining white supremacy. In order further to safeguard this concept, the gerrymander was frequently used. Legislative and congressional districts were set up with the definite purpose of insuring a Democratic majority. In 1882, for example, the legislature of South Carolina so gerrymandered that state that the Republicans could control but one of the seven congressional districts. The same device was used in arranging legislative districts. Another method used by the Democrats to frustrate the will of the black majorities in counties where Negroes outnumbered whites was that of centralized state government. So long as the whites stuck together, the Democratic control of the legislatures was assured. This made the highly centralized state government method very effective. In order to put this policy into effect, the legislature of North Carolina passed a county government law in 1876. This act provided for the election of justices of the peace by the legislature. In turn, the justices of the peace were to elect from three to five persons from their respective counties to act as a board of commissioners. Thus, the chief county officers were appointed rather than elected by the people.

Negroes continued to go to the Southern polls in the late 1870s and the 1880s, but their numbers declined steadily. For example, the number of black votes between 1876 and 1884 in South Carolina, Louisiana, and Mississippi suffered a drastic drop. The Negro vote was cut by one-half in South Carolina, by about one-third in Louisiana, and by about one-fourth in Mississippi.

The agrarian upheaval and the rise of the Populist party had a profound effect upon Negro suffrage and, in the long run, contributed much to the complete disfranchisement of Negroes in the Southern states. The economic distress of the region's farmers, coupled with the conservative and business-oriented leadership of the Bourbon regimes in the South, eventually inspired a widespread political rebellion. The poor white population began to assert itself and to demand a voice in the political controls of the section. It began to develop a new group and class consciousness, and to produce its own leadership. Often meeting with an inhospitable reception in the conservative Democratic party, the leadership of the upsurging white masses began to flirt with the idea of an alliance with the blacks as a means of crashing through the established order. The repressive activities against Negroes in the 1890s and early 1900s were stimulated not by fear of the Negro but by fear of the unity of blacks and whites. The Negro, by this time, was no longer a menace; he had been thoroughly suppressed.

Populism flared up in the Southern states, but only briefly. It had neither the force nor the leadership to overcome the deeply entrenched opposition of the ruling order. The agrarian revolt did precipitate many bitter fights between the white factions of the Southern states. During these political battles, both sides often appealed to the Negro voters in order to overcome the opposition. After each election, although both factions had appealed to and even used the black vote, the losing faction made definite attempts further to disfranchise the Negro and condemned the opposition for seeking the black vote. During these fights between the old party machines and the restless agrarians, election practices of the Reconstruction and "redemption" eras reappeared. There were riots at the polls, ballot boxes were stuffed, meetings were broken up, and repeaters were put into circulation. Ballots were thrown out on technicalities and, in general, the political situation in the South took on a very unpleasant odor. The rise of the Populists seemed to result in the fulfillment of the predictions of the old Democratic leaders who had often said that all their statutory provisions would be inadequate to keep Negroes disfranchised if a split occurred in the white ranks.

Thus, the Populist revolt furnished new reasons for dealing harshly with Negro voters. Effective—and legal—disfranchisement became an important factor in helping to reunite the white South in the wake of the divisions of the late nineteenth century. Beginning with Mississippi in 1890 and including seven other Southern states by 1910, ingenious disfranchising provisions were made a part of the organic law. These clever provisions circumvented the prohibitions of the Fifteenth Amendment and, on the surface, safeguarded the white voter. Many of the South's leading politicians contended that the admission of Negroes to the polls was tantamount to opening the door to all sorts of fraud. Those who subscribed to this view claimed that as long as there were black voters, they would be sought by the whites as political allies and oftentimes the methods adopted to gain their support would be corrupt. Therefore, the only alternative to corruption and fraud was the complete disfranchisement of the Negro and a return to white solidarity. In the light of these contentions and the seeming unanimity on the subject of Negro suffrage among white Southerners, one might have predicted that the disfranchising provisions would be passed with little or no difficulty. The fact is, however, that the campaigns were heated and the debates were long and extremely controversial. This situation resulted from the fact that the erstwhile Populists could not easily forget that the earlier restrictive legislation, which had been directed at the Negro, had been used to good advantage against them in their political struggles. With this in mind the whites who had been political irregulars saw in the new and highly complicated election machinery and qualifications the very imminent possibility that those in power would use the proposed devices to disfranchise any dissenter—whether Negro or white. But against the hard reasoning of skeptics who saw such dangerous possibilities, the experienced Southern Bourbon politicians hurled the ever-effective argument of "black domination." Although the fears of the opposition were never quite dispelled, race feeling triumphed, and the disfranchising amendments were adopted.

An examination of the disfranchising amendments adopted by the various Southern states reveals a striking similarity in the essential features of the acts. Each contains an educational prerequisite for voting, which is usually the ability to read a section of the state or federal constitution, and to write one's name. Poll taxes or other taxes had to be paid by the applicant for registration. It was necessary to register months ahead of elections, and a receipt for taxes paid had to be shown to registration and election officials. The property qualification was a new feature. This usually ran to two or three hundred dollars. One or more alternatives were usually provided for this qualification. Literacy was one of these. Another was the "understanding" clause, which usually called for the ability to interpret the state or federal constitution to the satisfaction of election offi-

cers. In some cases "good character" might qualify one for registration and voting, but it had to be substantiated by sworn testi-
monials, by proof of steady employment during a specified
preceding period, or by an affidavit giving the names of employers for a period of from three to five years. The property and literacy qualifications automatically eliminated large numbers of
Negroes, and the alternatives which were generally provided
were easily manipulated by the election officials so as to operate
to the disadvantage of black applicants. A further impediment
took the form of residence requirements and a list of disqualifying crimes, which were supposedly peculiar to the Negro's low
economic and social status. The crowning glory of constitutional disfranchisement was the grandfather clause, which was
the safeguard for the poor and illiterate whites.

As might be expected, the various disfranchising acts of the
Southern states have been the subject of numerous court battles. Time and time again, Negroes have sought to test the constitutionality of the disfranchising measures. Almost without
exception, the state courts in the South have tolerated and even
abetted the process of disfranchisement. Up to the year 1915,
the Supreme Court of the United States generally followed the
practice of the Southern state courts. The hands-off attitude of
the Northern people toward the discriminatory treatment of
Negroes in the South was reflected in its decisions. On numerous occasions, direct decisions on many of the Southern suffrage laws were evaded, and, instead, evasive and often technical constructions were placed upon the Fourteenth and
Fifteenth amendments by the court. Since 1915, the court has
shown some inclination to look beyond the letter to the spirit of
the law, but the Southern legislators have been crafty and thus
far have been able to discriminate against what they choose to
call the Negroes' characteristics rather than against them as a
race.

In the first three decades of the present century the Negro
vote in the South was negligible, as Paul Lewinson shows in
Race, Class and Party.[2] While not minimizing the importance
of the disfranchising amendments, it should be noted that the
most effective disfranchising weapon—and the one which has
had the most permanence—is not expressly formulated in the
laws of the states. This is the "white primary." The effectiveness

2. Paul Lewinson, *Race, Class and Party: A History of Negro Suffrage
and White Politics in the South* (New York, 1932).

of this color bar was detected early by white Southerners. During one of the debates on proposed disfranchisement clauses, an opponent of the proposal contended that they were unnecessary, since the white primary was already taking care of the black vote very effectively. Small wonder that the Negro, continually turned away from participation in the only real elections, and denied registration by "impartial" registrars, frequently made no effort to vote. In addition to these conditions, it was clearly brought home to even those Negroes who were still active in the most ineffective Republican party that they were not wanted in any political circles. This realization came with the adoption of lily-white policies by the party which has been traditionally regarded as the sole political hope of the black citizens of the South.

The severe rebuff given to the high hopes of Negroes in the period of reaction following Reconstruction led to disillusionment and ultimately to an attitude approaching resignation and fatalism. The last quarter of the nineteenth century was a period of decreasing political activity for Negroes, and black leaders sought to discover a new line and a new direction. This quickly took the form of a philosophy of conciliation, which involved a recognition of the supremacy of the dominant white population and of the inferior caste status of the Negro. The philosophy of the Negro in this period reveals itself as a somewhat strange admixture of futility and hope, and it was given its proper refinement through the lips of Booker T. Washington. The political aspirations of the Negro came to be regarded as chimerical, and he was directed to other channels of activity, such as the economic, in which he would be able through thrift, industry, and vocational skill to win for himself strength and respect in the community. The Negro reluctantly accepted his removal from political affairs and attempted to make the best of it.

Several exclusively Negro communities grew up in the South during this period. These were so uncommon, however, as to remain more or less freakish developments on the American scene, and their indifferent success has caused them to attract but slight attention. Perhaps their real significance is only to be found in the fact that there was no genuine encouragement for the creation of separate black communities by the white South. This might have been one form of compromise solution for the problem of interracial hostility.

The question might be raised as to why no more serious proposals were made for the repatriation of the Negro to Africa or his expatriation and settlement elsewhere. Why was there so much insistence on keeping the Negro in his place instead of thinking in terms of getting rid of him altogether, especially in view of the fact that he was no longer available to the South as slave labor but was thrown into competition with the Southern white worker in the open market? A good part of the explanation is to be found, of course, in the fact that the white worker who had to compete against the Negro had very little to say about Southern policy in this period, since politics was largely out of his hands. Those who controlled Southern politics were those who controlled the Southern land, and in their view the Negro was still very much needed if the cotton culture was to be preserved.

The thinking of the South in this period seems to have moved within an extremely narrow channel—simply that while the Negro must be "kept in his place" socially, politically, and economically, he should remain as an essential exploitable element in the Southern population. It might have been possible, in this era, to have created a separate Negro state or states, or to have set up separate black communities within white states, but it seems quite certain that any such proposals would have been vigorously opposed by those whites who held the political reins of the South.

THREE

Politics in the Contemporary South

POLITICALLY and economically the South is essentially an oligarchy. At no time in the region's history has the great mass of poor whites been articulate or influential. The voice of the South, as expressed through the Democratic party, has never truly represented any groups but the white middle and upper classes. The effective political control of the South has been in the hands of the large landholders, the bankers, and the powerful corporations. These are the groups that are responsible for the limited exercise of the franchise by both whites and blacks in the region and that profit from the position of strategic power which the South holds in national politics. These modern Bourbons have many influential representatives in the national government, including John N. Garner, Byron Patton Harrison, Harry Flood Byrd, and Carter Glass. The limited franchise in the South—the fact that so large a portion of the Southern white population itself is disfranchised—lends itself to oligarchical control. Legislators are largely subject to the will of these conservative influences, and this accounts for the fact that there is so little liberalism in Southern politics and so little progressivism in the field of social legislation.

In many counties in the South, politics are dominated by the few large landholding families. In other counties the dominating influence is the large corporations, the great mine operators, or the factory owners. In some instances these interests play a direct role in local politics; in others their influence is exerted indirectly. But in either case candidates are too often responsive to the will of the wealthy and the powerful few. In

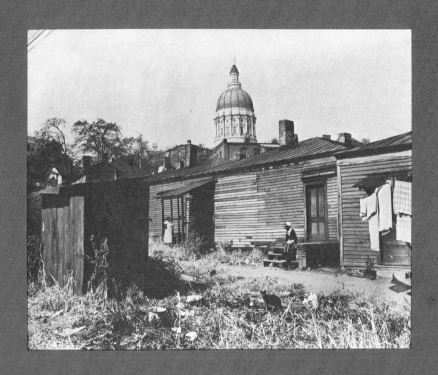

considering the controlling political and economic interests in the South, it is important to broaden the scope of our thinking to include the extent of Northern influence operative in the region. Speaking in economic terms, it may well be that the South is becoming a mere colony of the North. Certainly there is a vast amount of Northern capital invested in Southern enterprise and a great deal of absentee property-holding. It would be very revealing, I think, to make a searching inquiry of this kind. Northern competition and control operate through such concerns as the Georgia Power Company, the Tennessee Coal and Iron Company, and many of the public utilities, the banks, the railroads, the textile mills, and even the department stores and hotels. Such enterprises as the Georgia Power Company and the Coca Cola Company exert an important influence in Georgia politics under conditions made favorable by the various methods of limiting and controlling the franchise in that state, including the poll tax and the operation of the county unit system.

While on the subject of ruling interests in the South, I think it should be mentioned that an interesting study might be made of the influence of large corporations on race relations in the Southern region. For example, the Tennessee Coal and Iron Company in Birmingham, a subsidiary of United States Steel, has apparently engaged in rather crude attempts to keep the races divided. The company has made a vigorous appeal for Negro support through an organization known as the "Brotherhood"—a company union whose policy it is to attack the Congress of Industrial Organizations for "selling out on the Negro." A Negro newspaper in Birmingham has been subsidized by one of the large corporations, and its editorial policy has been devoted to an attempt to prejudice black workers against the activities of the CIO and to portray the subsidiary of the great corporation in a favorable light. Some effort needs to be made to determine whether the efforts of the unions in the South, especially the CIO and the tenant and sharecropper organizations, have done much to encourage the political participation of Negroes and poor whites and whether they have exerted much influence on such activities.

It would be easy to demonstrate the smallness of the vote in the Southern states, and I am convinced that, had we been able to make the analysis, it would have revealed that the vote in these states is confined largely to middle and upper class white groups. To an alarming degree, the white masses in the South are politically inert. Seldom in the states of the Deep South is more than 25 percent of the eligible electorate represented in any given election. Indeed, the outstanding characteristic of Southern political life is the very limited number of people who participate in it. Voting remains the privilege of the relative few, and this is true even when the Negro is left out of the calculation. Southern women seem slow to take advantage of the privilege afforded them by the Nineteenth Amendment, for reasons of indifference, inability to pay poll taxes, and a traditional attitude in the South that politics is not a woman's business.

In general, political processes in the South are loosely administered. There is often no real uniformity in practice, even within a given state, largely because of the unusual discretion vested in local officials and the amazing lack of supervision by the state agencies. In most instances the county official is virtually a law unto himself; his interpretation and application of the law determine its essential nature, and he is seldom challenged. All of this is decidedly true of the administration of the poll tax in the Southern states. The real basis for this chaotic condition in the political processes is to be found in the great decentralization of Southern politics, in the hegemony and power of the local "courthouse gangs," which rule over their county domains like feudal lords and whose leaders make a shameful and corrupt game out of the process of governing.

The most prominent feature of the administration of registration in the South is the amazingly loose and slipshod interpretation of the laws insofar as white registrants are concerned. The poll tax is a real burden on the white voters of the region, but the registrar is seldom an obstacle of any consequence. The registration officials are almost universally lenient and paternalistic toward the Southern white registrant. There would seem to be no good reason, barring the poll tax, why any white adult in the South—whether illiterate, feebleminded, or criminal—could not get on the registration lists and vote, if he so desired. Illiterates are commonly registered, and the registration officials often oblige by filling out the registration blanks and even signing the applicant's name, or permitting some third party to do so. In some instances absentee registration is permitted. There is scarcely ever any serious check on residence or age. In places where the law requires a statement of employment by the applicant, the provision is totally ignored. Unemployed persons, loafers, criminals—who are in some cases still serving terms—are registered, even where the laws of the state forbid it. Where character witnesses are required by state law —as in Alabama—the provision is ignored or openly scoffed at, since the registration official can "vouch" for the character of every white person in the county. The entire procedure, especially in the rural areas, is characterized by its extreme informality, its laxness, and its brazen disregard for the application of the law.

The poll tax requirement for voting in the Southern states makes a travesty of many of their elections. Political machines and individual candidates commonly buy votes by paying the poll taxes of those who will "vote right." This practice creates a large class of venal and mercenary voters who come to regard their ballot not as an instrument for the expression of one's political will, but as an article of commerce. The foundations of honest elections are thus undermined. Candidates without personal wealth or without machine backing usually have little chance in the elections, for the most effective way to get votes is to buy them. The amount of money expended in a given contest in some localities is controlled as if by a spigot: if the candidate for the particular office has serious competition, large sums of money will be used to pay up the poll taxes of supporters; if there is no opposition, or very little, no effort will be made to pay up the taxes. Thus, in a great many places there is a direct correlation between the intensity of election contests and the amount of poll taxes paid in. Yet it must always be kept in mind that there is no direct relationship between the extent of poll tax payments and voters' interest, since so much of the poll tax is paid up by interested third parties.

The fact that the Australian or secret ballot is so seldom employed in the South has made it possible for those who buy votes by paying poll taxes to check up on their investment. In most places in the South it is relatively easy to find out how a given person has voted. One of the most disgraceful by-products of the poll tax system in the region is found in the often large groups of hangers-on at the registration and polling places near election time who are waiting for an offer to have their poll taxes paid and their votes bought. A corps of habitual political panhandlers has been created throughout the South, a condition which must be considered a serious liability to democratic government.

The South is subjected to one-party government. It must be noted immediately, however, that this is not a one-party system on the fascist model, as some eager critics of the South loosely assume. For the Southern political system is highly decentralized and almost anarchistic. There is no dynamic and highly centralized political ideology in the South, whether democratic or totalitarian, nor is there even an efficient bureaucracy. The one-party system of the South expresses itself through the local political machines. These are the courthouse gangs, the county cliques, which are the main props of the Southern political structure as it exists today. The real venality of Southern politics is revealed in the operation of these gangs. Though they are technically subject to the controls of the county and state Democratic party committees, in their own domain they are generally supreme. By and large, they tend to make their own rules, and they are rarely well informed about the laws of the state that they are sworn to uphold. The men who sit in the seats of authority in the county courthouses of the Southern states are, on the whole, about as incompetent, provincial, and crude a company as can be found anywhere in the nation. In the courthouse gangs will be found the probate judges, the ordinaries, the county clerks, the registrars or members of the county registration committes or boards, the sheriffs, the beat committeemen, the members of the election committees, and the county Democratic party officers.

The county "rings" in the South are the units through which the state-wide machines operate. Politics with the courthouse cliques is largely a personal matter, and what factionalism there is results as much from personal rivalries as from conflicting issues. They are often corrupt, but their corruption is mainly in terms of petty graft. Politics is a game with them, and as a rule their garments of authority are worn loosely, except when it is necessary to put the black citizen in his place. The grip of the ring upon county politics is frequently so tight that even the Democratic primaries are mere gestures. Still, it should be pointed out that these county rings are sometimes subject to higher controls and exist at the pleasure of more powerful interests—large corporations, mill owners, or large planters. The very fact that voting is so limited in the South makes that section's politics unusually vulnerable to capture by those who possess great wealth. Other groups, such as the Ku Klux Klan and the American Legion, exert strong political pressure in some areas, while the church influence is strong throughout the Southern states.

The one-party system in the South is dictated by the presence of the Negro. The result is, of course, that the general elections are reduced to insignificance and party primaries become all-important. This means that it is impossible to have any real democratic process in the region, even for the white population, for the reason that the primaries revolve mainly about personalities rather than about issues. Thus the Southern electorate is inevitably less politically sagacious and well informed and more politically apathetic than that in any other section of the country. The South votes for men—Democratic men—but rarely ever for issues, unless the issue is defined in black and white.

The Democratic "white primary," operating under party rules stipulating that none but whites can vote in the party nominating contests, is enforced strictly in all of the Southern states except Kentucky and Tennessee and in a number of counties in Virginia and North Carolina. Thus, in the Southern states the Democratic party is, to all intents and purposes, the only political party insofar as state and local politics are concerned. In these states the nominations of the Democratic party for public office are virtual elections to office. The general elections are mere gestures. It is in these "white primary" states that the political rights of Negroes are sacrificed on the altar of white supremacy. The white primary has now become the most effective political instrument for the preservation of white supremacy and, therefore, the most effective device for the exclusion of Negroes from the polls in the South. The decision rendered by the United States Supreme Court in the third Texas primary case of *Grovey* v. *Townsend* (1935), upholding the use of the white primary in Texas, has given to this device a more or less definitive status. From these elections or primaries, Negro voters are barred either by a rule of the state or the local party organization. This disbarment generally takes the form of a declaration by the authorities of the Democratic party in each state that only white men and women are eligible for membership and are permitted to aid, through the primary elections, in the nomination of the party candidates. Since Negroes are denied the right of membership in the party and the privilege of participating in primaries, they are also excluded from all party proceedings, including conventions, caucuses, and mass meetings.

The origin of the white primary in the Southern states can be traced to the local or county party rules of the Democratic party which were common in the latter part of the nineteenth century as one means of excluding blacks from the old-fashioned precinct primary and from the newer type of local direct primary established by county rule for certain counties. It was only necessary to devise a local rule which would bar Negroes from participation in one or the other type of primary, since the state-wide and district party nominations would remain largely in the hands of state or district delegate conventions. In some instances, however, rules were adopted by state-wide party authorities. The early tendency was for the state not to concern itself with any of the rules for participation in party affairs and to regard these rules as purely party enactments. By the turn of the century, however, statutes were passed by state legislatures for the purpose of regulating party organization and activity. When the Southern states enacted state-wide mandatory or optional direct primary laws, which embraced more or less complete regulations governing the structure and activities of political parties and the requirements for participation in party primaries, the state party authorities in some states were recognized by law as retaining residual rule-making power supplementary to the statutory qualifications for party membership and for taking part in both the state-wide and local primary elections.

The main burden of Negro disfranchisement is borne by the traditional "one-party," "white-primary," "solid-South" states: Alabama, Georgia, Louisiana, Florida, Mississippi, Texas, South Carolina, and Arkansas. Here are found all of the ingenious devices for barring the black voter from the polls. Here are also found the frankest expressions of the determination to keep the ballot out of the hands of the Negro, by legal instrument if possible, by intimidation, terrorization, and force if necessary. The Negro issue is not kept out of politics, however, and the fear expressed is not a fear of Negro voting but of how the Negro might vote, or rather of how he might be voted, and by whom. But even in these states there is what may be called a token black vote and often a tendency to apologize for Negro exclusion from the real elections—the Democratic primaries —by insisting that the Negro is entitled to vote in the general elections. Only the most crass and hard-bitten will deny that the Negro should have this little privilege, even in these bastions of the Deep South.

While the Negro may exercise a very limited franchise in the South, his very presence is a dominating influence upon the region's politics. It is the Negro bogey that has frightened the South into its traditional devotion to a one-party system which is essentially the negation of democracy. The South—the white South—enjoys only a severely restricted democracy. Its range of democratic freedom in the realm of politics is always circumscribed by the self-imposed limitations of party choice. Only by blind loyalty to the Democratic party can the "Southern way" be preserved. Republicanism is heresy in the South, and the parties of the left are regarded as dire, revolutionary threats to Southern life. In no other section of the United States can such intense self-imposed political provincialism be found. The net result is a political naïveté and backwardness which leaves its indelible imprint upon regional affairs. The South pays a high price for its white supremacy in terms of a corrupt, undemocratic political system and extreme reaction in social legislation. In the final analysis, the nonvoting Negro remains the greatest single political influence in the Southern scene.

The Negro is often the essential vehicle of Southern politics. Though the "Negro issue" in any given campaign today is usually more imagined than real, it is a convenient handle for the campaign activities of many professional politicians in the South. The Southern mentality is receptive to "nigger-baiting," and so it becomes a legitimate instrument of political warfare in the region. There are many in the South today, however, who have grown wary of the Negro diversion. The South is slowly awakening to the fact that it has many problems that are immediately more pressing than its black one, and it is beginning to demand that its political representatives put all of their cards on the table at election time. In most places in the present South, the candidate must be "right" on more things than the Negro problem. Consequently, many campaigns are being pitched on a slightly higher level.

There are some "old-time" Negrophobe Democrats left, however, and they are unable to campaign within any other métier than that of the imminent black menace. Such regional stalwarts as J. Thomas Heflin, Coleman L. Blease, and James K. Vardaman set the pace for the political drumbeaters of racial hatred, and in Congress at the present time Ellison D. "Cotton Ed" Smith of South Carolina and Theodore G. "The Man" Bilbo of Mississippi are struggling manfully to preserve the traditional way. Bilbo is one of the most bombastic, but it is doubtful that any politician has ever been able to surpass "Cotton Ed" when he gets warmed up in the heat of a campaign back in the hills of South Carolina. Then, it is said, Senator Smith can really breathe fire on the Negro subject. His accounts of black brutes raping white women, presented to his breathless audiences with elaborate illustrations and his own picturesque sound effects, are considered masterpieces of emotional appeal and sure vote-getters—especially when the price of cotton is down.

Perhaps the most intensive use of the race issue in any recent Southern campaign was in the Smith-Hoover presidential struggle of 1928. In that contest both Republicans and Democrats in the South charged each other with "nigger-loving," and a flood of literature spread charges and countercharges over the region. The Southern press devoted a great deal of attention to this aspect of the campaign. In 1936 President and Mrs. Roosevelt came under the black cloud. Horror stories of the "capture" of the government by Jews and Negroes, of the Roosevelts accepting Negroes as social equals, were related, and pictures were printed of the President and his wife addressing Negro meetings, of them sitting on platforms with Negroes, and of Mrs. Roosevelt being "escorted" by black men. The Negro issue has also been prominently projected into the fight for poll tax reform in the South. It is always contended that repeal of the poll tax will lead to black domination.

The one-party system in the Southern states encourages the demagogues and incompetent lawmakers. The impression is widespread that the quality of Southern legislators by and large is of a very low order. I am convinced that this impression is quite justified. There is little evidence of any real statesmanship in the region, and it is notorious that the Southern governments are poorly, inefficiently, and frequently corruptly run. A careful appraisal of a group of Southern legislators, state and national, embracing their political records and histories, would provide documentary evidence of the quality of political leadership which the small-voting South cultivates. There is very little that can be done on the quality of contemporary Southern political leadership from secondary sources.

White Southerners employ many of the same defense mechanisms characteristic of the Negro. They often carry a "chip on the shoulder"; they indulge freely in self-commiseration; they rather typically, and in real Negro fashion, try to overcome a feeling of inferiority by exhibitionism, raucousness, flashiness in dress, and an exaggerated self-assertion. An air of belligerency, discreetly used when it can be done without risk, is one means of release for the individual who feels himself the underdog. A casual observation of the conduct of Southern lawmakers in the halls of Congress will be sufficient to demonstrate that Southern congressmen as a group are more abusive and indulge more in personalities and rough-and-tumble repartee than the legislators from any other section. What spice there is in the *Congressional Record* is furnished by Southerners, whether it be a Cole Blease, a Tom Heflin, or a "Cotton Ed" Smith delivering one of the notorious diatribes against the Negro (including a discourse on how permanent the Negro odor is), or a Huey P. Long giving one of his opponents a "dressing down" with enough insulting innuendo to have caused gun play in the old days (and, even today, enough to have gotten Huey's nose punched now and then, it was rumored). The Southerner is proficient, too, at conjuring up arguments to show how shabbily the South has been treated. Like the Negro, the white South holds out its hands for alms and special privilege.[1]

There are really only two ways of winning elections in the South. One way is to have the support of the big interests—the corporations, the landlords, and the investors—whose influence and power are so great that they can rarely be defeated. The other way is to win the vote of the poor whites and hillbillies by demagogic performances. In some instances, men like Hugo Black or Maury Maverick are able to gain election as independents, but not often. Since the elections hinge so much upon the contesting personalities in the Democratic primaries, it frequently happens that the individual who can harangue the loudest, who can arouse emotions best, who can put on the biggest show, or who can make the most fantastic promises wins the contest. Thus the South has produced some of the most notorious demagogues—men who stand for no principles, adhere to no political ethics, and aspire solely to power at whatever cost— in the history of American politics. It is inevitable that, under such conditions, the South should remain the strong seat of political reaction in the country, and that, despite its traditional allegiance to the Democratic party, it should produce those leaders within the party who are now trying to scuttle the progressive measures of their own party. It is readily admitted, even by many of the demagogues themselves in private conversation,

1. This paragraph is taken from Ralph J. Bunche's "Conceptions and Ideologies of the Negro Problem" (1940), pp. 71–72, one of the three other memoranda Bunche prepared for Gunnar Myrdal's use in writing *An American Dilemma*. The original typescript of this unpublished report, like the other Bunche memoranda, is located in the Schomburg Collection of the New York Public Library.—Ed.

that there is no longer any fear in the South of black domination. Yet the Negro issue is a handy one to fall back on, since it assures a ready response from the white masses. The irony of the situation is emphasized by the fact that there are many in the South who fear that if the black vote were released, it would fall prey to demagogues of the same stripe as those who now make political capital out of Negro-baiting.

Southern election campaigns retain much of the flavor of the "old days." There is a minimum of the subtle and sophisticated about them—they get down to the people and are a people's institution. They are supposed to provide entertainment as well as political education on the basis of which voters can later make their choices. They are occasions for "get-togethers." A Southern campaign "speaking" is a social event in most of the rural communities. Issues are never too important, but an ability to talk the language of the people, to appeal to them, to get them "worked up," is important to any candidate for office. Radio may be good enough for campaigning purposes above the Mason-Dixon line, but the Southern candidate still has to make the grand stump-speaking tours so characteristic of a more romantic age of American politics. Southern congressmen are notable for their lush oratory and extreme volubility. They have to be. They get plenty of practice in the hills and dales of the rural South. Music and liquor also play important roles in the more informal, intimate aspects of many Southern campaigns. Apparently firewater has as much appeal to the white Southern voter of today as it allegedly had for the black voter in the predisfranchisement days of the "black horror."

The Democratic "solid South" has always been a thorn in the Republican side. Here is an entire section of the nation where party politics is moot, where the issue is not between Republicans and Democrats but between Democratic candidates only. The Republicans have had no strong political roots in the region, except for the blacks who were willing to pay off in perpetuity the debt owed to the GOP for emancipation. Rarely are there any Republican primaries to vote in. Black Republicans cannot vote in the Democratic primaries, though white Republicans can—and do, quite generally. Thus, Republicanism in the South has largely reduced itself to a fight for control of party patronage when Republican presidents grace the White House. No Republicans, North or South, black or white, had any serious thoughts about making any Republican headway in the solid South—that is, not until the Hoover-Smith campaign of 1928.

Lily-whiteism in the South dates back further than 1928. A concerted movement had long been under way among white Republicans in the region to take control of the party organizations. This movement began to take rapid and effective shape in the 1920s. All it needed to complete its purge of the blacks was a nod from national headquarters. This it received with emphasis from Herbert Hoover in 1928. Hoover saw an opportunity successfully to invade the South in his campaign against Alfred E. Smith because Smith was remarkably vulnerable as Democratic candidates go. So Hoover Republicans were able to tilt with the Democrats on their own terms. The success of the Hoover invasion of the South in 1928 spelled the doom of the black influence in Southern Republican organizations. Lily-whiteism was given a great fillip, and today the Negro is largely on the fringe of Republican activity in the South. Perry Howard of Mississippi, the only remaining Negro national Republican committeeman, has alone been able to hang on. Patronage control is almost entirely in the hands of whites, and there are no longer any Republican "pickings" for the Southern Negro politician.

Partially because of Negro disgust with being "let-down" by the Republicans in this way and partially because of the attractive bread-and-butter appeal of Roosevelt Neal Dealism, the Southern black voter has deserted the Republican party in droves and now votes Democratic. Southern Negroes are finding that Southern white Democrats are no more forbidding than lily-white Republicans, and that actually there is more to be gotten out of the Democrats who control the South than could ever be hoped for from the Republicans. The shift required a difficult psychological adjustment for the black voter, who had long identified all of his troubles with the Democrats; but once made, it promises to be permanent. The Republicans find themselves confronted with a ticklish problem of strategy. The 1928 experience made a deep impression, but if Republican leaders repeat that experiment and endorse lily-whiteism in the South, they will run the risk of further offending the already sulking but strategic Negro vote in the North and West.

The lily-white Republican organizations in the South are usually small groups which have a very loose and informal existence. In most places they are held together by one man, whose interest is often dictated by his hopes for a trip to the national convention and a finger in the patronage pie when his party comes back in power. Rarely do Republican candidates appear on the ballot in the contests for local offices. It is only in the presidential elections that the existence of this minority political group is impressed upon the consciousness of the Southern communities. White Republicans follow their party allegiance only in the presidential elections; some of them have even won local offices as candidates in the Democratic primaries. Not a few Southern Republicans are ashamed to admit their party affiliation, for in many communities a white Republican is looked upon as something rather queer. But a few hardy souls come out bravely with it, even in the Deep South. It is rather difficult for a Republican to keep his heretical vote a secret in most Southern communities. It will be noted that in some places where the Republicans constitute a really threatening political minority, even the white Republicans encounter difficulties in getting fair treatment at the polls. Many Republicans think that repeal of the poll tax would be a boon to the GOP in the South.

The lily-white Republican movement in the South might actually be of some ultimate advantage to Negroes. That is, if the Republican party, as a white party, can attract to itself the large number of severe critics of the New Deal in the region, it may actually be an opening wedge for a two-party system in the Southern states. Ultimately, this would redound to the great political advantage of the Negro. There is some slight rumbling of this possibility in Georgia and other Southern states today.

For both historical and class reasons it would seem impossible for the Republican party to become a progressive force in the Southern region or to win a mass support. In the first place, the party is completely isolated from the white Southern masses in most parts of the region. The masses are in the Democratic party, and though that party is also largely controlled by business and landlord interests, the ordinary white voters are beginning to give evidence of a growing political consciousness and power that must be reckoned with in the future. This was demonstrated in the 1936 presidential election, when strong anti-Roosevelt forces were at work in the Southern Democracy; when the Roosevelts were widely smeared as "nigger-lovers"; when the Liberty League and other wealthy groups poured large sums into the South in an attempt to sell Alfred M. Landon with the slogan "Jeffersonian Democracy"; when many regular Democratic machines themselves were either tacitly opposed to Roosevelt or only lukewarm in his support. Yet those whites who were able to vote in the South gave the greatest vote ever for the Democratic ticket. In the second place, the Republican party in the South is completely identified with the wealthy banking, utility, and industrial interests and will never be able to command any mass following in the region under such labels. Finally, the GOP of the South has expressed very openly its contempt for the Negro and has deserted the one mass group that for historical reasons could give it loyalty.

It would be highly desirable to undertake a broad survey of the nature and extent of the newly developing economic and political liberalism in the South. This has not been possible in this memorandum, but I feel that we must call attention to this feature of the Southern scene, if for no other reason than that so many in the South today—whites and Negroes—bank so heavily on what this new liberal spirit will mean to general conditions in the region.

My own impression is that there is a tendency to exaggerate the importance of the new spirit of liberalism in the South, and to expect far too much of it. Yet this is undoubtedly one of the more promising trends in a section of the country so long identified with thoroughgoing reaction and provincialism. The new liberalism manifested by a still very limited group in the South is no revolutionary movement; but considering the soil in which it has had to take root, its very existence takes on the quality of a revolutionary break with Southern forms and traditions. The attitudes expressed by the Southern liberals of today are scarcely original with them. No one in the contemporary South is taking any stand that has not been taken in earlier periods, except, perhaps, the handful of Communists. Men like Governor Charles B. Aycock of North Carolina long ago covered most of the present liberal ground. But the point is that it is now safer and more respectable to utter such views. There have always been individuals in the South who were outspoken in their criticism of Southern practices and conditions. But these have been individuals. An emerging liberal force has recently begun to take formal and organizational shape. It has encouraged utterances and practices which could not have been made earlier. For example, in some of the white universities it has become rather common to have open and frank discussions of the Negro problem, and often with invited black speakers present. Interracial meetings are held in schools and public buildings. Liberal articles on the race problem are published by professors. The importance of the development of a liberal movement which makes its presence felt is the fact that it lends encouragement to the timid to do and say the things they have desired to do and say; it unshackles the large number of potential liberals who could not face the prospect of isolation and martyrdom in the community for holding more progressive ideas.

There are two main trends in the new liberalism of the South. One travels the road of interracialism in an effort through education and an appeal to Christian ethics to develop a new basis for understanding and tolerance between the races. The other concentrates upon the fundamental economic problems of the South and demands broad social and economic reforms as the solution to the ills of the long-suffering region. In some cases this new economic liberalism endorses fully the interracial approach; in other cases the tendency is to eliminate the Negro problem from immediate consideration as a mere concomitant of the broad economic dilemma of the South, which must be solved before progress in any other direction is possible. In still further instances, Southern economic liberalism finds itself unable to shake off the fetters of racial intolerance.

The dire racial problem of the South puts the liberal there to a severe trial. Quite understandably, he has a deep-seated emotional inheritance on the Negro question that cannot be easily overcome. There is a violent conflict between this emotional inheritance from the traditional regional background and the more rational demands of the newly-acquired liberal social philosophy. Even the most sincere liberal often finds it difficult quickly to revolutionize all of his habitual thinking on the racial question, and it is natural that he should frequently seek to escape from his psychological dilemma. Thus, there is a noticeable tendency for the Southern liberal to oversimplify the difficulties of solution and to brush the confounding Negro problem aside by adopting the matter-of-fact attitude that the race problem "will solve itself" whenever the South is able to solve its major economic problems. Or, to put it another way, there is no use in trying to do anything about the Negro problem until the South can work its way out of its economic morass. In other words, many Southern liberals of today resort to a kind of infantile economic determinism to which they ascribe magical qualities.

It is not without significance, however, that the contemporary Southern liberal can hold to his views and still retain respectability in the community—provided he does not get mired too deeply in the solution of the race problem. But once he gets smeared as a "nigger-lover," he loses caste quickly, and can no longer command respect for his opinions. All of his other liberal views on economic and political matters are then regarded merely as minor offshoots of his primary racial madness.

The Negro, on his part, allergic to the demagogic, white supremacy appeals, is quickly able to spot the Southern liberal, even when the individual retains a measure of anti-Negro bias. The Negro has come to realize that even a Democrat may be a "liberal"—and from the black point of view. Northern Democrats speak out boldly for Negro rights; Democrats of the border states tend to speak softly or to maintain a vague silence; while the Democrats of the Deep South, with only rare exceptions, employ traditional race demagogy. Even some of the New Deal liberals of the South have been guilty of this conformance with established political custom. This situation will change only with the growth of black and white unity in the labor organizations of the South, among tenant farmers, and ultimately within the Democratic party or some progressive offshoot of it—a unity that is found only in widely-scattered organizations and localities of the present South.

The new liberals of the South are coming from all walks of life. As yet, few have been recruited into the ranks of the professional politicians. But it is significant that a person holding broadly liberal views can win elective office in a section of the country that is still fighting the Civil War; that is still resentful and suspicious of "foreign ideas"; and that stubbornly clings to a political process which is fundamentally undemocratic for both white and black citizens. There have been only a few political liberals in the South in recent years; in this small band are included Justice Hugo Black; Mayor Maury Maverick of San Antonio, Texas; Senator Claude Pepper of Florida; attorney Brooks Hays of Arkansas; and the mildly liberal Lister Hill of Alabama, who succeeded Justice Black in the Senate and is finding it difficult to fill his shoes. These new political liberals have had to tread cautiously on the real question, lest they commit political suicide. The antilynching bill has been a particularly worrisome problem for them, and all of the elective liberals except Maverick have opposed it. Their explanation on such questions is that they are entirely and publicly liberal on those broad questions of economic policy which are of vital importance to Negroes as well as to whites in the South. They claim to be personally and privately liberal also on the Negro question, and may well be, but they argue that if they take a public stand on such matters they will only manufacture campaign weapons for their reactionary opponents, and that they will surely go down to defeat at the next election. Thus, they contend, they can do more good for the Negro in the South by keeping silent on the race issue, since Negroes will be much better off with representatives in Congress who work for progressive social legislation than with reactionaries there who are the lackeys of the vested interests.

The ranks of the newspaper editors have produced some of the outstanding new liberals of the South, and this is a particularly wholesome influence. These men, both big and small, are taking a much broader view of the region's problems. The columns of many Southern papers today give evidence of a deepening racial tolerance and a promising social consciousness. Many Southern newspapers now take a very advanced position on such questions as lynching, Southern justice, and Negro political participation, while manifesting a thoroughgoing progressivism on other regional problems, including the sharecroppers and unionization. Editors such as Virginius Dabney of Richmond, Jonathan Daniels of Raleigh, and Barry Bingham of Louisville are in the forefront of this development.

There is also a strong liberalism developing in some of the universities, including the University of North Carolina, which is far in advance of any other Southern educational institution in its progressivism. It is noteworthy that President Frank P. Graham of the University of North Carolina, a state institution, can serve as the head of the Southern Conference for Human Welfare, an organization of Southern liberals that has gone so far as to oppose racial segregation at its meetings. Perhaps the deepest significance of the conferences held by the SCHW is to be found elsewhere than in the adoption of resolutions. Its Civil Rights Committee, under the chairmanship of Maury Maverick, has conducted a vigorous educational campaign toward the elimination of the poll tax as a requirement for voting in the South. It has also had introduced into Congress the Geyer Anti-Poll Tax bill and has contested the constitutionality of the poll tax in its application to national elections in the courts. More important in any long-range view, perhaps, is the fact that these conferences have given Southern liberals for the first time a sense of solidarity and contact with one another. The conferences have also provided a long-needed national sounding board for the basic evils and problems of the South. It has given to the Southern Bourbon a solemn warning that the region can no longer be ruled in the traditional way without vigorous opposition.

Organizations such as the Coordinating Committee of the Citizens' Fact Finding Movement in Georgia carry on very useful educational work, particularly with regard to the political process. For example, in May 1938 the Coordinating Committee got out a pamphlet on the Georgia political system in which it attacked very courageously and intelligently the disfranchisement of one-third of the state's population—the black citizenry. In this publication it is pointed out that the Negro has been used in politics as a sort of club to hold the whites in line.[2]

Within such groups there is being created a broad reformist movement which covers all of the pressing problems of the South. Southern churches, too—especially the Methodist Episcopal Church, South—are playing an important role in this process. There are student interracial and liberal clubs. Led by the Southern Conference for Human Welfare, there is a strong bid being made for poll tax reform, and the schools are furnishing many supporters for the movement. There are numerous organizations throughout the South—and some of the most influential of them are women's groups—which are strongly on record against lynching. And there are authors such as Erskine Caldwell, Paul Green, William Faulkner, and T. S. Stribling who in their novels are boldly exposing and attacking the harsh aspects of Southern life. These are all influences of vital import to Southern thinking of the future, though their full effect will not be felt for years to come.

Nevertheless, there remains a more than ample portion of regional chauvinism among the Southern liberals. There is a great pride in the Southern culture even in liberal ranks. Many Southern liberals are still fighting a cultural war between the states. And, above all, it is important to realize that the liberals are still a lonely company in the South.

It cannot be doubted that the South does exercise political

2. This paragraph and part of the preceding one come from Ralph J. Bunche, "The Programs, Ideologies, Tactics and Achievements of Negro Betterment and Interracial Organizations" (1940), pp. 682–83, 704—another of the unpublished memoranda which Bunche prepared for Myrdal's *An American Dilemma.*—Ed.

influence in national affairs out of all proportion to its electorate. Even leaving the Negro out of consideration, the number of Southern voters is small in comparison with the voters in other sections of the country. Moreover, because of the relative ease in winning reelection, Southern members of Congress tend to hold positions of seniority. Since committee assignments are based upon seniority, it happens that, when the Democratic party is in power, most of the important posts on the strategic committees are held by Southerners. Even when the Democrats are not in power, the Southern reactionary leadership holds the strategic positions in the opposition. It is indeed a contradiction, which can be explained only in terms of the unusual stress of the 1930s, that the Democratic party was able to produce even a mildly progressive legislative program. It is attributable both to the astute and liberal leadership of President Roosevelt and to the severe crisis of the period that the most progressive legislative program in the nation's history should have been the contribution of that party in which the traditionally reactionary leadership of the South plays such an important role.

No one can prophesy what the future of the South holds. One might indulge in a bit of speculation as to what direction the future economic development of the region will take and what effect this will have upon the future political and economic status of the Negro there. Certainly there is the possibility that increasing industrialization in the South will lead to more and more class consciousness among Southern workers—both white and black—and that thus will be sown those seeds of factionalism and division that will ultimately smash the one-party system. There is no doubt that many in the South, including some influential congressional leaders, fear the breakup of the one-party system in the imminent future. They have no doubt that the class struggle is gaining rapid momentum in the South, and that this process will be accelerated as the working population moves from the rural areas to the industrial centers, and as the tenant farmers and sharecroppers, especially in the Southeast, find it increasingly difficult to maintain even their lowly status on the land. Whether or not the present efforts to include the Negro in the organizational activities of labor in the South succeed, it would seem certain that so long as the region retains its present political structure and continues even to pay lip service to its Democratic ideals, Negroes would gain from this tendency, if only as a result of contact with its backwash.

It would seem equally certain, however, that the ruling

classes of the South, whose vested interests are in the status quo, are not going to sit idly by and permit the work of labor organizers to engulf them in the real revolutionary possibility in the South—that of solidarity between white and black workers. It can be taken for granted that the ruling classes will employ the race issue and all other issues for all they are worth, and it may well follow that the racial situation will become increasingly disturbed in the Southern region and that the Negro may even lose what little political status he now has. Moreover, considering the present racial mores of the South, it must be assumed that, even if organized labor makes giant strides throughout the Southern states, it would only be after intensive union-fostered educational efforts among the workers that one could visualize the possibility of any large band of white workers in the South extending the hand of political brotherhood to their black fellow workers.

FOUR

Restrictions on Voting in the South

THE disfranchising devices employed in the South should be treated both historically and in terms of their present operation and effect. Attention should be devoted to such measures as the grandfather clause (which was finally outlawed by the Supreme Court); the white primaries (including the decisions in the Texas primary cases); the peculiar arrangement that exists in the ward clubs of South Carolina; the constitutional clauses, with their weird interpretations and variations; the character-witness requirements and their varied usage, especially in Alabama; property tests; disqualifying crimes; residence requirements; and the arbitrary requirement with respect to filling in application blanks accurately, including the "age trick" in Louisiana. Note must also be made of the exemption clauses, their effects upon Negro and white groups, and the use of alternatives. The analysis would not be complete if some attention were not given to intimidation and other extralegal methods of barring blacks from the polls. All of these aspects of Southern politics are revealed in the various chapters of part 2 of this memorandum. An effort is made to give a general picture of the Southern political process as it impinges upon the Negro, with particular attention to the looseness in the administration of registration and voting laws when applied to whites as against the rigid and severe application of the same laws to Negroes.

The registrars generally interpret the law for themselves. The result is a lax and easygoing attitude toward white registrants. In one state it is required that all members of the registration board be present when a registrant is accepted, but this is observed in the breach rather than the practice, and it is generally laughed at by the board members. It is a widespread practice for registrars to make out the applications for their white registrants "in order to save time" and also to save many illiterate whites from embarrassment. Literacy or constitutional interpretation tests are seldom administered to white registrants, though these tests are often given in most severe form to Negro applicants. Purging of the registration lists is generally a purely hit-or-miss affair, and in some counties little or no purging is done, even for crime. In some instances the names of people serving terms for felonies are kept on the lists by registrars who wish to avoid "having trouble" with these people when they are returned to society and wish to resume their citizenship privileges. Yet even prominent Negroes in the same community are registered, if at all, only through the indulgence of the registrar.

The members of the boards of registrars are themselves very mediocre people. In many cases they are barely literate. They know little or nothing about the law they are to administer, and for the most part take their responsibilities very lightly except when they are "troubled" by Negro applicants. In the rural areas they are usually people who have done some campaigning for the "right person." In big-city counties such as Jefferson, Alabama, where Birmingham is located, the chairman of the board of registrars will usually be a professional politician.

The registration procedure for white applicants is usually simpler in practice than is required by law. In many instances it is not even necessary for a person to sign his or her own name. It is rare that any white applicant is turned down, except perhaps in a large city such as New Orleans, where the administration of the law is more impersonal. In some cases white applicants may be rejected because they are thought not to be likely to "vote right." But, in general, Southern registration is no ordeal for whites.

Perhaps the greatest complication is the registration periods, which are fixed by law and, in such states as Alabama, technically come only at scattered intervals. But these provisions are not infrequently ignored, and, moreover, the registrars are often required to make things convenient for the registrants by going on circuit, as in Alabama, thus taking the registration books to the people. On the whole, however, the people take little advantage of this service, both because of lack of sufficient notice and because they prefer to use the occasion of registration as another excuse for paying a visit to the county seat.

The lack of any close check on the transfer of voters from one county to another frequently makes it possible for a person to cast ballots in two or more counties. This is now possible in Georgia, largely because of the indifference and inefficiency of the county registration officials. South Carolina has perhaps the most complicated registration system, since there are not only separate registration requirements for city, county, and school trustee elections, but also for participation in the Democratic primary. This last is provided for through "enrollment" in the Democratic ward or precinct clubs, which is merely a matter of signing the enrollment book, or having someone sign one's name in it. The so-called clubs are mere shadow organizations whose officers are responsible for the local enrollment books and for selecting delegates to the county Democratic conventions.

At one time the tendency was rather general in the South to apply the voting qualification tests—literacy and constitutional interpretation—to all applicants. Thousands of whites who could not slip under the wire by meeting such requirements, even when leniently applied, were enfranchised by a clever device employed in one form or another by most Southern states —the "grandfather clause." This provided that any man, or the descendant of any man, who had served in one of a number of specified wars (or, in some states, who had been a voter before 1867) was eligible to register and vote. This was a remarkable instrument, cut exactly to the South's needs, since it kept out Negroes and admitted even the most backward and illiterate whites. It was not difficult for any Southern white to dig up some kind of a soldier ancestor. The Supreme Court eventually declared the grandfather clause unconstitutional, and the South has now adopted the simple expedient of providing alternative methods of qualifying. But in the administration of the laws, the qualification tests are applied to Negroes only.

The registration of Negroes in some places in the South, even in the Deep South, is permitted without much difficulty, unless too many blacks present themselves during any given period. The white primary effectively prevents them from casting any real vote and there is often no serious objection by local whites to a token Negro vote in the general elections. This is not considered "dangerous."

No one knows how many of the approximately nine million Negroes in the Southern states are registered to vote. The number is more than it was a year ago, two years ago, or five years ago, but the increase has been slow. And in one instance a sudden increase of black voters brought threats of violence. But that was in Miami, Florida, in the most Southern of the "Dixie" states, which is at the same time the most overrun with Northerners. Typical Deep South states like Alabama, Georgia, South Carolina, and Mississippi have had slight trouble on this score because the number of Negroes registered there is negligible. (Yet Greenville, South Carolina, had a "Negro scare" last year.) Those Negroes who do register in these states are barred from participation in practically all elections that amount to anything. To a great extent, the ability of Negroes to get registered in any particular locality in the South depends upon the attitude of local registrars. A given registrar may be much more favorably disposed toward black registration than his predecessor or his successor. The general tendency, however, is for all Southern registrars to oppose wholesale Negro registration.

We can be quite sure that, if we except a few large cities such as Memphis, there is no large registration of Negroes in the South. But it is virtually impossible to say just how many Negroes are registered voters below the Mason-Dixon line. The only way to get an accurate estimate in any given county in the region would be to go to the courthouse and count the Negro names on the registration books. Even this might not be entirely accurate, for it has been found that these books are very carelessly kept. In some few instances, George Stoney even discovered that the telltale "colored" appeared after the names of white people in the registration records. The estimates given by the various county officials are often at wide variance, despite the fact that the number of Negro registrants is never large.

Negro efforts to be registered are usually described by the registration officials in the South as "trouble." Most of the officials simply take it for granted that black applicants ought to be rejected. All sorts of handy rationalizations are available to support this view. The registrars are also generally able to make very fine distinctions between the "types" of Negroes who present themselves, often admitting that certain of the "better class" blacks ought to be put on the books. There is a much better chance that a "big" local Negro will get on the registration lists than for a common, obscure Negro to succeed.

The basis for the decision of the registrar, with regard to Negro registration, is frequently explained in terms of how "the white people in the county feel about it." Often it is enough to justify rejection in the minds of the officials to explain that the people in the county—meaning the white people—

"wouldn't stand for it." Some Southern registrars are very boastful about the discretionary power vested in their office, and one went so far as to boast that he had it within his power to keep the President of the United States from registering if he should choose to do so. It will be noted, in going through the excerpts from the field notes, that Southern election and tax officials frequently prove to be very inconsistent in their statements, making one assertion to one interviewer and a contradictory one to another. Not infrequently the contradictory statements are made to the same interviewer.

The social situation and mores of the South create an atmosphere of essential intimidation for the Negro registrant who presents himself to what must always be presumed to be hostile officials—not to mention the fact that he or she must often run the horrible gauntlet of the leering hangers-on who habitually loaf about the courthouse offices in the Southern county seats. The very attitude of hostility manifested by the white population in many Southern communities is itself an intimidating factor operating to discourage Negroes from applying for registration or seeking to go to the polls.

Sometimes the registrars go to elaborate extremes in order to work out means of rejecting Negro applicants for registration. Lawyers are consulted in order to draw up lists of questions designed to make it possible "legally" to reject black applicants. The requirement that the registrant must produce two responsible character witnesses or endorsers, as in Alabama, is an effective means of limiting Negro registration. This qualification becomes extremely difficult when, by interpretation of the local officials, the Negro applicant is required to produce two white endorsers. It is also a simple matter for the white registrars to tell Negro applicants that the registration blanks have "given out," that it is "closing time," or that one or another member of the board is not present. In some instances the Negro applicant is told to fill out his blank and to file it, and that he will be notified when to come for an examination. Unless he happens to be a prominent Negro, no such notice is ever received.

There are many humiliations connected with registration, even when the Negro applicant has reason to believe that he will not be rejected. Frequently he will have to wait until all white applicants have been attended to. He may be insulted when spoken to by the officials, and he may have to listen to the intentional taunts of officials, clerks, and bystanders. He may be told several times to come back. The registrars customarily make favorable "presumptions" on behalf of white registrants, as, for example, with respect to the Alabama property requirement, while applying the provisions of the law quite strictly to Negro applicants. The same is true of literacy and constitutional interpretation tests.

Southern registration officials commonly explain the amazing absence of Negro names from the registration rolls by stating that blacks "just don't care to register." In many respects this is true. In the first place, Negroes are intimidated, afraid to step out of their "place," and reluctant to face the hostility of the registration office. In the second place, they realize that registration which permits voting only in the general elections is an empty gesture. In the third place, they can ill afford to pay the poll tax, and when they can afford it, they are not eager to pay out money for a meaningless privilege. The only true test of Negro voting interest in the South would be the Negro's attitude if an opportunity to vote in the Democratic primaries presented itself. Because of the significance of the white primary to Southern politics, it is customary for a great many Negroes in the South, even though extended the privilege of registration —which permits them to vote only in the general elections or, in some instances, in local elections—to take the attitude of "what's the use?" In those places where Negroes are allowed to register without much hindrance, it is difficult to say whether the absence of obstacles is due to the fact that few Negroes present themselves because of their indifference toward voting in the general election, or whether it is to be accounted for by the fact that the whites are willing to permit Negroes to register for such elections in the knowledge that the white primary will prevent them from playing any significant role in politics.

In some instances Southern registrars disclaim any intention to discriminate against Negro applicants, and insist that Negroes are treated in quite the same manner as whites. In a great many cases, however, the registrars frankly admit that differential treatment is given Negro applicants and that it is their intent, and the desire of the white community—a desire that they are more than eager to translate into action—to keep any large number of Negro registrants off the books. All sorts of technicalities are invoked to disqualify black applicants. It is frequently made clear that the Negro ought to have "better sense" than to try to register in such a hostile environment.

Those God-fearing Southerners who tremble at the trend toward increasing recognition of the Negro's political rights will take any doubting Thomas to North Carolina's magnificent capitol building in Raleigh and point knowingly to nicks in the marble steps. The places were chipped out, they will explain, by liquor kegs which the boisterous Negro legislators of Reconstruction days rolled down the steps. It is intimated that some of the legislators rolled down too, but whether they left any nicks is not recorded. Some of the stories enthusiastically related by the old-time politicians in the South, who claim to have engaged in "nigger vote buying" and "nigger vote stealing" in the "old days," are lewd and exciting. These men like to tell of the fights that broke out over the attempts to steal the "nigger vote," of how their black votes were bought with liquor and women, and of how they led the Negro voters along with music like the Pied Piper of Hamlin. High-jacking the other man's black voters was a vital part of this process. It is not uncommon to find Negroes in the South who accept the white man's picture of the horror of Negro domination during Reconstruction days and after, and who point, as the whites do, to the abuse of the ballot by the Negroes in this period as the explanation of black disfranchisement today.

Some Southern officials contend rather ludicrously that "clean government" in the South dates from the disfranchisement of the Negro and that the disbarment of blacks from the polls remains essential to the continuance of pure politics in the region. Some Southern election officers, however, are sometimes frank and honest enough to state that the way in which Negroes were "bought up" in the days before Negro disfranchisement is not a bit worse than the way in which white votes are bought up by poll tax payments today. Some go so far as to say that the buying up of votes today is much more flagrant.

Fraud in elections is an evil familiar to politics throughout the country. But the South, with characteristic ingenuity, has contributed some picturesque touches peculiarly its own. Votes are controlled and checked by registration slips, the "chain letter" system, vote buying, poll tax payment, double voting, vote stealing, "counting out" unfortunate candidates, employment of "agents" to sign up voters, and many variations of these methods. Whether or not all of the stories that one hears about vote stealing and "counting out" candidates in the South are true, they are told regularly enough, and by enough responsible people, to have some element of validity.

The number and power of black voters in the South is generally exaggerated fantastically, and stories of the "hundreds" or "thousands" of Negroes who are voting in one place or another go the rounds and are recounted daily among the ranks of the courthouse fence-sitters and tobacco juice–spitters. In the eight most hard-bitten anti-Negro-vote states—Alabama, Arkansas, Florida, Georgia, Louisiana, Mississippi, South Carolina, and Texas—there are certainly never more than 80,000 to 90,000 Negro votes cast, at a liberal estimate, and scarcely any of these are cast in the Democratic primaries. If the milder "border" states of Virginia, North Carolina, and Tennessee are included, another 100,000 to 115,000 black votes would be added. But the sum total of the Negro vote would be but a drop in the po-litical bucket even for these eleven small-voting states, eight of which are still poll-tax-ridden. Negroes constitute only 25 per-cent of the population of Arkansas, and though they are a ma-jority in not a single congressional district of that state, the threat of black political domination was employed effectively there to aid in the defeat of the poll tax reform movement. Louisiana did away with the poll tax requirement, and yet less than 1 percent of its Negro population votes. North Carolina has not had the poll tax requirement since 1920, and yet only a rela-tive handful (not over 50,000 by the most liberal estimate) of the Negroes in the state vote. Not many more than 1,500 Ne-groes voted in 1936 in the entire state of Alabama, despite the fact that some 18,000 Negro veterans are included in the state's blanket exemption of World War veterans from poll tax payment.

Perhaps the most effective of the special devices employed against Negroes is the literacy test—a test that is seldom ap-plied to white registrants. Negro electors are required to "read, write, and explain" any passage of the state or federal constitu-tion which the registrar may select—and to the satisfaction of the registrar. Since the registrar is the sole arbiter, any Negro can be disqualified, no matter what his training or knowledge may be. Negro college professors, some of them in Virginia, have been turned away from the polls under this procedure. The hopeful Negro applicant may be required to go out and get some responsible white man who will be willing to come in and vouch for him. This often means that unless a Negro has won a local reputation among the "responsible whites" for his timidity, tractability, humility, and general Uncle-Tomishness, it will be impossible for him to think of casting a ballot. If all else fails, the Southern community can always rely upon the very effec-tive instrument of intimidation. Usually, it would be enough to inform the individual Negro that the white community would not "think well" of his efforts to vote, or that it would not be "healthy" for him to attempt it. In some instances, as in Miami, the Negro population, under able organizational leadership, has refused to be intimidated and has thrown the challenge back into the teeth of such organizations as the Ku Klux Klan, which have tried to frighten Negroes away from the polls.

Emphatic notice must be taken of the insistently uttered "fear" of the white South at the possible consequences of Negro voting. When analyzed, this is found to be not a fear of Negro political domination through exercise of the ballot, but rather a fear, held by the "in" groups, that the black vote—that is, the Negro tenants on the plantations and the Negro employees in the mills and factories—would be used by the "outs" to bring about a shift in political power and control. Most of those we talked with in our interviews expressed the view that the white South is now in position to "take care of" the Negro handily enough and that there would be no valid fear of an independent Negro vote. Thus the fear is not one of black domination at all, but a fear of rival white domination, in a political game in which the Negro voter is only a pawn.

Among Southern officials the feeling is found, quite in accord with the well-established stereotypes, that the Negroes' efforts to vote are largely the result of the influence of "uppity" Negroes from the North. The attitude often expressed is that local Negroes would have better sense than to try. In other instances "Northern radical organizations," such as the NAACP, are charged with the responsibility for stirring up blacks and putting false notions in their heads. The conviction often seems great that the local Negroes, left alone, are quite content with things as they are and have no desire to bother with politics.

It is common to hear responsible white Southerners point to Memphis as a horrible example of what would happen if the Negro is given the vote in the South. They argue that the Negro is too poor and too ignorant to exercise the ballot intelligently and independently, and that he would be preyed upon by venal political machines. If pressed, some of them will go so far as to admit that the same argument applies to the poor whites in the South, and not a few of them really feel that the region would be better off if lower class whites also did not vote. A few are frank enough to admit that they are against the repeal of the poll tax for just this reason. Some Southern politicians are quite pragmatic on the question of Negro voting. Their sole objection to the enfranchisement of the Negro, they admit, is that it would increase the size of the electorate and thus make it more expensive for a candidate to get elected or for a machine to perpetuate itself in power, since there would be black as well as white votes to be bought. The objection of many politicians to the repeal of the poll tax is pitched on the same level.

Not infrequently there is violent contrast between the attitudes of officials in the same county toward the Negro vote. This is the case, for instance, in Macon County, Alabama, where Tuskegee Institute and the Negro Veterans' Hospital are located. Whites in the South often explain that, where there is resentment toward black registration and voting, Negroes do not attempt it for fear that they will stir up racial animosity in the community and that this will affect them injuriously in other ways. This is undoubtedly true, and it follows a well-established pattern used as a guide by many members of minority groups. The pattern is that rights and privileges should never be *demanded,* and may even be refused by minority groups when such action might intensify racial feeling.

The subject of the poll tax, if treated at all comprehensively, would constitute a large study in itself. An attempt is made here only to undertake an analysis of the poll tax in those states where it is retained as a qualification for voting, primarily in terms of its practical operations and its broad social implications for both whites and blacks.

Historically, the poll tax has long been in use in the United States—though not essentially as a voting requirement, except for a brief period at the beginning of the nineteenth century— and since the 1890s in the South. The tax, employed exclusively as a revenue measure, is still found in some of our Northern states, but it is to the eight Southern "poll tax" states where it is related to voting that our attention will be focused. Greatest emphasis must necessarily be given to the effect of the tax on the poor whites of the South. There is reason to suspect that the poll tax, as a voting qualification, was instituted not only with the intention of disfranchising the Negro, but with the conscious purpose of limiting the power of that great mass of poor whites which threatened the hegemony of the Southern ruling classes. As a result of the vigorous campaigns to abolish the poll tax in recent years, led by such organizations as the Southern Conference for Human Welfare, there is a considerable amount of data now becoming available concerning the effect of the tax upon the white population of the South.

The poll tax problem is closely tied up with the problem of machine politics. In the poll tax states, the machines regularly and frequently buy up votes by paying the poll taxes of the voters, and there are unquestionably many white people in the South who have voted regularly but have rarely paid their own tax. Since great numbers of the potential voters in the poll tax states are unable to pay their own taxes because of their low income, the political machines and the politicians who run them have the local voting situation well in hand, and need pay the tax only for enough voters to control the election. The cumulative feature of the tax in some states is particularly burdensome upon the voter, and there are instances of people who have had to pay thirty or forty dollars or more in order to be eligible to vote. There are other cases in which politicians have bought up blocks of poll tax receipts in advance and distributed them to their cohorts during the registration or election periods.

It is not unusual in the poll tax states for factories, and especially textile mills, to urge their employees to pay the poll tax, register, and vote. In some cases there have been deliberate efforts on the part of the mill managements to influence or even control the votes of their employees. Unless union organization is well entrenched, ordinarily a "suggestion" on how to vote from the foreman is enough to intimidate the workers. In some instances the companies have gone so far as to employ the check-off system in order to make certain that their workers are paid up. This practice is always explained as being done in behalf of the employee, who may thus reimburse the company in installments.

The poll tax, as a device for the perpetuation of a political machine, is closely linked with vice rings. This is to be expected, since the local political machines and the vice rings so often work hand in glove. Thus, the poll tax is a fertile source of corruption, political and otherwise. In a few cases this unwholesome product of the poll tax requirement has been exposed, notably in Hot Springs, Arkansas.

The poll tax in the South also has a direct bearing upon the election of delegates to the presidential nominating conventions. Only recently it was revealed that complaints had been made to the Senate Special Elections Committee concerning the nuisance of poll tax payments in connection with the naming of delegates to the national convention. How important this is in the national political process is demonstrated by the fact that Senator Robert A. Taft, when seeking the Republican nomination for the presidency, consistently refused to run in any of the states in which preferential primary elections for the presidential conventions were held, but chose to work industriously to "line up" the Republican delegations from the Southern states. The votes of these Southern Republican delegations— most of which are now completely lily-white—can be readily bought.

There are suggestions of a suspicious relationship between payment of the poll tax and Works Progress Administration employment in some parts of the South. Our field note materials have indicated that, in some places at least, local WPA officials have applied pressure to induce WPA employees to pay the tax and presumably to "vote right" in the forthcoming election. Data to prove a case of this wind is lacking, but it is certainly a question that can be seriously raised. In connection with this, it must be pointed out that there is virtually no such thing as the secret ballot in a great many Southern elections.

The poll tax requirement keeps the electorate small, and a small electorate is easily dominated by vested interests which are desirous always of maintaining the status quo. South Carolina, which is at present none too ably represented by Senator "Cotton Ed" Smith, has sent as little as 6.1 percent of its population to the polls to vote. The Southern demagogue has learned well the trick of posing as the plain and simple representative of "the people" while actually representing the entrenched interests of wealth and political power which alone are responsible for putting him in office. It is not without significance, also, that in spite of the much heralded fact that poll tax revenues are turned into educational channels, the poll tax states rank among the lowest in the nation in education. No other states are so backward with respect to social legislation as these Southern states. This is entirely understandable in view of the fact that the common men—the very people whose interests would be served by social legislation, by laws to protect labor, the sharecropper, and the tenant farmer—are precisely the people who find it most difficult to spare the money for the poll tax, and who are thus involuntarily disfranchised.

The poll tax is, of course, an additional barrier to the exercise of the franchise by Negroes in the South. It is not the only barrier, nor is it the most significant. Yet in most Southern states it imposes a discouraging burden on the use of the ballot in the only elections in which any appreciable number of Negroes are permitted to vote, that is, the general elections. But the general elections are ordinarily mere gestures in the South, and so depriving the Negro of the right to vote in these elections is not, under present political conditions in the region, depriving him of very much. It is something more than a mere catch-phrase to say of the South and its poll tax provisions that it is the registrar —and the Democratic party officials who set the qualifications for voting in the primary—who disfranchises the Negro, while the tax collector disfranchises the (poor) white man. Indeed, the fact that the poll tax can be employed to keep "undesirable" white voters from the polls is cited by many as a strong argument in favor of its retention. One of the most specious and cruel contentions is that which claims that one's willingness to pay a one or two dollar poll tax in order to vote is a sound test of good citizenship. Those who take this position in the face of known economic poverty of the South's millions willingly evade the question of ability to pay.

There is no fair test possible today of the political interest of the mass population of the South. It is quite impossible to gauge the relative interest or indifference of this population, both black and white, for the obvious reason that many thousands of voters in the Southern poll tax states are utterly unable to get their hands on the necessary cash with which to pay the tax. Thousands of others, who do handle some cash during the poll tax season, are simply unable to spare enough to pay the tax without cruel deprivation. In many families no member is "paid up"; in others one member, usually the head of the household, is or has at some time been paid up, but it cannot be afforded for the other members. It is a rare family of ordinary means in the Southern states in which multiple voting is found, except where interested third parties oblige by paying the taxes for them.

Certainly the poll tax disfranchises immeasurably more whites than blacks. For it is the poll tax alone that keeps the great masses of white voters from the polls, while the black voter is denied the satisfaction of casting even a bought vote (except in a few cities like Memphis, where the Negro vote is herded and voted by the political machine). Thus, for the most part, the Negro voter is spared the dubious pleasure of sharing in the political corruption so characteristic of the poll tax South.

Yet the Negro has a deep political interest in the abolition of the poll tax provisions. Not only would this promise the possibility of more liberal and enlightened state administrations and lawmakers in the South, through the enfranchisement of the masses of underprivileged whites, it would also promise to break the fatal grip which the small group of white Bourbons and their venal political henchmen have on the political and economic life of the region. The enfranchisement of the white masses would almost inevitably lead to the development of a vigorous and ultimately healthy political factionalism which would end the shameful one-party system. This would with equal certainty lead to the extension of the suffrage to Negroes. Wherever factionalism has developed among white Democrats (as in some counties in Texas), the Negro, even under existing conditions, has been invited to the polls, even to the extent of participation in the Democratic primaries.

Whatever the intent may be, it is easily demonstrable that the poll tax is not, in practice, a test of fitness for voting. It is a serious obstacle to the poor but honest voter, while the venal and unprincipled voter has easy access to the polls because his tax is paid for him. This is true in all of the poll tax states today, and statutes directed against such practices have proved ineffective. In Arkansas, Georgia, Tennessee, Texas, and Virginia, there is ample evidence of the common practice of selling poll tax receipts in blank and in block to fictitious persons or to agents, later to be distributed and used by or on behalf of the dishonest voter.

In spirit the poll tax laws are essentially suffrage laws. In the process of linking the poll tax payment with the vote, all of the poll tax states have enacted a number of statutes which have no ascertainable relationship to the collection of revenue, and which seem to have transformed the tax into a device for the disfranchisement of hundreds of thousands of voters of both races. In the assessment and collection of the tax, certain practices must be considered as especially significant. In the first place, it should be noted that it is quite usual in the South for those responsible for the collection of the tax to speak of it not in terms of its collection, but rather in terms of "selling" poll taxes. Bills for the tax, once it has been assessed, are sent out only in Arkansas and Texas, and, in some instances, in Virginia after three years.

On the basis of returns from questionnaires sent to the appropriate fiscal officer in each of the poll tax states, it must be concluded that the assessment of poll taxes—as officially reported—is made only against a very small proportion of the citizens in the age group liable. Strict enforcement provisions are retained on the statute books of Georgia, yet assessment of the poll tax is made against only about one-third of the assessable population, and collection is made from an even lower percentage. The significance of the poll tax requirement to the voting of women is interesting. In some states, such as Georgia and Arkansas, it would appear that women are given an especial inducement *not* to vote, since the law does not hold them liable for payment of the tax until they present themselves as voters. In Alabama, those women who do vote are held liable for payment of the tax only for the years since 1920. The close connection between poll tax payment and voting is demonstrated in the correlation it is possible to make between the varying interest in elections and the violent fluctuations in the amount of poll taxes collected. A valuable statistical analysis of this aspect of the problem could well be made, though I have been unable to tackle it.

It should be emphasized that the poll tax states do not enforce collection of the levies and that it is really a voluntary payment rather than a tax. Thus, the receipts from the poll tax in the eight Southern states requiring it as a prerequisite for voting are far below what they would otherwise be were it a capitation tax with enforced collection. The official figures on state suffrage tax receipts for 1936 are given as follows: Alabama, $306,675; Arkansas, $300,631; Georgia, $289,976; South Carolina, $255,419; Tennessee, $655,470; Texas, $1,685,244; and Virginia, $810,481. The figures for Mississippi were not available. The figures on poll tax collections indicate clearly enough that it constitutes both a small and a very uncertain portion of the revenues available to the public schools.

The two arguments most frequently encountered in support of retention of the poll tax as a qualification for voting in the Southern states are: (1) its abolition would lead to the undermining of white supremacy and bring on an immediate threat of Negro political domination; and (2) its abolition would lead to loss of revenue for the schools. When the fight to repeal the poll tax in Arkansas reached the legislature of that state in 1938, the specious threat of black domination was used effectively to defeat the repeal attempt. The front pages of Arkansas newspapers carried editorials warning of the black horror that would be visited upon the state if the poll tax qualification were abolished.

Yet there is, in fact, no basis at all for this argument. In the first place, those states which have the poll tax qualification for voting are also the states which, for the most part, have the closed, or "white," primary. These are one-party states, and the nominees in their primaries become the officeholders without contest. South Carolina has a relatively low poll tax, which is administered very loosely and is not a requirement for voting in the Democratic primary. Yet South Carolina has the lowest voting percentage of any of the Southern states, not because of the poll tax, but because of the complications of its Democratic primaries and ward club membership requirements. Furthermore, in the states which have abandoned the poll tax prerequisite, the figures indicate conclusively that there has been no significant increase in Negro voting after repeal. In North Carolina, for instance, the Democratic party, which has been the traditional "white party," actually made gains after repeal of the poll tax, cutting down the Republican vote from 42.7 percent in 1920 to 33.3 percent in 1936. There are counties in which the black population is larger than the white, yet the repeal of the state's poll tax has not brought about black domination of those counties.

As for the argument that the schools will suffer from loss of poll tax revenues, there seems to be no foundation for such a contention. In the first place, the revenues from the poll taxes are not large. In no Southern state does the poll tax constitute a significant part of the state revenue. Alabama collects as little as 67 cents from the poll tax for every one hundred dollars of its total revenue. Virginia secured 1.86 percent of its revenue from the poll tax in 1937. In no poll tax state does the amount of tax collected add up to 5 percent of the total appropriation made for education.

The poll tax, as a prerequisite to voting, is both a social and a political vice. Socially, it represents an open flouting of democratic principles. Politically, it has become a tool for corruption of the ballot by political machines, and it has failed woefully to produce a high quality of political leadership among the limited class in whose hands it restricts the franchise. Two significant attacks are currently being made upon the poll tax as a limitation on the exercise of suffrage: (1) through a suit in the federal courts attacking the constitutionality of the tax; and (2) through a congressional bill designed to permit voting in federal elections without payment of the tax.

Several conclusions can be made with respect to the poll tax. First, the poll tax, employed as a qualification for voting, is a development of the twentieth century and is peculiar to the American South. Second, the most significant result of the poll tax provisions has been the disfranchisement of great numbers of poor whites in the South. Third, the new constitutions in which the poll tax provisions were incorporated were not popular constitutions and in some instances were actually "put over" on the population. In Mississippi and Virginia, for example, the new constitutions were adopted by proclamation and were never submitted to the people for ratification. Fourth, in recent years vigorous efforts to do away with the poll tax restrictions on the franchise have developed in the Southern states. Fifth, the obstacles to abolition of the poll tax provisions by state action in many of these states are virtually insuperable. Sixth, the restraint upon the franchise imposed by the poll tax and the disfranchisement of Negroes by registration devices and the "white primary" are complementary. Seventh, the representatives of the poll tax states exert an influence in the Democratic party in Congress and in national affairs wholly out of proportion to the voting population which they represent. Eighth, the introduction of the "threat" of Negro domination as an issue in the poll tax fight is sheer sophistry. Dishonest Southern politicians utilize the Negro issue as a means of maintaining themselves and their machines in power. There is only one Southern state—Mississippi—which now shows a Negro population of as much as 50 percent, and that proportion is steadily declining. This would seem to be an effective answer to the alleged "fear" of Southern whites that Negroes, if allowed to vote in the South, would capture political dominance.

Statistical analyses in connection with poll tax payments and registration figures are made difficult by the fact that the local tax and registration records are in such bad shape. An analysis of change in the percentage of voting from one election to another might yield some evidence on payment of poll taxes by candidates. Election reports for Louisiana [which has no poll tax] give data on the number of registrations by county, by race, and by ability to write. A cursory examination indicates that there has been no large increase in the number of Negroes registered. A further investigation of increases in white registrations by county might be made in order to determine whether the repeal of the poll tax resulted in an increase of registration in poorer counties and among persons unable to write. Similar analyses might be made of changes in the percentage of voting in various counties in North Carolina and Florida following the repeal of the poll tax in those states.

Our treatment of disfranchisement in the South has been

based upon an analysis and a summary of constitutional and statutory provisions as to suffrage in the Southern states, in conjunction with the related data concerning practices obtained in the field studies. In this connection, we are interested in the incidence of voting requirements in an attempt to discover just what groups in the population exercise the franchise. To do this properly, it would be important in at least some selected counties from several of the Southern states to compare the general registration and poll tax figures with the figures indicating Negro proportions in the population, the extent of land tenure, the nature of the economic structure (including wage levels, per capita income, etc.), and literacy data. Unfortunately, we have been unable to do this—first, because of inadequate time and assistance, and, secondly, because of the difficulty in getting the required secondary data for the counties in which field work was done. Much of such data available is for regions instead of counties. This is the sort of analysis which remains to be made, however; and it should be made, for in this way we can show not merely which groups are really represented in the political process, and which are not, but also what possibilities there are for the excluded groups within the existing structure. Within the localities selected for study, an attempt should be made to show the composition of the governing caste and the basis for its control. In each instance it would be necessary to make a thorough analysis of the local governmental structure and of the tax structure. It would also be noted whether the locality or the state were responsible for schools, roads, relief, and the like. Since the sales tax is widely prevalent in the South, it too becomes an important factor in this equation.

The limited statistical analysis undertaken in this report is suggested by table 1 [from appendix 2 of the original memorandum], racial, educational, and voting percentages for selected counties from thirteen Southern states in the 1930s.

In the presidential election of 1936, 9,259,765 votes were cast in the seventeen Southern states.[1] There is no way of determining what the population of voting age in this area was at that time. But in 1930 the total population twenty-one years of age and over in these states was 22,175,151. In the elections of 1928 and 1932 an average of 8,080,587 votes were cast in the South. This means that what might be termed the *effective*

1. The eleven ex-Confederate states plus Delaware, Kentucky, Maryland, Missouri, Oklahoma, and West Virginia.

TABLE 1. RACE, ILLITERACY, AND VOTING PERCENTAGES FOR
SELECTED ALABAMA COUNTIES IN 1936

Counties	% of Negroes in total pop., 21 and over, 1930	% of illiterate in total pop., 10 and over, 1930	% of total pop., 21 and over, voting in 1936
I. Counties with more than 50% Negro pop., 21 and over, 1930			
1. Lowndes	82.6	29.9	11.2
2. Greene	80.6	35.1	8.6
3. Macon	80.3	19.0	8.8
4. Sumter	76.3	25.5	10.4
5. Bullock	75.1	21.3	12.5
6. Wilcox	74.7	28.5	11.4
7. Hale	72.9	23.6	12.7
8. Marengo	71.2	23.6	12.6
9. Dallas	71.0	24.9	8.9
10. Perry	70.6	22.6	12.3
11. Russell	66.5	25.8	17.8
12. Barbour	54.0	24.6	15.7
13. Choctaw	54.0	18.1	15.7
14. Autauga	53.8	22.0	16.7
15. Monroe	50.8	14.8	18.5
16. Montgomery	50.1	13.9	21.7
17. Clarke	50.2	15.3	21.1
II. Counties with less than 10% Negro pop., 21 and over, 1930			
1. Cherokee	8.1	10.0	26.6
2. Jackson	7.5	11.5	25.5
3. Franklin	6.2	7.0	42.2
4. Cleburne	6.1	10.6	29.1
5. Blount	4.1	7.1	35.2
6. Marion	3.8	6.7	30.7
7. Marshall	3.5	7.6	27.4
8. DeKalb	2.4	6.7	57.7
9. Cullman	1.1	5.4	29.5
10. Winston	1.0	6.3	39.7

vote, as distinct from the potential vote in the region, amounted to but 36.4 percent. In the United States as a whole, 52.6 percent of the population of voting age actually voted in these two elections. The effective vote of the South is far below that of the country as a whole and considerably lower than that of any other region. There is a wide dispersion in the effective vote of the several Southern states. West Virginia ranks highest, with 76.9 percent, and South Carolina lowest, with 10.6 percent. It appears to be generally true that the border states rank highest and the Deep South or, to be more exact, the black-belt states, rank lowest. Offhand, we could assume from the distribution that there was an inverse relation between the Negro percentage of the total state population and the effective vote. Without the aid of statistical devices, however, we cannot establish the extent of this relationship. Neither can we determine the relative importance of such other factors as educational level and economic status, both of which may also influence the effective vote either directly or indirectly.[2]

Our rough analysis, based on the use of simple, multiple, and partial correlation techniques, discloses that, when race, educational level, and economic status are separately correlated with the effective vote, they all show a very high degree of inverse correlation. If, however, race is held constant, there is an appreciable decline in the value of the coefficients of relationship between educational level and the effective vote as well as between economic status and the effective vote. Although there is a similar decline in the coefficients of correlation for race and the effective vote when education and economic status are each held constant, the decline is not as severe. This would indicate that of the three factors race appears to be the most significant in determining the effective vote. Conclusive proof of this is given when two factors are held constant. We can therefore conclude that the percentage of the population of voting age in the South which actually votes is definitely conditioned by the percentage of the total population that is black; more so than by either the extent of illiteracy or the extent of low-skilled labor among the gainful workers.

The field workers presented primarily impressionistic and very little factual data for the counties covered. In a more intensive study, the selection of counties for sampling should be diversified, both in racial ratios and in relative industrial and agricultural emphasis. The very definite objective aimed at here is to relate very closely the black and white franchise problems, and to demonstrate that nonvoting in the South is a broad derivative of the political and economic structure of the region, rather than a mere product of racial disunity.

2. This paragraph and the one that follows are part of appendix 3 of the original Bunche memorandum, pp. 1612–61. The appendix is entitled "Race as a Factor in the Popular Vote of the South."—ED.

FIVE

The Negro in Contemporary Politics

IT would be erroneous to assume that the Negro is completely disfranchised in the South. The pattern of race relations in that region is inconsistent and fickle, and this lack of uniformity is reflected in the attitudes of white Southerners toward Negro voting. It is true that the South is characterized by a general attitude of hostility toward Negro voting, but this is by no means exclusive or universal. There are sharp exceptions to the pattern in cities like Memphis, Chattanooga, and San Antonio. There are broad exceptions throughout the South with respect to Negro participation in the general election, though this is largely an empty gesture in view of the fact that the white primary system renders the general elections in a one-party state of little consequence. There are significant exceptions on a thoroughly broad scale with regard to participation in bond and municipal elections generally, and not infrequently exceptions are found with respect to Negro participation in the Democratic primary itself.

It is impossible to present any accurate or even nearly accurate estimates of Negro voting in the South. Factual data on such voting is extremely difficult to obtain. Rough estimates can be obtained through compilation of reports from Negro newspapers and other publications, and from the few books on the subject. In my opinion, a very liberal estimate would suggest that in the entire region there are not more than 550,000 registered Negro voters. Of this number, about 465,000 would be found in the eight so-called border states of Tennessee, North Carolina, Virginia, Oklahoma, Missouri, Kentucky, West Virginia, and

Maryland; and by far the largest proportion of these black voters would be concentrated in the five last-named states.

The nucleus of the solid South is to be found in the eight Deep South states where Negro disfranchisement is most complete and where the Democratic primary regulations are most severely exclusive—Alabama, Arkansas, Florida, Georgia, Louisiana, Mississippi, South Carolina, and Texas. Yet even in these states the Negro retains some vestiges of political power. In the city bond issue elections (which are nonpartisan) and in some of the state and county elections, his vote, though small, is not only permitted but sometimes actually sought. The records show many instances of such participation, but none has been quite as outstandingly fruitful as that which took place in Atlanta, Georgia, twenty years ago. In 1920 the schools of Atlanta were in very bad condition. The mayor and others proposed a bond issue of $4,000,000 for the construction of new schools, but this issue was defeated by a narrow margin. Investigation revealed that most of the Negro voters had opposed it. There were from three to four thousand Negroes on the voting rolls at that time, and some of them would have to vote in the affirmative in order to provide a constitutional majority. This matter was brought to the attention of the Interracial Commission, which was asked to find out why Negroes voted against the proposition. A conference was held with Negro leaders. Their position was that Negroes had no disposition to vote taxes which they must pay to buy white schools. Promises were then made that, when the issue was again submitted to the voters, Negroes would receive a pro rata share for black schools. The Negroes agreed to this. The issue was passed, and the black share was $1,250,000 out of $3,800,000. As a result of this action, Atlanta Negroes obtained the new Booker T. Washington High School and four elementary schools.

In Birmingham, Alabama, in recent years Negroes have begun to vote in the Democratic primaries, and in Texas, especially San Antonio, Negroes exert a relatively important political influence. The Bexar County Educational League, a Negro organization chartered in September 1939, supported Maury Maverick in his recent campaign for mayor of San Antonio. The Negro Progressive Voters League of Dallas, which was organized in 1936, claims to have corralled most of the city's black voters. It selects political tickets to support during councilmanic elections and stages campaigns for Negro registration. It was organized on a nonpartisan basis and insists that it is emphatically opposed to the individual approach to the Negro problem. One of its first major activities was to support the campaign of President Roosevelt for reelection in 1936. In 1937 it ran a "pay your poll tax" campaign. It now claims a membership of 7,000 registered voters out of a total registration of 39,000 in the city.[1]

The Richmond Democratic League is fairly typical of Negro political organizations in Southern communities. It claims to represent about a thousand Negroes and has been in existence over fifteen years. Its main activities are found in perennial campaigns that consist primarily of a few speeches and the singing of spirituals in meetings held at Negro churches. The object of such meetings has been to get the Negro to pay the poll tax and to vote. In recent years appeal has been made to Negro trade unionists in an effort to encourage their membership to vote. Recently the Richmond Democratic League held a "Swing Democratic Ball," and three hundred young people paid thirty-five cents each to do the jitterbug—and to hear a white alderman (a liberal city councilman) speak on the topic "Housing Needs for Negroes." On 1 August, 1939 the League held a four-hour "Legislative Conference" at a Negro Methodist church to which about twenty of the white candidates for nomination in the August primaries came. They came to listen to Negro leaders outline the legislative demands which were being made of white candidates seeking the black vote. Among the Negro speakers were a teacher, a lawyer, a social worker, a barber, and a labor leader, and each of the candidates responded. The audience was also permitted to ask questions. This was considered a very significant development in Richmond, in that white candidates for public office were thus publicly seeking the Negro vote and were required to make promises in the bargain.[2]

It is important to note the growing campaign to encourage Negroes to register and vote in such Southern cities as Miami, Savannah, Louisville, Birmingham, and Richmond. If the figures obtained for Negro registration in leading cities in Florida are approximately accurate, it would seem that there is much more extensive black registration in that state than is to be found in Louisiana, Mississippi, Alabama, Georgia, or South Carolina. It appears that both Negro registration and voting fig-

1. This description of Negro organizations in Texas comes from Bunche, "The Programs, Ideologies, Tactics and Achievements of Negro Betterment and Interracial Organizations," pp. 623–25. —ED.

2. See ibid., pp. 589–90. —ED.

ures have increased somewhat, though not greatly, in Florida since the repeal of the poll tax qualification for voting.

Despite the hardships frequently imposed by the registrars, there are increasing numbers of Negroes in the South who are demonstrating an amazing amount of patience, perseverance, and determination in trying to register, and who keep returning after rejections until they get their names on the registration books. Negroes in the South have even discovered that white men with whom they have business relations are often inclined to be quite sympathetic toward their registration efforts. Thus white business agents are not infrequently called upon to act as character witnesses for Negro applicants. In one case in northern Alabama, a town mayor who was also a wholesale grocer quite willingly gave a note of recommendation to a Negro grocer with whom he did business, which enabled this man to get by the local registrars without difficulty.

There is a strong difference of opinion among Negroes in the South as to the proper method to be employed in gaining increased registration for the race. Some prominent Negroes are content to go along with the customary method of getting a few blacks on the books through personal contacts with friendly and sympathetic whites. Others vigorously oppose this tactic as an uncertain "back door" practice which holds no promise for the Negro's political future in the region. These latter desire to make an issue, at every possible opportunity, of the Negro's denial, and they demand that Negroes be accorded the same treatment in the registration office as that given to whites. The efforts being made by Negro organizations throughout the South to give free coaching to Negroes in order to aid them in answering the questions put by the registrars is good civic education. Undoubtedly many of the Negro applicants have a better knowledge of the functioning of the state and federal governments than the registrars who put the questions to them and, for that matter, than most white citizens in their locality.

Labor unions in the South are in a position to play an important role in opening the registration books to Negro workers. An example of what may be done in this way is demonstrated in the activity of the United Mine Workers of America local in Walker County, Alabama. The deep-rooted prejudices of the Southern worker cannot be quickly overcome, but as labor unions develop in the South, there is a growing working-class consciousness and a tendency to identify black and white working class interests. Southern labor unions have begun to awaken to the fact that the white worker himself has been virtually disfranchised in the South. Any significant progress made toward better working and living conditions and toward progressive social legislation in the Southern states can result only from a politically conscious labor movement that will make its political influence felt and eventually wrest political power from the hands of the Bourbon oligarchy that has long controlled Southern destinies. In this movement a newly enfranchised black vote, if carefully trained and guided, can play a vital role, and there are increasing numbers of white labor leaders in the South who realize it.

Where the Negro votes in any significant numbers in Southern cities, the ugly head of machine control is reared. Thus the story of the black vote in places like Raleigh, Memphis, and San Antonio is not one of how the Negro votes, but of how and by whom he is voted. Negroes vote in Memphis. The machine of Edward H. Crump sees to that. It provides them with poll tax receipts, marked ballots, and bad liquor, and it herds them into the polling booths. It has even been suggested that Mr. Crump draws upon the handy Negro population just across the river in Arkansas. The use of the black vote by the Crump machine has had repercussions on Negro political status elsewhere in Tennessee. In their effort to overcome the dominating influence of Crump's power over state politics, white Democratic leaders in Nashville and Chattanooga have relaxed the white primary rules, and Negroes are beginning to participate in the Democratic primaries in those places. The eastern half of the state is traditionally Republican, and has always been accustomed to the Negro vote. As a result of these factors, the Negro in Tennessee is making more progress toward exercise of the franchise than in any other Southern state except Kentucky, where a Negro sits in the state legislature. But the percentage of Negroes in the population of Kentucky is below the percentage for the nation as a whole, and thus it is not typical of the South.

The Negro in central Texas is making his influence felt in local political affairs, but in this part of Texas the black population is relatively small, consisting largely of a class of artisans sandwiched between the poor whites above and the Mexicans below. In San Antonio, for instance, a larger percentage of Negroes than whites vote, though they do not always vote intelligently and seldom progressively. For more than twenty years —until just a few years ago—one of the most powerful political personalities in San Antonio, where the Negro population is 15 percent of the total, was Charles Bellinger, a Negro sportsman-gambler-racket boss. Under Bellinger's rule, the Negro vote was largely controlled through poll tax payment and machine domination. It was the hangover from this influence that kept the Negro population from voting solidly for the progressive Maury Maverick in his candidacy for mayor of the city, despite the fact that Maverick had been known as the only liberal congressman from Texas and one who had vigorously defended the anti-lynching bill in Congress.

The picture is different in southeastern Texas, however, where the Negro population is much larger and where Negroes are almost entirely excluded from politics. In this area—and this is the section of Texas that sent Martin Dies to Congress—are found all of the special devices and tricks employed to disfranchise the Negro. It is to be noted with regret that practically nothing is being done in behalf of, and little interest is taken in, the political disabilities of the great numbers of Negroes found in the small towns and rural areas of the South.

In some places in the South the Negro vote does constitute a balance of power in local elections, even though this vote is small. I think that a very revealing and important study could be made on the participation of Negroes in Southern municipal elections. This has been a fairly widespread phenomenon in the region and is usually the first opportunity given to Negroes to exercise the franchise. Ordinarily in these local elections, the white factions are fairly evenly divided along the line of those who want some improvement to be made by the money raised through bond issues and those who do not want to be burdened with the taxes needed to pay off bonds. In a situation of this kind, a small bloc of votes can control the result, especially where a specified percentage of the voters must vote on the bond issue in order to make the election legal. Thus it has often happened that the Negro vote has been enrolled in the struggle.

There is considerable evidence to prove that, even in some of the deepest parts of the South, local candidates are attentive to the black vote and even campaign among Negroes. White candidates sometimes bid openly for the Negro vote and employ Negro taxis to carry black supporters to the polls. Political rallies are sometimes held in Negro sections, and white politicians make campaign speeches and promises to the black voters. In certain instances as many as several thousand Negroes have voted in the city elections of Atlanta. Negroes in the thousands have similarly voted in municipal contests in Richmond, Durham, and Raleigh. Apparently the white populations of these communities were not unduly alarmed by this new activity on the part of Negroes, for there is no record of any serious protest made against it. On the other side of the ledger, however, was the attempt of the Ku Klux Klan to alarm and stir up the white population of Miami against the threat of black voting; a similar episode took place in Greenville, South Carolina, in 1939, when only a few hundred Negroes got on the registration rolls. There was some excitement last year surrounding the registration of about three score Negroes, mostly women, in Spartanburg, South Carolina, when a warning was issued that "the Klan will ride again."

In cities like Richmond, Durham, and Raleigh, the new Negro political interest in municipal elections is inspired and controlled by the city machines which have found a use for the black vote along the Memphis pattern. In Miami and Greenville, however, as in an increasingly large number of towns in the South, Negroes have organized their own movements to gain the franchise for their group, and are not yet subject to machine domination. In some of these instances, the Negro community has shown an adeptness for political bargaining and has got benefits for the Negro community as a result of its political activity.

Such instances do serve to counter the assertion that the Negro in the South has no interest in things political, though certainly there are enough forces at work in the region to justify him in an attitude of abject resignation toward his political status. It is quite significant, I think, that, given the smallest opening for a vote that counts, the Negro voter will appear in considerable numbers, often to the consternation of a white population caught napping. It may be important to the future political status of the Negro that, in a number of places throughout the South, the white population has been able to view without panic the spectacle of a black vote exercising a controlling power over election results. In several cases white candidates for important offices have desperately bid for the Negro vote. The "better elements" of the white population have sometimes turned to the Negro vote as a means of pushing desired reforms. In other words, when the Negro vote is needed badly enough, it is unleashed. Once the chains are loosened from the black voter in such cases, however, it has been found extremely difficult to chain him up again. The inexorable law of American politics is to get the vote, and once vote-hungry candidates taste a helpful vote, even if black, it is relished. While this sort of thing has not happened widely and frequently enough in the South to have become at all typical, it has cut a pattern, and there is good reason to assume that unless some very radical changes occur in the nation's political and economic structures as a result of the European conflagration, the pattern will become increasingly familiar to the political process of the American South.

One very large and very significant group of Negroes in the South has been having, in recent years, an unparalleled and unrestricted opportunity to express its will through the ballot. Not since Reconstruction days has any numerous group of Negroes had the opportunity to cast the independent ballot that is cast by the Negro cotton farmer in the cotton marketing quota referenda. Most significantly, many thousands of Negro cotton farmers each year now go to the polls, stand in line with their white neighbors, and mark their ballots independently, without protest or intimidation, in order to determine government policy toward cotton production control. These elections revolve about issues which affect directly the economic welfare of the producers, and these issues are much clearer to the voters than are the often obscure issues confronting them in the regular political elections. These cotton referenda are run off as regular elections, with regulations governing the eligibility of voters, voting booths, and the Australian ballot—features that are often lacking in the political elections of the Southern states in which the cotton referenda are held.

According to officials in the Agricultural Adjustment Administration, the role played by the Negro farmer in the marketing quota referenda in the Southern states has been very creditable, and in these referenda the black farmer has played a very active and decisive part. For example, in the November 1938 cotton marketing quota referendum, the Southern counties having the largest number of Negro cotton producers were the counties having the largest number of votes in favor of the cotton control program.

It can scarcely be doubted that the participation of Negroes in these elections and on an equal basis with whites is of the utmost social significance in the South. That such activities will tend to bring about a recognition by both white and Negro producers of parallel economic interests would seem clear. Participation in these referenda has given a great many Negroes in the region the first opportunity that they have ever had to cast a ballot of any kind. Moreover, it tends to accustom a great many whites to the practice of Negro voting. In these marketing quota elections, no attempt has been made to set up separate ballot booths for whites and Negroes, and all of the booths are mixed. There are three judges at every booth, and no serious racial incidents have been reported in the conduct of any of the elections. For strategic reasons, the director of the Southern division of the AAA has played down the fact of Negro participation in these elections in order to avoid the creation of a political issue. His interest has been in the success of the program, and this demands the most widespread possible participation of all groups. Thus, he has tried to avoid any publicity which would bring about political attacks upon this aspect of the program. He readily admits that the success of the program depends largely upon Negro participation.

The Negro has long been an issue in American election campaigns, both negatively and positively. In the South anti-Negro attitudes have been an important means of capturing elections. In the North, in those centers where the black population is concentrated, parties and candidates have often overexerted themselves in their efforts to demonstrate interest on behalf of and fairness toward the Negro. A rather peculiar racial twist is found in the political problems of the nation's capital. In the District of Columbia, whose population has no suffrage, the Negro issue looms large. For many years efforts have been made to win some form of suffrage for the district. These efforts have often been halfhearted, however, and never unanimous, because of the fear that the large Negro population in the district would wield a balance of power and dominate the elections. There are groups in the white population of Washington which are vigorously opposed to suffrage for this area and raise the bogey of a "black mayor" for the capital.

There is some evidence to indicate that the Southern politician who has national political aspirations, even though from the Deep South, is not averse to flirting with the Negro vote in the North. It was reliably reported at the 1939 NAACP annual convention in Richmond, Virginia, that Vice President Garner, who at that time had his eye upon the Democratic presidential nomination, invited a delegation of Texas Negroes, led by the editor of a Negro newspaper in Houston, to attend the Richmond convention and to exert an effort to bring the 1940 NAACP convention to Houston. It was said that enough money was provided to carry the members of this delegation on up to Washington and then to New York to visit the World's Fair. While in the nation's capital, the delegation is said to have met with the Vice President, and that it was authorized to make an announcement that $1,000 would be available for the purpose of entertaining the NAACP convention in Houston. The purpose of all this was to swing Negro influence to Garner, and the plan was that if the NAACP came to Houston, the Vice President would call the Texas state Democratic committee together and have it vote to let Negroes participate in the Democratic primary of Texas. I can personally verify that the Houston delegation was present at the Richmond meeting in large and vociferous numbers, and it did make a vigorous bid for the 1940 convention. But it seems that at the last moment Walter White got wind of the plot and immediately set to work to circumvent the effort. Almost at the last minute a spontaneous invitation was extended by an unorganized group of Philadelphians to hold the 1940 meeting in that city, and the Garner plans were defeated.

The Democratic white primary in the South operates upon a gentleman's agreement whereby the candidates are to abide by the decision rendered in the primary. But there have been instances where candidates, for one reason or another, have refused to keep the agreement and have opposed the successful primary candidates in the general elections. In some of these cases, as in Savannah, the defeated primary candidate has appealed to the Negro voters. This is an essential weakness of the white primary, and there is a growing conviction in the South that whenever and wherever the Negro is registered in any significant numbers, the whole primary system will collapse from its own inherent weaknesses, since narrowly defeated primary candidates will be attracted by the possibility of stealing the election with the aid of the Negro vote in the general election.

Indeed, there are an increasing number of people in the South—among them some very influential people and some keen observers—who believe it inevitable that within the reasonably near future a two-party system will develop in the region. They see a second or opposition party developing in response to the movement of population, the growth of industry, the increasing class consciousness of the workers of the South, and the tendency of the established parties to break up on ideological grounds. They realize, of course, that the development of a two-party system in the region will have a very significant effect upon the political status of the Negro. This is quite obviously so. It provides the main source of hope for the political future of the Negro in the South.

The attitude of the Southern political machine leaders toward Negro voting is also important to diagnose. As professional politicians, perhaps most of these men would have no compunction about calling upon Negroes to vote if they needed the black vote; but so long as the present political structure exists in most of these states, there is no need for it, since the white franchise is sufficiently limited to enable them to control it and to smother too serious factionalism. Not all machine leaders are as frank as the few who have indicated that Negro voting would increase too greatly the expense involved in machine control, since it is already necessary for them to pay up the poll taxes and buy the votes of many white voters. Sometimes white candidates in the South seek the Negro vote, but explain to black political leaders that they cannot afford to have an "open endorsement" of their candidacy by Negroes.

Where the Negro does vote in any significant numbers, white politicians often employ the effective strategy of creating several Negro political leaders whose intragroup rivalry splits the black vote into factions and thereby renders it relatively impotent. Where a Negro candidate runs for office with a fair chance of success, for example, it is a well established custom for white politicians to employ other Negroes to enter the race against him, thus splitting the black vote and making it possible for a white candidate to steal the race, even in an overwhelmingly Negro district.

Southern officials are often given to explanations of Negroes on the voting rolls of their communities by saying, more or less apologetically and sometimes even with a little pride, that this is due to "the fine type of colored citizens we have here." There are some in the South who feel that the Negro—at least the "cream" of the race, those who are best educated and best qualified—should be given some form of separate representation. Some Southerners, such as editor William Watts Ball of the Charleston *News and Courier*, advocate a black party and a black primary, in which Negroes would select their own representatives. It is sometimes advocated that Negroes be permitted to elect Negro representatives who would sit in the state and national legislatures in the capacity of advisory delegates with power to speak but not to vote, and with the responsibility of doing everything possible properly to represent Negro interests. The Union of South Africa has recently adopted a scheme of this kind as a form of nominal representation for natives in the Cape Province. It is, of course, purely a sop.

Some Southern officials declare that there are only two types of Negroes in the South who really want to register: one, those Negroes from "way back yonder" who registered and became accustomed to voting in the days before the disfranchising constitutions; and two, those Negroes holding jobs under the New Deal, who have been "required" to register or who feel that they are required to register. Numbers of righteous Southerners resent this intrusion of the New Deal, which they feel has tended to give the Negro false notions about his citizenship in the South. There are others who take the attitude that there is no particular objection to black voting so long as it is made certain that no Negroes will ever run for office. Other officials readily admit that Negroes might vote a good deal more than they do, since many of the devices employed to keep them from the polls would not hold up in the courts if the blacks were wise and courageous enough to use "smart lawyers" to challenge the practices in the courtroom.

There is undoubtedly a great deal of bewilderment in the minds of many Southern whites about the new tendency of Negroes to want to vote Democratic. Traditionally in the South it has been assumed that every Negro, if given the ballot, would vote Republican. Franklin D. Roosevelt and his New Deal have changed all of this, and many Southerners are torn between party pride in the fact that Negroes want to vote Democratic and traditional opposition to black voting. To many white Southerners, the New Deal, in its attitude toward Negroes, its "coddling" of them, is twentieth-century Reconstruction. Officials sometimes point, with a sort of embarrassed pride, to the fact that the handful of Negroes who vote in their particular county vote Democratic. Since there is no secret ballot in many parts of the South, the officials know pretty well how everyone in the county votes, white as well as black.

It is not without significance that in some places in the Deep South today it is possible for broad-minded white citizens of the community to take a stand in support of Negro voting without being eternally damned and ostracized by their white neighbors. In some instances, responsible whites have assumed leadership in getting Negroes to the polls, and have used the black vote, small as it is, as a bargaining lever with which to pry concessions from white candidates in the way of improved Negro treatment. There is often an element of the missionary spirit in such activity, however, and the white leaders usually take it for granted that all such efforts in behalf of Negroes must have white sponsors. If the South is changing in its attitude toward Negro voting, then the region is now in what may be called a transition stage in its thinking on the subject. It is changing from a previous attitude of absolute hostility toward black voting to a new tolerance toward a vote by that part of the Negro population that may be considered "safe."

The development of the lily-white Republican movement in the South and its effect upon Negro political status, both in the South and the North, have been considered in this memorandum. The Republican organizations in the South exist for the most part to provide delegates for the Republican presidential convention every four years. They are in no sense an opposition party except in scattered areas and in the border states. Their importance to the whites and blacks that make them up revolves around the patronage which is given in the form of postmasterships and other minor posts, and trips to the conventions. An example is provided by Perry Howard, member of the GOP national committee from Mississippi. Because of his shrewdness, his humility in the presence of whites, and his tractability among whites, he is fully accepted as a Negro leader by leading white Republicans. His rise to prominence was along the easy road of Republican party politics in Mississippi, where there are only a handful of Republicans and all of those are seeking Republican patronage. The test of fitness in that game is one's ability to play shrewd politics, and at that Howard is an expert. Once on top, he has remained there by playing his political cards well, "staying in" with the white folks, as he well knows how to do—it is often said of him that he is a better "lily-white" than a white Republican of Mississippi would be—and by a robust, all-out, Lincoln-freed-the-slaves, the-Democrats-be-damned brand of Republican soap-boxing.[3]

There is deep resentment among Southern Negroes at what they consider to have been the sellout of the Negro by the Republican party in order to advance its courtship with the Southern whites. Certainly a great many black voters in the South who support the Republican party do so only because there is no

3. This characterization of Howard is taken from Ralph J. Bunche, "A Brief and Tentative Analysis of Negro Leadership" (1940), p. 27, another of the unpublished memoranda prepared for Myrdal's *An American Dilemma*. —ED.

other party to give their support to, since the Democrats refuse to admit them to party membership. There are many older Negroes who are Republican because it is a well-established tradition for Negroes to vote so if they vote at all. As some frankly explain it, the Negro has more to gain in the South from supporting the Democrats—and in many places the Democrats are really more generous to Negroes than are Republicans, especially since Roosevelt II—but they vote Republican, nevertheless, because for historical reasons "no Negro can be a Democrat in the South and keep his self-respect." In not a few cases this self-respect is of less importance in the equation than the crumbs from the patronage pie.

The lily-white Republican organizations do not generally exclude Negroes entirely. There is no such thing as a pure white Republican primary in the South. In some states, as in Louisiana, the Negro Republican registrants are needed in order to give the party sufficient representation in the state to continue the party's legal recognition and keep its place on the ballot. The new "rotten borough" rule adopted at the recent Republican convention in Philadelphia will also encourage even the lily-whites to make some effort to court the Negro Republicans, since many congressional districts in the South will not be able to rustle up 1,000 white Republicans in order to be entitled to a delegate to the conventions. The Negro Republicans will be needed for padding.

The white Republican of the South is of quite the same breed as the white Democrat—though sometimes a mite less honest. By and large he has been and is as much opposed to Negro voting as the heartiest "cracker," but he has had more use for the black voter than has the Democrat. The Negro has been needed as window dressing for the Southern delegations to the national conventions and therefore is good patronage insurance for white Republicans. No Southern counties are any more inhospitable to the Negro than some of the traditionally Republican ones, as in northern Alabama and Georgia, for example.

The development of lily-white Republicanism in the South has been of no significance to the welfare of the Negro masses in the region. The fact that Georgia had two Negro Republican national committeemen meant nothing to that state's Negroes, except to that pitiful handful that groveled and slobbered at the patronage trough. The same applies to Mississippi. If lily-white Republicanism can lead to the development of real white factionalism in the South and an ultimate two-party system, the

Negro should encourage it. For in the long run the Negro masses of the South have far more to gain from the breakup of the solid, one-party South than from the hollow pretense of Negro Republicanism in a solidly Democratic white South. The Southern Negro is well rid of the patronage-bloated black lackeys of the black-and-tan days.

The sharp swing in Negro political allegiance from Republican to Democratic since 1932 is a noteworthy phenomenon throughout the country. Even in the South, where the Negro has more reason than elsewhere to reject the Democratic party, there has been a noticeable trend toward Roosevelt and the Democrats. It is to be seriously doubted, however, that this is a fundamental shift to democracy. Roosevelt beckoned the Negro, and he came, despite his traditional suspicion of the Democratic party and its Southern controls. The essential reasons for the Negro's political change of heart in the South are these: (1) the practical effectiveness of a vote cast in the Democratic primary as against a Republican vote cast in the general election, since the Republicans scarcely ever hold primaries in the South; (2) the development of lily-whiteism in the Republican party organization of the South; and (3) the liberalism and "forgotten man" appeal of President Roosevelt.

It is unfortunate that we do not have a clearer picture of Negro political status and activity in the border states, especially in Kentucky, West Virginia, Missouri, and Maryland. Except for a superficial treatment of the problem in Louisville, St. Louis, and Kansas City, Missouri, we have very little on any of these states, in all of which Negroes play a significant political role.

One of the most interesting problems in connection with Negro political status in the South involves the effort to test the alleged indifference and political apathy of Southern Negroes. Especially in the South is the impression given that the Negro has no political interests and no political ambitions. Any appraisal of the Negro's political interests would obviously need to be made in terms of the total milieu in which the Negro lives, including the constant pressure and repression to which he is subjected. The data at our disposal do not support any broad conclusions, but there is considerable evidence of Negro political interest in the South, and also of the ability of Negro organizations to arouse political consciousness among large numbers of blacks when it becomes possible to vote. The fact that, in the midst of the hostile attitude universally manifested toward black voting in the South, large numbers of Negroes do run the gauntlet of the registration officials and the election officers in order to cast what is quite frequently a worthless ballot would seem to indicate that the Southern Negro is not altogether listless in the face of the deprival of his fundamental rights of citizenship. On the other hand, there is a great deal of political apathy among Negroes, even as among whites, where voting is possible. Certainly the factors of Negro resignation and futility and the frequently expressed attitude that "politics is the white man's business" are important elements in the matter. It is rather common for leaders of Negro organizations in the South to charge that the Negro could vote to a greater extent if he would try harder and take more interest in doing so. Yet such attitudes will often be difficult to reconcile with the expressed determination of local registrars to keep Negroes off the voting rolls.

There are some Negro political leaders in the South who feel that if Negroes would only register in large numbers, even granting that the privilege of voting in the general election is a completely hollow one, the great number of available black votes would be bait for white candidates that they could not for long resist, and that in time this would result in white candidates bidding for the Negro vote. In this way they envisage the possibility of the Negro crashing into the white primary. Negroes in the South who turn to the courts to correct injustices done to them by registrars have frequently found the registrars quite alert. In both New Orleans and Birmingham registrars have forestalled possible adverse court decisions by registering Negro complainants before the courts heard their cases, thus rendering the cases moot.

There are not a few Negroes in the South who agree that the election officials are right in permitting only a few Negroes with property to vote. They take this stand on the ground that the relations with the "white folks" will be better if only the "highest type of Negro" votes. The idea is that the Negro must always avoid rubbing the white man the wrong way, and that at every possible opportunity he must put his best foot forward to the white man and impress upon him how well the "better class" Negro can conduct himself. Others, in resignation, take the accommodation attitude that the white people simply do not want Negroes to vote and that, therefore, blacks should not attempt to stir up any trouble about the matter.

There is a great deal of class feeling among Negroes in the

South, and it is not unusual for "upper class" Negroes—business and professional men—to take the attitude that the great mass of blacks, being uneducated and illiterate, are not yet ready to exercise the franchise. Not a few reflect the view that this black mass of uneducated people is a definite liability to the advanced members of the race, in that all Negroes are lumped together in the prevailing racial situation. Were it not for this crude black mass, they reason, the upper-class Negroes would be extended the privileges of citizenship by the whites without hesitation. A good many of these upper-class Negroes, far from expressing concern over the disfranchisement of their less fortunate black brothers, are proud of the fact that they are found among the chosen few in the community who are permitted to have the privilege of voting.

Many Negroes in the Southern states, especially the younger ones, charge Negro preachers with a good deal of the responsibility for the lack of Negro political activity. The Negro preacher, it is declared, either counsels his flock to stay out of politics altogether or else takes a totally indifferent attitude toward the problem. There are individual exceptions, of course, and some black ministers have played active and influential parts in Negro voting campaigns.

There are really very few, if any, Negro political bosses in the United States in the sense of an ability actually to deliver a significant Negro vote. Certainly there are no effective ones in the South. Most of the so-called Negro political leaders maintain their influence through personal contacts with prominent white politicians rather than on the basis of any mass following or an ability to command any significant vote within the Negro electorate. There is no Negro political figure in the country who can say that he actually has a following, though there are many who can buy up votes with the money of white candidates or machines.

The game of politics breeds some degenerate types of local leaders of both races. There are innumerable Negro hirelings of the political bosses, black and white, who will attempt almost anything for a handout. There are many stool pigeons, some professional and some voluntary and amateurish. There are Negro leaders who, either to curry favor with whites or to blast away at a rival leader, freely betray each other and their group. There are all sorts of racketeers who exert one or another kind of influence, and who are, when "in the money," sometimes quite liberal in their support of and donations to worthy Negro causes. Generally the local Negro leadership is so poor that, as one Negro citizen says: "What can be done about it? We got to have leadership. Somebody has got to come forward who knows the score and has the talent of persuasion and expose the bastards for what they are . . . lousy sewer rats, bloated with the blood of their own people. Before we can get to the real white ruling class enemy, we've got to first hack our way through a swarm of their black hirelings in our own group."[4]

No case can be made for the Negro vote as a great progressive bloc in any locality. Like the white vote, the Negro vote tends to be conservative, not very intelligent on issues, and rather easily bought. The charge is frequently made that the Negro vote is easily purchasable. We have no evidence to establish the fact that the black vote can be more readily purchased than any other vote. That many Negro voters are willing to sell their ballot for a price is indisputable. Many white voters are also willing to trade upon their voting privilege. It should be remarked, however, that in many places in the South, though only a handful of Negroes vote, this vote is the most independent in the community because white candidates do not bother to try to buy it.

Any analysis of Negro voting in the South ought to pay special attention to the age of black voters. The majority of the Negro voters in many Southern communities will be found to be those whose names, by hook or crook, remained on the registration lists from the pre–constitutional disfranchisement days. This category of Negro voters is rapidly dying out and has largely historical significance. It is much more important to know how many members of the younger Negro generations, who have come up under the new constitutions, are able to get their names on the rolls and to cast their ballots. We have no detailed data on this subject.

It has been possible to make only a very limited analysis of the extent to which the Negro expresses class and race consciousness in voting. Speaking generally, it appears that there is very little expression of class consciousness in Negro voting, whether North or South, for the simple reason that Negroes by and large have very little of such consciousness. Moreover, the Negro political leaders are usually much more machine and race conscious than they are class conscious. Race permeates Negro

4. This paragraph comes from Bunche, "A Brief and Tentative Analysis of Negro Leadership," pp. 89, 123. —ED.

life in this country in its entirety, and it is unquestionably a primary influence in Negro political motivation.

Attention also has been directed to the Negro attitude toward the overtures of the radical parties. These parties, and especially the Communists, have made serious efforts to win the Negro and have juggled their party lines in such way as to attract his support. Some Negro leaders, including William E. B. Du Bois, in the past have advised the Negro that it would be better for him to give support to the radical parties, even it if meant throwing his vote away, than to give it to either of the major parties which show so little inclination to do anything in behalf of Negro welfare. On the whole, however, the parties of the Left have been able to cut no appreciable swath through the black electorate. Their appeal to the Negro has not been great, despite the strenuous efforts exerted, especially by the Communist party. Whatever reception the radical parties have met among Negroes has been among the younger, urbanized intellectual leaders.

There are certain compensatory activities in which the Negro has engaged in lieu of normal political activity. Throughout the South there is a tendency to elect "bronze mayors,"[5] and to work up regular campaigns with posters and meetings in connection with their election. This is also tied up with efforts to stimulate Negro business. Moreover, all of the Negro organizations are usually ridden with politics and leadership rivalries. There is plenty of evidence that the Negro is a very political animal, and that his political urges will find expression in other channels whenever he is deprived of participation in the usual political processes.

There is a strong inclination on the part of many Negroes to regard the ballot as a prime source of black deliverance, and with many Negroes the right to cast the ballot is a symbol of equality of status. It is assumed, rather naïvely, due to a blind faith in the ideals of American democracy, that once the Negro gets the ballot, he can solve his problems with it—this despite the fact that the great masses of whites throughout the country, who have long been enfranchised, have been able to make but little progress toward solution of many of their own problems

5. "Bronze mayors" were Negro leaders chosen in mock elections to symbolize black needs and aspirations. The practice of electing "bronze mayors" reflected the political stirrings of many black communities in the urban setting of the 1930s. —ED.

with the ballot. The vote has become a fetish with many Negroes, but there is little evidence that social problems anywhere in the world are solved by fetishism.

The enfranchisement of the Negro in the South would be a great advance for black people, but it would still leave the major economic and political problems of the region unsolved, and these affect the Negro quite as much as the white citizens. The true significance of the ballot for the Negro in the South would be in the fact that this in itself would be a recognition of a new era in his progressive development toward full integration in American society. It would give him a new sense of responsibility and civic dignity, and, with proper guidance and leadership, it might well be that this Negro vote could be lined up in support of that small band of perspiring Southern liberals who are doggedly working for broad social reform.

Although the general pattern is for the Negro sections in our municipalities to be treated quite shabbily with respect to municipal services, it does seem evident that the black vote can be and is traded for improved facilities and services wherever the Negro votes in any significant numbers. In those areas in which the Negro is able to wield the stick of political power, his requests are much more attentively listened to and complied with. It is possible to illustrate graphically enough the significance of the Negro vote in national, state, and local elections. For example, in national politics, the antilynching bill has become a political football solely because of the importance which Northern candidates attribute to the black vote. In the present presidential campaign, it appears that the Negro vote will assume larger significance than ever because of the great importance now attached to the independent vote, which is expected to swing the election. The Republicans, who have now awakened to the realization that they can no longer depend upon the traditional allegiance of the black voters, have taken unusual steps to attract the Negro electorate. They have already employed a Negro publicity agent and have had a special study on the needs of the Negro made in connection with the work of the Glenn Frank Committee.[6] The Democrats are likewise beginning to employ measures to hold the newly won Negro support, and in this effort Mrs. Roosevelt is one of their strongest assets. Former Postmaster General James A. Farley got in a good plug for his party

6. Ralph J. Bunche, "Report on the Needs of the Negro" (1939). A copy of this 133-page unpublished study is located in the Schomburg Collection of the New York Public Library. —Ed.

in his unusually flattering speech at Tuskegee last spring in connection with the issuance of a commemorative stamp in honor of Booker T. Washington—the first time a Negro has been so honored. There is every indication that there will be much rivalry between the two parties and a lot of money spent in order to gain the Negro vote.

Negro political activity in the North ties up importantly with the Negro migrations during and after the World War, for it was these migrations that brought on the concentration of Negro population in the Northern urban centers. The outstanding characteristic of these new Negro populations, which found themselves in a strange environment in the North, was their political unawareness and innocence. Inevitably, they fell prey to the machine politics of the well-oiled political rings typical of America's urban centers. Each of the important Northern metropolitan areas with large concentrations of Negroes provides material for a graphic story of Negro voting experience. Only in Chicago has the history of Negro political life in the North been carefully traced; the story remains to be told for such centers as New York, Detroit, Cleveland, Pittsburgh, Philadelphia, Buffalo, Kansas City, Baltimore, and St. Louis, not to mention the very significant political role played by the black vote in smaller cities.

We are not so ambitious as to attempt to write these histories in this memorandum. The necessary data are not available to us, nor has there been time in which to do the job. We have tried merely a running account based, for the most part, on unpublished manuscripts and hastily prepared general memoranda compiled for us by selected individuals in the localities covered. It must be emphasized that any analysis of the Negro role in the machine politics of Northern cities should be related, as far as possible, to the experiences of other minority groups, especially the immigrant groups, and to that of the native white population. There is a great need for a series of analyses of Negro political activity in selected Northern areas based upon a fair grasp of the nature of machine politics in those areas, the relationship between machine politics and the Negro vote, and the part played by Negro political lieutenants and ward heelers operating in behalf of the machine. It is only for Chicago, in Harold F. Gosnell's *Negro Politicians: The Rise of Negro Politics in Chicago* (1935), that this has been attempted.

Unfortunately, it has been impossible for us to do very much concerning an essential corollary of the Negro in machine politics—the frequent tie-up between Negro politics and politicians and the underworld. We know generally that this is a relationship quite widely found, but we lack the specific data to do very much toward pointing up and illustrating the subject. For the most part, this underworld association reduces itself to the numbers and policy rackets and their numerous barons, to prostitution, and to petty vice. That there are broad patterns which might be derived from a close study of such activities I have no doubt, but in this study we lack enough factual data to describe them. There is some slight suggestion of the situation prevailing in Detroit, but my hopes for a considerable amount of such material on Chicago were not fulfilled.

We are lacking, also, in the close data necessary for an accurate consideration of the subject of gerrymandering in Northern cities as it affects Negroes. That this political device has been widely employed to the political detriment of black voters is generally accepted. Adequate documentation of the phenomenon for any particular locality, however, could only be provided on the basis of a close scrutiny of ward and district lines in Negro areas, Negro population figures for voting districts, and analyses of election returns by race. Such data for a number of cities, at least, would have been provided had it not been found necessary, for lack of funds, to give up the projected statistical analyses.

It is impossible to say, categorically, just how much political democracy actually means to the Negro unless it is also accompanied with full economic opportunity. That the Negro in a city like Chicago has received some considerable benefits from his political activity would seem to be incontrovertible. On the other hand, the fact that his economic opportunity has been fenced in by racial discrimination tends often to make opportunities for political participation something of a mockery insofar as the welfare of the entire group is involved. It is a striking fact in the history of American Negroes that, following emancipation, so little attention was devoted, either by government or by Negro leadership, to the economic welfare of this population. The Negro leaders were completely absorbed in the new political freedom. In their economic thinking, they were essentially petty bourgeois and thought that political emancipation had assured the group's wholesome economic future.

The analysis of Negro political status in St. Louis, Cleveland, and New York has been based almost entirely upon the research memoranda which we had prepared by reliable Negro citizens in these three centers. There has been no opportunity to expand the analysis beyond the limits thus determined, nor to make any careful check on the materials thus made available. Data for the Detroit and Philadelphia analyses came from field notes and unpublished manuscripts. The analyses here presented make no pretense to being intensive or thorough. This was quite impossible unless field work in selected Northern areas could have been undertaken. It was necessary, because of limitations of time and money, to make the choice between field work in the South and field work in selected Northern areas. When it became apparent to me that we could not afford to do both jobs, I selected the South without a moment's hesitation. The reasons for this decision were simple: the vast majority of Negroes still live in the Southern region, and nonvoting is a much more serious problem than voting. The Negro in the North votes. The story of how he votes; how he is voted; what his political attitudes are and how they are determined; the shifts in his political allegiance; the gains from political activity; the nature of his political leadership; and his influence upon the Northern and national political scene is an important and interesting one. I wish we could relate it in detail here.

But the fact is that the Negro voter in the North is much more thoroughly assimilated politically than he is economically or socially. The Chicago picture is quite typical, and Professor Gosnell has portrayed that well. The Negro voter, like the white, is preyed upon by the political machines. The Negro voter, through his political leaders, who are professional politicians and therefore self-seeking, expects a return for his vote in the form of improved municipal services. Where, as in Chicago, New York, Cleveland, Philadelphia, St. Louis, and Detroit, his vote is an important factor in determining election results, he does get improved facilities and services, though seldom in proportion to the real importance of his vote. Yet his vote is a voice that can command attention, and it gives the Negro of the North an effective lever that is almost entirely foreign to his black brother in the South.

All in all, the Negro voter in Northern communities takes over the established white patterns of political conduct and attitude. The Negro vote, no longer inseparably tied to the Republican party, is less a bloc vote than formerly, and must be carefully wooed by the political organizations. It is unfortunate that some real work could not have been done in this study on the extent and nature of the shifts in Negro voting in the North since 1928.

I would very much like to see some careful checking done on the thesis, as indicated in Chicago, that upper-class Negroes did not shift from Republican to Democratic, and that they are motivated by the prestige value of identity with the Republican party.

Another factor in determining our decision not to place too much emphasis here on Negro political activity in the North is the imminence of the 1940 presidential election. This election is highly vital to any real appraisal of the present trend in Negro voting. It will only be after the 1940 election returns are in and carefully analyzed that it will be possible to determine just how solid the shift of the Negro vote from Republican to Democratic has been. Will the black vote, which followed the bread and butter appeal of the New Deal from 1932 to 1936, return to the Republican fold? Both major parties are obviously devoting serious attention to the black vote—the Democrats to hold it and the Republicans to recapture it. The Republicans have traditionally paid lip service at least to the Negro cause as bait for the Negro vote, as the Republican platforms from 1884 to 1940 well illustrate.[7]

The major political parties employ all possible means of influencing the Negro to vote the "right way." One of the essential tactics involves purchasing the support of the Negro press. As the strategic power of the Negro vote in the North has increased, greater importance has been placed upon the distribution of party publicity and propaganda among the black voters. Large sums are set aside for Negro publicity. Negro publicity directors are appointed and the party campaign chests offer suitable inducements to the Negro press. A good many of the Negro ministers and lodge leaders in the North are important political figures, and during the heat of the campaign, church and lodge meetings are often converted into political forums. Not infrequently, candidates are "invited" to speak from the pulpits of Negro churches, and it is well known that many ministers and lodge leaders "cash in" on their efforts in behalf of candidates bidding for the Negro vote. In a recent conference of a large Negro church organization, a politics section was chosen whose duty it was to determine what party the church organization would support in the coming presidential campaign. Once this determination was reached, the decision was to be mandatory on all ministers in the organization. The presumption was clear

---

7. See pp. 1247–51 of the original Bunche memorandum for a summary of these platforms. —ED.

that the support of the organization would be sold for a sizable consideration—a fair deal in view of the fact that the influence of the church group among Negroes was great. This political activity of the churchmen and lodge leaders is not a peculiarly Negro but a typical American pattern.

It is difficult to assess the real benefits accruing to the Northern Negro from his political activities. Before 1932 the great concentration on presidential campaigns paid only small dividends to the Negro masses, though Negro political leaders often plucked juicy patronage plums. But the New Deal for the first time gave broad recognition to the existence of the Negro as a national problem and undertook to give specific consideration to this fact in many ways. The immediate gains from political activity have resulted from the strategic role played by the black electorate in municipal campaigns. Here the Negro of the Northern cities has been able to trade his vote for tangible results—better schools, playground facilities, sanitation improvements, hospital accommodations, police and fire protection, transportation services, and improved lighting and paving.

The question is often raised as to whether the Negro vote is or should be a solid bloc vote. It is not so now, and I do not believe that it should be, even assuming that it were possible to make it so. Nevertheless, the Negro vote assumes its greatest importance when it is voted as a single bloc and is able to hold the balance of power between opposing factions or parties. It has played a rather spectacular role in Chicago in this respect. This has been the real significance of the Negro vote in the North and West. It is easy to exaggerate the extent of this sort of Negro political influence, however. At the present time rather wild claims are made by some Negro leaders to the effect that the Negro holds the balance of political power in seventeen states. Actually, however, such claims are based not upon the effective Negro vote but upon Negro proportions of the population, and they assume that the black vote is a one-way or bloc vote operating in a no-man's-land between warring white political factions. One such claim states that there are 1,800,000 Negro votes in eighty-nine congressional districts located west of Columbus, Ohio, and in a three-hundred-mile area north and south of the Mason-Dixon line. These 1,800,000 votes are said to represent the strategic vote of the Negro. This is the area in which the Negro gave the support to the Republican party that helped to perpetuate that party in office with only minor interruptions for more than half a century. The point is, of course, that these figures are based not on the Negro voting population but on the Negro population of voting age. And to accept such contentions, one has to assume that every Negro twenty-one years of age and over in this area votes—an assumption that is palpably false. The fact that the Negro vote has been a very significant power in certain Northern areas is definitely true, and the strength of Negro participation in Chicago, Detroit, and New York bears this out, but such influence must always be carefully analyzed.

It has not been possible for us to work up any thorough account of the extent of Negro officeholding. Independent Negro candidates are rarely successful, even though the Negro vote may be a race-conscious vote; the machine power is usually too great for the independent to overcome. One of the most effective devices employed to defeat a threatening Negro candidate is that which encourages or buys multiple Negro candidates in order to split the black vote and permit the white candidate to win. It is significant, too, that successful Negro candidates for higher elective offices are sometimes the successors to retiring white candidates who have long been maintained in office as the friend of the Negro by black votes. Election districts are so drawn that the full force of the vote in the concentrated Negro population areas cannot be taken advantage of, and, consequently, despite the large black population in most of the Northern cities, it is virtually impossible to elect a Negro to Congress without considerable support from the white vote. The hope for a Negro congressman from New York depends upon the organization among the black electorate of sufficient strength to force the party machine to select Negro instead of white candidates for the office.

Although we have not been able to present an accurate and detailed description of the extent to which the Negro holds public office, it appears quite certain that the trend is toward a slowly but ever-widening horizon for Negro appointive and elective officeholders. The Negro has broken through a great many barriers in this respect, and it is not uncommon in many of the state legislatures, in municipal courts, and in city councils, even in the border states, to find Negro representatives. Most of the appointive offices held by Negroes have been dictated by reasons of political strategy. Many of the appointive officeholders, however, are individuals of unusual competence, and in training and ability are quite able to hold their own with the white appointees. The fact that Negro candidates can now undertake to run in many Southern localities without causing any particular community furore is in itself significant.

The great majority of attempts to return Negroes to elective offices have failed, but some of these contests have been surprisingly close. Such was the case in Dallas, Texas, in 1935, when a Negro, A. S. Wells, ran for the state legislature in a special election to fill a vacancy. Because this was a special election, Negroes were able to vote and to run for office. Seventy-three persons sought the nomination to fill this vacancy and sixty-three actually ran for the office. Wells, the only Negro in the field, placed fifth in this election—receiving 1,001 votes. The legislative seat was won by a white candidate with 1,844 votes. There were enough Negroes registered and eligible to vote to have enabled Wells to win, but only 40 percent of those qualified to vote actually went to the polls, possibly because of fear of the Ku Klux Klan terror. The Klan had published a leaflet warning Negroes to stay away from the polls and pinned these on the doors of Negro homes. In addition, Wells was a politician of the old school and did not have the unanimous support of the Negro people. He was not the best possible choice. Moreover, he was publicly antireligious, and this alienated Negro church followers.

Although the list of attempts to gain representation to elective offices is characterized by failure after failure, Negroes have enjoyed varying degrees of success in having members of their race given appointive positions. It is believed that the emergence of the Negro as a serious political factor has a direct bearing on the number and importance of the appointive positions held, and the field material tends to support this point of view. In the South it is found that, except in a few cases, the most promising situations exist in the border states.

It must be emphasized from the beginning that a study of the participation of the Negro in national administrative government is not merely the study of an isolated phenomenon. Its significance is that insofar as it portrays the participation of an important minority group in the governmental process, just in that degree does it show how successfully American democracy has worked with regard to that particular group. And it is realized that this in turn is related to the workings of democracy on the entire national scene when it is discovered that the entrance of the Negro into administrative government, as well as the innovations in the positions held, occurs in two great periods of upsurge in American democracy, namely, the Reconstruction and New Deal periods.

Although the emphasis here will be placed on the New Deal period, it is very important that some attention be given to the historical aspect of the subject. This is especially true of the era of Reconstruction and its aftermath, for this was the period of the greatest participation of the Negro in general national politics, and it was also in this period that the political future of the Negro was determined, was set, and was sealed. Until recent times this historical background of the Negro people was either willfully neglected or consciously distorted, since the story of their widespread involvement in Reconstruction politics was not in harmony with disfranchisement and the attempt to "keep them in their place." But because of the works of Du Bois and others, this story is slowly filtering through the walls of rabid distortion to become the cultural property of the Negro people. It is equally true, of course, that there is a strong tendency for Negroes, on their part, also to distort the story, and to grind the Negro side of the ax. Yet it is still possible for a newspaper writer to have a "Do You Know?" column concerning Negroes who have served in certain high governmental positions.

For convenience and clarity this subject has been divided roughly into three periods: the "pioneer" period, 1865–1900; the period of traditional appointments, 1900–1932; and the New Deal period. The justification for this division is the existence of certain peculiarities in each period as regards the type of men who participated, the kind of positions held, and the relation of the positions of those in them to the welfare of the general Negro population. It will be shown that the men of the Reconstruction period were national figures in political life and that they were sufficiently aggressive and politically able to take advantage of a favorable situation and enter into high positions never before held by Negroes. They clung to those positions, even after the death knell of Reconstruction was sounded, and thus set the pattern for future black appointments. During the second period these positions were to become traditional "Negro positions" to be held automatically by those in party circles who "delivered the vote." The professional politicians seemed satisfied to fight only for these positions and no others; as a result, they gradually lost major positions while others became modified. Finally, the positions held under the New Deal represent a radical break with the past because of their novelty and the entirely different character of the appointee, as well as the method of appointment. The first two periods will be dealt with only in order to throw light on the degree of participation, but the last period will be treated more fully, and an analysis of each significant position held will be made.[8]

The unusual entrance of Negroes into New Deal positions evoked widespread and varied comment. In the South, the *Georgia Women's World,* a hysterical anti-New Deal newspaper, printed pictures of Mrs. Roosevelt with Mrs. Mary McLeod Bethune and other Negro officials, and in its attempt to appeal to popular prejudices, claimed that the New Deal was advocating "social equality" and that Negroes were "taking over the White House." Among Negroes the reaction was equally varied. In his syndicated column, one venerable Negro educator maintained that a group of "handkerchief heads" and "Uncle Toms" had been brought into the government, while some Negro newspapers lauded the appointments as great steps forward.

The pitfall in evaluating these positions is the general lack of criteria for measuring administrative performance. To this may be added the novelty and short duration of these particular positions. When the New Deal found peculiar problems were arising from the impact of its expanded program upon a minority group, it called in "advisers" and "specialists" in an attempt to smooth out its difficulties. These Negro advisers were not brought in to be mere figureheads, but to aid actively in the prosecution of a socio-economic program. In some cases they were brought in only after blunders had been made and vigorous protests registered. If the stated purpose of establishing these positions was to integrate the Negro into governmental agencies and their services, then the evaluation must be centered around two questions: (1) to what degree do these positions represent integration into governmental agencies; and (2) to what degree do they aid participation of the Negro in governmental services? Although questions of personal initiative and alertness may arise, an objective analysis should be confined to the powers inherent in these positions, since most

8. These three periods and many of the major Negro officeholders are discussed in pp. 1359–1460 of the original Bunche memorandum. A summary of Negro officeholders for the years 1911–34, as mentioned in the NAACP's monthly journal, *Crisis,* is provided in chapter 17, pp. 1461–71, of the original memorandum. —ED.

of the appointees are highly conscious of the condition of their race and have made use of their power, in varying degree, toward bettering that condition.

The administrative position of the New Deal Negro personnel is quite varied. The weakest positions are those of advisers who are merely called in for advice and are responsible to division or bureau heads as well as to their immediate chief. The strongest positions are those in which the racial specialist directs an office or a division which is autonomous and on the same line with the other divisions in the agency. Excellent examples of the latter are the Division of Negro Affairs [directed by Mary McLeod Bethune] in the National Youth Administration and the Office of Racial Relations in the United States Housing Authority. These positions also have a voice in the selection of Negro personnel in their units, and in Mrs. Bethune's office their advisory power is exercised on a national scale. The small number of blacks in the two offices in the agricultural field is a special weakness, since Negroes are heavily concentrated in agriculture, and it is in this field that the greatest racial problems are found. The largest number of these appointments is in the emergency agencies, and therefore they may be considered temporary. Although some agencies are being continued or made permanent, there is no assurance of tenure, as can be seen by the drastic curtailments in the Public Works Administration in 1939. Out of a list of 103 Negro New Deal appointees, there have been 23 resignations and 3 curtailments. The resignation of over 20 percent is significant, since most have resigned in order to return to their former fields of endeavor, indicating that they attach no security or permanence to their positions.

In evaluating these offices, one should not lose sight of their relation to the administrative units within which they operate. Since it is a general administrative practice that subordinates are loyal to their chief and adhere to his policies, it is no surprise that there is found a significant correlation between the liberality of administrative heads and the latitude given to Negro advisers. Thus it was one of the foremost ideologists of the New Deal, Harold L. Ickes, who first established a race relations office in which the first objective measures against discrimination were also worked out.

The development of objective measures against discrimination in the administrative rules governing the allocation of funds represents a definite advance toward the guarantee of equality to minority groups and means that corrections can be effected before the passage of major phases of administrative activity. It also strengthens the administrative position of the race relations office. This leads to the question of the integration of the Negro into the regular branches of the administrative agencies, for this represents the ideal long-time trend. The majority of the present positions represent reactions to an undesirable situation, and supposedly, to the extent that these conditions are eradicated, will no longer be necessary. Therefore, the entrance of Negro personnel into regular positions not only supplements the special positions, but marks the beginning of the full integration of the Negro into administrative government.

The present distribution of Negro employees in the government is uneven and woefully inadequate. A majority of them are in custodial positions while the rest are in responsible places, but there is lack of employment in the typical positions which make up the great bulk of governmental jobs—the clerks, stenographers, and typists. In some agencies the advisers on Negro problems constitute almost the sole Negro personnel other than the custodial workers. In the USHA, in addition to those employed in the Office of Racial Relations, Negroes perform regular work in the technical, legal, management review, finance, and accounts divisions; they are also employed as reviewing and consulting architects.

Not only are Negroes in administrative government limited by handicaps inherent in the weakness of their positions and the traditional conservatism of administrative agencies, but their attempts to bring the services of their agencies to the Negro population are limited by certain factors which lie in the American social pattern. There is a wide gap between the concern of Americans for social advance and their concern for the miserable conditions of their fellow citizen, the Negro, and in the South there is hardly concern for either. Americans have been quick to respond to the attempts of the New Deal to regulate wages and hours, to pass housing legislation, to enact social security laws, and to enlarge federal aid to agriculture and education. But they have been slow to respond to governmental attempts to pass the benefits of this legislation to the Negro. Many of the contradictions in New Deal policy as it affects the Negro may be traced to this lethargy and to the strong, although waning, support it had to maintain among Southern Democrats.

Yet when the past is viewed, it must be concluded that these positions, with all of their handicaps, represent a distinct advance for Negroes. They represent the first feeble steps in a desirable direction—the full integration of the Negro into administrative government. If the Negro minority is to further this trend, it must seek to retain, strengthen, and make full use of these positions. Although the existence of such positions is no sure protection, it is doubtful whether hundreds of thousands of dollars and many services would have gone to black citizens had they not existed, and the personnel policies of certain advisers have achieved definite steps toward administrative integration. Interesting in this connection was a conference held in 1939 under the auspices of the National Lobby Committee to guarantee that Negro administrative assistants would not be laid off because of the President's Reorganization Bill No. 1, and to seek to insure equitable inclusion of Negroes in the new structure created by executive reorganization.

Finally, it should be emphasized that the struggle to strengthen the position of the Negro in administrative government is inextricably tied up with the general minority struggle for political, social, and economic equality. There is great danger that, in pursuing such aims, a minority group might concentrate on its own specific problems and forget the broader fight for social advance. If any lesson can be learned from history, it is that this constitutes social suicide. The men of the Reconstruction era made their advance by carefully and astutely weighing the general social and political forces at work. Today these forces are far more favorable to the Negro, and, even though the elements of reaction are strong, advantage can be taken of this situation to achieve a significant step along the road toward full integration of the Negro into national administrative government—and the broader frame of American politics.

SIX

Conclusion

NEGROES constitute roughly one-tenth of the total American population. This black section of the citizenry tends to diffuse itself increasingly throughout the country, though its great concentration is still found in the Deep South. In the decade of the 1920s, some 1,500,000 Negroes migrated from the South to the North, most of them settling in the industrial centers. Today approximately 32 percent of the total Negro population of the North is found in New York (327,706), Chicago (233,903), and Philadelphia (219,599). At least ten Southern cities boast black populations in excess of 50,000. This diffusion of the Negro population has converted the "Negro problem" into a distinctly national rather than sectional one.

The future of the American Negro is a problem of the national society. It is to be solved only through opportunity for development and through assimilation into the political and economic life of the nation. The Negro has for centuries contributed his labor, his intelligence, his blood, and even his life to the development of the country. He asks nothing from American society except that it consider him as a full-fledged citizen, vested with all of the rights and privileges granted to other citizens; that the charter of liberties of the Constitution apply to the black as to all other men. The Negro citizen has long since learned that "special" treatment for him implies differentiation on a racial basis and inevitably connotes inferior status. In a world in which democracy is gravely besieged and its very foundations shaken, the United States must consider seriously the implications of its own failure to extend the democratic process in full to some thirteen million of its citizens whose present status tends to make a mockery of the Constitution. The thinking Negro appreciates fully the difficulties inherent in the American social system. He recognizes that deep-seated social attitudes are not quickly changed. Yet it can be readily understood that, in a world in which dogmas of racial superiority and racial persecution assume an increasingly dominant role, the Negro views with great alarm the stubborn persistence of racial bigotry in America.

The Negro asks only his constitutional right when he demands that the laws of the United States be designed so as to extend their benefits to black as well as to white citizens, and that political parties, governmental agencies, and officials pledge themselves to extend the full measure of law and constitution to all men, regardless of race, color, or creed. Never since the Civil War has the Constitution assumed such vital importance in the ordering of the country. The future of the Negro rests with the future of democracy, and Negroes in great numbers now know that every blow struck in behalf of democracy is a blow for the black man's future.

It is to be noted, too, that there is a virtual identity of fundamental interest between Negro and white citizens. The Negro is learning rapidly that whatever relief is extended to the white workingman is reflected in improved conditions for the black laborer; that whatever is done for the white tenant farmer beneficially affects the Negro tenant farmer; that whatever housing provision is made for low-income whites will also ameliorate the wretched housing conditions of millions of Negroes, even though seldom in proportionate degree.

The great masses of Negroes remain disfranchised. But those Negroes of the North, East, and West who do vote have a much keener sense than formerly of the uses to which the ballot can be put. They know that the ballot is negotiable and can be exchanged for definite social improvements for themselves. There is no longer blind loyalty to one party, based upon traditional attachment. The Negro regards the vote as a new bargaining power.

The white voter ballots according to his individual, sectional, and group interests. The Negro votes on the basis of identical interests, but the social system of America dictates that he must give prior consideration to his racial group interests. So long as the dual social system persists in the United States, just so long must the Negro justifiably expect that political parties desiring his political support will devote specific attention to ways and means of Negro betterment in framing their platforms. The Negro finds himself in the uncomfortable position of decrying racial differentiation, while being compelled to demand it when important political policies are being formulated, in order to hold his ground in an uncongenial social milieu.

The Negro is a taxpayer and thus has a vital stake in the financial policy of the government. The black citizen, like the white, knows instinctively that the major share of the nation's tax burden is borne ultimately on the shoulders of the mass working and consuming population. The state of the nation's credit and the stability of the currency are closely linked with the Negro's struggle up the economic ladder. Taxes, especially the sales taxes of the Southern states, weigh heavily upon him. Certainly the Negro has strong reasons for hoping that national budgets will be balanced, that taxes in the lower income brackets will be lowered, and that a policy of governmental economy will be adopted. The Negro may wish for all of this, yet his very position in society creates an inescapable dilemma, in that he constitutes a disproportionate part of that section of the population which has survived during the past eight years only because of governmental largess. With conditions as they now are, the Negro has no alternative but to choose relief and relief work over tax reduction and governmental economy. It is either that or starvation for millions. In the face of such alternatives, the nicer subtleties of public "economy" arguments leave great numbers of Negroes untouched and unconvinced.

In a world in which narrow racial attitudes and dogmas have become so intimately identified with the policy of governments, and in which minority peoples are so sorely beset, our foreign policy is of vital import to the black population. The interests of the Negro, as of all minority peoples, are gravely menaced by the ravages of dictators who despoil democracy; who hold human liberty and equality up to scorn; who rape minority peoples; and who preach "Aryan" superiority as a religious creed. In the economic realm, the Negro as a low-income group is necessarily concerned that the United States pursue a balanced tariff policy which will reasonably protect the consuming public against exceedingly high prices for the necessities of life and yet preserve the traditional American wage standard.

For many years the Negro stood by the Republican party because of traditional allegiance to the "party of abolition" and its great leader, Abraham Lincoln. This party, it was thought, personified that strong central government which would protect the Negro against the excesses of the Southern states. It was only logical that the Negro should look askance at the doctrine of state rights. It is now rather bewildering to Negroes, therefore, to discover that the two major parties seem to have changed positions. The Republican party as the party of the opposition in the current campaign will need to explain carefully to Negroes this shift in position. It must give convincing, concrete assurances that in such vital matters as relief, social insurance, medical care, education, public employment, housing, and agricultural benefits the Negro will not again be thrown to the wolves (as he was after Reconstruction) and left, unprotected, to the not-too-tender mercies of a racially bigoted South. There is also the danger, not too widely recognized perhaps, that excessive centralization and bureaucracy in the national government may tend to cement the Negro in a permanent position of segregated inferiority in society. This tendency is already noted in the administration of the Federal Housing Administration and the Tennessee Valley Authority. Yet the Negro voter is apt to agree that even segregated, inferior benefits from the federal government are better than little or none at all from the states.

If democracy is to survive the severe trials and buffetings to which it is being subjected in the modern world, it will do so only because it can demonstrate that it is a practical, living philosophy under which all people can live the good life most abundantly. It must prove itself in practice, or be discredited as a theory. Democratic nations such as our own have an obligation to all mankind to prove that democracy, as a form of government, as a practical means of human relationships, is a working and workable concept. This America can do only by abandoning the shallow, vulgar pretense of limited democracy —under which some are free and privileged and others are permanently fettered. The Negro, and especially the Negro in the South, already has had too vivid an experience with embryonic fascism in the very shadow of democracy. Within our own gates are found intense racial hatreds, racial ghettoes, and racial differentials that saturate the political, economic, and social life of the nation.

It has been pointed out in this memorandum that the virtually complete disfranchisement of the Negro in the South at the turn of the century came, not through any fault of his own making, not because he was a poor citizen or was incapable of participating in political processes, but primarily because he was identified with a party to which the majority of Southern whites were opposed. The black citizen was the victim in a conscious, deliberate, and profitable exploitation of race consciousness by Southern demagogues and politicians. Already, in the South, political morality had reached a new low in the period in which Populism created divisions in the white society and Negroes were enabled to wield a temporary balance of political power. The South reacted by removing the Negro—a mere pawn— from the political scene, and by making itself solidly white politically.

This was, quite definitely, a severe rebuff and a source of serious disillusionment to the Negro citizen, who had built up high hopes of attaining the full stature of American citizenship. Negro politicians lost the opportunities for their careers, and Negro leaders generally were confronted with the ironical necessity of encouraging Negroes to become good and loyal citizens, even though they could not participate in the affairs of state. But such reactions and disillusionment were confined largely to the educated Negroes, to the leaders and the aspiring Negro middle and upper classes. That is to say, the disfranchisement of the Negro—or of the poor white by the poll tax today— is of more vital concern to those who believe in the preservation of democracy as the only way of retaining the real values in national life than it is of direct concern to the disfranchised themselves. The Negro in the cotton field who had never had the ballot missed it less than democracy needed him to exercise it.

In recent years Southern Negroes have begun to reenter politics, often through the Democratic party. But to date this has not extended much beyond the Negroes of the upper classes. The lower-class Negro, the working-class and peasant black of the region, is still politically virgin. In this he is joined by many thousands of poor whites.

When the Negro was disfranchised in the South, he was on the wrong side of the political fence. Recently in the South he has begun to get on the "right" or Democratic side, and this may be a form of voting insurance for him in the future, though such a development can by no means be predicted at the moment. There has certainly been a gradual easing of the barriers against Negro voting in the Southern region, with respect to both laws and opinion. This has encouraged the Negro to seek to regain his franchise. This trend is still largely restricted to the urban centers, but it does seem unmistakable. Still, the real test in the South remains in the Negro's ability to break through the white primary. All else is largely futile until this obstacle is surmounted. There are those who look to the Negro electorate as a great potential source of votes in support of liberal and reform movements in the South. But this hope is as devoid of foundation under present restraints on Negro voting as is the alleged threat of "black domination." The most cogent argument in support of Negro enfranchisement in the region today is that the potential black voter, like the white voter under the poll tax burden, is subject to the control of the white politicians who determine who and how many can vote, and thus keep the political power "on tap."

And by what means can the Negro hope to win the right to exercise the franchise? What can he expect from the Constitution and the courts? The simple truth is that, short of another civil war, the Supreme Court cannot enforce its decisions when they are confronted by a hostile public. Only an executive branch willing to back up the judgments of the court with the full strength of the armed forces could put teeth in such decisions. This is a major dilemma for the court, in that whenever it does present a fearless, honest opinion on some right of the Negro, it is likely to see that judgment widely flouted and made quite ineffectual, as in *Strauder* v. *West Virginia* (1880). In seeking escape from this dilemma, the court has often attempted to maintain its judicial dignity by paying lip service to the constitutional principles of protection and equality, while nimbly sidestepping the danger of running afoul of public opinion by countenancing not very subtle evasions of the spirit of the law. This resort to legal fiction in order to avoid social conflict is well illustrated in the case of *Grovey* v. *Townsend* (1935), in which Justice Roberts opined that justice for the Negro is served in Texas, when the Negro—excluded from the Democratic primary, which actually takes the place of the general election—is permitted to go through the useless exercise of casting a shadow vote at the general election.

The Negro should press with all vigor his fight before the courts for the full recognition of his constitutional rights. Court decisions, favorable or unfavorable, serve to dramatize the plight of the race more effectively than any other recourse; their propaganda and educative value is great. Certainly appeal to the courts is a useful tactic for an oppressed minority group, and it is fortified by the fact that the Negro cause is honest and just. But the problems of the Negro cannot be solved at the bar. The courts cannot uproot deep-seated social prejudices; they can never bring on a social revolution.

The so-called Negro problem in America is only incidentally a racial one. Many of its roots go deeper than race and are themselves embedded in the fundamental problems of economic conflict and distress which afflict the entire society. The primary interests of the Negro are inextricably tied up with the interests of the masses in the dominant population. Therefore, court decisions such as those upholding the Wagner Act, social security legislation, and minimum wage and hour enactments will in the long run do much to better the condition of the Negro. Every advance made toward lessening the conflict between labor and capital, between laborer and laborer, between white and black workers—in fact, any legislation designed to increase the security of the workingman's present and future—is of the most fundamental significance for the Negro and for all other minority groups in the United States. The courts can never save the Negro from an America torn asunder by industrial conflict and its inevitable by-products, racial intolerance and bigotry.

In these critical days of violent ideological conflict, when all thinking is confused and things political and economic are in a state of flux, it is important to the Negro's political and economic future here that he be clear in his own thinking. There is an annoying indifference among Negroes of all classes—from day laborers to the highest ranks of the intelligentsia—about what is transpiring in the rest of the world; and where thought is given to the subject, it is often distorted and confused. We may mention, for "laboratory" purposes and in attenuated form, a half dozen typical Negro reactions, often heard recently, toward the European conflagration and its threat to the Negro's future here:

1. Nazism or fascism is nothing new to the Negro, since he has always experienced it in the South anyway.

2. The Negro couldn't be any worse off than he now is in the Deep South. Therefore, an American fascism would make little difference to him.

3. American democracy is so imperfect, so hypocritical in its shabby treatment of the Negro, that unless it can quickly perfect itself and demonstrate its workability, it doesn't deserve to survive.

4. Even under fascism there would always be a need and a place for the Negro in America, since he is indispensable to the profit economy of the great American white middle class.

5. The war abroad is an "imperialist" war; the Negro and the United States should have nothing to do with it. Let us concentrate on achieving democracy at home; let us win freedom

and equality for labor and the Negro first; "the Yanks are not coming." (This is the "line" of the American Communist party, and it is being parroted by many Negroes who unknowingly fall into its subtle trap.)

6. The war is a white man's war and a good thing for the Negro. Let the white folks kill each other off and then the "black Aryans" will be the master race and rule the world.

Any attempt at logical thinking must be controlled by the answer to the very practical question: "What are the alternatives confronting the Negro today?" In the first place, he is not permitted the luxury of choosing between ideal systems. He is socially blind even if he permits himself to build his hopes in such a dream world. The Negro must take his immediate choices from imperfect, buffeted democracy, on the one hand, and totalitarianism, on the other. And this may be a privilege which will not long endure even in his thinking. Negroes are all too familiar with the many and serious shortcomings of American democracy; but they know, though they do not always recall, that democracy as a concept, as a way of life, has afforded them the sole basis for whatever progress they have made as a group since slavery, for the heroic struggle they have incessantly waged, for their aspirations in the future. Democracy, even imperfect democracy, has been the ideological foundation upon which Negro life has been based; it has been the spiritual lifeblood for Negroes. As an ideal, it has not progressed very rapidly in the world we know. But what else has the world to offer the Negro? If I were perched in a window on the top floor of a burning building and below me were some typical slit-mouthed, washboard-neck specimens of the Southern "cracker" type holding a net and yelling profanely: "Jump, you blankety-blank nigger!"—I would jump. I would resent the insult, resent the "crackers," and feel not at all happy about the fire that created the unpleasant situation. But I would indeed jump, and then having landed safely, proceed to "cuss" them out for calling me "nigger"—unless the fire happened to be in Mississippi.

The other alternative, as we have said, is totalitarianism—the authoritarian state, dictatorship. In terms of the immediate menace, this must be considered to be the brand of fascism peddled by Herr Hitler. Russian totalitarianism—the other side of the fascist coin—is significant to us now only insofar as the purge-drunk dictator Joseph Stalin sees it to his interest to support or oppose Hitler and the Soviet-Nazi pact. Hitler's nazism —National Socialism—is a world-revolutionary movement. It involves a revolution in the political, economic, and social spheres of modern life. This cannot be impressed too greatly upon contemporary Americans. It is the martial state in which all values are the values of war.

First of all, it considers constitutional democracy as an archaic, outworn political system, because of its inefficiency; its toleration of opposition within the state; its decentralization of power; its concept of individualism and the right of the individual as against the state; its devotion to concepts of individual freedom, liberty, will, and human equality. German fascism jettisons the democratic institutions of government—the legislatures, parliaments, and constitutions; the process of elective officeholders; the exercise of a free franchise by the people—and replaces all of these with a dictator, a ruler whom all must worship, whose mere word is law, and who governs with the mailed fist—a Hitler or a Mussolini. No opposition is tolerated, and dissenters are liquidated by means of the concentration camp and the firing squad. In the economic sphere, German fascism substitutes for private capitalism or socialism a powerful "planned" state economy. In the economic sphere, as in the political, all freedom is destroyed. The sharecropper or day laborer in darkest Mississippi has more economic freedom and, even if he is a Negro, more civil liberty than the Aryan worker of Germany today. In the social realm racial tolerance is decried by the fascist states as a fatal weakness of democracy. For the concept of human equality there is substituted the concept of the superior race, of the German or Aryan master and ruling race, which is predestined to rule the world. Thus, politically, economically, and socially under German fascism, there is created the essential slave state—a state to which obedience is assured through the frightfully efficient and ruthless operation of the gestapo or secret police.

And now, before this realistic backdrop, to comment briefly upon the specific Negro reactions previously mentioned.

First, the American South is not fascistic. The South is neither totalitarian nor highly centralized; it more nearly approaches the chaotic. It is prejudice-bitten and lacking in morality, but at the same time irrational in its treatment of the Negro. Life for the Negro in the South would be far harsher under a highly centralized, highly rational, and brutally efficient fascism which would give total, authoritative expression to the Southern doctrine of white supremacy.

Second, the Negro in the South—and in the North—would

be in a hopelessly distressing plight once there occurred in this country a complete destruction of the concepts of human rights, liberty, and privilege, and of the constitutional basis for their appeals to justice. That would create for Negroes an entirely new world, devoid, for them, of either rights or hopes.

Third, to say that if democracy cannot perfect itself and accord Negroes proper treatment they will have none of it, is, in these times, sheer nonsense and racially suicidal. It is not intelligent to think of burning down the barn in order to destroy the rats. This "all or nothing" position employs the liberty afforded by democracy to aid and abet, not its perfection, but its destruction in times of stress.

Fourth, Negroes cannot rely for their future upon the great American middle class. They must reckon upon the possibility that a total victory by Hitler in Europe would produce economic repercussions here that could throw the American middle class into hysteria and economic collapse. The neutralization of our huge gold stores, the loss of trade in Europe, and the necessity for astronomical sums for defense would all hit the Negro, as a marginal population, first, last, and most severely—if not fatally.

Fifth, white people have no monopoly on fascist ideology or on human exploitation. Black, brown, and yellow tyrants in a world in which white supremacy would be destroyed would be as ruthless as the present white ones. Changing the colors of the aspiring master races of the world is no solution to human suffering.

Sixth, the Communist position is sophistry of the cheapest variety. To say that we should ignore the imperialist war and bend all efforts to perfect democracy at home, in the world today, is deliberately to mislead the Negro, and to set a cunning trap for him. The Communists know that the Negro can always be enthralled by appeals for his rights. But the Communists, who are no longer radicals, want Negroes to forget that it was only a year or so ago that they were urging blacks to support, in their own interest, the fight for democracy in Spain—and they were right then. That was when Hitler and fascism were regarded as the twin forces of darkest evil for the liberty-loving, working masses of the world. But then came the Communist shift from the popular front line, the Soviet-Nazi pact, and now Russia and the Communists are on the other side. The vital war question for Negroes is *"who* will win it?" England, and France, before her collapse, gave recognition to the basic concepts of the democratic way of life, even though they were guilty of serious violations of the rights of certain subjects. But even now, during the war, African natives in British colonies are able to publish criticisms of government policy that would put a fine Aryan German worker in a concentration camp.

The Negro faces grave danger from the repercussions of a Nazi victory in Europe—less from the possibility of direct military invasion than from the penetration of Nazi ideology. Hitler also wages a total psychological war. To reassure ourselves on this point, we need only refer to his long string of broken promises, his brazenly false "reassurances" to Austria, Czechoslovakia, Poland, and the low countries, and, until now, his successful reliance upon the complacency and gullibility of the democracies. The United States has all the necessary raw materials for a native American fascism. It will suffice to enumerate them: racial intolerance; a badly functioning economic system, with widespread and continuing unemployment; a traditional admiration for things that work well and for spectacular successes; a naïve mass public, easily deceived, misled, and duped (witness our large crop of successful demagogues); a huge mass of wandering, futureless, discontented, and frustrated youth; a vast South in political, economic, and social chaos; a property- and profit-loving class that will grasp at any straw in a desperate crisis to salvage what it can of its vested interests. And against these factors, to hold the dikes against fascism, we have only what we are told is a traditional and determined love of freedom, individualism, and democracy, for which we will fight to the death.

And given fascism here, what of Negroes? Such an eventuality would be ominous indeed. The Negro is no longer indispensable in this country; he is entirely dispensable everywhere. He is increasingly a relief burden. There are conflicting viewpoints among Southern leaders concerning the question of the need for the Negro in the South. But the fact is that the Negro is not holding his own in employment, and even the South, as cotton culture wanes in one section or becomes mechanized in another, is suddenly awakening to the realization that it can travel its economic road without the aid of its black hands. There are no longer jobs that whites will not take and need. Fascism is a highly rational system. Its ends justify its means. And its ends are to organize the resources of the state for the benefit of the master race. The Negro is already virtually an alien race here. White supremacy under fascism or "one hundred percent Americanism" could seal his doom. Under a rational fascism there might well be: no education for the Negro; no government positions for the Negro; no licenses for Negro professional men; no business or automobile licenses for Negroes; no home or land ownership for Negroes; no legal rights for Negroes in the courts; no political rights for Negroes at the polls; Negro labor and concentration camps; registration of all Negroes; armband identification for Negroes of all shades; severe penalties for "passing"; decrees for the sterilization of Negroes; expatriation or exile for Negroes, as per Senator Bilbo; no Carnegie Corporation–sponsored studies of the Negro.

It is paradoxical that, in a democracy, nearly one-tenth of the citizens of the nation are refused the right of participation in the democratic process—not through lack of qualification, but solely because of color. There is an obvious and fundamental inconsistency between the South's insistence on "white supremacy"—as well as the tacit acceptance accorded it in the North —and the tenets of democracy.

The Negro in the South must meet all of the obligations of citizenship, including payment of taxes, but he is denied the privilege of citizenship. In no Southern legislature—with the exception of the "border" states—does the Negro have any direct representation. He has no voice in the selection of judges, governors, mayors, and other public officials who are responsible for the protection of his vital rights of life, liberty, and property. A great variety of ingenious legal devices has been conjured up by the Southern states to keep the Negro from the polls. The means employed to disfranchise the Negro frequently have serious social and economic repercussions for the entire mass population of the region. For example, the poll tax prevents poor citizens from voting in eight Southern states. Yet these same states load heavy tax burdens, in the form of sales taxes, on the backs of those least able to pay. Although the Southern Negro has been denied the franchise, his presence has diminished the real significance of the ballot for the white population of that section. For the white South has been compelled to adopt the one-party system and to vote solidly Democratic, and thus has had little opportunity to exercise voting choice except for personalities in primaries.

The inevitable objective of the Negro in the South is full citizenship rights. This embraces not merely the exercise of the franchise, but also the right to hold public office. It is certain, and there is no reason to deny it, that if the black ever gains the full right of franchise in the South, his next step will be toward office-holding. There are many Negroes qualified to serve as well as white officeholders now do.

There is need for a greatly strengthened corrupt-practices act which will contain specific provisions designed to protect the Negro in the exercise of the franchise, and which should declare the primary to be an integral part of the electoral process.[1] The names of political parties which in their nomination procedure discriminate on the basis of race or color, and the names of candidates nominated under such conditions, should be barred from the official ballot. The United States Department of Justice should investigate the registration and electoral processes of the Southern states, in congressional and presidential elections, as they affect potential Negro and poor white voters. The results of such investigation should be made public. The South should again be threatened with a reapportionment based exclusively on its white population, unless Negroes are allowed to exercise this constitutional right.

The Negro has always been subject to gross discrimination in government employment—in both civil service and non–civil service branches. While numbers of Negroes are employed by the government, they are generally restricted to menial and custodial tasks. Many well-trained young Negroes do not bother to take civil service examinations, for they know from experience that blacks have little chance of selection, no matter how high their rating. This results from the nature of the civil service appointment process, in which two factors are of special significance to Negroes. These are (1) the requirement of the photograph on the application for the examination and (2) the discretionary choice, from among the three highest applicants, which may be exercised by the appointing officer. There is a good deal of segregation in the government divisions, too. In non–civil service employment, Negroes customarily have been given some recognition, but only in the form of "political" appointments. These have been merely for purposes of wooing the Negro vote. Under the New Deal a few Negroes have been appointed as "advisers" on questions pertaining to the Negro, but the tendency has been for them to steer clear of the more controversial aspects of the Negro's problems in order not to displease political bosses and thereby jeopardize their positions. In

1. If the primary were declared to be an integral part of the electoral process, the exclusive white primary would be held illegal. —ED.

no single instance has a Negro been appointed to a really responsible, policy-forming position in the federal government.

The civil service should be greatly extended in government employment, and competitive examination should be the basis for the selection of all except head administrators in the permanent divisions. The federal government should adopt a broad policy of nondiscrimination in employment against any group because of race or color, on all projects controlled or subsidized by the government. The requirement of the photograph on civil service applications should be abolished, and identification should be by means of finger prints. Civil service appointments should be made strictly on the basis of rating, and the discretionary power of the appointing officer to choose from among the highest three should be abolished. All civil service rating lists should be made public, in order that candidates may be aware of their standing. Inquiries as to race or color appearing on applications for non–civil service positions should be removed, and such appointments should be made without consideration of race. Negroes should be appointed to responsible policy-forming positions in the government service. Negroes should be permitted to enroll in the Foreign Service training schools, and should be given wider and more responsible employment in the Foreign and Consular services. Employment in the offices of the District of Columbia administration should be placed under the civil service, in order that Negroes, who are almost entirely excluded from such employment, may have a chance at it. It is ultimately detrimental to the interests of Negroes to earmark certain political jobs for them, while excluding blacks from consideration in all others. Such a policy of segregated, "Negro jobs" should be discontinued. Negroes should be considered eligible for *all* jobs, in accordance with their training and ability.

Lynching fills one of the blackest pages in American history. It is an expression of mob law and constitutes a brutal violation of the fundamental principles on which the American government is founded. In its contempt for law and the law-enforcing agencies and in its barbaric manifestations, it has a degenerating influence on society. It is estimated that between 1889 and 1937 a total of 4,681 reported lynchings occurred, and unquestionably many more have gone unrecorded. This record of social perversion is bad enough, but the record of the attitude of law enforcement agencies toward lynchers is much worse. In the case of most lynchings, nothing is ever done to punish the murderers, though the identity of the ringleaders of the mob is generally well known to local officials. The states have demonstrated their complete inability or unwillingness to take necessary measures to cope with this evil. Thus the need for a forceful federal statute has been manifest for many years. The first such bill was introduced in Congress in 1920 but was never voted upon. Bitter opposition to it came from the South. The Dyer antilynching bill got through the House of Representatives in 1922, but it was stopped in the Senate by a filibuster led by Southerners. Since 1922 eight or nine other measures have been introduced in Congress. The solid Southern bloc insists that mob violence is the concern of state and local authorities, and it has bitterly opposed a federal antilynching law in any form. Efforts to put through a bill along the general lines of the Wagner–Van Nuys–Gavagan proposal should not be abandoned. Such efforts test the strength of the democratic process in the country, and any party pledged to a truly democratic program for the nation cannot ignore its responsibility in this direction. The Department of Justice should employ its excellent facilities to make a careful investigation and record of each lynching, and it should make such record public. When lynching parties cross state lines with their victims, the federal kidnapping law should be invoked.

In the final analysis, however, the political burdens borne by the American Negro cannot be legislated away. The roots of Negro disabilities reach deeply into the economic and political structure of the nation. Negro political ailments are merely symptomatic of more fundamental disorders in the economic system. These disorders cannot be cured by dabbing at the symptoms. The nation's economic house needs to be put in order. In the first place, it is useless to think in terms of full Negro citizenship so long as white and black citizens must engage in daily violent struggle for the wherewithal of life. This is the process that feeds fuel to the fires of race prejudice and perpetuates those mores which stand guard against Negro entrance to the polls. The economy must afford a far larger measure of security for all before the Negro can hope for much greater political advancement. This it can do only as a result of some far-reaching changes in the direction of a socialized economy—at least insofar as the production of the necessities of life is concerned. In the second place, unless the Negro is permitted to share in the fuller fruits of a more liberal and humane economy, political privilege will become sheer mockery. The black vote will never be influential enough to initiate in and of itself any radical changes in the economy. The ballot without bread would be a tragic jest for the Negro.

The Political Status of the Negro: A Survey Based on Field Interviews and Special Reports

SEVEN

Aspects of the Southern Political Process

THE three most salient features of the internal Southern political scene for our purposes are (1) the looseness and corruption in the region's politics; (2) the disfranchisement of both white and black citizens; and (3) the lack of any effective people's movements. It is proposed here to discuss only the first of these, with brief attention devoted to such matters as political controls, election practices, party machinery, the one-party system, campaigns, election fraud, and low voting percentages. These can be sketched only in broad and suggestive outline, primarily through illustrative data from the field notes.

Politics in Alabama counties, as in so many counties in the South, tend to revolve around local personalities. In Coffee County, for example, politics is said to be a straight question of "Carnley" and "anti-Carnley." Carnley is the probate judge, and it is said of him that "he thinks he can control any office in the county—and he's about right." There is always a small opposition vote against Carnley, but this vote is never well organized.[1] Dallas County is run by the "courthouse ring." The strength of the county machine is in (1) the hold it has over city and county patronage, and the way it has this pooled; (2) the lack of secrecy of the ballot; and (3) the lack of any attempt at opposition.[2]

1. George Stoney's interview with the chairman of the board of registrars, Coffee County, Alabama, April 1940. All quotations that are not specifically documented in this chapter are taken from Stoney's notes of interviews conducted in 1940. —ED.
2. Stoney's interviews with a former postmaster of Selma, Dallas County, Alabama, April 1940.

The probate judge and a few landlords dominate the politics of Lowndes County, Alabama, although, as one white voter in the county puts it, "there ain't much to run." There is little paying up of poll taxes because "most of the time there ain't nobody to buy." Since a sheriff could not, until 1928, succeed himself in Alabama, the sheriff of Lowndes County and his high deputy served in the job alternately for twenty years. When the sheriff died after the 1938 election, his wife was appointed to the job and the high deputy still runs the town. He will get the job again in 1942. The probate judge and his group all went in without opposition at the last election. The political races are so easy and so uncontested in Lowndes County that "they don't bother to come around and shake your hand no more."[3]

In Greene County, Alabama, local politics conforms to the usual pattern of the probate judge having a strong faction and all of the "antis" cooperating to beat him. Until 1932 the two factions were represented by the two local banks, because the candidates for probate were attached to each. One of these banks failed, however, and since 1934 there have been only two men elected who were not on the ticket of the probate judge.[4] According to the tax collector in Lee County, there has not been "a real hot election outside of the sheriff's place in ten years, to tell the gospel truth. Everybody knows how it's coming out." He added that a little group at Opelika controlled county politics with two exceptions: (1) the mills always elect the sheriff, and (2) the State Agricultural and Polytechnic Institute at Auburn is allowed one and sometimes both of the state representatives.

In Macon County, Alabama, there is said to be a political ring of landlords that now runs the board of control and that formerly was hooked-up with an ex–probate judge. There are four of these landlords, each of whom hires from thirty to forty men. Each of these men can swing at least one more vote and, in the words of the tax collector, "that means they have about 320 votes right there." In their combined plantations and places of business these landlords have about forty or fifty more votes, and "in one way or another they can vote over 400 any way they want to." This, in a county where the vote is as small as Macon's, represents great power.

It is necessary to have the okay of one of the county commis-

3. Stoney's interviews with several citizens of Lowndesboro and Hayneville, Lowndes County, Alabama, April 1940.
4. Stoney's interview with the sheriff of Greene County, Eutaw, Alabama, April 1940.

sioners to get on the Works Progress Administration in Madison County, Alabama. The WPA is the largest and newest bit of patronage in the county. The city patronage amounts to very little. The county patronage is not a solid bloc. Each holder of an important office has his own small group of job holders. The officeholders could get together, of course, and form an unofficial slate, but this kind of organization has seldom occurred in the county in recent years.

Politics in Bibb County, Alabama, revolve about the "ins" and the "outs", the "ins" being headed by the probate judge. The probate judge is in an extremely strong position because he has complete control of the poll tax machinery. He maintains a running record of those who pay the poll tax and notifies those of his friends who have not paid. He can cancel back taxes; that is, if a man owes back taxes for eight years, the judge can mark off four of them and permit him to pay the other four. This can be done because the judge and the tax collector can work together. As a matter of fact, however, it can be done without the knowledge of the tax collector, for the only record of how much in back taxes a man owes is on his individual card in the files of the probate office. If the probate judge marks off four years' taxes, no one—except, perhaps, the chief clerk who knows all the voters in the county—will know otherwise. When the taxpayer goes into the tax collector's office and pays the other four years, the tax collector has no records that show how much the man owes. He simply gives the man a receipt for the amount paid. The only way this fraud could possibly be discovered would be to check back for several years on the annual poll tax book ledgers into which all poll payments are put. If no record were found for payment and the voter could not produce a receipt, then indictment might be possible, but the poll lists are made up from the individual cards in the probate office, and if the probate judge marks those squares as paid, there would be no further inquiry. Moreover, there is no audit of the annual poll tax ledger. Payments could be entered in the book without any fear of detection. The Bibb County probate judge also pays up the poll taxes for some of his supporters.[5]

There is no strong political machine in Birmingham; that is, none that would compare with the Tammany or Crump machines. In Birmingham politics usually reduces itself to a struggle between the industrialists and their supporters and the anti-

5. Stoney's Bibb County notes, April 1940.

industrialists or "poor man's friends" candidates—generally with labor backing. The labor support has become important only in the past few years. Few of the big industrialists enter politics actively. They merely back one or another of the willing candidates who have the kind of farm-bred appeal it takes to succeed in Birmingham politics. Some industrialists have undoubtedly paid poll taxes for their employees. More of them, however, contribute to campaign funds and leave the dirty work to someone else, since the first method is too obvious. It is especially unpopular in Birmingham for a candidate to be known as a "corporation" candidate, though it is equally unpopular to be known as an out-and-out Congress of Industrial Organizations candidate. There are the usual evils of switched ballots, voting dead people, duplicating absentee ballots, and writing up the tally sheets incorrectly in order to steal elections.

Georgia politics is largely a matter of factions and a great deal of debauchery. These factions are political in nature, with no great variance in principle. For example, the Eurith D. Rivers group, formerly aligned with the Eugene Talmadge faction, is now violently opposed to Talmadge. There is no basic difference, however, in economic policies.

The political machine in Savannah is very real and has been active close to twenty-five years, though new men have come in to perpetuate it. It perpetuates itself by buying off the leaders of the opposition. A man may hear from his business associate that they are going to lose some important deals with firms connected with the machine or he may learn from relatives working for the city that they are going to lose their jobs if he does not stop his opposition. If this does not work, bribery is attempted. The man in opposition may suddenly get his taxes reduced or be told that there will be a certain opening six months from now.[6]

The political machine in Savannah and Chatham County politics is a combined city-county control group headed by John J. Bowen, city attorney and member of the firm of Abraham, Bowen, and Atkinson. Bowen seldom takes any public part in affairs. But Atkinson is chairman of the county Democratic executive committee and a member of the state legislature. The machine took over about twenty years ago and has never been seriously challenged since. It has lost a couple of state races—

6. Stoney's interview with a leader of the opposition to the machine, Savannah, Georgia, May 1940.

that is, the candidates it endorsed for governor or Congress did not get a majority in Chatham County—but it has never lost a city or county race. It has organized the town into district and precinct territories, with a captain for each. Its most notorious captain is Garfunkle, manager of the "Auditorium Box"—Savannah's business section where many people are voted from "business addresses" and where the total vote often goes higher than the actual number of residents. This machine is oiled by slush funds provided by all officeholders whenever there is opposition (city employees are also required to contribute when there is any heavy local opposition). A second source of support is contributions from concessionaires; these have been handled most discreetly. Slot machines are not allowed within the main part of town unless they are in private clubs; games must be well hidden and conducted without violence; liquor is sold on Sunday and after hours in the hotels and out in the suburbs (any indiscretion in Savannah brings quick withdrawal of this privilege); prostitutes must keep within prescribed limits, must not "travel," and must stick to one trade. A third source of sustenance involves "clips" from business firms. This is perhaps the most unfortunate part of the machine's operation. While one part of the city administration works to get business firms to come to Savannah (offering them such things as immunity from taxation), the other connives with real estate men for a part of the profits from sites, makes understandings with the managers about police protection, and the like. For example, the Union Bag and Paper Company, for its contribution, has the privilege of having its own police force, whose operations are free from public scrutiny. The sugar refinery and the paper company are allowed to violate the ordinances against polluting the river. In return, they not only chip in but also see that their employees support the machine with votes.

The Savannah machine is supported by city and county employees, benefactors through purchases, and their families. This is estimated as a standing figure of about 2,000 votes. The machine always holds both primaries and general elections for city and county offices, whether or not there is opposition. It could dispense with the primary when there is no opposition and save several hundred dollars. It runs the primary, however, because the managers and clerks at each box are paid five dollars apiece for the day's work. These people see that their families vote. The group is fairly stable, tends to look on this as its legitimate income, and thus stays regular. In addition, especially when there is opposition, campaigners, "checkers," and watchers are hired at five dollars a day. These jobs are handed about with less caution, for the people have no other duties than to hang around the polls. It is estimated that the combined strength of this vote, with the families for each, brings in another 800 votes. Votes are also bought. Votes are bought through the ward captains who befriend families in trouble, recommend them to relief agencies, etc. Each man is expected to have a certain following he can swing at any time. Cash is used to buy votes only when there is effective opposition. It is estimated that this group totals about 800 at the very least and can be expanded to 1,500 when necessary. The large transient population makes this possible. Finally, there is the illegal vote: dead people and people who have moved away, whose poll taxes have been paid by the machine; "ringers," people who vote under false names; and the like. Much of this has been cut out by the new board of registrars. Proof of the existence of this vote has been given by the fact that over 2,000 names have been struck from a list of approximately 15,000 by the new board in its term of office.

The machine seems to be handled with intelligence and with a thorough knowledge and understanding of the temper of the city. The city's white population is about 55 percent Protestant, 30 percent Catholic (mostly Irish), and 10 to 15 percent Jewish. Since the Jews and Catholics vote much more regularly than the Protestants, they get a larger share of the city and county offices. All groups are represented everywhere throughout the administration, however.[7]

In Augusta and in Richmond County, Georgia, there exists a very well-defined political machine under the control of the so-called Cracker Party, which for the past twenty-five years has dominated politics in the city. The Cracker Party probably had its origin during the tenure of Robert H. May, who was mayor of Augusta from 1879 to 1891. In the beginning, the Cracker Party was anti-Catholic, anti-Jew, and anti-Negro. It appears that during these early times Catholics had a firm grip on the politics of the city, and the Crackers were interested in breaking up this control. The members of the Cracker Party are Democrats, and in its ranks are now found Jews, Irish-Americans, and Catholics. There are influential citizens in

7. Stoney's interview with the chairman of the board of registrars, Savannah, Georgia, May 1940.

Augusta, however, who feel that the party has outlived its original usefulness. These critics claim that at present it has only one concern—a firm grasp on public office and the graft and spoils attached thereto. The prime purpose of its leaders is to remain in a controlling position in order that they can name those who hold the various offices.

A young lawyer who is fighting the Cracker Party through a "good government league" is thoroughly disgusted with the "buying and selling of votes in Richmond County which has become so flagrant that it is really beyond the pale of description." He is convinced that proper organization of those interested in good government in Augusta can turn the trick, but he is disgusted with the attitude of Negro voters who, he alleges, "voted right with the machine in this past mayoralty campaign, although they had the chance to vote for an independent candidate."[8] The Cracker Party does have some Negro allies. One of them is a numbers racketeer who is connected with "ring" politics because of the nature of his business, since he needs protection in order to escape the law. He attempts to manipulate the Negro vote behind the scenes. The program of the Augusta Good Government League is "to increase the use of the franchise regardless of race." It has tried to clean out the registration lists by abolishing repeaters, dead men, absent people, and transients from the rolls.

The Augusta *Herald* of 3 August 1939 asserted that one-third of the registration of the second ward was paid from funds collected from city employees. The setup at voting time is such that only an unofficial checker stands between the votes and the law. The checker of the opposition party has no one but himself. The booth is dimly lit. The chances of detection are slight. There is no dropping of the ballots before crowds. The ballot is numbered with a numbered stub, and the voter's name is on the stub. Therefore, anyone can check on a good proportion of the machine folks who stay away from the polls. According to the *Herald* of 4 August 1939, fresh evidence showed that a public official—who runs a sporting house—had corrupted the voting list in the second ward by getting people to vote twice. Two days later the *Herald* reported that the Taxpayers' League had alleged that the June 6 general bond election had seen repeater after repeater vote the names of people not living in the

8. Wilhelmina Jackson's interviews in Augusta, Georgia, February 1940.

city. An editorial entitled "Shall We Let Crackers Control Our Elections?" went on to say that the underworld vote is organized as a result of the permanent registration plan, by which one who is once registered is always registered and is able to vote as long as his poll taxes are kept up. It pointed out that the Crackers paid these taxes for many people, whether they were living, dead, or gone.

A member of the board of registrars in Waynesboro, Burke County, Georgia, explains that the reason for the very small registration list in that county is to be found in the lack of interest among the voters. He commented: "We should have 4,000. We could have, but the only time the people 'get out' now is when the ring routs them out, pays their poll taxes and votes them. They have to ride them into the polls and bring them back out again." He added that the people "don't have a chance to get interested" because they forget to pay their poll tax and there is no opposition to remind them. There is a "courthouse ring" in Burke County, and for many years the incumbents in office have met little opposition. This may indeed account for an unusual lack of interest in elections in this county. When opposition to the courthouse group does develop, the "ring" sticks together, rides the county collecting voters, and pays up poll taxes. An official in the county estimates that 40 percent of the people registered for the 1936 election had their poll taxes paid by political candidates.

In Bibb County, Georgia, Sheriff Jim Hicks, who is a good sheriff but a crude politician, controls the political machine by buying up 2,000 votes.

Until 1907, Charleston, South Carolina, politics had been in the hands of the old families—the "Episcopal crowd," as they were properly labeled, or the "Bourbons," as they have also been called. John P. Grace, an Irish-American politician with a powerful demagogic appeal, was elected mayor of the city in 1907. Thereafter, it was Grace's boast that he broke aristocratic rule in Charleston. Grace, says one Charlestonian, was a "good, straight businessman and one with considerable courage and originality." In politics he played a straight machine game, one that eventually got him into trouble. The Bourbons made a comeback in 1916, using a prominent Baptist layman as their candidate. But there was a great deal of fraud, and on the strength of this fraud Grace regained control in 1919. He gave Charleston paved streets before many other places got them, but he also nearly bankrupted the city. He also purchased a waterfront which the municipality still owns and loses heavily upon.

A year or so before the 1923 city election, Tom Stoney, a young lawyer fresh from the marshes of Berkeley County, and a group of young allies organized a movement to smash the Grace organization, which seemed in a position to dominate Charleston for many years to come. Vigorously attacking the graft and corrupt practices of the city machine, Stoney was able to rally support from many who were discontented with Grace's regime. Stoney managed to defeat Grace. He then proceeded to straighten up the city's finances and to revamp its government. The popular vote in Charleston has jumped from 7,478 in the first primary in 1928, when the enrollment was 13,000, to 23,239 in 1938, when the enrollment was 25,167. There was a slight increase in the white population of the county during these years.

Charleston city politics is much more tempestuous than its county politics, since the mayor of the town is always the head of its machine. There are, in both city and county politics, two levels of action. The first is a jostling for positions of leadership and control of the administration. This group has changed six times during the last forty years. Below this is a basic control group made up of neighborhood politicians, county officeholders, and the like; they have been in places of power since the 1890s. Most of the county's officials have held office for periods of fifteen to thirty-five years, through the major upheavals in the control group.

A familiar South Carolina saying is: "There is Charleston and there is South Carolina." The up-state population tells tall tales of the old city, runs down her people, and exaggerates the wickedness of her politics. Until Burnet R. Maybank, the present governor, assumed office, the highway board controlled the state, and this is rather true of several other Southern states. The highway board had secured the passage of an act giving itself exclusive right to the proceeds from the gasoline tax, and all of this amount was earmarked for maintenance. Nothing could break into this control. But two years ago Governor Maybank pushed through a law putting the appointment of district supervisors in the hands of the legislative delegations rather than the highway board. So far, however, Maybank and the legislature have been unable to find ways of diverting the highway funds to the general budget. Twice the state supreme court has ruled with the highway board, and it appears that it may take a constitutional amendment to make this change.

In South Carolina the state senator is a "little dictator" in each county because he sets the salaries of everyone in the court-house and is responsible for getting the county supply bill passed. This is why a senator who has been in office for more than one term almost always has the support of everyone in the courthouse. All highway department favors now come through the senator because he helps elect the district supervisor. Generally, the United States senators send their patronage through the state senators because the latter can give them the most direct support in a campaign. Next to the state senator, the sheriff is the most powerful man in most South Carolina counties. In Beaufort County, for instance, the sheriff has the power to pass up fines and to charge or not charge penalties. Even traffic violations and such come to his attention. As a result of his travels about, he contacts four or five times as many people as the ordinary courthouse official.

During the past quarter of a century or more, the White Municipal Party has controlled Tampa, Florida, politics. The men heading this party are leaders in the political machine led by Pat Whitaker, a lawyer who controls Tampa representation in the state legislature. Hillsborough County [in which Tampa is located] is said to be the headquarters of the "Bolitha" racket, a small-town Cuban numbers outfit. The unsavory reputation which the White Municipal Party and the Whitaker gang got because of their tie-up with the numbers racket has resulted in adverse community sentiment, even on the part of those who fear the Negro vote, and a strong desire to abolish the party and the white primary.[9]

The present Maverick administration in San Antonio, Texas, came into office on a fusionist ticket. Maverick's support came from a heterogeneous grouping of anti-Quin and liberal elements ranging from J. Frank Lapham, chairman of the board of directors of the Texas Oil Company, on the extreme right, to Emma T. Brooks, Communist state chairman, on the extreme left. This fusionist assortment of New Dealers, labor leaders, and anti-Quinites effected only the loosest sort of campaign coalition, and once the Maverick ticket was elected, it immedi-

9. Wilhelmina Jackson's interviews with leading officials of the Workers' Alliance, Tampa, Florida, 27 March 1940.

ately dispersed. In office Maverick has been the constant target of the ordinary and old-line politicians' attack. Without an organization of progressives behind him, he has floundered in pushing through his tax reform, which would have solidified his support with the mass population of San Antonio. His first reforms included relief, health facilities, city construction to make jobs, and so forth. He has attempted to blast the opposition in angry speeches which neither greatly impress his enemies nor reassure his hungry electorate.

The C. K. Quin machine that Maverick defeated represented the Bell Telephone, public utility, and pecan interests. It was Quin who introduced the John N. Garner for President resolution in the Texas Democratic state convention. In the May 1939 mayoralty election in San Antonio, the Garner machine wanted to shake off Quin because of the San Antonio political corruption which was attached to his name, but Quin ran for re-election anyway. He was defeated by Maverick by 3,500 votes. Eighty percent of the Mexican vote, from 20 to 30 percent of the Negro vote, 40 percent of the labor vote, and 20 percent of the assorted liberal and anti-Quin white vote put Maverick in office. The Quin machine, mainly through the efforts of Valmo Bellinger, had about four-fifths of the Negro vote behind it. The lieutenants in the Quin machine made a practice of buying up poll tax receipts in bulk, and in this company were numbered several Negro politicians, including Bellinger.[10]

The dominant political struggle in Virginia today—one that has its reverberations in local, county, and city politics—is that between the Governor James H. Price, or New Deal forces, and the Senator Harry F. Byrd–Senator Carter Glass, or anti-New Deal, faction. In Richmond, Mayor J. Fuller Bright, who until last year's election had held office in Richmond for the past sixteen years at the head of a reactionary local political machine independent of either the Byrd-Glass or Price factions, made his bid traditionally to the poor white vote on the basis of his record of "No Negroes on the city payrolls—city jobs for hard working white men."

Boss Edward H. Crump's Memphis political influence is felt way over in Chattanooga at the eastern end of the state of Tennessee, just as it is felt in every other county in Tennessee, because Crump controls most of the state patronage. Thus, every politician who is in the game for the business follows Crump.

10. James Jackson's San Antonio, Texas, field notes, February 1940.

In Hamilton County, Tennessee, the county boss and his machine find it possible to apply the "squeeze" not only to individuals but to such organizations as the American Legion, which is in politics in the county "up to its neck." The county machine can elect almost any fairly reputable candidate, but opposition can stir up a greater slush fund for the campaign. The candidates themselves put up part of the money for the campaign, but the machine also receives "contributions." For example, an assessment will be put on a man's property, perhaps one of the more wealthy citizens of the county. This man is then called up and told that the machine is running a particular candidate for office and that he is down for five hundred dollars.

> He will buck like hell and say he can't put up more than $250. That's all they expected to get out of him anyway. They can put the squeeze on them right regularly here, because there is new assessment every two years.
>
> I saw in the papers the other day where this George Hutchins, our local Coca Cola King, was receiving a salary of $76,000. He was the only Tennessean on the big money list. Well, you look up in the tax book, as I have when I issued the policy on his house, and you'll see he pays taxes on less than $5,000. I've been in that house and you couldn't refurnish it for less than $250,000, and it's assessed for less than one-half that. Of course, Hutchins is one of Church's [the county boss] big supporters. You wouldn't call him a politician. He's just practicing good business. He gets a whale of a lot more for his money than the merchant who gets consideration on his $20,000 store and kicks in maybe $50 every campaign.
>
> Eventually it's the taxpayers who support the machine, but they don't know.[11]

According to this informant, the Democratic machine in Hamilton County can depend upon a large number of its votes in advance. He explains that:

> They can count on the Negro school teachers. That's 300 right there. They used to vote the white teachers, too, but they can't do that so well any more. Then, there are 100 Negro janitors, and about 400 employed in the school system. Each of these has a part of his duty to qualify and vote four or five people in his family. Street cleaners and other sanitary work-

11. Stoney's interview with a former Republican member of the Hamilton County board of elections, Chattanooga, Tennessee, 26 January 1940.

ers make another 100. You can figure 2,000 controlled Negro votes at a minimum. Then, they've got ward heelers what control big blocks of them personally. Bill Grossman, a white bootlegger and gambler, is one. He runs the numbers racket and a lot of cheap dives in the Negro section of town. Bill is good for another 1,000 easy. Bill's for no party to tell you the truth. He's just a miniature gangster looking for profit and protection, and he'll vote for anybody who gives it to him. . . .

The fire and the police departments make up so many more machine votes. . . . In all, the city machine can vote about 6,000—rain or shine. The county machine can take about 3,000 more. We hardly ever have more than 18,000 votes in any county election.

Since we haven't the money to buy poll taxes, the Republicans have had to make a drive for the people over 50. At that we usually poll five to seven thousand votes and the Democrats nine to twelve thousand.

In Hamilton County, there is a close tie between the city hall group and the courthouse. This city hall-courthouse coalition forms a tight machine ring, and it is extremely difficult for any independent candidate to break through it.

There is a widespread absence of the secret ballot in the Southern states. Criticism of the custom of employing a numbered ballot in Alabama has led to the adoption of a "black sticker" which is supposed to be pasted over the ballot number in order to give protection to the voter. But the black sticker is still not widely used. Voting booths are frequently not employed at polling places, and often there are not even tables for the convenience of the voter—he must mark his ballot wherever he can.

George Stoney observed the balloting at the recent city election in Birmingham. At the city hall the election officials were all people over sixty. There were no watchers. The ballots contained the two names of the candidates for chairman of the city commission and a square at the bottom. In this square at the bottom was put the number of the ballot. *After* the person voted, the election inspector put a black sticker over this number and dropped it into the box. This same procedure was observed at the courthouse box. At an Ensley box Stoney observed the voting for some time. An Italian came in, got a ballot, went over to the window sill, and marked it. There were no booths for marking at any of the polling places Stoney visited, nor were there any tables except those used by the officials. The Italian voter folded his ballot and handed it back to the inspector. The latter spread the ballot wide open on the table, affixed the sticker, and said: "Now you've got a secret ballot." This after he and everyone within twenty feet had seen how the man voted!

A good many Alabamians are of the opinion that the black ticket, newly required as a means of protecting the secrecy of the vote, will achieve but little toward its purpose. As an ex-deputy sheriff in Lee County put it, "That ain't no more gonna stop me than nothing." For, as he explained, he and the sheriff had always checked up on the vote, had gone into the "vault" and marked them down, and they would continue to do so. In Marengo County the numbers on the ballot are used by election officials and others to check on how people vote. The voters have complained about it, but an officer of elections in the county states: "Naturally, they will. They promise two or three candidates for the same office they'll vote for them and then try to piss on them on election day. I look at every one of the ballots and nobody is going to stop me." In Etowah County, numbers are still used on the ballots, and one of the registrars states that "they should be. It hain't no secret ballot when you do. They can check right by that number and tell exactly how you voted." It is added that everyone knows this and that there is always considerable dissatisfaction with this feature at the polls.

Numbers are still used on the ballots in Cullman County, Alabama. The number is put on the top of the ballot and is, of course, no secret ballot as long as the number is there. One election official, a prosperous independent farmer, states that he has never paid any attention to how people voted though he knows that some of his colleagues have. Referring to these numbered ballots, he declares: "And they sit for a month up in the sheriff's office. You can't tell me *somebody* don't peep. . . . One man tears the number off himself every time he votes. We count his vote, but I don't know whether they would call it legal up at the courthouse." This same official says that about five voters he knows of are illiterates and about as many more ask help of the officials in marking ballots because of infirmity, disability, and so on. These ask any one of the inspectors to help them. The state law requiring two judges to watch is not enforced. Election officers are often asked for advice, he indicated, and in their primary elections it is generally given. In the general elections, however, the two Republican members and the others quarreled so much about this that they have "about stopped it.

We have to tell them they'll have to mark whatever candidate they like the looks of."

Marking of ballots by election officials and "hauling" to the polls are common practices in a number of Southern states. The county officials are pretty much a law unto themselves, and they ignore or enforce the election laws largely as they see fit. An old man who has worked as an election official for the past ten years in Gadsden, Alabama, states that he has had to help people mark their tickets because they are blind or crippled, or can't read "a heap o' times." He marks the ballots as they tell him and when they have no choices, "I generally always leave it blank."

In beat nine of River Bend, Bibb County, Alabama, the numbers are not used on the ballot. The voters in the beat were so vigorously opposed to it that a few years ago the practice was stopped. An election officer in the beat explained: "I know it's the law. The chairman of the committee came down and said he wasn't agona count a single one of our ballots that wasn't numbered. And, you know what we told him? We told him to go straight to hell!" Despite this defiance, the votes have always been counted.

The Australian ballot is not strictly enforced in Pickens County, South Carolina, because so many of the voters must have their tickets marked for them. Also, there are so many people voting in each place that there are not enough booths and no room for more. The county registrar observed that it is not possible to fool all of these illiterate voters, adding: "Some of them will fool you." She was working diligently for the election of the superintendent of schools, who is her neighbor, and was marking an old man's ticket, when, according to her story: "He let out a squawk. 'Yeah, you're a-markin the wrong one.' 'Hmph,' I said, 'I thought you said you couldn't see. . . .' That night I told the superintendent, I says, 'I did my best to get you a vote today, but the blind saw.' "

The lack of a secret ballot is a particular source of embarrassment to the white Republicans in the Southern states, who are often rather ashamed of their "peculiar" voting habits. In many places, election and Democratic party officials can come close to identifying every voter's preference, and especially do they delight in naming the Republicans.

There is no secret ballot in the general election in Pickens County, South Carolina, and the Six Mile Club president states that he considers that this makes little difference, observing:

"If I was a Republican, I wouldn't care. If I was in some business where it would hurt me, I just wouldn't vote. Naw, I guess I would vote with the crowd. There's no sense causing hard feelings over politics." The Australian ballot is used in the Democratic primaries at Six Mile, but that place does not provide the required number of voting booths. The boxes are set up at the schoolhouse so that there will be plenty of extra room to take their place.

There is no opposition in the general elections in Pickens County; general elections are mere formalities. There is no secret ballot, either. According to the secretary of the Pickens County Democratic committee, some of the Republicans try to hide the fact that they vote this way, but "Shoot! You can tell. Ain't no use of them trying to hide nothin'." He added that in this town everybody knows who they are anyway, and then he proceeded to name them. There is the old postmaster Marsh, the doctor from North Carolina who has a hospital out near Clemson, their families, and a couple of farming families who moved over from North Carolina. One or two of the mill executives also vote Republican.

Absentee ballots are another source of loose political practice. Absentee ballots in Pickens County are handled by the secretaries of the Democratic club. At the last election, about seventy-five absentee ballots were cast. In 1932 there were between seven and eight hundred; at this time there were many complaints of fraud. Since then, the Democratic committee has tried to keep the number down. This has been done mainly by warnings to candidates. The secretary of the committee states that if the law were strictly enforced, there would be fewer than fifty absentee ballots cast in the county. It is not required now that the absentee ballots pass through the mail. Workers for candidates are allowed to call for and deliver the ballots, and there is no adherence to the rule requiring a written application for an absentee ballot five days ahead of time.

There is no Australian ballot in the general elections in Sumter, South Carolina. According to the chairman of the Sumter County Democratic committee, "The tickets are out there on the table and you can pick up any one you want or all kinds." Admittedly, under such circumstances it is quite difficult to vote a secret ballot. But this is considered to be of little significance in Sumter. It is claimed that it is possible for a voter to split his ticket in the general election even on the printed forms given out by the party. The state law says that a ticket may be all printed, partly printed and partly written, or all written. The chairman of the Sumter County Democratic committee states that tickets partly printed and partly written are counted in the county.

There are no voting booths in Charleston. A voter marks his ticket wherever he can in the polling place. It is said that the only way a man could vote in secret in Charleston would be (1) either to call for all kinds of tickets, take them back in the corner, and then vote one—keeping the others in his pocket; or (2) to bring a ticket already written out—which, incidentally, is the only way one can vote a split ticket. This makes it all but impossible to vote secret, because it is known that "anybody who does that isn't voting straight Democrat." In Charleston the club rolls are padded and "they always are." The use of absentee ballots is the greatest abuse in Charleston politics. People vote them whether or not they are sick, out of the city, or what not. Some people apply for the ballots of others, mark them themselves, get the person to sign them, and bring them back in. Others get their ballots and sell them. This is the surest and simplest way of buying votes. It is said that about 1,200 absentee votes are cast in Charleston.

In the general elections in Saluda County, South Carolina, there is no secrecy about voting. The Democratic ticket is on the table in the polling place. "Once in a while" there is a batch of Republican tickets sent out. The voter comes in, marks the ticket, and puts it in the box. Everyone knows how he votes. In the primary, things are not very different. There are no booths, and the voters' home box is usually set up in a store. When it is warm enough, the polling table is set up under a tree beside the store. The voter takes the ticket, goes off by himself and marks it, or marks it "right there where everybody can see it, if he's the kind that don't care." A good many of the voters must have their tickets marked for them. These are not all old people. Many young women as well as young men have to call for assistance. Most people who have their tickets marked for them have only two or three people they want to vote for. After they vote for these, they tell whoever is assisting them, "put down whoever you voted for." The election managers do this. Especially in the choice of state officers this gives the manager a good deal of vote-getting power.

It is claimed that the Australian ballot is well enforced in the primaries in Greenville, South Carolina. There are the regulation number of booths—one for each one hundred registered voters—and only one voter can go in at a time. Of the several hundred voting at Mrs. Lucile D. King's box, she states that generally she has to mark only about half a dozen tickets. On the other hand, she says that at the mill boxes outside of the city limits more than a fourth of all ballots have to be marked by managers. In a general election, on the other hand, there is no secret ballot, and there is no use in trying to hide how one votes. If the voter tries to hide his ballot, everyone knows that he is voting Republican. Ballots—both Republican and Democratic—are sent out in the boxes by the election commissioners. The ballots are spread out on the table, and, according to the chairman of the county board of registrars, "You step up and pick your choice. There ain't nothing secret about it."

Numbers appear on the ballots in Greene County, Georgia. The justice of the peace in Greensboro is aware that this is an easy device for checking on how people vote. Although he claims never to have employed it, he was able to tell how every Negro voter in the last general election in his box voted.

There is no Australian ballot in McIntosh County, Georgia. It is said that it was tried once, but that it resulted in terrible fraud because the clerks and managers marked so many tickets that the grand jury decided not to use it any more. Now people can get "anybody" to mark their tickets. The customary method is for the candidate and the workers to get handfuls of tickets, take them out, mark them, and give them to their supporters as they enter the polling place. The clerks take these ballots, put a number on the back of them, and drop them into the box. By this method, it is claimed, it can always be known that those who pay for votes get them because they can stand at the door and watch. It is alleged that a few persons have been known to switch ballots after they got inside the polling place, but apparently this is not easy to do. A member of the county Democratic committee claims that "the old politicians" object to the Australian ballot on the ground that it would give the clerks and managers a chance to steal the elections. When the Australian ballot was employed in McIntosh County, the clerks were accused of using influence when they marked ballots for people, and it is estimated that almost a fourth of the voters had to have their tickets marked for them at that time. As it is now, however, the candidates mark the voters' tickets for them, and the chairman of the county Democratic committee declares: "I've seen them stand at the door and take a man's ticket away from him, and make him take one they've already marked in."

In Burke County, Georgia, the Australian ballot is not employed. Most people mark their tickets on a table set out in the open and everyone can see how they vote. It is not considered proper to try to hide one's vote. In Hall County, Georgia, numbers are used on the ballots. The ballots come printed, with perforated ends attached to a stub. When a voter applies, he is handed the ballot and his name is written across the stub. A tabular record is kept of each ballot so that if some are defaced or otherwise destroyed, this can be noticed. When the ballots are counted, the stub books are put into the box, out of curiosity's way. It is admitted that it would be fairly easy to check up on any one number, though it would be difficult in a district with a great many votes to check on many voters. It is said that after the election all ballots and stubs are sealed up in the boxes and placed in the safe of the clerk of the court, where they remain until the next election. They can be broken into only in case of a contest.

The facts all seem to warrant the conclusion that the secret ballot is not an essential principle in Southern "democracy." The following experience related by an election official in Hamilton County, Tennessee, is piquantly illustrative of this fact:

> The secret ballot in this county is the biggest farce I know about. When I was [the Republican member] on the election commission, I called out at the tenth ward fire house where they have the boxes. I had trouble first finding out who in the devil was the officer of elections. The man doing all the work said he was just a substitute. . . . There's two white doctors that owns most of that property out there, and they just about rule it. One of them was sitting in front of the fire hall, handing out ballots with instructions. The other brother was inside taking the ballots and putting them in the box.
>
> Finally the brother inside admitted that he was the officer of elections. I asked the fellow outside what right he had to be giving instructions and handing out ballots right there at the door. He evidently didn't know who I was because he said: "because I'm the goddamned biggest politician in this ward." When I told him who I was, he said I'd be lucky to get to a telephone. I started towards one on the wall and in a second there was a dozen firemen all around me. Then the doctor said he was marking the ballots for these Negroes because they

had bad eyes. He had examined their eyes and had the records in his office. All I could do was to make him get out of the hall and do it outside. The police wouldn't help.

The county machines employ all sorts of devices to control the vote, to pad it if necessary, to buy votes, to check on how bought votes are cast—all in order to keep the "ins" in power. Although voters are not supposed to be accompanied into the voting places in Georgia, they are so accompanied in some districts of Johnson County, especially in the Kite district. In other places the candidates usually try to arrange it so that a table can be put next to a window of the polling place where those selling their votes may mark their tickets in full view of the outside watchers. According to the tax collector, "It's got so bad here, we can't pay until we see them mark their tickets."

In Chatham County, Georgia, the board of registrars cannot put names on the voting list. It can only take them off and this has been its chief function. When the present board of registrars took over in 1936, it found that the Chatham County "ring" had the voting list padded with hundreds of names of dead people and people who had moved away, for whom it was continuing to pay poll taxes and whose names were voted. This was all handled by the tax collector, who is a key man in the machine. Each ward captain knows every voter on his list—those whom he can buy and those whom he can depend on, those whom he votes himself because they are dead. It is the duty of the ward captain to keep a card catalogue of these names, to check them with the tax collector each election time to see if taxes are paid, to visit the people who can be persuaded to pay their own taxes, and to pay up for the rest. It is said that voters who can be counted on as "regulars" often come to the tax window and, if they owe back poll taxes, are asked the suggestive question: "You were out of the state all that time, weren't you?"

An election official of many years' experience in Savannah asserts that an inspector can watch as many as forty men vote in one box. The inspector is given a list of the voters suspected of double-crossing or rebelling. When the voter comes in, the number of his vote is jotted down on a note pad. Then, when the votes are counted, the inspector watches for the number to appear in the count. Since the inspector usually checks the voter's choice for only one or two offices, this can be done in a glance. It is reported that it is the isolated persons punished that does the trick. Let two city-county employees or workers in a factory be fired after election time, and it is discovered by their fellow employees that they did not vote regular. Several hundred people will then be frightened into straight voting at the next election. The use of numbers on the ballot in Chatham County serves the purpose only of helping the machine in its efforts to coerce voters. It makes possible the employer's control of votes. The sugar refinery, the bag plant, and the gypsum plant are mentioned specifically as being guilty of this practice. It is also believed that there is checking-over of ballots at the courthouse, and it is known that this is done at the various precincts. "The numbered ballot is not only useless, it is absolutely vicious," declares one opposition leader.

About 70 percent of McIntosh County's tax in Georgia is paid by outside owners and corporations such as the Seaboard Air Line Railroad, the Union Bag and Paper Company of Savannah, the Pine Harbor Naval Stores Corporation, and R. J. Reynolds, the tobacco millionaire. The third district in the county is said to be almost completely controlled by the Georgia Power Company. The outside interests, we were told, do not interfere greatly with county politics, but they do play a very active role in district politics.

Even mild blackmail is sometimes resorted to in order to influence people to vote "right." For example, the chairman of the Ware County (Georgia) Democratic committee explains that county's large vote in the 1940 election as a result of the work of the sheriff's deputies, "who rounded up everybody they had anything on in the whole county. They'd say, 'All right now, if you don't vote, the next time we catch you in a hotel. . . .'"

The plaint is often heard in Georgia that people "have gotten in the habit of selling their vote," and this is true of Ware County. The chairman of the county Democratic committee told of what he considered to be a disgraceful episode at the Dixie Union precinct during the last election, where "about 100 of them [vote sellers] lay around there all day like a bunch of buzzards waiting. When it came about ten minutes to three [rural precincts close at three o'clock] and they saw they weren't going to get anything more, about 40 of them went in to vote all at once." Referring to the fact that, in a recent intensive campaign in Greene County, Georgia, one of the unsuccessful candidates —who owns the local bank, the gym, and the store in Shiloh— had registered and voted many old residents who had lived in Atlanta for the past ten or more years, the justice of the peace in the Shiloh district said: "I don't reckon I ought to allow it, but the boys was awful anxious to get him in, and you know how it is when a candidate comes from your district. You can't do much without making people mad."

In the recent election for sheriff of Hall County, Georgia, more women voted in the Quillians district than ever before. This resulted from the fact that the unsuccessful candidate came from this district and was known to everyone as a home boy. Intensive efforts to get out new voters were made. The candidates or their friend went to every house in the county and made up a list of all those who were not registered and were willing to vote if they were registered. They took these lists into the tax collector's office and, if they owed poll taxes and were not too far behind, paid them up. Then, these same lists were used when they sent out cars to collect the people and bring them to the polls. As explained by the justice of the peace of the Quillians district: "The registrars don't know if they're 21 or they've moved in the county, nor nothing. Most times they charge them a dollar and let it go." Many women in Hall County only vote every four years. After they become delinquent in the poll tax for a couple of years, the registrars take them off the rolls and then they register as new voters the next time. Sometimes they change their names; for example, they will first register as "Mary Lou Jones," then as "Mrs. T. H. Thompson," and perhaps a third time as "Mrs. Mary Jones Thompson."

The justice of the peace quoted above says that he has never refused to let a man vote even if he is not on the registration rolls, provided he can show a tax receipt for the last year required for Hall or any other county. "We have to *know him*," he added. He explains that this is done because he believes that the registrars often make mistakes and leave such people off the list. He states that about half of the people who vote at the Quillians box ask for help in getting their tickets filled out. Of these, about half are illiterate. Before the present law in Georgia was enacted, everybody had to pay *all* taxes before they were eligible to vote. Now it is necessary only to have paid one's poll tax. Some Geogians are afraid that if the poll tax were abolished, it would mean that people would again be required to pay all of their taxes in order to vote. All ballots must be marked in the booths provided in the polling places. In former times, however, the voters could come into the polling place, get a ballot, and carry it out "behind a barn somewhere" to get it marked by someone who paid for the vote.

It was not only Negroes who were lined up and voted like sheep in Georgia prior to the disfranchisement of 1908. An old mill worker in Gainesville, Georgia, who admits that there is still a great deal of vote-buying, though much less than there was before the voting booths were required and the Australian ballot instituted, recalls: "I can remember back there when I was starting in the mill, they'd line the mill people up and send them in to vote like they were so many nickels in a slot machine."

The enrollment procedure in the Democratic clubs of South Carolina is a terrible farce. There is no attempt made at careful checking in most places; the books are open and so loosely handled that almost anyone can take them out to get voters signed up. Signing for others is a common practice, and the only evidence of any strictness is in keeping Negroes off the books.

Park Place, South Carolina, is one of Greenville County's poorest suburbs, a community of WPA workers and itinerants. The enrollment in 1938 for Park Place was 412. The registration was 433 and included 5 Negroes. George Stoney interviewed the petty grocer in whose store the enrollment book is kept. This man has been president of the Democratic club a number of times. An inspection of the enrollment book indicated that there are many people who are signed for by other members of the family or by friends—since a large number of names appear in the book in the same handwriting. The book is carried around to the houses by candidates or their workers. The grocer explained: "I know it ortent, but they will do it." This club's enrollment is large because all of the people from the county home —inmates and employees who live there—are enrolled at this place.

A great many people require help in marking their tickets in Park Place. This is particularly true of the county home people. The grocer observed that "It's hard to fool them," because they take the dummy ballot out of the newspaper, get it marked the way they want it, and bring it to the polling place. Then they count down the names and tell the election manager which ones to scratch. These old people listen to the radio so much "till they might nigh know more than a man that reads the papers." Yet a large number of people cannot write and so have to have someone sign the enrollment book for them. It has been a custom in this club for the enrolling person to make a mark and have the other person signing it put his signature over it. Therefore, no witnesses are recorded on the book, and it would appear from the official record that no illiterates vote in this district. The Park

Place club is not a very large one. In 1938 there was a "big crowd" of about forty. Ordinarily, the meetings are attended by from fifteen to twenty people. There are no slates prepared at the meetings, and anyone who happens to be around may come in and vote, though a person is supposed to have been a resident of the neighborhood for sixty days. This is never asked about, according to our informant.

The story told by an enrollment committeeman to George Stoney is fairly typical of the stories told by the half dozen or so storekeepers in Saluda County, South Carolina, with whom Stoney talked about enrollment and voting. This man and the others interviewed are small merchants who know little about any politics except that in the county, and are not involved in it in any other way. Because their stores are conveniently located, the enrollment books are left there and they are designated as members of the enrollment committee. One of these store-keepers says that there is a steady stream of sixty or eighty people enrolling and voting at his store. The enrollment book re-mains at his store about half of the time during the six weeks in enrollment season. The rest of the time the executive com-mitteeman or someone else who gets his permission is carrying it around the community. The storekeeper states that he never pays much attention to it. Stoney's examination of the book indi-cated that several names had quite obviously been written by the same person.

The voting also takes place in this store or just outside of it. There are no booths. A voter can carry his ticket off to himself to mark it if he wants to, or he can mark it on the table provided. The storekeeper estimates that only six or eight of the group which votes at his store are unable to read or write. One of the election managers usually reads out the names of the candi-dates to each of these and the person names his choices. This is done "right out in public" so that there is slight chance of these illiterate voters getting cheated, according to this infor-mant. He concedes that some few of the voters do sell their votes, though this is not done at the store. The bargain is made when the candidate or his helper goes after the people to bring them to the polls. The storekeeper added: "This place used to be mighty bad for liquor in elections. We cut that out, though. I was kinda ashamed of that."

People in Saluda County are very "careless" about their voting system. It is virtually impossible to read most of the enrollment books and the registration books. All of the registrars are farmers who are much more accustomed to a plow than to a pencil. A member of the board of registrars who has often served as election official both for primaries and general elections told Stoney that he does not ask to see poll tax receipts or registration certificates for the general elections. Possession of the former is checked by finding the name on the registration roll. Possession of the latter is assumed. The Australian ballot is not used for either election in Saluda County. Boxes are set up on the porch or in the hallway of the schoolhouse. People go into the rooms to mark their tickets. In general elections there is seldom a Republican ballot available.

The people in Saluda County vote independently, but a candidate must do a good bit of "hauling" in order to get them to the polls. In a recent hotly-contested race, the county treasurer states that "the handouts" added up to eight hundred dollars for one candidate. This goes out in "favors" rather than in the form of straight vote buying, though there is still some of that, too. But a bag of flour, a new inner tube, some medicine bills paid—"it adds up quick," and it gets votes.

Corruption in Beaufort County, South Carolina, politics is of the petty kind. Candidates or their friends take the enrollment books around to the voters' homes (which is supposed to be against the rules), and they write people's names in them without permission. Then, on purging day, they bring in a list of additions. No one objects, because someone might object to one's own list. There is not a great deal of vote buying or use of liquor at the polls in Beaufort. All of the candidates have watchers.

In the average election, there are about a hundred absentee ballots issued for the Beaufort Democratic club and about ninety of them come back. This is for the Beaufort town box only. The provisions of the law are "construed very loosely." The applicant is supposed to apply in writing a specified number of days before the election. Actually, the applicants are allowed to come in person if they are leaving town and know what their address will be. Although the law requires that applicants be sick or have other binding reasons, a vacation is taken as reason enough in Beaufort County. Also, people who find it inconvenient to leave their work may vote absentee. Many candidates bring in the names of persons to whom they wish absentee ballots sent. One politician and officeholder always leaves a small fund with the secretary of the Beaufort Democratic club and the secretary of the county Democratic committee to pay registered mail charges on those absentee ballots sent out to his list. Though the law requires that ballots be returned by registered mail, few are. And yet they are accepted as ballots just the same. Sick people are sometimes served by a candidate or worker who may come by on the day of the election or before, take an absentee ballot out to the home, have it notarized, and bring it back. Few absentee ballots are cast by the Democratic clubs, other than the one in Beaufort.

The South Carolina political situation is perhaps less controlled by state-wide machines than that of any other Southern seaboard state. Thus, the Textile Workers Union of America, with less strength, has been able to do more politically in South Carolina than in any other coastal state. It is to be noted that there appears to be a great deal more freedom in voting and a great deal less fear about revealing how one has voted among the mill workers in Pickens County, South Carolina, than among the mill workers in the northern Alabama counties. The mill management in Pickens County apparently has been unable to project itself into the political scene as has been the case in Alabama. There is an individualism and an independence in voting among Pickens County mill workers that is entirely foreign to the northern Alabama mill areas. Nor does there seem to be evidence of any significant amount of vote-buying in Pickens County.

Politics in Sumter County, South Carolina, is said to be free of any taint of ring control. Almost anyone with appeal can get elected to the legislature. Courthouse offices, however, are harder to get, because the men now holding them are both capable officials and skillful politicians. There is considerable control exercised over the politics of the city of Sumter. A group of businessmen in the town are reported to have been able to pick the candidates for office over a period of years. They get together in informal sessions a week before the primary and say, "It's your turn this time."

While not so important as in Charleston, the precinct and ward clubs in Greenville County, South Carolina, are considered worth fighting for. For several years after an abortive attempt by the anti-Smith Democrats to capture them in 1928, the ward clubs remained in the hands of the neighborhood hack politicians, who worked first for this candidate and then for that. They might be called "free-lance ward heelers." There is no political control group in the county, nor is there any one man in the city of Greenville for whom all will jump when he snaps his fingers. There is in Greenville, however, a group of fifteen or twenty prominent men who get their way most of the time; they can chisel from the police petty privileges that are irksome to the ordinary citizen. This does not constitute any serious threat to freedom, however. The greatest trouble in Greenville is its political apathy. Greenville has had for years one of the worst legislative delegations in the state simply because the "decent" people do not take the trouble to persuade a worthy candidate to run.

Under Alabama's absentee voting law, people who have lived in other places for as long as fifteen or twenty years are still permitted to vote absentee. Some of them have been out of the state that long. A man who has not lived in Bibb County for twenty years, but who has kept his vote there and has been casting an absentee ballot, came back to the county in 1940 and is now running for probate judge.

In Madison County, Alabama, the voting of dead people's names or the names of people who have moved out of the county is said to be common. The same is true with the duplication of absentee voters. Most of the "big money" is put out by candidates. The present chairman of the Madison County board claims to have personal knowledge of this because of his numerous experiences in running for office in the county. In 1936 he ran for circuit clerk: "I got beat because I wouldn't buy votes. I had a chance to get in the ring. They came to me and said it would take so much. I didn't have it to put out—and wouldn't have put it out if I'd had it, so I got beat." In 1938 he was an inspector at his precinct box. He was not supporting any candidate at this time and says he determined that:

> By God! I'm going to see a straight election at this box if they kill me.
>
> They didn't much like it, but I stuck there all day long. I saw to it that every man who wanted to, voted a secret ballot. Course, a lot of them don't want to. Most of the time, people selling their votes will frame up with a bunch and they'll promise him so much. When he goes into the polls, he lets one of the people serving as officers see the way he votes or maybe lets him mark his ballot for him. That fellow winks out the window to let the man with the money outside know the voter did what he promised.

According to the provisions of the state law, however, an election official can mark a ballot only when the voter is physically unable to mark his own, and then it is supposed to be done in the presence of two of the officers.

There is no secret ballot in Madison County, for in addition to the difficulty people have in marking their ballots secretly, there is the number on the back of the ballot. The chairman of the county board of registrars states that he has been an official at several ballot countings and that he knows these numbers were used to check on how people voted: "When you've got from 50 to 200 votes in a precinct and a man maybe buys 10 or 15, he's bound to notice how they voted, even if he don't want to know sometimes." When a voter comes in, a number is put down beside his number, and this number is called out. A second clerk checks his name off the poll list and puts that number on the back of his ballot. It is a simple matter for an officer to jot down a few numbers on his cuff or the palm of his hand or a slip of paper; then, when the ballots are counted, number "44 or whatever one he's looking for is staring him square in the face." Since the ballots have to be gone-over several times to complete the count, the officers have plenty of time to do their checking.

Next to the use of the numbered ballot, the misuse of absentee ballots is perhaps the worst evil connected with elections insofar as white voters in Madison County are concerned. To secure a ballot, a legal voter simply needs to write to the judge, stating that he "expects to be out of the county" that day. When he receives the blank ballot, he marks it "or somebody marks it for him," and it is returned and put in a special absentee box. A list of the names of those who have voted absentee is made up, and a copy is put in each box when it is sent out from the courthouse. The clerks are supposed to check off all such names in their precinct registration books before voting is started, but they seldom do this.

In all elections, everywhere in this country, it is important, in the interest of fairness to the candidates, to check on the election officials. It is a frequent practice in the South for candidates to have "representation" among the election officials. In many places it is held that this is the only way in which the candidate can protect himself against being cheated out of the election. It is very important in Bibb County, Alabama, for instance, for a candidate to have adequate representation among the election officers. A large percentage of the voters are either too old, too unlearned, or too lazy to mark their own ballots. A local editor estimates that approximately 25 percent of the ballots in the county are marked by election officials.

A member of the Democratic executive committee of Cullman County, Alabama, who works at the polls every election, states that he is often asked by people to help them mark their tickets. When they name the men, he always marks the ones they say. Very often they name only their choice for county officers, congressmen, president, governor, or legislator, and say: "You fill in the rest." When this happens, he declares, "Naturally, I mark the ones I'm for." He explains that this happens in every polling place, adding: "That is why it is so important to have the backing of the people who work at the polls. I don't mean anything crooked, either."

In Jefferson County, Alabama, the board of registrars does not seriously try to enforce the provision requiring employment for the greater part of the year preceding registration. It is considered also that, in the limited time allowed for purging, the board could not take time to check the list of voters carefully in order to purge those convicted of felonies. The board has purged only those they happened to hit upon or were told about. When illiterates were registered, it would be without inquiry into their property holdings. According to a former member of the board, "We made sure they were good citizens. That's all." This informant estimated that in this county alone there are fully 10,000 improper names on the voters' list, but he refused to estimate how many of these voted regularly: "I wouldn't be quoted on this for anything, but we've got a class of foreign vote here that will lie like anything. A Greek or a Syrian will tell you the truth, but an Italian will lie even when he doesn't get anything out of it."

The textile mills in Madison County, Alabama, though they operate under cover today, have always been politically active. In earlier years they would present regular mill slates. Later, when such firms as the Lincoln Mill at Huntsville were making people pay their poll taxes out of their pay envelopes by the check-off system, the mill had the slate posted and "suggested" that employees vote for it. But with the coming of the labor unions, the mills have been much less open in their political activities. Their main participation now is in donating to the campaign funds of favorite candidates. There have been incidences in the past years, however, in which the company would fire men who did not vote "right." One informant, the manager of the Lincoln Supply Store, gave the names of four men who were given extended layoffs for this offense.

As the president of the Lincoln local of the TWUA explains it:

> Before, they had a habit of telling you to come by the over-seer's office. They'd have a ballot stretched out there marked like they wanted you to vote. They wouldn't out and tell you you had to vote that way, but they'd say, this is the way the management thinks you ought to vote because it will be for the best interest of the business.

This same informant opines that far fewer workers pay the poll tax now than formerly did in Lincoln, simply because the mills used to make them pay. He adds that the union had asked the management of the mill to take poll taxes out for the employees, but the mill refused, stating that it was not now its policy to do so. The attitude of the mill has changed, of course, since the unions beat their pickets in 1934. The first poll taxes were taken out of the pay envelopes by the mill company in Lincoln in 1927, and there were over three hundred registered voters in the community at that time.

A member of the Alabama legislature from Madison County states that in such places as Hazel Green (Lowe's Plantation), tenants must vote as the landlord says. To quote him: "I've had them to tell me, 'I want to vote for you, C.J., but I can't. If they find out, they'll drive me off the place.'" The numbers on the ballots are used to check up on how people vote in almost every precinct. In almost every election, after the official burning of the ballots, lists of names of those who voted and how they voted on major offices are "for sale." The legislator also said:

> One thing I often worry about is whether people suffer more for voting for me than I can help them when I'm in office. I don't know what these other fellows have been telling you around here, but I'm giving it to you straight. This is the meanest election country [sic] on the face of the earth. I don't see a way in the world out except to have the federal government take over supervising elections and clean the mess out. We're going to come to that eventually.

This candidate complained of the difficulty he had in getting his representatives placed at the polling places, but added:

> I have the promise of the county chairman this time, though, that he will put two women on every box. Maybe they won't do some of the things they have been doing with women around. . . . This will not stop them from paying up poll taxes for people. Last month I sat in this store and watched them bring them in from the country in car loads.

He added that the biggest politicians in the county—that is, the ones who put up the most money—are not so much interested in candidates as in issues. They put up money, and the men who meet their requirements for performance on those issues get their financial support. He emphasized that Madison County is getting into the hands of fewer and fewer landlords and that it has been going this way for twenty years. The cotton program has accelerated this process. The most important political influence in the county is found in two or three of the largest landholders, who play behind-the-scenes politics. County politics tends to be controlled by these large landholders, while the cotton mills devote much more interest to city politics.

In 1930, Democratic white primary rules which were decreed either by state or local party authorities were in effect in at least eleven Southern states. In the rules of four of these states—Alabama, Florida, Louisiana, and Mississippi—the primary election statutes specifically recognized the state executive committees of political parties as the authorities vested with the power to add to the statutory qualifications for participation in party primaries. The Alabama statute provides that: "Every State Executive Committee of a party shall have the right, power, and authority to fix and prescribe the political or other qualifications of its members, and shall, in its own way, declare and determine who shall be entitled and qualified to vote in such primary election." The statute of Florida declares that the state executive committee "may by resolution, declare the terms and conditions on which legal electors shall be declared and taken as proper members of such party." The Louisiana law permits "further qualifications prescribed by the State Central Committee of the respective political parties." The Mississippi enactment provides that a voter may participate in a party primary if he "is not excluded from such primary by any regulation of the State Executive Committee of the party holding the primary." The Arkansas statute makes no declaration as to the authority of party officials to make rules of membership, but the Democratic state committee, with the authorization of the Democratic state convention, enacted a white primary rule. Thus, in five Southern states a state-wide rule establishing the Democratic primary as a white primary is enforced.

In three other Southern states—South Carolina, Texas, and Virginia—the white primary rules have been enacted by the Democratic state conventions. The statutes of these three states specifically recognize the right of the party to add qualifications, though they do not specify the state party convention as the agency for making such rules. The South Carolina law declares only that: "Except as herein provided, the primary election shall be conducted in accordance with the party rule." A provision of the Texas statute recognizes the state executive committee as the rule-making authority in matters of membership, but the existing white primary rule in Texas was the act of the state Democratice convention. The Supreme Court of the United States, as well as the highest court in Texas, has recognized in this body an "inherent" right to enact such a rule. In Virginia, also, the law has given political parties rule-making power to fix "other requirements" for participation in party primaries. Georgia forbids participation in all primaries to anyone "who is not a duly qualified and registered voter . . . and who is not duly qualified in accordance with the rules and regulations of the party holding the same." The "party authorities" are granted the right to make additional requirements. In North Carolina the law makes no mention of the power of the party to fix rules of membership, but the Democratic county organizations make such rules. Similarly, in Tennessee the Democratic county organizations make rules in a majority of the state's counties, and it is said that a few counties in Kentucky have had Democratic white primary rules, though apparently none now exists. It should be noted that in North Carolina the white primary rules are not universal. In the border states the tendency is to permit full participation by Negroes in the Democratic party primaries.

The Democratic white primary rules are ordinarily brief. For example, the Arkansas rule states that: "The Democratic party of Arkansas shall consist of eligible and legally qualified white electors, both male and female, who have openly declared their allegiance to the principles and policies of the Democratic party." The Louisiana Democratic primary rule reads: "That no one shall be permitted to vote at said primary except electors of the white race." The Texas rule states: "Be it resolved, that all white citizens of the State of Texas who are qualified to vote under the constitution and laws of the State shall be eligible to membership in the Democratic party and as such entitled to participate in its deliberation." The Virginia rule declares that "All white persons who are qualified to vote at the next ensuing general election"—and who are otherwise permitted to vote by the Democratic party—"are hereby declared to be members of the Democratic party of Virginia."

The South Carolina rules have certain unique features. The state statute governing the primary provides, in the first place, that membership in the Democratic party may be acquired only by registering as a member of a township or ward Democratic party club, which affords the privilege of participating in the party primary. The law makes elaborate provision for the organization of the clubs and the rules of the state Democratic party supplement these provisions with respect to the details of structure and procedure. The rules provide that:

> The qualifications for membership in any club of the party in this state, and for voting at a primary shall be as follows: viz, "The applicant for membership, or voter, shall be twenty-one years of age, or shall become so before the succeeding general election, and shall be a white Democrat."

It was once required that:

> Every negro applying for membership in a Democratic club, or offering to vote in a primary, must produce a written statement of ten reputable white men, who shall swear that they know of their own knowledge that the applicant or voter voted for General [Wade] Hampton in 1876, and has voted the Democratic ticket continuously since.

But this provision has recently been stricken, and the rule states clearly now that only white Democrats may belong.

County white primary rules are enforced only partially in Tennessee and North Carolina, and no longer at all in Kentucky. In Tennessee only local white primary rules are found, and Negroes are definitely admitted to the Democratic primaries in Memphis and to a lesser extent in Nashville and other municipalities in the middle and eastern parts of the state. In North Carolina Negroes are admitted to the Democratic primary chiefly in the western counties, and the only white primary rules are those made by individual county organizations. But in the rest of the states of the solid South, state-wide white primary rules prevail, and with relatively few exceptions these rules are strictly enforced. The prevalence of state-wide rules fixing the primary as a "white" affair during the past quarter of a century or more is responsible for the extreme degree of uniformity in the process of excluding Negroes from participation in these Southern elections. But this uniformity and universality in the application of the principle of exclusion is a comparatively recent phenomenon.

In recent years the constitutionality of the white primary regulation has been challenged in both state and federal courts in Arkansas, Texas, and Virginia. The basis for the seeming validity of the white primary rules in the states now employing them is to be found in the fact that they have all been enacted by the Democratic party authorities and not by the state legislatures. Yet there is definite legal significance in the fact that, in most of the white primary states, the primary election laws either directly specify or implicitly recognize some agency of the Democratic party as the authority vested with power to fix qualifications in addition to those stated in the law for participation in party primaries. Moreover, in at least half of the Southern states using the white primary, the direct primary as a method of nomination is mandatory, at least for the Democratic party, and the organization and procedure of the party as a whole are in varying degree determined by state law. Even in those states where the primary system is optional, the laws of the state go into considerable detail in determining the structure of the party choosing to employ primaries. Still more significant, perhaps, is the fact that in at least half of the Southern states employing the white primary, the administration of the primary election is vested in the regular election officials, and in more than half of these states the state itself pays the expenses of running the primary. Such facts are the basis for raising serious constitutional and legal questions concerning the fundamental nature of political parties in this country, the extent to which they retain their original and traditional character of voluntary association, and the basic interpretation of a statutory provision which deliberately delegates supplementary rule-making power to a subordinate, nongovernmental party agency. The most important question of all, of course, is whether or not a primary itself is an election, or at least a preliminary stage of an election, rather than a mere preelection nominating procedure which, though regulated by law, retains its private character.

White supremacy is given symbolic expression in the official emblem of the Democratic party of Alabama. This emblem, described in the following excerpt from an Alabama newspaper in 1904, appears on the ballots used in the Democratic primaries for the state:

> The amended election law of Alabama requires that each political party, making nominations to be voted for at a general election in this state, shall select and adopt an emblem

> or device which shall be printed at the head of the ticket in the columns respectively for the nominees of each such party. In compliance with the provisions of the law, emblems adopted by the Democratic, Republican, Populist, Prohibitionist and Socialist parties have been filed with the Secretary of State.
>
> The Democratic emblem, filed by Chairman [Hugh S. D.] Mallory, in accordance with a resolution of the State Executive Committee, . . . consists of the picture of a lusty game cock, with head high and a look of defiance to everything and everybody showing a disposition to oppose him.
>
> Above his head, on a scroll, are the words: "White Supremacy" and underneath: "For the Right."[12]

The elaborate stationery of the Democratic executive committee of Jefferson County, Alabama, with headquarters in Birmingham, carries in the upper right hand corner an engraving of a red gamecock, above which is a scroll reading "White Supremacy" and below which is a scroll reading "For the Right."

In Georgia the official Democratic party designation of its primary is the "Democratic White Primary."

South Carolina has a unique means of excluding Negroes from participation in the Democratic primaries—one that is a little awkward, to say the least. The system of enrollment in Democratic clubs is used as the basis for determining party membership and ability to vote in the Democratic primaries. Any white person in South Carolina may "enroll" in the appropriate Democratic club merely by signing the enrollment book for the district in which he resides. This makes him a "Democrat" and entitles him to participate not only in the periodic "reorganization" meetings of his club—and these are mere gestures —but to vote in the Democratic primary.

The date of Democratic club reorganization meetings is set by the state rule. The time and place are fixed by the president of each club. Anyone may take part in these reorganization meetings who is eligible to vote in the particular box at the time. One need not have been enrolled for the previous election. It is within the discretion of the club's president to allow or refuse to allow spectators at these meetings, but, of course, Negroes are never admitted, should any be bold enough to come. At these meetings delegates to the county conventions and an executive committeeman are picked. Each club is entitled to one delegate

12. Editorial in the Greensboro *Watchman*, April 1904.

for each twenty-five persons who cast a vote in that district in the first primary of the previous election year. Clubs also pass resolutions at their meetings. They may also petition the committee or the convention for the right either to join another club or to divide themselves into two clubs.[13] Thus, each Democratic club is allowed to run its own affairs. Although the clubs are supposed to stay within the state rules, there is no attempt to check up on this unless someone protests. The executive committeeman names the polling place. The stores and other places accommodating the polls get no pay. Neither do the members of the enrollment committees appointed by the president of each club.

Three days after the enrollment closes (the date is set by the date committee), the executive committee meets to consolidate the rolls and purge them. The main job is to check duplications, but this is not done too thoroughly. No names are added at this time. It is to be noted, however, that often some names are added later through the provision allowing the circuit judge to order additions. Scarcely more than half a dozen names are purged for other reasons each time. Most of these are people who have not lived in the county long enough or who do not live in the county at all. Efforts are made to transfer people registered in the wrong clubs, but they are not able to do this in many cases. These people are allowed to vote by going back to their own club. All people either purged or changed from one district to another are given notice by registered mail. Seldom are there any protests. Neither is there publication of those stricken or of the entire list.

Following this, a certified copy of the list is made and filed in the clerk's office where anyone who wishes may see it. Candidates or citizens are privileged to prepare a challenge list for the coming election. No members of the general public appear at the purgings by the committee. There is no rule against this, but the public just does not come. Ordinarily no challenging is done until voting time, but there are a good many challenged votes each time. The main claim is lack of residence or improper enrollment. Most cases are settled when either one or the other of the parties does not show up. Others are passed on by the committee when it sits to certify returns.

The Democratic primaries in Charleston are conducted under

13. Stoney's interview with Mack Wells, secretary of the Greenville County Democratic committee, Greenville, South Carolina, June 1940.

a special statute passed in 1915. One of the requirements of this law is that all Democratic club rolls, after being duly purged and certified by the county committee, must be published in the newspaper together with addresses. After this publication, a sufficient time must be allowed for names to be challenged. The expense for this must be borne by the county executive committee. One of the requirements governing the party primaries in Charleston is that one voting booth must be provided for each one hundred enrolled voters. Another requirement states that the clerk of each enrollment committee must be paid so that the list may be kept clean. As a result, the cost of elections is high. This means that the entrance fee for candidates must likewise be high, and this tends to cut down the amount of opposition. Charleston public officials usually die in office. The present sheriff has served continuously since 1918, the supervisor for over fifty years, the auditor for about thirty years, the treasurer since 1922, the coroner since 1928, and the probate judge since 1916.

Each ward in the city of Charleston has two and sometimes three Democratic clubs. A person in a ward may choose any of the clubs he wishes to join. To join, he simply puts his name on that particular enrollment book. The purge committee makes sure he does not put his name down twice. The rural districts have only one club each, so the voter has no choice there. All clubs meet on the fourth Monday evening in April at eight o'clock sharp. All meet at the same time so there can be no roving bands. Only those are admitted to the clubs who have signed the club roll for the preceding primary election, two years before. As soon as the president calls the club to order, someone for the administration offers a full slate of officers, delegates to the county convention, and so on. There is a motion to accept this, and, unless there is opposition, the motion is approved and the meeting is over for another two years. If there is objection, the objector or objectors may offer another slate. The city and county employees in Charleston attend the ward club meetings more regularly than most other people. Few others take any interest, because they have no importance except as a convenient way of getting elections conducted. The administration has one person in each of the clubs to whom it looks for leadership and who is expected to take responsibility.

An important question with respect to South Carolina is whether the state laws relating to the qualifications of voters are of any real significance in view of the power given to the Democratic party to make its own rules for the primaries. The difference between the numbers voting in the primaries and the general elections in South Carolina is far greater than in Georgia or Alabama. That may be because South Carolina is more completely a one-party state, having no Republican counties, or it may be because of the peculiar primary laws with the Democratic club institution. Instead of interparty rivalry, typical of a normal political situation, the one-party system in the South which is articulated through the Democratic primary gives rise to bitter personal rivalry and factionalism which often finds angry expression. In such instances, however, the clash is usually between personalities rather than issues. In many places the one-party, white-primary system leads to a complete stagnation of political life, and candidates merely succeed themselves in office year after year without healthy opposition.

Just as South Carolina has a unique institution in its system of Democratic enrollment and ward clubs, so Georgia has a peculiar institution in its county unit basis of representation in the state legislature. Since the votes of Georgia counties in the state elections are computed on a unit basis, the candidate who receives the most votes in a county receives its unit vote. Thus, just as in the present method of electing the president of the United States, it is possible for a Georgia candidate for state office to receive a majority of the popular vote and still lose the election. Georgia's numerous counties are thus given a direct representation in state affairs. Moreover, the rural counties are thereby enabled largely to dominate the cities of the state politically. The county unit rule was first pressed by the agricultural workers and farmers in self-defense. But the system was subsequently seized upon by individuals who saw in its operation an opportunity for political power.

Georgians are divided into those who bitterly condemn and those who vigorously defend the county unit system. The system gives some measure of political power to the rural people who do not have the economic power to combat big interests. It does tend to keep the big city rings from controlling state politics. On the other hand, it gives an entirely disproportionate influence to small-voting rural counties, while penalizing urban counties with large populations. It also permits candidates in congressional elections to win with less than a majority of the vote. There is no question but that the urban political machines in Macon, Atlanta, and Augusta are bad and constitute a dangerous threat to the interests of Georgia's rural population. Yet Gene Talmadge is a child of the county unit system.

The justice of the peace in the Montezuma district, Macon County, Georgia, gives the typical defense of the county unit system in Georgia:

> It don't look fair when you first think about it—some fellow up in Atlanta saying that some rube out in the sticks can vote and his vote will count ten times as much as mine. If it were not for the county unit vote, machines could be built up in Atlanta, Savannah, and Macon that could corner the state house officers, and they'd forget about us out here.

The defense of the system, though it works to the detriment of urban Georgia, is sometimes obtained from city leaders. One prominent antimachine leader in Savannah states that he supports the county unit system because:

> I'm a "cracker." I believe the boy ten miles off the highway needs nine months school worse than the boy with the dust-paved streets in front of his house. The country people have no other way of protecting themselves from the big interests who control the machines in the cities. Without it, Georgia would be ruled by a machine dictatorship. It is almost this now. Big interests control Macon, Columbus, Albany, Atlanta, Savannah, and Augusta. They could easily combine forces to rule the state if popular vote settled things. In the big cities, what have you got? A lot of foreigners, Northerners, Italians, wops of all kinds. Take half the politicians in these towns and you'll find they're some kind of an outsider. A cracker don't seem to thrive in politics in the city.

This man admits, however, that the unit system does throw power into the hands of men like Talmadge; but, bad as this is, he prefers taking such a risk to having worse befall the state.

In appraising the Georgia political system, there are some good and some very bad features. Perhaps the best feature of the state's election system is its excellent absentee ballot law as contrasted with the practice in Alabama. While this absentee ballot law is not administered with equal rigidity throughout the state—it has been noticed to have been rather loosely administered in Putnam County, for example—it is a good law. The number of absentee ballots cast in Georgia is so small as to make the kind of fraud suffered in North Carolina, Virginia, and other

Southern states impossible. It should be noted that the gubernatorial race in North Carolina in 1936 was actually decided by absentee ballots; the election was so bad that the legislature provided that absentee ballots would no longer be valid in the primaries. Another good feature of the Georgia election system is the year-round registration, with a central place for it and a definite person responsible for it. This eliminates the uncertainty typical of voting in Alabama and Tennessee, which causes so many people to be kept off the voting lists in such states.

In Johnson County, Georgia, Stoney ran into a sort of "Trouble in July" situation in that practically all of the officials of the county were off on fishing trips and one of the county bums was sleeping in the judge's tobacco quid–littered courtroom. When Stoney asked this loiterer if he votes, he replied: "Once'st anyway" at every election.

The separation of state and county primaries in Georgia serves a good purpose. This gives the people of the county a chance to pick men on their own merits and according to the needs of the county offices, without considering the actually irrelevant connections these county men have with state politics. The fact that in most counties members of the legislature and county committees are elected in the state primary rather than in the county primary strengthens this connection.

On the other hand, this separation of state and county primaries has left the door ajar for some malpractices. It is the beginning of all of the independence in county elections that makes such a jumble of Georgia politics. The calling of a primary several months before the men take office is extremely hazardous. In Johnson County, for instance, the primary comes more than a year ahead of time. If a sheriff is defeated in February, let us say, he has until January of the next year to wreak his vengeance. The early primary also cuts off any chance for people to consider candidates and to get others to run against incumbents. All these objections, however, could be cleared up without combining state and county primaries. The county primary could be set for June 1 all over the state and would work out excellently. In Alabama, almost every county officer is lined up as a Bibb Graves or a Frank Dixon man, and his chances of getting reelected rest as much on the strength of his faction in the county as on his past record. Georgia is not completely free of this, but it is much freer than Alabama.

There is much evidence of fraud in Southern elections. For

instance, in Gadsden, Alabama, a woman florist from an old plantation family tells of how her brother was "counted out" of his race for mayor of Gadsden. She claims that this information came to her from three different men who were present at the meeting where the arrangements for stealing the election were made. This caucus decided that it was desirable to defeat her brother and that it would take about 250 votes in the large city box to do it. Two women clerks volunteered to do the job. Counting the votes at this place was usually an all-night job, and at about midnight it was suggested that the clerk take the ballots over to one of their homes and have some sandwiches and coffee, while continuing the counting. This was done and, while the officials were occupied with food, one woman switched the 250 ballots.

An ex–deputy sheriff in Lee County, Alabama, explained how the present sheriff was elected by "stolen votes" in his campaign of 1938. This informant admitted that he had voted eighty-seven dead people, whose names are still on the lists, by absentee ballot. This act, he thought, was justified by the fact that there was a great deal of thievery in that election. The sheriff, whom he was supporting, had control of the courthouse box and the brothers of the sheriff had control of the mill box at Pepperell. After some of the workers had voted in the box at Pepperell, they were carried to the courthouse, where they voted again. The sheriff, he added, had a "bunch of dumb women" acting as officials who "couldn't tell a mill hand when they saw one." They found the men's names on the qualified list and went ahead and voted them without asking where they lived. It is alleged that the sheriff spent over $8,000 winning that race. The ex–deputy sheriff thought the office well worth it, for he felt that the sheriff would "pick up that much on the side from bootleggers." He added: "I'd give $8,000 any day in the week to be sheriff if this county was dry."

The superintendent of education for Macon County, Alabama, emphasized the importance of money and the bought vote in Macon County elections, philosophizing:

Money buys everything in this world. . . . It has bought elections in this county for the last thirty years. I know; I've been in them. But I suppose it buys elections all over the country. . . . The politicians pay back poll taxes. . . . I've seen them pay as high as $36 for one voter. . . . Then, they have to pay for their votes after they get them qualified. . . . But the man who can't pay $1.50 for himself can generally be bought pretty easily anyway.

The commissioner's race usually brings out a big vote in Madison County, Alabama. An officer of elections at Owens' Crossroads in that county explained that the race was so hot that:

> The candidates called them down and paid their poll tax for them. That's what's a fact. . . . I seen them pay up as much as fifteen dollars for a fellow, and I say it's a good thing, too, because there's so many people just ain't got that much money—folks on the WPA and all. They wouldn't be able to vote unless somebody helped them.

This man thinks that most votes in his precinct are bought. He explained how they check to be sure people voted the right way. The man who wants to sell his ballot lets one of the election officials see him mark the ticket. If he marks it right, he is given a "little blue bead" which he exchanges for the sale price after he gets through voting.

The clerk in the office of the probate judge in Madison County estimates that one-third of the county's vote is "bought." In fact, many of the voters have to be bought twice—once with poll taxes and again with the payoff at the voting box. He gives a graphic description of how the arrangements are made to pay poll taxes:

> Mighty near every few minutes the last two weeks of January somebody's a comin' up to the counter and askin': "Kin you look up and see how much I'se behind in my poll tax?" You go ahead and tell him, and then he wants to know how much his wife or his neighbor owes. "He stopped me coming to town and asked me to find out for him." You tell him all that and then he'll say, "You mind puttin' that down on a piece of paper so's I won't fergit?" The next day or so he'll come back with the money, saying he got stopped by the same people coming to town. Hell! There's no way in the world to prove he's not telling the truth, but I know good and well half of them are lying. I've even carried men to town in my car that'll come in and tell a lie like that to me at ten o'clock.

This rather cynical observer added that he knows Madison County "like a book. It's a bunch of sharecroppers and textile workers, and illiterates—black and white. Them that's got a vote sells it, by God, because they need the money. It's got so any man's got to spend a lot of money to get elected. I don't care if he's Judge Butler or Jesus Christ." Neither does the sheriff of Madison County have a very high opinion of the quality of the county's elections: "I don't know how they are where you come from, but elections are pretty rotten around here. Nothing's done to the boxes or anything like that, I don't think, but there's a many a vote bought right here in this courthouse."

A WPA worker in Huntsville, a former sharecropper, paid his first poll tax in 1940 at the suggestion of his WPA foreman. The amount due was $13.50. He put up $7.50 and "a fellow gimme $6.00." (He would not say who.) "Oh! just some fellow that's a-runnin'." One responsible observer estimates that 1,700 of the usual 7,500 votes cast in Madison County can be bought and are bought at each election. Of these 1,700, a candidate might count on about 75 percent turning out to be "good." The others would double-cross. With this number of bought votes, it is comparatively easy for a man with any kind of a following to get in office if he has the money. In 1938 a candidate running for tax collector was reported to have spent $10,000 in his campaign and yet lost because half of the people he paid voted against him. This happened because of the candidate's inexperience and because he did not know how to spend money effectively in a campaign.

A good many of the textile workers in Madison County now sell their vote. Prior to 1934, and before the workers were organized in unions, the textile companies had largely controlled the voting of their employees. Before 1934 few candidates "ever bothered to come to see us. They know'd we was in the bag," declared one worker. But in recent years the candidates have commenced to come with two dollar bills, and the feeling among many union leaders is that until this habit of selling the ballot can be broken, the union "had just as well stop talking about backing anybody."

The procedure for purchasing votes and checking upon bought votes in Madison County is to let one of the election officials see the voter mark his ballot—there are no voting booths, merely open tables. This official gives a poker chip to the voter who marks his ballot according to his agreement; the voter later exchanges the chip for two dollars at a nearby store. Until the last primary, when vigorous objection was raised against the practice, the identification numbers on the back of the ballots were used in Dallas as a means of checking on how people voted. At the last primary, the officials at the ballot boxes left these identification numbers off the ballots.

The estimates of the number of bought votes in Bibb County, Alabama, run high. It is said that from four to five hundred out of a total average county vote of about two thousand votes are bought in each election. Saw-millers and miners are reported to be the most frequent offenders in this respect. Until the passage of the federal wages and hours law, miners received only 92 cents a day for twelve hours of work, and they regularly sold their vote as a means of supplementing their income. The political action committees of the CIO now find it difficult to convince these workers that they should vote for principle rather than money.

According to a candidate for probate judge this year, Bibb County politicians practice the trick used rather extensively elsewhere—that of insuring the buying of votes. By this practice, a voter makes a bargain with an agent outside of the voting place. The voter obtains his ballot and permits a confederate—who is an election official—to see how he marks his ticket. This official gives the "okay" sign to the man on the outside and the voter gets paid on his way out.

The following items quoted from the Centerville *Press* of 16 June, 1938, give some insight into the nature of Bibb County politics:

T. C. Mitchell of Camp Hugh, Beat 3, Box 1, Bibb County, Alabama became angry at the polls Tuesday as he voted and seized the ballot box, threw it out the window at the polling place and then went on the outside and broke the box open, and destroyed some of the ballots. The election officers there brought Mitchell to Centerville where he was placed in jail and a new ballot box was secured and the voters at Camp Hugh completed their voting.

Eighty-eight votes had been polled before Mitchell destroyed the box. These votes were not counted Tuesday and will be turned over to the County Democratic Executive Committee for them to decide what to do about the matter. It is the general opinion that this box will be thrown out completely and none of the 88 votes counted for either candidate. . . .

Mitchell was said to have been drinking some, but was not drunk. It is not known definitely what he became angry about as several different versions of the incident have been told in Centerville.

Several citizens went to Montgomery Wednesday to consult the Attorney General about the matter and we understand that the Attorney General stated that he did not know of any law under which Mitchell could be prosecuted due to the fact that the law "does not contemplate such acts" as happened at Camp Hugh Tuesday.

The allegation is made that the angered man saw an election official peeping at his vote. The man was released without punishment and the ballots were thrown out since no contest would have been decided by that marginal vote.

A second item from the Centerville *Press* concerns absentee voting:

Walking into the voting place in Peyton County Courthouse, Tuesday afternoon, three men told officers at the polls not to interfere while a fourth man grabbed the county's absentee ballot box, containing 741 ballots, and handed it out the window to a confederate who drove away in an auto.

Sheriff J. R. Hody said the absentee ballots were "kidnapped" shortly after noon when all but three of the poll officials were having lunch. . . .

Sheriff Hody said he was told the men entered the voting place in the probate office and that three of them warned the officers against action while a fourth produced a sack, put the ballot box in it and handed the sack . . . out the window. Each of the five men were identified by the poll officials as prominent Chilton County citizens, the sheriff said. No arrests had been made late Tuesday night.

Commenting on the large number of absentee ballots cast in the election here Tuesday, a leading Chilton County citizen said the usual number of absentee ballots cast is approximately 300.

Disappearance of the absentee ballot box followed the election campaign here in local run-off races. Focal point of election heat here has been in the state senate race.

The editor of the Centerville *Press* stated that this trouble arose because the opposition had stuffed the absentee ballot box. When it was stolen, they knew they would be in for a hot court battle if they raised objection, so the whole matter was dropped. No absentee ballots were counted for either side.

Johnson County, Georgia, is supposed to be a bad county for vote selling. The Negro secretary of the Johnson County Republican committee, a small farm owner, told of several white workers on the adjoining plantation who bragged about how much they got for their vote in a recent election. One family he saw got in the poll worker's car in rags:

> That man didn't have no hat on atall. He had a hat wa'n't as good as this 'un I got on, so he wouldn't wear it. You should have seen him come back! . . . Bran' new overhauls, one of these here flashy straw hats with a ribbon around it. . . . The lady, she had a new hat on too and she yelled out she had a new dress under her arm. . . .

After relating several such episodes, this Negro informant remarked that this kind of thing was exactly what the white people claimed they disfranchised the Negro for doing. "You know, they say he vote for a plug tobacco or a quarter. . . . It looks like the whites are doing the same thing, 'cept it cost somebody more money."

While George Stoney was in Hall County, Georgia, the trial of United States Representative B. Frank Whelchel on charges of selling postal appointments was being held in the federal building in Gainesville. Whelchel is from Hall County—a poor boy, educated in Gainesville and trained in law in a local office. He climbed the ladder rapidly. Representative Whelchel was first sent to Congress in 1934 by a majority of a few votes. In 1936 he failed by over two thousand votes to get a majority in his district, but he did get a majority of the county unit votes. Most of the prominent people in Gainesville with whom Stoney talked admitted privately that Whelchel was guilty as charged. These included the tax collector, the clerk of court, the editor of the newspaper, and the biggest druggist in town. But they could not see that he was doing anything that was not all right as far as Georgia politics go. The farmers and mill people in the county with whom Stoney talked also thought Whelchel guilty, and they felt he ought to be punished, but not by the federal men coming in and disgracing their home town with such a trial. The federal prosecutor tried his best to adapt himself, but there was a tremendous amount of local sentiment against him. The decision of the local jury, acquitting Whelchel after the judge had indicated to jury members that the defendant had admitted taking the money, was a farce, and it merely proves that Georgians, at least in Hall County, would rather be cheated than have the government help them out with the prosecution of the people who are cheating them.

In Savannah, Georgia, the group headed by John J. Bouhan pays the poll taxes of poor whites when their votes are needed. The machine keeps them paid, according to the editor of the Savannah *Morning News*, "because it never knows when it will need them in a campaign or bond issue." A cargo checker told Stoney that he was approached when he was in "a bad way" and "they come around and said they'd give me $5 and furnish gas if I'd drive for them." This man worked all election day, calling on addresses the ward manager gave him and bringing people to the polls. When he would find that people had moved away, he would report back to the ward captain, who would have him call at "a certain house" where he would pick up "two men or two ladies, or one of each, whatever was wanted." He would take them to the polls, and they would vote the names of the absent people. If the people he called on said they were not coming to vote, or were reported out of town, the same thing would happen. On election morning, he had been furnished with a list of people to pick up during the day when he could spare the time. These, he said, were people the administration had paid taxes for and who vote regularly. Most of them were women or older people who hung around the house all day.

The tax collector of Johnson County, Georgia, prefers having help come from the clerks and managers of election. A clerk, he explained, can give a candidate a great deal of help "in the ordinary kind of way" by suggesting the candidate's name when voters are marking tickets. Also, the clerk can serve as an inside checker in watching people mark their ballots, and forty or fifty dollars spent among clerks will bring much better returns than an equal amount spent buying votes outright. His experience has taught him, he volunteers, that to give the men a little something at the start and to promise them so much more if they carry the box—that is, "pay on performance"—produces the most effective results.

It seems to be common knowledge that there is a great deal of vote selling in Johnson County. A member of the county board of registrars related several specific instances of this as follows: (1) A man brought six people in from his farm and wanted to get two dollars apiece for their votes. The candidate (the informant's boss) refused, saying that he had spent so much on the election that he was not going to spend another cent if he never got elected. The man got angry and threatened to take his people back home before he would have them vote for nothing. (2) A young man for whom the registrar had high regard came into the office of a county official for whom she was doing some extra work. He wanted five dollars for his vote and that of his wife and one other person. He got it. (3) Another man came to the same official and, because the official would not buy a new tire for his car, got so angry he cursed him out openly in the office and threatened to campaign against him, as he did.

One of the election officials in Crescent, a little store community in McIntosh County, Georgia, states that, though he sees to it that the ballots do not get out until the morning of elections, still "nine-tenths of the people bring in their tickets already marked." He adds that a great many of them are marked by people who have bought this privilege. "It's bad here. These whites around here aren't much account. They don't own nothing and they don't care much what happens to the county so long as they get their drink of liquor." He estimated that at least half the people who voted at this box last election had been made eligible by having someone else pay their poll taxes.

The chairman of the board of registrars in Ware County, Georgia, considers one reform very badly needed; namely, the removal of registration and poll tax payment from the office of the tax collector, who is "an interested party to the election." In the 1940 elections it is said that "a terrible time" was had "keeping straight records." The tax collector of the county put on a great many people who could not be identified or checked upon. "Marked tickets" are still allowed in Ware County, though there is a modified form of the Australian ballot with booths, election officials, and so forth.

It is common knowledge in Gainesville, Georgia, that a great many people in the mills vote double. They vote at the mill box and then go to the courthouse and vote again. Moreover, it is reported that many people vote the first time for a dollar, regardless of what their age is. They give their names to a friend who registers them as twenty-two and pays their poll tax. Unless the tax collector knows the individual personally, he says nothing.

The registration slip requirement in Tennessee is almost as vicious as the poll tax requirement. Only the four large counties of the state require these registration slips. Ward heelers take up these slips when they register people so they will have something to bargain with when they contract with the political leaders. As the president of the American Newspaper Guild in Chattanooga put it to Stoney:

These fellows that don't have nothing else to do, they hang around these little stores around registration time and persuade some fellows that don't have no more than they have to do, to go down and register for them. When he comes out, the fellow will say, "Here, better let me have that." And he'll take his registration certificate. Lots of them don't take nobody but people over 50. They don't have to have poll tax. There's a lot less trouble about voting them. But, anyway, they go to a candidate, and they say: "How much you give me for these seventh or tenth [or wherever they're registered for]?" If they're on the poll tax bracket, the candidate's got to match every one with $2.00 for a slip, too. Lots of honest candidates get milked that way, 'cause half the time the damn ward heelers sold them votes to half a dozen people.

Once one of those bastards got your slip, he don't turn loose neither. He'll wait right outside the poll until you come out and he'll take it up to vote you again next time. Course he'll give you maybe 50¢ or a drink for your trouble. It's many a thirsty soul on these damn streets that would go to more trouble than that for a drink.

The campaigning in Bibb County, Alabama, is on a very "folksy" level. For several weeks before election day almost every cross-roads community will hold some kind of entertainment, given by a church society or a PTA, at which the candidates will speak. The pianos and extra blackboards and library books for the county schools are frequently paid for by money made at these pie suppers or oyster stews. Some of the candidates hold their own "to-dos." One candidate for probate judge in Bibb County held three such "to-dos" within a two-week period. He provided no refreshments, but gave his crowd a "speaking" and string band music. "That always gets a crowd," he claims. This candidate holds that the most effective way to campaign down there is to "go and sit with people" because they want to feel that they know a candidate and that their vote for him will be "appreciated." A good many votes, it seems, are bought with a few dollars and liquor distributed on the night before the election. "You'll always have that, and you can't do much about it," he said.

It makes "a good deal of difference," too, whether or not a candidate has been made favorable to him at the box. This is true, in the first place, because so many country people are in the habit of talking over their tickets with the officer of election. They will stand at the table and argue about whom they ought to vote for. If they are undecided, an election officer can do some very effective electioneering for the candidates he favors. Also, among many of the voters there is always the hope of reward for voting for someone. They have made no bargain for their vote, perhaps; but they promise to back a candidate, and they want the election official to see how they vote in the hope that word will get back to the candidate in order that their vote may "count for something." There is a great deal of semi-illiteracy in Bibb County, also, and old people especially are in the habit of asking somone to assist them.

Attempts to introduce precinct voting clubs such as are used in New York and Philadelphia have failed in Birmingham except among the farm population. Jefferson County campaigns must have the flavor of a country barbecue if they are to be effective. Congressman Luther Patrick was elected because he appealed to the "nostalgia of the homesick country people who lived in Birmingham." Patrick sponsored a radio program of "corn pone philosophy" in his campaign. Birmingham politics split on the "ins" and "outs" basis. The chairman of the county board of registrars says that "any man who is in the courthouse can usually count on the support of the other men there unless he's completely obnoxious." The political organizations seldom form slates. The slate idea does not meet with popular favor among the voters, and it is a political handicap to be accused of being on a "slate."

The main method of campaigning in Madison County, Alabama, is to make speches at all the pie suppers, barbecues, and ice cream suppers given by the PTAs, church societies, and schools. Food is usually sold at these functions. In addition, every really ambitious candidate makes a house-to-house canvass. In the words of the Madison County board of registrars chairman, the candidate "backslaps, baby-kisses and bites a chew off the same plug with every farmer from here to Tennessee, and, if he has enough two-dollar bills, he gets elected."

In Greene County, Alabama, is found the usual pro- and anti-probate judge factionalism. Personality plays a great part in the campaigns. There are a few pie suppers and other affairs found in many Alabama counties during the campaign period. Most of the Greene County candidates spend the bulk of their time in Eutaw, the county's main trading center, and they see the voters there. Three of the large landowners in the county take considerable interest in politics. Each of them controls about twenty or thirty votes, which may be coerced votes. It may be that the people vote with their employer because they see that is where their "best interests" lie.

An example of how a campaign is conducted and the vote lined up for a particular candidate in a Southern city is presented in the campaign of Estes Kefauver, a Democrat running in a special congressional election in Chattanooga in September 1939. The group of labor leaders and "progressives" campaigning for Kefauver had every voter in the city listed on a card with his race, address, poll tax standing, membership in organizations, telephone number, and responses to questions put to him on the Kefauver race before the election. All of these cards were cross-referenced in categories such as telephone subscribers, church members, American Legion, union affiliation, other organization, party, and so on. The system was set up on the "Cincinnati Plan," a political reference scheme developed a few years ago to beat the machine in that city. Most of this work was done by volunteers. During the campaign, several different types of form letters were written to the various organizations and interest groups, and cross-referenced in the files. A few days before the election, four girls polled all telephone subscribers with a series of questions "nicely framed" so as to get an indication of the way they were going to vote. The result deviated from the actual results of the election by less than 3 percent, precinct by precinct.

In Beaufort County, South Carolina, an important function of the county Democratic committee is to arrange the "circus." Before the primary, the committee plans a public meeting in each district, at which all of the major candidates are invited to speak from the same platform. The local committeeman usually presides and arranges details of the affair. These meetings do not amount to a great deal. Campaigning in this county is done personally for the most part. As one officeholder puts it: "You've got to build up a following by shaking people's hands."

Campaigns in Johnson County, Georgia, are highly personal affairs. Each candidate tries to cover the entire county and shake every voter's hand. The schools and churches put on barbecues, pie and cake suppers, and the like, and candidates are asked to come and make short talks. A renter in Johnson County told, with a glow of satisfaction, of the way candidates have been tricked when they have tried to buy votes indirectly. For instance, he gloated over the way a politician was tricked by a local grocer. The politician, assuming the grocer was for him, gave him a keg of liquor to distribute with his compliments on election day. He brought it in the night before. The boys around the store saw it. When the candidate had gone, the storekeeper locked up the keg and did not open it until after election day. This made the boys so angry that they all voted against the man.

There is no machine in either Hall County or Greene County, Georgia. Each man in the courthouse, at least as far as the public is concerned, runs his own race. Thus, local politics is a matter of personal contacts. Few speeches or rallies are held, and candidates try to meet each voter personally through house-to-house canvassing. In Greene County it is an "unwritten law" for every officeholder to be given two terms, or eight years. Most officeholders stay in for twelve years.

Filing [entrance] fees in the Southern states tend to run high. In some cases they run to as much as five hundred dollars for the office of tax collector, as in Chatham County, Georgia. In Georgia the filing fees are used to pay the expenses of the primaries, while in Alabama the state pays for the primary elections. In the latter state the filing fee is a source of great graft, though the fees are low. In some South Carolina counties the fees are low, but the entrance fees for Charleston County are so high as to discourage candidacies. In a recent contest for sheriff in that county the entrance fee was two thousand dollars. Yet this selective principle does not seem to afford the South a very high quality of local officials.

The low caliber of the election officials in Alabama; the lack of any qualifications, except affiliation with the Democratic party, for such positions; the constantly repeated complaints made by the higher county officials about the inability and even the illiteracy of the election officials; and the fact that these jobs are usually handed out at the rate of two dollars per day to those who have no jobs and "need money," is a fairly typical picture of the election officer throughout the Southern region. A member of the board of registrars in Burke County, Georgia, explains that he never went to school until he was nine, and then for only a few months; he says he "can't read much of anything correct now."

The chairman of the Sumter County, South Carolina, election commission points out that in the county races, each man is his own politician, that "we have some good ones," and that that is why they hold office so long. He gives a picturesque description of the county officeholders:

> We've got a blind coroner [true], a cork-leg supervisor, a sheriff that's so old he can't hardly get around [true], a one-legged Jew auditor, an auto mechanic for a superintendent of education, a clerk of court who's as old as the hills, and a woman probate judge who isn't a lawyer [all true], but I'll have to admit they're all damn good politicians and pretty good officials.

The low salaries paid to members of the legislature in South Carolina and the fact that they meet for almost half of each year account for the rather poor caliber of men running from the wealthier counties. In 1936, for example, Greenville's delegation—according to the respectable, enlightened, but rather conservative "good government" people in that city—was made up of shyster lawyers looking for bribes, ill-equipped small merchants elected because they happened to have been former textile workers, and other misfits. Eventually a reform movement was launched. The so-called Greenville County Council's community advisory body held several forums and round tables on county and state government. Out of this grew two movements. One was the Good Government League. Its sole purpose was to get out the vote, the theory being that if "all the people" voted, the free-lance ward heelers and their following would be beaten automatically and good government would triumph. This league was started in the early part of 1938 and worked both during the enrollment period for 1938 and the city enrollment and registration periods for 1939. The league's "all the people," however, did not include Negroes, and its leader does not hesitate to state that the organization had nothing whatever to do with the attempt of Negroes to register.

The second movement came indirectly from the Greenville County Council. A few leaders, inspired by the council's work, organized quietly to take over the large city Democratic clubs and a few of the rural ones. A major objective was to get the county convention to work in the state convention to amend Rule 32 so as to require party loyalty only in local and state elections. A second objective was to put their own men in control of the voting at these large wards and put their men in as executive committeemen. This was in preparation for the running of a slate of legislative candidates in the fall primary. The group succeeded in capturing the important clubs, mostly because it took the "enemy" by surprise. It passed resolutions against Rule 32 in most of the large clubs and got enough delegates to the county convention to get a similar resolution put through there. It named a controlling minority of the county executive committee and named a majority of the delegates to the state convention. The latter delegation was responsible—or as responsible as any other in the state—for getting Rule 32 changed by the 1938 convention. This delegation was made up of a group of conservatives, mostly anti-New Dealers, with a powerful minority of Republicans sprinkled in. Their fight against Rule 32 was made for no such idealistic reasons as the freedom of the ballot—though the result was the same. They did succeed in getting control of the main boxes and thus encouraging an abler group of men to run for the legislature. While the present group cannot be called liberal, and while some of its members have proven themselves to be antilabor, both the CIO leaders and liberals in the state admit that they are much better than the old set.

Miami, Florida, politics tend to be personal. As one prominent Miami citizen puts it:

> Personal squabbles between six or seven mediocre personalities constitute political leadership here. . . . And the virtual dictator which the Florida Governor is—having power either to accept or reject nominations for sheriff, state's attorney, county prosecutor, school board members, justices of the peace, and constables—combines with the fore-mentioned factor to make a pretty distasteful political picture.[14]

Miami has had some unpleasant experiences, with particularly bad officials as city commissioners. The last set of commissioners was put out of office by recall. At the present time a vigorous controversy is raging over the issue of the tie-up between the city commissioners and the Florida Power and Light Company. The primaries in Miami are, of course, white primaries, and victory in them is equivalent to election. Campaigns in the city are not very intense as a rule.

The effect of the provisions of the Alabama constitution of 1901 has been to limit radically the number of white voters in the state. A careful study of the poll list from a majority of the counties in Alabama suggests that the number of white registrants in the state is slightly less than 400,000. Since there are approximately 950,000 white persons twenty-one years of age

14. Wilhelmina Jackson's interview with a member of the editorial staff of the Miami *Herald,* Miami, Florida, March 1940.

and over, considerably more than half a million white Alabamians of voting age are not exercising the privilege of the franchise.

When the question is raised as to why Alabama's vote, and particularly that in counties like Etowah, is so small numerically, the usual first response is "the large Negro population." This population is commonly referred to as "almost half" of the state's population—a phrase used by virtually everybody who talks about the Negro vote unfavorably. Many others say "half" or "over half," but in Etowah County there are not so many Negroes, nor is the percentage of blacks in the state itself as large as such statements would indicate. In Etowah County there is a large shifting population of people who come in to do construction work and then move on without attempting to qualify for voting. Moreover, a number of the farming people, including the sharecroppers, do not qualify. In discussing the sharecroppers in Etowah County, an Alabama state senator told Stoney: "A high percentage of the adult white people in this county . . . well, I wouldn't say they are no good, but I will say they aren't capable of making intelligent political decisions. And when they are in that class, I tell you, I think it is a good thing they do not vote." Furthermore, only a small percentage of women take an active interest in politics. As the Etowah senator states:

> Very few of them would bother to vote unless their husband or their brother or their son persuaded them to. Most women aren't interested in politics, and I think if they aren't interested, it ought to be their privilege to stay at home. What right have we to force them to take part in politics when they aren't so inclined?

The same allegations as to lack of interest are made against the participation of Negroes.

The source of greatest weakness in Birmingham politics is the small number of voters. A city election attracts only 15,000 to 28,000 voters to the polls, in a city with a population in excess of 300,000 and with a registered voting strength of about 40,000. Jefferson County has almost half a million people—of whom 40 percent are Negroes. The top county vote is about 45,000 out of a total registered vote of some 60,000. The small voting group, quite aside from the limited registration, is due to the lack of real issues in most campaigns.

The small vote plays an important role in Georgia county elections. The state primary election in 1938 polled only

312,000 votes. Only about one-third of the potential voters—
white and black—are registered, and only about one-fifth of
these vote. Poll taxes for approximately 175,000 people were
paid in Georgia in 1938, while only 312,000 people voted.

The vote among white people is unusually small in Burke
County, Georgia, though it is difficult to find a clear explanation
for it. A check of the list of qualified voters made up for the fall
primary in 1940, complete and certified, gives the following
totals: women, 687; men, 936; or a total of 1,623. In the town
of Waynesboro the registration is 359 men and 337 women. In
one rural district there are 35 women and 29 men registered; in
another there are 8 women and 34 men.

The election returns indicate that the total vote in Augusta,
Georgia, is low. The city is subject to one-party machine control. For example, in the election for mayor in December 1939,
the city's first general election since 1912, there were two candidates—the nominee of the Cracker Party and an independent
critic of that party. There were 3,665 votes cast, of which the
machine candidate received 3,468 and his opponent 175.[15]

The vote of women in Gainesville and in Hall County, Georgia, is exceedingly small. The county ordinary feels that the
main cause of this is the poll tax. Women get behind three or
four years in their poll tax and never can pay up. At a recent
election, a great many women voted, but only because the candidates paid their taxes for them. According to the county ordinary: "It was awful the way they did this. It might be good in a
way, because they wouldn't have gotten to vote otherwise, but I
can't see how this is much different from plain out buying votes.
. . . All of them do it, and they do it every time. I know. My husband was in it for 18 years."

McIntosh County, Georgia, has very few voters. As a general
rule, not more than 500 persons vote in the state primary, and
in off years this goes down to 350. Nevertheless, McIntosh
County has two county unit votes, as compared with Atlanta's
60,000 votes and six county unit votes. Before the white primary was institutionalized in Georgia, it was the Negro who
was manipulated, but now it seems to be the white voter who
is "hauled." The last county primary in McIntosh County
brought out the "biggest vote in history since the niggers quit
voting," according to the court clerk in Darien. It was a fight

15. Twenty-two of the 3,665 voters apparently failed to vote for either
candidate in the mayoralty race. —ED.

between two factions in the county that "went out and shook the bushes" for votes. It is said that the candidates for sheriff were leaders in seeking votes and that they paid up poll taxes "as high as fourteen dollars for one man."

In South Carolina the percentage of white people voting in the Democratic primaries is much higher than in either Georgia or Alabama. There is also much more community freedom and lack of control in South Carolina; that is, within the Democratic primary. But in the general elections there is an exceedingly small vote. Charleston newspaper editor William Watts Ball says that the white male is "a thoroughly habituated voter and always has been. The white woman votes as her husband does." He states that the maximum potential white vote in South Carolina is 500,000. The vote in the primary of 1938 was 344,000. In the general election for that year it was very small. In the 1936 presidential election—the largest ever—it was about 114,000. When Miss Jackson asked officials at the courthouse in Charleston to see some of their records on general elections in order to determine the voting strength, they laughed and said: "Why, we don't even keep a record. You'd have to get them from the capital. Nobody votes at all hardly after the primaries."[16]

Few people in Lawson district, Charleston County, bother to vote in the general election because, in order to do so, it is necessary to go all the way to Charleston for a certificate. Yet a commissioner for that district feels that the general election is the election that the best people ought to vote in because it puts them on the jury list and also it is the "real" election. He adds: "The trouble is you got to give people something before they'll vote. They don't get nothing for the general election." There are no Negro members of the Lawson district Democratic club, though the Negroes in the district vote Democratic in the general election.

Durham, North Carolina, has a population of 52,037, and 18,717 of these are Negroes. The voting-age population numbers 31,169, of whom 11,302 are Negroes. Durham election returns for the past decade indicate that the total vote is low but increasing. Only in national elections is there a sizable vote. In the 1932 Democratic primary there were only 5,417 votes for United States senator and 2,360 for governor. In the 1932 general election for the representative in Congress from the sixth

16. Wilhelmina Jackson's Charleston field notes, 12 April 1940.

district, only 8,134 ballots were cast. In the general election for the sixth district congressman in 1936, 11,710 votes were cast. In the city election for mayor in 1929, there were 3,818 votes. For the same office in 1931, there were 2,516 votes; in 1933, 7,077 votes; in 1937, 6,027 votes; in 1939, 4,348 votes.

EIGHT

Southern White Attitudes toward Politics

WHILE many expressions of Southern attitudes toward politics, and especially the Negro issue, are recorded throughout this memorandum, I have thought that it would be useful to assemble in one place some representative samples of such attitudes. There is a widespread spirit of discontent with contemporary politics in the South. Potential voters are bitter because the poll tax keeps them from the voting booths; many are contemptuous of the type of officials chosen under present conditions; others are resigned or indifferent. There is also a wide variety of attitudes expressed toward Negro voting, ranging from extreme hostility to rational support of the idea.

A typical expression heard from the poor whites throughout the South is: "No, I don't vote. I don't care nothing about it. Whoever they elect, it's all right with me. I'll have as good as the next one." It should be noted, however, that this indifference is often feigned and results from the individual's shame at his inability to pay the poll tax and thereby qualify for voting. In interviews with the white man on the Southern street it is not uncommon to hear such statements as: "Listen! Politics is the rottenest thing in this world. Don't you never have anything to do with it. It will make a liar out of you quicker'n anything I know of." How widespread are such attitudes, and what relationship do they have to the ideological and psychological foundations for a democratic society here?

The expression "A man ought to vote; that's about the only right a poor man's got," occurs repeatedly in the interviews with whites in the South. Another expression frequently repeated is: "You know, a heap of folks will pay more to vote agin a man than they will to vote for him." A great many of the poor white women interviewed by George Stoney indicated a belief that politics is not a woman's affair, and in most cases their husbands shared in this belief.

The county ordinary in Ware County, Georgia, described the election in that locality as "crooked as hell. Any man that gets elected has got to keep both eyes open. We don't have that Australian ballot, and it wouldn't make much difference if we did. You still got to watch your clerks and managers. When I ran the first time, they almost stole it away from me."[1] A retired deputy sheriff in Ware County, in boasting reverently of the fine qualities of the former sheriff, included among them the following: "He killed a man for every year he was in office, and he served 16 years. He never killed no white man. They was all niggers he killed."

The *Citizen-Georgian* of Macon County, Georgia, in an editorial of 5 November 1936, attacked the absence of a secret ballot in the state.

> The present method can hardly be called a secret ballot because friends, relatives, supporters, and sometimes even the candidates themselves, literally stand over the voting booths, making it impossible for a person to mark his ticket without several persons knowing for whom the vote has been cast.
>
> Certainly the massing of political workers in and near the voting places, handing out cards and handbills, should be stopped. The voters must run through a line of political workers to get to the voting box. This aggravating practice would be stopped under the Australian system.

One white small-farm owner in Greshamville, west of Greensboro, Georgia, in an old plantation section that was finally abandoned completely, foresees a Roosevelt dictatorship in the offing. He was willing to see it come, however, and in his opinion it should "put every man on fifty acres, build him a house, furnish him tools, and then put a man over him that will make him work. . . . give him what he needs to live on. That's what you're coming to. Let's start it and be done." To quote the

---

1. George Stoney's interview in Waycross, Ware County, Georgia, May 1940. Unless otherwise indicated, all quoted passages in this chapter are taken from Stoney's notes of field interviews conducted in 1940. —ED.

secretary-treasurer of the Greene County Democratic committee, who is also editor of the Greensboro *Herald Journal:*

> The trouble with Greene County is that we have had too many large plantations. Too many white men sat around town on their "fannies" while the nigahs did all the work. The nigahs didn't know how to look after things, so they let the land wash away. When the boll weevil came, there was nothing left. We can't go back to the old cotton system. We've got to make the people live at home on the farms, and you can't do that with the plantation system.

A textile worker in the Chicopee Mill at Gainesville, Georgia, states that this year several of his friends were registered for the first time and that they had their poll taxes paid by the candidate for sheriff. He thought this shameful, since all of these men could well have afforded to pay the tax themselves: "Some folks think it's all right to gouge a politician for everything you can get. I don't."

The conservative Gainesville *News*, in an editorial on 17 January 1940 discussing the action of the Hall County Democratic executive committee, which ordered a county primary to be held some nine months before the induction of the successful candidates into office, takes occasion to deny the need for a primary in the county election:

> As previously stated in these columns, there is no real necessity for a primary at all. Only white Democrats choose our officials whether the voting be in a primary or at a general election and since we long ago excluded the negro from voting, there is, at least to our mind, no justification in assessing those who wish to offer for public office an expense that many can ill afford to bear.
>
> We have seen the primary abolished in our city as a useless bother and expense; now let's abolish it in our county.

Stoney observed that in all of his interviews in South Carolina he heard fewer than a dozen people make the statement: "There's a class of white people that oughtn't to vote." This statement, on the other hand, was heard time and time again in both Alabama and Georgia. Perhaps the absence of this feeling in South Carolina is due to the fact that there has been no poll tax requirement in the primary, and that the popular vote in the primary has been a great deal freer and larger than in the other two states.

An editorial in the Charleston, South Carolina, *News and Courier* of 10 February 1940 reads as follows:

If the southern white people could and would take into their heads the simple fact that presidents and vice-presidents are elected by the electoral college, they would be masters of the American political situation.

The presidential electors, not the people, choose the president and vice-president.

South Carolina has eight electors, one for each senator and each congressman. Thus, while its population is less than one-seventh (its white population is about one-twelfth) of the population of New York, it has more than one-sixth of the power of New York in the electoral college.

Nevada's population is not quite one one-hundred and thirtieth of New York, but it has one-fifteenth of the number of New York's electoral votes.

So, all the smaller states have disproportionate weight to population in electing the president and vice-president by reason of the equal senatorial representation.

Now, when both northern parties, Democratic and Republican, unite in Congress against the South in Negro legislation, why does not the South resort to the electoral college for its protection?

The Constitution gives it the protection—why not use it?

If, as is probable, the North and West shall divide between the two "major parties" this year, eight South Carolina electors might dictate the choice of the president and vice-president. Ten or a dozen southern states acting together could get everything they want through the electoral college. One might control.

The states of the North and West are divided. There are northern states—Vermont, New Hampshire, Delaware, Connecticut, Maine, Idaho, Oregon—that . . . now see eye to eye with South Carolina in respect to state rights. Was not Mr. Borah of Idaho the staunch friend of states' rights?

Why are the southerners tying themselves to the great . . . "pivotal states" in which the negroes in the cities have the balance of power in elections?

The white South holds the commanding trumps and has only to play them to put an end to this continuing attack of the northern congressmen upon it.

The chairman of the Madison County, Alabama, Democratic committee claims to be a crusader for clean elections in the South. He states:

> I'm from North Georgia. . . . As a boy, I saw elections and bad ones. I saw fifty niggers voted in one precinct, then hauled over and voted again in another precinct. I saw them, and white men, too, bribed by a drink of liquor to vote for the crookedest men in the county, and I saw good men have to use the same tactics to save the county from ruin. I developed a horror of crooked elections and I made up my mind when I took this job, I was going to see that we have straight elections.

He thinks that "the Democratic principles are carried out better in this county than in almost anywhere else in the country. . . . Why, there's as much difference between Tammany Hall and the Democratic party of Madison County as there is between a nigger and a white man."

People in the northern "white" counties of Alabama complain about the way the "Black Belt" has them "hog-tied." As the tax collector of Cullman County puts it: "One little county down there, Wilcox, hasn't got a thousand votes and it's got a senator. Up here, we got one senator for Cullman, Blount, and Winston Counties. Cullman alone this next time will vote close to 10,000."

Stoney made a series of interviews in a squalid little settlement just outside of Cullman, Alabama. While it may not be said, perhaps, that these people are typical of Alabama, they are certainly representative of a large group in the state and regional population. For this reason, and because of their statements in response to questions about voting and the poll tax, I quote these interviews in full.

After you make the second (and last) signal light on the highway that is Cullman's main street and pass the sawmill, the road slopes gently down to the creek and then moves up, curving away over Grandview Ridge to north county farms. The town side of this narrow valley is occupied by a lumberyard, filling station, and scrap heap. On the other side are bottom land corn fields. As the road begins cutting into the ridge, one side rises almost to a cliff, making a handsome platform for a heavy spreading brick and concrete dwelling for the sawmill owner. The other side hollows out below the road, and in an old field with ridges half a dozen crazily-built houses sit in disorder. This little settlement has no name. It was started two years ago when a lawyer owner agreed to sell small strips of land to the present residents for from ninety to three hundred dollars, letting them pay ten dollars a month.

The first house I came to was a two-room affair with a porch, supported behind by piles made of pine logs driven in the ground. Some of them had been made too short, so an assortment of wood blocks, pieces of iron, and the back of a scrubbing brush had been shoved in between them and the house floor. The structure was of raw, smelly new pine, one board thick, with light showing through the knots in places. An attempt to cover the inside with tar paper had been given up for lack of material after one wall was covered. Wads of newspapers had been stuffed and nailed into cracks showing in other places. Bright new curtains were at the windows, and the front room had a definite air of being "prettied up"—boudoir doll on bed with lacy skirt, narcissus in duck-back china container, etc.

The young mother—nursing her fourth baby and sewing at the same time—listened while Stoney talked with the grandfather, huddled up to the little iron stove whose pipe ran out a hole at the top of the wall. There was no chimney. Both grandpa and mother seemed proud of their new house. It was built by the missing father the summer before. He is a WPA worker. Until this last year, they all sharecropped in the northern end of the county. They admitted it got pretty cold during the big snow. "You'd keep that stove red hot and water'd freeze in a bucket on the other side of the room." Grandfather, mother, and the four children all "stayed in bed" during most of it.

The wife knew nothing about voting or politics. "Pa's the voter in the family." Grandpa liked this. He had been voting thirty-six of his fifty-seven years. He had lived in Tennessee until the World War, paying poll taxes and voting there. Since the war, he has been sharecropping in Alabama and voting free, because of war service. No one else in the house votes. His son has never paid poll taxes and is too far "behind" to "get right" now. "I told him to go on down to the courthouse when they was apayin' up so much fer people here last month, but he said he wouldn't." Why? "I don't know, just said he wouldn't." The wife said she might vote if her husband could ever afford to pay both of their poll taxes (he is thirty-two, she is twenty-seven), and she "got interested." Right now she was much more interested in "getting this here house paid for, now we built it." Stoney said he thought it was a fine place. She believed him and pointed out the cement-edged well (with all the family's foot prints and initials on it), with more than wifely pride as she told him how handy her husband was about doing things.

The second house looked worse, because it was no better built and was one year older. The raw pine boards were water-stained. The windows, obviously scavenged from some other building, were sagging crookedly. The house sat better on the ground, though, and there was a chimney. For this one's builder had used the site and remaining chimney of a burned house. "Some WPA workers built it, I think," the woman inside explained. "The roof leaks since the snow." The battered iron bed was jammed up at the front door so that only half the passage was clear. "We had to move it there because we got rained on every place else." She laughed, a thin, immature girl-mother, with a snuff stick in her mouth. They had lived in the house— she, her husband, and the three children—for only a month and a half. They had moved from Vermont (ten miles west) when her husband got a job in the sawmill. They had been sharecropping before. She looked forward to the spring, when her husband, "who can build a house good as a carpenter," would be fixing up the house; when they would have money to fix it up; and when she could get to "putting in a garden" in the acre of ground they have been given permission to use farther down toward the creek. This lady was the one who told Stoney about the lawyer and the purchase plans. The WPA workers had "got the 18 months" and so had to "turn in" their interest and move. They are buying the quarter acre of land and the house from the lawyer for ninety dollars, and they get the use of that acre of land in the bottom free. Neither this woman nor her husband votes; they never have. "We never had the money, so we never thought much about it," was the only answer Stoney could get.

On the back of this house was a lean-to, made of this year's timber. It had no window, and the only entrance was to the outside. Stoney heard a voice inside, and he knocked. "You don't want to fool with her," the woman he had just been talking with yelled through the back of the house. "Who is it? Let me see," came from the inside. He pushed aside the slabs that formed the door. An old woman sat hunched in a broken chair over a cook-range that well-nigh filled up one end of the lean-to. Her skin was so discolored, or dirty, that it was hard to tell her race. She was scooping beans from a pot on the stove, mashing them to mush in a broken saucer, and lapping them into a toothless mouth with her tongue. The woman on the other side called again: "She's crazy. She don't know nothing," and laughed. The old woman kept muttering as Stoney closed the door.

A man named Hall lived in the well-built, newly painted one-room cottage that stood proudly on its brick pilings in the midst of this colony. He told Stoney about the old lady. She had come there the winter before. He thought she was some kin to one of the WPA men. He was not sure. Anyway, they had built her a lean-to to live in. He himself had bought the stove for her, and the women of the colony, first one and then the other, helped look after her. Someone carried a bucket of water to her every day, and first one and then another would "throw in her washing" with theirs. When any of them had any leftover food, they would take it to her, and she got a "few beans and dried fruit" from the welfare department. "They come by and leave something every two weeks." He said that "nobody thought much about it," when the WPA workers left her there and he "hadn't heard" any complaints from the newcomers about having her stay on their property. "She ain't botherin' nobody."

Hall had built his own house with the help of his brother, who came from the other side of town to help him on Sundays and after work. Both of them work in the band-saw factory. He has been paying on the house and the two acres of ground that go with it for a little over two years, and figures he will have paid the three hundred dollars plus interest by the time this year is out. Hall's wife does not vote. "She never says nothin' about it if she does," he laughed. "Course, you can't never tell what a woman'll do when you ain't around." He had voted the first time three years ago and did not figure it was "worth the money." He said almost every man who worked at the band-saw factory "but me" had his poll tax paid by someone else this time. A foreman there was the go-between. "I could have got it, too. I didn't." Why? "Well, I figured I'd paid it up myself when I voted before and I might as well wait 'til I could pay my own way again." After a long conversation about the decadence of political morality in the county, he concluded with: "They say it's all right when both sides are doin' it an' you could vote either way. What do you think? I jus' don't think it's honest anyhow." When Stoney asked Hall how many children he had, he glanced in the house and counted five. He is twenty-nine and his wife is twenty-eight.

Back of Hall's "state inspected and approved" outhouse (there is a notice nailed up inside) and across a couple of shallow trenches dug to keep the water from washing down from the road is a fourth house: two rooms, unpainted, second-year weathered pine, completely unadorned. But this house was well built, too. Its roof is a sturdy tin, and its front door fits snugly without sticking. A sawmill worker built this house, a sometime carpenter, his wife explained. She apologized for doing her washing on Sunday and for looking like this. "When you got babies, you can't worry about Sunday," she remarked. She and her husband were both thirty-six years old. They had seven children. Neither of them had ever voted. She "never knew what it was all about." Her husband "talked about it sometime," but she was sure he had never voted. She did not know exactly why he did not. She "guessed" it was the poll tax, after Stoney explained what the poll tax was!

Facing away from the road and surrounded by a low hedge, Mr. Weldon's house hardly seems part of the colony. Well-pounded paths to the back doors of those closer to the road show there are ties. The house has three rooms, sitting close to the ground at an angle. There are flower beds bordered with upturned pop bottles along the sides, and two old tires on either side of the front steps form a place for flowers in the sandy yard. Weldon said he and Hall had built about the same time. His house was twice as big as Hall's and cost him half as much. He figured the total cost was not over $60.00. His one acre of land is costing him $175.00, and he has almost paid for it. "Pretty cheap for a home," he bragged. When he makes the last payments, he hopes to paint it and then start double-sealing it on the inside. Three of them plan to wire their houses together this next summer. All of those in the colony use kerosene lamps rather than electricity, though the Alabama Power Company has a line a few hundred yards away along the highway. He laughed scornfully at most of the houses around him. "That goes to show what happens when people who ain't carpenters try messing around."

Weldon is a carpenter, working "off and on" with the Cullman Construction Company. He is not a union carpenter, and there is none in town. "I wish we did have [a union]. They might pay us half what we're worth." He told of going to Birmingham and trying to get into the union there. They would not take him. He could not get work otherwise, so he came back to Cullman. He said he had written "a couple of times" to Birmingham, asking them to send up "papers" so they could start a union in Cullman. No answers came. "I believe in unions all right. You can put that down if you want to [referring to Stoney's notebook]. I don't care who knows it, either." He has five children, one by a former wife.

Weldon had registered at age twenty-one in Morgan County. He paid poll taxes and voted there for two years. He moved to Cullman and has not voted since. He is now thirty-four years old. His wife, twenty-four, does not vote either. She has never registered. "I was aimin' to get her registered and vote this last time. It'd be a hellova lot cheaper, wouldn't it? But she wouldn't do it. She said she wouldn't vote unless I went in there with her and I don't reckon they'd let me do that if I wasn't votin' myself, would they?" He thought "they ought to fix it so a feller could pay up." In fact, he thought "they ought to do away with that poll tax everywhere. I seen in the papers that they ain't but eight states that's got it. Hell, Alabama's got every tax they ever thought up. It's a wonder they don't charge you to piss. I bet they would, if they could tie a meter on you!" He laughed and began talking about schemes they might work out to put slot machines in privys and make you put in a token every time. Almost everyone in his construction company votes, or will vote this time. Like Hall, he said he had a chance to have his back taxes paid up this time, but "didn't take it up." Why? "I just didn't." He thinks he will if they offer it to him next time.

Down almost on the flood line of the bottoms sat the last two houses of the colony—two rooms each, with front porches, tin roofs, and pilings made of stacked pine logs. The steps and the porches look newer than the houses, whose white has faded considerably. They sit [on the same lot] within ten yards of each other, though there is ample room on the clearly marked-out lot (by drainage trenches) for more space between them. These houses had been moved "on a telephone pole truck" from half a mile down the road, Stoney was told. They used to be sawmill houses.

Stoney found a pleasant, stringy-haired wife cleaning up around the sheet-metal stove where the several children were making a big mess lighting matches and rolls of newspapers by putting them up against the stove's red-hot sides. "My husband and her's yonder [pointing to a slightly older woman lying across the bed reading a pulp magazine] are brothers. They moved these here houses down the road themselves." They bought the lot together, and the two families are practically one. Both men work as truckmen for the Carter Wholesale Supply Company.

> Naw sir, I never did vote [she is 27]. My husband [30], now, he and my brother-in-law went up to the courthouse last time and registered. They was aimin' to vote, and they went up to the courthouse to pay their poll tax, and it was too late.

She thought they would pay up and vote next time. "Some of them said if they would, they'd help them out some."

To Stoney's question about her interest in voting, this woman answered: "I got my three children to look after." The other woman rolled up from her reading with a good bit more interest: "*I* want to vote. Are you fixing up about it?" Stoney explained. She was too eager with her story to be disappointed. "My husband's talked about voting ever since I can remember. He was going to vote this time, but he couldn't get the money together in time. When he does, I'm going to make him save up for *me,* too." She laughed as the other woman "pshawed" and spanked her with the broom handle. She admitted that it would be expensive, for she is now thirty and her husband is thirty-six. "We're paying our half on this place, too. It makes it hard getting together that much money at once." But she thought her husband ought to vote, just the same. "If you don't vote, you ain't no citizen," she said several times, as though it was the single thing she had remembered from a school teacher's civic lesson many years before. "I've got a boy comin' on fifteen. I'm not going to have him raised up like we are. When he comes twenty-one, I'm gonna see he starts out right. When *he's* twenty-one, he's gonna *vote!*" When Stoney expressed surprise at her having a son that old, she answered: "Lord, boy, how old you think I am? I'm goin' on thirty-one years old, and I got four more young'uns besides him." When Stoney mentioned that only one person in this settlement voted, the older woman laughed: "We're new here. Maybe the politicians ain't found us yet."

Woodside, South Carolina, is a mill village outside of Greenville. It is the one box completely controlled by the local of the Textile Workers Union of America. In 1938 Woodside had an enrollment of 725. Of this number, 129 were recorded as being illiterates and having someone sign for them. The registration for general elections is 265. No Negroes are registered.

The president of the textile workers' local at Woodside stated that he was "all for" having the Negroes of Greenville register, and he admitted helping out "what little I could" in the efforts made by blacks in the city to register in the summer of 1939. "Nigras," he said, are taxpayers and citizens and are entitled to vote "by our American principles." He did not believe that Negroes would vote solidly with labor when they do get the ballot. It would, however, help them to get "their rights." And, since most Negroes are "the working class of people," labor would benefit. Those in the textile unions could not say anything about this. Practically no Negroes work in that field. If they started talking about this, it would "split our membership wide open," and they cannot take the chance.

The Ensley Italian Club in the suburbs of Birmingham, Alabama, has about four hundred members, all of whom must be qualified voters and registered Democrats. Members of the club who owe back poll taxes and lack the money to pay up are loaned funds from the club treasury. The Italian secretary of the club explained that it was run "under the rules of democracy." In his broken English the secretary explained his attitude toward the several Negroes in the beat who vote regularly.

> We don't mind about the nigra. They vote. All right; we no bother him. We like a nigra in his place. We are Southern, you understand. The Italians in the North, they may feel different. Down here we live Southern. We are Southern.

A textile union man in Lee County, Alabama, explained that:

> Over in Georgia, we even had the niggers in the union— them that worked around the plant. We had to do so's they wouldn't work no cheaper than the whites and beat us out of jobs. . . . That's the trouble with this town. People work niggers all the time. Every one of them new houses out yonder is being put up with nigger carpenters, and they've even got a nigger contractor. . . . That's the trouble with the whole damn South, is niggers.

One attitude encountered fairly frequently among poor whites in the South is that the Negro, especially the Negro farm owner, is being illegally treated when he is denied the right to vote, and there is a feeling that the big whites are letting some of the better-off Negroes vote even in primary elections in a state like Georgia. In contrast to this attitude is the feeling by a great many other poor whites that the black man is being unduly favored by the government benefit programs; that the Negro has no business even thinking about voting; and that in *this* region they would be scared to try. Their attitudes toward Negro voting, in contrast with their rather solemn attitudes toward the immorality of selling the vote, present an interesting moral pattern.

William Watts Ball of the Charleston, South Carolina, *News and Courier* thinks that:

> There is more likelihood (and there are some signs of it now) of the breakup of the Democratic party in the South. There is agitating in this state among labor people such things as Huey Long, share the wealth, the CIO, Labor's Non-Partisan League, and so on. When the question of racial prejudice as between white and Negro arises, however, the white textile workers in the state will be the last to combine politically with the Negro.

But Ball went on to admit, in the interview on 30 October 1939, that:

> If it ever comes to the point where, because of the radical political tendency of white textile workers who constitute about 22 percent of the white population, the Democratic primary is threatened in South Carolina, then it will be "pull Dick, pull devil" between the white conservative population and the white radicals for the Negro vote.

The chairman of the Jefferson County, Alabama, board of registrars puts it this way: "When the cotton mill people and the tenant farmers and the Negroes begin to take part part in the political life of Alabama, things are going to be radically different." The difference will "depend on whether it is the rabble who are voting or the sturdy working men."

The Hoover-Smith campaign of 1928 projected the Negro into unusual prominence in Southern politics. Both Hoover and Smith were charged with being Negro-lovers. For example, the Montezuma *Georgian,* in an editorial of 11 October 1928, declared:

> Certain supporters of Herbert Hoover have made complaints that Smith followers had brought up the Negro question in the presidential campaign. In retaliation, the Hoover followers charge Al Smith with appointing Ferdinand Morton, a Negro, as Civil Service Commissioner in the Harlem District in New York City, who they claim has a white stenogra-

pher. The good Atlanta Democrats have looked into the facts of the matter. The facts show that the Harlem District is composed largely of Negroes, about 200,000; the office held by the Negro is a Civil Service appointment. The appointment is made by the Mayor of New York City and one with which the Governor has nothing to do; the appointment of Morton was made by Mayor [John F.] Hylan, a political enemy of Al Smith. The white stenographer referred to is also a Civil Service officer. . . . A white woman can work for a Negro if she wants to. The question raised at first was as to whether white girls would be or had been compelled to work by the side of Negroes. That is far different from a white girl choosing to be a Negro's stenographer.

The Savannah *Morning News* of 11 September 1928 carried an election day advertisement addressed to the voters of Chatham County, which attempted to pillory E. D. Rivers, a candidate for governor, for an alleged statement that he made to the effect that he would "vote for the blackest Negro in Georgia before he would vote for Al Smith." This statement was allegedly made before meetings of the Ku Klux Klan at Waynesboro and Miller, Georgia. A four-column advertisement in the 5 November 1928 issue of the *Morning News* vigorously attacked the efforts of the Smith supporters to raise the race issue, stating in part:

> *This Negro question is very foolish. The people of Georgia are not* afraid of Negro domination. They do not need the politicians to keep down Negro domination for them. The people of Georgia can do this themselves. . . .
> *There is no Negro question in the South. The only Negro question* left in America is the mixed dance halls licensed by Tammany Democrats in New York; the mixed public schools with Negro teachers teaching white children in New York; the Negro policemen and other officeholders under Al Smith —TAMMANY DEMOCRACY in New York.

A paragraph from the 15 September 1928 issue of the *True Citizen,* the county newspaper at Waynesboro, Burke County, Georgia, which fought vigorously against Hoover in the 1928 campaign, reads:

> Where a man conscientiously has his scruples about an issue, there is excuse, but when a set of selfish individuals, guided solely by partisan acts to insult the South . . . by

spreading its "niggarized" Republican propaganda to a party that has always held a white man above a black man; a party whose nominee has never willed or ordered that white American ladies be forced to work alongside of inferior black Negroes, here we say it is time to call a halt.

The Negro was made a political issue in Madison County, Alabama, in the Hoover-Smith campaign. A great deal of feeling was stirred up against both candidates by local campaigners who accused Hoover of "dancing with a nigger" and Smith of passing laws insuring them race equality. J. Thomas Heflin did some campaigning in Madison County and, of course, employed the race issue, but since that time it is said that there has been very little such activity.

An editorial in the Charleston *News and Courier* of 5 November 1928, in the midst of the Smith-Hoover presidential campaign, declared:

In Illinois, Indiana, Ohio, Pennsylvania, New York, Missouri, Kentucky and a few other states, the Negro vote has great weight.

Republicans and Democrats do what they can to get the support of the Negro in the North. There is no doubt about that. The Republicans usually get the support of the Northern Negro. The Democrats would get it if they could.

The principal difference between the two parties in respect of the Negro vote, is that the Republicans insist upon the right of Negroes to vote in the South and the Northern Democrats—now, as always—are insistent that the Southern white people be left . . . in control of the affairs of their state.

Never with a Democrat in the White House does [sic] or will the dangers of the appointment of Negroes to office within the South arise.

If we should have two white parties in South Carolina and in other Southern states, both will try to get Negro support. Therefore, Negroes will be protected in voting. That is about as plain as it is that two and two make four.

But the Negro vote should be an important part of the vote of a successful party in South Carolina. Negroes will not be denied a share of the office. Mr. David Lawrence has brought to attention that once Negroes are voting in numbers in the South they, in combination with Northern Negroes, may hold the balance of power in American affairs. . . .

Those white people who withdraw from the national Democratic party will make the breach that will admit the Negroes to the polls. When they split the party, they and they alone will be responsible for the result. . . .

The results will not be pleasant. In this state, are nearly as many Negroes as white people. Twenty-five years ago, Negroes were still voting in South Carolina town elections. Liquor and beer flowed freely when even fifty Negroes voted in a town having 500 voters. So great was the corruption, the disorder, the shame, that all the towns were compelled to adopt a white primary plan and keep the Negroes out of politics altogether.

The dirt, the filth, the "wetness" of those elections would be repeated on a state-wide scale if 100,000 or 50,000 Negroes should vote in general elections.

When the Negroes were voting in South Carolina, the Negro women were not voting. The *Negro women* will have the ballot if the Negroes begin again to vote.

The Greenville, South Carolina, *News* of 3 September 1928 carried an editorial entitled, "A White Man in the Wood Pile." It devoted itself to an attempt to answer the question as to who was behind the organization of Georgia Negroes for Al Smith. It referred to a story appearing in the paper that reported a meeting in Georgia of a number of Negroes who formed an "Al Smith for President League," and suggested that the incident had the ring of political machination because Southern Negroes were not in the habit of holding voluntary political meetings. All political meetings of Negroes, it went on to say, had been called at the order of Republican leaders, but the Negroes of Georgia had decided that their salvation lay not in the Republican but in the Democratic party. The editorial went on to point out that this incident had to be considered in the light of two important developments: (1) the veritable flood of propaganda inundating the South to the effect that the Democratic party of New York was a Negro-loving party, receiving most Negro votes, and appointing an army of Negroes to office; and (2) the maneuver of the Republican party in appointing only white men as presidential electors—something that had not been done since the Civil War. The editorial suggested that the purpose of all this was to drive as many Southern Negroes into the Democratic party as possible, hoping thereby to persuade the Democrats that their party had become more friendly to Negroes than were the Republicans, and thus to make it appear that Negroes had jumped the party. The Republicans hoped in this way to induce as many white people as possible to become members of the GOP. The aim of the Republican party, concluded the article, was to cause unrest and to break Southern solidarity.

The Negro issue flared up in Jacksonville, Florida, in the 1928 campaign, stimulated by a charge made by the local Hoover club that Tammany Hall had appointed a Negro to an important office. A paid political advertisement appeared in the Jacksonville *Journal* of 2 November 1928, above the signature of the Democratic executive committee; it was entitled "Let's Do the Job Right." The following is quoted from this advertisement:

> If Negroes were appointed to office in Tammany Hall, where were they appointed? In the North. Where does the Republican Party perform its similar "noble experiments"? In the solid South. What party appointed [William D.] Crum, a Negro, as Collector of Customs in the Port of Charleston and waged a bitter fight to keep him in office by virtue of ad interim appointment over solid South objection? The Republican Party! What party appointed to office of Deputy Collector of the South's leading port, New Orleans, [Walter L.] Cohen, a Negro, and required the white people having business with that office to deal with him? The Republican Party! What party recognized as its National Committeeman from Atlanta in the Empire State, Ben Davis, a Negro? The Republican Party! What party recognized in Tennessee as one of its two Republican bosses, one Bob Church, a Negro? The Republican Party! What party recognized as its National Committee-woman from that same State a Negro woman, M. Williams? The Republican Party! Facts are facts and the fact is that ever since the Civil War, the Republican Party has tried to degrade the South while the Democratic Party has been the friend of the South, of white civilization, of white government in the South.

On 7 November 1928, following the election of Hoover, an editorial appeared in the Jacksonville *Journal* under the title, "To the President Elect." Among other things, this editorial stated:

If the Negro question could be eliminated, it is understood that the South, as now constituted, would divide almost as naturally and strongly on the question of Democracy and Republicanism as do other sections of the nation. In the opinion of many, such a division would be helpful to the South, stimulate its political and economic thinking and get for it a more important consideration in the national councils of both great parties.

Jacksonville Negroes relate that when the present governor, Fred P. Cone, was running for office and campaigning in Duval County, he observed in a radio talk: "When I'm elected, anyone can come to State House and my home, and I'll have two of the blackest niggers in the state ready to greet you." It is also said in Jacksonville that in the city election of 1939, following a heavy registration of Negroes upon the heels of the poll tax repeal, one candidate for city council campaigned on the issue that "I'll put niggers out. Their heavy registration evidences their ingratitude."[2] This candidate won.

There has been a concerted effort afoot in recent months in Miami, Florida, led by the magazine *Miami Life*, to raise again the race issue in the city's politics. Wesley E. Garrison, chairman of the Republican club of Dade County, is being vigorously attacked in the columns of *Miami Life* for his "Negro loving" tendencies. For example, the issue of 9 March 1940 states:

> The man who easily qualifies as Miami's No. 1 Villain, the tax shark who tricked thousands of Negroes as well as whites out of their property before the slow moving legislature could protect property owners from such vultures—Wesley E. Garrison—starts a new chapter in perfidy. "Gone With the Wind" must have given him the idea. His technic's [sic] the same as the carpet-baggers. "Mister" the Negroes to distraction! . . . Poses as their kind brother, . . . pretends to be showing them the light, the way not only to equality, but to dominance! . . . Work up a reputation as a big power in Darktown . . . so that if, and when, a Republican is elected president, Wesley E. Garrison may get somewhere!
>
> Note the circular we reproduce on this page. It's "Mister" Garrison along with the colored "Misters"—and the magnani-

2. Wilhelmina Jackson's interviews in Jacksonville, Florida, February 1940.

mous Garrison even allows one of his colored "brethren" to have top "Mister" billing!

Up north, even among Negroes, such things are recognized as cheap artifices of politicians who don't hesitate to sell the Negroes down the river once they're in. Up north Republican spell-binders no longer are able to enslave the colored race by "mistering" them, such servile hypocrisy immediately arousing suspicions. . . .

Maybe, over in Darktown, the people don't have illusions of black supremacy and maybe they appreciate the fact that they constitute less than one-fifth of Miami's or Dade County's population.

Those who read know that it was the carpet-baggers who caused their ancestors much misery in the reconstruction era over the South. They won't forgive this greedy schemer for putting Miami colored folk on the spot at this particular time when "Gone With the Wind" is stirring up many vivid memories among Southerners!

The *Miami Life* of 16 March 1940, asserts:

The equality campaign among Negroes of Tax Shark Wesley Garrison isn't doing Republicans of Dade County any good. The other night passengers on a 17th Avenue bus ordered the bus halted and got out. A young Negress had cursed the white passengers because another Negro had been told to take a seat in the rear of the bus.

Following the unprecedented voting of Negroes in the Miami municipal election of 1939, a drive was initiated to amend the city charter in an attempt to exclude Negro voters from participating in city elections. Sam B. Solomon, who was responsible for getting Negroes out in the 1939 election, wrote a letter of protest to Governor Cone, from which the following is quoted: "Attention called to . . . [the] bill to amend city charter which has now been passed by both Senate and House and awaits only your signature. We wish to protest passage . . . which would be an open and direct violation of Fourteenth Amendment of our National Constitution."[3] This bill, which provided for "a nonpartisan primary for white people in Miami city," was signed by the governor over the protest of both the Negro Citizens' Service League and the American League for Peace and Democracy. A columnist for the Miami *Herald*, in "Behind the

3. Solomon to Cone, 11 May 1939.

Front Page," wrote concerning this bill on 12 May 1939: "Passage by the House and Senate of Florida's Legislature of a local bill restricting voting in the Miami City primary to whites is a gesture of futility, even if the Governor signs it and the bill becomes a law."

The local politicians have attempted to discourage Negro registration and to use it as a means of stimulating the white population into more active participation. It is said that some eight years ago a candidate for mayor of Tampa attributed his victory to the fact that he ran on a platform which promised the Latin people in Ybor City that, if they put him in office, he would wipe "niggers" out of the sanitation and street cleaning departments and replace them with Latin workers. It is reported that the Latin section voted heavily for him.

The special election for president of the city commission of Birmingham in 1940 was fought out on the unpleasant issues of "political equality for Negroes" and "who was responsible for having the Southern Conference come here [to Birmingham]?" These questions were raised by an opponent of W. Cooper Greene, a former postmaster of Birmingham who had slightly assisted the organizers of the Southern Conference for Human Welfare in setting up their 1939 meeting. Greene's opponent, W. B. Houseal, distributed leaflets which carried the following message:

> To the white voters of Birmingham: I favor the strictest segregation of white people and Negroes. That means that I will use all my influence to stop the disgraceful condition on our one man street cars and buses which forces white people to use the same entrance as Negroes.
>
> This condition must be remedied and I pledge myself that it will be done.
>
> I ask your vote and influence if you agree with me.

Greene answered the Negro equality charge merely by stating, "I am a Southerner," and he ignored the second question. He won the election by an overwhelming majority.

Sam Houston Jones, recently successful as a candidate for governor of Louisiana over the Earl K. Long machine, was attacked during the campaign as a "nigger lover" because pictures and articles praising him appeared in two Negro weeklies—the *Louisiana Weekly* and the *Sepia Socialite*—both of which featured Jones as the "white hope of the race." Jones went on the air to "defend" himself by declaring that he was no "nigger lover" and boasting that he was mainly responsible for Negroes' not being able to vote in Louisiana now.

The reaction to the influence of the controlled Negro vote in Chattanooga politics is indicated in the following excerpts from the Chattanooga *News:*

> Boss Walter Robinson and his herded Negro voters, the City Hall's payroll army and the many agents, representatives and servants of special privilege achieved another victory at Tuesday's polls. Both by their own unparalleled efforts and by their success in raising false issues to delude the masses of voters as to the real issues of the campaign, they have succeeded in reelecting Mayor Bass. . . .

> Let us consider for a moment the machine's constant strength. To begin with, competent political observers placed the City Hall's payroll vote at some 3,500. Machine officials put people on the payroll not to serve the public, but to perpetuate their own grasp upon the public purse. Employees thus placed upon the taxpayers' backs, are expected to vote their relatives and friends for the master of the machine. Tuesday's election demonstrated that this payroll army did its duty to the boss.

> To this 3,500 city payroll vote one must add the purchasable Negro vote to insure the retention of which Bass' ward heeler, Walter Robinson, was put upon the city payroll. Four days before the election, Bass' Negro ally proudly and publicly boasted that he had 3,500 Negro votes in his pocket and that these votes would be safely voted for his boss. Robinson made good his boast.

> To the payroll army and the Negro mercenaries, with their 7,000 votes, must be added the important group of voters influenced by the public utilities, contractors, supply sellers and other special interests which have received and expect they will continue to receive favors from Mayor Bass and the other recipients of special favors too numerous to count.[4]

> . . . The complaints against Robinson appear to have risen by the fact that the fourth ward, dominated by the Negro boss, did not come up "right" for certain Democratic candidates in the recent election, although these candidates claimed to have provided Robinson with campaign funds. One reason advanced for failure of the colored ward to back the Democratic candidate was that Robinson, a Repub-

4. Chattanooga *News,* 18 March 1931.

lican, was a candidate for state committeeman and had to appear "regular."

Robinson has had a reputation among politicians who have used him as being loyal and has never been known to "doublecross" candidates from whom he had received money.[5]

. . . Robinson, for a number of years, has been a truant officer in the city's colored schools. The information that Robinson has the finger of the Democratic candidates of the last election pointed towards him, came from high official circles yesterday. This, perhaps, is the first time the Negro ward leader has been "put on the spot" by such a large group of influential politicians. . . . Every Democratic candidate lost heavily in Robinson's Fourth Ward as well as others in which the Negro leader had appointees who had influence with their race.

In all, the Democratic nominees are reported to have placed approximately $2,200 in the Negro precincts and some of them, after the votes were counted, suspected that some of the money they contributed for use in the colored precincts must have been used against them.[6]

The Negro is only rarely a direct issue in Durham, North Carolina, politics. A rather unusual twist occurred in 1938 in the case of Oscar Barker's candidacy for the state senate. Barker wrote to about a dozen Negro women, urging that they support his candidacy. He made the mistake, however, of addressing these women by their first names, the letters reading "Dear Ethel," and so forth. Some Negroes in Durham have photostatic copies of these letters. The Durham Committee on Negro Affairs became incensed over this "insult," contacted Barker, and obtained an apology from him. Barker's opponent, however, did not let the matter drop and used the story of Barker's apology to the Negroes as campaign material to win white votes.[7]

Ellison D. "Cotton Ed" Smith of South Carolina regularly employs the Negro issue in his campaigns for office. In his 1938 campaign for reelection to the Senate, he justified his conduct at the 1936 Democratic convention in Philadelphia—when he walked out on the convention while a Negro preacher led it in

5. Ibid., 25 August 1934.
6. Ibid., 27 August 1934.
7. Wilhelmina Jackson's interview with the treasurer of the North Carolina Mutual Insurance Company, Durham, North Carolina, 18 November 1939.

prayer—by saying: "I don't mind a nigger praying for me spiritually, but I object to his doing so politically." Paragraph six of Senator Smith's 1938 platform read: "Support Cotton Ed because he is opposed to Communistic influences which dominate C.I.O., an organization that lobbied for the anti-lynching bill and favored putting Negro workers side by side with white workers in factories."[8]

The following editorial in the Jackson, Mississippi, *Daily News* of 24 August 1938 presents a fine illustration of the use of the Negro issue as the basis for an appeal to the white population:

> Every Negro in Mississippi who has two or more gray hairs in his woolly head should be in favor of Paul Johnson's plan to pension all persons over the age of 65 at $30 per month.
>
> Golly, wouldn't that be water on the wheel for Sambo, and likewise Aunt Mandy!
>
> It would mean plenty o'possum, sweet potatoes, and watermelon throughout all the days of their lives.
>
> Every Negro in Mississippi over the age of 50, and likewise his wife, would immediately proclaim themselves 65 or over, and thus eligible for pension.
>
> You couldn't disprove it, either. Records of our Bureau of Vital Statistics do not go back far enough to do so.
>
> When considering a Negro's age, you must take his or her word for it, and they are all notorious for claiming to be older than they really are.
>
> At the very minimum of reckoning, Paul Johnson's old age pension program would cost $18,000,000 per year and Negroes would get fully half of it.
>
> Uncle Sam *would* insist on that.
>
> The Federal Government would not put up its pro rata unless Negroes were placed on equal footing with white people.
>
> You don't need a lively imagination to get a picture of the future.
>
> Indiscriminate old age pensions for whites and Negroes alike would paralyze labor conditions in this State.
>
> It would mean deserted farms, abandoned factories, homes without servants, suspension of practically every kind of outdoor work, and a reign of idleness that would make the depth of depression look like an era of boundless prosperity.

8. Quoted in the Columbia *State*, 22 August 1938.

Pleasant prospect, isn't it?

And all because a loose-tongued and irresponsible politician is running at large in Mississippi.

Move around the Negroes, Mr. John Voter, and listen in on what they are talking about. Here is a typical remark:

"Lawd, Gawd, I shore does hope dat man Johnson gits 'lected. I'll be rite down to de cote house de next morning to git de pension fo me and my ole 'oman."

"No more work in white folks' homes for Mandy!" shouted a fat and perspiring mammy who couldn't possibly be more than 55, yet she claims to be 70.

If Negroes had the voting privilege in Democratic primaries, they would go to the polls next Tuesday with the view of voting for Paul Johnson.

The Greenville, South Carolina, *News* of 7 July 1939, carried an article headed: "Ku Klux Declare Klan Will Act in Negro Registration Here." In the same issue of the *News*, the following notice appeared in the classified advertisement columns: "Fiery Summons—All Klansmen are called to action regarding white supremacy. Read the article in the Greenville *News* of July 6 regarding Negroes registering for city elections. Contact headquarters, P.O. Box 1511." And again: "White citizens: Are you interested in white supremacy? Read the article in the *News* regarding Negroes registering. Do you know the group backing this movement?" Fred D. Johnson, leader of the Ku Klux Klan, was quoted as saying:

There has been a growing interest in the Klan in recent months. Many white citizens who are not members of the Klan have asked me what the Klan will do about the Negroes registering and have pledged me their loyalty and support. The Klan maintains that the white race is and should remain what God created it—supreme—and that a complete segregation of the races is necessary, and that the white men advocating this move are more to blame than the ill-advised Negroes who have followed them. Those men who are advocating racial equality are no friends of the Negro. This movement is being sponsored by the NAACP which operates out of Phillis Wheatley Building—a project carried on under the Greenville County Council. The Workers' Alliance, a communistic group, are also behind the move.

The Klan investigation committee will make a thorough investigation of this movement and at the proper time, and in the proper way, will act.

A Richmond lawyer and former member of the Virginia legislature observes: "We have a tremendous submarginal white population, and we could not afford to allow radicalism to develop among Negroes—notwithstanding their ofttimes justifiable grievances—because of the possible effect it might have on the poor whites."[9] The congressional campaign of 1938 in Portsmouth is a fine example of how the race issue is sometimes used in Virginia politics—and also of the operation of the Byrd-Glass state machine. Colgate W. Darden, Jr., the voice of the machine in the second district, was running for Congress against Norman R. Hamilton, anti-New Dealer and editor of the Portsmouth *Star*, who had defeated Darden in 1936 and who was running for reelection. In gratitude to his Negro supporters in the election of 1936, Hamilton set up an imposing campaign headquarters for Negroes on Portsmouth's Effingham and High streets—the center of the city's Negro district. Negro girls received fairly lucrative secretarial positions, and Negro voters were much impressed. Darden and his managers pounced upon this Negro setup as excellent campaign material. Photographers were employed to take pictures of the Hamilton Negro headquarters, and a special circular was published, of which 10,000 copies were distributed in all of the poor white sections of Portsmouth, and in the outlying rural regions where the small white farmers lived. Captions such as these were used: "Look, Hamilton's a nigger lover!" "See, the niggers are set up better than your own people by him," and "If you vote for Hamilton, niggers will be teaching your children soon." Thus, despite Hamilton's congressional record of strong support for general social relief in his district, the Darden forces, by appealing to the racial prejudices of the poor white voters—many of whose poll taxes were paid by the machine—turned sufficient votes from Hamilton to win the election. Hamilton states that he knows that this was "one of the things that cost me the elecion."[10]

The secretary-treasurer of the Greene County, Georgia, Democratic committee repeats the tale his father told him of the days when the Negro was a bought vote in Greene County. Now there are about fifty Negro voters in the county. Formerly, these black

9. James Jackson's interview, Richmond, Virginia, October 1939.
10. Wilhelmina Jackson's interview with Hamilton in Portsmouth, Virginia, September 1939.

voters were under the leadership of a local Negro doctor. Until 1932, in order to get a postal appointment, it was necessary for one to pay this doctor in Greensboro, get his endorsement, pay a Negro in Athens who was a district leader in the Republican organization, get his endorsement, and then pay a Negro Republican in Atlanta and get his endorsement. This is proof, according to this man, that even the best-educated Negroes are for sale. Moreover, he considers it "mighty funny" that the Negro, who has by inclination always been a Republican, should be turning to the Democratic party that does not want him. He said to George Stoney, "You ask any nigger on the street who's the greatest man in the world. Nine out of ten will tell you Franklin D. Roosevelt. Roosevelt's greatest strength is with the lower element. That's why I think he is so dangerous."

The Negro question was a factor in the 1938 senatorial race in Georgia when President Roosevelt vainly attempted to purge Senator Walter F. George. Senator George went about speaking to the effect that the President had been "ill-advised" by such men as Thomas Corcoran, Benjamin Cohen, and the rest of the "left-wing brain-trusters," as well as by Clark Foreman, whom the Senator built up in his speeches as a sinister traitor to the Southern tradition. Foreman's connection with the Interracial Commission was whispered about in the crowds, and this "made one of the neatest niggah-baiting tricks you ever saw."

In discussing the present status of the Negro in the United States and the country's need for him, Senator Theodore G. Bilbo of Mississippi has said:

> You must understand that after the Civil War, the niggers were very low down. They just couldn't take care of themselves. They had no independence. They were just the cheapest laborers. The white laborers had to compete with them. Because of that, the South got to be a low wage region. Its industrial development was retarded. Because the white man was accustomed to think of the nigger as doing the labor, it became part of the Southern culture that labor was despised.
>
> What has happened since, however, is that the white people are multiplying themselves so much that they are forced to drive the niggers out of labor. This trend is now tremendously enhanced by the Wages and Hours Law. The real importance of this law is that it puts up the wages and by that makes it possible for the white man to grab the nigger's job. The niggers are just put out of business in the South.

In the Northern big cities and also in the big cities of the border-line, the niggers are segregated and there is nothing for them to do. The employers don't want to have them, and the unions want to keep them out. In the North, nobody does anything for the niggers because of idealism. If it was not for the vote, the nigger would be nothing in the North.[11]

Senator Pat Harrison of Mississippi, in discussing Senator Bilbo's proposal for the expatriation of American Negroes to Africa, stated emphatically to one of our interviewers on 16 February 1940:

The removal of the negra from the South would mean the economic collapse of the South. The negra is one of the largest and most important factors in our labor supply. By training and tradition, the negra is better adapted to the Southern type of agriculture. . . . With respect to his working ability, his goodness, and his trustworthiness, the negra can't be beat.

According to Harrison, white supremacy is no longer a practical issue in the South. He observes:

There is no longer any real fear of black domination in the South, though Southerners are always aware of the fact that they were once threatened by it. But, this is a hangover from the old days and it is only used now by some politicians in their campaigns. Right now, so far as the people of my state are concerned, if the status quo was maintained and agitators and reformers don't come in and try to cause trouble, there is mighty little fear of the negra. Of course, an ignorant or uneducated negra, like an uneducated white, is more readily inflamed than an educated person who thinks carefully through things before he acts. White supremacy is merely used as an appeal for votes, and I haven't heard it used that way there for a long time, because the whites down there are perfectly safe.

Senator Walter F. George told us on 9 February 1940:

In the Southeast, the negra is an indispensable part of our civilization. He is not only engaged in agriculture, but also in other lines. Those who have the best interest of the

11. Gunnar Myrdal's interview with Bilbo, Washington, D.C., 8 April 1940.

South at heart really regard the negra as an intensive part of our civilization and an important factor in the development of our section of the country. There is no real sympathy in Georgia for proposals such as Senator Bilbo's for the removal of negras from the country; that is, there is no sympathy for such proposals among thoughtful people and the better class of people. Only extremists would advocate this. Many who seem to advocate it, do not actually mean it.

Continuing, George declared:

There is no practical merit in any proposal to remove the negra population from the country. It would be a definite setback to the Southeast. We couldn't replace the negra in the South with citizens of like understanding of our culture and problems.

Senator George insists that white supremacy "is no longer an issue among the better elements in the South. There may be occasions in one locality or another, when friction and conflict develop and where the issue may be raised, but we know today that the negra is no longer a threat."

Liberal forces working for poll tax reform in Tennessee have tried to show the lack of substance in the contention that the Negro poses a threat in state politics. According to a statement prepared by the Tennessee League of Women Voters—"Democracy Versus the Poll Tax: How Will Tennessee Decide?"—there are no congressional districts with potential Negro political dominance. There is only one state senatorial district, the thirty-first, with potential Negro political dominance. There are only two counties, each of which has one representative in the legislature, with potential Negro political dominance. There are no incorporated towns or cities of 1,000 population or more with potential Negro political dominance. There are only three counties—Fayette, Haywood, and Shelby—with a majority of Negroes in the county districts.

In an interview on 13 February 1940, Justice Hugo Black expressed the opinion that white supremacy "is only a political issue in the South now." He feels that there is only scattered fear of Negro domination in the South—in places where the ratio of black to white in the population is high. It is in such sections that the greatest tension between the races is found, and that could be true if such a population ratio occurred in New England.

Some expressions of the viewpoints of a few well-known Southern liberals are herewith reproduced.

In the opinion of Maury Maverick of San Antonio, Texas, the diffusion of the Negro population throughout the country would have an important effect upon race relations. He thinks that race relations are better in San Antonio than elsewhere in Texas or the South because there are comparatively fewer Negroes there. He feels that a movement should be developed to break up the big Negro concentrations in the South and transplant them over the country, because the colored people "can't win anywhere when they are in a majority." The Negro, he thinks, has a better chance economically and in terms of his civil liberties when he is in a minority. He points to the black minority in San Antonio and contrasts it with the status of the Negro majority in Mississippi and the economic plight of Negroes in Harlem. Where there are a whole lot of Negroes, states Maverick, the whites consider it their business to supply the whites with jobs first. To quote him directly:

> There never has been a lot of Negroes here. When my grandfather came here, his father sent him ten slaves. My grandfather didn't want them, but there wasn't anything else for him to do but keep them—he couldn't fire them. Why, I got a cook here who gets nine dollars a week and her Thursdays off and she doesn't do a damn thing but cook. Economically, colored people are better-off here. Besides small Negro population, a factor in making for better race relations is that we have had some white men here who have been good to the Negro. For instance, banker Breckenbridge gave money to the St. Phillips Junior College.
>
> My folks were fairly liberal on the race question. In 1911, a colored boy [Lee Johnson] killed a cousin [Dr. Maverick] of mine. A mob formed at the jail to lynch the boy, but my dad and other men went before the mob and urged them to go away.
>
> The Mexicans have been and are more exploited than the Negroes here. This is due to the language variance plus the traditional "gringo" contempt for the Latin American. The main thing both Negro and whites have got to do is to cut out the lying to one another when they meet or make a speech, or ask for something. We got to cut out the "I love Marse Tom and all da white folks," "Old Black Joe is just like one of the family," "We love the darkies," and so on, and

when we meet, talk straight from the shoulder, plain facts. When I ran for Congress, Day [the opposition] said I was for social equality; that I was going to have Aunt Jemina and Ole Black Joe come in my parlor, turn over the furniture, and piss in the corner. I don't give a damn about the social equality of the Negroes having some economic equality. I don't care where they have to sit on a streetcar. What I am concerned with is their having a dime in their jeans to get on the streetcar with. The Mexicans have social equality, but what has it got them when they can't enjoy economic equality? The attack that the Negroes should make in the struggle for their rights should be from the standpoint of the self-preservation interest of the whites. That is, that they must have adequate health facilities and equal wages in order that the health and wages of the whites will not be lowered.[12]

In a speech delivered in Atlanta on 11 January 1940, before students of the Georgia Institute of Technology, Mayor Maverick pointed out that the greatest problem of the South is the Negro and that white Southerners should decide now to give the Negro "full economic justice." For, he asserted, "If the Negro has a low standard of living, a high prevalence of disease, it has a direct effect on white people. As for social equality, Negroes do not even talk about it. I know what they want is groceries; a chance to eat and live."

Barry Bingham, the liberal Louisville newspaper editor, declares:

I believe the future progress of the Negro in the South will go forward in just such proportion as he can achieve: (1) better educational opportunities; (2) trade union organization; (3) legislation designed to relieve the abuses of the farm tenancy system; and (4) common action with the masses of average southern whites. I think the poll tax issue constitutes the ideal meeting point for white and Negro Southerners at the present time.[13]

The attitude of Virginius Dabney, the liberal editor of the Richmond *Times-Dispatch*, is summed up in the following re-

12. James Jackson's interview with Maverick, San Antonio, Texas, February 1940.
13. James Jackson's interview with Bingham in Louisville, Kentucky, January 1940.

port of an interview with him.[14] Dabney sees a trend in the South toward increasing participation of the Negro in all forms of Southern life. There will be general improvement in education, participation in labor unions, and political involvement. There will also be setbacks. There will be ups and downs, but the long-run development will consistently be in the direction of progress. Within a century or so, Dabney feels, the Negro will be much more nearly equal in his political and social status than is the case now. As for the principal obstacles in the path of Negro progress, he cites economic competition, especially on the lower level, with the white society. The Southern liberal, he contends, will tend to rationalize Negro employment on the basis of broad social justice. That is, even though the skilled black worker might be depriving white workers of their jobs, the liberal would be compelled to take the position that society must be so ordered as to treat all people justly and to give all an opportunity to work. Dabney points out that the white liberals of Richmond have been consistent in urging the increasing employment of Negroes by the city. Another obstacle in the path of Negro progress is that of the doctrine of race superiority, which must always guarantee priority to whites.

Dabney also considers the frequent tactlessness of the Negro groups and organizations as an obstacle to the race's progress. He cites as an example the case of the Citizen's Defense Organization, which is led by Samuel Kelly, a Negro, and which, in 1939, appeared before the mayor's committee of Richmond and vigorously demanded that changes in policy be made. The demands related primarily to a more just treatment of Richmond's needy—Negro and white—by the Social Service Bureau. Dabney states that this demand was couched in terms which were designed to make certain that the organization would not get what it was demanding. It was a dictatorial, inflammatory approach. Dabney feels that the tactics of Negro organizations are apt to produce the best results in the long run only if they assume a firm, but noninflammatory attitude. They should be dignified and should present their cases without stirring up undue antagonism in the community. He feels that the interracial commissions follow an effective approach to the problem, since they decide their policy carefully and try to do things with

14. Dabney was interviewed in Richmond on 18 October 1939. The Bunche memorandum does not identify the interviewer. —ED.

the least friction. Editor Dabney is convinced that the NAACP was unwise in fighting against the intermarriage laws in several states. He thinks that this was an issue designed to stir up antagonism against the more important objectives of the NAACP, and that it neglects the fundamental issues for a matter of lesser importance. For even had the NAACP been successful in its attempt to get the anti-intermarriage laws abolished, nothing significant would have been gained.

The Richmond editor believes that a fight conducted by Negro organizations in the South on the political front will undoubtedly arouse a great deal of opposition from whites; nevertheless, this is a fight that ought to be made, because, he says, Negro citizens should try to enlarge their public participation in every sphere of activity. The enfranchisement of the Negro would tend, it is true, to give nourishment to the many corrupt political machines of the South, but this would be similarly true of the reenfranchisement of the poor whites in the region who are now unable to vote because of the poll tax and other requirements. Dabney believes that the answer to this objection is that there should be more strict requirements with regard to literacy and other qualifications for voting, but that no man should ever be required to pay any fee for the privilege of voting. Dabney believes that most can be hoped for from the upper classes of both races in the attempt to solve the race question. He thinks that the lawyers, doctors, teachers, and businessmen are the most liberal elements in both groups. As he sees it, there is not very much progressive thinking among the masses of people—either black or white. He does not think it possible that the poor whites can be led soon to identify their interests with the interests of the Negro. He says that those who believe this is possible are guilty of wishful thinking.

With regard to the significance of organized labor to the Negro, Dabney holds that ultimately this will be a great boon for Negroes—that is, the Negro's participation in the processes of organized labor, assuming that it will be possible for blacks to overcome the present widespread resistance to their membership in unions. He feels that the participation of Negroes in the processes of collective bargaining will be of utmost significance to Negro progress. He also feels, however, that the immediate reaction to the increasing efforts of Negroes to participate in the union movement will result in unfavorable conditions for the Negro race. Dabney holds quite strongly that the efforts of radical organizations in behalf of the Negro have been very harmful to his interests. He alleges that Southern whites have no fear of what might happen should the Negro, in large numbers, be brought into the radical ranks. However, he does feel that the resentment of whites against Negro involvement in the radical groups is due to the arrogance and the extreme demands made by such organizations on behalf of blacks. The typical reaction of whites to such demands is: "Well, if this is the way they're going to act, we just won't give them anything." He feels certain that such tactics have alienated from the Negro some very good white friends.

Richmond Negroes point out that, though Dabney has always taken a very favorable attitude toward the NAACP, after the 1939 NAACP convention in Richmond he wrote an editorial in his paper in which he took exception to a speech by Charles Houston at the convention and indicated that the speech was "to much for me" in that it suggested social equality.

Julian L. Harris is the son of Joel Chandler Harris, the author of *Uncle Remus*. His wife, Julia Collier Harris, is a well-known literary critic and biographer of her father-in-law, and she comes from an aristocratic Southern background. She and her husband have spent much of their lives in New York and in France, and are both well known in literary circles. They consider themselves modern and subscribe to the preachments of Sherwood Anderson. While editor of the Columbus, Georgia, *Enquirer-Sun*, Harris was awarded the Pulitzer Prize for his outstanding work against lynching—his newspaper was eventually bankrupted because of this effort. The following excerpts from Stoney's casual conversation with the Harrises during the evening of 30 January 1940 in Chattanooga will give some idea of the confusion and contradiction in even their thinking.

Julian Harris fought vigorously to get the Southern Conference for Human Welfare to hold its 1940 meeting in Chattanooga. He does not agree, however, that Negroes and whites should sit together at the meetings of the conference, nor does he see why they would want to. He does say, however, that they should be allowed to if they so desire, but basically he thinks that all of this is rather artificial in the same way that he believes the interracial commissions are artificial. He declares:

> Negroes and whites will get together when they have the same economic and intellectual interests, and when they get together on any other basis than that, it is artificial. . . . The unions have been meeting black and white for years—

the miners have. They didn't say much about it, but they did, and that is the secret of a lot of the good relations Negroes and whites are having. . . . They just don't talk about it. I have a Negro writing for us on this paper.[15]

Harris went on to explain that this Negro reporter is a good newspaperman whom he hoped to put on the regular staff soon. When the Negro reporter was first hired, the city editor raised the question as to where he would work. Harris told him that the man would be placed in the office with the other men and nothing was to be said about it. He has gotten along well and the issue concerning him has never been raised.

The problem of "race equality" troubles the Harrises. Harris thinks that young liberal Southerners might well associate with Negroes "on an intellectual basis," though Mrs. Harris was dubious, inquiring: "What if you brought some of these young men [Negroes] into your home? Would you want them to meet your sisters? If they are so attractive as you say, that kind of thing inevitably leads to intermarriage, and you wouldn't want that, would you?" Both of the Harrises were quite convinced that very little "cross-breeding" now goes on in the South. They had the queer impression that most of the present crop of mulattoes are produced in Boston. Yet they admired greatly such men as Clark Howell Foreman and Arthur F. Raper, whom they described as "evangelists of the gospel of race equality." Their admiration would seem to be based primarily, however, on the heroism of the fight of these men rather than on the principles for which they are fighting. Harris was severely critical of the Northern intellectual Negro. He thinks that Walter White and the NAACP representatives generally are "exhibitionists" and that White is no Negro anyway; or, at any rate, he would be white if he did not get more satisfaction out of being a Negro leader.

Mrs. Harris is one of the leaders of the Southern Women's Committee for the Prevention of Lynching, and her husband has a record extending back thirty years for vigorous fighting for improved conditions for Negroes. Yet both of them are thoroughly convinced that the Negro is a separate creature and must be kept "in his place." Harris expressed great admiration for Booker T. Washington (whom his father first introduced to the public at the Cotton Exposition in Atlanta—this was Washington's first public appearance before a white audience

15. The paper referred to is the Chattanooga *Times*. —ED.

and Harris's father was severely criticized for it) and his ideals. He also had praise for Dr. Rufus E. Clement of Atlanta University, for his independence and for not being a "white man's Negro." But Harris condemns all Negro leaders who claim that their race expects them to fight against segregation, because as a whole, "every intelligent Negro in the South understands the situation and is proud to keep himself separate with his race." On the other hand, he contended that "down deep inside, the Negro wants a little social equality. I know them. I was raised with them. They're sly—br'er rabbit was the Negro, you know." To which Mrs. Harris added, "Of course they's sly and clever. Every slave race is. They have to be."

It is usually accepted that there is more liberalism on the Negro question in North Carolina than elsewhere in the South, and it is explained that this is due to the fact that there have been a number of white people in the state who are interested in Negroes as people—such personages as President Frank P. Graham of the University of North Carolina, for instance.

NINE

Voter Registration
in the South

LAX administration by the local officials, especially with regard to absentee ballots, primary registration, and presentation of registration receipts, is quite general in the South. Sometimes this results from the indifference of registration officials, sometimes from outright connivance in corruption, and sometimes from both. The names of dead people are frequently voted. There are complications in connection with registration procedure, which is often extremely informal, except where Negroes are involved. Registration lists are inaccurate, poorly kept, and frequently padded. Purging of the lists is a hit-or-miss process. Election officers are of a low intellectual—and, often, moral—caliber. In the following pages some aspects of registration procedure as it affects white registrants in the Southern states are considered.

In Madison County, Alabama, registration periods are as follows: in odd years, thirty days between October 30 and December 31, the exact days to be determined by the members of the county board. This is the period in which the registrars go over the county and spend a day at each precinct. This period is advertised by three insertions in the newspaper, plus at least two posted notices at each precinct voting place. The registrars usually spend eight hours at each precinct, though there is no rule about the amount of time they must spend or the hours they must keep. In even years, there is a regular registration period of ten days, beginning the fourth Monday of January. This is held at the courthouse and is the time of the heaviest registration. For six days, beginning on the first Monday in January,

the registrars sit to purge the list, and then, on the second Monday in February, they sit to hear complaints from those who are served notice that they have been stricken. Actually, in Madison County the purging takes much longer, for, according to the chairman of the board of registrars, "I guess if you had three men who knew what they were doing on the board, it would be all right, but one of these men on with me can't read worth anything and the other one can't write so you can read it."[1] Finally, every year there are five days of registration (at the courthouse) beginning the first Monday in July. These latter registration periods are not advertised because they come at regular times. The newspapers generally carry news stories about them, however.

All of the members of the county board are Democrats. No effort is made to have bipartisan county boards in Alabama. The members of the board receive a stipend of five dollars a day but no reimbursement for mileage driven on the days regularly authorized. The chairman receives the same amount as the other members. The committee also has the responsibility for putting up the notices at the precincts, and for this the members receive five cents a mile, but no daily allowance. This procedure in Madison County is the general procedure for most counties in the state, though in the urban counties there are some variations. Jefferson County, for example, has a full-time registrar with an office and a secretary. In Alabama, registrars can be removed from office at any time and at the pleasure of the appointing board (the governor, state auditor, and commissioner of agriculture and industries), and without cause.

The purging of the election list in Madison County is described as an exceedingly difficult task. First, the registrars get the list of all death certificates given out by the board of health. These certificates provide only the name and the place where the person died. He may not be a resident of the county or, as in most cases, he may not be a voter. Thus all the registrars have is a name, which may not be correctly given; so they must check through the whole poll list. They have no record of voters who die outside the county, so they must rely on their personal knowledge. Then, they get a list from the probate judge of those people who have been committed to the insane hospital, and these are checked off. From the circuit clerk they get a list of

1. George Stoney's interview in Huntsville, Alabama, February 1940. Unless otherwise indicated, all quoted passages in this chapter are taken from Stoney's notes of field interviews conducted in 1940. —ED.

those convicted of crimes listed in section 182 of the code. The chairman of the board states that at the last purging "there were only four, and two of them were murderers. You seldom find a person who is convicted of crime to be a qualified voter. I think that's the best proof of the quality of voters in Madison County." The chairman does not recall anyone's ever having been disfranchised in the county because he was convicted of wife-beating or petty larceny or vagrancy.

The biggest problem of the registrars is that of checking off those people who have moved permanently from the community. Alabama's law gives a person the right to an absentee ballot so long as he does not establish a residence in another state. There is no means to determine when a person plans to vote absentee. It is admitted that there are a great many names of people on the list who are dead or who have moved out of the county and do not vote absentee.

According to the state law, those stricken from the list are to be given notice by the sheriff in time to appear before the county board at its regular session in February, to show cause why they should not be striken. Also, the names of those removed should be published in a paper of general circulation in time for the people affected to appear and defend themselves. Excepted from both of these provisions are those people who are dead, those convicted of crime, those who have moved permanently from the county, and those committed to an institution for the insane. "Hell!" said the chairman of the Madison County board, "that's all there are." So, he publishes no names; the sheriff serves no notices; and the board merely sits all day catching up on its back work. In January 1940, 450 people were purged from the list in Madison County, of whom 338 were dead, 108 had moved out of the county, and 4 were convicted. All of those convicted were white men.

Practically all of the registration in the county is done at the courthouse. The chairman of the county board told George Stoney: "We'll go out to one of these county precincts and sit around all day and not register a man, and then when we come up to the courthouse, fellows from that very spot will come in a-flockin'. We're another excuse to come to town." The hours at the courthouse are usually from 9:00 A.M. to 4:00 P.M., though it is claimed that sometimes it is 6:00 or 7:00 P.M. before the registrars are able to get away. It should be noted, however, that the "too late" or "office closed" excuse is readily given when Negro applicants appear.

In Huntsville, the county seat, the registration is done at the courthouse. In other places the registration generally occurs at the polling places, including drug stores, country stores, barber shops, and schools. In one place the registrars "sit out in the middle of the road and take them as they come. I take a card table along and spread out. Last time we sat out on the edge of a bridge all day and not a soul came. Good thing it happened to be a pretty day." The storekeepers receive no compensation for allowing the board to meet in their places. Most of the store-keepers are glad to have the board, both for the company it gives them and the trade it attracts. There is a reluctance to use schools for registration, both because of lack of room and because parents have said that they do not like "having such things around their little children."

The chairman of the Madison County board states that a few people are turned down every period mainly because they are illiterate or not mentally competent. He says that a vast number of people come in to register who can scarcely write their names. To speed up the work and to make possible the legibility of applications, he and one other member of the board fill out the applications for the people, asking them the questions orally. They do have to sign their names, however. If a man cannot do that, he is given the constitutional test. The chairman cannot recall anyone passing this test who could not write his name. Several attempts to register mentally incapable people come up each registration period. Some candidate or cam-paigner will bring such persons in. If the applicant cannot answer the questions orally, the registrars refuse to register him. It takes about fifteen minutes to register each person. Age is taken on affidavit only. But if a false statement is made on this and it is discovered, the person's name is simply left off the list of qualified electors. He can then come in and protest to the probate judge in an attempt to get it straightened out. Yet, apparently, no one has ever been prosecuted for such perjury. This misrepresentation of age is quite common, because the word has circulated that people who become twenty-one be-tween October 1 and February 1 can vote one time without pay-ing a poll tax. Many applicants come in and give their birth dates to fit in with this position. The mistake, if found at all, is usually discovered when applications are transferred to the registration books and it is found that the applicants were mixed up in their arithmetic. It is said that about a dozen such cases came up at the last registration period in Madison County. The chairman of the county board insists that at least one witness who has known the applicant for a minimum of twelve months must accompany him. "I don't care if I've known him all my life."

The law requiring a person to have had employment for most of the year preceding registration is, according to the chairman of the board,

> out of date since woman suffrage. You couldn't deny a woman the right to vote because she didn't have a job, so you can't deny a man the vote for that reason. I never refuse to register a man on account of that, but I stress it and stress it hard when I go over their applications. Sometimes I make a man think I'm not going to register him for that reason. You see, I like to think of registration as a kind of quality test. People ought to have certain responsibilities.

According to state law, there is to be no registration except on the appointed days and in the appointed places. It is illegal to register a man in any other place except in his home precinct or at the courthouse. The registrars, however, receive calls from many people who wish to be registered out of season, especially those who apply for state jobs under Alabama's new civil service law, which requires all applicants to be qualified voters.

There is no state supervision of registration or of the work of registration board. The board sanctions are judicial and final. They are an examining board, and if two of the three members agree that a man is either fit or unfit, then their decision stands. If they turn a man down, he can appeal to the circuit court and get a writ of mandamus. Then the solicitor of the state would be required to defend the actions of the board without cost to itself or the county. The chairman cannot recall that any such action was ever taken in the county. No manuals or instructions are issued from the statehouse. Members of the board are "assumed" to know what their duties are, yet most of them do not know, including two of the members of the Madison County board.

The Bibb County registration periods are quite typical in Alabama: ten days in January, five days in July in even years, and five days in July and thirty days between October 1 and December 31 in odd years. Polling hours are from 8:00 A.M. to 3:00 P.M., and the three registrars sit the full time. When they travel around to the mining camps, they often start at ten o'clock in the morning and work until 4:30 or 5:00 in the afternoon, in order that the men can register after they come off work at four o'clock. They sit for six days in January in even years to purge the voting list. The registrars are paid five dollars per day, and one of them receives five cents per mile for tacking up notices of registration at the polling places.

The polling places are varied. Three of them are located at company commissaries in the mining camps. The registrar explains that "these are the only public buildings. That is where the men hang out and the most natural place for them to come." Two of the registration and voting places are small-town city halls. One is a school. Three are on church grounds. The registrars never go into the church. "When it's cold, we have to stay in the car," one of them said to Stoney. One polling place is in the courthouse, three are in country stores, and one is "on the side of the road." Registration is often done from the car. The registrars receive no state supervision, nor do they get any instruction from the state. As one registrar puts it: "We are supposed to read the law and figure it out for ourselves."

The registrars in Bibb County generally fill out the application blanks themselves, asking the people the questions. It is explained that this is "so much faster." The registrars fill out the whole blank, including the questions about the witness. The witness is usually the storekeeper or, perhaps, one of the registrars themselves. Very rarely do the applicants for registration bring a witness with them, and the registrars have required this only in a very few cases when people hesitated so long over the question that the board suspected their statements concerning length of residence. The registrars do not test a person's ability to read and write, providing he can sign his name and answer the questions "intelligently." During the past two years, only two white people have been denied registration. One of these did not have the proper residence requirements, and the other was so obviously mentally unbalanced that the registrars voted unanimously to refuse him. The question about "occupation" is filled out very loosely. If an applicant is unemployed, the registrars put down the work he does most often or has done last. The board members never employ the property qualification.

The office of probate judge of Bibb County takes no initiative in purging the voting list. As the probate judge himself puts it, "If we see somebody on there and we know he's dead, naturally we mark him off." The judge admitted that the voting list is cluttered with many people who have permanently moved from the county. These people could not be removed because they "might take a notion" to vote absentee, which they have a right to do so long as they do not establish a residence elsewhere.

In Coffee County, as in most Alabama counties, few people are registered when the registrars travel around to the beats. The polling places are schoolhouses or country stores. The only apparent qualification for registrar is that a man must be "a Democratic elector." In Coffee County the board of registrars sits the regular periods and one extra period—a ten-day period every January (instead of every other January) which is called for by the county commissioners. The registrars usually write out the applications. For people known to the registrars, many questions are left blank. At a recent registration period in Coffee County, the chairman of the board told us, eight applicants (white) were turned down because they were illiterate "and worse," despite the fact that "the sentiment's against refusing to register a man unless he's plumb out crazy." Also at a recent registration, one candidate for office brought in a woman of ninety-five to register for the first time and with her was her daughter of seventy-two, who had never cast a vote. Both of these applicants were allowed to register, although neither could write her signature legibly. The registrars never employ the constitutional test or the property test for white registrants, and the question concerning employment is ignored, unless for special reasons the registrars are not sure about the applicant.

The voting lists are not purged very thoroughly. The registrars get the names of the dead and the insane from the probate judge. They check with people at the beats as they travel around, and when people are reported to have moved permanently from the county, the registrars have the sheriff notify them that they are being purged. No one ever appears to protest a purge. It is admitted, however, that the absentee ballot law makes it almost impossible to purge the list accurately.

The registrar at Tuscaloosa, Alabama, states that often when people come in to register and find out that they must pay up a good deal of back poll taxes, they say they do not wish to do this. In such cases, they are asked not to register, so that their names will not "clutter up" the record. Some known illiterates are registered when they have property, and the only evidence that others are illiterate is that they cannot sign their names. Formal constitutional tests are not given, although, as one registrar remarked, sometimes members of the board try to "question a few niggers when they come in."

A member of the board of registrars of Etowah County, a

woman and grocery store owner, comments on registration qualifications as follows: "I don't register them that can't hardly
read and write at all. Some of the others have, and I don't kick.
Most of the time, they's feeble-minded when they're that-a-way
anyway." This registrar refused two or three applicants at the
last registration period who were trying to register as having
spent some years out of the state. They were refused because
they could not give either street or town addresses for the years
they had been away. She commented: "They's lyin' an' they
know'd it. They's lyin' to get out of paying poll tax. You know
goddam well if a man lives in a place five years like he says he
does, he ought to know the name of the town, at least." It is
admitted that the state provision that the applicant should have
had employment is not enforced. She confessed: "I didn't know
nothin' about that. I registers WPAs and unemployeds and
loafers and everybody else that comes in and's got the other
qualifications." As to witnesses to the applicant's identity and
the fact that he has been in the county for the last twelve
months, officials in the courthouse are usually employed. "The
probate judge or the tax assessor signs a lot of them. I sign a lot
of them, myself, especially boys and girls who live around here
that I've watched grow up. . . . If folks didn't bring nobody into
town with them, they go out on the street and grab the first one
that comes along. They don't have no trouble about *that*."

According to the law of the state of Alabama, all three registrars have to be present in order to make the registration legal,
and two of the three must agree that a candidate is eligible. One
of the registrars of Etowah County, in commenting upon this
provision, explained: "If we lived up to that law, we'd have to
call time-out every time a body had to go to the bathroom. Hee,
hee, hee. . . . Lord, ain't it crazy?" Generally, two of the three
registrars are present, and two always sign the application. They
do not require the applicants to write out their own applications,
however, because "Lord, if we did, we'd never get through. We
got to be able to *read* all that mess." All the applicant is required
to do is to answer the questions and sign his name. Another
board member says, "We register almost anybody. And . . .
people in this county are so ignorant. So many of them can
hardly write their names." This registrar recalled four people
for whom she had to "hold their hand while they made the
cross." All of these were white property owners. Since the registrars will fill out all of the blanks for the people, she does not
know exactly how many others are only able to sign their names.

The number of women registering recently in Etowah County has increased, according to one of the registrars; not primarily because women are becoming more interested in politics, but because employers are insisting upon it. States the registrar: "You can't hardly get a job in none of these big places but what they ask if you're a legal voter. The telephone company, Sears and Roebuck, Kresge's . . . all of them." The reason is said to be "labor trouble. These agitators come here and get the people all stirred up. They know if something ain't done to stop it soon, we're going into communism sure as the Lord."

An inspection of the registration blanks in the office of the probate judge in Gadsden indicates that most of the blanks are made out in two handwritings, which seems to establish the fact that the registrars do make out the applications for the registrants. It is also noted that the person who "vouches" for the white applicant is usually either a member of the registration board, the probate judge, or someone else in the courthouse.

In Cullman County the registrars do not bother with filling out the second sheet of the application for registration. This second sheet is the one on which information about the witness is to be given. The registrar in Cullman County states: "We just tear that off and fill out the front and back of the other sheet." "Ordinarily" the registrars fill out the applications themselves, asking the applicants the questions and having them sign the form. During the last registration period, however, the registrars let the applicants take the blanks home and fill them out themselves, because of the overwhelming number of applicants. The registrars even arranged for two WPA workers to help those who could not complete the blanks themselves. No witnesses are generally required when a person appears personally before the board, nor is there any test made of a person's ability to read and write. If the applicant can sign his application, that is enough. If he cannot, then "we take his word" about the amount of property owned and the fact that he pays taxes on it. During the recent registration period, says the registrar, "we was in such a hurry, then, we would sign it ourselves if they couldn't."

Purging the voting list is considered quite a problem by the registrar in Cullman County. Back in the 1920s, the board decided to clear the list and to notify everybody on it whose name was in doubt. The criminal list was checked carefully and people were called in from the beats to give advice about those who had moved or died, and postcard notices were sent to every person whom they had considered striking from the list. One of the present registrars explains what happened:

I made more enemies in that one week than in all the rest of my life. Some of the people had moved to somewheres else in the county. We had not aimed to purge them 'til we knowed they was gone, and we said so on the card, but they came in just a-cussin'. That purging law's all right for a city like Mobile or Birmingham where you don't know everybody, but here the least little thing you do, folks get mad.

In Cullman County they purge for crime very seldom—only for murder or other serious crimes. If a man is sent up for a year or two, they are afraid to purge him for fear he will be out and have his citizenship restored before election time, "and come up to my place raising hell." Since 1926, the registrars here have sent out no notices about people being purged, and they do not sit to hear complaints.

In Hale County little attention is paid to the matter of getting people to register and pay poll taxes except by the candidates for office. Registration occurs in the city hall, the courthouse, country stores, and in "precinct houses"—small wooden huts resembling tourist cabins. There is no state supervision of the work of the registrars. The chairman of the board says no one is registered unless the registrars think that he can fill out his own application. Two applicants were refused on this ground at the last registration period. They were discovered when they could not sign their names. Ordinarily, however, the registrars fill out the blanks for the people and have them sign. It is only when an applicant is not known that a witness is required, and this happens very infrequently, for if the board members do not know the applicant, then the people around the precinct do. Unemployed persons are registered. If the applicant has no job at the time of registration, his latest employment is put down on the application blank. Purging of the lists in Hale County follows the procedure in other Alabama counties.

In Dallas County, Alabama, the usual procedure is followed with regard to registration. The registrars do not require that the whole application be filled out. No witnesses are required unless there is some doubt about the person's identity. The registrars fill out the blanks for their applicants, and signing their names is the only proof of the applicant's ability to read and write. There is no supervision by the state, and the registrars are guided by the rulings of the attorney general.

In Lee County during the rush period the office frequently stays open until seven or eight o'clock, taking as many people as come. Country stores and schools serve as registration places for the rural beats. In Auburn registration is at the courthouse. Because so many workers at the cotton mills desire to register, the registrars take a certain number of days off each registration period to sit in the offices of the two textile mills and accept registrations. Word is left at the courthouse that if anyone comes in to register during this time, he should be sent out to the mills.

About half of the people registered in Opelika are mill workers. They move in and out so much that the registrars have a hard time keeping up with them. The bosses at the mill work vigorously to get the men to register, pay their poll tax, and vote. It is customary for the foremen at the mill to act as witnesses for most of the workers. As one of the local registrars says, "I know a world of them lie to us [about the length of time they have been in the state] but you can't argue with them when the bookkeeper swears they have." As each man registers, the bookkeeper of the company asks him, "Do you want to pay this yourself or do you want to have the mill take it out?" Practically all of the men have said that they desire the mill to take out the poll tax payment. The registrant then signs a paper handed to him by the bookkeeper. Moreover, the foremen "answer half of the questions" the mill workmen are asked when registering.

In Lee County the registrars write out the blanks for almost everyone, though occasionally "someone who's real good with a pen" fills out his own. All of the registrants are required to sign for themselves, however. The witnesses must be people the registrars know personally or the witnesses must appear in person. Except for the mill people, this almost never happens, since the registrants ordinarily name someone in the courthouse.

The only educational test given to white registrants is the ability to sign one's name. One of the registrars can recall having turned down only one man solely for reasons of illiteracy. This was a mill worker who was brought in at the last registration period. When the man was asked to sign his name, he answered that he did not know how. The fellow worker who had brought him in tried to protect him by stating: "There's something the matter with your hand, ain't there?" But the honest registrant denied that anything was wrong with his hand.

The aspiring Negro voter is often a source of embarrassment to the Southern registrar. The registrar, however, has it within his power—by subterfuge and device—to protect himself and his fellow whites against this menace. One of the registrars of Lee County speaks very frankly:

> We never used any of those things [referring to the constitutional and other tests] against a white man. I'll just be honest with you. We have had a good little bit of trouble with niggers. . . . Way back in 1920, when I was on the board before, we had a world of nigger women coming in to register. There was a dozen of them, I reckon, come in one registration period. We registered a few and then we stopped. . . . Oh! We put them off. . . . Tell them they had to bring in white witnesses. . . . Tell them how much poll tax it was going to cost them. . . . We got that pretty well weeded out now. Not many come around. I don't think more than one come in the last two years.

In Lee County the probate office claims to do its best to keep a record of all deaths, removals, transfers, insanity commitments, and so on, to furnish the registrars when they purge the voting list. Yet the probate office does not strike people from the roll without the consent of the registrar. The probate judge for the county declares: "I know a dozen people on that list right now who are dead, but it's against the law for us to remove them without the board's permission."

In Macon County, Alabama, the registrars fill out the applications themselves on the excuse that "it saves time." The whole blank is filled out and the people are required to produce one witness in person. Only infrequently, however, does any applicant bring in his own witness. No one is denied registration because of unemployment. If the applicant is unemployed, this is merely noted on the blank.

In Jefferson County the chairman of the board of registrars is a full-time county employee and holds a position of some importance, for he has the power of appointment over a staff of from eight to ten clerks. Although appointed by the governor, his salary and the expenses of his office are met by the county. The office of the board of registrars handles all of the details of registration, makes up the poll tax list, records the poll tax payments, fixes the beat line, and decides all questions concerning the voting eligibility of citizens of the county. In most Alabama counties, this last function is performed by the probate judge. The salary of the chairman in Jefferson County is five thousand dollars a year, and the office is regarded as an important political plum. The incumbent in the office was the campaign manager for Governor Frank Dixon in his first election contest and was his manager for Jefferson County in the last election. He is a professional politician and spends much of his time in directing campaigns of candidates in the county races.

The chairman of the board estimates that there are from twenty to twenty-five thousand poll tax payers in Jefferson County, but neither he nor the tax collector keeps a tabulation, since both of these officials work on a salary rather than a fee basis. The number of those paying or of those on the qualified list is not kept. It is estimated that there are from sixty to sixty-five thousand certified voters. The registrar is supreme. He makes no reports to the probate judge and his work is not checked.

The board of registrars sits for registration during all of the periods required by law and for certain special periods; every "off" year between October 1 and January 1 it spends seventy-five days (instead of the usual thirty days) in traveling about the beats and registering people. A full day is usually spent at each precinct. A relatively small group of people is registered on these rounds, but those who are registered in this way would find it difficult to come to the courthouse for registration, because some of the beats are as far as thirty-five miles away. The board chairman points out that "it is a service to a small group of people." In every even year beginning on the fourth Monday in January, the board devotes ten days to purging the voter list. In even years, also, there are six ten-day periods of registration beginning the second Monday in April, the fourth Monday in June, the fourth Monday in July, and the first Monday in August, October, and December. In odd years, in addition to the seventy-five day registration period, there are forty extra days—falling in ten-day periods beginning the first Monday in February, April, June, and August.

During the country round, or when there is no special registration rush, the registrars generally fill out blanks for people as the applicants answer the questions. On those days when there is a large number of applicants, the people fill out their own blanks and the board checks on them later. An effort is made to examine every new voter personally, though on rush days this is impossible. The test of the applicant's ability to read and write is seldom administered as such. If a person does not show sufficient intelligence in answering questions, or if he cannot sign his name, then the board investigates him further. The chairman explained to Stoney: "We turn down people we think can't mark their own ballot." Between 1 October 1939 and March 1940, the chairman estimates, half a dozen illiterates were registered, all of whom had property qualifications. There were undoubtedly a great many more registered who would find it impossible to write anything but their name.

Purging the voting list in a city the size of Birmingham is a huge task. For the most part, the board members rely upon the health department death records and the insane. As they travel about, they go over the voting list with old residents. In the words of the chairman of the board: "We purge people here in the office every day. We get letters asking that their registration be changed to another county or state. . . . Thousands of voters are on the list who no longer live in Jefferson County or who are dead, but we can't strike their names off unless we have some kind of proof." The registrar admitted personal knowledge of well over one hundred names that should come off the list and admitted that only a new registration could clean up this situation. But this new registration cannot be arranged, because the people who reregistered in 1901 were promised that they would never have to register again. People who registered under the grandfather clause are carried on the rolls. Very few voters have been purged for crime. During the last purging none was purged for this reason because the clerk of the court failed to send the dockets down.

The board chairman in Birmingham thinks that the voting lists will be clean by 1942. The board struck the names of over 2,000 dead people from the rolls at the last purge. Some of these people had been dead for as long as twenty-five years. Purging of the dead from the lists is performed daily and newspaper accounts are checked. Many names of dead people were discovered on the lists when 27,000 postcards were recently sent out notifying people that their precincts had been changed. Relatives phoned in or otherwise notified the board of many deaths.

No persons are indicted for making false statements on their applications. The registrar takes their word unless he suspects that they are not telling the truth. He merely questions them and, if he is still suspicious, requires them to produce evidence and a witness. The registrar points out that a great many people and "especially the Italians" lie about the time spent in the state. This is done in order to get out of paying the poll tax for back periods. The registrar feels that there is nothing to be done about this except to take the applicant's oath. Sometimes the applicants trip themselves up in answering the questions. When they do so they are registered anyway, although they are cautioned about the danger involved in such acts. Unemployed people are registered without question. In fact, "unemployed" is often put in the blank left for statement of occupation.

A great many people who have just reached twenty-one, the voting age, register if their birthdays come after the poll tax period, because in this way they get a free vote. Anyone refused registration by the board may appeal to the circuit court without cost to himself. The chairman of the Jefferson County board states that he always explains this to each applicant who is rejected. Yet, to his knowledge, no board has ever had its decisions reversed by the court. Several cases have been appealed, but the board had registered the people before the cases came to trial. At the time of Stoney's interview, the cases of eight Negroes— who had been denied registration by the previous board—were on file.

Since Jefferson is the governor's home county, he has been given the right to appoint all three members of the board of registrars. Besides the professional politician who serves as chairman, a well-known Presbyterian pastor and a prominent lawyer—both men of considerable reputation in Birmingham —serve at the regular compensation of five dollars per day. It is amazing that there is no direct supervision of this registration work by the state. The chairman of the board is merely required to send in a typed list of all people registered, with their precincts indicated. The attorney general sends to the registrars rulings on any questions which cause them difficulty. They are also furnished copies of all decisions made for other boards and copies of any changes in statutes or new statutes. Other than this, the board relies upon the state code for its instructions.

In Burke County, Georgia, all people registering are required to sign the registration book in person and in their own hand. If the person is white and illiterate, the tax commissioner reads the oath to him and the person who brings him in signs for the applicant. Illiterates, it seems, are always "brought in by some politician."

The tax collector of Johnson County, Georgia, does not demand that all persons who register come in to sign the registration book in person. A sister or a mother or a candidate can do this for them. The tax collector explains that this does not make a great deal of difference since he has to make the signature for so many of the applicants anyway. The tax collector has never used the literacy or character tests, and he adds: "To tell you the truth, the qualifications for a voter have got down pretty low in this country. Party politics is mighty crooked in this county. There's lots of trading and trafficking." One of the registrars says that no one is ever purged from the voting list for crime. Several whose names are on the current list are either in jail or out on parole.

Although the members of the board of registrars have signed their names to it, the current registration roll for Johnson County is admittedly not accurate. None of the tax defaulters for one year back, and in some cases for two years back, has been struck from the list. The reason for this is said to be the fact that the ordinary, the tax collector, and the clerk were supposed to make up a list of the tax defaulters and file it with the registrars by April 20, so that the latter could have a chance to notify defaulters, who then would have fifteen days in which to appear and get paid up. There are two new members of the board of registrars—one of them a young lady—and they did not know anything about their duties until the chairman, who has served for many years, instructed them after May 5 "to get busy." Then the judge and the solicitor, both of whom are interested in the district-wide race this coming fall, told them that they could not legally strike these defaulters because they had not been notified. But at least one member of the board— the young woman—considers this to have been a frame-up, because, she contends, all five people involved knew about the law, including the chairman of her board. She feels that they deliberately let matters slip because the same thing had occurred in a neighboring county, and those in Johnson County needed to have an enrollment equally as large in order to have any chance in the district elections. Thus, in Johnson County, they took the rolls drawn up for the county primary of November 1939, for which 1938 taxes had to be paid to vote, added to these all those who had registered since the county primary, whether or not they had paid the tax, and then the solicitor added a few names that did not appear on the registration books.

In Macon County the tax collector registers all of the people on the books. Unlike some other counties in Georgia, the registrants are all required to come into the registrar's office and sign the book. All except women registering for the first time and people just becoming twenty-one are required to take the oath. The county tax collector expressed shock at the suggestion that people in other counties are registered without having to make a personal appearance, exclaiming: "Good Lord! If it was that way, I could put a couple of hundred people's names down on the books myself, pay up their poll taxes, and haul them in and get elected to anything I wanted to."

In Dougherty County the secretary to the tax collector does most of the registering. It is said that all applicants are required to come in person and sign the register. If they cannot sign for themselves, the tax collector or his secretary signs for them, and it is admitted that this practice is quite common. The literacy, character, and educational tests are never employed, and it is claimed that "no difference" is made in the treatment of Negroes and whites. Few Negroes apply for registration, however, and those few come "when some president of one of their organizations gets after them." It is estimated that there are over five hundred Negro names on the registration books in default on poll tax payments. Voting lists are made up separately in Dougherty County for the county primary, the state primary, and the general election. The county primary comes before the closing date for qualification for the state primary. Few people qualify after this date, however. The Negro list is added for the general election.

Everyone who registers in Ware County is required to come in and sign the book in person, says the tax collector, "unless it's a wife, or a sister, or somebody like that," or a person registering for another person of close kin "if I know them." The literacy and character tests are never used.

In McIntosh County the tax collector requires all people registering to appear in person and sign the registration book. If the registrants cannot sign for themselves, the tax collector does so for them in their presence. It is claimed that there is no difference in treatment between whites and Negroes in this respect.

In Chatham County it is said that every person registered is required to sign the registration book in person, the exception being that when a married couple is transferring from one district in a city to another, the husband or wife may sign again for the other. There must be an original signature, however. Women are required to reregister when they change their names. The tax collector admits that he does register people who cannot read and write. He reads the oaths to them and then signs for them. He has had to refuse, he says, only about fifteen persons during his term in office. These were people who could not give satisfactory answers about their age, place of residence, time in the state, and so forth, and he alleges that this is the only kind of test given anyone. He states that there has been only one appeal to the board, "and that didn't get to first base." This was the case of a man who had not been in the state long enough.

In Greene County people need not come into the registration office to sign the books and be registered as voters. Most voters are registered by candidates or their workers who supply the names and approximate ages. No proof is required of age, time of residence in the county, literacy, or character. Payment of poll tax is the full requirement. The tax collector of the county declares that he has never administered any of the tests provided and claims to register Negroes just as he does whites. He says that, in fact, he encourages Negroes to register so that he can get the poll tax. He estimates that about thirty-five Negroes are qualified voters. In 1938 about forty Negroes were designated on the voting list. Of this number, only about fifteen are said to vote. Some of them are too old to pay the poll tax. During the registration year 1939–40, the tax collector has registered six Negroes, all of whom are property owners and appeared in person. The registration in the spring of 1940 was the largest in the history of Greene County. Over three thousand dollars in back taxes were collected, and "two thirds of this was paid by the candidates."

It is admitted in Greene County that the registration lists are cluttered with many "duds." Many names noted for purging by the justices of the peace had to be left on the lists because the people were still paying taxes in Greene County while living elsewhere; were living in another county and paying poll taxes there, but had not asked for a transfer; were over tax age; or were dead, but no definite proof of death could be gotten. A member of the board of registrars is satisfied that many of these people who have moved to adjoining counties have been registered there without getting a transfer. With primaries coming at different times, voting in two or more counties is not difficult.

The three members of the board of registrars of Greene County are paid three dollars a day and work as long as necessary. This bill is met by the county. During the past year they worked a total of nine days.

The following appears at the top of a page in the registration books in Georgia:

I do swear, or affirm that I am a citizen of the United States; that I am 21 years of age, or will be on the _____ of _____ of this calendar year; that I have resided in this State for one year, and in this county for six months immediately preceding the date of this oath, or will have so resided on the _____ of _____ of this calendar year; that I have paid all taxes which, since the adoption of the Constitution of 1877, have been required of me, except taxes for this year; that I possess the qualification of an elector, required by the Constitutional Amendment adopted in 1908 and that I am not disqualified from voting by reason of any offense committed against the laws of the State. I further swear, or affirm that I reside in the _____ District G.M., or in the _____ Ward in the City of _____ at no. _____ on _____ street. My age is _____; my occupation _____.

Those entitled to permanent registration under the law as amended on 10 August 1913, include:

All persons who have honorably served in the land or naval forces of the United States in the Revolutionary War or in the War of 1812, or in the War with Mexico, or in any War with the Indians, or in the War between the States, or in the War with Spain, or who honorably served in the land or naval forces of the Confederate States, or of the State of Georgia in the War between the States; or

All persons lawfully descended from those embraced in the classes enumerated in the subdivision next above; or

All persons who are of good character and understand the duties and obligations of citizenship under a republican form of government; or

All persons who can correctly read in the English language any paragraph of the Constitution of the United States or of this State and correctly write the same in the English language when read to them by any one of the registrars, and all persons who solely because of physical disability are unable to comply with the above requirements, but can understand and give a reasonable interpretation of any paragraph of the Constitution of the United States or of this State that may be read to them by any one of the registrars; or

Any person who is the owner in good faith in his own right of at least forty acres of land situated in this State, upon which he resides, or is the owner in good faith in his own right of property situated in this State and assessed for taxation at the value of $500.00.

Under all of this are blanks for the following: date registered, name, age, white or colored, soldier, descendant of soldier, good character and knowledge of duties of citizenship, education, owner forty acres of land or five hundred dollars personal property, post office, occupation, transfer to, and transfer from. Those not entitled to register in Georgia are the following:

> Those who shall have been convicted in any court of competent jurisdiction of treason against the State or embezzlement of public funds, malfeasance in office, bribery or larceny, or any crime involving moral turpitude, punishable by the laws of this State with imprisonment in the penitentiary, unless such persons shall have been pardoned.
> Idiots and insane persons.
> No tax-collector shall allow any person to sign his name in the voters' book unless he is satisfied, at the time, that the taxes due by said voter are paid, and that he is otherwise qualified.

The tax collector in Hall County, Georgia, who assumed office in 1930, does not recall ever having refused to register a white person. He explains that he started to do so at one time when a man brought in the name of his brother who was known to the tax collector to be half crazy. He did not refuse registration, however, because he was afraid that the brother would get angry if he told "this on him right here in front of everybody." The man never voted, as he died before the next election.

Although there is a board of registrars in Hall County, the tax collector does practically all of the registering and most of the rest of the work. The board is made up of an old man who is the Republican member, a seventy-odd-year-old school teacher, and a retired merchant. The members of the board are appointed by the judge of the superior court at the suggestion of the county officers. The Republicans have no chance to nominate their representative on the board. The Republican member of the board in Hall County has served for fourteen years and never fails to vote in the Democratic primary.

In Hall County the principal duty of the board of registrars is purging the voting list. This is done before each election, beginning the day after the closing date set for registration and tax payment. From the voting lists are taken the names of all of those who are delinquent in taxes. This is done by the collector of taxes. The dead are also struck from the list, and these names are obtained from the justices of the peace who hold the elections in the rural districts. No certificates from the health department are checked, however. Those who have moved out of the county are taken off the list only after a transfer is received or no tax payment is shown—or when somebody is confident they are dead. The county ordinary sends a list of those who are insane, and the clerk of the court sends a list of those convicted of crimes. Not more than half a dozen are struck from the list for criminal conviction at each purging. Only those who have committed felonies are removed. Whenever possible, people whose names are struck from the list are notified by mail. Those who have moved from the county must give permission before the registrars can strike their names from the list.

People may register at any time merely by coming into the office of the tax collector or the registrar and signing the book. In the case of the county primary, the Democratic committee— and, in other elections, the state law—fixes the last date on which people may register to vote in the election. Those who register after this date are put on the books but not placed on the voting list until the next time. There is a separate registration for city elections. Until recently the state law provided that a person must pay *all* county and state taxes in order to vote. During the depression, however, this has been changed to allow persons to pay only poll taxes.

It is not necessary to appear in person in order to register. In Hall County no tests are given. If applicants do appear in person, they may make a mark in the book and have someone else sign for them. Most people are registered by a candidate or by a brother, husband, other relative, or "friend." Candidates often come into the registration office with long lists of names. Ages are given only approximately. In former years, the registrars were provided with small slips containing a voter's oath which the applicants had to sign. But this has been done away with since 1930. Now the voters' names are recorded in the book as the people give them. While this is perhaps not legal, it seems to be the common practice all over the state.

Anyone who moves into Hall County and wants to register is first required to get a transfer from the county of previous residence. This transfer is a regular form and on it is the statement that the person has paid all poll taxes due to date. Few tax collectors in Georgia who issue these transfers, however, bother to look up the record or to answer the question regarding the poll tax. The reply of the applicant is usually accepted at its face value even though this blank remains unfilled. Thus, people who have transferred their residence to Hall County may start voting by paying up all of the taxes owed since they moved into that county.

The tax collector in Putnam County requires all people to come in and register in person, except perhaps the wives or daughters of men who are registering, though he knows this is not legal. However, he takes the position that this is justified in a town as small as Eatonton. The literacy or character tests are never employed. The tax collector states further that he has signed the registration book himself for a number of men, knowing that they would be "embarrassed before people" in not being able to sign for themselves. "You see, a good citizen making a good living that can't write hardly or read—a lot of people didn't get a chance like you and me—you hate to make them feel bad."

The Greenville County, South Carolina, board of registrars sits to register on the first Monday, Tuesday, and Wednesday of each month. When the books opened in January of 1938, however, the board members stayed on duty full time for almost three months. According to the chairman of the county board, everyone must appear in person to get a registration certificate, and everyone is required to take the literacy test. The registrants are asked to read a short passage of the constitution, but the chairman states that she does not ask them to explain it because "there's plenty I don't understand about it myself." Only a few applicants have been turned down.

The chairman told Stoney that she does not try to get proof of age or residence from the registrant. There is no way that this can be done, she explained, and she admits that many "get by." She cited one case which brought her into court. A school trustee's election was being contested on the ground that one girl who voted—casting the deciding vote—was underage. It so happened that the girl registered with her mother. The chairman explained: "Her mother said she was 21, and gracious goodness, who am I to argue with a woman about how old her own kid is?" Another time the chairman was taken to court in a trustee election contest. A man had applied for a duplicate receipt, then found his old one, and at that point "thought up the smart trick" of erasing his first name and putting in that of his wife. Registration certificates must be thirty days old to be good for an election. The chairman of the board had to testify in court that the last name was in her handwriting and the first name was not.

To vote in the Greenville city primary, one must enroll with a special enrollment commissioner who has no connection with the official city setup. He is employed by the city Democratic committee. To enroll for the primary, one must also show a registration certificate from the county and be on the poll tax list. To vote in the Greenville city general election, no literacy test is required. It is assumed that the registrant has stood such test when he presents the county registration certificate which is required. The registrant is also supposed to present a county tax receipt showing that the poll tax has been paid. No display of a voting certificate is required for voting in the primary. The primary and general elections are "completely separate." They are kept this way, according to the secretary of the Greenville County Democratic committee, "so we can keep the Negro from voting. We have no quarrel with the Negro. He has a right to vote in the general election if he wishes. We do not object to that."

The present chairman of the board of registrars in Pickens County, South Carolina, was appointed in 1938. She is a woman, and the other two members of the board are men. She states that when people apply for registration, she makes them read and write or show tax receipts for three hundred dollars worth of property. She declares that she knows Pickens County and almost everyone in it, and "I know who to ask if they can read and who not to. Plenty of them have to say 'no.' " When they do, she does not let them register, adding: "One has come in three times now."

Until a recent state supreme court case invalidating the Democratic registration, the practice in Pickens County was for one person to bring in a bunch of names and get receipts for everyone. Now the county registrar makes the applicants come in person. She does not require them to show their poll tax receipts, however. It is the poll holders who require this or who are supposed to, though, according to the registrar, they do not do so, except in trustee elections. These elections and the primary, the registrar says, are conducted decently, but the general elections are "a joke."

The town general elections in Pickens County are admittedly not very carefully handled. According to a former general election commissioner, the city clerk, together with a registrar, ordinarily writes out the town certificates and sends them around to people's houses. The same is true of the city primary in Easley, where the former election commissioner lives. He declares that before the last election they brought a certificate for him, for his wife, and for his daughter—all written out and signed.

Registration for general elections in Sumter County, South Carolina, comes the first Monday in each month. If the demand is great enough, the board of registrars goes back on Tuesday and Wednesday. Early in 1938, when the new registration began, the board spent almost a month at this job. At this time the civic clubs were putting on a drive to get people to register and were receiving cooperation. The county paid the board members extra for this. Although the legal hours are fixed, the board often sits later so that working people can come in and register.

The Sumter board does not require that people show their poll tax receipts to register, for, as the chairman of the board says, "that's the business of the poll holders." It is because the poll tax receipts are not required that so many people have signed up. The chairman admits that any white person who is twenty-one years old or over is registered without question. It is only once in a great while, when the board members are suspicious, that they try to check up on residence. Since the applicant is not required to do any writing in the official process (all writing is done by the registrars, and the voter's signature is not required either on the stub or on the receipt), they "assume" that every white man can read and write.

The enrollment book for one of the big ward clubs of Sumter is to be found at Dr. Lawson's drugstore near the center of town. According to Dr. Lawson, the book was just brought there and left. This is the first time it has been put in his store. People may come in and register any time the store is open; that is, from 7:00 A.M. until midnight. He will give the registrants curb service, but he will not allow the book to be taken any farther away from the store than that. These are the instructions the county chairman gave him when the book was brought around. No one looks after the book. It lies on the counter and people come in and sign. Dr. Lawson said that he thought it was all right for a husband to sign for a wife and the other members of his family, although he "wouldn't want to let it go much further than that." He makes no attempt to check up on ages, residences, and so on, though he knows almost everyone in the ward. This is left up to the committee on purge day.

A member of the board of registrars of Saluda County stated quite frankly that he does not know very much about his work as registrar. He got the job as a favor from the state senator for whom he had worked in the campaign. He merely does "what the clerk told me" was necessary when he took office. When the new registration period started in January 1938, this member of the board and his colleagues spent several days in the courthouse renewing certificates. Now, the registrar goes in once a month to check up on things. Few people come in to register, and those who do can get their receipts from the clerk. He is not supposed to give them out to anyone except those who are called for jury duty and who are in a hurry, but he does not bother about this. People in the county have registered very well, although most people have done so in order to be on the jury. Women register because they come along with their husbands. With reference to the Negro registration, he added: "We had a half a dozen niggers to come in." They were required to read a portion of the constitution and to write it out, and to answer certain question about it which the clerk gave to the registrars. None of the Negroes was turned down, which the registrar thought due to the fact that the Negro community had sent "the best ones in there first. When they found out what they had to do, they went out and told the rest," so that now Negroes "don't come in unless they can pass." It is frankly admitted, however, that white people are never tested by the registrar because "we was never asked to."

The clerk of the county court, when asked if the poll officials do not ask to see the registration certificates in the election, exclaimed: "I'd hate to be a manager and ask one of these farmers for his registration certificate or his poll tax receipt. Boy! You'd get run out of the place. People in this county—they won't stand for red tape in any form." People in the county register, not in order to vote in the general election, but so they can vote for school trustees and be drawn on the jury.

Because of a state supreme court decision in 1939, a bit more care has been used in writing up the certificates. Formerly, an executive committeeman would hand in a bunch of names, and receipts would be written out for him to take back to his neighbors. Often, only one of the registrars would sign them, or the clerk of court would write them up himself. Now, however, efforts are made to get people to apply in person. They need not wait for the first Monday in each month, though. The clerk has the board sign two or three dozen receipts ahead of time, and he fills them in when people apply. This is done when people are called on jury and either cannot sign their old receipts or have ones that are not signed by all three registrars.

In Beaufort County, South Carolina, there are twelve districts or precincts for primary elections and nine for general elections. The latter are set by state statutes. The former are set by the county Democratic committee. In Beaufort County the primary election districts conform to township lines as much as possible. There are definite boundaries so that a voter has no choice as to where he will vote. In the primary he must always vote with the Democratic club in the district where he lives. The district Democratic clubs do all enrolling and this is completely separate from registration. Each of these Democratic clubs meets on the fourth Saturday in April of election years to "reorganize." Anyone who has lived within the district for sixty days and who is a white person at least twenty-one years of age may attend and vote. The president of the club appoints an enrollment committee of three members whose duty it is to see that all eligible voters in the community put their names in this book. The book is furnished by the state Democratic executive committee—a large ledger with pages alphabetically tabbed, each page containing spaces for the date (seldom filled), signature of voter (if the voter cannot write, a place for his mark and for the signature of the person signing for him is provided), age, occupation, and address. Enrollment books are open for six or seven weeks. The time is fixed by the state Democratic executive committee. The local newspapers always give two weeks' notice of the opening date and run large notices every week during the period telling where the voters may find the books, etc.

None of the club officers in Beaufort is paid. Generally one member of the enrollment committee is a merchant, and the book is left in his store. Technically, each person is required to sign the book in person, though in actual practice this is not done. Three days after the closing date, all enrollment books are brought into the courthouse by the Democratic executive committeeman. Here the committee divides itself into four committees, covering the four parts of the county, which go over the books—striking out duplications; transferring people who they find have signed the wrong book; and considering protests, though protests are seldom made. After the list is purged, additions are made. Committeemen from each district hand in names, and a motion is usually made that a request be handed to the circuit judge to include these names on the qualified list of enrolled voters. In 1938 sixty-six names were added in this way, but this practice is not followed in most South Carolina counties. These additions were apparently people who had failed to sign the books and had asked the executive committee-men to include them. According to the rules, they are supposed to be ill, away from home, or to have some other good excuse. There should be fewer of these during the current year, for the state committee has arranged an absentee blank for enrollment.

At each box there are two or three managers and a clerk who are selected by the executive committeemen and approved by the chairman of the executive committee. There is no provision for giving candidates representation on this board. Each candidate is allowed one watcher at each box and one or more watchers at the ballot countings. All returns are counted in public.

In the primary, state and county ballot boxes are set side by side. One is painted white and the other yellow. The corresponding tickets are printed on white and yellow paper. Both boxes are supervised by the same election officials. A voter gives his name. It is located on a certified enrollment list previously typed out in alphabetical order, which gives name, age, occupation, and address. The voter's name is checked on this list and is written out by the clerk on a tally sheet. He is given two ballots—one for the county and one for the state—and goes into the voting booth. It is claimed that the Australian ballot system is strictly enforced in Beaufort County. After the voter has voted, he folds his ballots and hands them to a manager, who tears off the numbered tabs at the top along the perforated lines, puts the ballot in the box himself (or has the voter do it), and files the two tabs. After the election, the votes are counted in the districts by the managers and clerks. Results are put on tally sheets; these are put in the boxes; they are locked and brought to the courthouse by the executive committeeman. If there are challenged votes, these go into special envelopes. Each is sealed up separately, and there is no counting of them until they are passed upon by the executive committee when it sits to declare results. Absentee votes are secured by voters from their club secretaries. They are returned to him. He brings them sealed to the club, opens them in the presence of the managers and clerks, dumps them folded into the box, and mixes them up.

In Beaufort County nothing is required of a voter in the primary except that his name appear on the certified copy of the enrollment list. No registration or poll tax receipts are required. There is no attempt at supervision of the district clubs. The chairman of the Beaufort County Democratic committee affirms emphatically that there are no Negro members of any district primary club in the county.

Certificates of registration for voters are issued in Beaufort County to those applying on the first Monday in each month. No certificates are issued within thirty days prior to an election which is not a primary. All three registrars come together and write out these certificates as people come to the courthouse. The applicants must show their poll tax receipts for the previous year. It is claimed by the chairman of the county board of registrars that the literacy or property tests are enforced "strictly. We do that to keep down the niggers. We have no trouble here with that. All talk you hear about niggers voting is in up-country. Down here we're seven to one, and we don't have any trouble. Colored people know it's going to be settled in the primary and they don't try to register. They're not interested in that." The chairman admits, however, that he never asks a white man whether or not he can read and write. He does require all Negroes to read a section of the constitution and to write out a part of it, unless they have previously had a receipt, in which case the Negro applicants are allowed a new receipt without test.

After the certificates are issued, the names of voters are written into books in alphabetical order—one book for each general election district. These books are used for elections and are also the official lists from which jury lists are picked. This is why Negroes are identified. There is no place in the book for this identification, but in Beaufort County "col." is written beside each Negro's name.

The state committee in South Carolina has recently ruled that a new enrollment for the primary must be made every two years. Until 1938 there were primary enrollments every four years, with revisions and additions made each two years. Things would get so confused in Beaufort County, however, that the chairman of the county Democratic committee often had to call for a new enrollment every two years anyway.

Actually there is no qualification for voting in the Beaufort County primary except age and residence. Criminals are allowed to vote if they are not behind the bars. The town banker in Beaufort, jailed for embezzlement in 1926, came back after his term and ran for mayor. His citizenship had not been restored, but nothing was said about it. He was given a place on the Democratic primary ballot and received seventeen votes.

According to an enrollment committeeman at Shelton, in Beaufort County, the Democratic primary enrollment book which is kept in his store does not require any of his attention.

People sign up as they please. At the time of Stoney's visit the book was "out," as the executive committeeman was taking it around to people in the district, a practice that is customary in that district. The enrollment committeeman seldom attends his district club meeting and all the club does, he says, is hold the election. The elections are held in his store. The poll holders and delegates to the convention are "about the same ones every time."

An interview with a druggist who is a member of the local enrollment committee indicates the laxity with regard to registration for the primary in Beaufort. He explains that all he does is take the enrollment book when the chairman of the party brings it around, spread it out on his counter, and keep the pencil sharp. Most people come in and sign without ever seeing him. He has served for fifteen years or more—ever since they brought the books around and put them on the counter without asking him. He contends that the information in the books is accurate, except for the ages of women—most of whom put "21 plus." The rules say that each person must sign in person, but in practice this is not required. One member of a family can sign for all the rest. Or, if "you know someone is sick or can't come down, you can put his name on the book. I wouldn't let just anybody do it. You know—if they're responsible and I know them." The druggist lets anyone register who is of proper age and has lived in the state for two years. He never asks them about the latter requirement unless he knows they have not. Then, if they have put down their names when he was not present, he does nothing about it, leaving it up to the committee to correct it. He recalls only two such cases in the past five years.

To illustrate the informality of the enrollment in Beaufort County, a county representative related that a Negro minister had signed up without anyone knowing about it. He had just slipped in and put his name down in the book when no one was looking. The county representative comments: "We didn't know it was a negro so we let it pass. He had the nerve to come in and try to vote!" A former mayor of Beaufort was at the polls at the time. He went over and told the Negro "if he knew what was good for him, he better get out and stay out." The man left.

All matters pertaining to general elections in South Carolina —municipal, state, or federal—are governed by statute. According to the state law, cities of a certain size must have elections every year. Those of a slightly larger size must have a general election every two years. Larger cities must have general elections every four years. To vote in these city elections, one must obtain a special city registration certificate—a new one for each general election. Requirements for obtaining this certificate are: (1) the presentation of a county registration certificate; (2) a poll tax receipt for the preceding year; (3) meeting all requirements for registering in the county; and (4) in addition, having resided in the city for four months and in the ward or district for sixty days. These certificates are issued by three "supervisors of registration" appointed by the mayor. They start working ninety days before the general election, and their books remain open for two months. Voters are supposed to display their certificates to vote. These supervisors are supposed to give representation to the different political parties or factions. The records in the office of the clerk of council of Charleston show that there were 2,502 white people and 52 Negroes registered for the city general election of 1939.

In Charleston the city general election is conducted by three election commissioners appointed by the governor. By a special act passed in 1877, the election must come on the second Tuesday in December. The three-man board of commissioners appoints three managers for each polling place "so that each political party shall be represented." The general election means absolutely nothing in Charleston city politics.

In the county, the general elections are conducted by a three-man board of commissioners appointed by the governor. These men, in turn, appoint the precinct election officials. Registration is handled by a three-member board of registrars appointed by the governor. All of these men receive a small fee, and the governor usually appoints whomever the state senator recommends. There is no attempt to give the minority party representation on any of these boards.

Although the registration board for the general elections in Charleston must meet in its office once a month to list those who have registered and to accept all comers, anyone who wishes to can get registered "almost any time of day or night" by seeing the chairman of the board at his drugstore on King Street. The colored registrants in the registration book for the general elections are plainly marked "col." In the city of Charleston, on the basis of the registration from 1 January 1938 to 1 May 1940, there were 7,920 white persons and 362 Negroes on the books. In the county districts there were 4,302 whites and 200 Negroes. Thus the totals for the county are 12,222 whites and 562 Negroes eligible for the general elections.

According to the secretary of the Charleston County Democratic committee and the chairman of the board of registrars, the enrollment system for Democratic primaries in the county operates as follows: the books are kept open from June 11 to July 23. Three days after this, the lists are compiled and published in the newspapers. Three days following the publication is the purge date. This is done by a subcommittee of the county executive committee. Any person who wishes to do so may appear and bring charges. In 1930, when candidates John P. Grace and Thomas Stoney were battling over the solicitorship and the state senatorship, several hundred names were purged. Many people lost their tempers and the old bitter factionalism rose up again.

The "leaders" in each ward work hard to get their people to enroll and to come to club meetings. Now they are requiring that people sign the enrollment books for themselves. This is being done to avoid the accusations made in 1938 that there was padding of the rolls. This has reference to the Maybank-Manning gubernatorial campaign of 1938, in which Colonel Wyndham Manning, the defeated candidate, charged that Burnet R. Maybank stole the election through padding the club rolls in Charleston.

A person has his choice of the Democratic clubs within his ward. When he enrolls, he takes an oath that he is not enrolled in any other clubs. Many duplications are found, however, when the rolls are consolidated. People thus found are notified by registered mail to appear before the committee and are given their choice of clubs (that is, if they registered in two clubs in the same ward) or are put in the club where they reside (if they registered in two clubs in separate wards). According to the chairman of the board of registrars in Charleston County, all except women are required to show either a poll tax receipt or a record of exemption for registration. Everyone must read the oath, and the chairman states that it is surprising "how many people in this town can't read or write. I mean white people. They come in here well dressed, looking fine." He says that he has turned down a good many white people as well as a good many Negroes on this count. He seldom applies the property qualification, for few of those who cannot read and write are able to show tax receipts on property valued at as much as three hundred dollars.

There is no longer any poll tax payment required for registration in Louisiana, but the poll tax receipts for the two preceding years (that is, for the present year and the one immediately preceding) must be obtained in order for the person to be eligible for registration. For current registration, as an example, poll tax receipts can be obtained by anyone and without any qualification or payment. Once the poll tax receipts are obtained, the applicant must appear at the registration office. The clerk then presents the applicant with a printed card. This card cannot be taken away from the office and the applicant must fill it in. If the applicant is illiterate, he must answer the questions, and the clerk will write them in. Then he must mark the card with his "X." The answers to questions must be absolutely correct. Although the questions on the card appear very simple, there are many applicants who make mistakes.

The registrars in New Orleans are appointed by the governor. The New Orleans office maintains a large staff of clerks—there being one for each ward. In referring to the experiences of Negro applicants, one of the registrars said: "There are only a few niggers who know exactly when they were born or where they were born, or even where they were living."[2] Answers to the questions on the application card are regarded as an elementary educational test. According to the law of Louisiana, if the applicant fails to fill out the card accurately, the clerk is forbidden to explain his error to him. The applicant can return day after day to fill out new cards, but, says this registrar, he usually gets tired and quits trying.

Cards which are incorrectly filled out by applicants are preserved in the office of the registrar until such time as the applicant is registered. The applicant has the privilege of appealing to the court when rejected at the registration office. The judge of the court to which the appeal is made can call for the incorrectly filled-in registration cards as evidence. Ordinarily, according to a New Orleans registrar, the judge will merely ask the complaining applicant to fill in the card and will decide upon the matter then and there. The registrar takes the position that it is foolish to give votes to Negroes, because they only sell them.

The Louisiana constitution also provides for the employment of a constitutional interpretation test as a means of qualifying. Yet one of the present registrars in New Orleans states that, during the five years he has held office, he has never applied this constitutional understanding test to anyone—white or black.

2. Gunnar Myrdal's interview in New Orleans, 13 November 1939.

The qualifications for voting registration in Baton Rouge, Louisiana, include a two-year residence in the state, one-year residence in the town, six months residence in the ward, three months residence in the precinct, and demonstration of ability to read and write. People who own property but who cannot read or write can have someone else register for them. Persons over sixty may register without signing the poll books. People must register at least thirty days prior to the date of the election. They must be white in order to vote in the Democratic primary.

The registration books in Raleigh, North Carolina, are ill-kept and undated, and many mysterious signs appear behind the names. These are the records, however, which determine who can and who cannot vote in Raleigh.

In Mississippi the registration qualifications are as follows: (1) residence in the state for two years; (2) residence in the county and city for one year; (3) American citizenship by birth or naturalization; (4) interpretation, upon request, of sections of the state constitution, or reading of the same; (5) reading the oath of office out of the registration book (this pledge is written in sentences which continue on the second page, an arrangement designed to confuse the applicant for registration); and (6) payment of the poll tax two years prior to the election year in which the applicant offers to vote.

The registration certificate or slip as employed in Hamilton County, Tennessee, acts as a bar to free suffrage and is exploited by petty ward heelers. As the chairman of the Hamilton County Democratic committee puts it, "little sniveling ward heelers" register people, collect their certificates, and then go to candidates and offer to vote them for so much. "They're nothing in the world but leeches on the people running for office. They call a bunch of people in to register who don't give a damn. . . . They come to a candidate I know as much as $500 off a single man on a ticket. . . . Lots of times they sell to both sides. . . . If I was running for office, I wouldn't give them a dime." It is said that often the ward heelers do not deliver the votes they promise. The practice is illegal, of course, both for the man who collects the registration certificate and for the registrant who thus gives up his certificate.

The chairman of the Hamilton County board of elections explained:

We don't vote heavy in Hamilton County. Nobody cares much about elections. I don't know anything about your grandfather clause. It may be in effect in other counties in Tennessee, but in this county, and in the three other big city counties, we have a new registration every two years. Then, 20 days before election, we must hold what they call a "supplementary registration" for three days. That is when the bulk of people generally register. About 26,000 is top registration, I guess, and most elections don't draw more than 15,000. Bond elections come to around seven or eight thousand. . . . You can vote in the city election, either a bond election or a regular election, if you own property there, even if you aren't a resident.

There are three judges at every registration place in Hamilton County. If these judges suspect a man ought not to be permitted to register, or if any of the three thinks so, they stamp "disagree" by his certificate. The voter is entitled to appeal to the county board of elections. This board hears the evidence, and if it feels that the appellant is qualified, it writes "void" under the "disagree." Only one such vote has been contested in the last five years. Hamilton County has a new registration every two years and has no form of permanent registration whatsoever.

Voting registration qualifications in Knoxville, Tennessee, are the following: one year of residence in the state, six months' residence in the county, supplemental registration twenty days before election, no educational qualifications. Election officers or a private citizen may mark the ballot for a blind or feeble person. The payment of the one dollar poll tax for the year immediately preceding the election not later than sixty days prior to the day of said election is required. In order to vote, one must be a naturalized or a native citizen twenty-one years of age or over. Those over fifty are exempt from the poll tax payment, and those just becoming twenty-one do not have to pay it.[3]

In order to discover the real nature of the Southern registration laws it is necessary to analyze their application to Negro registrants rather than to white, since it is only with respect to Negroes that the laws are strictly administered by the local registration officials.[4]

3. James Jackson's Knoxville, Tennessee, field notes, November 1939.
4. At this point in the Bunche memorandum, the author and his assistants included a careful summary of the registration and voting qualifications, as provided by state statute, in seventeen Southern and border states. See pp. 367–435 of the original typescript. —ED.

TEN

Negro Registration

THE following materials provide some documentary evidence of Southern registration practices as they affect Negroes. The testimony here presented is primarily from two sources: (1) the practices and attitudes of Southern registration officials as gleaned from their own testimony to interviewers; and (2) the experiences of Southern Negroes in their efforts to register as related to interviewers. As a purely arbitrary classification, the material is presented by states and counties—this was the only classification that time would permit. It would have been much more desirable to break down and reintegrate these materials under topical categories, but this simply could not be tackled within our rigid time budget.

The application blank for registration in Alabama constitutes a literacy test in itself. It is so worded that it would cause considerable difficulty for the average applicant if he were required to fill it out himself and without aid. It must be kept in mind, however, that in Alabama it is the general practice for registration officials to fill this blank out for white applicants, while Negro applicants, if they are fortunate enough to be given the chance, are required to undertake it themselves and without assistance. The application can be rejected, and often is, if errors are made.

In Birmingham, Alabama, until the past few years, prospective Negro registrants were required to have two white endorsers, though in some instances one such would be enough, providing he carried sufficient prestige. Depending on the reputation of the whites, telephone calls could be made or letters given to satisfy this requirement. Actually, however, the only requirement of the Alabama law is that a registrant produce a person who can testify that he has been in the state two years, the county twelve months, and the precinct or ward for three months. The two essential voting qualifications in Alabama are: (1) to read or write any passage of the constitution, providing the applicant has been working the greater part of the preceding twelve months; and (2) to own or pay taxes on three hundred dollars worth of real or personal property (or, if married, for either of the parties to own such property). Ordinarily, in the case of white applicants, qualification can be gained under either of these provisions. When white applicants appear who cannot read or write, it is usually presumed that they own three hundred dollars worth of property. Negroes, however, are given a registration blank to fill out and are told:

> "You will hear from us—you will get a letter or card, requesting you to come in and meet the board"—but nothing more is ever heard from the board. In some cases, however, a few cards are actually sent out, and the Negroes come before the board and are asked such questions as: "Are you a Communist?" "Do you own property?" "Why do you want to register to vote?" "Do you belong to that radical Negro organization?" (meaning the NAACP). On other occasions, a minor mistake in filling out the card will be pointed out, or the individual may be asked to name certain officers of the state or the members of the President's cabinet, and so on.[1]

But the laws of Alabama make it easy to appeal from the decision of the registrar and to have one's voting qualifications determined by a jury. No bond is necessary, nor any other security for court costs. The judge can instruct the jury only as to qualifications fixed by law. Mandamus proceedings can be instituted free. Arthur D. Shores, a young Negro lawyer, has been actively engaged in a fight to break down the barriers against Negro suffrage in Birmingham. On 15 June 1939, Shores filed six petitions for mandamus on behalf of Negroes who had been refused registration. There is, however, a catch in the Alabama law, in that if the appellant has not been refused *formally* by

1. Interview with Arthur D. Shores, Birmingham, Alabama, 18 November 1939. The interviewer is not identified in the Bunche memorandum. Unless otherwise indicated, the quoted passages in this chapter are taken from the notes of field interviews conducted by George Stoney in 1940. —ED.

the board, he cannot come to the court and say he has been refused. The registration board is permitted thirty days to give formal notice. If the appellant appeals before this period is up, refusal cannot be proven, but if he appeals after the period is up, the appeal is too late. In this case, the judge arbitrarily denied the six mandamus petitions. Then Shores brought proceedings under the state statute providing for appeal. Before the case could be heard, however, all six of the petitioners were registered, and it became impossible to find one who had been denied registration.

The Birmingham *Post* of 16 June 1939, carried an article entitled "Judge Bars Action on Negro Votes," which described as "almost without precedent" the action of circuit judge S. Russell McElroy in refusing to issue a mandamus writ commanding members of the board of registrars to show cause why they had refused to allow six Negro citizens to register as voters. The judge would not comment on his decision. Petitions for the writ set out that "white citizens are registered forthwith, while the petitioners have been refused registration because of their race." Named as defendants in the documents were Sam Hawkins, Lucy McCall, and A. M. Romeo, members of the registration board. Quite significantly, the Birmingham *News* of 14 July 1939 carried an article which indicates that, in spite of Judge McElroy's adverse decision, the appeal to the courts was not without effect. The *News* article stated that the names of several Negroes, including the plaintiffs in the mandamus suit, had been added to the Jefferson County registration lists recently. But Sam Hawkins, chairman of the board of registrars, denied that the litigation was responsible for the action. "As I recall," Hawkins was quoted as saying, "these Negroes applied just about the time our registration period closed for June. There was no refusal on the part of the Board to accept the registrations—it simply was delayed because of the time required to check on the qualifications of the applicants."

In a letter to United States Attorney General Frank Murphy on 7 August 1939, Arthur Shores explained what happened:

As Chairman of the legal redress committee of the Birmingham Branch of the NAACP, I am writing to acquaint you with a matter affecting the denial of certain civil liberties of Negroes and to solicit your help therein.

During the last period held for the registration of qualified electors in this County (Jefferson) there was practiced gross discrimination, and arbitrary refusal of Negroes, until a petition was filed in the court to compel registration. After this petition was filed all petitioners were registered. As a result of this court action several school teachers were called in by their superintendent and requested to withdraw their petitions or be dismissed. There have been attacks made upon me both personal and from the standpoint of employment in order to curb my activities in the courts regarding the civil rights of Negroes.

The registration books will open again here on the 9th of August through and including the 17th, and we are anticipating further movements on the part of certain reactionaries to curb the Negroes' efforts to register and vote; hence we are asking you if you will kindly have someone from your department to be on hand as a casual observer to the doings at the register's [sic] office so we may be guided in bringing whatever action necessary to protect these fundamental rights.

The Attorney General's office requested Shores to present "the facts and circumstances surrounding the situation" to the United States attorney in Birmingham.

The following is a copy of a petition to the Alabama courts filed in 1940 by attorney Shores on behalf of a Negro who was denied registration by the board of registrars of Jefferson County.

Your petitioner, William Boswell, respectfully represents unto your Honor as follows:

1. That he is a bona fide resident citizen of Jefferson County, Alabama, and is over twenty-one years of age.

2. That he is a citizen of the United States, has resided in the State of Alabama for more than two years, in the County of Jefferson for more than twelve months and in the 9th Precinct of Jefferson County, Alabama for more than three months immediately next preceding the filing of his application for registration on the 31st day of January, 1940.

3. That he is able to read and write any article of the Constitution of the United States in the English language and that he has been regularly employed for the greater part of the twelve months next preceding the time he offered to register.

4. That he has never been adjudged guilty of a felony or

any other crime, that your petitioner further avers that he is not an idiot or insane. Petitioner further alleges that by reason of the allegations hereinbefore made, he was in all particulars on the 31st of January, 1940 a duly qualified elector of the said State of Alabama according to the laws of the State and as such was entitled to be registered as an elector.

5. Your petitioner further shows that under the provisions of the laws of the State of Alabama, the Board of Registrars, duly appointed and qualified to register qualified electors and composed of Rufus Bethea, Sterling J. Foster and Herman A. Whisenett, held sessions at the court house of said county for the purpose of registering all applicants who were duly qualified, and that during the session and on the 31st day of January, 1940 when the said board was in session as provided by the laws of the State of Alabama, your petitioner made proper legal application to the said Board to register as an elector. That the said Board during such registration period and on the 31st day of January, 1940 declined and refused to register your petitioner.

6. Petitioner further states that during such registration period the said Board of Registrars has unlawfully combined, confederated and conspired together, and have formulated and devised various schemes and plots whereby they have prevented and still prevent the Negro residents of Jefferson County, including your petitioner from being registered; and petitioner further states that as a result of said conspiracy, it has become the general, habitual and systematic practice of the said Board of Registrars, these respondents and their predecessors in office, to refuse to register Negro residents and citizens of Jefferson County, Alabama including your petitioner, and to deprive them of their rights of suffrage solely on account of race, color and previous condition of servitude.

7. That as a part and parcel of the said conspiracy of the aforesaid Board of Registrars and in furtherance thereof, the said Board of Registrars invented, devised and set in motion and operation various schemes, tricks and artifices and have used every subterfuge to prevent the registration of Negroes and to deprive them of their fundamental and constitutional right of suffrage, to wit: said Board of Registrars would conduct examination of Negro applicants including your petitioner, behind closed doors, said examination consisting

of extraneous and irrelevant questions not pertaining to the qualifications of an elector. That even after admitted satisfactory answers to such questions the said Board would arbitrarily refuse to register Negro applicants, including your petitioner.

8. Further, that said Board of Registrars in its refusal to register your petitioner was acting under color of custom and usage in said Jefferson County and State of Alabama, that such refusal to register your petitioner is contrary to the provisions of the Constitution of the State of Alabama and violates the rights of your petitioner under the Constitution of the United States and the 14th and 15th amendments thereto and the laws of the United States enacted pursuant thereto.

9. Petitioner appeals from the decision of the Board of Registrars in denying him registration, under section 384 of the Code of Alabama of 1928, that his qualifications to register may be determined by a jury.

PREMISES CONSIDERED your petitioner prays that this Court will allow his appeal, and that the question of his right to register as a qualified elector of the State of Alabama be adjudicated, and for such other and further relief your Honor may think proper.

As a result of a voting drive by Negro civic organizations in Birmingham in the spring and summer of 1939, several hundred Negroes (probably the largest number since the disfranchising constitution of 1901 was adopted) presented themselves at the courthouse as applicants for registration in August and September. The men and women were given blanks to fill out in the usual manner, but instead of receiving their registration certificates they were told that they would receive some word from the board of registrars by mail. Dozens of them later received cards asking them to report again before the board at a specified period. Arriving at the courthouse, the applicants were ushered into a private room open only to the three members of the board and were questioned closely from ten to twenty-six minutes. During one entire session of the board, no Negro applicant was certified, although the applicants were all literate, none had prison records, and some were property owners and high school graduates (one school principal was included). On this particular day only two members of the board were present. Some records of what occurred are here presented.

J. C. Gandy, a steel worker, literate and active in civic organizations, was asked the following questions: "How many branches are there in the government?" "Name them." "Who is the head of the government?" "How many different types of courts are there in the state?" In answer to this question, Gandy answered: "The Fourteenth Amendment granted me my right to become a citizen and voter." No comment was made on this answer. He was asked what schools he had attended and whether or not civics had been taught in these schools. Finally, he was told that he was disqualified under Section 382 of the code of Alabama (1923). In answer to his remonstrance, he was told that he could either come back the following January or appeal to the courts. He could have a jury hearing, the registrars informed him, without cost; then, if he wished to appeal that decision, he could go to the circuit court, the next higher court, and the supreme court. Gandy still asked whether he had answered the questions to their satisfaction. The questions, the board said, were correct except for one. "We have no prejudice against you," one board member added. "But we won't pass you this morning. Come back when the books open in January." On coming out, Gandy announced his determination to try again. "They haven't turned one rock so far as discouraging me," he declared. "They've just made me more determined."

Oscar Roberts, a literate steel worker and active in union and civic work, was admitted and questioned as follows: Where had he attended school? To what grade had he gone? Had he studied civics? He was asked whether he owned forty acres of land; when the answer was given in the affirmative, he was told to show his last tax payment receipts on the property. What sort of government do we have in this country? Is it a dictatorship or a democracy? Roberts answered, "It is supposed to be a democracy." He was given a copy of the United States constitution and asked to explain the section referring to the election of Senators and Representatives. He read the section, then explained to the board, "When I came to Alabama, I didn't come as a law student. I came as a worker." He was asked about the procedure followed when a suspected criminal is arrested and a jury trial must be held. Finally, he was told that he was disqualified by the board. When he asked upon what grounds, a member read from the Alabama constitution the section giving the board of registrars power to reject applicants. He was further told that he could come back in January or exercise his right of appeal to the courts.

J. Peterson, a miner, was admitted and held briefly. He was first asked what references he had to show the board that he should be registered. He asked what was meant. The question was repeated in the same manner. Peterson proceeded to show that he was a property owner. Asked to give proof of this, he produced his tax receipts. At the end, Section 384 of the code was read to him and he was dismissed without being certified.[2]

In 1936 a Birmingham Negro named Hosea Hudson attempted to register. He applied at the courthouse with a group of three Negroes. A few whites were present at the time. He was given a registration blank to fill out, was relegated to a seat some distance away, and was given no assistance in answering the questions. When the blank was completed and handed in, he was asked to stand in back of the room and not to help any of the other colored men who had come with him. Meanwhile, the whites in the room were assisted by members of the registration board, who filled in their questionnaires for them and immediately gave them registration certificates, indicating that they were accepted by the board as voters. Hudson was told to go home and that his certificate would come through the mails. Knowing from past experience that he would never hear from the board, he immediately invited an attorney to file a petition to make the registrars tell in court why he was not registered. The judge refused to consider the case. The certificate was subsequently mailed after the case had been filed. "Have you voted since?" "No," he replied, "I haven't been able to pay my back poll tax." The tax in his case amounts to twenty-four dollars.

Marion E. Jackson, a native of Georgia, has lived in Birmingham twenty-one years. He is a young man who recently received a bachelor's degree from Morehouse College. At present he is employed at the Birmingham *World* as an associate editor. He is a member of a social club of young men, of the NAACP, and of the Jefferson County Young Negro Democratic Club. He describes his attempts to register in Birmingham:

> I went up to the office of the board of registrars to vote. When I went there, they handed me an application blank. I filled out this with all of the answers properly replied to. It was then turned in to the desk clerk. A few days later I received a card to appear before the board of registrars of Jef-

2. These Birmingham accounts are taken from Edward Strong's field notes, May 1940.

ferson County. I responded to this card and found six or seven other Negroes waiting in an anteroom on the fourth floor of the courthouse. This was not the office of the board of registrars; it was a special room that they had selected for this meeting. I was the last one to arrive and I had an opportunity of questioning the folk going in and those coming out. Each person told me that the first question was to name all of the Bill of Rights. After they had explained this, they were given a portion of the Constitution to be read. Then the members of the Board told each one to turn his face out of the window while they talked. After they came out of this conference, they brought the people back and read to them some statute on the registration book and then stated that they were not qualified to vote but that they could contest the decision of the registration board in court.

I majored in political science and American history. So, when the board asked me to name the three divisions of the government, I gave them to them. . . . Then they asked me to name some of the powers of the President. I told them he had the power of ratification [sic], appointing, confirming, and so on. Then I told them that the House of Representatives had the power of appropriation and to pass laws. They then told me, "Yes, you are doing pretty." One fellow then wanted to know if I owned any property. He then asked me if I had $100.00 worth of clothing. They concluded by asking me to read a portion of the Constitution of the United States. I read a portion . . . and then they asked me to turn my back and look out of the window. When I looked around, they told me that the board had not seen fit to pass me, but that I could contest the action of the board in the Alabama courts.

When the next registration period began, I registered again and they told me to go out of the door and go down the hall where the board was sitting. Incidentally, this was on the same floor with the office in which you make out application blanks. This was the last day the board was sitting during that period and there was a large number of colored and white people waiting in line to see the board. At this time, I was asked the identical questions as asked on the previous occasion. They told me that before they read the Alabama law whether there was anything I wanted to say for myself. My answer was yes, and that I desired to read a portion of the on the power of the registration board—they asked me Constitution to them out of a history book which I had carried along. I read five pages of the American Constitution. This took about thirty minutes. In the meanwhile, the line in the hall had increased to about 100 people. The chairman of the board asked me if I had not read enough, so I asked him had the law prescribed a law which said a person might not talk in his own favor. The answer was no, and I continued to read. The chairman of the board stopped me again. He told me that if I stopped a few minutes, they would take another vote of application. I stopped and turned my back to the window as I had done on a previous occasion. They had about a ten minute discussion; then the chairman of the board told me that I had passed the examination of the board, and he wrote on a slip of paper a three and some dashes, indicating that I was to pay poll tax for three years back.

Another Birmingham Negro, who has been rejected by the registrars three times, relates:

I was at the courthouse filling out my blank to register to vote, and my real estate agent came in and asked me, "Moss, can I help you any?" The man in charge told me that that was against the law. I have been up there three times and had never received my registration certificate. I think they let so many by at a time, and should you be in the number you just get by. I would have been glad to pay my back poll tax, but I've never heard from them.

The following is an extract from a letter written by a group of young Negro miners who attempted to register in the small mining community where they worked. No Negroes before had even attempted to register in the community of Belle Ellen, near Birmingham. Word had spread beforehand to the whites that the men, members of a civic group, were planning to register. The registrar was seated in a car in front of the office when the men arrived. When the Negroes approached, they were asked to come up one at a time; the registrar proceeded to quiz each person, not bothering to leave the car. Their letter tells the rest of the story:

We went to the polls to vote November 6 [1930] but didn't pass our registration because of these questions: ... (1) How many articles and amendments are there in the Constitution? (2) What is meant by *non compos mentis* when it is applied to a citizen in legal jeopardy? (3) Name the amendments in rotation. (4) What is meant by habeas corpus?

In an attempt to aid Birmingham blacks in their efforts to hurdle the obstacles to registration offered by the board of registrars, the Southern Negro Youth Congress of Birmingham offers a free tutorial service, designed to prepare Negroes for the questions fired at them by the registrars in the constitutional tests. A set of questions and answers on registration, here reproduced, was worked up and distributed in the Negro community.

1. What does it mean "to register"? "To register" means to file formal application to have one's qualifications passed upon as a prerequisite to voting.

2. Why is it necessary to register? It is necessary for one to register to see if he has the necessary requirement as set out by the state laws.

3. Who can register? Everyone who is a citizen of the United States and the State of Alabama may register, providing he or she is 21 years of age; has not been convicted of a crime; has been working; if he or she can read and write any passage of the Constitution of the United States; if a person cannot read or write but owns real estate or personal property valued at $300.00 or more or is married to someone who owns that amount of property may register. A person does not have to posses both qualifications.

4. When do you register? The books for registration will be open in Birmingham from November 16 to December 30, inclusive.

5. Where do you register? The place of registration is at the county Courthouse on the first floor.

6. If I haven't paid my poll tax can I register? One may register before he pays his poll tax, in fact it is the best policy to register and then pay poll tax.

7. How long must I have to live here in order to register? One must have lived in Alabama two years, in the county one year and in a precinct or ward three months before he can register.

8. If I can't read or write can I register? One may register if he can't read or write providing he owns property or is married to someone who owns property valued at $300.00 or more.

9. What makes me a "bona fide resident"? If you have lived here the prescribed time and intend this shall be your home.

10. Do war veterans have to register? War veterans have to register but are not required to pay a poll tax.

11. What shall I do when I go to register? Request a blank for registration and fill it out and return it to the Board of Registrars.

12. What kind of questions will I be asked? Usually no questions other than what appears on the blank is asked.

13. What must I know about the U.S. or the state Constitution to register? The law requires that you should be able to just read the Constitution if you do not own property.

14. How will I know whether I have been registered? A certificate of registration signed by the members of the Board will be given to you.

15. Is there any law to protect me if I am threatened with losing my job for attempting to register? There are ample Federal laws to prosecute a person who threatens to fire one for attempting to register, as well as law giving one the privilege to sue for a breach of contract.

16. Must I bring witnesses in order to register? Witnesses are not necessary for registration.

17. What shall I do if I am not registered? If you are not registered, report that fact to the investigator of the NAACP, Mr. E. O. Jackson the chairman of the Legal Redress Committee or the NAACP Atty. A. D. Shores.

18. Is it ever necessary to register a second time? It is not necessary to register a second time unless you change counties.

19. After I have registered am I entitled to vote? You are entitled to vote after registration when your poll tax is paid.

20. Who can vote? All persons who have registered and have paid their poll tax.

21. After I have registered and paid my poll tax how soon can I vote? At the very next election of any kind.

22. Where can I get additional information on this subject? From Mr. E. O. Jackson, special investigator and field secretary of the NAACP and at the office of the legal adviser of the NAACP, Atty. A. D. Shores.

The chairman of the Jefferson County board of registrars states that, according to the law, the board can make no difference in the treatment of Negroes and whites, and "so long as I am in this office, the law will be carried out." He estimates that there are between eight and nine hundred Negroes who are qualified voters, though he could not estimate how many others are registered.[3] He stated that there were approximately nine hundred Negroes registered in Jefferson County following the 1901 constitution—a much larger percentage of both the voting population and of the Negro population than at present. This change in ratio he attributes to the actions of past boards in refusing to register Negroes. A check of the registration records, however, revealed that during the registration period from January through July 1939, the previous board had registered 1,966 people, of whom 79 had been Negro. During the first period of the new board, 1,054 people had been registered, of whom only 7 were Negro. And during the second period they had registered 1,691, of whom only 4 were Negro. When confronted with these figures, the chairman of the board tried to explain by claiming that not so many Negroes had come in to register recently. But, when pressed for a more accurate statement, he admitted that some 175 had come in, and he revealed that during the two previous periods "a Negro organization" had brought 400 people up to the office at one time and 200 at another time. He also admitted that the United Mine Workers of America had brought over 200 Negro miners into the courthouse at Bessemer when registration was proceeding there. Although practically all of these Negroes were turned down, the chairman conceded that during the two registration periods in which he had served only 25 white people had been rejected.

Yet he insisted that the Negro is treated justly. "I don't know how the other boards did it, but we give every Negro who comes up here a fair test." He explained that the Negro applicant is asked to read a section of the constitution and to interpret it. If it happens to be the preamble of the constitution, he is asked such questions as: "What does domestic tranquility mean?" The registrar explained that very few Negro applicants had been able to answer this question, but that he did not reject them on the basis of one question. He had prepared, with the help of a lawyer, a whole series of questions. If it happened to be the second section of the constitution they were asked to read, the applicants would be asked to explain the functions of the three branches of government. The chairman obviously felt that he had worked out a perfect method from a legal standpoint for disfranchising the Negro.

The total number of Negroes identified as such on the quali-

3. Stoney's interview, Birmingham, Alabama, March 1940.

fied voting list of Jefferson County is as follows, by year: 1928, 419; 1936, 549; 1938, 712. The number of Negroes registered between the printing of the list in 1938 and 1940 was 166.[4]

A former clerk who served for three years in the registrar's office in Birmingham gave the following description of the methods of dealing with Negro applicants for registration. Negroes would be given applications when they came in. After they had filled them out, they were told that the office would notify them when to come back for examination. All of these applications were checked by the clerk with the criminal dockets. If the applicant had failed to mention on his application that he had been convicted of crime, no matter whether it was a felony or misdemeanor, his application was thrown out. If it was a felony and he noted it, the application would be discarded even if his citizenship had been restored. The clerk explained: "You know, when you check all the drunk cases and everything, there's hardly a nigger in town that isn't on the books." These Negro applicants were never notified. If they inquired, the court records would be cited and this was enough to frighten them into silence. A second inspection of the files picked out all of the schoolteachers, doctors, lawyers, and a few businessmen. These were notified to come on a special day set aside for their examination. The others were given examinations only if they raised too much disturbance. Those picked for examination were given very slight tests and almost all of them were registered. Those who raised objections were generally given very severe examinations and few of them would pass. This clerk thought that the reason the present board of registrars is able to eliminate practically all Negro applicants is because it is giving all of them the severe examination. He said that the old method of elimination had been worked out before "the nigger lodges began stirring up their members. I'm glad to see this new board keeping them out better. You've got to some way. If you don't, these damn politicians are going to start going out and saying 'Mr. nigger, I want your vote.'" And, with this, he spat in disgust.

A former member of the Jefferson County board said that

4. These figures were obtained by Stoney from the county board of registrars, March 1940. They do not agree with the estimates Arthur D. Shores made in the interview of 18 November 1939, cited above. Shores thought that, by the fall of 1939, three thousand Negroes were registered in Jefferson County, two thousand of them having been added to the rolls in 1939. On one occasion, he said, some three hundred Negro miners came to the registration office at once and were all registered. —ED.

black applicants for registration were taken care of by simply having them file applications. When the time for their examination came, the board sent for all of those whose applications indicated that they might be qualified. A list of questions on the constitution had been drawn up. To make things legal, these same questions were also used in examining a few whites whom they required to take tests. In this way, the board was "fairly successful" in preventing Negroes from registering. However, it was explained with regret that more and more Negroes are being educated to the point where they can pass any reasonable test. This woman warned: "It's a thing we are going to have to face. I don't know what we are going to do about it. I am strongly in favor of keeping the cumulative poll tax. It is the only thing in the world that will save us."

White Southerners are facile at conjuring up the awful things that would happen to the South should the Negro get the vote. A Democratic official in Jefferson County pointed out that if such were the case, Negro voters would be bought at "fifty cents a head" and "herded like sheep" into the polls as they had been herded before 1901. He expressed the belief that only the cumulative poll tax and strict registration would serve to keep Negroes out, because "So damn many of them are being educated by the state now that you can't keep them out by the literacy test. We've found that when they get educated, they tend to become radical." This informant expresses the belief that if Alabama did away with the cumulative poll tax, "thousands" of Negroes would be brought into the border counties of the state and voted by "industries and labor unions—it don't matter which." He charged that the "labor unions" are getting to be so powerful in Birmingham, especially among the Negroes, that it will take eternal vigilance to keep them in check.

A barber who is a beat committeeman for one of the larger boxes in Ensley (an industrial community on the outskirts of Birmingham and the home of a large steel mill), and who is also an officer in the Ensley Italian Club, was shaving a white man from Cullman County while discussing politics in Jefferson County. He mentioned that there are several colored voters in his beat, that they take a great deal of interest in elections, and "hardly ever miss." The man from Cullman then remarked, "They ought to kill every one of the bastards that does." The Negro shoe-shine boy was working on the Cullman gentleman's shoes at the moment. The barber asked "Shine" whether he had ever managed to get registered. The young Negro fumbled uncertainly, uneasy under the harsh stare of the man from Cullman, and replied: "Naw sir, we had a meeting up to the Masonic Lodge Hall [the location of the Birmingham NAACP] and they told us all to go register. I went down there and filled out some old blank they give me. I ain't heard nothing from it."

The Negro recording secretary of the Birmingham Negro Smelter Workers' local registered on 6 December 1939. He relates that in his examination he was asked—among others—the following questions:

1. What form of government do we live under?
2. Name the three branches of government and tell the function of each.
3. Name the two houses of Congress. Tell how the members of each are elected.
4. How is the number of representatives determined?
5. What is the Bill of Rights? Name some of its provisions.
6. From what country did our form of government originate?

He states that after he had fully answered all of these—which took some twenty minutes of oral examination—he was told to step aside. He moved away about twenty feet. The registrars conferred for a few minutes and then told him that he was "unanimously passed." As he put it, "That meant I could vote as soon as I paid $21 poll tax." And he paid that tax the next day. This man had been filing completed applications every year since 1934.

His wife accompanied him to the examination and was tested following his success. The registrars would not let him stay in the room during her test. She informed him that she had been asked about the same questions and thought that she answered them correctly, but she was rejected. She is a graduate of a Negro college in Mississippi and taught school for several years. She was told by the registrars that they were not refusing her because she was from Mississippi; they also said that she "knew a lot more about the Constitution than most people who came up there, and if she would come back the next time she ought to be able to pass." Her husband, the recording secretary, had had no schooling above the sixth grade, but had studied for two years in the WPA adult education class held in a Negro church in Birmingham, and this had given him the knowledge necessary to answer the questions put to him.

Another Negro—a man of forty-nine—who had accompanied these two to the examination had an unsuccessful quest. He, too, thought he had answered the questions all right, and he had also studied in the WPA school. When he was rejected, the registrars told him that they would be glad to give him a list of the questions, and that he could take his case before the court if he was not satisfied with the treatment accorded him. He was given no reason for being turned down. As he describes it, "They told me to come back in April and I could try again." In answer to the question as to whether he would do so, he said: "Sure I am. I'm going up there till they get so tired of me they'll put my name on the book just to get shed of me. It might be best for me not to get registered for a couple more years, anyway. It'll take me that long to save up the poll tax I owe."

The head district organizer of steel workers in Birmingham, although engaged in a campaign to register the Negro members of his union, expressed some reservation about the general right of Negroes to vote. This organizer, a Welshman, had chosen and schooled twelve Negro members of the union for registration. Previously he had sent more than a hundred Negroes to the Bessemer courthouse to try to register in one day. They were turned away by the registrars with the excuse, "out of blanks." He was sure that the twelve Negroes subsequently selected and trained knew more about the constitution "than the registrars themselves." The Negro schoolteacher who tutored them got through, but all twelve of these black applicants were turned down. Said the district organizer: "I'm not so sure about this question of the Negro voting. It's all right for us and the men in the union. We know they will vote with us, but how about those in the black belt around these plantations? They can't help but vote the way their landlords want them to vote. . . . I don't know whether I think it's a good thing or not."

The CIO in Alabama has been encouraging the poor white worker to pay his poll tax and has also begun to devote its attention to the political plight of the Negro. One local of the UMW in Walker County, organized in the Alabama By-Products Coal Corporation, borrowed $1,100 from the First National Bank of Jasper; it first compelled every white member to register, with the local advancing the poll tax, and then compelled every white member who had paid his poll tax to carry one Negro to the registration office and to help him qualify. The local advanced the Negro's tax. It is claimed that 485 whites and Negroes were registered in this way—of whom 267 were

Negroes. This occurred in 1937. Since then, it is further claimed by a CIO representative that seven large locals in the state, with a total membership of more than six hundred each, have adopted the same policy. Prior to the adoption of this practice in Walker County, only two Negroes and only 4 percent of the poor whites voted there.

The ability of Negroes to get registered in Tuscaloosa, Alabama, varies with the registrars. Some of these are favorable, while others deliberately make difficulties. All of them, however, have objected to wholesale Negro registration. Negro war veterans must qualify like any other black registrant, though this is contrary to law. According to two prominent Negroes, a few years ago it was possible "to get the names of a number of Negroes we wanted registered, take them into the office, and they would mail out the registration certificates. We've always endorsed our own people though they turned down some of the applications at times; if we brought too many, they'd hold us up, stall for time, and so forth." On occasion, when the registrars in Tuscaloosa have desired to stop some Negro from registering, they have applied the constitutional interpretation test. One Negro applicant, it is alleged, was told that he would have to recite the Constitution. The Negro went on to recite the Gettysburg Address, and the registrar said: "That's right. You can go ahead and register."

Negroes do not vote in the Democratic primaries at Tuscaloosa. All of the Negroes registered are said to be Republicans. A few years ago one Negro actually voted in the Democratic primary. In order to do so, he employed a white lawyer when efforts were made to stop him; when the lawyer accompanied him to the polls, he was allowed to vote. Negroes in Tuscaloosa do not state their party affiliations when they register. It is said that attempts are made to require black registrants to meet the three-hundred-dollar property qualification in order to register. Thus an ordinary Negro has no chance. The more advanced Negroes, it is claimed, are even encouraged to register, and the superintendent of education has invited Negro teachers to register. Negroes are encouraged to register, asserts the chairman of the local board:

> I tell the other members of the board we can get the poll tax out of them [Negroes]. I always have trouble about this with the new members. What I do, generally, is to call a meeting and explain the thing to them. I tell them the kinds of

niggers we got voting now, and I tell them how much poll tax we collect, and I generally don't have much trouble after that.

In 1935 the Tuscaloosa County superintendent of schools sent out a letter stating that all teachers—white and black— would have to have their poll taxes paid or their contracts would not be renewed. This threat was not carried out, but it frightened a large number of teachers into paying up. The chairman of the board of registrars states that he sent word to the Negro teachers that the board would hold a special night for all those who wished to come to register. This was done, he explains, to save them "embarrassment" and only after it had been noted that some of the Negro women teachers had shown signs of uneasiness when they had come in earlier. It is said that at this session the superintendent of schools came up and helped the Negro teachers fill out their blanks. No constitutional tests were given.

According to this registrar, only three Negroes are known to him to vote in the Democratic primary, and "they're good old niggers. Nobody fools with them." He does not think that other Negroes try to vote in the primary and feels quite sure that they would not be welcome. They do vote freely in the city elections, however, which are nonpartisan. He states that he has heard no complaint from the people in the county about Negroes voting and assumes that this is because Negroes do not vote in the primaries.

Not a great many Negroes apply for registration, however. Only about half a dozen were registered during the last ten-day period when over eight hundred people were put on the registration books. All of the Negroes who applied were accepted. All of these except one—an ex-soldier—were schoolteachers. The chairman of the board reports that, while some 10,000 whites are registered in Tuscaloosa County, only between 150 and 200 Negroes are on the registration list. This, he explains, results from the fact that Negroes "just don't care to register." He claims that he has never turned down a Negro applicant for registration. In a recent thirty-day registration period, he asserts, not a single Negro appeared for registration. Negroes in Tuscaloosa contradict this.[5]

It became increasingly difficult for Negroes to register in Tuscaloosa County after the split some fifteen years ago with

5. Gunnar Myrdal's interview, Tuscaloosa, Alabama, 17 November 1939.

the Republican "lily-whites." It became necessary for Negroes to go to one or another of the registrars at night and make bribes or promises of help in order to get registered. The two election boards prior to the present one made the Negro registrants memorize the constitution. Since the new chairman came on the board, however, things are reported to be somewhat easier. If the chairman of the board is not present, Negroes do not try to register, for the other members always try to hold them up. But even with the sympathetic chairman, Negroes find it impossible to get registered the first time and are told to come back. The chairman has registered several Negroes "after hours" who have been refused registration by his colleagues. In general, it is said, Negro teachers and veterans are now accepted without much question, whereas previously they were given examinations. Yet Negroes in Tuscaloosa wish that they might be registered in a "legal way," and there is a feeling that all who have been registered could be denied the right to vote if they were challenged. The wish is often expressed, too, that Negroes might register "without having to depend on favors."

It is estimated by Negro leaders that there are about five hundred Negroes on the registration books in Tuscaloosa County and that about three hundred are qualified to vote. The other two hundred can't pay up their poll tax. There are a great many other Negroes in the county who might be able to vote. For instance, there are a good many Negro veterans who could vote without paying taxes, but who have not registered. This is especially true of Negroes living outside of the city in the county. These Negroes, however, apparently cannot see any advantage in voting in the meaningless general elections. The Negroes in the city have the municipal elections to interest them.

Negroes have been regularly refused permission to vote in the Democratic primary. They are all "supposed to be" Republicans, though, actually, most of them vote Democratic now. Two or three Negroes do vote in the primary, but there is some doubt as to whether their votes are counted. About a dozen Negroes try to vote in the primary at each election. They call themselves Democrats and insist that they have a right to vote. They are generally held up, however, told that they must go to see this or that official, and are stalled off until the polls are closed.

In the city elections in Tuscaloosa, Negroes claim to hold a balance of power, for the city races are nonpartisan and often very close. This is the only time there is any semblance of real opposition to Negro registration shown by the general public—

in the registration period just preceding the municipal election. During these periods, when two or three Negroes go in to register, there is always cursing and mumbling among the white people in the halls. As a result of this, the chairman of the board of registrars has asked Negroes, if possible, to try to register at other periods, when there is less feeling.

The Civic League in Tuscaloosa, which is the chief Negro organization in town, carries on an active program of civic education among blacks, consisting mainly of encouragement to Negroes to register and pay their poll tax. There is also a Negro voters' organization which meets just prior to each election. Its main job is to get Negroes, especially young Negroes, to vote. When municipal elections come up, each candidate is invited to come before this group and speak. These meetings are never publicized. The leaders of the group interview each candidate about his intentions on matters affecting Negro welfare in the town. Following these meetings, the group holds a general discussion and the club selects the ticket it will support. These endorsements are kept as secret as possible, for the hint that a white candidate has received the promise of Negro support is often used in whispering campaigns against him.

The tax collector of Bibb County, a cotton-growing and mining county, is perhaps a fairly typical example of the Alabama courthouse official. George Stoney found him standing behind the elbow-high desk, rubbing his two-day growth of beard, spitting a stream of tobacco juice over a pile of tax ledgers into the sawdust bed of the stove, wiping his mouth on the sleeve of his gummy sweater, and readjusting the battered hat which he always keeps on in the office—while agreeing to give Stoney a few minutes of his "very valuable time." A good-natured man of not more than thirty, he seemed glad to talk with Stoney in order to break the monotony of chatting with the courthouse loafers and the shriveled old tax assessor who shares his office. The tax collector, whose office is in Centerville, was eager to tell Stoney about the "old nigger miner" who had come into his office and paid up $13.50 in back poll taxes. Only three Negroes had paid the poll tax. He referred to the Negroes sympathetically as "good old niggers" and stated that about twenty-five of them were registered for voting. The others, he said, could not pay their poll tax. He pointed out that a great many Negro miners had been trying to register, but added: "They been holding them out. I don't think they're gonna get away with it much longer. We got enough white men in the county to take care of them if they get out of hand. The reason they are fighting it so hard—just between you and me and the gatepost—is because them are CIO niggers." Of the twenty-five Negroes registered in Bibb County, two or three are schoolteachers and the others are old settlers. The few who vote do so in the Democratic primary as well as in the general election.

A registrar of Bibb County explained that there was some "trouble" about Negroes trying to register in the mining district town of Belle Ellen at the last registration period. It was said that about a dozen Negroes came in and tried to register. The registrars permitted all of these Negroes to fill out the blanks, and the registrars went back to that beat the next day to give them a special examination. Only one of them passed the test, however. The list of questions on the constitution was made out by the probate judge. This informant added, rather sympathetically:

> They studied, too. One of them was especially smart. We registered one old nigger who came in by himself. A second one was registered this past time—an old farmer, also a war veteran—but, we very seldom have one to apply. They're not interested in that kind of thing around here. I think those at Belle Ellen tried to register because somebody got after them.

Shelby Johnson, chairman of the Negro Voters' Club of Huntsville and operator of the "Grand Shine Parlor," is recognized by local whites as one of the "leading colored men" in town. He first registered as a voter in 1919 after he had "tried quite a few times." He kept going to the courthouse by himself or with one or another white man, but it was no use. Finally, he got three leading white men in the courthouse to go in with him and the registrar took him in. Since then he has been trying to help other Negroes to register. In the case of one of his recent successes, he had to go to the registration board four times before he finally got the man put on the books, just before the registration period closed.

Johnson states that he knows one of the Huntsville registrars personally and likes him "as a white man." But, he notes, the registrar carries on a policy that has been maintained for years in Huntsville—to register just a few Negroes to show that the county is within the law. He recently registered one of Johnson's friends "as a personal favor to me" and told Johnson when he did so "not to bring any more Negroes up there for another couple of years." Johnson, his wife, his son, and his daughter all vote, and, when they do so, it is in the Democratic "white" primary and in the city elections. They have had trouble at the polls only once, and that was in 1934 when "a man ran us away from the polls with a stick." He remarked that he and his wife did not "bother" to go back down to the polls at that time. They pay the poll tax.

Johnson explains that most Negro schoolteachers in Huntsville have not tried to register because "they are afraid for their jobs," and the same applied to the teachers at the A. & M. College. Nevertheless, a good number of Negroes in Huntsville have been trying to register for several years, but have always been turned down. He adds:

> You go up there, and they might tell you the blanks have given out or it's closing time. Most of the time they just walk out on you. The law says, they say, that all three of the registrars must be there before they can register a person. This isn't so, because I've seen them register white people when only one is there; but just as soon as they see a Negro coming, one of them gets up and walks out, and that's the end of it.

Shelby Johnson tries to get at least one Negro registered each registration period. And he knows the routine well. First, his Negro applicants are handed a blank—if the supply has not accidentally run out as it did on one occasion. The whites were allowed to use blanks that had been spoiled before, but the Negro he had with him on that occasion had to come back. Then they are told to fill out the blanks. For whites, the registrars fill the blanks out themselves. By the time the Negro has filled out the blank, one of the registrars has slipped out and they cannot legally register, they say, because all three of the registrars are not present. The Negro is then told to come back later. When he does, it is "after closing time." Closing time may be anywhere from two o'clock in the afternoon on. Or the officer may look over the application and claim to find mistakes in it. He cancels the blank and tells the applicant he must come back and try again. If the Negro applicant refuses to leave when the third officer steps out and decides to wait until he comes back, the registrar (a) temporarily closes the office, forcing him to leave, or (b) ignores his application entirely, making him wait around until all whites are served and, incidentally, until it is "too late" again. Meanwhile, remarks are often made to try to intimidate, or, more often, to embarrass and ridicule the applicant and any people who happen to be with him. Johnson says that Negroes in Huntsville are often left off the poll list, especially new registrants. He does not know whether this is intentional or not, and, in any case, he has never known Negroes to have trouble getting on the supplementary list when they have appealed to the probate judge.

A registered Negro voter in a northern Alabama mill town explained the procedure whereby it was possible for him to get him son registered by exercising his personal friendship with a registrar.

> When I carried my boy up there to be registered, he told me to go home and he would see me later. That night he came down here and registered him here in the shop. He took a chance. It's against the law, and I hope you don't let this get out, because I don't want to get Mr. _____ into any trouble. He told me he wanted to see my boy registered, but he didn't like to have Negroes hanging about where they were registering people. He said the other registrars didn't like it, and the public might not understand. . . . I wish my boy hadn't had to register that way. You can't enjoy your privileges when you get them through the back way like that. . . . We don't want to see Negroes in office. Things are in a bad enough mess as they are without us making them any worse, but we do want a little protection.

The circuit judge of Madison County is rather circumspect in his discussion of Negro registration and voting in the county. He told Stoney:

> No, there has been no effort on the part of anyone, to my knowledge, to register the Negro citizens. Some of them have registered themselves—some few—I don't know how many. I have heard the registrars talking among themselves, and I judge from what they say that they would not be friendly to Negro registration. Of course, they cannot prevent a man from registering, according to the law, solely on that ground. I hope they do not do this, but I cannot say.

The Republicans have shown no interest in the Negro vote in Huntsville.

A Negro teacher in Madison County, who has been teaching since 1920, is a registered voter. He explains that when he first registered, he was "a young man and didn't mind pestering them to death." He went to the registration office three times and every time one of the registrars would walk out. Then the others would say that they could not register him until all three of the registrars were present. Finally, he got a letter from the superintendent of schools and got one of the courthouse officials to go in with him. They then signed him up, explaining when they did so that it was done "for the sake of the principal" and "so they would be complying with the law." But they added that they would not register any more Negroes that year.

In 1928 this man fell behind with his poll tax and did not qualify for voting again until 1940, when he paid eighteen dollars in back taxes. He proudly displayed his poll tax receipt. He voted first, he explained, because the president of the normal school at that time had urged him to try it. He paid up so much back poll tax this year because he has come to believe more than ever that Negroes must vote to secure their rights. His wife does not vote. He took her to the registration office a couple of times, but each time one of the registrars "walked out on her. She got disgusted and won't go up there any more."

Another Negro teacher, who had lived and voted in Indiana and Missouri, ran into a stone wall when he attempted to register in Madison County. He first tried to register in the county in 1937; the county officials refused to accept a transfer from Missouri because that state does not require the poll tax. He explained his experience in these attempts to register:

> I got into the office sometime after 3:00 o'clock. A school teacher, you know, can't go to town in the middle of the day. They told me I would have to get some qualified voter to vouch for me. I went out and got lawyer Grayson [a white man, trustee of the normal school and referee in bankruptcy]. When we got back, they said it was "closing time," but the clock said it was a little after 4:00.
>
> In 1939 I tried again—three times. At the first attempt I stood around for quite some time before I could get their attention. They were busy writing in their books, sharpening their pencils and straightening up the papers on the table. After a while I saw that I was being evaded. One of them stepped out to get a Coca Cola, and before he came back, the second man went out. Finally, I went up to the chairman, John Hampton, and told him I wanted to register. He looked up at me and asked: "Who sent you here?" I told him, no one. He said: "What makes you think you can register?" I told him I thought I was qualified. I said this as politely as I knew how.

Then, he asked who would recommend me. I gave him the names of several influential persons in town who had promised to help me: the superintendent of the city schools, Mr. Todd of the Risin Bank. . . . He said I would have to have them in person.

I went out and in ten minutes, I was back with Mr. Brewster, a white man who works at Humphrey's Pharmacy. The chairman tried to get Mr. Brewster off to one side and whisper to him, but I heard enough to know he was persuading him not to sign for me. When he told Brewster he would have to put his name on the application, he said he had better not do that. I guess he was afraid they might put his business on the spot.

I went and talked the matter over with Superintendent Brown [white superintendent of schools]. He expressed eagerness to recommend me. He implied he would sign my application, but preferred to do it in his office. Mr. Hampton would not let me take out the application.

The second time I tried was a day later, carrying with me a qualified Negro voter, Mr. Patterson [a filling station owner]. They were all busy when I got there and before they got around to me, it was "closing time" again. Other people were still registering, however. I asked two of the registrars when closing time came. One of them told me it was 3:30 and the other said 4:00 o'clock. Finally, they told us we would have to get out, and they closed the door. I waited around and noticed a white couple walk in. . . . I went around to the other door and walked in. I found the board registering these two people. In the meantime, my witness had gotten a white person to come in with him. He is a clerk from Judge Butler's office, I think. He insisted that I be registered. Even at his insistence, Mr. Hampton would not register me. He said it was too late.

The third time was a week or so later. I carried Dr. Cashin, a qualified Negro voter, with me. Finding that I was going to be persistent, the chairman gave me the answer he should have given me the first time. When I asked him for an application blank, he said: "You're a school teacher, aren't you?" "Yes," I said. "And, you're supposed to have some sense." I told him I might not have as much as many people think I should have, but that I thought I was qualified to vote. "Do you know the purpose of the Constitution adopted by the state of Alabama in 1901?" I told him I did not know to what specific matter he had reference. "I'm going to tell you. It was adopted for the purpose of disfranchising the Negro." "For that reason you are not going to register me?" "I think not." That was the end of it. I told him I was going to take up the matter in the court and walked out. Next time, I'm going to take a lawyer with me. We're going to push this thing through.

This man believes that there are "a great many people— white and black"—who are not qualified to vote in the county. He states that he has seen white people registered who could not write their names: "They would have to hold their hands while they made the cross." There were 109 Negroes registered in Madison County in 1902. This is the top figure for this county; 1908 saw a few more registered, and then scarcely a Negro was registered until 1919. A few more were then able to register, until 1924, and then there were none until 1930. In 1902 there were a number of Negroes registered in the rural boxes, but now there are only four.

A Negro teacher in the Negro high school in Huntsville has tried twice to register. His first experience was two years ago, when he was told that there were no blanks available. On his second attempt, during the registration period for 1939–40, the office was "closed in my face." He is not very enthusiastic about registering now because it would require him to pay twelve dollars for delinquent poll taxes. Three of his fellow teachers vote, but two of these are absentee voters in other parts of the state. He explained that, while the teachers talk about voting, they have the feeling that it is hopeless to try. The women teachers dislike the treatment they expect to receive when they make the effort, and the men find it difficult to raise the poll tax money. As he put it, "It's hard to pay Alabama poll tax on an Alabama standard of living."

The principal of the Negro high school at Huntsville, E. Z. Matthews, first registered in Sheffield in 1917. His wife was also registered there. In 1937 he tried to transfer this registration to Randoph County, where he was teaching. The probate judges in both places agreed, but the board of registrars of Randolph County refused. The board explained that no Negro had registered in that county since 1902. Eight Negroes were on the books from that date. Thus, it was necessary for the Negro principal to transfer his vote back to Sheffield and vote absentee. He has not yet attempted to transfer his vote and that of his wife to Huntsville, though he intends to do so.

Matthews related that when he first went to vote, the registrar flatly refused him, saying he had never registered a Negro before. He was principal of the school at Sheffield at that time and appealed to a prominent white politician. This politician wrote across the application, "Please register Professor Matthews. He is all right." After that, according to Matthews, "The registrar was the height of politeness because I had the backing of the strongest men in the county. That's the only reason most of us get on the books."

It was not this easy to get his wife registered, however, although she became one of the first two Negro women in Sheffield to register. There was great fear, he explained, that many Negro women would come and register in 1920 because they did not have to pay back poll taxes. He and his wife went to the registrar's office at 1:30 P.M. The registrars refused to take them until about 5:00 P.M. Then, finding that she was a schoolteacher, they stopped asking her about the constitution. The two of them kept sitting there until about six o'clock. The registrars wanted to lock the door, but they kept sitting there, so a registrar went over to the desk, wrote a couple of minutes, and shoved a piece of paper in Mrs. Matthews' hand. "What's this?" Matthews asked him. "Damn you," said the registrar. "That's it!"

Another Negro schoolteacher in Madison County was registered in 1937, but has never voted due to inability to pay the back poll tax. He would have had to pay $13.50 in order to vote this year. He is the son of Huntsville's best-known Negro citizen, the messenger and porter in the Risin Bank. Consequently, he states, he had "no trouble" when he went to register, because his father was so well known. He went to the registrar's office

> a couple of times, and Mr. Hampton [the registrar] put me off, so I went to the mayor of the city and got a statement from him. When I got back, Mr. Hampton said it was closing time, but when he read the note from Mr. McCollister [the mayor], he said it was all right. He asked me a few questions about the constitution and made me fill out the blank without explaining what he wanted in the places. I did that all right. Then he asked me if I owned enough property to vote. I told him I was paying taxes on an automobile. He made me go get a statement of taxes on that and then gave me my certificate right off.

This Negro teacher's father, the "respected colored citizen," had registered in the early 1920s. He said that he had had no trouble because two men at the bank where he is employed went over with him. He pointed out that at that time the Negro vote was especially important to these men because they were fighting the Ku Klux Klan. They found that, of the three or four hundred members of the Klan, only fifty were registered voters. There were that many Negro voters. The "men at the bank" let the candidates know this and helped end the power of the KKK in local politics. The older man, David Kelly, explained that he thought the registrars were right in letting only the Negro with property vote. It is better for relations with the "white folks" if only the "highest type of Negro" takes part. "Then they'll see how well we can conduct ourselves." He also said that Negro voters now accept a certain amount of responsibility for the welfare of other Negroes in town, and they are looked to by the whites. If a great many Negroes start voting, especially the "wrong kind," Huntsville will be "as bad as Chattanooga."

The Reverend Z. K. Jackson, who is the Negro pastor of the M. E. Church in Huntsville and who moved to Huntsville from Gadsden a year and a half ago, had his vote transferred in December 1939. One of the registrars lives near the Reverend Jackson and knows his personally, so there was "no trouble" when he had his registration transferred. He is also a war veteran.

Governor Bibb Graves made a speech to the schoolteachers of the state over the radio a few years ago, urging all of them to register and vote. Following the speech, Negro teachers in Randolph County—and in several other Alabama counties— tried to register. Three of them in Randolph County were turned down flatly by registrars who had been appointed by Governor Graves.

In Macon County the chairman of the board of registrars declares that the only "trouble" the registrars have had is with the orderlies from the Veterans' Hospital at Tuskegee. The middle-aged lady who is serving as chairman of the board and is now in her first term admits that she knows little about it, and she states: "Honestly, it's awful the way they are doing. Oh! They come in and they say they have been here two years when they haven't. They are not really intelligent Nigras like the ones out at Tuskegee, you know. We have to ask them a lot of questions about the Constitution and everything to keep them out." These questions on the Constitution, she explained, were made out by state senator Watkins Johnson, chairman of the county Democratic committee. The chairman admitted that she had to learn the answers to these questions herself! But even this device did not work too well, she averred, because "most of the boys knew a lot about that. I think they had been studying." So the registrars began to require all of the Negro applicants to have three hundred dollars worth of property on which they pay taxes in Macon County, and even then two or three of them got by because they owned cars.

There has been trouble for Negroes attempting to register in Macon County all along. One of the most active Negro political leaders, Archie Yates, recites some of his experiences in taking other Negroes regularly to register:

> First, they started making you get two witnesses to vouch for you—two legal voters. When we got that easy, they made us get two white witnesses. I started putting pressure on people who I trade with, and they signed for them all right. Then, they started saying we had to get two white people who worked in the courthouse. Then was when we started putting pressure on candidates we'd supported. Now, they'll let us sign with about anybody. . . . They've started this year asking a lot about the Constitution. They found out we know about that. One doctor from the Veterans' Hospital scared them to death. He started rattling it off from memory so fast they couldn't stop him for five minutes.

Other Tuskegee Negroes who have desired to register have studied the Constitution and find no difficulty in answering the questions. Quite lately the registrars have begun to require that everyone have property—even soldiers who have discharges —and Yates exclaimed: "I know that's not legal!" Consequently, he never likes to take anyone to the registrars' office who does not have both education and property. He does not encourage the orderlies from the hospital to go, because they have no property and are not well known in the community. He states: "They get turned down, and it's bad for our record. A lot of them got turned down last time. They weren't all high goods."

Yates says they had to "get after" the principal of Tuskegee in order to persuade him to register. Now that he has registered, it is thought that it will be easier to get other Negroes from the Institute to try. In former years there was a small group of "old Republicans" at Tuskegee Institute, and the county Republicans would make regular pilgrimages to the Institute before the presidential campaigns in order to enlist the support of this group. Yates claims that the Negro vote in Tuskegee has been a controlling factor in recent town elections—this, despite the fact that less than a hundred Negroes are registered. Those Negroes who are able to register, however, are permitted to vote in the white primary.

The present tax collector, who was elected in 1938, came out to Tuskegee, asked for the Negro vote, and promised to treat Negroes well if elected. At this same time a candidate for state senator, an attorney from the town of Tuskegee, publicly stated that he did not want the Negro vote. He called upon the county Democratic committee to seek a court injunction to prevent Negroes from voting in the primary. The Democratic committee, however, refused the request, and the candidate was defeated. Most of the Negro votes at Tuskegee come from the ranks of the war veterans.

At the last election for tax collector of Macon County, the incumbent saw—at three o'clock in the afternoon on election day—that he needed votes, and his supporters hired the Negro taxi in the town of Tuskegee to bring black voters to the polls. Negroes came for the ride, but they had already promised to vote for the man who now has the office. It is claimed that, in return for the black vote, the Negro has gotten better treatment in the courthouse. He is no longer pushed aside to make room for white customers but is taken in turn when he comes to pay his taxes. It has been possible to find whites to vouch for Negro registrants as a result of business contacts with them. Insurance agents, car salesmen, and so forth, are usually willing to vouch for black registrants for fear of losing Negro business.

In Union Springs, Bullock County, Alabama, Dr. and Mrs. Smith are Negroes who have recently succeeded in registering. Dr. Smith is a dentist and runs a grocery store. It cost them over fifty dollars to register, but he states that he did not mind paying that amount. "That is nothing to pay for American citizenship. . . . A man is not a citizen of this great country unless he votes. Do you know that?" Dr. Smith, feeling this way, had gone to the former probate judge of the county several times to ask his aid in getting himself and his wife registered. The judge had refused, stating that people in the county would not like it. The present probate judge is his friend, however, and when he went to see him, he was told that it would be all right if he could get the backing of some other white people in town. Then Dr. Smith got the mayor's endorsement. With a grin and a wink, Dr. Smith said: "The mayor is my friend. He's a wholesale grocer." The registrars asked no questions. They had him fill out his blank and his wife's, and then said they hoped that the Smiths would always be as good citizens in the future as they had been in the past.

Dr. Smith knows of no other Negroes in Union Springs who have tried to register. He feels that a few of the educated Negroes in the town could be registered if they tried. The principal of the Negro high school had said that he might lose his position if he tried to register. Dr. Smith is of the opinion that it is not the poll tax nor even the registration difficulty that is keeping other Negroes from registering, but ignorance, since "most Negroes don't have sense enough to vote." He added that he "did not think they ought to try until they are educated," though "it's all right for us who are ready for it." As Stoney noted, Smith seems to have much more interest in being one of the only three Negro voters in town than in trying to increase that number. His wife, a near-white mulatto, also thought that there were "not many more people around here who would know how to vote." The wife's main concern was over the fact that when the list of Negro voters was published, the designation "Mrs." had not been placed beside her name, nor "Dr." beside his, as it is done in Montgomery. The third Negro voter in Bullock County is an elderly retired schoolteacher. The Negro chauffeur of one of the registrars states that he was not permitted to register when he had suggested it because "niggers don't vote much down here. . . . They don't let us, that's all."

In Montgomery County, Alabama, an entirely different process is employed for the registration of Negroes and whites. It is admitted that the reading and writing test is never used by the registrars who make out the blanks for most applicants, as the questions are asked orally. The applicants must sign their own applications. Ordinarily, only the first two sheets are filled out; the third sheet—for witnesses—is left blank, except in a very few cases where the registrars have reason to doubt the veracity of the applicants. For the registration of Negroes, however, everything is different. Negro applicants are required to fill out their own blanks. One of the registrars explained: "They can't take it outside to fill it out. We make them fill it out right in front of us." Then they must have two white people, qualified voters, to sign their blanks. A very few of the Negro applicants bring their witnesses with them. Most of them give the names of two people who they think will sign for them. These are instructed to go out and get the white people, and have them come in to sign personally. The applications are held throughout that registration period and then destroyed if the signers do not appear. Few of the signers appear, it is said. When they do appear, these white witnesses are questioned—unless they are prominent people—about how long they have known the Negro seeking registration, how long they have known him as a resident at his present address. If the witness has not known the applicant for most of his life, his signature is rejected. Since so many Negroes in Montgomery have moved in from other places, it is particularly hard for them to find suitable witnesses. A registrar described this process with many illustrations, citing one case after another where Negroes had failed to get on the books because of its application.

This registrar also told, with a good deal of color and emotion, of the "eloquent plea" made by a group of prominent Negro doctors and educators before the registration board. They were requesting that Negro voters be allowed to act as witnesses for Negro applicants. The registrar, an elderly preacher, indicated that he sympathized with these men and praised their ability, but cautioned: "You know that wouldn't ever do. I think every white person at that meeting admired those men for what they done with themselves, but you know what that kind of thing would lead to."

The Negro Civic and Improvement League, Inc., submitted the following tactfully worded petition to the county board of registrars in 1938 in an effort to ease the harsh registration requirements applied to Negroes. The petition declared:

That the Negro Civic and Improvement League Inc. of Montgomery, Alabama, represents a large group of Negro citizens, who are embracing the principles of good citizenship, observance of law and order and are ardent supporters of both the federal and state constitutions. While the leadership of the organization is selected largely from the ministers, teachers, business and professional element of our race, the membership is made up of an appreciable number of the common folk who are intensely interested in the welfare of our great state and in the educational, civic and political improvement of the Negro race.

We are deeply grateful for the many considerations which your race and this board in particular have extended our race, we believe that much more good can be accomplished by your sympathetic consideration of this petition.

1. It is the custom of the Board of Registrars to require two

white persons to come in person and endorse or recommend all Negroes who make application for registration. This requirement seriously handicaps many eligible Negro citizens from becoming registered because of their inability to get their white friends to make the sacrifice necessary to appear in person. There is also the embarrassing aspect of not being able to use reputable members of their own race who are themselves qualified voters.

2. It is reasonable to expect any one who vouches for or recommends one for registration, that they should know something of the character, education and integrity of the individual and their interest in community welfare. It is obviously true that white persons have rather limited opportunity to know our race in such a manner.

3. In Jefferson, Mobile and other counties in the state Negroes are registered and voting in much larger numbers than in Montgomery where our state capitol is located. The white citizens of our county often aspire for positions in the state and federal government which is within the gift of the electorate but Montgomery's colored electors cannot contribute much to the success of a Montgomery County candidate as compared with the Negro electors of other counties because of the few that are qualified.

Although the county board of registrars granted a hearing to the league's leaders on 18 July 1938, it would not agree to change its practice in requiring two white endorsers of Negro applicants for registration.

The Negro population of Montgomery has thus had considerable difficulty in getting on the registration rolls. About sixteen Negro war veterans were taken to the registration office, but only two were able to get through. One of them was spoken to very roughly, and he left in humiliation. The first time the president of the Negro normal college attempted to register— this being before he was well known in the community—he was told that there was no blank to give him. A couple of years ago, however, he registered without any difficulty. After getting registered, he encountered two young Negroes who asked him to go into the office and aid them in getting registered. He did so, and the woman at the desk became very irritated, asking him pointedly if he knew "what he was doing for these boys."

Some two or three years ago there were about 265 Negroes registered in Montgomery out of a black population of 29,000.

At the present time, however, there are less than one hundred Negroes on the registration rolls, due to failure to pay the poll tax. About four years ago Montgomery Negroes tried to vote in the Democratic primary and approached the county Democratic committee on the subject. They were told by the secretary of the committee that the Democratic party "is a private party, like a social club. We can take in or reject whoever we please. In other words, it is for white people." Until two years ago the sheriff, now no longer in office, would turn Negroes back during registration periods by yelling at them: "Go back, you can't register." Practically all of the Negroes who are registered in Montgomery come from the upper ranks of the Negro society. It is well known in the city that the white population is willing to permit a "token" registration of this kind.

Two prominent Negroes in Montgomery went to register in 1939. One of them filled out the blank and was asked to bring two responsible white citizens up to the registration office to endorse him. Although the president of a local bank had endorsed this Negro applicant, he did not get registered. It is said that this requirement of the white character witnesses was started in Montgomery only in 1937. Until that time, responsible Negro citizens might be used as character witnesses. In fact, it is said that on one day in 1936 two prominent Montgomery Negroes remained at the registrar's office all day as endorsers of Negro registrants and were able to put through 156 Negro voters. Following this episode, however, Negro endorsers were no longer acceptable at the registrar's office.

A Negro member of the American Legion (it is said that there are approximately 1,500 Negro ex-servicemen in Montgomery County, and these do not have to pay poll tax) tried to register at Montgomery many times. On one occasion he presented his American Legion card, but was told to get two white citizens who would not only endorse him, but who would vouch that he would vote for no ticket other than the Democratic or Republican. Apparently there was fear that he would vote a Socialist or Communist ticket. The applicant resented this and refused to follow these instructions. He went in to see two "big white men," but they were too busy to accompany him to the registration office. One of them, however, connected with a very large furniture company in the city, telephoned the registration office and tried to endorse him in that way, but was told that this was unacceptable. He would have to come up and sign on the dotted line. This was in 1937. A prominent Negro also tried to act as endorser for him, but was refused. A Negro came to Montgomery from Tuscaloosa County and presented his registration certificate from his home county, and was told to "go on back to Tuscaloosa to vote."

The superintendent of education in Montgomery County some four or five years ago made it known that he desired that all teachers—white and colored—be registered voters. The local press printed this news and gave it a good deal of attention. On one occasion thereafter there were thirty Negro teachers waiting to register at the courthouse. It was the last day of registration, but they were told to wait and were left waiting after four o'clock when the office closed. Then a white official came out and told them: "Go on home. You girls needn't worry about it, you won't lose your jobs." The teachers are still not registered, and the superintendent of schools has said nothing more about it. In 1921 a Negro letter carrier thought that his uniform would see him through the registration procedure, but the registrar of the county told him when he explained his desires: "If you don't stay out of here, I'll show you how far that uniform will carry you." He kept going back, however, and finally was able to get two acceptable white men to vouch for him and was registered.

In the three terms that the present chairman of the board of registrars of Coffee County has been serving, only one Negro applicant for registration has appeared. This was a man who had recently moved into the county and wanted to have his vote transferred. The registrars persuaded him that it would be better if he voted absentee in the other county. "We told him how people in this county feel about it, so he decided to take our advice." It is thought that there are still four or five Negroes on the voting list in Coffee County—those who have been on for a very long time and who are now very old and never vote. The chairman of the board says: "We aren't troubled with that here. The people wouldn't stand for it. Now, I recognize that some niggers are capable of voting a lot more intelligently than a lot of white men who do vote. They are the exceptions, of course, and I believe they've got sense enough to know why white people don't want them to vote." The chairman can remember when the landlords brought their Negro tenants to town in wagon loads back in the 1890s in Tuscaloosa County and "voted them like so many sheep. They'd do it again if you let them." This expression of fear of the Negro vote, so often repeated, is thus not a fear of the Negro vote per se, but allegedly of the Negro voter as a weapon in the hands of unscrupulous or untrusted whites.

In Dallas County a Negro "radical" was refused registration two years ago. This man had been one of the lieutenants in the "Communistic" attempts to "cause trouble" on plantations in Dallas County. He had come into the registrar's office, it is said, "sneering like he didn't much care." The registrars asked him if he could read; he replied "not much," and gave the same response as to writing. The registrars then asked him if he knew anything about the Constitution, and he replied that he knew a little. Then, according to one of the registrars, "We showed him enough to let him know we could keep him out so he didn't try to register. He walked out. . . . This is the only time we ever tried to scare a man."

The "trouble" on the plantations referred to was an attempt to organize a sharecroppers' union. Again, according to the registrar, two white men—one from New York, the other from Philadelphia—came into Dallas County and started "stirring up" Negroes out on the plantations. A couple of meetings had been held, and then a white citizens' committee was formed. The sheriff accompanied this citizens' committee of about forty members to the Negro church where the white organizers were addressing a group of Negroes. The armed members of this committee disarmed the speakers, took them outside the church, stripped them, and beat them in the light of a fire so that the Negroes could see what they were doing. Then they took them to the county line and let them go. Said the registrar: "They didn't beat them hard; just enough to humiliate them and show the niggers what they thought of these white men by beating them before niggers."

It is estimated that there are about twenty-five Negroes qualified to vote in Hale County. Three of these have registered during the past five years. One Negro, who was registered two years ago, discovered that he owed thirty some dollars in back poll taxes and never paid it up. In the 1939–40 registration period another Negro registered but failed to pay the fifteen dollar back poll tax owed and thus could not qualify for voting. Another Negro applicant attempted to fill out his own application but gave up in the middle of it. The registrars of Hale County require Negroes to fill out their own applications, to give references, and to have those references come in and sign for them. No Negro schoolteachers in the county are qualified voters.

The chairman of the board of registrars dismissed the subject of Negro voting with the comment: "Niggers around here aren't interested in that kind of thing."

In 1938, and also at the last registration, the names of Mr. and Mrs. Joshua Owens—who run a small Negro business— were left off the voting list, as were those of almost all other Negro voters. Mrs. Owens pointed out that it had cost her husband thirty-six dollars and her fifteen dollars to get registered and pay their poll taxes in 1930. This couple had been able to vote in the November election of 1938 (though their names were left off the poll list) only because they went to the office of the probate judge and got a slip.

Negroes are not allowed to vote in the Democratic primary. Owens had tried in 1936. The primary official talked with him a long time and told him that, if he once voted for the Democrats, he would not be allowed to vote any other way in the future, etc. Owens still insisted, however, stating that he had voted for Roosevelt and would do so again. The primary official then pointed to the "white supremacy" emblem, told him that the primary was not supposed to be for him, and asked him if he wanted to be the cause of any "misunderstanding." Owens then walked out of the polling place in disgust. Since then Negroes have been omitted from the poll list. Negroes are not allowed to vote in municipal elections either, since these are partisan and are under the primary system.

It is said that the Negro community of Attalla, an industrial community on the outskirts of Gadsden, in Etowah County, Alabama, had some sixty Negro voters in the old days. Practically all of these had registered in 1902 or shortly thereafter, but the registrars would accept no more black voters until 1936. Most of the older voters have died out, and now there are seven Negro voters, with perhaps three others registered who are behind with the poll tax and so are not qualified.

Cady Lipscomb, Negro cafe proprietor of Attalla, was registered in 1939 and, to qualify for voting, had to pay poll taxes amounting to thirty dollars. In describing his experience at the registration office, he states:

> When I first went in there, they wouldn't wait on me. They was so piled up with white folks, they told me to come back. When I went back again, he [the registrar] says, "So, I see you've come back." I says, "Yes, sir." And I stood back right polite like. They didn't ask me to sit down like they have the

white folks when they ask questions. I don't mind that. I'd a-stood outside and hollered to get registered, but they was awful nice to me. I was dressed up sorta nice, you know, respectable like. . . . He asked me where my white man [witness] was. I told him he came in with me before and left, but I could go get him. He asked me if I got property and I showed him my receipts. "And I'm heir to $3,000 more," I said. "I don't care how much you're heir to," he said. . . . I don't think he liked to register me much.

The registrar asked Lipscomb the questions and wrote the application himself, which is the practice only when registering whites.

But a friend of Lipscomb, an ex-serviceman, had been refused at the registration office. He recalls: "They told me I had to be a property owner. The first time I went up there, they asked me to give references back for 20 years. I did that. I got a man to come up there that had known me for 40 years. Then, he [the registrar] asked me if I had any property. I said 'no.' He said, 'Then, you can't register.'" The person who had vouched for this Negro applicant was a white WPA road foreman. This experience had occurred during the first registration period; but the veteran did not give up, and during the second registration period he made three further attempts—all unsuccessful. In his first attempt during the second period, he was told that it was after closing time. The second time he went to the office to see the judge, who had promised to help him and who went in with him and whispered to the registrar. The registrar then asked if he had a witness to testify for him, but the foreman was not with him at this time, and he was told that he would have to come back again with a witness. On the third attempt, he went back with the foreman but found the judge busy and unable to come over to help him. The registrar flatly refused to register him, saying that he was not going to register any Negro who could not show property qualification.

This Negro veteran explains his interest in voting as follows: "Well, I'm getting on 52 years old. I've seen a lot of this county, and I've seen it bad. I want to be a citizen of this place before I die, and maybe cast a vote to better conditions around here. Look at this bunch [pointing to a group of young Negroes who were lounging about in the cafe]. We can't go on like that-a-way. You know that yourself." He also pointed out that he had made many applications for civil service jobs, as an ex-serviceman, and felt that he had always been turned down because he is not a voter. This man had been trained for three years at Tuskegee as an electrician. Lipscomb indicated that he had had no trouble getting white people to vouch for him because the salesmen who solicit his trade in the articles he sells in the cafe were all willing to help him out. Lipscomb's brother-in-law had also gotten registered and had to pay thirty-six dollars in back poll taxes. He thought this poll tax payment entirely unjust, not so much because of the amount, but because it made him pay "for something I didn't get to get," indicating that he considered the poll tax to be a payment for voting rather than for support of the schools.

Homer Battle, a Negro barber in Gadsden, Alabama, works in a shop that serves only whites. He is a registered voter. He got registered without much difficulty when a local white florist signed his papers. As he explains it: "I could have gotten lots of other white people, but I didn't want to embarrass them." He was required to show a receipt indicating that he was paying taxes on three hundred dollars worth of property. In his case, it was a receipt for an automobile tax. He had been trained at Tuskegee, and one of his teachers there had impressed upon him how much more the Negro might get if he registered and voted. He pointed out that:

> If we had 50 more Negro voters here, we could have a fine place fixed up for the Negroes in this little town. They have five playgrounds for white children and not one for the colored children. . . . I don't mean to say anything against our city officers. We have a fine bunch of white officers. They come in here to get a shave and I know all of them personally. They're nice to me, but they can't do much for you if you aren't a voter.

Battle has aided other Negroes in Gadsden in getting registered. He thinks, however, that Negroes are "wasting their strength" in getting people registered who are too far behind in their poll tax. He is of the belief that the registrars agree among themselves to register a certain number of Negroes each registration period. He also believes that Negroes have made "trouble" for themselves by encouraging people to go up to register who are not qualified—that is, who have not got three hundred dollars worth of property. During the past year, for instance, Battle himself took the son of one of the wealthier Negroes in town to the registration office. When the young man was asked for his property receipt, he displayed those for his father's property. The registrar refused to register him because he had no property in his own name. Battle thinks that it is "wrong" for the courthouse to ask Negroes to pay back poll taxes "when they didn't enjoy the privilege of voting those years."

Battle votes Democratic and votes in the Democratic primary. He says: "People come in here before elections, asking me to vote for first this one and then that one. I always take their cards and say, 'Yes, sir. Yes, sir.' I have to do that, you know, to be nice to people; but when I get there, I vote for the man I think is best."

Young Negroes are discouraged from voting because of the poll tax, and they keep hoping it will be modified or repealed. Among the class of Negroes in the South who are interested in voting, this hope that the poll tax will be repealed or modified, insofar as its cumulative features are concerned, is very great. It is estimated that there are about eighty Negroes registered in Gadsden, but only about fifty of these are on the qualified list, since the others have not paid up their poll taxes.

A Gadsden Negro undertaker, born in Alabama, is a member of the American Legion and saw service in the last war in France. He moved north with his family when young and first voted at twenty-one in New York City. He first voted in Alabama in 1927 in Birmingham. He was refused registration at first, but then he went to the commander of the American Legion for Alabama, who signed his application. At this same time forty-nine other Negro ex-servicemen were trying to register, but only two of them were successful. This man's wife is also a registered voter and had to pay $18.50 back poll tax in order to get on the qualified list. The undertaker had no trouble when he transferred his vote from Birmingham to Gadsden, because he was already a registered voter in Alabama, had property, and is an ex-serviceman. He realizes that Negroes in Gadsden have no chance to register unless they own property, and he suggests that the temporary exchange of property might be a means of getting around the registrars. He is especially disgusted at the way some of the white candidates try to get the black vote once the Negro gets on the roll. He referred to one candidate for the city commission, who came around to him and "honked his horn till I had to go out to his car to talk with him. He went up to Dr. Abbott's and sent somebody up to his office, and had him come all the way down to the street to talk to him. Hell! I'd buy white folks to vote against a man like that."

J. C. Shinault, an elderly Negro voter in Attalla, had registered in 1902. He explains that there was no trouble in registering in this early period, since he was a property owner and had
been active in politics before then. Professing to be an "independent" in politics, he generally votes in the Democratic primary, but in the general elections supports men on both tickets
according to his inclinations. He knows of no effort ever having been made by Republicans to aid Negroes in registering in
this section of the country. Now seventy-three years old, he
has been voting since he was twenty-one. He recalls having
made speeches in the campaigns of 1896–98 and in the "big
fight" just before 1901.

A member of the board of registrars in Gadsden observes:
"We do have a few Negras who register and vote. I think about
ten have registered since I have been on the board. They are all
property owners and good citizens, but we have to have some
way of preventing others from taking advantage of us."

One of the members of the Etowah County board is a woman
who runs a grocery store down in the hollow of North Gadsden,
on the border line between "nigger town" and the hill down below town and the railroad track, where some of the "less desirable" poor whites live. Most of her trade is with Negroes. Her
name has appeared on the applications of several Negroes who
have registered for voting in the last five years, and she has had
the reputation, among both Negroes and whites in the community, of being "very fair" about letting Negroes register. She
explains that not many Negroes vote in Etowah County

> because not many can qualify. We got school teachers that
> can read and write a lot better'n most white people. When
> they can, I don't think it's right to keep them from voting. I
> don't believe the law was made to disqualify them that's fully
> able to meet all the requirements. We got several niggers here
> in town that's good citizens and they register and vote. I
> think it's a good thing. I think if a nigger gets an education,
> he's as good a citizen as anybody else; besides, the money
> [poll tax] goes to a good cause. Every cent of it goes to educa-
> tion, and it educates his young'n just the same as it educates
> mine.

With regard to the applications of three or four Negro registrants which she signed, this registrar says: "Yeah, I signed for
this undertaker around here and his wife. They're good citizens.
They trade with me here, and I know'd them since they move

here. I signed for a colored school teacher. I know a good nigger when I see one. I was raised up with 'em. Three-fourths of my business is with 'em." She estimates that there are about forty Negro voters. She emphasizes that the registrars do not take just anybody's signature for Negro applicants. "It's generally a prominent lawyer or a businesswoman, or one of the registrars." When asked if another Negro voter might sign for a Negro applicant, this registrar responded:

> Lord, no! We wouldn't take *their* word. There ain't many that gets by me, I tell you. They have to be mighty *good* niggers to get by *me*. I don't want you to go tellin' nobody that, cause they'll think I'm discriminating when I'm not. I've been in nigger-town doing business for the past twenty years, and I've learned to tell between 'em. I ain't discriminating. If they can show where they're good citizens, I'll sign for them myself.

It is to be noted that this woman, who says she likes "niggers," is the most liberal official to whom prospective voters may turn in Etowah County. With this double responsibility on her shoulders, it is interesting to note her attitude toward the race question as indicated in the following story which she related:

> I was a-goin' up to Long Island to see my sister, and I know'd they didn't do things like we did up there, but I forgot all about it, you know. Well, I go into a railroad car and I see a coal black nigger a-settin' in almost every seat. Well, I turns around to go out, thinking I'm in the wrong car and I see a white man comin' down the aisle at me. "I guess we both got in the wrong car," I said to him and he laughed, fit to split. "Lord," he says, "I know'd you was from the South the way you come a-runnin'. Well, you just as well set down," he says, "cause you're gonna have this 'till you get back across the Mason-Dixon Line." [This man sat with her all the way up so she would not have to run the risk of having to sit next to a Negro.]
>
> Comin' back I was a-travelin' by myself. When I got in the car, I noticed there was a nigger in almost every seat and when another one'd get on, he wouldn't go sit with the other niggers. He'd go sit by a white woman. Look to me like they did it a-purpose. Well, I made up my mind no nigger was gonna sit by *me*, so I sits cross-wise and puts my feet up to take up the whole seat.

The conductor came by and told her she would have to put them down. She did so, but took out "a long fork knife I always carry in my pocketbook when I'm travelin' and laid it on the seat." She added that she would have used it "on any nigger that tried to sit next to me." She told the conductor this and he said he could do nothing about the situation. The thing for her to do, he advised, was to hail the first white woman to come on the train and have her take up the seat. When the seat next to her was almost the only vacant one left, a little woman going to Baltimore got on the train and agreed to save her from the supreme humiliation. The Southerner swore, with many a laugh and slap on her heavy thigh, that she would have "stuck that knife as far as it'd go" into "any black nigger" who might have tried to sit down next to her.

Refusal to register Negroes in Etowah County dates back to 1901, the year of the new constitution. Alabamians can recount endless stories concerning the "menace" of the Negro vote prior to the 1901 constitution. The postmaster in Alabama City in Etowah County, for instance, tells how his father helped haul Negroes "from one polling place to another, and the nigger vote was the deciding factor. Whoever could buy that up generally got elected. He [father] hated to do it, but it looked like it was necessary. The constitution of 1901 cut out all that." In the first registration after the new constitution, stories are told of how Negroes were rejected. For instance, one Negro brought documentary proof that his grandfather, a white man, was indeed his grandfather and had voted in 1860. He was "run out of" the polling place. Another Negro had been trained by a group of Republicans for the literacy test. He memorized the first sections of the state and national constitutions and began to recite them from memory at the polling place. He also had tax receipts to prove that he owned forty acres and three hundred dollars worth of personal property. Finally, he was refused registration when the registrars persuaded the white man who had come to sign his application to withdraw.

The chairman of the board of registrars of Etowah County states that not more than five or six Negroes have been registered since he has been on the board, though several others had "offered." He does not believe that Negroes ought to be allowed to register unless they pay taxes on five hundred dollars worth of personal property or own a home. He has refused to register all who could not show receipts for this amount, stating: "If you want my personal opinion, I think there are damn few niggers that ought to vote in any election. You can't show me more than two in a thousand who're not gonna vote for the first person who gives him two bits." Before the present chairman assumed office, according to his version, there were

> people on the board who didn't give a damn. They got pretty lax. The word got out among them [Negroes], and we had them coming in in droves, wanting to register. Well, I just told them they had to show me receipts or get a written statement from the tax collector's office that they owned $500 worth of property, or they couldn't register. There was damn few that could qualify. When they learned I meant business, they stopped coming, most of them.

The chairman admitted, however, that if these Negroes had gotten a lawyer and challenged him, he would have had to register them, "but they didn't come back."

When one of the registrars of Cullman County first came on the board of registrars in 1922, there were only two Negroes registered, and only four have registered since then. A friend of the registrar's who was with him when this statement was made—an accountant and American Legion leader who speaks with a decided German accent, was outraged to hear that the registrar had registered Negroes under the same rule as he did the whites. Said the registrar, defensively: "Hell, I can't do anything else. They've all got property and they've got a high school down in the colony [the Negro settlement]. They can read and write as good as you can." The registrar admitted, however, that he made the Negro applicants fill out their own applications, adding: "Under the law that's all you can do." The German inveighed bitterly about the "damn niggers. Dey stink. By George, ef one come around my place, I'll run a poker up his ass. . . . I can't stand to see the black bastards around." Referring to a Negro employed at the Cullman Hotel, the German added: "He won't stay here long. Some night somebody will run the son-of-a-bitch out of town."

It is said that there are only about 150 Negroes registered in Decatur, Alabama, and many of these never vote, through failure to pay up the poll tax. Those who do vote are permitted to vote in the Democratic primary, however. Since the Scottsboro case, Negroes have been called for jury service on both grand and petit juries, though they seldom actually sit on the jury because the lawyers utilize their challenges to keep them off.

Whenever Dr. Newlyn Cashin, a prominent local Negro, endorses a Negro, he can usually get registered. This is after the Southern pattern, for Dr. Cashin, who was born in Decatur and has been practicing medicine there for many years, is a typical example of the Negro middle-class black in the small Southern town who can command the ear and a certain amount of respect of the responsible whites in the community. According to Dr. Cashin, white candidates in Decatur have often sought the small Negro vote, and, in one instance, a candidate tried to buy the Negro vote with whiskey and food but was unsuccessful in his quest.

It is said that Negroes in Mobile had considerable difficulty in getting registered from 1935 until 1939, when a new board of registrars assumed office. About four years ago, Dr. Belsaw, a prominent Negro citizen of Mobile, took a well educated Negro minister down to register. The minister filled out his application, and then the chairman of the registration board informed him that he would have to interpret the United States Constitution. Some random passages from the Constitution were read to him, and he gave an excellent interpretation of them. Then the chairman of the board asked the following questions: "Under what form of government do we live? In how many branches is it divided? Who was the fifteenth vice-president of the United States? Who was the fifth attorney general of the United States?" The minister was unable to answer all of these questions, of course, and the chairman then told him: "You don't know the history of your country, and you cannot be registered." We were told that, except for this one registration board, which held office only for four years, the boards in Mobile have been fairly lenient toward Negroes. The new board promises to follow in the lenient tradition. Dr. Belsaw asked the registrar why he wished to be "so hard on this man—you know he's qualified to vote." The registrar replied: "Now listen, doctor, you know this law was passed to keep your race from voting."

Dr. Belsaw conducted down to the registration office another Negro, who informed the registrar that he wished to register under the property clause. The registrar said: "Do you own $300 worth of real estate?" The applicant replied: "Yes, sir." Said the registrar: "Well, how do I know you have?" The registrant answered, "I can show you my deed." The registrar: "That doesn't mean anything—it might be mortgaged." Applicant: "Well, I can go over here and get the records and show you there's no mortgage—it's mine." Registrar: "Aw, I haven't got any time for that—get out of line." The applicants for registration in Alabama, it should be noted, can take their option of the several ways of qualifying for registration. It is said that this same registrar informed a local citizen in Mobile that the reason he was not registering Negroes was because "every nigger that registered becomes a Holcome nigger, and I'm against him." Holcome is the local machine boss. In Mobile the only endorsement requirement is that of one qualified voter, and this endorser may be either white or Negro. However a registrant qualifies, the character witness must be produced.

Buford Boone, an editor, gives in an unpublished article a graphic description of the experience of one Negro at a Georgia registration office:

Take Ed Drummond, for instance. He's a young Georgia Negro who attended school long enough to hear a suggestion that, to be a good citizen, the Negro should take an interest in his government. And he heard that no citizen can be genuinely interested in his government unless he exercises the right of franchise.

Drummond reaches 21 and decides to register and vote. He goes to the awesome courthouse, where the tribunals grind away most of the time they are in session on cases against Negroes. He's a little ill at ease, because some message from the cautiousness and meekness which have been instilled in his being tells him he may not be doing quite the right thing. But it's too late to turn back.

"What do you want, boy?" someone on the inside of the tax collector's office asks.

"I just want to register so I can vote."

Then he gets the works. Since he's only 21, he doesn't have to pay poll tax. He says he has no criminal record—so far, so good. But wait.

"Do you understand the duties and obligations of citizenship under a republican form of government?" he hears.

"What do you mean by that?"

"Just what I said. Do you or don't you?"

"I don't know exactly. . . ."

"Well, do you own forty acres of land or $500 worth of property?"

"No-sir."

And if that isn't enough to discourage the applicant, he gets another test. He is required to read correctly any section of the Georgia or federal constitution, or he may be required to write any section when it is read to him. The man behind the counter is the sole judge of his success or failure. Usually the decision is negative.

"You can't qualify," he is told. A Negro graduate of Harvard University heard the same verdict in a Southern state a few years ago.

While there is no obstruction to the registration of Negroes in Atlanta, a spirit of intimidation is evident in some Georgia counties. It is felt that Negroes in a small county where the racial patterns are fixed would find shotgun parades, and so forth, if they tried to register in significant numbers. John W. Dobbs, a black political leader in Atlanta, estimates that there are approximately 2,100 Negroes registered in the city as of 1939. In 1936 there were less than 1,000. The incumbent tax collector of Fulton County has been very fair about Negro registration, as was his predecessor.

The Atlanta Civic and Political League was organized at a mass meeting held on Lincoln's birthday in 1936. The stated objectives of the league, which in recent years has been the most active Negro protest organization, are as follows: (1) to get ten thousand Negroes registered; (2) equalization of teachers' salaries; (3) appointment of Negro policemen and firemen; (4) appointment of Negro physicians and nurses in the city hospital; and (5) more parks and playgrounds for Negroes. The leadership of the league considers one of its most effective achievements to be the publication of a report worked up by a fact-finding committee detailing the discriminations against Negroes in Atlanta. The league contributed its support to the defeat of a bond issue to raise Atlanta's contribution to a WPA civic improvement program in 1938. The league opposed the issue because only a small sum had been allocated for Negro schools. The bond issue was voted down by a narrow margin, and the Negro vote, inspired to opposition by the league, was an important factor. On one occasion, when the league was holding a mass meeting in a Negro church, several cars full of unhooded white men attempted to intimidate the meeting by charging that Negroes were hatching a plot against the white people. The police were called and the whites were dispersed.[6]

6. This paragraph is comprised of statements from Ralph J. Bunche, "The Programs, Ideologies, Tactics, and Achievements of Negro Betterment and Interracial Organizations" (1940), pp. 609–11. —ED.

In an interview on 4 November 1939, Miss Josephine Wilkins, president of the Georgia League of Women Voters, expressed doubt that the registration of a large number of Negroes in Georgia would serve to break the white primary unless there were very special circumstances, such as the allegation of fraud. It is her opinion that if the white candidate broke the gentleman's agreement and ran in the general election, he would have no standing in his party and, except for very special circumstances, could not carry his white vote, obtained in the primary, to the general election. Ben Davis, a former Negro national Republican committeeman from Georgia, thinks that the white primary can be broken only if Negroes register "in such large numbers as to make whites bid for the Negro vote."

Until quite recently, there has been no difficulty in registration for Negroes in Savannah, Georgia. Until the appearance of the Young Men's Civic Club, Negro registration in Savannah fluctuated between 500 and 1,100 names, though it is estimated that the Negro registration should be in the neighborhood of 15,000. After the YMCC became active, Negroes began to be subjected to a requirement making them recite provisions of the constitution in order to qualify. In Savannah the only active Negro organization with a political purpose is the YMCC. Organized in October 1938, under the leadership of a young working-class Negro, it has as its sole purpose the registration of Negroes for voting. The organization is somewhat unique among Negro reform groups because its leadership is not selected from the elite and because its initial efforts were directed toward enlisting the support of the local Negro longshoremen's union in its registration campaign. In the words of George Fuller, its president:

> We had about thirty people in attendance at our first meeting. . . . We selected representatives to appear before all organizations with our message. We set up a registration committee. Then we set up districts and put out handbills two or three days in advance, announcing meetings in the several districts. On the day of the meeting we would take a band down to the meeting hall. We covered the city like this and got good crowds—250 to 300 in each district. Then we held general mass meetings in one of the Negro theaters. From the outset we stuck to one objective—registration of Negro voters. We held meetings once a week in each district—in churches, poolrooms, anywhere. Negro registration here is

now about 700 [an increase of some 300]. . . . We have set up an institute for the purpose of training our people how to qualify, and we don't let anyone go down [to the registrar] now until they have been through us.[7]

The Savannah registration list completed for use in the 1940 state primary and general election listed 729 Negroes and 14,395 whites, or a total of 15,124 registered voters. The tax collector estimates that about 35 percent of this total are women. He informed Stoney that he makes no difference in the registration of whites and Negroes. This does not seem to be borne out by the facts, however, for he declares: "We never had much trouble until two years ago. A bunch of them came up. Some of them looked like they were 35 or 40, saying they were 21. A lot of them got by before we caught up with it." Following this episode, he began requiring that Negroes show some proof of age—an insurance policy, a birth certificate, or a copy of a school certificate—and he claims that "this stopped the big rush. Niggers aren't going to pay poll tax to vote." Otherwise, he says, there is no difference in treatment, for "we're not allowed to make any difference."

The explanation given to Dr. Myrdal for the registration of so many whites and of so few Negroes is that: (1) whites are better off, more responsible (and thus can better afford to pay the poll tax), and have more interest in doing so; (2) more whites were soldiers in the World War or had ancestors in former wars; (3) whites have more property, and thus the poll tax is more easily collected; (4) whites, on the whole, are better educated and can meet the education tests better. The tax collector admitted that the education test is not always necessary with whites, because more whites have property assessed at five hundred dollars, more whites are veterans or descendants of veterans, and more whites are known to be of good character.[8]

The tax collector indicated the significance of the Constitutional reading and writing test with regard to any attempt by a large number of Negroes to register in Savannah, pointing out that one's ability to fulfill that requirement "depends upon the speed with which you read," explaining: "If I read a long paragraph as fast as I can read, I bet you can't write it." The tax collector felt that these methods of keeping any large number of

7. From ibid., p. 607. —ED.
8. Gunnar Myrdal's interview with John Cabell, tax collector, Savannah, Georgia, 1 November 1939.

Negroes away from the polls would hold up, first because of the effectiveness of the speedy reading technique, and secondly, because, as he explained it: "These middle-class, upper-class Negroes have the same contempt for the lower-class Negroes as we do. They don't want them to have the vote. There are class differences in the white society, but nothing like the stratification in the Negro community."

It is well known in Savannah that the tax collector does "make things a little hard" on Negroes, although the chairman of the board of registrars, a Jew and a Republican, said to Stoney: "Every darky that's really entitled to vote is on that list." He added that any Negro who can read the oath, who can write his own name, who can furnish proof of age and some proof of residence, and who has all poll taxes paid can get registered in Savannah. The tax collector, however, does make Negroes certify their age more often than others, refuses to register those who cannot read and write (while white illiterates are allowed to register because of the grandfather clause), and refuses to grant concessions on poll taxes to Negroes. On some occasions, asserts George Fuller, the registrar has required the applicants to read a paragraph of the constitution, commit it to memory, and repeat it to him with the book in his hand.

In Darien, Georgia, there has been considerable difficulty for Negroes, due to what are called the "tricks." For instance, until a few years ago, anyone was allowed to register in McIntosh County who paid three dollars in back poll taxes. The Negro school principal had taken a good many Negroes up and had them registered by paying the three dollars. When election time came, the names of these people were often not on the list. The registrars had ruled them ineligible because they had not paid up all back poll taxes.

In Macon, Georgia, in the spring of 1939, there were only 37 Negroes registered. In November 1939, as a result of some organizational activity, there were 320 Negroes registered in the city and a total of 450 in the county. About 80 percent of these were women. It is said that it was difficult to get Negroes registered, not because of white opposition, but because of the apathy and inertness of the Negro population itself. For the city registration, the books are open only every other year, and the period of registration is from January 1 to April 15. The county books are always open. The white primary has been a discouraging factor to Negro registration. Negroes have feared that they would have trouble if they went to register. They were afraid that the whites would come out to investigate homes, property, and so on.

The tax collector of Bibb County explained that the qualification which requires the reading and writing of the Constitution for registration in Georgia is not so simple, because he requires a "reasonable definition." He commented: "I can keep the president of the United States from registering in Macon if I want to." As an example, he referred to the Supreme Court jurisdiction clause of the Constitution (Article III) and explained: "God himself couldn't understand that. I myself is the judge. . . . It must be written to my satisfaction." The tax collector warned: "If we didn't have a law to stop niggers from registering, we should have to make one."

In Macon County few Negroes have applied to the tax collector for registration in recent years. The tax collector admits that Negroes are the only people to whom he applies the literacy test. He has Negro applicants read the oath, but he does not recall turning down anyone.

The tax collector of Burke County estimates that there are eighteen Negroes qualified to vote in the general election in that county. There is a difference between the treatment of Negroes and whites in registration for voting. Negroes are required to be able to read the oath themselves and to sign their own names, though these requirements are not made of whites. Three Negroes have applied for registration in Burke County since 1938, when the present tax commissioner assumed office upon the death of her husband. All three of these Negro applicants have been professional men. It is said that Negroes in this county are not required to have property if they can pass the literacy test. The tax collector claims to be at a loss to explain why more Negroes do not register. People may register without paying the poll tax. Voting among women of both races has been slow since something of a rush in the middle 1920s. Another member of the board estimates that there are twenty-eight rather than eighteen Negro voters in the county. "They aren't interested in voting here," he added, and most of them have never tried. Since 1928 this registrar has not heard of any Negro applicant's being turned down, and he feels that voting in the cotton elections is "making them think about it more," though certainly this has not been shown in the number registered thus far.

It is said that Negroes have no trouble in registering for the general election in Statesboro, Georgia, and that about a hundred are on the registration books, as compared with three thousand whites. Negroes cannot vote in the Democratic primary. White candidates make no bid for the Negro vote since they do not need it in the general election. Nor is there any bid for the Negro vote in local bond issue elections. In 1938, for example, a fifty-thousand-dollar bond issue was voted in Statesboro for paving streets and for building a white gymnasium, and the Negroes in town did not know anything about it. Even the Negro property owners did not go to the polls. Dr. Van Buren, a staunch Republican, thinks that Negroes can break into the white primary only as a result of bloodshed or some such drastic action. There are thirty thousand people in the county, fourteen thousand of whom are Negro. The registrants are designated by race on the registration roll. There have never been more than fifty Negroes voting. These Negro voters are the "old timers." During the eight years in which the present tax collector has held office, only about fifteen Negroes have been registered. Since the poll taxes are collected only when there are property taxes to be paid, a number of Negroes have paid the poll taxes without registering.[9]

In Hall County, according to the tax collector, Negroes are registered just as whites are. The literacy and property tests are not administered to them. Very few Negroes now register, however. The tax collector estimates that fewer than ten have registered since 1930, when he assumed office. The reason for this lack of Negro registration is said to be the white primary, which bars Negroes from participation in any important election. It is also pointed out that there would be a "great deal of bad feeling" if Negroes should try to vote in any but the general election. Since the candidates bear all expenses for the primary, they have no difficulty in keeping the Negro out of them.

There are three Negroes registered in the Shiloh district of Greene County, and they all vote, but a justice of the peace adds: "That don't make no difference. They can't vote in the primary. Not in my day, you won't see it." Three Negroes are registered in the White Plane district for general elections, but they seldom come to vote. White Plane is one of the best farming sections in Greene County, and most of the farming is still done on fairly large plantations with Negro croppers. The justice of the peace of White Plane thinks that if the poll tax were repealed, more Negroes would try to vote. Even if they can vote

9. Myrdal's interview with the tax collector, Statesboro, Georgia, 2 November 1939.

only in the general election, he thinks that it is dangerous, for the New Deal Democrats or some other "radical" group could run a separate ticket in the general election, and with the "reliefers" and the other "out-for-all-they-can-getters," they could get a majority in Georgia. Then chaos would break loose, for "the class of people we've got in elections now is bad enough—the class of white people, I mean."

In Greensboro, the county seat of Greene County and the largest town in the county, the names of five Negro men appeared on the 1939 voting list. No Negro names appear on the 1940 list because it was made up for the Democratic primary. A Negro farmer near Greensboro who has been on his 165-acre farm for thirty-two years used to vote but does not bother now, for, he states, when he goes to pay his poll tax and tells the registrar he wants to register, he is told: "You don't need to register."

According to the registration roll in Johnson County as compiled for the fall, 1940, primary and general elections, there are 2,196 white males and 2,094 white females, or a total of 4,290 whites registered, as against 11 Negro males and 2 Negro females. These 13 Negro registrants are listed as from Bray district. Those Negroes on the rolls and identified as Negroes are listed as "Mr." Negroes from Wrightsville and one or two other places are not identified as Negroes on the registration rolls. The total black registered vote in Johnson County by general estimate is about thirty. The Johnson County tax collector says very few Negroes register and that those who do are generally applicants for some kind of state or federal job requiring registration. He states that he registers these Negro applicants "like anybody else."

There are no serious efforts to keep Negroes from registering for the general elections in Augusta. Chairs are even provided for Negro registration workers during the days that the books are open, so that Negroes may be encouraged to vote by their own race as they come in and go out of the courthouse. But the Democratic primaries are for whites only, and unless independent candidates run, the Negro vote in the general election following the primary counts for nothing. According to an unpublished survey recently made, from 1914 to 1936 there were 804 registered male Negro voters in Augusta. Approximately 154 of these are dead and 57 others out of town, leaving 593 registered Negroes in 1936. In July 1939, 210 were actually eligible to vote. Between 1920 and 1936 there were 442 registered Negro women voters in Augusta. The number who have not paid taxes or have left town or have died is 301. According to the Augusta *Chronicle,* 372 Negroes are now eligible to vote.[10]

The tax collector of Ware County declares that the only difference in treatment between whites and blacks in the registration process is that all Negroes are required to come in in person to register and to sign the book. They must sign it themselves, so that the tax collector can "see they can write." If whites cannot sign, on the other hand, the tax collector will sign for them. A member of the county board states that at the time of the last general election there were approximately three hundred Negroes registered in Ware County.

The most recent state to abandon the poll tax is Florida. When the necessity for paying the annual levy as a prerequisite to voting was swept away, Negro registration began to increase. When a city election came up in Miami in May 1939, the city had the largest number of Negroes in history on its voting lists. Resentment flared up in hostile demonstrations that had the Miami police department's nerves on edge for two or three days. On the night before the election, hooded riders in automobiles with hidden license plates patrolled the principal Negro residential sections. The robed men, identified as members of the Ku Klux Klan, put the torch to oil-drenched crosses on street corners. Nooses dangled menacingly from automobile windows and one dummy was strung up bearing a sign, "This nigger voted."

But the Miami Negroes were not intimidated. Under adequate police protection, more than a thousand went to the polls and voted. Separate booths and boxes were set up for them, but when the ballots were counted, the public learned that the Negroes had voted just about the same as their white brothers. There was no disorder at the polls.

According to the city registrar, the approximate number of Negroes registered for city elections is 1,050. The registrar of Dade County estimates that, as of 4 November 1940, there are 1,947 Negro registrants in the county, as compared with 54,347 whites. For some twenty years only 50 Negroes had been registered voters in Miami, but with the active campaigns staged by the new Negro leadership a great increase in Negro registration occurred last year. According to Samuel Solomon, who sparked the campaign to get Negroes to the polls, the Negro leaders appealed to the Ministerial Alliance of Miami and pro-

10. Wilhelmina Jackson's interviews, Augusta, Georgia, February 1940.

vided the ministers with cars so that it would be relatively easy for them to go to the polls.[11]

Sam Solomon, a young Negro undertaker, heads the Negro Republican Club of Dade County, Incorporated, which claims between three and four hundred members. Its main purpose is to register Negroes as Republicans. Negro women affiliated with this group organized a corps of "Good Morning; have you registered Republican?" boosters. Solomon attracted nation-wide attention in 1939 by defying the threats of the Ku Klux Klan and leading Negro voters to the polls. On 9 March 1940, he sent out the following letter on the stationery of the Negro Republican Club. It was entitled "A Personal Letter to You from Sam B. Solomon."

> . . . when I returned here I thought at least 5,000 of you would have registered; instead I found less than 2,000 had registered to vote in the coming election. You know I am will-ing to fight for you, your rights and privileges. But what can I do when the names are not recorded on the registration books to back me up?
>
> If my people do not go to the ground floor of the Court House and register, I'll be a foolish man to open my mouth —no matter what happens to you.
>
> This is not my fight alone. You must help me.
>
> Do me this favor: Register at once if you have not. Have every person in your house register, all of your employees and friends.
>
> If you do not register 10,000 strong, I'll have to give up the fight for the rights of Negro people.
>
> What is your answer? Let me know, please.
>
> Yours for greater opportunities for Negroes.[12]

There are some prominent white citizens in Miami who openly encourage Negro voting. For example, an editorial in the Miami *Herald* of 12 May 1939, reads: "Miami's elections are conducted on a nonpartisan basis and under these circum-stances, a negro cannot be excluded from voting." The editorial and news columns of the *Herald* following the municipal elec-

11. The description of Negro registration in Florida is based on Wil-helmina Jackson's interviews conducted in 1940. —ED.

12. This paragraph is taken from Bunche's "The Programs, Ideologies, Tactics, and Achievements of Negro Betterment and Interracial Organi-zations," pp. 616–17. —ED.

tions of 1939 were highly sympathetic to the efforts of the Negro leaders. A columnist in the *Herald* wrote on 10 May 1939:

> During the unlamented city election campaign, some of the candidates and their henchmen accused me of wanting to clean up slum conditions in Negro town as a gesture toward getting the Negro vote for candidates who bore the *Herald* endorsement. The gentlemen who made those assertions knew better, of course. . . . As long as the slums are allowed to remain ignored in Negro town, just so long will the threat of epidemics hover over the whole Miami area.

According to Solomon, some white employers would call him up during the campaign to get the Negro voters registered, to check as to whether their domestic servants were registered to vote, and to assure him that they were doing their part to get them to register.

Figures obtained in the office of the supervisor of registration for Duval County in 1934 indicate that there were 487 Negroes registered as Republicans and 587 registered as Independents, or a total of 1,074 registered Negroes in the county. This, as against 34,100 whites registered as Democrats, 425 whites registered as Republicans, 188 as Independents, 2 as Socialists, and 1 as Prohibitionist. At that same time, there were 24,825 whites *qualified* to vote as against 582 Negroes. In 1936 there were 1,624 Negroes registered as against 46,274 whites. In 1938, following the repeal of the poll tax qualification, 47,110 white Democrats were registered, 325 white Republicans, and 41 white Independents, as against 8,105 Negro Republicans and 1,076 Negro Independents.

There seems to be a great deal of interest in voting among Jacksonville Negroes, and intensive campaigns urging Negroes to register for voting are sponsored by and conducted by Negro organizations and leaders. The editor of the white Jacksonville *Journal* openly urges Negroes to get out and vote. As a result of this, he has lost a good deal of advertisement in his paper and some of his circulation. He seems to be generally sympathetic toward labor and minority groups. In an interview on 27 February 1940 he said: "I've been called a Communist because I speak in Negro churches and before Negro groups on such problems as slum clearance, organizing into unions, registering, and voting." A white woman, Mrs. F. W. Traynor, is active in efforts to get out the Negro vote. She states: "I've always believed Negroes should vote, and I feel they haven't because they didn't know that they could. I tell those with whom I come in contact to vote because that's the only way in which they kin get their rights. No, I don't publicly urge them to do so."

Although the registration of Negroes in Jacksonville is now heavy, it was not very great in previous years due to the poll tax requirement, which was two dollars a year and cumulative for two years. Now, however, although the Negro registration is heavy, Negroes do not vote in significant numbers because of the lily-white primary. The supervisor of registration for Duval County informed Miss Jackson that "Negroes are all of them Republicans in Florida, not Democrats." Several Negroes claim that on various occasions they were told that Negroes are not allowed to be Democrats in Florida.

Because of the heavy Negro registration of 1938 in Jacksonville, the precinct lines were changed, and considerable confusion was evidenced among the potential voters of both races when they came into the office of the election officials to find out where they must go to register. The registrar himself was observed to be confused, because on each of these inquiries he or his secretary had to go into a huddle over the map to find out where certain street locations placed a voter. Miss Jackson noted that the Negroes were accorded polite answers by the supervisor and his secretary.

Perhaps the most important attempt to break through the lily-white Democratic setup in Florida took form in the Sylvaneus Hart case of 1934. Hart petitioned the fourth judicial circuit court of Florida for a writ of mandamus to compel the registrar to register him as a Democrat. The court's ruling was negative, on the ground that: "The State Executive Committee of each political party may, by resolution, declare the terms and conditions on which legal electors shall be declared and become members of the party preparatory to voting in the party primary." Since this case, according to Leonard Lewis, Hart's attorney, no further attempt has been made to break the exclusive policy of the Democratic party in Florida.

Fewer than five hundred Negroes are registered in St. Augustine, Florida, although the 1930 census lists 2,111 Negroes over the age of twenty-one. The city government in St. Augustine is nonpartisan, and this affords the Negro an opportunity to participate in municipal elections. In 1939 a contest was sponsored by the Negro Civic Alliance of St. Augustine in an effort to interest young Negroes in political participation. Prizes of from five to twenty-five dollars were offered to Negro youths who would bring in the most registration certificates. As a result of this campaign, some 250 additional Negro names were added to the registration books. The Civic Alliance also devoted itself to a campaign to interest preachers in the organization of a ministerial alliance which would aid in the registration movement. The Negro population is concentrated in the fourth ward, and, according to the figures obtained from the office of the city registrar, there were 577 registrations in the fourth ward in March 1939.

The voting booth for the fourth ward in St. Augustine is located in the office of Mr. Butler, president of the Civic Alliance, and he states that both whites and Negroes come in and vote together quite harmoniously. The voting booth for precinct 19 in the county and state elections is also located in his office.

In St. Petersburg there were 20,136 registered voters as of 15 August 1939. Of this number, 723 were Negroes. The largest Negro representation was in precinct six, in which there were 420 Negro registrants out of a total of 3,835. According to the 1930 census, there were 40,425 people in St. Petersburg, of whom 7,416 were Negroes.

In Orlando, Florida, the Negro registration is very low. There are not more than 80 Negroes registered out of the 4,705 Negroes over twenty-one, according to the 1930 census. The Orange County Tax Payers' and Voters' League, which has existed for only one year, is attempting to get Negroes registered and is offering a five dollar reward to the pastor who gets the greatest number of people registered. Negroes in Orlando claim to feel repercussions of the trouble about black voting which occurred in Miami in 1939, and the whites are giving evidence of hostility toward Negro political participation.

For the Tampa city elections of 1939, 1,330 Negroes were registered. Some Tampa Negro leaders have waged a vigorous registration campaign since then, and it is estimated that some 2,500 Negroes are now registered to vote for the general election of 1940. Negroes vote in the municipal general elections as well as the congressional and presidential contests. It is only in recent years that Tampa Negroes have begun to evidence an interest in voting, and this appears to be due to the insistent urging of their leaders, especially those in the NAACP headed by President Strachan. It is said that in 1934 scarcely a hundred Negroes were voting in Tampa. Some white citizens in Florida, mainly members of trade unions acting through their community medium, the Community Improvement League, urge Negroes to vote in Tampa.

In New Orleans, Louisiana, Negroes have had considerable difficulty in getting registered. One prominent New Orleans Negro, in his first effort to register there, was told by the clerk that he had miscalculated his age because he had computed the age without considering whether February had twenty-eight or twenty-nine days. On another occasion, this same Negro—although he had registered on three previous occasions—was turned down at the registration office four consecutive times. On the fifth time, a white clerk who knew him let him register without difficulty.

In the 1936 registration period in New Orleans three Negro members of the executive committee of the NAACP attempted to register and were turned down because of incorrectly filling out their cards. These men went to a Negro lawyer and filed mandamus proceedings. As soon as the cases were filed, the registrar called the lawyer and told him that his clients could be registered without going through with the court case. The Negroes, however, told their lawyer that they preferred to fight the case through, though none of them had sufficient money for it. Later, the assistant attorney general called the lawyer and arranged a conference with the parties in the case. In that conference this Negro lawyer, who is now deceased, was threatened, and his Negro clients thought it necessary to protect his career. They conferred with the registrar and told him that they were interested in getting Negroes registered. He then promised that after the primary he would register all "intelligent Negroes" that would be selected and sent to him. On the whole, however, the professional and business Negroes of New Orleans were not greatly interested. Immediately after the primary the registrar asked the NAACP leaders: "That we not embarrass his office by bringing too many Negroes from any one ward—that we distribute them among wards. We brought 21 to his office and he registered only five."

The secretary of the newly organized Urban League in New Orleans failed several times in his efforts to register in 1935. On one occasion, a druggist promised to see the white ward leader about the matter and to try to get a note from him which would permit registration. This note was obtained and was addressed to the registration clerk for that ward. The note read: "Register this man, he is with us." When the Urban League secretary went to register, however, the clerk for that particular ward was ill, and the man who was in his place "suggested that I come back to register at a date in February, which was after the election. I told him there would be no need of registering then. I went back several times and the same man was there, so never got registered." One flagrant instance of failure to register a Negro in New Orleans is that of a young Negro college student who stood in the registration line behind a white person who did not know how to fill out his registration card. The Negro helped him fill it out, and the white man was registered while the Negro was turned down.

A Negro pastor in New Orleans attempted to register more than a dozen times in one year without success. He was determined to register, however, and continued to go back to the registration office. On one of the occasions, while waiting for his turn, he saw one of the clerks take out a card and fill it out completely for a white applicant. When the Negro minister filled his card out, the clerk threw it back to him as "wrong." The minister then spoke very loudly and exclaimed: "Do you mean to tell me that you turned me down after you have just filled out this white man's card without him touching a pen?" The Negro had spoken so loudly that the attention of a policeman was attracted and the minister related his story to the officer. Surprisingly, the clerk admitted that he had filled out the card for the white applicant, and the officer then said: "This man has something on you, and you had better register him." The minister was then registered.

A New Orleans Negro, who resembles a white man and is employed in the department of public welfare, went into the registrar's office in the fall of 1939 to register. He filled out his card and returned it to the clerk, who hurriedly checked it, wrote out his registration certificate, and handed him the book to sign. Just as the Negro began to sign his name on the register, the clerk jerked the book from him and said: "There's a mistake here. You can't register. You've made an error." The clerk apparently had at the last minute seen the telltale designation "colored" on the man's card.

A. P. Tureaud, a Negro lawyer in New Orleans, was refused registration there in 1934. He described his experience in an interview on 14 November 1939:

The deputy registrar of voters of the seventh ward had me fill out an application. When I did so, he looked at it and said, "It's wrong," and tried to retain it, but I snatched it out of his hand and called a policeman to whom I told what had happened. The clerk then refused to give me another card. I went to Mr. Gregory [the registrar] and he came out with me until I filled out another card, and then I was told that that also was "wrong." I returned to the office the next day and the same thing happened. I again saw Mr. Gregory and told him that he had better register me or I would mandamus him. Gregory told the clerk to give me another card and go ahead and register me. Later, I endorsed a note for this clerk and he told me: "You know, Tureaud, I don't want to do this to you. I know you can qualify if anybody can, but we have to do this on orders from above."

In New Orleans it is possible for a few prominent Negro leaders, who are in the good graces of the white population, to get a few Negroes registered. This is on a purely personal basis, however. As a Negro physician puts it:

There is wide belief among whites here that the Negro is not prepared to exercise the rights of citizenship. This is based on the concept of the Negro which whites have gained through their experience with Negro domestics. So, when I say to the white registrar that a particular Negro is not of this type, they will register him.

In Opelousas, St. Landry Parish, Louisiana, two Negro doctors—Dr. Terrence and Dr. Donatto—attempted to register prior to the election for parish officers. This was after the repeal of the poll tax in Louisiana in 1934. The registrar, Paul Fontenot, sent them to the sheriff's office. The sheriff, in turn, sent them to the judge of the circuit court, who sent them back to the sheriff. When they went back to the sheriff's office, one of the sheriff's deputies gave them a long lecture, telling them how long he had known them and how anxious he was that they would not get into any "trouble." The sheriff told them that he would issue poll tax receipts if they got registration certificates. They obtained the required registration certificates from the registrar, but the sheriff insisted that he had no authority to grant them poll receipts. The following day, a young Negro electrician named John Deshotel attempted to register and was bloodily beaten in the sheriff's office.[13]

13. This incident and those in Louisiana that follow are based on James Jackson's field notes, February 1940.

These two physicians had no organization, but were merely acting on the supposition that Huey Long's statement that anyone in Louisiana could vote applied to them also. After Deshotel was beaten up, the two doctors—as well as Deshotel—made no further efforts to register. Deshotel was the target for the sheriff's attack rather than the two doctors because he was relatively unknown and was not a very important figure in the community, whereas the two Negro physicians had large personal followings and a violent attack on them might have resulted in stirring up the Negro community. This is said to have been the last effort of Negroes to vote in St. Landry Parish. The county clerk of the parish and the Opelousas tax assessor informed James Jackson that there were no Negroes registered to vote in St. Landry Parish.

The registrar of voters in Baton Rouge allegedly makes it very embarrassing for Negroes to register. He has the privilege under the law—the understanding clause—to ask any question he wants to ask. One Negro leader in the Baton Rouge community declares:

> I don't know of anyone here who has had any trouble registering—such a relatively few have attempted to—but it is common knowledge that no Negro will be allowed to vote in Port Allen [a town in West Baton Rouge Parish]. A man told me that when he went up to register, the registrar said to him: "Now, listen, boy, if you just insist on registering, I'll register you. You got a right under the law, but I tell you, you've got to live here, and you'll be pointed out as an uppity nigger. So, if I was you, I'd forget it. Besides, your one vote won't count none nohow—don't you know I would lose my job if I let a whole lot of Negroes register? I'd register you and maybe two or three others, but it won't get you nowhere. So, why don't you forget it, huh?"

It is said that there are very few parishes in the state of Louisiana where Negroes are allowed to register. Only in the two or three large cities are they permitted to register without difficulty.

In North Carolina, the North Carolina Committee on Negro Affairs is the most active organization on behalf of Negroes. This all-Negro association, organized in Durham in March 1936, has branches in Charlotte, Greensboro, Winston-Salem, Raleigh, and Durham. It is a mild pressure group, and its first meeting, called just before a Democratic primary in the state, had as its keynote the larger participation of Negroes in the election campaign. It began with a strong political consciousness, as indicated by the following statement: "There was an apparent common understanding that politics, whether local or national, exerts a more or less dominating influence over the recognized sacred rights of all men."[14] Since its inception, the organization has broadened its program to include a fourfold objective—the improvement of the educational, economic, socio-civic, and political welfare of the Negro in the state. In politics efforts are made to stimulate the exercise of the franchise by Negroes, to encourage the registration of qualified black citizens for participation in the various elections, and "to centralize all civic organizations throughout the state by encouraging affiliation with the North Carolina Committee on Negro Affairs, to the end that the Negroes of North Carolina will present a solid front for the solution of our common problems."

At the present time Negroes in Durham encounter no difficulty in registering. But there have been instances in the past when registrars gave Negroes considerable trouble in registering. For example, the Durham *Sun* published stories in 1933 concerning the attempts of Negroes to gain the removal of a city registrar. The articles relate that the Legal Redress Committee of the League of Independent Voters informed Chairman Purcell of the Durham County board of elections that J. E. Polk, registrar for East Durham, discriminated against Negroes attempting to register in that area. Registrar Polk required only Negroes to read, write, and interpret long sections of the Constitution. Polk was openly antagonistic toward the protest of the Negroes and had M. Hugh Thompson, a Negro attorney who was protesting the registration procedure, forcibly ejected from the precinct. Subsequently, Polk was removed, and Durham Negroes have had no great difficulty in registering since.

It is said now in Durham that the present registrar is so obliging that he brings his registration book up to the office of the North Carolina Mutual Life Insurance Company and registers its Negro officials at their desks. Of the 11,302 Negroes of voting age in Durham, approximately 3,000 are registered. Only approximate figures can be given, because separate registration

14. From Bunche, "The Programs, Ideologies, Tactics, and Achievements of Negro Betterment and Interracial Organizations," pp. 597–98. —ED.

lists or racial identifications do not exist. The total city registration in 1939 was 22,815.[15]

According to a city hall list for Greensboro, 291 Negroes were registered voters in 1935. It is variously estimated that at present there are anywhere from 810 to 1,002 Negroes registered. It is claimed that an old white man who was registrar in precinct five even goes up and down the streets registering Negroes and helping them to write their names. This is quite a different story from that told by Watson Law, who relates that in Greensboro in 1909, after he had read and interpreted the constitution, which "I'd studied for a long time, I forgot to cross my 't' and dot my 'i' in equity and they threw it out. I'll never forgit the word *equity*—never. I went back, though, and they finally registered me." When Wilhelmina Jackson visited the chairman of the county board of elections, in an effort to get figures on Negro registration, she was told that: "There hasn't been a registration in so long here, that I guess we have more dead people voting in Greensboro than any place else in the state."

Several means of refusing registration to Negroes of all classes have been used at Winston-Salem, and this over a long period. It is said that when the authorities are challenged, a few Negroes are registered. But when they are not challenged, even though many Negroes may appear for registration, few are accepted. The result is that relatively few Negroes now attempt to register. For example, the editor of the "Colored Notes" section of a Winston daily told the following story:

> When I came back to Winston in 1917, the registrar refused to register me, and so I made a speech: "I have just returned from the war, fighting for democracy and now I come here, and democracy in its elemental form—the vote—is denied. Oh, no! I wasn't scared over there and now I'm not scared, and I'm here to stay until you register me."

Another Negro—a local businessman—complained:

> They wouldn't allow my dortor to vote—I rushed down there and told the blame fool that he never would have as much sense as my dortor and that he better let her vote. When she went back, one of those red-faced crackers said to her,

15. All of the material pertaining to North Carolina in this chapter is based on Wilhelmina Jackson's field notes, November and December 1939.

"Ain't you the same girl that was here this morning?" The other snapped out, "Let the girl register." I was so mad then that I decided to stay and help others of my race get through. I stood in the door and one of them came up to me and told told me to move. "Move," I said. "And you a paid servant of mine—not on your life."

A white physician in Winston-Salem recalled that several years ago, during registration, a Negro woman was standing in line in front of him. When she got up to the registrar's desk, the official immediately asked her whether she knew the secretary of the local chamber of commerce, and when she said "no," the registrar thereupon informed her that she could not register. According to the white physician:

> My blood boiled. I reached over her and said "see here, I don't know that man and you better register me. But I'll 'know' because I'm a white man. It's no honor to know him, because he's nothing but a debauch and drunk. Let this woman register."

And the woman was let through. A Negro labor union member was refused registration: "The registrar asked me to recite the Preamble of the Constitution. I knew that. I had been studying the Constitution for five or six weeks. I read it too fast for him, and then he ast me to write what I read. When I wouldn't do it, he said: 'Suit yourself.' "

A Negro woman, who has been a city school librarian for twenty years in Winston-Salem, was subjected to a severe test by the registrar. Here is her story:

> He asked me how old must a governor be? How are tax laws drawn up? And so forth. But I came home and went back. I failed again. This time he had the nerve to call me "dumb," and I said, "If so, then your city has been paying me for twenty years for being so dumb." Upon that he registered me, cautioning me to be quiet. I wasn't, but the hundred or so that I contacted to go and register did not even try.

A professor at the Winston-Salem Teachers College was refused registration at the last registration period.

According to the chairman of the Mecklenburg County board of elections, there are 25,000 people registered in Charlotte, and approximately one-fifth of this number are Negroes. The Negro voting population is concentrated in ward two, box two, where

1,404 people are registered; ward ten, box one, where 786 are registered; and ward eleven, where 1,574 are registered as of 8 November 1938. The chairman of the board says there are several hundred other Negro votes scattered throughout the other wards.

Many more Negroes are said to be trying to vote in Charleston, South Carolina, now than there were in the 1920s because "the churches and preachers and the schools and all kinds of organizations are after them about their rights." The Democratic party nationally is also lending encouragement to Negro voting, and the chairman of the board of registrars thinks this is bad and is opposed to it. He says that "most" of the Negroes in Charleston County vote the Democratic ticket, but he insists that no Negroes in the county vote in the primaries or are members of the Democratic ward clubs.

The most serious obstacle to the Negro vote in Charleston is the white primary. In most local elections all candidates are unopposed and Negroes take an attitude of "what's the use?" The poll tax, although small, is a serious handicap, because Negroes in general are too poorly paid to afford this assessment. Since only a small number of Negroes attempt to register, no serious effort is made to stop registration. No specific effort has been made on the part of either white or Negro groups to enlist the black vote in Charleston in a particular local campaign or on a specific local issue.

Mrs. Lucile D. King, the chairman of the Greenville County, South Carolina, board of registrars, complained: "We've had a lot of trouble about niggers registering. You must have read all about it in the papers. Yeah, Lord! It was a mess!" In explanation, the chairman stated that a few "educated nigras" and "some white people, I think," were back of it. She said the white lawyer who played a leading role in this move to get Negroes registered was an ambitious young fellow who wanted to be mayor. So few people vote in the general election that he thought he could "slip in" and take the place. The people came to her because they had to have county registration certificates before they could get city ones. Nothing came of it all, she continued, because few voted and "they all voted one way." "I let them register," she remarked, adding that she turned down two or three because they could not read and write.

The Klan got after me too. You know that. Yeah. They had two or three niggers out front showing them how to do—

you know they're awfully ignorant about things like voting and all. So the Klan, they published warnings in the papers and they rode around this town like a circus parade. A federal man came here to see me about it about two months ago. He asked me if they had bothered me. I told him exactly what happened.

The day after the first group of Negroes came in, the chairman of the county board received a letter from a young lawyer in town warning her that she had better enforce the law strictly against Negroes. It told her to come to his office, where she would receive instructions. She called him up, told him her office was in the courthouse, and that he could come over there if he wanted to see her. He did come, with another young lawyer. They had the law all typed out. She took them to the county attorney. He read their digest and told them that Mrs. King had this already, and that if the Negroes were qualified to register, she had to register them. And she observed: "And I did." Mrs. King noted that not more than 350 Negroes have come in to date, but that there was a "big fuss" about it up to the time of the city election in 1939. Since then she has had very few to apply. She said she expected a few more to be coming in before the presidential election. The general impression in Greenville is that Mrs. King has been "very fair" in her handling of Negro applicants, and there seems to have been little trouble in getting Negroes registered there.

The city police of Greenville are said to work "hand in glove" with the Ku Klux Klan, and it is charged that most of the patrolmen are themselves members of the Klan. Quite significantly, one of the candidates for sheriff of Greenville County at the coming election is a known Klansman. Another candidate for the same office attempted to join the Klan, but the first candidate had him blackballed so that he would not split the Klan support. A local white lawyer states that he has had his own difficulties with the KKK because of his activity in behalf of Negro registration in Greenville. During the registration of Negroes last summer, he says that he received several warnings from the Klan. It was the Klan, he asserts, which caused his previous landlord to make him move his law office. His last experience with the Klan was in court. He was defending a Negro and was examining the jury. He asked one prospective juror if he was a member of any organization having the suppression of Negroes as a part of its program. The judge interrupted, asking him to be plainer; so he asked the man if he was a Klansman. The judge quickly recessed the court and called the lawyer back into his office. The judge told him, "You don't want to ask that question." The lawyer answered: "If you were a Negro and were being tried, wouldn't you want to know if your jurors were Klansmen?" The judge did not answer, but warned him it would not be good for him if he asked that question. After the session, the lawyer was met in the corridor by a Klansman who attacked him with brass knuckles. He fought back. He was arrested and charged with assault and battery, disturbing the peace, and trying to destroy public property. The case was dropped. The lawyer then tried to sue his attacker but the case was "no billed."

The president of the Better Government League in Greenville, an enhusiastic student of suffrage and suffrage extension in politically apathetic Greenville, emphasized very pointedly the fact that his movement had nothing to do with the attempts of Negroes to register in Greenville in the summer of 1939. Most of this effort, he explained, was newspaper talk. He blamed the whole episode on two white men who, he said, wanted a group of "darky votes to control." This is what would happen should more Negroes vote. He thought it better that "the darkies" take no part in the election. He does not think that the "better class" of Negroes is interested in the vote, and the other Negroes would not be if white men did not get after them about it.

A careful check of the general election registration books for all of the Greenville city wards (most of the Negroes in Greenville County live inside the city) and the books for about half of the Greenville County districts, including those with large Negro populations, revealed that only 324 Negroes had been registered in the county from January 1938 through the enrolling days of June 1940. This figure has been variously reported by others, however, as from approximately 600 to as high as 900.

There is no legal requirement that race be indicated in the registration books in Greenville. But, because these same lists are used for making up jury lists, Negro voters are usually marked as such and, therefore, the lists are fairly dependable guides. In the Greenville registration books, all Negroes are identified clearly with a "col." beside the name. The registrar in Greenville told Stoney that she believes that every registered

Negro was identified, and she estimated that there were not more than 350 on the list. Of the 324 Negroes who were thus identified, 297 were from inside the city limits.

In Columbia, South Carolina, there are two types of registration for voting. One is for the Democratic party primary and is called the "club enrollment"; the other is for the general election. The names on the Democratic club roll can be used for the general election registration. This separate registration is a device which keeps the Negro out of politics, since Negroes are not enrolled in the Democratic clubs. The Democratic party club roll for Columbia had 11,158 names in 1938. It was flatly stated that this number did not include any Negro names. It was not possible to secure general registration figures, our investigator being told that it was necessary to obtain these when the general registration board is in session. However, leading Negro citizens of Columbia estimated that there are approximately a thousand Negroes registered for the general election in Columbia—probably an overly optimistic estimate.[16]

Some Negroes who present themselves for registration at Sumter are given a test. The chairman of the board of registrars states: "Most everyone [Negro] that comes in is either a school teacher or a preacher or some kind of a business person. We don't ask them. . . . Some of the others, we do, but I don't think we've turned down a half a dozen since I've been on the board." In 1936 in Sumter there was a

> big registration of darkies. It was for the president's election, you know. I think mighty near all of them voted for Roosevelt, too. There were some from this Republican bunch too, I think. . . . Some people came in there when we were working and said: "You better be careful the way you register up all these niggers." I told them that if a darky's got the qualifications, the law says he shall register, so I'm going to register him.

The chairman expressed the belief that some "school men" and some members of the Joseph W. Tolbert faction were encouraging Negroes to register. Since the 1938 registration books were open, however, not more than twenty Negroes have registered, according to the chairman of the board. Of all the names on the books between 1928 and 1938, when the new registration was

16. Wilhelmina Jackson's interviews, January 1940.

called, he estimated that not more than 450 or 500 were Negroes.

Negroes are not identified on the registration books by race. The chairman explains this by saying: "I thought about it, but the other board didn't do it, so we haven't been." He explained that the jury commission could avoid taking Negroes for jury service even though Negroes are not identified by race on the registration books because there are enough people who look over the list before it is drawn from to make sure no Negro names get on it. He felt sure that no Negro had served on any but federal juries in Sumter County, because, in his opinion, no names of Negroes are put in the hat from which the names for jury service are drawn.

Negroes have had no trouble in getting registered in Sumter in recent years. The willingness of the registrars to cooperate has been continued since the 1938 registration began. Most of the Negro vote, which is confined to the general election, comes from the Negro college and from the Negro schoolteachers in Sumter.

The treasurer of Pickens County is certain that there are not more than "six or seven" Negroes who have registration certificates in the whole county, and that three of these are in the town of Pickens. These three do not vote in the city general election, although they have that right. They are said to be Republicans and friends of "old man Marsh," the former postmaster and white Republican who, according to the county treasurer, "is one of them Republicans a man can trust"—by which he meant, apparently, that Marsh stayed Republican after the 1932 landslide and has never tried to hide his political affiliation. Few Negroes ever vote in Pickens County. The chairman of the county board of registrars, who was appointed in 1938, has had only one Negro apply for a registration certificate. He received it. The others, she explained, either are not interested or "don't know they can vote." A few in town do know it, but "don't fool" with it. She explained that it is not the Negroes only who are illiterate. It is the mill people and the farm people, too. Most of them come out of the hills, where the schools are bad now and where, twenty or thirty years ago, they were nonexistent.

Negroes are reported to have no trouble in getting registered in Newport News, Virginia. The main difficulty is to get Negroes interested. In 1928 there was a Negro block of 1,098 voters. Now it is estimated that there are between five and six hundred Negro voters. It is claimed that the Negro was able to exert real political pressure when there were a thousand black votes. As a result of this pressure, Newport News Negroes obtained a new elementary school. Even now, with only some five hundred votes, the white candidates are eager to get Negro support, but the Negro vote is not solid. Approximately 820 Negroes, as against approximately 5,600 whites, were registered in Newport News as of June 1939. In 1937, 5,781 whites paid their poll taxes, as against 826 Negroes.[17]

As of 31 December 1938, 2,833 Negroes were registered in Norfolk, Virginia, as against 38,349 whites. A teacher of history in the Negro high school of Norfolk states that teachers in his building, who are compelled to pay the poll tax, still do not register for voting. "They just don't bother about it." A Negro political leader in Hampton, Virginia, was asked the following question when he attempted to register in 1928: "What constitutes the twenty-seventh judicial district of Virginia?"

In the cities of Virginia, especially in places like Richmond and Norfolk, Negroes now encounter little difficulty in registration. This was not always so, however, and it took a successful court fight to break down the registration barriers against Virginia Negro voters. The main obstacle to their voting in the general elections now is the three-year cumulative poll tax requirement.

In Hampton the County Civic League has been organized for some twelve years. Its broad program embraces general civic improvement, but its main activity centers around the participation of Negro voters in the election campaigns. It claims to control some five hundred Negro votes of the five thousand voters of the county. Its meetings are chiefly devoted to the task of educating Negroes as to voting qualifications and notifying them as to the due dates for poll tax payments and registration. It is claimed that the Negro vote holds the balance of power in Hampton, and that the white candidates bid for the support of the Civic League. The League gets but meager support from the Negro elite.[18]

In Petersburg there is a League of Negro Voters whose ob-

17. These figures and those that follow on Virginia are taken from Wilhelmina Jackson's field notes, October and November 1939.
18. This paragraph and the three that follow are taken from Bunche, "The Programs, Ideologies, Tactics, and Achievements of Negro Betterment and Interracial Organizations," pp. 593–96. —ED.

jectives are to stimulate interest in voting and to urge payment of poll taxes. This is a federation of local Negro organizations. According to its president:

> We adopt the technique of house-to-house campaigns, using students and others with leisure time to make the canvass. We also distributed a leaflet explaining how to register and how much poll tax to pay. We have devised a system of collecting poll taxes by installment. Our campaign has been measurably successful. In 1932 there were only fifty-two Negroes qualified to vote. Today, in 1939, there are 395 qualified Negro voters. We have received no opposition from whites—on the contrary, several candidates for office have approached us and encouraged our activities. We have been so concerned with the technical details of mechanically making a quantitative improvement in the Negro vote that we haven't yet presumed to analyze candidates and issues from the standpoint of giving direction to our voters.

In Portsmouth there was a Civic and Welfare Club which was organized by Negro water-tenders at the Navy Yard in 1931, with the purpose of forming a central political organization for Negroes. This organization broke up in 1935, however. In the words of its organizer:

> I began this organization in 1931 with the idea of the best colored men heading it—lawyers, doctors, preachers—these were the men I wanted to head it. . . . I wanted the group small —about fifty leading citizens—to go to the front and fight for the colored man's rights. The issues on which we organized and for which we planned to use our ballot were: schools, proper highways, sanitation, street lights, community centers and recreation centers. . . . We were going to work hand in glove with the city administration. Before the end of 1935, someone had written to Washington and reported my activities. I was written to from Washington to stop my activities or my job would end. I had to get out of things. . . . The Civic and Welfare Club died.

The breakup of this organization really revolved about its attempt to control all federal appointments for Portsmouth Negroes.

Newport News boasts a number of independent Negro organizations, including the Negro Citizens' Voters League, a Young Men's Democratic Club organized in 1932, a Young

Colored Men's Democratic Club organized in 1936, the East End Voters League, the Citizens' Voters League, and the Newport News Negro Republican League. The two Negro Democratic clubs are pro–New Deal. The Citizens' Voters League is the oldest Negro organization in Newport News. Formerly it was headed by a Negro stevedore and was originally called the Negro Republican League.

In Vicksburg, Mississippi, during the month of February 1939, a bit of vote consciousness was stirred up among Negroes. On the initiative of a Negro doctor and a Negro beauty parlor operator, seventy-five Negro women, members of a Negro women's Republican club, went down to the registrar's office in a body and registered. No efforts were made to prevent them from registering or to discourage them. A flurry of excitement went through the white community, however, and several Negro employees in white families were asked: "What is behind all of this? What do you want to vote for?" This was significant only as an evidnce of Negro voting interest, since the Mississippi white primary effectively debars Negroes from the only significant voting in the state. According to A. W. Wells, the president of the NAACP in Jackson:

> Negroes don't receive any encouragement from the registrar when they go down to seek to register. They invariably ask you why do you want to vote, and they ask you to interpret the Constitution. If you hesitate in reading the state oath which has lines that continue on across the next page, they slam the book in your face and tell you you're disqualified. Sometimes they tell you this anyway. About 100 Negroes vote in general and special elections. Only two or three vote in the primaries, and they are old figureheads in the community.[19]

There are about 8,000 registered Negro voters in Tulsa, Oklahoma, about equally divided as to Democratic and Republican affiliation.[20] There are several Negro organizations: the Tulsa County Citizenship Council, an organization initiated by the chamber of commerce to get out the Negro vote; the Young Negro Democratic Club, which is a typical ward club without principle or political perspective; the Young Negro Voters League, which is very similar to the Young Negro Democratic Club; and the Jefferson Political Club, which is a slush-fund or-

19. From James Jackson's field notes, February 1940.
20. Ibid., March 1940.

ganization whose main efforts are devoted toward obtaining patronage.

In Oklahoma City the Negro Democratic Central Committee organized the Negro vote and brought it into the Democratic camp. This organization was soon split into two factions, however, and just recently these two factions have come together under the Negro Democratic Clubs of Oklahoma—an organization headed by a Negro "millionaire" oil man. This group is designed to function in local elections and primaries, as well as national elections, and to effect organizations on a county, ward, and precinct basis through the medium of ward clubs.[21]

The Little Rock Civic Association has an educational program for the purpose of getting people to register and vote in the general elections. It is headed by a Negro teacher. It has been preparing an attack upon the white primary. There is also in Little Rock the Arkansas Negro Democratic Association, organized in 1928 for the specific purpose of mobilizing the Negro vote for the 1928 presidential election.[22]

According to the official figures released by the Davidson County, Tennessee, election commission on 21 August 1939, a total of 45,458 voters (including those in Nashville) were registered, of whom 6,911 were Negroes. For the city of Nashville, the official registration aggregate was 29,907. In Nashville the fourth ward has an overwhelming Negro majority. The ninth, eleventh, fourteenth, and sixteenth have Negro majorities, while the fifth, thirteenth, and fifteenth wards have slightly less than half of the registrants as Negroes. There are large Negro minorities in the second, sixth, eighth, tenth, and seventeenth wards. The following is a breakdown of those eligible to vote in the heavily populated Negro wards of Chattanooga, where the Negro vote is controlled by the local machine.[23]

Wards	Precincts	Negro	White
12th	4th	395	—
4th	4th	663	37
7th	2nd	420	102
7th	1st	239	261
3rd	1st	145	65
2nd	1st	30	638
5th	1st	136	374
8th	1st	91	179

21. From Bunche's "The Programs, Ideologies, Tactics, and Achievements of Negro Betterment and Interracial Organizations," pp. 621–22. —Ed.

22. Ibid., p. 621. —Ed.

23. James Jackson's field notes, October 1939.

ELEVEN

The Poll Tax

THERE seems to be little room for doubt that the entrenched interests of the South in the late nineteenth century were fearful of the possible union between poor whites and Negroes, and that this possibility of a united people's movement impressed them as a revolutionary upsurge that must be crushed at all odds. The poll tax legislation lent itself admirably to this purpose. It made it possible for the region to maintain its white supremacy doctrine and at the same time to keep away from the polls not only Negroes, but those underprivileged whites who constituted a new threat to the hegemony of the Southern ruling class. Some white Southerners were quite aware of the role the poll tax requirement was destined to play. Some of them even came out boldly and stated that the poll tax would be an important method for getting "rid of the venal and ignorant among the white men as voters." It is ironic that the support of the poor whites and the "hillbillies" was enlisted by the conservative interests of the South, not only to vote the Negroes out of politics, but to vote *themselves* out as well!

The poll tax qualification for voting was inserted in the Tennessee constitution of 1870, but was not effectively applied under state statutes until 1890. Virginia experimented with the poll tax qualification between 1875 and 1882, but abandoned it under the criticism of a governor who stated that it "opened the flood gates of corruption." Florida introduced its poll tax requirement in 1889, followed by Mississippi in 1890, Arkansas in 1892, South Carolina in 1895, Louisiana in 1898, North Carolina in 1900, Alabama and Virginia in 1901, Texas in 1903, and Georgia in 1908.

The poll tax takes an awful toll of the South's voters. Eight states—Alabama, Arkansas, Georgia, Mississippi, South Carolina, Tennessee, Texas, and Virginia—still retain the tax as a prerequisite for voting. These eight poll tax states had, according to the 1930 census, a total potential voting population of 11,606,406. Yet in the 1936 election, one of the most hotly contested in recent years, a total of only 2,679,473 votes were cast in those states. This was only a few thousand more votes than were cast in the single state of Pennsylvania—nominally a Republican state—for the Democratic party alone. The potential voting population of Pennsylvania—that is, the population of voting age—numbers only 5,827,000. In other words, less than one qualified voter in four cast a ballot in the eight poll tax states, while in the other states of the Union almost three out of four of the adult population voted.

The accompanying map of the South indicates the states in which the poll tax is retained as a qualification for voting and gives the percentages of adults who voted in the presidential election of 1936.

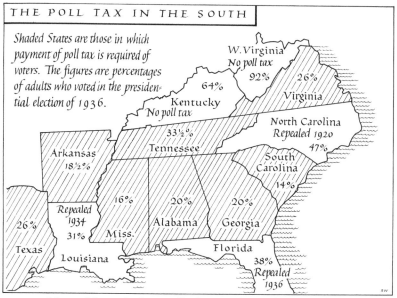

THE POLL TAX IN THE SOUTH

Shaded States are those in which payment of poll tax is required of voters. The figures are percentages of adults who voted in the presidential election of 1936.

W. Virginia
No poll tax
92%   26%
64%   Virginia
Kentucky
No poll tax
North Carolina
Repealed 1920
33½%   47%
Tennessee
South Carolina
Arkansas   14%
18½%
16%   20%   20%
Repealed
26%   1934   Alabama   Georgia
31%   Miss.
Texas   Florida
Louisiana   38%
Repealed
1936

Adapted from the Louisville *Courier-Journal* of 9 April 1939.

The payment of a poll tax was a qualification for voting in eleven states—all in the South—in 1920. From 1896 to 1916 the combined vote of these states shrank 18 percent, while the adult male population increased 50 percent. North Carolina repealed the poll tax as a qualification for voting in 1920. This resulted in an immediate increase in the popular vote. During the years 1916 to 1932 the vote actually increased 142 percent in that state. The states of Kentucky and Tennessee have just about the same population, but whereas Kentucky, where voting is not bound by the poll tax, cast 911,000 votes in 1936, Tennessee, with its poll tax prerequisite, cast a vote of only 473,000. The abolition of the poll tax requirement in Florida and Louisiana resulted in immediate increases in voting in those states. In Florida, for example, the special election in 1937 following the repeal of the tax showed an increase of 65,000 votes over the previous voting averages, while in the following Democratic primary voting was double that of the former averages in the state.

According to Barry Bingham, publisher of the Louisville *Courier-Journal,* "as many as 64% of the white adult voters have been disfranchised in the poll tax states, and in every one of those states, more whites than Negroes are barred from the ballot box by the tax." Bingham points out that not only do several of the poll tax states make the levy retroactive, but that they also

> require the payment of the tax months in advance of election day, and only the most wary citizen is likely to remember to pay up in time to save himself from disfranchisement. That is only one of a welter of restrictions that serve the sole purpose of confusing and confounding the would-be voter, to such an extent that in Arkansas and Virginia, for instance, it is not unusual for a citizen to require the services of an attorney before he can assure himself of a vote.[1]

It is typical of the states requiring the poll tax as a qualification for voting that the tax must be paid at a date which is determined by and is usually well in advance of the election. In Alabama the tax must be paid by February 1; in Arkansas, by October 1; in Georgia, six months before the election; in Mississippi, by February 1; in South Carolina, thirty days before the election; in Tennessee, sixty days before the election; in Texas, before February 1; and in Virginia, six months before the election. Not only does this set a trap for the unwary voter, but it requires the voter to safeguard his franchise at a time

1. "Do All Americans Have the Right to Vote?" Louisville *Courier-Journal,* 9 April 1939.

when interest in an election is at its lowest ebb due to the fact that the campaign has not even started. Moreover, it should be noted that the deadlines for the payment of the tax usually come in mid-winter, when cash is very scarce in the rural areas and when tenants and sharecroppers, who generally live on the credit system, possess none at all. George C. Stoney, in referring to the Texas poll tax technique, observes sagely:

> Paying a poll tax in February to vote in November is to most folks in Texas like buying a ticket to a show nine months ahead of time, and before you know who's playing, or really what the thing is all about. It is easy to forget to do, too, and here is where the politicians are obliging. They buy up as many poll tax receipts as they can before the books close, keep them on file and pass them out to their "owners" on election day—with instructions, of course, and an extra dollar or so for sweetnin'.[2]

The poll tax provides a serious medium for the corruption of elections. For many years, political machines have followed the practice of buying up poll tax receipts in large blocks and herding these bought voters into the polls in order to keep the political boss and his lieutenants entrenched in power.

In Hot Springs, Arkansas, a corrupt political machine shockingly abused the poll tax as a means of maintaining itself in power through alliance with the vice ring which it protected. A legislative investigating committee probed into the Hot Springs situation in February 1937. The testimony given before this committee is said to have disclosed the manner in which votes were cast through the purchase of poll tax receipts by some of the city's high public officials, and the pressure which the mayor of Hot Springs brought to bear on city employees to compel them to vote for the incumbent officials.

> . . . a certain citizen of Hot Springs testified that he had been present at a political meeting attended by Hot Springs police officers, firemen, and a selected group of citizens friendly to the machine, and that after Judge Ledgerwood of the municipal court opened the meeting Mayor McLaughlin stated that he expected 10 votes from every person present and advised them to get out and get poll taxes for 10 voters, but that if they could not do this themselves, then perhaps arrangements could be made to get the poll taxes.

2. Stoney, "Suffrage in the South. Part I: The Poll Tax," *Survey Graphic,* 29 (January 1940): 5.

This man also testified that one of the employees was asked if he had his poll taxes, and he answered, "No. I will get my own poll tax and vote for who I please." To this Mayor McLaughlin replied:

"Now, there is a man who can vote for whom he pleases, but after this election we are going to know how he voted and there will be some man to take his place. Now that applies to the drug stores and other business. The man that don't co-operate with the administration and vote right—that is, don't vote right for his boss—he will be boycotted in business. Get those poll taxes—down at the office you will find a slip there authorizing poll taxes for you. And I want those filled out. . . . I want you to bring them up so I can turn to them at any time and see just what we need.

"They had those pink slips and were handing them out on every corner," concluded the witness.[3]

In Chattanooga, Tennessee, the same administration has been in power for the past twelve years. Before each election, racketeers, bootleggers, and numbers and policy barons pur-chase large blocks of poll tax receipts as partial payment for the protection given their illicit enterprises by the city administra-tion. They provide fleets of automobiles for the political ma-chine in order that floating voters may be carried from one polling place to another to make use of the poll tax receipts which have been thus bought. Thus, there has developed a close relationship between the city administration and the vice ring, and the city suffers from a continually festering sore of corrup-tion and graft.

This is one of the evils of the Southern political process with which the Negro has little to do. As one Alabama informant put it, "Nobody ever goes so far as to pay a nigger's poll tax." This is quite true in Alabama and would be equally true for Georgia, Mississippi, and South Carolina. Some exceptions are to be found in Tennessee, especially in Memphis, and occasionally perhaps in Texas. But on the whole the Negro must pay his own poll tax, if it is paid at all. And when he does pay it, the only privilege granted is participation in the hollow general elections, if indeed that is not denied by action of the registrars.

Not only is the poll tax a great source of fraud in elections; it puts a premium on nonvoting. In Montgomery County, Ala-

3. *Congressional Record,* 76 Cong., 1 Sess. (5 August 1939), Appen-dix, pp. 4124–25.

bama, for example, the candidates for probate judge, "who are usually wealthy men," ride out into the countryside and persuade people to vote for them by getting them to sign up to have their poll taxes paid. The law allows a man to pay poll taxes for another so long as he does it without intending to influence his vote. This law is obviously almost impossible to enforce or even to interpret. Most of the states still adhering to the poll tax voting requirement have laws against anyone paying another person's poll tax. Yet it is a notorious fact that this is common practice in virtually all of these states. Authorities throughout the poll tax South condone these violations. Questionable practices associated with the poll tax qualification, other than the outright buying of the vote by payment of the tax, include discrimination in the granting of exemption from poll tax payment, misdating of poll tax receipts in order to give the appearance of payment of the tax within the required period, and employment of the check-off system for the tax payments of employees in mills and other industrial plants.

Complaints that "wholesale payments of poll taxes" were being used to influence selection of delegations to the national party conventions were filed with the special Senate Elections Committee in April 1940. Senator Guy Gillette of Iowa, chairman of the committee, was quoted in the Washington, D.C., *Sunday Star* of 14 April 1940 as saying that "no one factor could be used more to influence the election than these poll tax statutes. For instance, in a state with a poll tax of $2.50, boosters for a presidential candidate could go in and swing an important block of votes by spending $5,000.00."

The effect of the poll tax on voting in the South now has a direct significance for the continuation of the Southern region's great influence in the councils of the Democratic party. The eight poll tax states exert an influence in Congress and in national affairs out of all proportion to the population which they represent. Approximately 18 percent of the present House of Representatives and 16½ percent of the present Senate represent the oligarchical one-party, minority-controlled poll tax states. More important still, however, is the fact that chairmanships of the congressional committees are determined by seniority membership in the party in power. Half of the chairmanships of the twelve most important House committees are currently held by representatives from the small-voting poll tax states. The same condition exists in the Senate. It should be noted that the tenure of the congressmen from a poll tax state is, on the average, much longer than that of non–poll tax state congress-men. It is not uncommon for a congressman from the poll tax states to be elected with as few as five thousand votes.

The poll tax acts as an obstacle to Republicans in those Southern counties in which they have a chance to win political power under fair election procedures. For instance, in Hamilton County, Tennessee, Republicans charge that the poll tax has prevented them from winning the county. They are placed at a disadvantage due to the fact that the Democrats, "selling" poll taxes in the trustee's office, are able to exert great influence over the nature and extent of the vote in the county. A prominent Republican in Hamilton County explains that, while he is not in favor of the complete abolition of the poll tax, he is in favor of having it levied just as any other tax is: "The way it works now, it absolutely defeats the entire effort to have honest elections. The minority party has no way of raising revenue enough to qualify its people. If they did away with the poll tax, Tennessee, I know, would be listed in the doubtful column and this county would go Republican."[4]

The poll tax is very convenient for the Hamilton County machine politicians; they can look at the registration books, calculate how many votes they will need, and then go out and buy them up. This would seem to explain why in frequent instances there are large registrations and yet small votes in the elections. People register, expecting to have their poll taxes paid for them, and when the machine finds no need for extra votes, their taxes remain unpaid and they are disqualified. One Republican said to Stoney:

> The biggest benefit the tax payers of this county could receive is the repeal of the poll tax. It's not the only evil, but it is the biggest. If they would enfranchise everyone, regardless of color or creed, then I don't believe they or any other machine could control a majority of the voters of this county. I know because I went into politics. A bunch of us did in earnest. I had a house-to-house canvass made of every place in the fourth precinct of the twelfth ward [Negro], and we found 2,600 people of voting age. There weren't 400 of them registered. . . . You give me $30,000, and I can carry this

4. George Stoney's interview with a former member of the county board of elections, Chattanooga, Tennessee, 26 January 1940. Except where otherwise indicated, the quoted material in this chapter is taken from the notes of field interviews conducted by Stoney in 1940. —ED.

county for any man you name, if he has any decent name at all.

About $5,000 of it would go to support an organization. A paid organization is absolutely necessary. The rest would go to buy poll taxes and to buy votes.

First, I'd get every voter and person eligible to vote in the county on card indexes, with cross references and everything. I'd have about 80,000 cards. . . . I could make some kind of appeal to every group, enough at least to get a good share of the independent vote. With the poll tax, almost anybody who knew the town could do it.

The amount of the poll tax is $1.00 per year in three states, $1.50 in two, $1.75 in one, and $2.00 in two. In Arkansas the $1.00 tax is doubled in case of failure to pay. Sometimes receipts are required not only for the current year, but for previous years. In Virginia receipts for three years preceding are required. In Alabama the would-be voter between the ages of twenty-one and forty-five may be required to show receipts for every year that has elapsed since he was twenty-one. The only persons commonly exempted from poll taxes are veterans, disabled persons, and the aged. In South Carolina the requirement applies only to men.

Questionnaire returns received by the Division of Labor Standards of the United States Department of Labor, sent out in accordance with a resolution adopted at the Third National Convention on Labor Legislation, show unmistakably that many workers, farmers, and tenants in these eight Southern states are prevented from voting because of inability to pay the poll tax— a restriction which has been felt with increasing severity since the depression began. The questionnaires further reveal that the poll tax is keenly resented both as an undemocratic device and because it actively interferes with the election of candidates favorable to labor. The central labor union in a small Texas town says that the poll tax requirement has blocked the frequent efforts in Texas to ratify the child labor amendment. Again, it is reported that the secretary of an important Virginia central labor union writes: "Practically all labor legislation for the past ten years has been defeated both in the House of Representatives and in the Senate of Virginia due to the influence and vote of those legislators from sections of the state that have a low labor vote; the lower classes being not able to pay poll taxes." From Tennessee a labor official writes: "In every election, we find hundreds of workers who have registered but cannot vote because of lack of two dollars." In some towns in Tennessee, the burden is even heavier because of the addition of a tax levied by municipalities as well as the state tax. The secretary-treasurer of a Georgia central labor union writes that he has personally "come in contact with a large number of working people who would have voted all the way down the line for the New Deal if they could have had the $1 to pay the poll tax." The editor of a liberal daily newspaper in Virginia writes: "I think it is true that Virginia's backwardness in the adoption of social and labor legislation is attributable, in part, to the highly unreasonable restrictions which have been placed around the franchise."[5]

In Tennessee, Texas, and particularly Virginia, there have been prolonged and strenuous efforts at repealing the poll tax requirements. These efforts have failed because not enough sympathetic members in the state legislature can be secured. In Tennessee poll tax repeal bills have been introduced at session after session of the state legislature for the past fifteen years, but without success. Recent campaigns to repeal the poll tax requirement have been successful in two Southern states—Louisiana and Florida. It should be noted, however, that the Louisiana legislature did not perform a clean job on the tax, since it left a requirement that the voter must produce a poll tax certificate obtainable without payment of tax, which many of the Louisiana electorate still confuse with the old poll tax receipts.

The alleged fear that the abolition of the poll tax will open the floodgates of black political power is now often employed in the South to discredit the efforts of those who are striving to achieve some measure of democracy for at least the white population of that section. For instance, an editorial of 3 November 1939 in the Tuscaloosa, Alabama, *News* employs the threat of Negro domination as the basis for opposition to repeal of the poll tax:

> This newspaper believes in white supremacy, and it believes that the poll tax is one of the essentials for the preservation of white supremacy. It does not believe in a Democracy with a small "d", because it knows this country never has had such a Democracy and never will have such a Democracy as long as white supremacy is preserved. . . . If it is "undemo-

5. United States Department of Labor, Division of Labor Standards, news release, 26 October 1937.

cratic" to argue for white supremacy—as it certainly is—then we plead guilty to the charge.

Comparatively few people pay the poll tax in the poll tax states. The chief influence of the tax is a negative one, since no effort is made to collect it except from property-holders and others who wish to vote. As a revenue measure it would provide far more funds if it were divorced from its connection with voting and if its collection from all adults were to be strictly enforced. The Montgomery *Advertiser* reported on 28 March 1940 that:

> A tabulation released . . . by Comptroller I. C. Heck, shows that 181,496 Alabamians have paid $467,392 to exercise their voting franchise in the state primaries and the presidential election this fall.
>
> The 181,496 voters, who renewed their suffrage, is considerably short of the more than 300,000 who voted in the last gubernatorial primary. What makes the difference is the exempt status of a great number of voters over 45 years of age and war veterans.
>
> This becomes immediately apparent in Montgomery County, where this year, 6,950 residents paid $15,112 in poll tax. . . .
>
> The poll tax is $1.50 a year, but Alabama law—the only one of its kind in the nation—makes the arrears cumulative. Thus, if a voter has not paid for two years and wants to begin voting again, he must pay two years' back tax, plus the $1.50 for the current year.
>
> In election years, there is a tendency to pay up the arrears. This year in Clarke County, where most citizens are eating and sleeping politics, 3,564 voters have paid up. The average cost of requalifying was $4.86. One family alone paid $108. Approximately 6,000 expect to vote in May and November.
>
> In Cullman County, where the Democrats have to fight hard against the Republicans, it costs 5,431 citizens an average of $4.53 to requalify.
>
> "In Clarke County," said Comptroller Heck, "some payments were as much as $36."

In several Alabama counties the amount of taxes paid by voters and politicians reflects the existence of "hot" county races. In the absence of interesting campaigns, or in off-election years, a large part of the population lets its franchise lapse.

The main reason for the strong support for the poll tax in Alabama and the reason behind the recent defeat of a legislative measure to modify the poll tax is said to be the "race situation." The Negro vote would be small in the northern part of the state, but in southern Alabama it would possibly be the "deciding factor," and white people "do not want this influence" in Alabama politics. An American Federation of Labor leader in Gadsden favors, and thinks that most local members of the union favor, the poll tax, providing it is not cumulative. He takes this position because he believes that the tax helps to keep Negroes "down" in the southern part of the state. There is no fear of Negro voting in northern Alabama, where blacks are in the minority, but the registrars are considered wise in following the policy of allowing only Negroes who have property to vote. It is estimated that ten Negroes in Etowah County pay the tax. The tax collector observed that "one nigger came in the other day and paid up $36."

In Etowah County, as elsewhere in Alabama, some people are favored in the office of the probate judge by having part of their poll tax "checked off" and having to pay only the remainder of it. This can be done easily without the state's knowing anything about it, for all of the auditing that is done is by tax receipts taken from the tax office. People who pay back poll taxes go to the office of the probate judge and get a statement saying how much back tax is owed. This record is kept on individual cards. The tax collector does not question this, but issues a receipt for the amount paid. His records go back to the office of the probate judge and there payment is marked down on the individual cards. Those paid up are filed in the "qualified voters" drawer. The judge could take out one of these cards, make a few pencil marks on it, and cancel several years' back taxes without even his secretary knowing it, unless she was familiar with every single voter in the file.

The poll tax is admittedly the factor which limits voting in Etowah County, since "it mounts up till people just can't pay it." Yet it is considered a good thing because, as a member of the county board of registrars told Stoney: "It keeps a lot of illiterate people and them that's inclined to be radical away from the polls. There's just lots of them ['radicals'] in Etowah County. . . . This is a regular nest of them. They'd run the county, too, if they got a chance to vote themselves in. They'd ruin our county."

A state senator from Etowah County is of the opinion that the poll tax is a good thing for the following reasons: first, it goes to the schools; second, if a man lacks enough interest in the welfare of his community to make a "free will offering," then he is not the kind of a voter the state should have. It ought to be cumulative too—first, because it would not be "fair" to those who have been paying "all these years" to let the others by; second, the adults who pay it are really paying for the old schooling which they have already enjoyed—they are not paying for the privilege of voting; third, if a man only had to pay in the years when he wanted to vote, then it would be definitely a "political tax." The senator then went on to state his philosophy of voting:

> I   am not one of those men . . . who gets excited about the small number of people in Alabama we have voting. If people do not have interest in the issues, I think they ought not be persuaded to vote by a group of party workers. Besides, with 25 percent of the people voting . . . you are bound to get the best minds of the community and the best judgments in that 25 percent. It gives you a pretty good cross section of the intelligent people. . . .
>
> I think people make a mistake when they say voting is a right. If you will look back into the early history of this country as I have, I think you will agree with me that those men meant for voting to be a privilege. They set up our country on this theory that voting is given by the state to the individual as a matter of grace.

A collection of loafers in the sheriff's office at Elba, a courthouse town in Coffee County, Alabama, were in agreement that the poll tax is important because it "keeps the niggers" from voting. They understood that there was no danger in Coffee County, of course, since they could "handle" the few they had there, but it was the black belt which worried them. They felt that if it were possible to pass a law keeping the Negro from voting, repeal of the poll tax would be a good thing. Unless this could be done, however, it would be better not to take the chance. One member of this group, a sawmill worker, did not like the idea of women voting either, since they only vote when they are "kin to a man that's running."

It is an accepted fact that candidates pay the poll taxes for a great many people in Coffee County, though they give the money for it to the people directly. Said the clerk in the office of the county tax collector:

> I know they do. Of course, if somebody pays, we haven't

got a right to ask him where he got it, but bad as the crops were last year, I know the people couldn't have paid it themselves. Some people brought in ten and twelve dollars that hadn't seen that much money in a whole year. We run a farm, and a lot better one than most people, and we lost money last year.

The Alabama mills at Enterprise "registered some of their employees" for the first time this year. At the time for poll tax payment, the superintendent of the mill brought down the poll taxes for fifty of his employees and explained that he was taking it out of their wages, adding that he was going "to have all of them registered by next time."

A dozen or so white farmers were interviewed by Stoney at the Centerville courthouse in Bibb County. They were in favor of poll tax revision to the end that the cumulative feature of the poll tax should be done away with, though they did not think in terms of its total abolition. They all feared that the complete elimination of the tax would raise the dangerous problem of "niggers voting" and that if the poll tax were removed entirely, Negroes would be voting "in droves." They would tell tales of what happened back in Reconstruction days. None of them, of course, had any firsthand knowledge of those days, but it was "my father told me" or "I hear tell," etc. It would appear that the Southern demagogues have told this Reconstruction horror story over and over again, until it has become both a dogma and a historical certainty to these people.

The tax collector of Bibb County estimates that about 10 percent of the poll tax collected in that county is paid by mail. He explained that no effort is made to determine whether the tax payment comes from the person to whom the poll tax receipt is made out. He readily admits that candidates and, perhaps, companies or employers help the people pay the tax. To quote his picturesque language: "When a person you know ain't got a dime in the world comes in here and puts out six dollars, you know damn well *somebody* slipped it to him." The tax collector receives 2½ cents per name for receipts issued.

A committeeman in a UMWA local in Bibb County stated that he owed fifteen dollars in back poll taxes for the year 1939–40. He had made arrangements with a man in his local to "do the best he could for me," and this man went to the county probate judge and "got me right" for $10.50. This same man made similar arrangements at that time for eight other union members.

The informant displayed the certificate, which was marked paid for the years from 1933. The probate judge had marked "out of state" on his card for three of the years.

The politicians in Bibb County are satisfied with the poll tax. They are afraid that the vote "might get too big" if the tax were repealed. But there is no real "danger" of the Negro's getting to vote in large numbers in Bibb County should the poll tax be repealed. This is because Negroes are eliminated by the registrars.

The editor of the Centerville *Press* is against the repeal of the poll tax or the elimination of the cumulative feature because he believes that there are already enough people in the county who sell their votes. He declares:

> I see them coming to town the Saturday before election. They go to this candidate and pick up 50¢ and they go to that one and hit him for 50¢. It's got so now no smart candidate will give them anything unless he gets to see them mark their ticket. . . . If the tax were repealed, it would cost $10,000 to elect a probate judge. As it is now, the men in office have to spend most of what they make to stay there. This means that any man who can make a living in any other way doesn't fool with politics. I've been working across from that court-house for over twelve years and I know those fellows.

It is not the poll tax that is preventing a great many Negroes from voting in the South. As one Negro voter in Huntsville, Alabama, says:

> We have a number of intelligent, educated men and women here who would be glad to pay that amount of money if they could get registered. They would be willing to pay that much just for the privilege of saying they are full-fledged citizens. There would be at least a hundred who would register if for no better reason than to keep up with the Joneses.

The provisions allowing poll tax exemption for disability in Alabama have often been so abused as to result in "open scandal." The former law provided that anyone so disabled that he could not make a reasonable living at the profession or calling for which he was trained was entitled to exemption. Under this provision the exemption list in Madison County had always been high, sometimes running around four hundred. In 1936, with the commissioner's race coming up (this is always the most heated political race in the county), extra votes were being sought. Following the example of politicians in neighboring counties, certain of the candidates in Madison began bringing in their supporters who, according to the probate judge of the county, "had bad coughs, broken fingers, lumbago, or were hard-of-hearing." The number of exemptions reached about eight hundred before the books were closed.

Under the new law, however, a person must be "totally and permanently disabled" in such a way that he cannot earn a living; and, in addition, he must sign an affidavit saying that he has not had five hundred dollars worth of property within the last tax period. This has cut the total number now receiving exemption in Madsion County down to 150. People can register in Madison County without paying the poll tax, and a good many of them do. Some of these people hope that they will be able to get the money needed to qualify for voting. Others register in the hope that they will find some candidate who will pay their poll tax for them. Still others anticipate special exemption for disability. Responsible people in the county all agree that the poll tax is the main reason for the small vote. The circuit judge believes that the county should have a voting population three times as large as at present.

The president of the Textile Workers Union of America local in Marymack Village, a mill village about four miles from Huntsville, cannot vote because he is behind in his poll tax. He has been in Huntsville since 1918, but never registered until 1936. But by that time he was unable to pay poll taxes. He is forty-one, and thus owes in the neighborhood of thirty dollars for back taxes. He has a large family, none of whom vote, and buying that vote would be "like buying a house." He finds it difficult to urge other men in the union to pay their poll taxes and vote when they know he does not. Yet layoffs, strikes, and shutdowns have made payment actually impossible. The Marymack Mill workers are said to be notorious for selling their votes. In a recent campaign when the politicians tried to cut the two-dollar fixed price, they formed an informal brotherhood union and forced the price back up to two dollars.

From 1927 to 1934 the three textile mills in Huntsville were very active in politics. Two of the three mills required that their workers pay poll taxes and register. The tax books were brought to the office, and the workers paid or had it taken out of their pay envelopes. The mills, of course, encouraged their workers to vote "right." But this practice was stopped in 1934 when, after the first spurt of union organization, the employees voted solidly against the mill ticket. Since that time the vote in the mill boxes has declined sharply. Strikes, lockouts and curtailments, and the lack of compulsion have caused most mill people to fall behind with their poll taxes, and elections find them unable to exert the power they could have. They were, however, very active in the 1936 campaign, and in 1938, despite a lockout that came in the midst of the poll tax season and lasted through the voting season, they conducted a political program that has won the respect of politicians throughout the county. Under labor's Non-Partisan League, all three of the union locals held mass meetings before both of these elections, worked out their tickets, and issued sample ballots.

The Huntsville unions have urged their members to pay their poll taxes, but they have been able to carry on only a halfhearted campaign, because the workers simply did not have the money. Mat Williams, a "good union man" in Huntsville, says that the only good he sees in the poll tax is that "it's the only thing in the world I know of that makes a man glad when he gets to be 45." Williams, an ex-serviceman, like all other ex-servicemen in the union, votes regularly. But his wife does not vote, because she cannot pay her poll tax. He threatened to "pay it up" when several other union men were trying to save up money enough to "buy" their wives the vote, but then he got "hard up" and could not do it. Out of the fifteen or so men who "swore at the last election" they were going to enfranchise their wives, only two did so. It would cost Williams eighteen dollars to pay his wife's poll tax, and he explains that "one vote will have to do" until his boy gets three years older. This one vote is for a household of five.

"Politicians" pay other people's poll taxes for them "a-lots" in Madison County. This year, on the last day on which poll taxes were collectible, the tax collector's office stayed open until after midnight. The corridors were filled with people "hanging around, waiting for some candidate to pay their poll tax." The tax collector commented that every incumbent running for re-election was absent from the courthouse all that day, leaving the clerks to face the music while they hid from the clamoring voters.

The chairman of the Madison County board of registrars believes that it is right that the poll tax should be voluntary and a qualification for voting, because the act of paying is proof that a person wants to help support the schools, and this is "as good a test as any" of a man's fitness to vote. No one is required to show his registration certificate or his poll tax receipt at the polls in Madison County unless his name does not appear on the certified list. If it does not, and if he has these two slips, he can vote anyway, providing he takes an affidavit that he is a qualified voter. If anyone should challenge a voter, he is permitted to go ahead and vote, providing he takes the challenge oath.

The tax collector of Lee County states that about 60 percent of the employees of the Opelika Mills Company and a much higher percentage of those working in the Pepperell Manufacturing Company plants pay poll taxes. The workers in these textile mills pay their poll taxes "through the office." They are "signed up" at the payroll window and the amount is taken out of their pay envelopes. The voting is done in the company-owned recreation hall. Managers of elections are foremen and "people from the probate office." The foremen are known to be "big politicians" and to have much influence over the hiring and firing of men. Although the payment of poll taxes is more or less a voluntary proposition, according to the tax collector, one of the textile companies "drums it up" among its employees.

There are over four thousand property taxpayers in Macon County, Alabama, but only some eight hundred poll tax–payers. The tax collector of the county explains that this may not be understood "unless you know how many niggers we got." He estimates that perhaps fifteen Negroes pay poll taxes, including the president of Tuskegee Institute, who had been a registered voter in Texas or some other state "out that way." Most of the other Negroes who vote are veterans or over age. The tax collector admits that a great many poll taxes in Macon County are paid by the candidates. He tells of numerous cases in which a man would come into his office and pay the poll tax for eight or nine people—tenants on the same place, neighbors, people who work in the same store, and so forth. "I know a lot of them had it furnished, but that's none of my business to ask." He estimates that "from 20 to 40 percent" of the poll tax collected in the county is paid with money originating from political sources. In answer to a question about the number of tenants who vote, he replied: "Right smart of the tenants are voted." The probate judge estimates that "about 20 percent" of the total poll taxes collected each year is paid by candidates, though, he adds: "Nobody ever goes so far as to pay a nigger's poll tax."

The chairman of the Macon County Democratic committee
—who is also a state senator—expresses the view that the poll
tax is a good thing:

> It keeps out a certain class of white voter who isn't really
> competent to vote. In this county, and in some others, it pre-
> vents those Negroes who might want to vote for the money
> they might get out of it, from trying to register. . . . I know it
> doesn't keep out all those who might sell their votes, but it
> does keep out a great many. Some poll taxes are paid by the
> candidates, I know. It is done on both sides in a great many
> counties, just as it is here. It is never done only by one side.

It should be noted that the poll tax is the important factor in ac-
counting for the small number of women voters in Alabama.

This state senator also describes the method used to kill the
reform bill in the last session of the Alabama legislature: "We
[the leaders of the opposition] told the men from north Alabama
that its repeal would allow the Negroes to vote. We told the men
from south Alabama that it would increase labor's vote. By
playing labor and the Negro against each other, we had no
trouble in killing it."

The paying of people's poll taxes by candidates or their
"agents" in Cullman County has become an open scandal. The
poll tax has been paid recently in three ways: (1) it was given
out directly by the agents for candidates to one member of a
family who paid the tax for several members; (2) it was given
directly to the people who were then required to bring back receipts showing they had paid their taxes; (3) lawyers, acting
on behalf of the candidates, went about and solicited permission
to pay up people's poll taxes. The person thus benefited was
asked to sign his name to a statement giving the attorney power
to act as his agent. Attorneys, then, with long lists of names,
went into the tax office and handed over large sums of money.
These lists were checked with the probate judge's office beforehand to ascertain exactly the amount of back tax owed.

An election official who is also a county Democratic executive committeeman in Cullman claims to know personally "at
least fifty people" who have had back taxes paid this last season
by one or another of the candidates for probate judge. He states:

> One man came into the office—a nice fellow, I've known
> him for years—and he says: "I want to ask you some-
> thing. . . ." A supporter of one of the candidates had offered

to pay half of the $36 back poll taxes which he owed if he would pay the rest. The man wanted to do this, but felt he would be obliged to vote for the particular candidate, though the man had asked for no promise. This man was asking the election official what to do. He states that he wanted to vote for the other candidate, and so I told him to wait a minute. I went back and phoned up _____ and told him about it because I knew he was paying them up, too. _____ said "You send him up here, and we'll fix him up." And he went up there, and _____ paid the $18.

An election official in Cullman County, alluding to the huge poll payment made this year, estimates that "at least 2,000" people had their poll taxes paid for them and that it was done by "both sides." In describing how this was performed, he relates:

My boy, there, got his tax paid up by _____. I'm ashamed to say it, but he did. He's 23, and he hadn't paid his tax to vote, and I was after him about it one night when another fellow was over here. He said, if he'd go home with him, his daddy could fix it up. Well, my boy went home with this friend, and they went up to the courthouse together, and got right. I told my boy he ought to be ashamed of hisself, doing a thing like that, but he swore he didn't promise nobody how he was going to vote; but he knowed the man was aworkin' for _____, and you know, yourself, if a man puts out for you, you're bound to feel obligated.

This official hesitates to favor poll tax repeal for the following two reasons: (1) south Alabama might then be in danger of Negro domination. Cullman people have no such fear because they have no Negro population. Even so, they would be affected in state affairs by what transpires in southern Alabama. (2) It might turn a "whole mob" of voters loose in the big centers, to be "bought and paid for" by the unscrupulous politicians. He pictured Birmingham becoming another Kansas City. He spoke of a recent campaign in Cullman County in which the payment of people's poll taxes by others became so flagrant that: "It was done openly. It got so bad towards the last, people began taking from both sides. I know one fellow who said he owed twelve dollars. He collected from both sides, got a receipt and showed the same receipt to both paymasters."

The poll tax payments in Cullman County have been large

this year (1939–40) because of the intense interest over the
1940 election of the probate judge and the attempt of the Democrats to oust the Republican incumbent. The sheriff of the
county admits that many of these payments have been made by
the "political group," and though he does not have "definite information about where it's coming from, . . . I know it's not paid
by the people themselves in lots of cases." Although there have
been no convictions on charges of one person's paying the poll
tax for another in Cullman County, the practice is traditional
and of common knowledge. One prominent candidate, in speaking of this matter and referring specifically to a recent election
in the county, states:

> The parties interested in this election have put up about
> $15,000 this year . . . which came directly out of two candi-
> dates' pockets—one on each side. There is a great deal of
> sentiment about the poll tax in this county. I don't think peo-
> ple ought to have to pay anything for their vote, and a great
> many other people think the same thing. As long as you do,
> you are going to have candidates paying people's poll taxes
> for them, and what one does on one side, the other's got to do.

The registrar of Jefferson County, Alabama, estimates that 25
percent of the registered veterans in that county are under forty-
five and thus receive exemption from payment of the poll tax.
There are between 10,000 and 11,000 veterans on the certified
list, of which some 8,000 are active voters. The registrar himself is a big American Legion man and is said to deliver the
Legion vote. He estimates the total number of exemptions in
the county, including those excused because of disability, active
war service, national guard affiliation, and the like, to be approximately 3,600.

It is common practice in Alabama for men to register in a
new county and to be put on the books and given a clean poll
tax record on their word that they had already paid up. It also
happens that many probate judges will excuse a person some
or all of his back taxes if he is moving to another county to vote,
as a sort of "last favor." It is likewise common practice for people to register in a new county and to claim that they are over
age or exempt. When this claim is presented, many probate
judges do not bother to write back for records to see whether or
not the applicants have paid all taxes due. There are "any number of cases" where people have moved from Montgomery
County, owing from one to twenty years back poll tax, and are

now voting in the counties of their new residence without having written to the office of the judge of probate in Montgomery for a transfer. One possible explanation for this looseness is the fact that probate judges in the other counties see in the new voter a new supporter and do not bother to write back for records.

The tax collector in Birmingham is admittedly not very strict about observing the deadlines for the collection of the tax. He states that "when people tell me they honestly forgot it, and when I know every penny of it goes to the school, I don't see hardly how I can refuse to take their money."

The indications, however, are that this was a means whereby the tax collector could save a friend, for it was noted that the clerk did refuse to take the money of several people who offered it beyond the deadline. The tax collector believes that everybody knows when poll taxes are due, since all of the papers carry on campaigns, run streamer heads about it, and help the League of Women Voters in their drive to get people "paid up." To make it easier for people to pay the tax, the tax collector establishes poll tax booths over the county for a week or so before the deadline. About twenty-five of these booths are set up each two years, and they are manned by deputized League of Women Voters members, beat committeemen, or anyone else who can be trusted.

In Birmingham the Democratic party makes no effort to get people to pay their poll tax. Individual candidates do, however, and some candidates pay the poll tax for the people. Many of the business concerns insist that their employees pay the tax. Some of the mining companies formerly paid the taxes for their employees by the check-off system, but this practice has been discontinued "since they got unions." There is no difference in the tax requirements for men and women in Jefferson County, except that women's taxes are cumulative only from 1920. All decisions about exemptions are made by the registrar. The tax collector of Jefferson County finds no fault with the poll tax law. He states: "We here in Alabama are satisfied with our poll tax law." He admitted that it was "not much good for keeping the Negro from voting," but he defended the tax on the ground that if a man is not willing to pay $1.50 for schools, he is not "the kind of a citizen we want to vote." The chairman of the county board of registrars believes that without the poll tax requirement, politics in Jefferson County would be in a dangerous way. The miners shift about so much, the large population of construction workers drifts so extensively, and so many thousands of people migrate from the county that great numbers could easily be herded to the polls by a machine were it not for the poll tax—or so the chairman thinks.

Much of the poll tax in Montgomery County is paid through the mail, not merely by absentees but by city people who do not like to stand in line. The tax collector merely "assumes" that people who send in the money are the same as those who have signed the registration books. In Montgomery, the telephone and the power companies have someone in their offices bring in poll taxes for their employees in the different divisions. The tax collector assumes that this is taken out of the pay envelopes of the employees of these companies. He notes also that several of the "large mercantile establishments" warned their employees that poll taxes must be paid by a certain time, and that they have someone from their office come into the office of the tax collector to check on the employees midway in the tax collection season. The actual payment of the tax, however, is made by individuals. The tax collector observes that few men in Montgomery County dare announce their candidacy for public office before the close of the poll tax season and that those who are rumored to be candidates "get worried to death by people after them to get their poll taxes paid."

Members of labor unions in such textile towns as Dallas, Alabama, point out that they can catch the young people and register them, but that it is almost hopeless to try to get people past thirty registered, since they cannot afford to pay the back poll tax. The treasurer of the Dallas local of the TWUA states that he and his brother are the only ones in a household of nine who vote. His wife, a woman of twenty-seven, does not vote because of the poll tax. He adds: "I've got a sister-in-law that's dying to vote. She's 29. She's got my no 'count brother and three young'uns to feed. . . . That $14.50 would last her two weeks board bill on the whole mess."

The clerk of the election commission of Hamilton County, Tennessee, was very emphatic in his explanation as to why it would never be possible to do away with the poll tax requirement for general elections in that county. In answer to a query as to why this would not be possible, he replied heatedly:

> Why? And have some big, black son-of-a-bitch sitting up in the courthouse sending white men to jail? That's what would happen if the niggers started voting heavy here.

They'd have a black commissioner at City Hall—some sporting black reared back like God Almighty. No, Sir! Son, I'm not for that! I'm a Southerner and a Democrat. I was born and bred in the South, and that kind of thing ain't in the blood that runs in *my* veins. We had niggers on our farm. A nigger mammy carried me around when I was a baby, but you start saying a nigger's on equality with me and that don't go with me. No, siree! They outnumber the whites around this town and if we didn't have the poll tax, they'd out-vote them.

After admitting that quite a number of Negroes are permitted to vote, this same representative of Southern officialdom continued:

Soon as they start trying to do away with that poll tax, they're gonna have trouble. Some black bastard'll vote himself into City Hall and there'll be a race riot sure as hell. It's done it before. That's what we ought to have—something like that to kill off about three-fourths of the son-of-a-bitches. Got too many of them around here anyway. They're getting away with too much now. . . . Hell! They've got schools and libraries, and such as that as good as the whites. We ought to kill off about half of them and then put them back on the farm like it was in slavery time. That's the only way to do it. Hell! The way they talk now, you'd think any one of them black bastards as good as a white man.

This man was equally vigorous in his opposition to public health service and relief benefits for Negroes. He also vehemently denounced those "no 'count whites" who complain about the poll tax, especially those folks who "don't pay a cent of taxes; but that two dollars's for schools, and they're sending six or eight young'uns. That's the kind that kicks most about the schools, too. They ain't got sense enough to see how much the state's a-givin' them." The mayor of Chattanooga is also very clear in his attitude toward the poll tax. He stated, in connection with a question concerning the poll tax, "Yea! What you want to do, repeal it and have the niggers in this town bond us to death? They'd have this town in the poorhouse in two years. They don't pay taxes, so they don't care how much you spend."

In Hamilton County a "certified list of poll taxes paid" is made out each spring, printed, and sent in to the secretary of state in Nashville. In the early fall a supplementary list is made out in the same way. There is no racial identification in these certified lists. The poll tax is thought of as a unit tax of two dollars. Although the law calls it a one dollar state tax and a one dollar county tax, the amount is assessed as a lump sum. It is recorded on the county tax books only, turned over entirely to the county, and not audited by the state. The only state check is through the "certified list," and this is little more than a formality. Special elections are generally exempt from the poll tax requirement. No poll tax has been required for voting in the Hamilton County Democratic primary for more than a decade. The Republicans hold only county conventions. Poll tax slips are demanded of all those who vote in the elections in August. These elections are a combination of the county general election, the Democratic state primary, and the Republican state primary.

Only haphazard efforts are made to collect back poll taxes in Hamilton County. As the assistant trustee of the county explains it:

> You see we're supposed to collect it, but you always can't. Mr. Richardson [county trustee] at the first of the year he says "you got to get that poll tax." And, of course, we're strict at first. But it's just like it was in school, you know. They're strict on one thing for a while and then they are not so strict. When a man comes in to pay his taxes, we make up the bill and then we always ask him about his poll tax. Lots of people begin to argue. They say they're exempt or they live out of the state, or they don't vote anyway. Of course, if that's so, we don't bother them. The rest of the time we try to talk him into it. Of course, he can't vote unless he's paid his last year's poll tax. He knows that already without us telling him. But, that don't mean much to a lot of people.

As to the right of issuing a tax receipt for other taxes, if payment of poll taxes is refused, the assistant trustee explains that:

> Well, we're not supposed to, but most of the times we do, especially when they argue about it or when we're right busy like in February or March. Some people, they kick about paying poll tax because they think it's just something the politicians get, but when they find out it's for schools, they generally pay up. Lots of people pay up for the past few years. Maybe they don't have money for that before. When they think that this is about all they pay during their life for an education—something like $60.

The tax collection officials in Hamilton County apparently

exercise discretion in the amount of persuasion they employ on different people toward the payment of the poll tax:

> We always try to go easy on those people we know can't afford it, but if it's somebody we know's just trying to beat the county, we generally make him come back when he feels like paying. Lots of them do, too. Course it's pretty hard to make a nigger pay his poll tax. Of course, the school teachers always pay their taxes, and they vote. . . . But take an old nigger that don't own nothin' but a shanty that he pays $1.72 tax on. It's pretty hard to make him pay a poll tax.

Among those exempted from poll tax payment in the county are people over fifty, the physically handicapped (these must have a certificate from the county physician to be exempted), and people without state residences (as shown on the tax records). Veterans are not exempt in Tennessee.

Two episodes witnessed in the tax collector's office in Chattanooga are suggestive of the nature of poll tax administration in the South. In one instance an attempt was being made to "sell" the poll tax to an elderly farmer, who refused to be moved by the argument that "this is the only way you pay the state back for your schooling, and all you pay them is about $60 during your life." The farmer growled that he "never had no $60 worth of schoolin'." After prolonged argument, the farmer refused to pay the tax, and the tax official refused to give him a receipt for the rest of his taxes. The farmer went out very angry. The tax official commented: "He'll be back Monday. Just you watch. Imagine a man owning a farm worth $10,000 fussing about paying $2.00 poll tax."

In the other instance a bewildered middle-aged woman had commenced to pay taxes on property owned jointly by herself and her sister. The sister had always paid the taxes before, but was now ill. This was the first time this woman had ever paid taxes of any kind. Not having been billed for the poll tax, and the bill for the property having been sent to the other sister, she claimed to know nothing about it. To the tax collector's questions, "Haven't you ever tried to vote?" and "Haven't you ever thought about it?" she replied, "I don't bother about it." The tax official brought out a receipt for the tax and said he hoped her sister would be feeling better soon.

Schoolteachers in the county have little choice about paying the tax. As the county superintendent puts it: "We see to it that all the teachers pay their poll taxes. They can't get a contract until they do. Yes-siree, the teachers and everybody connected with the schools help do their best to keep up the schools." Any man can come in and buy poll tax slips for all of the members of his family. The clerks in the collector's office merely take his word for it.

The 1935 Tennessee Valley Authority election in Hamilton County, for which the poll tax requirement was waived, demonstrated the great increase in voting over the election to which the tax requirement applied. This indicated quite clearly that many more people do vote when no poll tax slip is required.

With reference to the allegation that certain labor unions in Hamilton County had bought poll tax receipts for their members, allowing them to pay on installment into the union treasury, the chairman of the county board of elections says:

> They're not supposed to, but I know they do. I guess the labor unions are guilty just like the rest when it's in the politician's interest to allow it. Of course, the trustees are supposed to uphold the law, and the law says it's a crime to pay poll taxes for other people, but they do it. They've done it for years. Why, they just put down the money and buy up a whole book of them.

The "vote herders" know some time in advance whom they can vote, and

> they're not taking such a big chance. They know whose vote they've got. It's mostly the underworld element, you know. They're afraid not to vote or to do anything else these fellows tell them, because when they get into trouble, he can help them out or he knows something on them. So, these herders, they register them, take up their certificates and buy poll taxes to go with them, and the fellow who votes don't see it till election day.
>
> There's a lot of talk around here about doing away with the poll tax. Right here in this town, there's a big sentiment against it. I'm against that, myself, and I'll tell you why. It would put the nigger in power. We've got a large Republican group here, and the nigger would be the balance of power. . . . Not that I'm against the nigra, understand, but ninety percent of his vote is a controlled vote. If he voted where his benefit lay, I'd be all for it, but he don't.
>
> About 90 percent of the nigras are nominal Republicans, and I guess they'd vote that way if they weren't balked by first one bunch and then the other.

As to the political use of poll taxes in Chattanooga, an experienced labor leader and campaign manager in local politics avers:

> Anything they tell you up at that county courthouse about not selling poll taxes to these ward heelers is barefaced lying. They buy up back-dated poll taxes after the books are supposed to be closed. . . . They never keep a record of receipt books. . . . I've seen them erase names and have people vote —two and three of them—on the same receipt. . . . In some of the wards, the Republican is bought off, or he's so drunk it don't make any difference to him. . . .
>
> What they do is, they take a whole book of extra receipts and put down the money for it. If they have to show an account of it, the money is there; if they don't after the election, they get it back. . . . I've seen men with whole fistfuls of poll tax slips and registration certificates, handing them out at the door of the polling places and taking them up when the people come out.

The trustee is an important county office in a county such as Hamilton, despite the fact that he does not assess taxes and has no judicial function, primarily because he does "sell" poll taxes. The following testimony by a local Republican suggests why:

> I'll tell you a story. I come from back up in the hills here, and when I was coming along as a young fellow, my father was elected trustee of the county on a Republican ticket. He was the only Republican in the courthouse when he was elected, and he was the first one elected in 14 years. Well, sir, he served three terms [legal limit] and before he got out, every single person in the courthouse was Republican. My father was a church-going, God-fearing, upright man. He never stole a dime or cheated a man out of anything. He didn't know anything about it—I guess he suspected—but, anyway, me and my brother handled the poll taxes out of his office, and we did just like the other crowd when they was in, until we had every JP's [justice of the peace] court in that county, and I can say it right out: the most common use of the poll tax in that county, in this county, and in every other county where the poll tax is a requirement for voting, is to control the election either through block purchase or bogus tax receipts.

It would seem difficult to employ "bogus tax receipts" when a certified list of people who paid the tax is printed. But it is explained that two lists are made out, or at least this was the practice when our Republican informant was a member of the board. One was the certified list, and this was not used at the polls; it was replaced by special typed lists, numbered and sent out to each precinct. On these typed lists were more than six thousand payments for which the county had actually received no revenue. Thus, in addition to the illegal purchase of poll taxes, these "bogus slips" were also in circulation.

The chairman of the Hamilton County Democratic committee has no doubt that the repeal of the poll tax would increase the vote enormously, but the politicians favor the tax because:

> It gives them a smaller field to work. . . . And they can control the vote better that way. I'm telling you these things because I like to think of myself as a little progressive. . . . But, by virtue of my holding a state job, I'm almost a part of that machine. You've got a bunch of men in there—I'll tell it to you straight—who want to control things for themselves. Not that they're selfish. . . . Yes, by God, it's because they're selfish! They want things to go their way, and they don't care about the poor devils who vote.

The machine politicians are for the poll tax because it serves their interest so well. As a political reporter for the Chattanooga *Times* states:

> The only damn reason they keep the poll tax is so they can control the vote—keep it small and control it. I've watched this thing 15 hours a day for 15 years now, and I know that for a fact. But, if they have the registration receipts, it won't be a hell of a lot better. Of course, the machine wouldn't know so well where it stood. They'd have to spend more money.

A former chairman of the county election commission and present editor of the *Hamilton County Herald* says of the poll tax:

> Sure, it makes all the difference in the world. We had a good example of it in the power election a few years back. The legislature passed a bill on taxing—on taxing the people— and we voted 27,000 here in the city of Chattanooga. They wouldn't have voted more than 18,000 at the outside, without it. . . . The poll tax is supposed to go to the schools, you know. I don't think very much of it gets to the schools, but it's a good way to keep a lot of the riffraff away from the polls. It's a

handy way for the politicians to keep in power, too, but it does keep a lot of people who don't have sense enough to vote from being herded.

In Virginia the poll tax is kept on the books first of all to prevent Negro domination or office-holding in the black belt counties of Dinwiddie, Amelia, Nottoway, Brunswick, and Prince George, and secondly to prevent the state from falling into the hands of the poor white semi-illiterates, who are living in want on a plane with the Negro and who share most of his grievances against the state government.

Although Negroes encounter less and less difficulty in registering and voting in Virginia, the state's poll tax of $1.50 per year, which is cumulative for a three-year period, is a restriction on black voting. It is equally restraining upon poor whites, of course. This requirement strengthens the Byrd-Glass state machine in Virginia, for the poll taxes of the poor whites are paid by machine men and those of Negroes by so-called "leaders" whose function it is to corral the Negro vote. In a political address published in the Portsmouth *Star* of 3 August 1938, B. A. Banks declared that the Byrd-Glass organization "dominates the state from the mountains to the sea with the weight of its dead hand; its tentacles in the shape of local machines, are found in every city and county in the state."

Figures obtained from the city treasurer's office of Norfolk reveal that the following poll tax payments are recorded: 1937 —18,309 whites as against 1,578 Negroes; 1938—19,201 whites as against 1,785 Negroes; 1939—18,329 whites as against 1,448 Negroes. According to one Negro political leader in Richmond:

> The poll tax keeps most Negroes from voting, as it does most white folks. If you miss a year paying your $1.50, it adds up each year for three years. Then you owe about $5.00 [penalty is added for delinquent payment], which you must pay *six months before the date of the primary election.* Then, you have to register. Registration is simple. You just write your name, address, and date of birth on a slip of paper the registrar hands you. He doesn't have to tell you what to write, however, and that's the joker in the deck. They used to mail everybody a notice when their poll tax was due, but they don't do that any more.[6]

6. James Jackson's interview with Roscoe Jackson, president of the Richmond Democratic League, Richmond, Virginia, October 1939.

The Southern Planter, a magazine with a wide circulation in the rural areas of Virginia, has carried on a vigorous campaign against the poll tax as a qualification for voting. In the following passages from the issue of January 1938, it debunks the argument that the tax in its present form is an important aid to education.

The outspoken defenders of the voter poll tax are, as a rule, quite insincere; for, in clever speech, they voice their desire for the tax as a pillar of support for the public schools; but, in their hearts, they cherish it as a sort of central wheel in a vicious political machine—a device for keeping the electorate small and readily controllable. Clothed in the guise of the defenders of education, they smugly decline to discuss the issue further than to pose the question: What would our free schools do without the revenue from the poll tax?

Our answer to this poser is: Have three times as much revenue for the schools by disconnecting the tax from elections. Treated strictly as a tax, the yield of the poll tax would be three times as large, and its burden far more equitable. For one-third of the adult population of Virginia the public schools and local treasuries now receive, on a four year average, about $700,000 annually; from the other two-thirds they receive nothing; but if poll tax collections were made fair and equal upon all persons over 21, they would receive more than two million dollars.

The majority report of the Committee on the Study of the Capitation Tax as a Pre-Requisite to Voting, representing the Young Democratic Clubs of Virginia, defends Virginia's poll tax law, declaring that:

It has been pointed out to us that other Southern states have abolished the poll tax and thereby increased the number of persons participating in elections. We again revert to our former position, has this resulted in any better government? The State of Virginia possesses a government inferior to none, and we submit without fear of contradiction, that the men in public office, on the whole, are of a higher type than in any other state in the Union.

It has been argued that there are many who cannot afford the poll tax, but with the thousands of dollars spent annually on tobacco, cosmetics, and similar luxuries by the great mass of the people, it is felt that it is not hardship, but a lack of any real sustained interest in the functions of government for which the poll tax is spent, that prompts the cry of unreasonableness. . . .

The majority of the committee recommends that no change be made in the present laws of Virginia respecting the requirements for voting.[7]

A strong minority report criticizing the above position was submitted.

A former general election commissioner in Pickens County, South Carolina, fails to see anything vicious in the poll tax, since it is only a dollar a year and one does not have to pay it in order to vote in the primary. But he does think that "it's a little hard to make a Negro pay it when he doesn't get a chance to vote." In Pickens County the poll tax is collected along with a one dollar road tax, which is charged to all males in the county between the ages of twenty-one and sixty. In a very few cases the county treasurer collects the two separately. This has been done when candidates for school trusteeships wanted to pay up people's taxes so they could vote. Many of them are said to do this. When people move out of the county, no attempt is made to follow up on them with respect to poll tax collection, and if a new person comes to the county, no effort is made to see whether or not he paid the tax in his last place of residence.

The mills in Pickens County help with the tax collection. For example, the Central Mill at Central and the Glenwood Mill at Easley will pay all taxes for their employees and take them out of their pay in weekly installments. They do this for road, poll, and personal taxes. The mills do this, however, only with the permission of the workers. The county treasurer states that the mills make no check to see if their employees do pay their taxes. Apparently, the mills are trying to avoid having to bother with garnishment, since wages are garnished for taxes. But these are the only two mills in the county that follow this practice.

There are about a thousand people exempted from the poll tax in Pickens County because of disability. As the county treasurer understands the law, it states that a man must be 50 percent disabled to be exempted. If the man is a veteran, the treasurer demands to see his government rating of disability; otherwise, he takes the county doctor's word about it or will "look for myself." The county doctor is very lenient, and, as the treasurer says, after all "if a man's sick and down and out of work, he's

7. *The Virginia Democrat* 5 (July 1939): 5.

'bout as bad off as a man that's got one leg and drawing a little old government pension."

Few people are required to show their poll tax receipts in general elections in Pickens County. In fact, the county treasurer knows of no cases where this has been required. Everyone is asked for the poll tax receipt in the school trustee elections, however, and these are definitely affected by the poll tax requirement. In the city elections both county and city registration certificates and poll tax receipts are supposed to be displayed. But the treasurer declares that he has never shown his and that he knows of no one who ever has. It is necessary to be registered with the city registrar, however. The city registrar will "take your word" for the fact that you have poll tax receipts and county registration certificates.

In Charleston County, South Carolina, 10,514 people paid poll taxes up through the deadline of 15 April 1940. The rest go "on warrants" to the sheriff, and he turns them over to the magistrates. The magistrates collect from about 2 percent of those sent to them. Neither they nor the sheriff take the time to follow them up. This means that the poll tax is not very rigidly enforced in Charleston County. There is no road tax to attach to it. The county treasurer of Charleston County thinks that, in view of the lack of enforcement of the tax, the amount collected is surprisingly good. Many people, especially country people, are said to register so that they may serve on the jury. Regular jurors get three dollars a day and grand jurors five dollars.

There are a good many Negro property owners in Charleston County—this is characteristic of the low country. All of these pay poll taxes and many of them register also. Few of them vote, however. The treasurer of Charleston County states that he does not think that "voting ought to have anything to do with it [that is, with the poll tax]. I look on it as an educational tax. That's where all the money goes. A good bit of our poll tax comes from people who don't pay any other kind of tax, and they may have four or five children in the public schools." The chairman of the Charleston County board of registrars is very much opposed to any change in the poll tax law because "it saves us from having a great big nigger vote." Furthermore, if the poll tax were not required, the juries would be "half black."

The treasurer of Charleston County declares that there is no block paying of poll taxes by politicians or by anyone else in the county, and that no industries or other employers aid in the collection of the tax. In the first instance, there is no point, since general elections are mere formalities in the county.

The county treasurer of Greenville County recognizes that the number of road and poll taxes charged on the digest "isn't half what it ought to be." The reason it is not larger, according to the treasurer, is that he has no way of locating people without property. No check is even made of the auto license applicants. There are no arrangements with employers for help either in collecting or in making up the digest. Rural people pay much better than those in the city because in the rural areas the school trustees help make up the digest. Most poll taxes are collected from people paying other kinds of taxes. No one pays it to get on jury lists, since people may register without paying the tax. The county treasurer does not think that poll holders enforce the requirements about showing poll tax receipts at general elections except in the case of school trustee special elections. Since people who do not have property to seize are difficult to collect from, and since the amount is small, they simply do not bother with it.

The poll tax is an important factor in South Carolina politics, especially in city politics, despite the fact that it is not a prerequisite for voting in the Democratic primary. For instance, one must have his poll tax paid to vote in the Greenville city primary. It is especially important in Greenville County, because it is not strictly enforced unless one wants to vote or owns property. John Culbertson, a white defender of Negro enfranchisement, reports that when he wanted to get settled-up to vote in the Greenville city election of 1939, it cost him eight dollars. He did not know what made the bill so high, but thinks that a part of it was for street tax, a part of it interest, and a part probably execution fee. He points out that all of this has the same effect as a cumulative poll tax. Only 1,822 votes were cast in the last Greenville city primary in 1939, and Culbertson attributes this ridiculously low vote to the poll tax.

For the year 1939 there were 2,985 road and poll tax bills posted on the tax books for Beaufort County, South Carolina. Approximately 1,700 of these were collected in the office. Another 250 will be collected by the magistrate, and the rest will be collected by the sheriff. The digest for road and poll taxes is made up from the previous year's books with reports from the deputies in each district, and with the school trustees and the sheriffs and deputies adding to it each year. The tax is seldom cumulative. According to the county treasurer: "Unless we know that a man has been deliberately trying to beat us out of it, we don't charge him back tax." Often the cost of collection of the tax is more than the amount collected. Collection is forced, just the same, because it makes general collection that much easier. At the present time about 95 percent of the poll taxes and road taxes are said to be collected in this county. Since about 1932, only about ten people have been put on the road to work out their road and poll taxes. This can be done in a period of two weeks. About half a dozen people each year, who are said to be making a deliberate effort to avoid payment, are forced to pay the ten dollar fine in addition to costs.

About one hundred people in Beaufort County are exempt from the poll tax because they are "physically incapable of making a living." They obtain a doctor's certificate or "we know them to be entitled to exemption." The county treasurer uses his own judgment on such matters since there is no strict rule.

The poll tax has no connection with the Democratic primary in Beaufort County. The only election in that county where the poll tax is important is in the Port Royal municipal election. Port Royal has no primary, and, according to the laws of South Carolina, to vote in a municipal general election, a person must have a municipal registration certificate. A new one must be secured for each election. To secure one of these, a person is required to show a county registration certificate, plus a poll tax receipt for the previous year, and in some places he must show a city tax receipt as well. Beaufort has a municipal primary. Rules for voting in this election are the same as for the county primary. Technically, a person is supposed to show his poll tax receipt in order to get a registration certificate, but, according to the county treasurer, this rule is not enforced.

Thus, since the general election is meaningless in Beaufort County, the poll tax has little effect upon county government. The county treasurer estimates that there are about half a dozen white Republicans in the county and two dozen Negroes who vote—all of whom are assumed to be Republicans. Negroes are charged poll taxes just as whites are, and this practice is defended on the ground that Negroes receive "more than their share" of the police and welfare service, school facilities, etc., and pay little tax.

The Southern apologist for the poll tax usually waxes sentimental in pointing out that the revenue from the poll tax all goes to the support of schools. This is a part of the sales talk for the tax. In fact, however, the tax makes no significant contribution to educational revenue—for the reason that it is a regulatory rather than a revenue measure and in the very nature of its operation cannot contribute important revenues to the school treasuries.

The poll tax does cut down the number voting in general elections in Beaufort County, for it is the requirement that receipts must be shown rather than the amount of the tax that affects the voting. Until some ten years ago, poll tax enforcement in Beaufort was lax, but now the officials are "bearing down" on people, and it is estimated that about 90 percent of them pay it.

Women are not subjected to the poll tax requirement in South Carolina. When these provisions were passed, the idea was to make it difficult for Negroes to vote. When the presentation of tax receipts became burdensome to whites, however, the poll tax receipt was substituted. When women got the suffrage, the poll tax requirement was not extended to them.

Poll tax exemptions are handled loosely in Sumter County. If a man comes in who looks like he is totally disabled or unable to support himself, the county treasurer will grant him an exemption. The special deputy does the same thing if he finds a person in this physical condition for whom he has an execution. No doctor's certificate is required. The county treasurer estimates that there are a "couple of hundred" in Sumter County who are thus exempted.

The treasurer of Sumter County is very sympathetic toward people who are unable to pay their poll tax, allows them to pay it in elaborately worked out installments, and never fails to ask after the health of the crops. He reports that $3,711.40 (including interest at 1 percent per month) was collected in Sumter County for poll taxes on 1939 digest before the books were closed. The rest has been put on execution and will be handled with a special deputy in charge of past-due taxes. The most a person can pay for the poll tax in Sumter County is $1.50. The county has a road or street tax of $2.00 that is collected along with the poll tax, although the two may be paid separately. All property owners except women are forced to pay poll taxes. All others are required to pay "if you can catch them." The treasurer explains that "South Carolina has this voluntary system of taxation."

The poll tax is said to be hard to collect in Saluda, South Carolina. In the first place, it is allegedly difficult to get the people on digest for it who do not have other property, and in addition, the county districts are thinly populated. Until April 15, people may pay their poll taxes at the office of the county treasurer. Until that date they pay not in excess of $1.07. When the tax goes into execution, however, there is a $1.25 fee added —$1.00 of which goes to the special sheriff's deputy who is responsible for all delinquent taxes. Twenty cents goes to the treasurer for making the execution. Since half of all tax receipts in Saluda County go on execution, the slightly larger proportion of poll taxes going into execution is not surprising. There are half as many dog taxes paid in the county as there are poll taxes.

The state of Arkansas witnessed an intensive campaign for the passage of a law repealing the poll tax in 1938. This campaign for repeal was mainly directed by Brooks Hays, the national Democratic committeeman and present counsel to the Farm Security Administration. Reactionary forces in the state, however, used the bogey of Negro domination and also spread rumors among the population that the repeal of the poll tax would greatly reduce the available money for schools. Opponents were able to defeat the bill for repeal. Only one daily paper in Arkansas, the Jonesboro *Daily Tribune*, favored the repeal legislation.

Brooks Hays connects the fight for the repeal of the poll tax with the fight of the Negro to end his disfranchisement. According to him, there exists no articulated sentiment within the Democratic party which would support a move to permit the Negro to vote and to participate in the Democratic primary. He feels, however, that many Democrats will support a move for the abolition of the poll tax and, thus, through the active participation of the Negro in this struggle, the basis can be laid for a more effective attack upon the white primary. He thinks that the abolition of the poll tax would give opportunity for the Negro to demonstrate the potency of his vote in bond issues, national elections, general elections, and in support of independent candidates. When the white politicians are thus impressed with the significance of the Negro vote, they will seek that vote.[8]

The poll tax has contributed greatly to political graft and corruption in Arkansas politics. There is no secret ballot in Arkansas. The long ballot is used in all elections. The ballots are issued in duplicate. They are numbered and the voter must sign

8. James Jackson's interview with Brooks Hays, Little Rock, Arkansas, December 1939.

them after they are marked. The duplicate is put on record and the other one is deposited in the ballot box. The April 1939 ballot for municipal offices in Little Rock was almost the size of a newspaper, and it was necessary to mark it in the open on the desk of the election officer.

Such obstacles to the free exercise of the franchise in Little Rock have been highly effective in defeating the democratic process and in reducing the number of voters to a relatively small number. For example, in the 1937 general election for mayor of Little Rock, only 357 votes were cast, and in the primary held prior to this election fewer than 3,000 ballots were cast. In the 1939 mayoralty election, only 1,700 votes were cast.

In Georgia the poll tax is collected along with all other taxes. Record is kept of it on the same books. It appears as a notation on all forms made out for drawing up property, land, and other kinds of taxes, and when a man has other taxes, his bill includes this notice. Otherwise, no written notice is given to him that he owes poll tax. If a man once declares that he owes the poll tax or ever once pays it in the county, then he stays "O.D." ("on digest," meaning that declaration is made that tax is owed so far as poll tax is concerned). The main way the tax collectors get wind of people who owe the poll tax and who do not declare it is through the work of the school boards of the different districts. All local districts levy a special local tax that goes to the schools in that district. The poll tax also goes to the schools, but not in that way. It is sent to the state and is prorated back to the counties just as they pay it, and put into the grammar school fund. This fund is divided as other moneys are, between white and Negro schools. However, since these special local taxes for schools are levied on personal property as well as other property, and the school boards comb their districts quite thoroughly, many people who have not declared themselves for the poll tax are thus revealed. This holds true only for whites, however, since Negroes have no such local special tax because, if they did have, they would be entitled to a share of the local school tax.

In Georgia all males of twenty-one or over and all women who have ever registered to vote are supposed to pay the poll tax. In Hall County the tax collector claims that he enforces this law, and it seems that he does—as regards women, at any rate, for when a married woman is registered, the tax is put in her husband's name. Daughters living at home have their taxes included on their father's bill. Until recently, a woman could come in and ask that her name be removed from the registration list and thus have the dollar charge stopped, but this cannot be done any more.

In checking over the poll tax receipt and registration books in Newton County, Georgia, the tax collector estimated that there are approximately four thousand white persons in the county who would be liable for payment of the poll tax. Only 2,707, however, were actually charged with the tax. The explanation for this is that if a person has failed to pay the poll tax for a period of several years, the tax collector is not inclined to charge him with it. About two thousand actually pay the poll tax in this county. People over sixty years of age can become qualified voters without payment of the tax. Thus between 2,500 and 3,000 white people in the county are qualified voters. The tax collector estimates that about two thousand Negroes in the county should be liable for payment of the tax. Actually, however, only 314 Negroes are charged with it. Of these, the tax collector states, only about two hundred pay the tax. This official says that Negroes are just as anxious to pay their poll tax as whites when they are charged with it. But very few of the Negroes follow up their poll tax payment with actual registration. The tax collector estimated that only some twenty-five Negroes in the entire county were registered. These Negro registrants come from two categories: the old Negro families who have memories of past political participation and desire to continue to vote; and the more wealthy Negroes in the community who look upon registration as a form of social prestige even if they are not permitted to vote. Both the poll tax and registration books carry separate printed columns marked "colored."

The tax collector of Newton County is very emphatic in his allegation that he has never attempted to keep a Negro from registering, providing he has paid his poll tax. When asked how he could then explain the fact that so few of the Negroes who have paid the poll tax are actually registered, he stated: "Negroes just don't have the nerve to come up and ask for registration. They feel that they could not and should not register."[9] The tax collector further admitted that Negroes are definitely discouraged by the white people of the community from appearing for registration.

In Hall County, Georgia, the total amount of poll taxes col-

9. Gunnar Myrdal's interview in Covington, Georgia, 7 November 1939.

lected for 1938 was $4,283. The total number of people listed on the rolls used by the poll officials in the March 1940 primary was 7,551, of whom 1,395 were listed as sixty or over. The county tax collector, when asked how the remaining 6,156 were eligible voters when the total tax collected was only $4,283, and much of this was back taxes, explained that he did not know. A part of this was accounted for by the number of people who had transferred from other counties (and having paid up all taxes there). Another part, perhaps a large part, was accounted for by the number who were twenty-one this year and thus did not have to pay, or women who were registering for the first time. It would seem certain, however, that a number of people in this county must have voted without paying any poll tax, though they were legally obligated to do so. According to the tax collector, the only people who are under any pressure from their employers to pay the poll tax are the schoolteachers.

The last day of assessment of the poll tax is December 20, and the payment period begins October 1. The payees have until May 5 to pay the tax in order to vote in the state primary and in the general election following in September or November. Seven percent interest is charged on all back taxes. If a person fails to return his tax by December 20, *even if he is on digest,* the collector has a right to charge him fifty cents extra for issuing a feoff. Actually, however, the tax collector in Hall County does not charge this fee, and the bailiffs "seldom, if ever" are called upon to collect poll taxes. States the tax collector of Hall County: "I could charge that and make a couple of thousand dollars right easy-like every year, but it would make everybody mad. You know, we got a lot of poor farmers in this county. Every little quarter or fifty cents comes hard. If you can cut it down, it's that much more they've got to spend for overhauls."

In Hall County no receipts are issued in blank for poll taxes. This is not necessary in view of the fact that the display of receipts is not required at the polls. In order to vote, a person must appear on the list of qualified voters. So little value is attached to the poll tax receipt that people often tear up or throw away their receipts, especially those in the cities. There is no payment of poll taxes outside of the tax collector's office, except when payments come in by mail, and there is very little of this. There is no law requiring the tax collector to make his circuit as in Alabama.

There have been no distress sales or garnishment of wages for poll taxes in Hall County, though this is possible under the law. Negroes who pay property taxes and buy automobile tags and the like are charged a poll tax whether or not they are registered. Most of the others have no property that could be seized. There are no school trustees to help the tax collector keep tab on them, and few Negroes register. Actually, only Negro property owners are forced to pay the poll tax, unless they are registered.

While Stoney was in the office of the Hall County tax collector, he noted the following: (1) a man came in, paid the poll tax for his wife, daughter, and six other people whom he had looked up beforehand (none had the same name); (2) a stenographer came in and paid the tax for six people in her government loan office; (3) the tax collector's brother stood yelling out the door or window at people who were passing, telling them to come in and pay taxes—"come on and slap down a dollar so you can vote."

In Hall County a person cannot register if he owes poll taxes. On the other hand, the practice seems to be to charge no person, white or black, male or female, any poll tax unless he is a registered voter. A Gainesville election official estimates that repeal of the poll tax would increase the local registration by at least four thousand. A good part of this increase would be women's votes. But the rest, this official declares, would be "a lower-class element who have no property, no money, and no responsibilities." These votes are said to be the "bought votes." If the poll tax requirement were repealed, all of them would have to be bought, according to this man, and he is therefore against repeal.

A small farm owner in Hall County points out that not only does the poll tax take the vote away from many poor people, but it makes it difficult for the poor man who wishes to run for public office. In illustration, he noted that in the recent county primary, one of the candidates for the office of sheriff:

> didn't have the money to put out like Bell, and he lost. I worked for Lawson and I know. We registered everything in this district that was 21 years old and had two legs. If they didn't owe more'n two years' taxes, we paid it up, but we couldn't go no higher. Bell was a payin' them as high as six and eight.

The wife of a poor sharecropper on a plot just north of Gainesville states that her husband votes most ever time when he ain't behind in his taxes. This last time he lacked a dollar and a half paying it, so he didn't get to vote. He went up there to vote, thinking it was all paid. He owed five dollars and a half, and Charlie Bell [brother of the sheriff] said he was gonna pay it up for him. I don't reckon Charlie had it all to pay. . . . I voted. First time. Charlie Bell, he registered me, and he said I could vote without it costing nothing, so I did. They say I'll have to pay if I ever vote again.

She explained that she would vote again "if somebody pays for me." She thinks that her husband votes for "whoever he is ast to."

In Hall County it is said that candidates who pay people's poll taxes "don't know how people are going to vote—or whether they are or are not. I've seen it happen many a time that you give a man money to pay up his poll taxes, and he'll never pay them." Some candidates guard against this by taking the money to the tax collector themselves. The candidates employ go-betweens in the paying-up of poll taxes. As a textile worker in Gainesville describes it:

They don't yell out they'll pay poll taxes. Everybody'd be on them, but after they talk to you a while and know you're for their man, and you say you can't vote cause you haven't paid your poll tax, they say they'll fix you up. . . . Hell, naw. They don't give *you* the money. They run it in themselves.

Candidates pay poll taxes for voters to such an extent that the tax collector of the county estimates that it runs into a "fair proportion of all that is paid."

According to the checklist of registered voters used by the tax collector in Johnson County to inform candidates and others of who has and who has not paid up poll taxes during 1939–40, it was discovered that 1,311 of the total number registered are either one or two years behind in taxes. According to the stated requirements of this county, anyone can register who pays taxes back to the last registration. In commenting upon this situation with regard to the poll tax, a member of the county board of registrars observed:

Trouble is, in this county there are so many people on there [registration rolls] who haven't got the money to pay up them poll taxes. They got in the habit of depending on the candidates to pay it up, and it got to be where it was a terrible drain on them. It wasn't so bad when they paid up 25 or 50, but times have got so hard there wasn't enough money in for them to put out for all them people. It was too much.

It is said that the poll tax keeps few people from voting in Johnson County. The tax collector makes out lists of all who are registered and who owe the tax, and the *candidates* take these lists out, bargain with the people, and come back in and pay up the taxes themselves. The editor of the Wrightsville *Headlight,* the county weekly, advises that: "They ought to do away with the poll tax. Things would be a heap better off if they would get rid of it and tighten up on the election laws to cut out so much of this vote buying. They was doing it so much here in this last primary till it got to be a regular business."

Exact figures on poll tax payment in Richmond County, Georgia, were not available, but Wilhelmina Jackson secured the following figures during her visit to the tax collector's office on 13 February 1940: number charged for poll taxes—1,605 Negroes, of whom about 75 percent have paid the tax and 1,500 are registered; 8,696 whites, of whom about 78 percent have paid the tax and 14,000 are registered in the county.

In Greene County, Georgia, the poll tax is collected from all Negro property owners, automobile owners, and any other Negroes the tax collector can get on his records. In a recent election in this county, an agreement was reached between the contestants and the tax collector to the effect that anyone who paid four dollars or who had it paid for him would be allowed to register regardless of how much poll tax he owed.

A warehouse checker in Greensboro stated that he and his wife did not vote in the last county election because: "We was behind with our poll taxes. I've been a sick man. Every cent I could get together went for medicine or doctor bills, or something or other. I just didn't have the money to pay it." But he explained that he and his wife had always voted before. Referring to the big vote in the last county election in Greene County, he continued:

> There always is every four years. The candidate pays up people's poll taxes. I don't believe in such as that. It ain't right. You know it ain't. . . . You're not a citizen if you don't vote. They ought to think about it when they vote, too. They ought to realize the privilege they got of electing the people that rule over them. . . . But just a heap of folks can't get up the tax. . . . 'Course the county's got to get taxes from somewheres.

As FSA renter in Greshamville who in order to vote at a recent election had to pay a back poll tax of three dollars, half of which was paid by a candidate whom he was supporting, explained that his wife did not vote because:

> Her taxes wasn't paid. She owed four dollars, and I didn't have that much money to put out. Floyd Freeman [one of the candidates] come by here talking, and he said he'd see they was paid. Well, I didn't see after him about it, and I didn't go up to the courthouse and hang around, begging somebody to pay them—I'll be damned if I'll ever do that—so they didn't get paid. Her name wasn't on the list when it come out. If you've got to know the truth about it, that's it.

As if to excuse himself, he added: "There's plenty around here who *did* go begging and then voted against the man what paid it." This he considered the lowest trick of all. As for voting regularly, he commented: "I got other things to spend that money for. I got seven mouths to feed."

When asked if candidates pay up poll taxes for voters, the tax collector of Greene County exclaimed: "Oh, yes! They're right nice about that." His assistant interposed, "You don't quote that." To which the tax collector responded: "Why not? There's no law against it, and if you stay in town ten minutes you can find it out. I guess a fourth of the poll taxes I collect are paid with money that comes from one candidate or another."

In Chatham County, Georgia, no one is up "on digest" for poll taxes unless he has other taxes to pay; then the poll tax is added to the regular tax bill. Otherwise, the poll tax is issued on a separate receipt and never appears on the digest. Actually, therefore, it is not assessed. No one is charged the poll tax unless he owns property or is registered, or both. Unregistered people without property are not charged. The tax collector of the county claims that all male property owners, Negro as well as white, are required to pay the tax. No bills or notices are sent out about the poll tax, and no notice other than the regular advertisement concerning all taxes is given in the papers. In earlier years the registration board used to send out notices in April warning people that they would be struck from the voting list if payment of the poll tax was not made, but this practice was discontinued when the courts ruled that failure to pay a poll tax automatically disqualifies a voter and that no notice is required in order to purge him. Thus, people owning property receive the reminder when they pay their other taxes. Non–property owners can go on for years without knowing or being reminded of their delinquency.

The poll tax is charged cumulatively from the time when a man becomes twenty-one or from the time a woman first registers. It has never been the custom in Chatham County to charge either feoffment costs or the extra penalty fee for late payment. When the sheriff collects poll taxes as a part of a poll tax bill, he does charge a feoffment on the whole bill. The sheriff can force a person to pay only seven years' poll tax as a part of a total tax bill, but in order to qualify to vote, citizens must pay all poll taxes, since this is considered not as a legal tax debt which would be affected by the statute of limitations, but as a qualification for voting comparable to the literacy test. The largest poll tax collected by the tax collector, as he recalls it, was twenty-four dollars, though each year a number of people pay from eight to ten dollars in back tax. It is admitted, however, that a great many people in the county "get by" without paying the full amount of the tax by claiming that they were out of the state.

The relatively small vote in Savannah is explained by the chairman of the Democratic county committee as a result of the poll tax. In commenting upon the poll tax, he stated: "It keeps a lot of trash out. . . . It keeps a lot of good people out, too. I know a lot of women who registered eight to ten years ago, and now they can't vote because they don't feel like going back and paying up that poll tax." While admitting that something ought to be done about it, he reflected that "it might turn things over to the WPA." Poll taxes are cumulative in Savannah. If a man desired to register at age fifty, he would have to pay up poll taxes from age twenty-one. Women, however, are in a more favorable position, as they need not pay poll taxes until they first register. Following their registration, however, they are required to pay. Thus there is no prior poll tax qualification for women.

It is admitted in Chatham County that the machine does pay up "a certain number" of poll taxes. Each man in the ring, disclosed one county official, "is supposed to keep up his following —maybe 50 or 100 votes he can carry all the time—if he's a big man." This man says that "not more than 20 percent" of the poll taxes are paid in this way.

No attempt is made in Macon County, Georgia, to collect poll taxes from unregistered people unless they pay other kinds of taxes. Negroes who own property and pay taxes on it are required to pay the poll tax just like others, whether or not they are registered. The only exemption made in Macon County, as in Chatham, is for the blind. Until the present registrar assumed office, the tax collector is reported to have generally "used his discretion" about putting people on the tax list. Few people were ever required to pay more than one or two years in back taxes, and even now, it is said, not everyone is obliged to pay the extra penalty and feoffor's fee. The sheriff and the tax collector frequently leave off their fifty cents fee for friends. Since it is their own loss, nobody else can complain, and it makes good political capital.

The tax collector feels that the poll tax law ought to be stricter than it is and that 1940 taxes ought to be required in order to vote in the 1940 elections, on the assumption that "any man who thinks enough of his vote will pay that." In order to prove his point, he took out a registration list and pointed to the names of people whom he considered as undesirable voters. Most of these people had registered either at twenty-one or during an intensive local primary camapaign when, so he said, somebody had paid up their taxes. This class of people seemed quite numerous, in his estimation, and among his remarks concerning them were these: "No good." "WPA loafer." "She's got a bastard baby." "Five boys in the family, and they buried their daddy without getting him embalmed." "Been to the pen twice." None of them should be permitted to vote, he declared.

The sheriff of Macon County explains that the list of voters in the county this year is very short because of the poll tax. Many people have got behind because there have been no lively county contests. The sheriff adds: "They won't pay until 1942 or 1944 and then come in expecting some candidate to pay it up for them. Well, they needn't be coming to me, because I've paid my last poll tax for *anybody*." The sheriff admitted that he had paid a few poll taxes because "everybody else that has run has paid up a few, too," though he believes that the practice is not so frequent in Macon County as in other Georgia counties. He says that some Talmadge supporters had paid up back taxes this year and that he could call names if he wanted to do so, pointing out that: "They're getting ready for the governor's race. I told them they were wasting their money. Talmadge is going to carry this county anyway."

The Macon County tax collector admits that the poll tax restricts registration and that this explains the small vote in the county:

A lot of farm women vote once and don't pay up their tax. It gets up to six to eight dollars. It's too much. They don't vote any more.

In this county—in every county for that matter—you've got two classes of people. You got people who will vote the way they think they ought to and you got another class you can buy with a dime. I think we ought to keep this bunch out of elections all we can.

Arguments advanced against the repeal of the poll tax as a qualification for voting in Georgia are the following: (1) it amounts to very little, almost any person can save up this amount; (2) if the poll tax were repealed, the state would return to the old requirement that *all* taxes must be paid—this would cripple the men who are considered most able to vote; (3) it would throw open the polls to a "lower element" that is too much in politics already—vote buying would increase and there would be more instead of less corruption; (4) "you've got to keep the nigah down. The only way you have now is the white primary." If admitted to free voting, the Negro would be swung into the general elections, and chaos would follow.

The registrar of Macon County, a young cotton broker, fears removal of the poll tax would strengthen rabble-rousers like Talmadge. He is a strong supporter of Senator Walter F. George, and he warns: "You don't know the ignorant class of white people we have got in Georgia. You don't have many of them in North Carolina, I don't think. You spend more on education. I believe in that. Maybe education will do it." He then went on to describe what might happen if "that crowd" were turned loose, and he thinks it is a happy thing that this group is the most "violent nigger haters." Only this, he believes, would stop their collaboration in a revolutionary force. "We're getting them in that mood now," he added. "If this New Deal keeps up much longer—and then we have to cut it off right quick . . ."

In McIntosh County, Georgia, people are "supposed to pay poll taxes all the way back," but it is said that this rule "is not quite in force." Although it is not clear just how the rule is "not quite in force," a partial explanation seems to be the fact that the collector is apparently always willing to consider that a prospective voter has just come from out of the state if that voter is on "his side." No penalty fees or feoffor's charges are made for the poll tax in this county. There are no rules against the paying up of poll taxes by third parties, though the county Democratic committee once talked about such a rule. It was simply taken for granted that such a requirement could not be enforced.

The last election in McIntosh County was hotly contested because of the appearance of a "new faction" in the county, and it is estimated by the chairman of the county Democratic committee that one-half of the money paid for poll taxes in McIntosh came directly from the candidates or their supporters. The clerk of the court in Darien cited a cogent argument used in this county against any change in the poll tax law. Without the poll tax, he says, the candidates for office would "get these bastards back in the swamps and get them drunk, and haul them in here by the dozens. They do about that bad now."

When a person registers in Dougherty County, Georgia, he is put "on digest" for the poll tax. The people on digest are sent notices in November that the poll tax and other taxes, if they owe them, are due. The tax collector states that "we do this when we have time." No interest or penalty charges are made for poll taxes in Dougherty County. No great effort to collect poll taxes is made except in election years when, as the tax collector described it, "we pull them in here from the street and knock them in the head to get right." No one is charged a poll tax who does not pay property taxes, unless he is registered. Women property holders are charged only when they are registered. Negroes are charged only if they have property or are registered. There is no effort to collect tax from other defaulters. The sheriff collects poll taxes only when they are a part of a whole tax bill.

As for back poll taxes in Dougherty County, there seems to be considerable vagueness. The tax collector states that most people "get by with paying three or four dollars," though he does not make it clear how they get by. He states that in the tax year 1939–40 one woman in the county paid thirteen dollars in back taxes, and a man who registered for the first time paid fourteen dollars. In Georgia there are many transfers from one county to another, and in Dougherty County, at least until 1936, no formal transfer was required—only the oath that the person had paid all back taxes. The tax collector indicated that this accounted for the great increase in registration in the county in 1932. He says that in election years people are allowed to "pay their taxes to the candidates." These candidates bring in "long lists" of people who have given them their tax money, and these are checked off prior to the closing of the books. Candidates usually bring in these lists on the last day. This practice is permitted because "so many people don't have time to bring it in themselves."

It is admitted that candidates in Dougherty County pay a great deal of the poll tax for voters. In the sheriff's race in 1932, for instance, "one man put in about $900, and the other man, five to six hundred dollars. Why not? They both had it, and it all goes to the schools." Continuing, the chairman of the board of registrars indicated how the poll tax payment might be used to get rid of an "undesirable" officeholder:

> Last year the town had a mayor we wanted to get rid of. He was one of these railroad men; been in four or five years. When the CIO came here and tried to organize out at the textile mill, he went out there and tole them to join and come up to the city hall. He'd give them anything they wanted. A lot of us didn't think it was his place to do a thing like that. We don't want any CIO in this town. I don't think $900 would touch the amount we put in. We got everybody out; women and all.

The registrar added that he put one hundred dollars into the kitty himself.

While interviewing the manager of a combination grocery and lunch stand on the edge of the mill village in Albany, Stoney counted fourteen men and five women over twenty-one who came in during a little more than an hour, and not one of whom was a qualified voter. This was explained by the manager of the stand as follows: "They are not paying their own poll taxes, and the sheriff's not paying them up this year because nobody was against him." Ordinarily, it was explained, the sheriff pays up the poll taxes each four years for the people in the mill village, and they have come to depend on this. Until 1932 the sheriff simply put up one dollar for each. After the election, they were marked off the registration books, and were registered the next fourth year as new voters at one dollar a head. But that was broken up in 1932, and it cost the sheriff "plenty" to get elected that year. The explanation given as to where the sheriff could get the money to pay up all these taxes was that the "courthouse pool" to which "all the whores and gamblers and after-hour liquor merchants" contribute "was the source," and that "it don't cost anybody much that way."

The tax collector of Putnam County feels that the worst feature of the poll tax is the way it discriminates against the "best" of the "poor people," stating that a man "that ain't worth nothing" will register and "fish around" until he gets someone to pay his poll tax, or will "slide around" until he gets out of it. The honest poor people, "especially women folks," will not register because they fear the payment of that dollar annually and are too honest to try to get out of it. He named twenty or more people who he knew would vote if the poll tax were not in effect. These, he said, had all been offered payment of their taxes by candidates; "everybody has this year."

The tax collector states that he knows this because: (1) many people come in inquiring about how much they owe, explaining that "so and so said he was gonna help me out with that"; (2) one worker for a candidate this year came in with a long string of names, found out how much they owed, and wrote a check for thirty dollars to cover the amount right there in his office; (3) he has done a little of it himself. The way it is done is that a man says he would like to vote for you but hasn't got the money right now to pay the poll tax. He will have it in a week or two, but too late to pay up before the deadline. So you let him have it, knowing that if you do, you "might" get a vote. If you do not, you have much assurance that you will not get a vote. And, if you either ask for or accept repayment before the day of election, you are sure to have lost a vote.

The chairman of the Putnam County Democratic executive committee is against poll tax repeal because it would let in a great many people who have "a price on their vote," and there are enough such people on the list now. Moreover, so many old people would get on the list, if the tax were eliminated; now they are behind in their taxes—so far behind that they cannot pay up. He would do away with the exemption law for sixty-year-olds because he sees a real threat from the old age pension supporters. Also, there are so many WPA recipients, FSA clients, and so forth, that it is difficult for a freeholder to have much say now. He would change the law so that freeholders would be exempt from the poll tax. He thinks every person who considers himself "important enough" to vote should be able to dig up a dollar. If there are "some good people" who can't get up the money, "if they are really worthy, they won't have any trouble finding somone who will give them the money." Those who cannot pay the dollar are, in the main, the kind of people who have no right trying to dabble in the affairs of state. He doubts that many "decent" people in Georgia want the tax repealed.

It is not merely as a means of keeping the Negro from the

polls that the tax is defended in Georgia. There are many people who think, like the chairman of the Democratic committee in Ware County, that the poll tax is a commendable means of keeping unwanted white voters from the polls or, as he put it: "There is an element in this county, you might call it the slum of the population, that should never vote." The chairman of the Macon County Democratic committee favors the poll tax because its repeal would "let in a class of voters that will sell their vote."

The board of registrars in Ware County has ruled that anyone who pays five dollars can become eligible no matter how much back poll tax is owed. This was done because "so many people got behind during the depression—good people—and they couldn't pay up." Even this five dollar figure is cut down for people over sixty who register owing several years' tax. Thus, says the chairman of the board, a man of sixty-three will have to pay two dollars, a man of sixty-five will pay one dollar, and a man of sixty-six will pay nothing.

Sometimes rather subtle distinctions are made in Georgia between the types of people whose poll tax is paid for them by willing candidates. The general assumption is that anyone who really wanted to vote and who does not owe too much back poll tax can get it paid for him, at least in a county such as Ware. There is a breed of what might be called poll tax "runners" or agents who work on behalf of candidates and who advise prospective voters on how to get their poll taxes paid. One such agent in Ware County draws distinctions between those who are honest and want to vote, but cannot because of lack of funds with which to pay their poll tax, and those who are virtually professional vote-sellers:

> A lot of people can't afford to pay up their taxes, . . . and they don't know how to go about getting helped out. I know all those fellows up at the courthouse. . . . A lot of people really ain't able to pay. . . . I don't mean the kind that hangs around and begs people to pay their tax. That's the kind you got to buy with a drink of liquor on election day anyway. They ought to disfranchise every one of them. I mean a lot of people are really hard up.

The ordinary in Ware County acknowledges that there is a "lot of poll tax paying," but he is emphatically opposed to any repeal of the tax:

> If you did that, a man would have to have $10,000 to get

in office in this county. It might work all right in central or north Georgia, because they don't have the voting population we've got down here, with all this lumbering and turpentine. They liquor them up here bad enough as it is, but if everybody'd vote, it would be awful!

In Ware County the poll tax is not collected, except from those who have property and from those who are registered. Non–property-holding citizens who do not register are never charged with the tax. This applies to Negroes and to whites. There are no distress sales or sheriff collections for the poll tax unless it is a part of another tax bill. No penalty or feoffment fees are charged. The tax collector explained that it has not been customary to assess such fees in Ware County. He acknowledges that the poll tax is "so crooked. . . . Why, my lord, . . . this last time—hell, every time as far as that goes— they'll come in here with a list of seventy-five or a hundred names and pay up their taxes. I've seen them pay as high as $350 at a trip." The tax collector added that everyone did it and that he had done "a little of it" himself, because "a man's got to." Continuing, he explained: "But the way they buy votes here is worse than that. You pay up a man's taxes and then you've got to watch him like a snake or somebody else will come along with a drink of liquor and he'll vote for him." There is also "a certain kind that waits around to see who's giving out the most money. Sometimes I think it might be better to charge five dollars or maybe twenty-five dollars to vote if it would keep that kind from voting." This man was the only incumbent defeated during the recent elections in Ware County.

The tax collector of Burke County states that candidates often pay up poll taxes for voters in that county. In most instances the money is given to the voter individually and he brings it in to pay up. The Vestel Lumber Company of Sardis, the county's only industry, requires that all of its employees pay their poll taxes. The tax commissioner assumes that the company gets the permission of its employees and takes money out of their wages. This assumption is based on the fact that foremen have brought in the total amount for the men, and then the company has asked her to bring the registration books out to the mill so that employees may sign up. This she did, and she explains that she has also carried the books out to school and to celebrations in order to "accommodate the voters." The poll tax is not charged to propertyless people in Burke County providing they do not register, because: (1) they cannot be found, and there is no method for seeking them out; (2) it would cost too much to have a deputy run them down; and (3) they would have nothing to seize for payment once they were found.

In commenting on the operation of the poll tax in the South and particularly in Mississippi, Senator Byron Patton Harrison said in an interview on 16 February 1940:

> Of course, John L. Lewis and the Southern Conference, and Mrs. Roosevelt and the President are all against the tax, but the people of my state all feel very well toward our poll tax law because the money from it goes for education. Personally I am for it, and I think there is no chance for its repeal. It all boils down to the fact that localities know their own conditions better. I am for the poll tax because I think it makes for good elections. We have fine and clean election laws and elections now in my state. Some Northern states are lax in their election laws, and they let people vote who haven't had much residence and who don't pay any taxes, and who were just foreigners a short time ago; but in Mississippi we are much tighter in our election requirements, and we are better off. Look at Louisiana and the trouble it has had with its elections since it abolished the poll tax. Of course, my opposition to the repeal of the poll tax is based on the premise that a locality knows its own problems best and how best to deal with them.

It is not only the issue of the preservation of white supremacy that accounts for the stubborn resistance against the organized efforts now being made to remove the poll tax as a voting qualification. The political leaders of the poll tax states favor retention of the poll tax qualification because, having been chosen by a limited electorate, they do not care to risk the uncertainty of a political contest in which thousands of new voters would participate. Moreover, there are interests in these states which desire that political power shall remain in the hands of the "upper class" of property-holding voters rather than in the "unsafe" and "irresponsible" hands of the illiterate and propertyless masses. The disfranchised white masses themselves, to be sure, have been—at least until quite recently—indifferent, apathetic, and inarticulate.

The total vote in such states as Arkansas, Mississippi, and South Carolina is so small as to warrant the charge that these states are ruled by an oligarchy, and of course this oligarchy is unwilling to vote itself out of power. Repeal of the poll tax in most of the eight states retaining it as a prerequisite for voting can be accomplished only by amending the state constitution. In Virginia and Tennessee constitutional amendment requires passage of a bill by two consecutive sessions of the legislature and then ratification by a majority vote at the polls. The rotten borough domination by the black belt counties in Georgia, Alabama, and South Carolina makes it virtually impossible to obtain favorable action against the poll tax requirement in the legislatures of those states.

In a public statement supporting the poll tax repeal amendment (No. 26) in Arkansas in 1938, Brooks Hays explained that he was in support of the proposal because he believes that "it is wrong on principle to place a fee on the right to vote, but chiefly because it will contribute something to the elimination of fraud and corruption in Arkansas elections." Hays went on to point out that what has been happening in Arkansas is that organized political groups are purchasing poll tax receipts in blocks in every election and giving these receipts away to their friends who will vote "right." He called attention to the fact that in every election for many years in Arkansas the newspapers of that state have been filled with reports of election contests in which the practice has been made a matter of public record. He observed further that in the very year in which the repeal amendment was being considered, two candidates were barred from public office in Arkansas because it was proved that they had purchased and distributed several hundred poll tax receipts in the course of the campaign. "Thus," said Hays, "we are actually enfranchising the dishonest person who is willing to boodle, but we are disfranchising a multitude of honest people who have too much honor to permit someone to pay their poll tax."

In a letter of 9 September 1938 to Hays, concerning his proposal to repeal the poll tax in Arkansas, President Roosevelt wrote: "I am glad to know that there is such a general move in those states which still have poll taxes to repeal them altogether. They are inevitably contrary to the fundamental democracy and its representative form of government in which we believe."

Those who are struggling for poll tax repeal are thus confronted with major obstacles. Moreover, there is no doubt that the real significance of the tax is not widely understood by the Southern man in the street. The movement for repeal has not yet struck a mass appeal in most sections of the South. An or-

ganizer for the Steel Workers Organizing Committee in Chattanooga points out that both labor and Negroes are handicapped
by the poll tax:

> Repeal that and you will let thousands of working people
> get a chance to say what the government ought to do. It's the
> only way to stop politicians buying poll taxes. . . . Most unions
> can't afford to play around with poll tax receipts. I know of
> only one local in the last few years that paid poll taxes out of
> the treasury; that was a small but very active local of the
> movie operators. Of course, we urge all our members to buy
> their poll taxes, but a lot of them can't afford that two dollars.

The Southern Planter, in its February 1938 issue, declared:

> In Virginia efforts to repeal the poll tax, which amounts
> to a property qualification for suffrage, are being met as they
> have been met elsewhere with noisy political threats that
> such repeal in the South would mean that white voters would
> be overwhelmed by Negro voters in some sections of the State.
> Fortunately North Carolina, as Virginia's "Nighest neighbor,"
> can testify to the emptiness of this threat.

This publication also observed:

> Those who would prefer government of money rather than
> government by men will hide their hatred of democracy be-
> hind any phrases and arguments in Virginia as everywhere
> else. But if there are any men in Virginia honestly afraid that
> poll tax repeal would mean an overwhelming of white voters
> by black counties, let them be reassured. There are more Ne-
> groes in North Carolina than there are in Virginia (918,647
> to 650,165), but poll tax repeal has not even rippled the race
> question in this State, but it has set white men free from a poll
> tax which denied citizenship to poverty.

In discussing the operation of the poll tax in the South,
Justice Hugo Black of the United States Supreme Court stated
in an interview on 13 February 1940:

> It is always wise to give a reason for what you do. There
> were a number of people who sat in the Alabama convention
> in 1901 who thought it best to restrict the privilege of voting
> to a small group in the state. This convention was ostensibly
> called to disfranchise the Negro, but its real purpose was to
> keep the white franchise restricted and to maintain the oli-

garchy in power. This same group would not hesitate to call upon the Negro vote if it was necessary to preserve their power today.

Continuing his discussion of the poll tax, Black stated:

The poll tax is a heavy weapon with which to restrict the ballot so as to make it hard for a man with my views to get elected. I would have had a much easier time had there been no poll tax law. The abolition of the poll tax would not greatly affect the status or the franchise of the Negro in the South, but it would enfranchise a great number of white voters, and would make it possible to secure much more liberal-minded representation from the South, representation which is closer and more expressive of the will of the population of the South.

President Frank P. Graham of the University of North Carolina has aptly written:

The struggle for political democracy has, in historic stages, centered in the battles for the right to vote as basic to the American system of local-state-Federal cooperative self-government. Denial of the right to vote on the grounds of property, race, and sex have given way before the advance of common men and women along the rough road toward democracy. Across this road the poll tax stands as a surviving barrier to the right to the participation in self-government of Americans even now disinherited in the land of their fathers.[10]

10. *The Poll Tax* (1940), p. 4. This was a pamphlet issued by the Southern Conference for Human Welfare and the American Council on Public Affairs.

TWELVE

The Negro at the Polls: The Inner South

Many Negroes in the South resign themselves to an accommo-dationist attitude that the white people simply do not want blacks to vote and that, therefore, Negroes should not attempt to stir up any trouble about the matter. Others, as this chapter will show, are less passive about the Negro's traditional political status. Some Southern Negroes are advocating that the Negro support the Democratic party for pragmatic reasons, since that party controls the South and whatever the Negro may expect from political action must come through the Democrats.

The differential in registration treatment between white and Negro voters is often rationalized by white officials, as we have seen, and even in such way as to warrant extending the fran-chise to selected Negro voters. In one Alabama county, for in-stance, the board of registrars requires Negro voters to meet property qualifications while white registrants are not so re-quired. This is justified as "good practice," in that it does away with the "fear" of Negro domination while extending to the "best of the Negro citizens" the opportunity to cast a ballot. Not in-frequently the view is expressed by responsible whites that "re-spected" black property owners and taxpayers are apt to be permitted to vote even in the Democratic primary, since this will serve to aid the Negro in acquiring a "feeling of civic responsibility."

One example of "liberal" Southern opinion was voiced by Justice Hugo Black in an interview on 13 February 1940. He expressed the view that the ultimate fulfillment of Supreme Court decisions relative to Negro rights must depend upon their

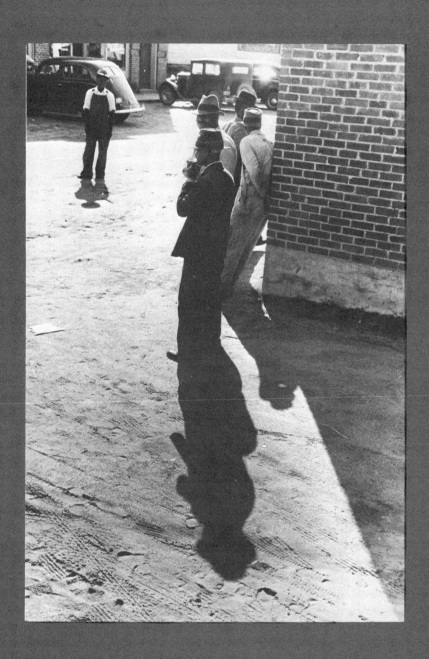

agreement with the mores of the community. He does feel, however, that some types of decisions, such as those he wrote in the recent Louisiana and Florida cases, do have some practical significance to the people of the states concerned. This is true because all states do wish to be able to obtain convictions in their courts and to feel certain that these convictions will not be set aside by higher courts. Yet a court decision affecting the rights of an individual in a particular election contest would not necessarily cover all elections and, consequently, Supreme Court decisions have less importance in this field, as is indicated by the Texas primary cases. The Supreme Court decisions, however, do have significance in charting new frontiers for groups whose rights are abused and in aiding them to move forward in their attempt to win their constitutional rights.

Justice Black went on to stress his belief that the importance of voting to the Negro in the South is overemphasized. In his estimation, there are many more important problems confronting the Negro in the South—especially the economic ones—than the ballot. As a matter of fact—and he stated it bluntly—great numbers of Negroes in the South are not yet ready to vote. They have not had the advantages of education, economic opportunity, and the tradition of freedom which would make it possible for them to vote intelligently. He stated that this is similarly true of great numbers of whites in the South. His personal feeling is that such people would be ready game for corrupt and demagogic politicians.

The really important thing in Black's estimation will be our ability to maintain the channels of communication open and free, to give people an opportunity to say what they think, to put health, education, economic opportunity, and contentment of the many above money and corporate interests. To quote him:

> The real core of the problem is economic and that must be worked out before anything significant along other lines can be hoped for. Give the poverty stricken South economic opportunity and opportunity for education, and the race problem will work itself out. Many people, unfortunately, ignore the economic nature of the problem and in raising other and relatively extraneous issues unconsciously play into the hands of corporate interests that are eager to keep people from understanding the real nature of the problem.
>
> When it serves their purpose to do so, the corporate interests of the South utilize the race issue by inflaming the poor whites against the Negro. For example, this was done in the

fight against the Wages and Hours bill, and the representatives of the corporate interests were telling the white workers that this was an attempt to bring about equality between the races and to elevate the Negro to the detriment of the white workers.

Few Negroes have voted in Alabama since 1901. According to the official registration figures in 1908, 3,742 Negroes were registered. Although there have been no official figures since that time, Professor Charles W. Edwards, in addressing the first meeting of the Southern Conference for Human Welfare in November 1938, estimated the maximum number of registered Negro voters in Alabama at that time at 1,500. This figure may now be too low by perhaps five hundred voters, due to the recent increase in Negro voting in Birmingham. Despite the severity of its registration and election laws toward Negroes, there are some breaks in the uniformity of the state's exclusion pattern. There are instances in which Alabama Negroes even vote in the state's "white primary." In some few places Negro voters have played an important role in local elections. The fear and rivalry between "black belt" and northern Alabama counties is an important factor in determining white attitudes toward Negro voting. The northern Alabama or "white" counties, with limited Negro populations, have no fear of Negro domination but do fear the manipulation of the potentially dangerous black vote by the white populations of the black-belt counties.

It is estimated that there are some three hundred Negro voters in Tuscaloosa County, Alabama. There have been Negro voters for a long time as a result of "the type of colored citizens we have." The probate judge admits, however, that "the registrars keep them out all they can. . . . They make them memorize the Constitution and things like that. . . . Not more than five or six Negroes vote in the Democratic primary."

The chairman of the Etowah County Democratic committee considers the Negro as a voter unimportant one way or the other. Those Negroes who do vote are permitted to vote in the Democratic primary. He states: "They aren't supposed to. It's against one of the fundamentals of the Democratic party, but they do and nobody cares much. There's not much restriction on niggers registering here, I don't think. When you go a little deeper into the black belt, you'll find it, I expect."[1] The Repub-

1. George Stoney's interview in Gadsden, Alabama, February 1940. Unless otherwise indicated, the quoted passages in this chapter come from Stoney's notes of field interviews conducted in 1940. —ED.

licans of Etowah County have made no move to have Negroes register, and this informant suspected that they would be "the last" to make such a move, since they are already suspect on this point. Continuing, he added: "We have some mighty good Negro citizens in this county. They register and vote, and are fully qualified to do so." It is admitted, however, that the number of Negro voters is small, mainly because the board of registrars makes different requirements for them. They must own property. Whites are registered whether they have property or not.

The views of an Alabama state senator on Negro voting are revealing. Referring to the Negro voter in Etowah County, he said:

> Yes, we have a few. They are respected property owners and taxpayers, and I think they vote in the Democratic primary. This is perfectly all right, I think, for those who have the qualifications. They are taxpayers, and I think it helps them to get a feeling of civic responsibility. . . . We have been carrying the Negro too long on our backs. He must learn to carry his own weight. You may not like it, and I may not like it, but they have got to learn to take care of themselves at the polls as well as everywhere else. Do you know how much we pay to educate nigras in this state and how little we get back from them in taxes?

The senator agreed that the registrars of Etowah County are doing "absolutely the right" thing to register only those Negroes who have property. These, he indicated, "we can depend on to vote with the more stable element of the population. They have something to lose."

It is estimated that there are fifteen qualified Negro voters in Greene County whose names are designated on the poll list, though they rarely, if ever, vote. Some of these have been on the list for a long time and have paid up their poll taxes or are exempt. A few, perhaps, were put on by the probate judge without the necessity of paying the poll tax so they could be used in the drawing of juries. No Negro has served, however, and it is suspected that if one's name is drawn, the judge excuses him. This is done to meet the constitutional objections raised in the Scottsboro case.

The chairman of the Greene County Democratic committee has been in Alabama and in Greene County for only six years. He comes from Wisconsin. Concerning the lack of Negro voters in Greene County, he commented: "I was worried about that when I first came down here, and when I go home to Wisconsin every summer, people always ask me about that. They don't seem to realize that these Negroes down here are not like those few up there are. They lack the mental capacity to act intelligently."

The editor of the Greene County *Democrat* is afraid of the Negro vote, for the county has a Negro-white ratio of four to one. Therefore, he is against any change in the poll tax law irrespective of the revenue it brings in, which—admittedly—is "not a drop in the bucket." It is, however, a safeguard against Negro voting. He thinks that the registrars would be rushed if the poll taxes were abolished. There would be court cases and, finally, they would be forced to register Negroes. He anticipates that this last will happen in the next ten years, anyway, and when that happens, the cumulative poll tax will be the black belt's only defense. To quote him: "Oh! We can control the niggers all right. If we can't do it one way, we'll do it another. But I tell you, . . . I saw that happen once. It's not a pretty sight. I don't want it to happen again." He went on to tell of how his father had bought Negro leaders, persuading them either to keep their followers away from the polls or to get them to vote Democratic —this in the 1890s.

Notice should be taken of the highly exaggerated stories concerning the large number of Negroes who vote in this or that place. These stories travel about from one courthouse to another and are believed almost as firmly as those about Reconstruction. For instance, almost any Alabamian outside of Jefferson County will state that there are at least five thousand Negroes voting in Birmingham—a gross exaggeration.

In Hale County, Alabama, Negro voters since 1932 have not been given special identification on the voting lists, and since 1936 all except three have been left off entirely. A Negro businessman and his wife, who were registered in 1930, have been left off the list since 1938. This couple was able to vote in the November election of 1938 only because they went to the office of the probate judge and got a slip. Negroes are not allowed to vote in the Democratic primary. They are not permitted to vote in municipal elections either, since these are also primaries.

Concerning Negro voting in Marengo County, an officer of elections in that county, in the presence of a number of Negroes, including two Negro women, stated: "There ain't a fuckin' nigger in this end of the county who'd so much as go near a ballot box."

The sheriff of Dallas County says: "We haven't got but

twenty-five niggers in the county who vote, and all but one of them are Democrats." The sheriff states further that these Negroes vote in the Democratic primary.

> Of course, they [the registrars] keep them down as much as they can . . . discourage it. . . . A nigger friend of mine came to me the other day, a doctor up here at this hospital, and he said, "Mr. Kennedy, I've been knowing you for a long time, and I'd like to help you out and vote for you next time. Will you help me?" You know what I told that nigger? I told him to get that kind of thing out of his head. I told him I would appreciate his support a lot more if he stayed where he belonged. . . . Some of the niggers out on my place come to me with the same thing. They said they'd been voting in these AAA elections and they'd like to vote for me. Well, course, most of those niggers have been with me for twenty-five years. Everyone of them would vote for me, but I told them to stay on the farm where they belong.
>
> This AAA voting is giving them ideas they can become regular voters. I think it's dangerous. If we didn't have the poll tax, they would vote, too. I don't know what would happen. Two years ago they had a bill up in Montgomery to let people pay two years back and vote. I went down there personally to get it defeated. . . . Oh! I'm not afraid for myself. Every voting nigger in town voted for me.

One Negro in Dallas County has been voting the Democratic ticket since he registered in 1926. He advises those Negroes who are able to get on the voting list to vote Democratic, because "If you need help, you don't go to a Republican senator or mayor or sheriff, you go to a Democrat. If any favors come to you, they've got to come through a Democrat or not at all." This man, C. J. Adams, states that he has met with no opposition to his voting in the primary since 1926. Before 1926, however, he had tried "many times" to register and, on one occasion, he was "run out" of the courthouse by men who said that they had orders not to register Negroes. He says that now there is no opposition offered to those Negroes who go to register, "if they know a few things and talk like they are intelligent." In his opinion the poll tax is the big thing keeping Negroes from voting, because those who do become interested always have from ten to twenty dollars back tax owing. On election days, Adams usually takes most of the Negro voters to the polls himself. The ladies especially, he notes, feel uneasy, though he knows of no instance in which they have suffered insults. He believes that at the last election the Negro vote in Selma elected Sheriff Kennedy, who won by only five votes and who received a solid vote from Negroes.

An ex–deputy sheriff in Lee County expressed the belief that many Negroes could vote if they wanted to try, since they have both property and education: "I think they don't know about it, or they're scared." He did not believe that they could be legally kept from voting. As an active politician, he felt that the Negro vote would make no difference to him, though "I don't want none of them running for office is all." About the only change in local politics that would result from Negro voting is that "it would cost more money to get elected," just as it would if the poll tax were repealed.

The probate judge of Lee County estimates that twenty Negroes vote in that county. He professes to have no idea why more Negroes do not vote and thinks that few try to vote. The Negro has never been a factor in local campaigns, although Tom Heflin "talked about them a lot, and he had a big following in this county."

In addition to the qualified Negro voters in Lee County, there are another twenty whose names are on the books but who are ineligible to vote because of their failure to pay the poll tax. A Negro dentist in Opelika registered to vote in 1912, and he was one of the first Negroes to vote in Lee County after the 1901 constitution. This man referred to the "horrible" days before 1901 when Negroes were voted in "droves" and when they were "given liquor and penned up at night in the jail so they could vote them the next morning." He attributed the desire of whites to take the vote away from Negroes to the fact that "most of them were too damn ignorant to know what it was all about." The few Negroes who vote in Lee County do so irregularly. None, apparently, has ever voted in the Democratic primary. Nor have Negroes ever voted in the city elections. The dentist points out, however, that many Negroes "have the property and education" to qualify them for voting if they would try, but he assumes that they "don't see any use in it."

The tax collector of Lee County states that "very few" Negroes vote in the county. Those who do, he claims, vote in the Democratic primary as well, though this is contradicted by Negro testimony. He observed: "You don't hear nothing about them," and expressed wonderment that more of them do not try to vote, adding:

I don't see how the registrars could keep them out if they want to. There's lots of them who can read and write and understand the Constitution and are a lot better educated than either one of us is. . . . I guess the better-class nigger must know, when you get right down to it, that the better class of white man don't want his vote, so he don't.

The leader of the Negro voters in Tuskegee and Macon County reports that there are eighty-eight qualified Negro voters in the county, though a check of the registration list reveals only seventy-four. The group most active in encouraging Negroes to register and vote is the Tuskegee Negro American Legion Post. The first principle of the American Legion is citizenship and the right to vote, so the Tuskegee group is "going after it." For the first time in Macon County, white candidates in 1938 turned attention to the Negro vote. Two candidates for one office fought for it, although

one of them wasn't man enough to come out here and ask for it. He tried to grab a man on the street and whisper in his ear. . . . The other man came right out here and talked with us—face to face. He told us he didn't want no public endorsement and we knew why, but he did want our vote, and he promised to protect us if we gave it to him. He went to see every single Negro voter, and he got it. . . . We defeated the tax collector in 1938 [he lost by 22 votes].

Most of the Negroes who vote at Tuskegee vote the Democratic ticket and participate in the Democratic primary.

The circuit clerk of Macon County thinks that the Negro vote is getting "worrisome." He warned: "We hold it down all we can, but we got this Veterans' Hospital and the Institute here. They're educated, and they've got property, and there's not much you can do." He added that the number of qualified Negro voters had stayed in the neighborhood of forty or forty-five for a long time, but it had begun to jump in 1934. However, he feels that the probate judge will be able to "hold it down to under 200 for a long time," and that this should be no serious cause for worry. He admitted that those Negroes who do vote now vote independently. More than half the Negro voters of Macon County are veterans.

The superintendent of education for Macon County estimates that two hundred Negroes vote in the county. Most of them, he thinks, are professors at Tuskegee Institute or doctors at the

Veterans' Hospital. In commenting upon them, he added: "They are good voters, too. When you go out there to talk to them, all they ask you for is little local things, and if you treat them as you should, you get their vote. That's all they want." This informant is sure that the Negro vote in this county is not bought; to the contrary, he believes that it is about the most independent vote in the county. He takes the position that here should be no objection to the intelligent Negro's voting: "They are going to vote with the white people, except when they want something special in a local way, and that is all right, too. They are entitled to some things. I don't know how you feel about it, but I think they are."

A young white lawyer who was present during this discussion and who dismissed Macon County politics quickly by stating flatly that they are "a bought and sold proposition" stated, with regard to the Negro vote, "I guess the registrars keep as many of them out as they can and still be fair." If the Negroes were not careful, the lawyer remarked, the landlords would begin registering their Negro tenants and voting them against the Tuskegee group, and then the Tuskegee group "would be sorry they ever started it."

The chairman of the Macon County Democratic committee, who is also a state senator, declared that Negro voters in the county are allowed to vote in the Democratic primary without any opposition, and he believes that it is "a good thing to have them vote in the primary. Maybe they will want to stay and will never want to vote Republican again." When the state Democratic executive committee issued its call for the primary, this senator says that he saw to it that the local committee dropped the word "white" from its legal advertisement. He expressed the conviction that there is "an exceedingly fine group of Negro voters in this county. They are professors at Tuskegee for the most part. They have never caused any ill feeling. I have never heard any real objection to their voting, certainly not within the committee." Other Negroes, however, are kept from registering by the registrars whom the senator "advises" on this point. That is, as he explained it, he calls to the attention of the registrars all parts of the law which they may use against "those whom they think will not make the highest type of citizens."

The Macon County tax collector estimates that there are about sixty-five Negro voters in the entire county, as against two thousand white voters. In order to obstruct Negro registration, the tax collector requires a white endorser for every Negro registrant. He states, quite definitely, that in the Veterans' Hospital at Tuskegee and at the Institute itself there are more than a thousand Negroes who are much better qualified to vote than the average white voter in the county. He adds, however, that it would be a great misfortune if these Negroes were permitted to vote, stating that Tuskegee Institute has been traditionally very cautious about encouraging Negroes to vote, because Tuskegee realizes that its security depends upon maintaining the goodwill of the whites in the county. The tax collector declared flatly that in the event Tuskegee Negroes attempted to register in great numbers, Tuskegee would be destroyed—intimating that the whites in the community of Tuskegee and in the surrounding area would burn the institution down. He also added that all of the whites would leave the town of Tuskegee should it become politically dominated by the Negroes and Tuskegee Institute.[2]

The Negro manager of a resettlement project in Alabama criticizes the Tuskegee faculty members for their lassitude and timidity with respect to voting. He thinks they are "too cloistered." He relates that about two years ago a candidate for sheriff in Macon County, running in the 1938 race, tried to make an issue of the Negro vote. The only eleven candidates refused to take up the challenge, however, and this man was defeated—largely by the Negro voters. He described his experiences with voting in Savannah, Georgia, while he was teaching at the Georgia State Normal School there. He organized a Negro Democratic club in Savannah, despite the fact that the chairman of the Democratic committee there tried to dissuade him by asserting that Negroes could not vote in the city primary election. At the very next primary he went to vote early in the morning and was refused. He insisted upon his rights, however, and, after talking with him for half an hour, the manager of the election agreed to let him vote, but warned him not to send any other Negroes there. He went back, however, and brought twenty other Negroes, all of whom voted. The members of his club in other precincts had similar experiences, though many did not get to vote. Then the chairman of the Democratic committee came around to see him after the election, warning him that he would be horsewhipped out of town unless he stopped this work. Although he ignored this threat, he was never molested.

2. Gunnar Myrdal's interview, Tuskegee, Alabama, 9 November 1939.

There are no Negroes on the Notasulga beat voting list in Macon County now. According to the beat committeeman, there used to be "three or four good old niggers. I reckon they could vote now if they took a mind to." Although the Negroes who were eligible in Notisulga beat seldom voted, some of them have served on juries. The beat committeeman pointed out that "we got to do that since this Scottsboro raping case." He remembers, however, only one instance in which a Negro has served on a really important case, and relates: "I watched him sitting there. He was scared to death. He didn't do nothing at all. . . . That law don't amount to nothing."

An independent Negro farmer near Notasulga told of a recent conversation he had with another Negro farmer down the road who owns about two hundred acres of land and who had been on the voting list in the county until 1928. This man said he had not complained to the probate judge about being left off the list after 1928 because he decided the white people "didn't want him to vote" and he "didn't want to do nothing that would stir up no trouble. It's all right for Negroes to vote in Tuskegee because they have education and they have the Institute there. Up here, people are different." The tax collector stated that he did not mind people at Tuskegee Institute and the Veterans' Hospital voting. In the first place, this is an independent vote, and in the second place, it could never grow very large. But he is afraid "that the landlords and plantation owners will start registering the niggers on their places. They do it with the white ones right now. By God! I know they pay their poll taxes."

The probate judge of Macon County holds that the Negro vote "is getting to be a serious menace." It has been increasing steadily since 1936. They come from the Veterans' Hospital and the Institute, and he states that "over a hundred of them" were registered last year. This is an exaggeration. The judge complained that the Negro registrants were not given the constitutional test. "They could have kept them out this way, but the registrars didn't have sense enough to do it. You can't go out and oppose them in public, because they will get mad and all vote against you." Then he added:

> Now, you can go out and talk to them and get some of their vote. You can at least keep it away from somebody else. . . . Yes, they vote in the primary. People call them Republicans, but you can't refuse them a ballot when they swear they're Democrats. We advertised in the white primary, but

they don't pay that any attention . . . but I think a lot of them vote Republican in the general election. Most of them are inclined that way.

The fact that the elections in Macon County are ordinarily unusually close apparently places exaggerated importance upon the handful of Negro voters in the county.

The Macon County sheriff feels that the Negro vote situation "is getting bad. We ain't had no trouble yet, and I hope we don't. There might be if they turn them loose, but I don't think they're going to do that right yet." He thinks that Tuskegee and the Veterans' Hospital could "control things here if they want to, unless the registrars keep them out. I think there ought to be a law about putting two big nigger things like that in one county." The sheriff did not think that the Negroes were holding meetings or organizing their vote, although his deputy thought that they could do so and no white men would know anything about it. To this the sheriff responded, "Yeah. A nigger's a nigger, and he always will be. They're clannish as hell. They do a lot of things they don't tell you about." He knew of only two candidates who had gone out after the Negro vote, and "one of them even went out there [to Tuskegee] and shook hands with them and begged them to vote for him." When asked if he had indulged in such practice in his campaign, he exclaimed "Hell, no! I wouldn't ask a nigger to vote for me if I never got elected."

The chairman of the Madison County board of registrars at Huntsville, in discussing the Negro vote, stated flatly that he does not "encourage their registration." He explained that he had lived in this neighborhood when it was represented by a Negro schoolteacher. This Negro representative, it was said, did have some sense, in that he went to the state legislature with a white representative and told the white man that, since he did not know anything about all that was going on, he was coming back to Madison County to teach school and for him to send the per diem along every month. "He had sense enough to know he didn't belong in the legislature."

A Negro voter in a small Southern town like Huntsville is something of a marked man. As one informant in Huntsville puts it, "When a nigger votes, almost everybody in town knows about it. Besides, they're the most prominent ones in the county. I think they're going to start letting a whole lot more of them register now to out-vote this WPA bunch." Of the Negro vote in Madison County, the probate judge says: "We've got about fifty to sixty in the county voting—property owners, good citizens, too." He continued: "They don't seem much interested. They're pretty much contented with things like they find them around here, I guess. One or two of them registers his boy or his wife once in a while, but no white men have tried to register any around here that I know of since the new constitution."

The typical Southern attitude toward Negro voting is not confined to men. For instance, the wife of the probate judge in Madison County recited the following:

> I was at a state meeting of Democratic women last year and a lady . . . was telling us they didn't have a poll tax in South Carolina and they didn't have any trouble with niggers voting. Oh! There was an old judge there—it was the funniest thing! He was from one of the black belt counties—probably had been sitting in the office for twenty or thirty years—you know, one of those counties where his family runs the whole place and he never had to work for the office. Well, he got up and said he'd tell how we handled the niggers down in *our* county. When they come in to register, we make them read the whole Constitution and explain every section!
>
> Hee-hee-hee, lawd, there was some woman from the North visiting . . . and she got up and just *screamed*. She thought that was just terrible. "You don't let them vote at all?" she wanted to know. This old judge sort of back-watered a little at that, and he said—rolling his eyes all around and looking up at the ceiling like he was about to bust laughing: "Oh, yes! We register them if they're *qualified*. Oh, yes!" I like to *died* laughing at him.

The circuit judge expressed the thought that more Negro citizens do not vote in Madison County because they are afraid "it would raise the racial issue." This he considered to be a wise view for them to take. He regretted the necessity of it but thought they were correct in assuming it. The cynical and outspoken clerk in the office of the probate judge explained why there was so little Negro political activity in the county: "They don't take much interest. That's why there's so few. I guess the old nigger knows the same white man's gonna be president and sheriff right on. It don't matter whether he votes or not. So, he says he just as well let the white folks elect him." The reaction of the chairman of the county board of commissioners to the disfranchisement of the Negro is: "Well, I didn't disfranchise the nigger, and I'm not going to enfranchise him."

Although all the evidence and testimony collected in Madison County points to the contrary, the chairman of the county Democratic committee insists that no Negroes at all vote in the Democratic primary, because "the Democratic primary is a white primary in this state. Only qualified white electors, the law states, are eligible to vote." He has a fear of the Negro vote. "Look at Memphis! And we'd have the same conditions around here if we let the nigger vote. I guess we have about the best bunch of darkies around here you'd find anywhere in the South, but if they voted the way they do in Memphis, it would be the same thing."

The chairman of the Madison County board of registrars estimates that possibly one hundred Negroes are registered in the county. The registered Negroes, he states, "are all pretty well educated. Some of them are college graduates, and all of them are good citizens." He adds that there has been little effort on anyone's part to get the Negro in Madison County to register. A few younger Negroes are beginning to attempt to register. He told of registering a young Negro college graduate recently, the son of a legal voter "and a pretty good old nigger at that." He also explained that several Negroes had tried to register on "false claims." One of these had been a man "from Tennessee" who could not prove that he had been in the county the proper length of time. It is said that the whites in Madison County do not try to register Negroes, though it could be done. But the chairman of the board of registrars warned: "Suppose I try to register the dozen niggers on my place. I could do it and vote them like I want to, but the next year some other man might have them, and he could do the same thing against me." Since the white people know this, they do not desire to see the Negro vote.

A Negro voter and operator of a shoe-shine parlor in Huntsville said he registered and voted despite great difficulty because:

> First, I thought it was the duty of every citizen to register and vote. Then . . . people treat you different when you vote. I've noticed it. 'Course they treat me *too* nice sometimes. I wish they wouldn't, 'cause I know I'm going to have to pay for it. I shine a couple of pairs of shoes and press a couple of uniforms free almost every day. . . .
>
> It's not that we Negroes want any kind of equality with you whites. All we want is peace and quiet, and security and a chance to make a living like the rest of the people. We want

to be let alone, and I don't believe we can get these things unless we have something to say in electing public officials.

There are about eight or nine Negroes in Bibb County who vote, out of some twenty-five who are registered. After the 1901 constitution went into effect, there were fifty or sixty Negroes who voted regularly. All of these were landowners or schoolteachers. Since then not more than half a dozen Negroes have been registered. The probate judge declares:

> We had some trouble about that here a while back. Some of the men in these mine unions tried to register some of their nigger members. They knew they could control them, you know. One of the registrars came to me and asked me what they were going to do about it. I told her to ask them this one question and I bet not a one of them could answer it. If they couldn't, she had a right to refuse them. I told her to ask them what the Constitution meant when it said that the right of habeas corpus shall not be denied.

The judge got a big laugh out of this one and explained that only *one* Negro got by.

A rural mail carrier and his wife in Bibb County, who because of his steady income are representative of the upper middle class in that county, were opposed to the poll tax and to the numbered ballot. But on the question of Negro voting, the wife volunteered: "Oh! It may be all right for a few nigger school teachers and doctors to vote, but not all of them. Nuh-uh, it won't do." And, her husband added: "The people won't stand for it."

While in Birmingham in March of this year, Stoney visited polling place no. 9–1, the box near the Negro housing project where about 175 Negroes cast their ballots in the election of the chairman of the city commission. This box was in a white barbecue stand and was placed on the counter. Two women acted as election officials. While Stoney observed, about one-half dozen voters—all Negroes—cast their ballots. All of them were well dressed and came either in taxis or large autos. All were treated courteously, even though they had to move through a row of white loafers. One of the women officials was unusually kind to the Negro voters. She explained that she thought it was a shame that there could not be some way worked out so that all of the "intelligent" Negroes could vote. She realized, she stated, that Alabama had to be careful because of the people in the black belt. "I don't know how it could be worked, but when I see these smart nigras come in here and vote, I just wonder." The other woman official, an older woman, was much less liberal on the question, and took strong exception to the first woman's "radical views," saying "Lawd, honey. You don't know what you're talking about. You don't know niggers. Now, I like 'em in my kitchen and all like that, but when they commence to messin' in politics, I thinks it's the time to halt." A white patent medicine salesman, who was hanging about the place, agreed completely with the second lady: "If you don't watch out, you're gonna have the same kind of niggers you got over in Miami. They know now, by God, they can control an election, and they've got the police department scared. . . . They'd just as soon stick an ice pick in you as look at you." This salesman had traveled widely over the South and had collected an unbelievable number of rape case anecdotes, about a dozen of which he proceeded to tell, to the silent delight of the white loafers in the place, including three boys of less than ten years. Whenever a Negro voter came in, he would break off in his narration, resuming as soon as the voter marked his ticket and went out. The liberal lady official did not want to hear the stories at first, but after two or three she listened as intently as Stoney and the rest.

The small Negro vote in Cullman County, Alabama, now enters the Democratic primary. Cullman, a northern "white" Alabama county, has its own method of treating the Negro problem. This method is suggestive of the location or reserve policies employed so extensively to solve the native problem in Africa. In Cullman the Negroes are entirely off by themselves in little colonies. They have their own lands, their own churches, their own schools, and their own stores. In Hansville there is only one Negro resident. As one Cullman official puts it, Hansville

> takes the same attitude toward them that is taken in Cullman. That is, it doesn't like them around. Every five or six years a few—maybe a half dozen—collect in town one by one, working on the railroads, brought in as servants or something. Then something happens and they all leave. Less than two years ago, here, a half-drunk white man met a Negro in an alley at night. The Negro had no way to defend himself against the white man's pocketknife and was cut up pretty bad. All the other Negroes left town.

The approximately two hundred registered Negro voters in Montgomery are "mighty high-class, intelligent people." Most of them are Republicans at heart, explained federal district judge Charles B. Kennomer, but vote Democratic because they have no other choice. Wherever Negroes are being registered in Alabama, he asserted, the registrars are making certain that they vote Democratic. The judge charges that when he ran for Congress in the fifth district in 1920, he carried five of the seven counties then included in that district. Etowah, his home county, "cheated" him out of the election by seven hundred votes. About forty Negroes were registered in that election, and all of them were registered to vote against him. After the election, most of these Negroes were removed from the rolls. The judge estimates that there are between 2,000 and 2,500 qualified Negro voters in the state of Alabama, 80 percent of whom vote the Democratic ticket. Republicans have made no effort to register Negroes in the past dozen years, and no Negroes have appeared at the Republican state convention during the last decade, because "the more thoughtful Negroes who really are Republicans decided it would be better for the party if they stayed away."

The chairman of the county board of registrars in Montgomery indicated her attitude toward Negroes and Negro political participation in the following terms:

> All niggers—uneducated and educated—have one idea back in their mind—that they want equality; but look on them for yourself. You don't mean that we could have them in our churches, that we could bury them in our cemeteries, that we could have in our schools and in our homes any more than we could have apes or other animals. They have, of course, a "soul" and there is a place for them. Take common white workers—mill hands—they are also different from us and have a different place. It is just the same with Negroes, only more so. It is necessary to keep the Negro from voting, for voting would lead to social equality. The niggers are in the majority in this county and in Alabama. They would take over the power in the state. The white people are never going to give them this power.[3]

In Georgia, Negroes are to all intents and purposes totally disfranchised through the operation of the white primary system. Only in some city elections, where there are no primaries, does their vote count at all. Yet the voters' lists seem to show many Negroes who are qualified voters. The tax collectors' lists

3. Myrdal's interview, Montgomery, Alabama, 11 November 1939.

show still more who pay their poll taxes. Georgia would probably be a good place to base a suit on the primary question, in view of the Georgia registrars' practice of omitting all Negro names from the lists of qualified voters for primaries. This seems to make the exclusion official and public, even though the primary expenses are borne by the party. In Georgia, it should be noted, the exclusion of Negroes is much more complete, especially in local politics, than in Alabama. The reason is that in Georgia the primary is paid for by the candidates rather than by the state or county as in Alabama. On the other hand, because the courts have ruled that Negroes cannot be excluded for reasons of color, Alabama is much more strict about registering blacks.

In discussing the political status of the Negro in Georgia, Senator George observed in an interview on 9 February 1940:

> In the Southeast, the negra has the status of general citizen. There is a political discrimination or what may seem to be discrimination. Actually, there is no racial prohibition against voting in Georgia, but you must understand that Georgia is a one-party state with a primary system and that the practical effect of this system is to exclude from voting those who are not members of that party. The negra can participate in all general elections, including local bond issues, and so forth, whenever the negra becomes vote-conscious and really wants to vote. All of the southeastern states are one-party states, and these states fix their own primary laws without interference from the national government. It may be right to say there is discrimination, but this is not entirely racial discrimination. For example, there are some 60,000 white Republicans in Georgia, and since they are not in the majority party, it could be said that they also are discriminated against. We have in the Southeast the only one-party section in the country. My home county is a rural county, and there are some negra voters in my county. There are some good negras whom I know well and who have always voted in the primaries of my county. These are not many, of course, but there are a few. I presume they still vote, though I have been out of touch with local affairs for several years now due to my work in the Senate. I know they always used to vote.

Senator George stated it was his belief that the Negro will "eventually be admitted to the Democratic party." Continuing his observations, he said:

You know, there is a poll tax in the South, and that is a factor that affects the Negro voter. The negra feels that there is no need to pay the poll tax since he is not permitted to vote in the primary which is the controlling election. I don't believe we are far from the time when there will be two parties in the South. Another party is growing up in the South, due to the movement of population, the development of industry, the infiltration of people with different ideas. This will certainly change the political status of the negra, and there will be a new understanding between the races.

In 1937, when the state beer and wine law was before the voters, Ben Davis, a former Negro Republican national committeeman from Georgia, was approached and asked for an estimate of the total number of black voters in the state. Davis quoted a figure of 10,000. He was a "wet" and was sent out "gumshoeing" in sixty-five Georgia counties to win Negro support for the beer and wine law. The law won by eight thousand votes, and he claims that the "wet" interests give Negroes credit for having won the election.

Negroes vote only in the general elections in Chatham County, Georgia. No Negroes vote in the Democratic primary. The chairman of the county Democratic committee claims to recall that, when Negroes voted in the city election in 1913, before a primary was declared, both opposing factions got Negroes drunk in different parts of the town. "They got them 'liquored up' and lined them up with guards on each side with baseball bats." Continuing, he explained: "Of course, we are supposed to have a democratic form of government, but I have an idea the writers of the Constitution were thinking about an educated democracy." Now, he says, the mayor of Savannah handles Negro representation through an informal advisory group made up of the best-educated Negroes in town, and "this takes it out of the barroom." This informant expressed "disappointment" with the educated Negroes. In a special election a few years ago, he was interested in the Negro vote and called together a group of "the best nigras in town" to talk about getting support for his candidate. He comments: "Do you know the first thing they asked me? They wanted to know how much I was going to pay them. That made me so mad, I told them I wasn't going to pay them a damn cent, and I walked out. I don't know whether they voted with me or against me."

The leader of the opposition to the Chatham County machine

feels that the Negro vote is "too small. We have a mighty good class of niggers here. We've never had any race trouble to speak of. I think it would be all right for some of them to vote in the white primary. . . . I don't think they have as much to do with things in the town as they ought."

The tax collector of Bibb County points out that, according to the law of the state, if a Negro declares himself a Democrat and is registered he has the right to participate in the Democratic party primary, since the law does not permit the party to make color distinctions. However, if "in practice a Negro tried to vote in a Macon primary, he would be asked what in hell he wanted."

The Negro chairman of the Burke County Republican committee ascribes the lack of Negro voting in the county to a number of causes: (1) the poll tax which many Negroes cannot pay. (2) Fear—there has been so much talk about threats to Negroes that many are afraid to try to vote, but, in his estimation, this fear is groundless so far as registering in Burke County is concerned. He claims that he has not had a person turned down for registration in the past twelve years. (3) Indifference —the preachers in the county preach "stay out of politics." Only one preacher in the entire county is registered. The schoolteachers show no interest. Negro leaders refuse to show others by their example. (4) Misuse of the franchise in the past. At one time there were between twenty-five and fifty Negro voters who took part in the city elections at Waynesboro. Their votes were bought individually by the candidates. At the last county Republican convention there were twenty delegates, all Negro, several of whom were not registered voters. Almost all of them were old men.

It is estimated that there are about 120 Negroes qualified to vote in McIntosh County, Georgia. Of these, about one hundred live and vote in Darien. They are permitted to vote in the city elections. Since the Darien city election does not attract more than four hundred votes at the outside, this gives the Negro ballot a powerful influence. The whites are planning to destroy this influence by making the Darien city election a primary election, from which Negroes will be automatically excluded. From 1870 until 1908, McIntosh County sent a Negro to the legislature. There were Negro mayors and Negroes in courthouse offices. They were Republicans and made arrangements with white people in the county so that they too had a chance at these jobs. White people who agreed to treat them fairly received their support. Things worked out well until the disfranchisement of the Negro all over the state in 1908. The white people did not object, so it is said, until the county was held up to ridicule by all the rest of Georgia. The state legislature sent white men from other counties into McIntosh County to act as registrars, and by this means they disfranchised so many of the Negroes that the whites took control and they have had complete control ever since. Rapidly thereafter came the loss of federal power. Lily-white Republicans now control the GOP in the county.

Darien is a small community of about a thousand people divided equally between Negroes and whites. According to the tax commissioner, registration lists are reviewed every three years in the county. There are 115 Negroes registered in the county, and 143 Negroes have paid the poll tax. The chairman of the McIntosh County Democratic committee is opposed to the proposal that the Darien city election be changed to a primary in order to eliminate the Negro voters. He states that, as chairman of the school board in Darien, he has found them most helpful. The Negro leader, who is the principal of the Negro high school, "lines them up" for the candidates he favors; that is, "the conservatives." Since the Negro voters constitute the balance of power, they thus insure the continuation of this administration, and the county chairman spoke with considerable respect of this leader and of the Negro population in general.

In Crescent, a small store community in McIntosh County, there are a couple of Negroes who vote in general elections, and an election official remarked: "And they voted the Democratic ticket last time." He stated that he happened to know this because, "man, you can tell, the way they run things around here." He explained that, because of the numbers on the ballot and because there are so few votes in this box, it is "hard not to notice how people vote." Moreover, he added, "they go into the boxes" in the courthouse and check on everybody.

The following excerpts from Wilhelmina Jackson's interviews with Negro workers on Butler Island, off Darien, are probably rather typical of that section. Mrs. Waters: "Yes, I register, but I do not vote. I just don't have time. You see, I always be working at voting time and all like that. . . . I tell you I been trying to get on WPA for some time. Yes, I think Mr. Roosevelt is just fine." Another, a girl named Sarah, stated: "I don't vote, but what I got to vote for? Slavery days done come back. My mama didn't know. They didn't have to buy their own food, you know." A pulpwood worker: "Naw, I don't vote. Black man ain't got no right. Even Negroes serving on the juries are so old that they can't get out of their own way, and all they can do is 'yes' the white man." Negro fisherman: "No, I don't vote. I didn't pay my taxes. Tain't much use anyway."

An examination of the official qualified list for 1940 in Ware County shows that there is a total of 3,032 white men and 2,698 white women, or 5,730 white names on the list, as against 144 Negro men and 109 women, for a total of 253 Negro names. All but six of the Negro voters listed reside in Waycross. The active Negro vote in Ware County is estimated by a justice of the peace at two hundred, "and when they start voting, it's a mess! A whole bunch of them came up to vote in this Justice of Peace election, and they were so impudent. Gracious! You would have thought they were low-down white people the way they walked up to you." The chairman of the board of registrars estimated that there are about 250 Negro voters in Ware County, and it is said that there is no difference in the treatment of Negroes in registration.

> A lot of those old people [Negroes] got on a few years ago when they thought we were going to have a vote on old age pensions. The rest are employees of the Georgia Power Company most likely. A couple of years ago there was a movement to take a vote on having a municipal light system here. The power company registered them up to vote against it.

A number of key Negroes in Waycross were employed to round up the black vote, and they succeeded in getting six hundred Negroes on the books. The special election was then called off. According to one of these Negro workers, "The Georgia Light and Power Company gave me $300 to pay these Negroes to get them to register. I spent all but $11.50, and all but one of the Negroes I asked to register registered. I won't call his name."[4]

The chairman of the county Democratic committee says that in the recently called general election for justice of the peace in Ware the Negroes all stuck together and voted for the same person. If that person had received any substantial white vote, he would have been elected, and by a minority made up of Negroes. "Their so-called leaders lined them up, and they voted like sheep. That is what always happens. I know every time we start to have a bond election, they go out and round up the nigras." This

4. Wilhelmina Jackson's interview, Waycross, Georgia, 20 February 1940.

man is not "against having a few of the educated" Negroes vote, but he believes that the "vast majority" of blacks have no business with a ballot in their hands. He related that several of them—"good old darkies, they didn't mean any harm"—had tried to vote in the recent primary and that "some white man had told them there was an election, and they came around, and asked if they could help him out. We didn't get mad. We said that this was a little election we were holding amongst the white people and that they'd get their chance in the fall." At the same time, however, he praised the "race harmony" in Waycross, the interest Negroes take in caring for their sections, and particularly how they assume responsibility for redecorating their wing of the county hospital.

The official voting list for Dougherty County in 1932 showed that there were 4,283 whites and 92 Negroes eligible to vote. In 1938 the list of qualified voters in the clerk's office indicated a total of 3,238 white people and 200 Negroes who were eligible to vote. The latest available data on the number of qualified Negro voters in Dougherty County, based on the qualified list for the special general election on 6 June 1939, is 72 Negro women and 157 Negro men, or a total of 229 Negroes as against 3,741 white people.

The chairman of the board of registrars in Dougherty County states that Albany has a "good nigger vote" which he estimates at between two and three hundred, adding: "They're property owners and taxpayers. They're mighty good citizens. We're not going to have them voting in our primary, but we don't keep them from registering and voting for president." The registrar admitted that this gave the Negro voters no political power, yet it did give "the good ones a chance to show the white people they want to pay their taxes to help support the schools." Continuing to expand his philosophy on the Negro question, he observed:

> You know, we've spent a fortune educating the niggers down here. The nigger race has come a lot farther than the white race in such a short time. You just look back at slavery times and count up. It hasn't been a hundred years. It's wonderful, and it's all due to the credit of the Southern white man. The Yankees haven't done a damn thing for the niggers, and we'd be a lot better off if they'd leave us alone to handle things as we know how to. . . .
>
> The nigger has saved us from the CIO. Did you know that? Yes, sir, if it hadn't been for the nigger, we'd have all the

Italians and the foreigners they've got up North. We don't want the CIO down here—not in this town, we don't.

There was a time when the Negro had a strong vote and a powerful Republican organization in Dougherty County. A Negro political leader in Albany, a former chairman of the Republican committee in the county, relates what has happened to the Negro vote, and presents his philosophy of Negro political participation as follows:

> My people are very easily discouraged. When the white man does something that seems to cause them trouble, they interpret it to be prejudice. They are afraid they are going to get in bad. So, they say they aren't going to fool with it. . . . We used to have a good Republican party here. It was controlled by the Negroes. I was chairman for many years and attended the state convention for this district.
>
> In his heart, every Negro is a Republican. He was raised that way. Abraham Lincoln gave him his freedom, and the Negro has always been grateful for that act. . . . In his heart, every white man in the South is a Democrat. He was born that way, and when you see a white man who was born in the South voting Republican, you know he is after the spoils and nothing else.
>
> We had control of the Republican party in Georgia until Harding's time, and we were in the majority until Mr. Hoover's election. When the nomination of Mr. Smith motivated many white people to turn away from the party of their birth, Mr. Hoover's advisers told him that there was a chance for the Republicans to gain a foothold in the South if they would make the Republican party a white man's party. Mr. Hoover mistook the unpopularity of Mr. Smith for his own popularity and the popularity of his party. He thought the Republican advance in the South could be made permanent by putting white men in control. That is what he did. Since then, the Negro's voice in the Republican party has dwindled. The other day in Atlanta, only four Negro delegates were named for the convention out of 14. We used to send a fifty-fifty delegation every time, even when the Negroes outnumbered the whites five to one. . . .
>
> This has discouraged Negroes all over the state. I have stopped trying to work with the Republicans here. We are not welcome, there, but I keep telling my people that there are more important things. Don't worry about who is going to be

president. Local, city, county, and state elections are the important things. You must qualify and help to name the men who are going to rule over you as sheriff, chief of police, mayor. . . .

They come complaining to me about the white primary. I tell them it is all right for the Democrats to hold their white primary if they want to. Negroes have no place there. That is their own business. I tell them when they complain, that they could break it up if they would. Negroes are over 50 percent of the population in this county. If they would qualify as they should, they could be, if not the majority, the balance of power. If the whites would nominate someone in their primary who was obnoxious to the Negroes, they could go to some other white man and say: "Look here, we would like you to run against that man. We will throw our support to you if we can expect certain reasonable services in return."

There is always a white man willing to run independent if he thinks he has a chance of being elected. He doesn't care whether it is black votes that elect him or white ones. There are always some white men who have enough friends to carry them with the help of the Negroes. . . . One election like that would break up this white primary. The Democrats would be afraid to hold one.

It doesn't matter to me now whether we have a Democrat or a Republican in the White House. I think the Negroes will fare just about as well under either.

Negroes are said to have no trouble qualifying for the vote in Albany, and there has been a gradual increase in qualified Negro voters in recent years. The most difficult barrier to Negro voting is the poll tax.

There are about thirty Negro voters in Putnam County. Most of them are "government folks," WPA teachers, and so forth. "They were afraid they would lose their jobs if they didn't register. The government wanted them all to be citizens. They were teaching about the government, I guess, and they don't feel like citizens unless they're registered." This informant, the tax collector, indicates that he "stopped" several of these prospective Negro registrants when he told them it would put them in debt to the county for one dollar a year for the rest of their lives. He says that those Negroes who do own property "pay their taxes a heap better'n white folks, and if they can't pay, they come down to make a settlement instead of trying to lie out of it like most white folks." The tax collector thinks that "niggahs would be all right voting if the whites was what they ought to be. That was the trouble before. White fellows wouldn't leave them alone."

A justice of the peace at Rockville in Putnam County states that he is not afraid of the Negro vote and that a few Negro landowners now vote in the county. He does not understand why more do not vote, observing: "I've been reading in the paper where they're getting scared around here." He explained that Negro voters used to be treated rough around the polls, and he supposes that they have not forgotten. He thinks, however, that Negroes ought to vote on the same plane as whites, because: "They get educated like the whites; and, the ones around here, I'd as soon have them vote as a lot of the whites. . . . I don't think there'd be any trouble if the whites would leave them alone."

The registrar of Macon County, Georgia, declares that no Negroes vote in the Democratic primary in the county and that he has succeeded in cutting down their number considerably by a rigid check on poll tax payments. He is against all Negroes voting and thinks that only "smart niggers" vote. He feels sure, however, that no Negroes in the county are denied registration, though actual registration is done by the tax collector. On the basis of the registration for the 1940 election, there are 1,214 white persons eligible to vote in the county primary and 1,418 eligible to vote in the state primary; that is, 204 more people paid the poll tax after the county primary. On the general election list, only 27 Negroes are eligible to vote, and 42 are listed as in default of payment of the poll tax. According to the registrar, the few Negroes who do vote are voting for the New Deal "since Roosevelt became Santa Claus." The chairman of the county Democratic committee believes that the fewer Negroes who vote and the better the poll tax is enforced, the cleaner politics in Macon County will become.

In the Englishville district of Macon County, the poorest section of the county, the justice of the peace reports that there have been two Negro names on his voting rolls for several years. One of them died a year or so ago, and the other is in default on poll taxes. A white "rehab" farmer, in discussing Negro voting in the county, declares:

> They don't vote in any of the regular elections around here. . . . Well, I guess some niggers are better qualified to vote than a lot of white people. They keep up with the state officers and

all. I know I don't keep up like I should. I guess if they'd go lettin' them vote again, they'd vote kinda like the white people told them to. These big landowners on some of these big farms around here might start hauling them to the polls. . . . I don't know. I know two or three niggers they wouldn't haul. A lot of them they would.

A white farm owner in the Ideal district observes: "We don't have the class of niggers here that would want to vote." He explains that these here "know what's good for them," and so do not try.

Comparing the present with the past, a member of the board of registrars in Greene County comments:

> You talk about the way they used to buy up the niggahs. Pshaw! It's not a bit worse than the way they buy up the whites with poll taxes now. I'd like to see them do away with all this primary tomfollery. I was in politics back when the niggahs voted, and we never had any talk about "black domination." I ran, and I got every single niggah in the county to vote for me. I could do it again. . . . If a man had so much land and so many niggah families on his place, he had that many votes. Now, any one of these croppers out here being supported by this New Deal can vote as much as a man like me. Why, I've got 5,000 acres.

Upon hearing this, this man's wife interposed: "What do you mean? You wouldn't want *me* down there mixed up with a lot of darkies around the polls, would you?" To which the registrar responded: "Well, that's what I say. I agree with you, I don't think women have any business in politics."

A justice of the peace in Greensboro, Georgia, and a former tax collector in Greene County, recalls his first exploits in county politics as a "nigger stealer." He explains that the big plantation owners would drive their Negro hands into town in wagon loads. The game was to try to steal them away from him before he had time to vote them. This was done by liquor, by music, and by women.

In Wrayswood, a farming section of large plantations along the western extremity of Greene County, the 1939 district qualified list carried the names of five Negroes, one of whom has since died. He owned one hundred acres. Another is a renter over tax age, and the other three own two-horse farms. They vote regularly, but only in the general elections. When the justice of the peace was asked whether Negroes who are moving back into this district under the FSA program might begin voting, he took it as a challenge and fired back: "What's the difference? Every nigger is another vote for Roosevelt."

A white sawmiller in Greshamville, a farming area west of Greensboro, believes that Negroes in Greene County are taking advantage of the FSA program and that "the niggers in this county are shooting way ahead of the white people, and you can't blame them. I hate to see it in a way, but I know I'd do the same if my skin was black. They're going to own this country some day. By God, if they do, they'll earn it!" He works whites and blacks together on his jobs with little trouble, pays them the same wages, and favors educated Negroes in the jobs because "you can tell him what to do and go off and leave him. . . . You can reason with him." He thinks that the Negro will be voting again in Georgia in the near future and comments: "What do you think about that? You know I lie in bed at night and think what would happen if they did." He states that he can just remember the time when "the plantation whites was riding the niggers to the polls." While reflecting, he expressed the wish that "when the niggers do start voting again, I hope it's the better class first. If they don't watch, we're liable to have the same trouble we had last time."

Union Point is a cotton mill and trading town in the northeastern part of Greene County. The 1940 qualified list carried no names of Negroes because it was made up for the primary. The 1939 list carried the names of five Negro men. According to the justice of the peace, one of the Negro voters is "farming for the government [that is, FSA] right across the road. Why, 'cose he votes for the New Deal when they give him six or seven hundred dollars' worth of equipment to farm with and him not putting up a thing." The justice of the peace states that at the time of general elections these three Negro voters "come in every time. They're mighty polite. . . . Always with their hats in their hands. I haven't got any kick there. . . . Naturally, they vote for the New Deal, because give a nigger a little sweetnin' and he'll vote any way." The great plaint of this man is that "you can't get a nigger to chop wood or wash clothes any more. It's past history! They're working for the government." Storming against the government agencies, especially the WPA, the FSA, and the CCC, he raged:

Who are they helping? Tell me, who are they helping? A

lot of sorry, damn niggers! They put them out at this CC Camp where they spend their time scouting around in the woods trying to hide from work. They put them on this W.P.A. and let them go to sleep on their shovels. They put them out on these farms with a brand new plow and a good mule, and a hundred dollars' worth of seed and fertilizer, and let them waste it.

In Gainesville, the Negro vote has been steadily decreasing. The older Negroes are dying off, and the young ones are not registering. The reason for this is said to be because they see no use in paying the poll tax to vote when they can vote only in the general elections. Referring to Negro participation in the Democratic primaries in Hall County, the secretary-treasurer of the county Democratic committee states: "Niggers have been ruled out. It's our private affair, and we don't invite them in, and that's that." A poor white farmer, after pointing out that only a few Negroes vote in the general election in Gainesville, and not in the primary, commented:

> They voted a long time ago before they had any primary, I think. You know, I don't know what you think about it—this is a funny thing for me to say I guess you'll think—but I don't think that's just right. Niggers pays taxes the same as we do. There ain't much difference in us when you get right down and think about it. We all eat and we all wear clothes, and we all rot when we die. . . . Lots of people are prejudiced on the nigger. I ain't. I was born in the South, and I'm a Southerner, all right, but it don't look right to me.

George Stevens, a seventy-two-year-old Negro businessman in Gainesville, has been voting since he was twenty-one. He was born in the upper end of Hall County, the son of a slave who could read and write. He was taught to read and write by his father. When he was twenty, he recalls, some white men came up from town and talked him into coming down to Gainesville and helping them with their political campaign. He did help them each election for several years. These white leaders, together with himself and other Negroes, would get Negroes from all over the county, keep them in the Negro Odd Fellow's Hall all night before election—"keep them up all night laughing and chewing plug tobacco and as much liquor as the white men would give them." Stevens described this as a grand frolic. The next morning they would all file out, go down to vote, and then go home to sleep it off. He asserts that things happened this way "for 10 or 15 years," but then he realized after a while what harm this was doing to his race. He tried to get other Negroes interested in voting more intelligently. He and one of the teachers in the Negro school were making a small beginning when the disfranchisement of 1908 came. Following 1908, Stevens and the few Negroes who reregistered—he estimates something over two hundred—went into the Republican party.

At present Stevens thinks there are some forty Negroes eligible to vote in Hall County. Of these, approximately thirty-five are over sixty, and not more than half of them actually vote. When Stevens sent his assistant up to get registered recently, he was refused. The man at the desk wanted to know why he wished to register. The assistant replied that he wanted to be a citizen. The registrar told him that he could be a citizen without "messing with voting." The assistant then explains: "I looked at him and left. I didn't want no trouble."

Stevens himself votes occasionally in the city elections in Gainesville and believes that three or four other Negroes do also. There is no city primary. Recently a candidate for sheriff called at Stevens' shop and asked him to vote for him in the primary. Stevens says: "I had know'd that man all his life. I know'd he would be good to the colored folks. I wanted to vote for him. I went up there, and they told me I wasn't on the list. That was like a slap in the face to me . . . me, who'd paid taxes in this town all these years. . . . I'll never try that again."

There is a tendency among old-timers in the South to date the beginning of "clean politics" with the disbarment of the Negro from the polls. For instance, the clerk of the court in Gainesville claims that politics have been "reasonably clean" in Hall County since 1906 and 1907. He recalls that in that period he was a young fellow engaged in carrying people to the polls:

A little money and a little liquor, and you could carry every nigger in town. We'd get a bunch of niggers and keep them locked up in the Odd Fellow's Hall all night—feed them peanuts, cheese, and crackers, and give them just enough liquor to keep them happy. . . . Get a string band in there to supply a little music. The next morning we'd march them out like a bunch of convicts and vote them. Before the days of the Australian ballot, they used to take them from one county to another. *I* never did that.

The tax collector in Augusta, a member of the "Cracker Party," informed Miss Jackson that there are about thirty-five Negroes in the city who actually participate in the so-called "white primary," though he was not very explicit on this point. There is a feeling among a number of Negroes in Augusta that the grip of the underworld on the black masses is so strong that, even if allowed to vote in all elections, the Negro vote would find it extremely difficult to be intelligently independent.

There are 344 Negroes registered and qualified to vote in the Brunswick, Georgia, elections. According to an elderly Republican leader in Brunswick:

> Sometimes the Negro vote counts here. A few months ago we had an office opened for reelection—tax commissioner. There were 2,000 registered voters in the city—Negroes and whites. It was realized that Negroes actually held the balance of power. A half dozen men came to see me on reelection. We cast our votes for Exley, who won the election (filling an unexpired term). If we could get a thousand votes, we could break up the white primary. Last week the Republican club put on a campaign to register as many Negroes as possible, and formed a young men's and young women's club in order to get a pretty sizable number around the handicap of poll taxes. No, we have no Democrats among our local Negroes who vote, yet we all voted for Roosevelt in 1932 and 1936. Three or four years ago the lily-whites and the Republicans got together. Under the Hoover regime, we had a postmaster here—Smith—who went right out to replace all of the colored carriers. . . . The state-wide lily-white movement affected Brunswick, too. Today, we have two factions here—the lily-whites and the colored Republicans. This is our main reason for turning against Hoover.[5]

It is said that of the three-hundred-odd Negroes registered in Brunswick, only about fifty-five actually vote. The Negro longshoremen in Brunswick are organized but are not politically active. The shrimp workers and power workers are not organized, and labor is not a potent political factor. Some efforts are now being made by Brunswick Negroes to organize Negro women and Negro youth. It appears that the younger Brunswick Negroes are no longer blindly loyal to the Republican party

5. Wilhelmina Jackson's interview, Brunswick, Georgia, 16 February 1940.

and that the advent of Roosevelt and the New Deal has caused a number of them to switch political allegiance.

Judge Orville A. Park, writing on the Georgia political system for the Coordinating Committee of the Citizens' Fact Finding Movement, deplores the disfranchisement of the Negro:

> This disfranchisement of the Negro is thoroughly undemocratic and is more hurtful to the white than it is to the Negro. In a democracy all citizens must be equal before the law, and political opportunities and political privileges must be accorded alike to all. It is said, of course, in justification of the present system, that the great mass of the Negroes are ignorant and venal, having no knowledge of or regard for the duties of citizenship. The same may be as truly said of a very considerable proportion of the whites. There is no more reason why an ignorant and venal white man should vote than that his brother in black should do so. All of us know that there are intelligent, upright Negroes who understand and who would appreciate the duties of citizenship and exercise the right of suffrage with equal intelligence and as consistently as the white man does. It can but be humiliating to such Negroes that they are denied all participation in the government solely because of their race. What incentive is there for the Negro to improve himself, to learn the problems of Government and to be prepared to participate therein, when all participation is denied him?
>
> We have used the Negro as a sort of club to hold whites in line. We talk of Negro domination when all of us know that there is no fear of such domination. It was a great mistake when the Reconstruction government after the War gave the ballot to all the Negroes. They did not know how to use it and they fell easy victims to designing politicians. It would be a mistake now to let all Negroes, regardless of qualification, intelligence or character, vote, but we cannot justify the denial of the ballot and all participation in public affairs to Negroes of intelligence and character who have demonstrated that they are good citizens, and there are many such.[6]

It is estimated that not more than 1,500 Negroes now vote in the entire state of South Carolina. The decline of Negro political participation in this state has been attributed to two main causes: (1) intimidation of the Negro at the polls and

6. In *The Georgia Political System,* May 1938, pp. 10–11.

(2) the institution of the formal Democratic party, with its ward club system. George Stoney was unable to find any Negro members of the primary ward clubs in South Carolina. Many of the older Negro voters, however, do seem to be voting Democratic, partly because of the New Deal and partly because they are disgusted with Joseph W. Tolbert, a prominent Republican leader who has played for Negro support.

Although not an active factor, the Negro is an influence in South Carolina politics. As the editor of the Columbia *State* puts it:

> Directly, the Negro is a negligible factor in South Carolina politics. Indirectly, and as a backdrop, the Negro is the most powerful political factor in South Carolina. Candidates' whole activities are based on the predicate that Negroes might get something, and one of the main appeals in their campaigns is keeping the Negro out of affairs of state.[7]

The Charleston *News and Courier* takes a stand against the participation of Negroes in politics on the same basis as whites. The following is quoted from Wilhelmina Jackson's interview with William Watts Ball, the old-time editor of the *News and Courier*:

> You want to know about nigroes in politics? Well, they aren't in politics now, but they have had a history of political participation which, up until 1877 and the inauguration of Wade Hampton as Governor, was quite great. After the election of Hampton, due to a bit of gerrymandering, a Seventh District was created including Beaufort, Berkeley County, Richland County, and so on. From this "black district," as it was popularly called, came the nigro congressman, Robert Small. At this time, too, there came into being the "eight box" law which, in effect, was a literacy test. One was a box for federal officers, one for state, county, and so on. Of course, if one could not read, he wouldn't know who to vote for, and he wouldn't know when he voted wrong nor when his vote was thrown out. This kept quite a few nigroes out. Of course, I have no doubts but that the ignorant whites, who it would have caught, were just voted on in. Despite these handicaps, nigroes were voting in collaboration with greenbackers and Republicans in 1882—a Methodist minister and two nigroes

7. Wilhelmina Jackson's interview, Columbia, South Carolina, January 1940.

ran on an independent ticket in the up-country for state legislature. They didn't win.

Now, there came into existence Tillman, a man who sought
to gain power in the state—elected Governor in 1890. There
was held a constitutional convention, one of the results of
which was the famous alternative clause—property versus
education as a prerequisite for voting. Immediately, of course,
this disfranchised the vast majority of nigroes, although I
have no doubt but that numerous allowances were made for
the poor whites. The Supreme Court upheld this law. Nigroes
were dealt a severe blow by this. Their feelings hurt as years
went by, the nigro vote became less and less until finally it
reached the place it has now, where only 1,500 votes were
cast in the entire state. The law of the Democratic party, that
only people who had relatives who voted for Wade Hampton
in 1877, I do not believe is fair, because most of the nigroes
voted for Chamberlain—Hampton's opponent. What happened to the seventh district? It disappeared in the census,
and the heavy migration destroyed it anyway. Now, I believe
nigroes should be in politics. In the first place, let me say this.
I do not believe in Democracy with a small "d". I believe in
Democracy with a large "D". Only the best qualified in both
races ought to participate in politics. The nigroes should
have a black party with a black primary. You know, the
Democratic party in the South is strictly a racial party. They
should release "tieless" Joe and the Republicans entirely. The
membership is kept small so patronage distribution won't
have to go but so far. This cream of both races, voting in their
separate primaries, would make politics approach something
near good.

Now get this straight. I like nigroes. Why, when I was a
boy, I played with little nigroes on my grandfather's plantation, and when I go in a public place, I want a nigro servant.
White servants leave something lacking. I don't like to face
them. Yes, the nigroes are good at nursing, cooking, and so
forth, in the mass, but the cream should do the politicalizing.

In the opinion of Tom Stoney, an ex-mayor of Charleston, the
New Deal is no kin to the old Democratic party because it has
done three things which are against the basic principles of the
older organization: (1) it has betrayed the old stand on the
tariff; (2) it has turned its back on state rights and has endorsed
the centralization of power; and (3) it has taken the Negro into

the body politic. With regard to the last, this warning was issued.

I don't blame the nigra for trying to get in. I have done everything in my power to give the black man everything that he should have. But, I tell you, we are coming on bloody times when he becomes a part of our voting public. I say, I don't blame the nigra for trying, but I shudder to think what will happen when we return to the days of Reconstruction. We are going to have more and more trouble with him as times go on. Personally, I have nothing against the black man. But, I think God must have had something in his mind when he made one race black and another white. If he hadn't intended for there to be a difference, he would have made one yellow race.

Stoney stated that the few Negroes who vote in the general election in Charleston would not number three hundred and that, until they had started voting Democratic, their votes were "seldom counted."

According to the clerk of court in Charleston, there are between eight hundred and a thousand Negroes registered in Charleston County out of an approximate total registration of ten thousand. Negro preachers in Charleston, as a group, are only mildly interested in black political participation, though two of them actively encourage it. A few whites, mainly identified with the Tolbert Republican faction, covertly urge Negroes to try to vote. Negroes estimate that about 1,200 Negroes are now registered in Charleston, a considerably larger number than officials report.[8] It is related that when John P. Grace was mayor of Charleston some years ago, he contacted a prominent Negro on the quiet and asked how many Negroes were registered. When Grace discovered that there were only 328 Negroes registered, he responded: "I'm sorry. I can't use 328. It will do me more harm than good. The Negro is a political nonentity."

The strategy of the NAACP in Charleston is to get Negroes registered whether they vote or not, so that the black vote will loom as significant. It is felt that when it does, the white candidates will bid for it, and that this will tend to break up the Democratic primary. There has been no restraint placed on the registration of Negro women in Charleston. A Democratic politician in Charleston states quite frankly that he has no objection

8. Wilhelmina Jackson's interviews in Charleston, South Carolina, 11 April 1940.

to Negroes voting in the party primary, but that they already have the poor whites to buy. The Negro vote would greatly increase the cost, and he is afraid that the machine could not bear it.

This tendency of the Negro to permit himself to be bought politically is often condemned as a fatal weakness. For example, Dr. McFall, Sr., a prominent Charleston Negro, said in an interview on 28 October 1939:

> In an election of a board of assessors a few years ago—ten men to be elected—a primary was not held. At that time, about 600 Negro votes could be used and would have meant election of the men receiving the Negro vote. A group of Negro leaders, representing this vote, held a caucus and selected a slate, extending a complimentary vote to the men selected. Three men, prominent in the Democratic party, were to be given unqualified complimentary support. Others were to be questioned as to their attitudes toward the assessment of Negro property, for there had been some abuses in such assessments. One of the members of our caucus decided to support a slate other than the one selected by the caucus for a twenty-five-dollar contribution from a white group.

In the northern part of Charleston County, in the corner between Berkeley and Dorchester counties, is Lincolnville—an almost entirely Negro community. Lincolnville is a settlement on the railroad, an incorporated village of some three hundred people today. The village was established shortly after the Civil War when it was given a charter, and since that time it has had a municipal government completely manned by Negroes. At one time, it is said, the village had almost a thousand inhabitants and boasted some two hundred voters. Now the vote has dwindled to forty-nine. In general elections, Lincolnville is included in the Lawson precinct, and registration in that precinct, as of May 1940, was sixty-nine whites and forty-nine Negroes. The population of the village has dropped because of the loss of the phosphate mine. The village must—according to state statute—hold an election every year. To vote in this election, a person must get a special municipal registration certificate. Negroes in Lincolnville give out these certificates. But in order to get a certificate, one must show a county registration certificate plus a poll tax receipt. In order to get one of these, it is necessary to go to Charleston on the first Monday in the month, and Lincolnville Negroes have found that after this lengthy trip it is often necessary to wait about the office for many hours. As one Negro storekeeper in Lincolnville put it: if one "behaves himself," he "can get a registration certificate at Mr. Burk's drugstore in Charleston." The young people of Lincolnville are moving out in order to get work in Charleston or are going North, and the older people are dying off.

Lincolnville Negroes do have some slight voice in county affairs, and this is expressed in the election of school commissioners for their districts. Three of these commissioners are elected in a general election. Since there are almost as many Negroes voting in Lincolnville or in Lawson district as there are whites, they have effective power. Recently the chairman of the school commission tried to switch the voting for the commissioners to the Democratic primary. The Negroes of Lincolnville got back at him by voting solidly against him the next time. Although he was not defeated as a school commissioner, he did lose the chairmanship. Lincolnville Negroes claim to have the best rural Negro school in Charleston County. It has two hundred pupils and nine grades. Lincolnville has its own town constable, and Negroes boast of the fact that "we don't have any of this business of a sheriff's deputy entering a house without a warrant or anything like that."

On the Sea Islands off Charleston, Negroes have little political privilege. On Edisto Island it is said that only fifteen out of three thousand Negroes are registered to vote. On James Island thirty out of six thousand are registered. And on John's Island it is said that only twenty-five Negroes are registered, and, of these, only seven or eight vote.[9]

In Greenville only a handful of people vote in the general election. In October 1938 there were only thirty-five Negroes in Greenville County qualified to vote. Yet the white press played this figure up as though it were a significant number. Early in the spring of 1939, a number of Negro organizations in Greenville began to devote attention to the Negro's political status. It was discovered that there was general ignorance among Negroes about their disfranchisement. The NAACP, the Youth Council of the NAACP, the Negro Division of the Greenville Council, and other groups began to get active. In the spring of 1939, at the annual meeting of the Interracial Commission held in Greenville, Arthur F. Raper spoke on the white primary and

9. Wilhelmina Jackson's interviews in Charleston County, South Carolina, 24 January 1940.

the poll tax and stated that not until these two evils were removed would Negroes get out of the rut they are in. Following this meeting, the Greenville County Council held a mass meeting at Textile Hall at which Mary Bethune spoke. The keynote of her speech was "get representation." In May and June of the same year, the Youth Council sponsored two forums on youth and democracy, and these meetings were announced through the papers. At this same time, the Greenville County Council began to agitate for a housing project for the city. The federal government had earmarked $800,000 for the Greenville project, and Negroes had worked very hard for it. They had circulated a petition to which they had attached six hundred signatures. But the whole movement was defeated because of the opposition of the organized real estate interests in the city. The agitation for a Negro park was continued. All of this activity stimulated Negro registration. In May of that year, sixty-five Negroes were registered. In July forty more were registered, and another hundred were put on the roll before the closing date. The Negroes had the idea of flooding the general election and sponsoring an independent candidate.[10]

Sensing this, the white population became excited. They saw that the CIO, the Workers' Alliance, and possibly some disaffected whites were beginning to cooperate with the Negroes. An extensive underground movement began. The president of the Workers' Alliance was arrested three times in one week. The Ku Klux Klan became active and in late October of that year took a war veteran out and beat him badly. Fifty Klan members went after a Negro professor and invaded eight Negro homes in search of him. The Greenville newspapers contributed to the hysteria by running such headlines as "Registration Among Negroes Increases" and by printing pictures with such captions as "Only a Few of Many Negro Women Registering." An editorial in the Greenville *News* of 7 July 1939, entitled "General Election Voting," observed: "If Negro citizens find it worthwhile to take an active interest in voting in this general election, certainly white citizens should realize the wisdom of performing their civic duty at the ballot box. . . . For our elections have been characterized by the casting of only a handful of votes." The intimidation efforts of the Klan and of other groups in Greenville apparently attained their purpose, for less than a tenth of the registered Negro voters were out on general election day.

10. Wilhelmina Jackson's interview with R. O. Johnson, Greenville, South Carolina, 3 February 1940.

Since the 1939 episode, work in behalf of Negro voting in Greenville has gone quietly. Negroes are urged to go in and register one or two at a time. According to the chairman of the board, Negroes are not coming, however. But there have been some first signs of Greenville's recognition of the needs of its Negro citizenry. An announcement was recently made that two fully equipped playgrounds for Negroes would be built with WPA money and the newspapers printing the story emphasized, with comment, that these playgrounds would be just like those for the whites.

The Negro in Greenville has always been an important force in local politics, not as an active voter, but as a bogey. The strength of this must be fully realized before the community uprisings that followed the attempts of a handful of Negroes to register for city elections in 1939 can be understood. According to Joseph Dokes, a student of the Negro in Greenville:

> Of the 250 Negroes who are qualified to vote in municipal elections here, all have to have two registration certificates. The approximately 600 Negroes registered for county, state and national elections have to have only one receipt; those registered and qualified for municipal elections have to possess property tax receipts within the city. Some of these Negroes vote in the general election for Democratic nominees; in the state and national elections, they are divided—some voting the Republican, some the Democratic ticket.

With regard to the 1939 episode, the same source writes:

> Even though there were 250 Negroes who qualified for voting in the municipal election in September 1939 in Greenville, only 54 of them voted. All of these voted for the Democratic nominees for municipal offices. In the same election, of the 2,224 registered voters of the city, only 551 persons voted. This was a greater number than is usual for the general elections in the city.

The president of the South Carolina League for Progressive Democracy (Labor's Non-Partisan League) states that the League had nothing to do with the attempt to get Negroes registered in Greenville in the summer of 1939. Expressing his personal view, he argues that the Negro can get what he needs, and can get it much better, in other ways than through the vote. He feels that labor really has nothing to gain from Negro exercise of the franchise, although he believes that if labor "got in," the Negro could look to it for a "square deal." The TWUA organizer for Greenville admitted, however, that his organization did get involved in this attempt of the Negroes to register. Since the Workers' Alliance, which gave the strongest backing to the movement, used the TWUA office as headquarters, the TWUA "got smeared." "Personally," this organizer said, "I think the niggers ought to have the right to vote. They're citizens, like everybody else. I'd do most anything I could personally to help them get it." Yet he felt that he could not jeopardize the welfare of his union for this. He could see no immediate advantage for the TWUA in having Negroes registered, but added: "Sooner or later, we've got to get them because we're not going to have enough by ourselves."

A prominent Greenville Negro who votes because it has been "a tradition" in his family to vote believes in Negroes' registering and asserting their political rights, but he says they must do this in "a dignified way." This man had no stomach for the efforts made in the summer of 1939 on behalf of Negroes in Greenville. He feels that this movement for Negro enfranchisement was backed by the "wrong people"—the Workers' Alliance and "that bunch." Almost everyone who was registered for the first time, he states, was a relief worker or unemployed. There was not a really well-established Negro in town behind the movement except "Jim" Brier, head of the NAACP. Brier, he states, was really the worker for the entire movement. It was Brier who put the Negroes out in front of the courthouse to direct the people coming in to register. "That," said this man, who is head porter at the Greenville Hotel, "was alright for 1866, but now if Negroes need that kind of help, they shouldn't be trying to vote."

Professor Brier was pushed out of his place as school principal for his NAACP activities before the registration fight began. During the registration fight, Brier received many notes from the Ku Klux Klan, but managed to escape without harm. The Negro porter would give Professor Brier credit, however, for being the only Negro Republican in the state who has really worked to get his people enrolled: "Too many of our race are content to be the only one. They rather pride themselves on being the only one." Brier went to the Republican national convention at Philadelphia as a member of the Hambright faction, led by Greenville's richest banker, George Norwood. Brier's "pull" with Negro delegates from other states helped the Norwood group gain recognition over the Tolbert faction at the convention. This may mean that Professor Brier will have Norwood's protection, if not his support, when he returns to Greenville.

It is said that many Negroes in Sumter voted for Roosevelt in 1936. No Sumter Negroes have ever tried to vote in the Democratic primary, however, other than two "Wade Hampton" Negroes. The Sumter *Item* of 4 November 1936, reported: "President Roosevelt received a considerable portion of the negro vote cast in South Carolina, reports from election officials today indicated. More negroes than usual voted in a number of South Carolina counties this year, though no special check was kept of the part they played in the election." Only a few Negroes vote in the general elections. The town of Sumter has two lively but small Republican groups. The Tolbert faction is "all niggers" in Sumter, says the chairman of the county Democratic committee. The other faction is "lily-white" and is made up of people from Missouri who came to Sumter to set up cooperage plants, some people from Virginia who established businesses in Sumter, and other out-of-staters. The chairman emphasized that only one native-born South Carolinian "is connected with that bunch." He did have a good word for some Negroes, however, commenting that the town has had some "mighty good niggers," including a Negro physician (whom he referred to as "nigra" instead of "nigger") recently deceased, a retired Negro mail clerk, and several others whom he called "mighty decent citizens."

In Columbia one man has dominated the local political scene for the past fifteen years—Mayor Owens. His long service in office has enabled him to build up a powerful personal political machine. Mayor Owens is convinced of the wisdom in the non-participation of Negroes in politics. The only elections worth mentioning in Columbia are the primary elections. The Republican vote is of no consequence. Campaigns are intense during the primaries but are not even conducted during a general election, when little voting is done. Some Negroes in Columbia do vote. The voting is confined, however, to local bond issues and to presidential elections. Negroes in Columbia do not evidence a great deal of interest in voting since they are excluded from participation in the Democratic primary, which is the real election. The feeling seems to be that they are parties to a farce when they participate in the general election.[11]

There are only about one dozen Negroes in Columbia who vote in the general elections. Negroes do not vote at all in the Democratic primary, for in the *Democratic Party Rules*, section

11. Attitudes based upon returns on questionnaires and Wilhelmina Jackson's interviews with five Negro civic leaders, Columbia, South Carolina, 24 January 1940.

7, there is this statement concerning Negro voting in the party primary:

> Every Negro applicant for membership in a Democratic Club or offering to vote in a Democratic Primary must show a written statement of ten reputable white men, swearing to their own personal knowledge that applicant voted for General Wade Hampton in 1876 and has voted Democratic ticket continuously since then. For every Negro so voting, a note shall be made, put in the ballot box and manager of elections shall keep it separate from all other votes and turn it in [with general voting report].

The secretary of the Richland County Democratic club stated that there are no Negroes now living in Columbia who could comply with those regulations.

In 1934 Dr. Mance, a Columbia Negro, registered as a Democrat. He encouraged other Negroes to do the same, and finally nearly a hundred Negroes got on the roll. About a week and a half before the primary election was held, however, all of these Negroes received a card asking them to come and show cause why their names should not be purged from the Democratic club roll. When the Wade Hampton clause was read and when it was asserted by the reader that most white men could comply, Dr. Mance argued that white women—if registered—would also have to be purged because in that year they were not constitutionally eligible to vote. The names of the Negroes were purged, however, and Dr. Mance and several others took the case to court. In the meantime, the primary was run off and the court held that the Negroes bringing suit were too late in so doing, as contests of that nature must be brought a reasonable time before the primary is held. Their objections that they were sent cards too late were to no avail, and the case was thrown out.[12] Subsequently, the Democratic rules were changed, and section 7 now reads: "Any *white* man—21 years of age and over—may apply for membership in this club and vote in the Democratic primary."

There are some prominent whites in Columbia who feel that Negroes should be permitted political participation. The editor of the *Free Press* reprinted in that paper an editorial from the Charleston *News and Courier* endorsing the Negro vote. The

12. Wilhelmina Jackson's interview with Dr. Mance, Columbia, South Carolina, 18 January 1940.

Reverend Clyde Helms, chairman of the Social Service Commission of the Baptist Churches of South Carolina, submitted a report and a resolution at the last Baptist state convention stating that the right of Negroes to participate freely in elections should not be denied. This report read:

> In most sections, the Negro is denied the ballot. Everyone is agreed that wholesome restrictions should be placed about the ballot, but every citizen who is qualified to vote should be permitted to do so. There is good reason to anticipate social upheavals in any commonwealth in which a minority group —composing 45 percent of its population—is denied the ballot simply because of its color. No race can attain its highest development where its qualified members are denied a voice in the management of public affairs.

On the other hand, one Columbia white minister has been quoted as saying: "I would wish for a shotgun and a tree when nigras started voting and the precise aim to pluck them down one by one as they tried and dared to cast a vote."[13]

Dr. E. C. L. Adams, a retired white medical doctor in Columbia who owns a 2,500 acre plantation several miles outside of the city and employs some forty Negroes as day laborers or renters, permitted Wilhelmina Jackson to visit his place and to interview some of his workers. Miss Jackson was admitted into the home of Dr. Adams on the plantation, was invited to have a meal with him, and was permitted to interview his Negro workers without anyone else being present.

The first of the Negroes interviewed was Buster Hubbard, a day laborer on the farm—a man of about thirty-five who had been working for "Doc" Adams for the last fifteen years. When asked whether he had ever voted, he replied: "No'm, we doesn't vote a-tall out here." Asked whether he had ever desired to vote, he said: "Wal, guess I wouldn't mind it, 'cordin to what it 'tis." In response to the query whether he had ever seen a newspaper, he replied: "No'm, never have yet." And, when asked whether he had ever listened to a radio, he replied: "No'm, has no lights." Asked for his opinion of President Roosevelt, however, he became voluble and said: "Swell man, Mistuh Roosevelt, he is Negro fren 'cause mos' people out here is renters and Mr. Roosevelt 'low so much a year to rent crops and give us peas and

13. Quoted for Wilhelmina Jackson by Professor G. Croft Williams of the University of South Carolina, Columbia, South Carolina, January 1940.

food for cotton and all." Concerning Senator "Cotton Ed" Smith, he replied: "Don' like him a little bit. If'n I recollects correctly, he said niggers kin live off'n twenty-five cents and fifty cents a day. For that you kin git clothes off'n that, but not food. You and family would be naked or slight your stomachs, and where there's children, you gotta feed 'em. No'm, I don't like Senator Smith a little bit." When asked whether he thought the vote would better his status, Hubbard replied: "Folks in Nort' has privilege to vote, reason they's so far ahead of our colored folks in the country, and 'specially in Sous Caolina."

Nero Brown, an old one-eyed Negro, when asked whether the Negro workers on the farm ever discussed politics, replied: "Yes'm, 'specially we colored folks gist together and talks about Senator Smith. He's a mean white man to us colored folks." When asked whether the Negro workers admired Roosevelt, Brown replied: "Yes'm, and eff'n we cud vote, we wouldn't vote for anybody else but Mistuh Roosevelt, but no one out here ever tried to vote. We's mostly scary, that's it. We'd rather go on and do the best we can." When asked whether he had read a news-paper or heard a radio, Brown replied: "No'm, 'cept when I goes to Columbia, and I goes right sharp on Sat'days." Asked if his preacher ever talked about politicians, Brown said: "Yes'm, he thinks Senator Smith's a fine man. But ef'n I cud vote, I'd just vote for Mistuh Roosevelt; he's a fine man."

The next worker was "Thad" Gibson, an old man of about seventy-two, who said of Franklin D. Roosevelt:

> Roosevelt has done more for colored people than any other president in this community. He give us our first school—a three-room WPA school. He give us teachers . . . for our chil-dren. He give us food when we was hungry and our children hot WPA lunches in school. Tain't no use talkin' 'bout politics. Our folks down here don' even know what 'tis and if they cud vote tomorrow, they wouldn't know how or what they was votin' for. They's that ignorant.

A young day laborer of about twenty-seven or twenty-eight named Milton Washington, when asked about Senator Smith, said: "If you tend to your business everything will be all right. I don' let him cross my mind." About Roosevelt, he said: "Purty good, I reckon. I never wuked on WPA yet and never had any dealings with presidents, anyhow." Concerning a desire for vot-ing, he commented: "It never has done drove 'cross my mind about votin', 'cause I never voted and don' know nothin' 'bout what it is. I just want what's comin' to me Sat'day night so's I can give my mother some food and go to Columbia."

The next worker, Peter Epps, a man of about forty who was partly a WPA worker and partly a day laborer, stated that: "Negroes shud vote for Mistuh Roosevelt if they kin." Asked whether Republicans meant anything to him, he said: "Never heard of it." When asked whether the Negroes on Adams' farm ever talked politics, he said: "They's talked more politics since Mistuh Roosevelt been in than ever befo'. I been here twenty years, but since WPA, the Negro sho' has started talkin' 'bout politics."

The overseer on "Cotton Ed" Smith's plantation, about four miles outside of Lynchburg, South Carolina, observed: "Nigras don't vote here 'cept for farm parity payment. Gits right much outta that, too. When you git down to it, white folks don't know nothin' 'bout votin' out here, either." One of the day laborers on this farm—who said that she received $1.00 to $1.50 a week "'cordin' to the weather" and that her working hours are "sunup to sundown"—replied when asked about voting: "Never has. Doesn't want to. Not so far as I know's any good come of it." When asked what she thought of the WPA, she replied: "I never jined that club, yet. Don't know much a-tall about it." None of the several day laborers and sharecroppers interviewed by Wilhelmina Jackson on the plantation knew anything about voting, political issues, or even about the WPA, nor did they know anything about Senator Smith except that he did go to Washington quite often, probably because "he's got plenty of money and time," though contending that he was on the farm a great deal of the time too.

There are no more than five or six Negro Republicans who vote in Saluda County, though perhaps a few more have at some time registered, especially since the attorney general has made the ruling that Negro names must be put in the jury box. The names of Negroes are placed in the federal jury box and a former chief commissioner for Saluda County states that he saw one Negro from the county serving: "He sat up thar and didn't hurt nothing at all. He's a good old nigger—minds his own business. I'd about as soon have him up there as most white men if I was being charged." This man went so far as to state that he would not mind seeing some of the Negroes vote, because: "We've got some mighty good niggers in this county. They've got a limit to the amount of vision and all like that, I'll grant you, but they're honest and steady as you'll find."

A member of the board of registrars of Saluda County says that when Negroes came in to register, he would ask them which district they wanted to vote in and that "every one of them said they didn't want to vote. They said they wanted to register because they thought it was a help to the government." Negroes are also made to show poll tax receipts and registration certificates at the polls. According to the county clerk, "if a nigger votes here, he's got to show his credentials." Six Negroes are now registered, but only one of them is under sixty-five and thus eligible for jury duty. He has never been drawn, however, "and never will be." Expressing his views on the Negro vote, the clerk declared:

> I don't think a nigger's got any right to vote. They never contributed a damn thing to the community. All they do is live on it. Look at the schools they get out of us. Their taxes wouldn't pay for them in a hundred years. . . . Hell! I'm glad to see them going North, and a pile of them have gone from this county.

> I'm getting a stack of letters every day from some of them in New York and Detroit and all over wanting birth certificates so they can get their working papers. I'll see them in hell before I'll send a damn one of them anything.

Continuing, he observed:

> I wouldn't lift a little finger for them unless I get my fee for it. . . . Lie around. Won't work in the fields any more. . . . Too *good* for that! All they want is WPA or go to work in the sawmills. . . . Oh! You'll find one good one in a hundred or two. One or two of them are pretty good farmers. . . . You could count them on your hand. . . . I'm glad they are going North. . . . Good riddance.

An elderly Negro in Saluda who is a faithful follower of "tieless" Joe Tolbert, and who has been taken to Republican conventions by Tolbert, has done his best to get "something started" among Negro voters. The older Negro voters, he states, kept dying off, and he could not recall there being more than a dozen Negro voters since he was a boy. He is now fifty-nine. By 1936 there were only two Negro voters left in the county—himself and his wife—and so then, he declares: "I got busy and commenced working me up a bunch to go register." He got ten or twelve who said they were willing and most of them—eight—

were registered in 1938, when the new registration began, but not that many voted because

> they got discouraged. . . . James Bush, who had worked in the Ford repair shop for a dozen years, got fired. His mother— an undertaker—was not bothered. Ella McGraw, a school teacher, was warned by the authorities that she had better not "mess with such as that." Raney Hurley, a Negro land-owner out in the county, received a hike in taxes.

Two others were the reverend John Davis and the reverend John Williams—both of Ridge Spring. One of these men was "warned." One other was a janitor in the bank—one of the best-known Negroes in the town and a good friend of the mayor's. He also was fired. "The mayor said he was surprised. He said he'd always liked him, but right there, he ruint hisself when he started foolin' with votin'. All that got people discouraged."

The last time this informant carried tickets (ballots) to the polls, he got in trouble. One of the poll holders told him that he was too late and that he should have given those tickets to the chairman of the commission the day before. The Negro objected that he thought a man could bring in the tickets any time and that a voter had a right to bring his own tickets to the polls indi-vidually if he wished. The poll holder "wanted to know who told me that. If I'd 'a said Joe Tolbert told me that, he would have run me out, so I said: 'You all white folks say so.' One of them jumps and says he going to get a law book. Humph! He run out that door and he run right back. Didn't go no place and a'sayin', yeah, that's right."

At the last registration, this man got two Negroes registered —the two ministers—who had no property. This is the first time he had tried this because: "I know'd it might be trouble, so I says, let's wait to about 1:30. Don't never approach a white man on an empty stomach if you want him to do you a favor." They went in at 1:30 p.m. and got registered. As for the young Ne-groes in this county, "all they study about is getting out. They don't want no land. All they want to do is go North."

In Beaufort County few Negroes vote and these only in the general election. They are "mostly old people. The young fellows have got better sense than to start anything like that." The clerk of court in Beaufort County states that he has issued general election certificates of registration to Negroes who have applied on "off" days. He has done this, however, only for "good old darkies" whom he knew. He does not see, he says, why "we shouldn't let some of those darkies vote." He mentioned several whom he considered "good friends—mighty good friends"— and "I don't think it would hurt a bit in the world to let a few of them come on in to our primaries." Up through April 1940, eighteen Negroes were registered for the general election, and the clerk of court predicts that not more than forty would be registered for the 1940 elections in the county. Negroes have never voted in the primaries here. According to a prominent Negro leader in Beaufort, all of the "voting Negroes" in the county are Republican, while a few of the "talking" ones are Democrats.

According to the wife of H. G. Fisher, an undertaker:

> Only the old folks in Beaufort are foolish enough to hope . . . and to think how far we went when I was young. We used to be the public officials here . . . now all they will give us is jobs as street cleaners. . . . A white man is janitor of the courthouse. They won't hire a Negro if they can avoid it. No wonder the young people are going North. They want to go where they have more privileges.

This Negro woman recalled the days when she went to school with white children and the daughter of her mother's master was the teacher.

The city manager of Beaufort believes: "We are going to have some more trouble about Negroes voting; we had a sample of it last time." He told the story of a Negro Baptist preacher—a Southern Negro educated in the North—who tried to vote in the Democratic primary. He was greeted by a former mayor of Beaufort with the question: "What do you want, nigger?" When the Negro preacher said that he wanted to vote, he was told to "get out and stay out if you know what's good for you." The city manager warns that: "We can expect this from now on." He felt that there would be no trouble from local Negroes, but that the ones coming down from the North will cause trouble. The local schoolteachers also are "getting ideas. They are telling the students they ought to take their rights." The city manager is "against this kind of thing—at least, not for a long time."

There are six or eight Negroes who vote in Pickens County, and all of these vote either in Pickens or in another town box, according to a former general election commissioner, who added: "They better not try voting in some of these country places up around these mills." He explains that no larger number of Negroes vote "because they aren't interested." He does not think, however, that anyone would "bother them" in the town of Pickens, although the old feeling against Negroes and Republicans remains very strong there.

This man, who is now a school trustee, referred to the threat of a school strike which occurred last spring. He thought a Negro preacher was back of this. "I don't know whether he's an agent of this Association for the Advancement of Colored People or not. I wouldn't be surprised. We've had trouble with him once or twice before. The colored people themselves don't like him. He keeps them stirred up all the time." He reports that most of the Negroes from Pickens County are leaving for the North: "Any cornfield colored girl who gets a little experience as a servant will pick up and leave for Nashville or Washington or Philadelphia [mocking their pronunciation of the city names], where they think they're going to get higher wages." He has a Negro girl in his house now who went up there and came back, and he says she found out it was not so nice. He did not know, however, whether he was going to keep her or not, because "she's spoiled now." He concluded: "I'd be satisfied to see them all leave. I'm sick and tired of seeing white men standing back from work because they think it's a nigger's job."

The secretary of the Pickens County Democratic committee estimates that there are ten or twelve Negroes who vote in the county. All except one of these vote with the Republicans, and this one is said to be the courthouse janitor. "He's what you call a white man's nigger. . . . Killed another nigger and got life for it. . . . Got a pardon from the governor. . . . Been working here ever since. He'll do anything for a white man, but he sees that a nigger keeps in his place. . . . Don't have much to do with them. They're afraid of him." This Negro votes Democratic, and "he says he wouldn't vote Republican for nobody." The secretary asserts: "No sir! No niggers vote in any primaries in *this* county."

No Negroes vote in the Six Mile, South Carolina, box, and the president of the Democratic club at Six Mile thinks that not more than two or three Negroes vote in the entire county. The attitude of the young president of the Democratic club at this rural community is that there are too many ignorant votes cast now, and if all the Negroes voted it would be much worse. He observes: "Oh, I believe in educating the nigger. I do believe in that. It looks like when they get educated, they're more reasonable like. . . . They're just as polite and nice and intelligent as any of us are." This man stated that he was less certain that the local people would "stand for it" than that the Negroes, if they got the vote, would try to "do something wrong. You can't tell what you'd get into. . . . Funny thing when you come to think about it. Supposed to be a free country and all. The Constitution says they can vote in a general election, don't it? . . . I guess there's an unwritten law."

According to the census, out of a total population of 63,864, Orangeburg County has 40,640 Negroes. In Orangeburg Negroes have a chance to vote for local officials because there is no primary for the municipal elections. However, rather too typically, the small number of Negroes who do vote in city elections can be bought by promises of small payoffs and favors. It is said that, for the most part, the Negro intellectuals in Orangeburg do not vote. In 1939, for example, only two Negro teachers voted in the trustee election. It is stated that the ease with which Negroes can register in Orangeburg makes the low registration figure appalling. It is further observed that "with ten possible exceptions, the 125 Negroes registered to vote in Orangeburg's city elections are the ordinary Negroes."[14]

Not more than a few hundred Negroes vote in the entire state of Mississippi. A few of them are old Negro aristocrats, and a few are young schoolteachers. Negroes are completely barred from the Democratic primary in this state. Mississippi presents perhaps the darkest picture of frustrated Negro political effort. Here exclusion devices and intimidation reach their zenith. About the only ray of political light to which Mississippi Negroes can turn is reflected by Perry Howard, the nation's sole remaining Negro Republican committeeman, who for years has resided in Washington, D.C., and not Mississippi, and who has been aptly described as "a better 'lily-white' than a white Mississippian could be."

Senator Harrison of Mississippi has stated that: "Under the laws of Mississippi, the nigra can vote now in the general election if he can meet the qualifications of the constitution." But as to the possibility of the Negro being permitted to participate fully in the electoral processes in the South, the Senator declares that, though education will help, the old tradition persists about the period when the Negro controlled the state legislatures: "The nigra is satisfied down there from a political standpoint. In my state, the nigra has played no part in politics for forty

14. Wilhelmina Jackson's interviews, Orangeburg, South Carolina, 1 February 1940.

years and has no desire to do so. We are all content to leave the situation alone as it is."[15]

About a dozen years ago in Vicksburg, in a special election for mayor, Negroes had an opportunity to vote. Dr. W. J. Holsey was running against Judge Henry. A Holsey supporter campaigned among the Negroes. The vote was about 1,700 for Holsey and 1,500 for the judge. Later, Dr. Holsey—in a speech of welcome to a Negro convention at the YMCA in Vicksburg—said that the Negro vote was the margin of victory in his election. A lawyer named Ewing acted as intermediary between the Negroes and the mayor and succeeded in getting several streets paved and a few street lights put up in the Negro sections.[16]

According to Dr. S. D. Redmond, chairman of the Republican state central committee in Mississippi and a prominent Negro politician:

The Negro's status in Southern politics is dark as Hell and smells like cheese. There is an unwritten law in the state of Mississippi that not enough Negroes shall be allowed to register to jeopardize white supremacy. The poll tax is the most effective instrument, along with the registration procedure, for disfranchising the Negro. The catch in the poll tax law is this—you must have paid the tax before the proper time for two successive years prior to the election in which you offer to vote. The poll tax assessment is $2 per year. In addition to this, you must pay a street tax of $1 if you are a resident of the town or city. The property qualification for registration and the grandfather clause were removed in 1936. . . . In spite of the elimination of the grandfather clause and the property qualification for voting, it is nonetheless well nigh impossible for any mass registration on the part of Negroes in Mississippi. The registrar, who is also the circuit clerk, is the final arbitrator in determining the applicant's ability to read and write, and interpret clauses from the Constitution. The registrar here in Jackson has been quoted as asking such questions as this: "How old was Christ when he was born?"

On one occasion, a Negro applicant went up to register. Said the registrar: "Get the hell out of here, nigger, before I take something and knock you in the head. You niggers are

15. Interview with Senator Byron Patton Harrison, Washington, D.C., 16 February 1940. The interviewer is not identified in the Bunche memorandum. —ED.

16. James Jackson's interview with Dr. Owens, a Negro Republican leader, Vicksburg, Mississippi, February 1940.

looking for trouble. What you want to vote in a white man's election for? You think you are equal to a white man, don't you?"

I sent out letters to the county clerks in all Mississippi counties, seeking to determine the number of registered Negroes in the state. None replied to my letters. Subsequently I telephoned several of them and these are some of the replies: From Sharkey County in the Delta: "Don't allow niggers to register in Sharkey County." From Madison County: "Seventy-five niggers registered in Madison County." From Vicksburg: "About 300 colored people registered in Vicksburg." From Lincoln County: "Only one nigger—Burwell Jackson who died five years ago—has been registered here as far as I know." From Copiah County: "About twenty-five niggers registered in Copiah County." From Humphreys County: "None. You know we don't allow niggers to register in Humphreys County." From Forrest County: "Only four of 'em registered here." From Newton County: "Five niggers here." From Yazoo County: "Only three niggers vote here, thank God."

Of course, you know that nomination in the Democratic primary is tantamount to election. No candidate dares challenge the primary nominee in a general election. He would be definitely *persona non grata*. . . .

Back in 1890 or thereabouts, after they'd accomplished the defeat of the Reconstruction Government, a constitutional convention was called to change the Reconstruction constitution of 1868. At this convention, there was one Negro who will be remembered in future histories of Mississippi as the Judas of his people. This Negro was Isaiah T. Montgomery, from Mound Bayou. Montgomery betrayed his people by voting for Section 240 of the infamous Constitution of 1890 which wiped out the political liberties of the Negro people and the vast masses of white people. Montgomery was lionized and acclaimed by the Bourbons for this betrayal.[17]

Negroes have had no voice in the political life of Louisiana since 1896—the year in which the primary election law was passed. Throughout the entire state not more than two thousand Negroes are eligible to vote. The registration difficulties have proven great, and the registrars have succeeded in keeping all but a small number of blacks from the polls even though

17. James Jackson's interview, Jackson, Mississippi, January 1940.

poll tax payment is no longer required for voting. Most of those who vote are in New Orleans.

Louisiana is the one Southern state which publishes official registration figures with a racial breakdown. The official statement of registered voters in the state as of 21 March 1936, reports the following totals: white males—382,005; white females—256,528; colored males—1,737; colored females—270. The report also states that of these totals, 582,317 whites wrote their name as against 1,931 colored, while 51,492 whites "made their mark" as against 15 Negroes. Negro voters were registered in only sixteen of the sixty-four parishes. The bulk of the Negro registration is from two parishes only: Orleans (New Orleans), with 889 Negro males and 113 Negro females, or a total of 1,002 registered; and East Baton Rouge, with 590 Negro males and 146 Negro females, or a total of 736 registered. It is doubtful that many more than half of these registered Negroes actually vote, however.

The Negro masses, as well as the white masses, were solidly behind Huey P. Long in Louisiana. It is claimed that he did not discriminate against Negroes in providing free school books, that he put Negro nurses in the hospitals and Negro servants in the state capitol, and that he refrained from referring to "niggers" in his campaign speeches.[18]

18. Interview with Dr. Hardin, a Negro leader, New Orleans, Louisiana, 13 November 1939. The interviewer is not identified in the Bunche memorandum. —ED.

THIRTEEN

The Negro at The Polls:
The Outer South

NEGROES can now register and vote without much difficulty in
Virginia, especially in the urban centers. There are no accurate
statistics available, but it is estimated that some twenty thousand Virginia Negroes now exercise the franchise. Perhaps
three-fourths of these are Democratic voters and cast their ballots in the Democratic primaries. The poll tax, with its three-
year cumulative clause, remains as an important restraint upon
Negro as upon white voting in Virginia. It is not unusual in this
state for political candidates to bid publicly for Negro votes.

In Richmond in 1936 there were 30,177 citizens eligible to
vote, of whom 1,527 were Negroes. About a thousand Negroes
are in political clubs, centered, for the most part, about the
Richmond Democratic League. Since 1920, Richmond Negroes
have not been an important issue in determining elections, but
the situation is now changing. For example, in the 1936 Dudley-
Bright campaign for mayor, Bright turned the tide in his favor
at the last moment by a whispering campaign among the whites
that Dudley was going to put Negroes on the city payroll and
discharge one-third of all white policemen, firemen, street cleaners, and so forth, in order to give jobs to "niggers." The charge
was false, however, for Dudley, though supported by Negroes,
had neither the wish nor the need to bid so highly for a mere
1,500 Negro votes.[1]

Chesterfield County, Virginia, has a population of about
22,000, of whom 6,000 are Negroes. The largest Negro vote

1. James Jackson's interview with Roscoe Jackson, president of the
Richmond Democratic League, Richmond, Virginia, October 1939.

438

polled in the county in recent years was between three and four hundred in the August primaries of 1939. There have been some obstacles to Negro registration and voting in this county. H. H. Price, an elderly Negro resident, recalled in an interview with James Jackson:

> In 1924, when I moved my residence from Richmond proper, the registrar refused to accept my transfer, but when I threatened court action, he acquiesced. In some districts of the county they require Negroes to answer a lot of illegal questions. Vote qualifications are simple enough if you have paid your poll tax. It is difficult in some districts where Negroes are thickly populated—they ask a lot of illegal questions.

Price, who has long been active in politics, expressed it as his view that the

> Negro should center his energies in local politics and local issues. We have fooled around all these years, bickering in national politics and got nothing because we ain't enough to count in national elections. We must build up from a position of strength in local politics—that is, county and city elections—and on local county bond issues before we can gain any hearing in national politics. . . .
>
> The secret of Negro success in the South as a whole lies in effecting an alliance with the whites. Not the whites in any general sense, but those he comes in contact with on the job, at the county postoffice, at the general store; he can talk to them and not be afraid—he does already on every subject in the world but united political action. In the meantime, if Negroes will qualify and vote, and vote unitedly in their own interests, they could hold office right now with things as they are.
>
> There should be 11 Negroes in the Virginia House of Delegates and two seats in the Virginia Senate, reckoning it on the basis of the 1930 census. Negroes are a majority in 22 counties, and in 39 counties are equal in number to the whites. . . .
>
> In the fourth congressional district of Virginia—but for Petersburg and Hopewell—Negroes would be in a majority. John M. Langston was elected to Congress from this district fifty years ago, and the population balance has not altered much since. With only a handful of white voters supporting your man (if all the Negroes *voted*), you could send an-

other to Congress. If the Negro could get a little cooperation in this district from whites, he could achieve many things.

This Virginia Negro declares that: "In 1936, Negro opposition defeated a bond issue for a $40,000 jail in Chesterfield County. We demanded a school bond. Didn't many whites vote—those that did voted against it. Poor people don't vote for jails."

In Norfolk the "administration" forces are led by the clerk of the corporation court, who has a forceful and gruff personality and who has held office for a number of years. A number of the upper-class Negro business and professional men and women lead the "administration" supporters in the Negro community. There is also a strong antiadministration group among the Negroes of Norfolk who have organized an independent Democratic league in a revolt against the Norfolk machine. Negroes here vote in all elections—local, state, congressional, presidential, and primary. A good many of the upper-class black citizens of Norfolk feel that the Negro population, in general, does not evidence much interest in voting. It is said that Negro preachers do not urge Negroes to vote, though other leaders do. Some of these leaders are inspired by factional affiliation as pro- or anti-administration, and others by force of belief that the vote will help. Some white politicians also urge Negroes to vote.[2] Some of the upper-class Negro women, when they presented themselves for registration, were asked difficult questions and were refused registration upon their failure to answer them. Their cases were prosecuted by a local Negro attorney, and they were registered.

The population of Portsmouth, Virginia, according to the 1930 census, was 45,704, of which 18,849 were Negroes. But only some 1,300 to 1,400 Negroes vote. Yet even this small number of Negro voters, if consolidated as a bloc vote, could hold the balance of power in congressional and municipal elections. The Negro vote in Portsmouth is not a bloc vote, however, for two cogent reasons. The first of these is the nature of Negro political leadership. There is a Negro leader for every fifty black voters, and each of these leaders is at the other's throat in the mad scramble for the meager monetary rewards that can be won from small-town politics. The other reason is to be found in the

2. Wilhelmina Jackson's Norfolk memorandum, October 1939. Unless otherwise noted, the quotations in this section on Virginia are taken from Miss Jackson's notes of field interviews conducted in the fall of 1939. —ED.

fact that in Portsmouth there are two important political factions—the Glass-Byrd-Darden group, backed by the DuPont millions, and the Hamilton-Price group, pro–New Deal and backed in the past by the Planters fortune (the peanut king). Thus the Negro vote never becomes a bloc vote, but is split between these two factions and is, therefore, no serious threat to Portsmouth.

Negroes in Portsmouth vote in all elections. Their right to vote in the Democratic primaries was established by the case of James C. West of Richmond in 1930. In this case the Negro's right to participate in the Democratic primaries in Virginia was clarified and upheld by the circuit court of appeals of the fourth judicial district. In the first few years following this favorable decision, however, Portsmouth Negroes did meet with discriminatory practices on the part of registrars and judges of elections. Two types of restrictions were applied to Negroes' voting rights. The first was a catch question asked by the judge of elections. Upon going to cast his ballot, the Negro voter would be asked whether he had voted Republican or Democratic in the last general election. If the answer was Republican, he would be prevented from casting his ballot. A Negro attorney in Portsmouth claims that: "They attempted in the primaries of 1931 to keep me from voting because, in the last election, I had voted Republican. However, I took my case to court and was given the privilege to return to the polls and cast my ballot." The second type of voting restriction was based purely on race. On occasion Negroes were merely prevented from voting in the primaries in direct contravention of the decision in the West case because they were Negroes.

Difficult questions and inconveniences of other types were employed in efforts to stop Negroes from exercising the right to vote in the Democratic primaries. Three Portsmouth Negroes relate their experiences. Charles Butts, a Negro singer:

After paying the required poll tax for the primaries of 1931, it became necessary to apply to the registrar for registration. I knew beforehand that Mr. Parker, the registrar, was a violent Negro-hater. He had made up his mind to keep as many Negroes out as possible. He gave me a plain slip of paper on which I, myself, had to make out a form and fill it out. Then I had to give it back to him and if it pleased him, he'd register you, and if it didn't, he'd keep it, refuse to register you and never tell the reason why. Three times I went to be registered and three times I was refused. The first time, my form was all right, but he asked me how many signed the Declaration of Independence and who was president of the Senate (at the time of my registration). These were civil government questions which one doesn't know unless one is in school constantly. I didn't know, and I wasn't registered. The second time I went to the polls, the registrar told me the "sun was down" and so I wasn't registered. The third time, I hadn't signed my name enough times on the blank form he gave me and I wasn't registered. I knew the machine was run at that time by Dr. Brooks, who was anti-Negro, and so I figured it would be best for me to take a politician along with me the last time I went. I took our ward leader, a man who was "in the know." I was registered this time. I almost got out of the notion of voting, though.

Mrs. Samuel E. Johns:

Parker was registrar at that time, 1931. He hated Negroes, I knew, but my husband convinced me that I should get qualified to vote, so I went to get registered. He gave me a blank form to fill out and in court, but not at the polls, said I had failed to sign my name at a required place. He also, at the registration counter, asked me how many signed the Declaration of Independence, and my answer was wrong. He didn't register me. In court my lawyer, Mr. Melvin, asked the judge if he could ask Mr. Parker a question. The judge told him yes, whereupon Mr. Melvin asked the registrar how many signed the Declaration of Independence. Parker couldn't answer. The judge gave me the privilege of going back to register without further difficulty.

Miss Quintella Brown, a schoolteacher:

I failed to put Norfolk County behind Portsmouth, Virginia, on the blank form when giving the facts of my birth. I was refused on those grounds. I took the case to court and won, however. Even now I have trouble directly at the polls, for they attempt to put my ballot in the box for me. I will not let them do this, however.

In at least two of the wards in Portsmouth—Harrison and Jefferson—the Negro vote controls the councilmanic elections. Half a century ago there were Negro councilmen, commonwealth attorneys, municipal judges, and tax collectors in Portsmouth. Today, however, the only city office of any consequence held by Negroes is that of probation officer, held by Mrs. W. V. Jennings.

In 1935 Portsmouth applied for a change in its city charter so that elective councilmen would be chosen by wards instead of at large. The whites opposed to the change immediately raised the cry that the change would make it possible for Negroes to sit as administrators of the city. Two Negroes did run for the city council. One of them, a Dr. Johnson, recalls:

> I ran for city council in the municipal election of 1936. This was the first time in forty-five years that a Negro had done such a thing. It stirred up the city, so that not only the Negro papers but the white papers as well wrote about it. The petty town politicians got warm about it. They thought I should have "consulted" them about my candidacy. One of these offered me $100, which a white man had given him, to sell out, but being a man of principle, I naturally refused it. In my campaign, I made it a point to ask for those things which Negroes needed, such as free textbooks, better streets, roads, and so forth. I also made it a point to go around to the various civic leagues in the wards in a bid for their support. But they had been forewarned or bought, and attitudes of coldness and hostility met me. Some of the papers ran letters and articles in which some of the Portsmouth people characterized me as a political "goat." These were answered by me in firm tones in the Norfolk *Journal and Guide*. I said that the general criticism which was levied against me as being premature in my efforts was ill-founded; that the Negro, even if he polled only one vote, had to make the step forward in those sections where conditions were favorable, and the Harrison ward, due to the predominance of Negroes, was certainly such a section. I ran to prove the point that Negroes weren't asleep politically. I lost, but hope the point was proved.

Dr. C. C. Somerville, a Negro preacher, was the other black candidate in 1936:

> In 1936, in looking over this town's history, I found that for forty years no Negro had taken a position in the government of the city of Portsmouth. No policemen, no patrolmen, nor constables were Negroes. When I found this out and saw that I was eligible for councilman, I applied from the Jefferson

ward; my application was accepted, and I was listed among the candidates. I was the only Negro that applied from the Jefferson ward. The white papers made a note of the fact that I was a candidate. I did not attempt to campaign. I simply contacted my friends and relatives. None of the Negro organizations in town supported me. When the votes were counted, Dr. Johnson and I both had the same number— eight apiece. This appeared to me as a very strange thing, so I'm going to run again in 1940. This time, I'm going to make a bid for the support of Negro organizations in Portsmouth.

The stories related by Johnson and Somerville do not give the complete picture, however. Dr. Johnson does not have a large practice in Portsmouth, and Dr. Somerville was the stormy petrel in a factional dispute which split the congregation of the second largest Baptist church in the city. Many Portsmouth citizens feel that their candidacies were clouded. Political leaders such as Thomas Reid and Norman Hamilton charged that these two Negroes were paid to enter this race; that the machine politicians gave them fifty dollars each in order to build up a case against the return to the ward system.

Newport News has a population of 34,417, of whom 13,281 are Negroes. Of the total population, 21,872 are of voting age and 8,250 of this number are Negroes. It appears that the voting percentage in Newport News is not very high. Newport News Negroes vote in all elections and on all issues. The Negro community of Newport News has apparently evidenced a great deal of interest in voting, especially when issues concerning their welfare are at stake. The usual charge is made that Negro ministers, as a whole, do not urge their congregations to vote, while other Negro leaders do so. White candidates for office openly urge Negroes to vote and frequently speak at Negro meetings. White groups, such as the Young Democratic Club, deputize Negroes to get out the vote for their candidates at election time. The Negro voters of Newport News give their main support to the Democratic party. There is quite extensive political organization among them.

According to the 1930 census, as corrected to include a subsequent annexation of 1 January 1932, the total population of Petersburg was 30,074, of whom 12,802 were Negroes. In this population, 3,013 whites and 395 Negroes were qualified to vote as of October 1939. In 1932 there were only 72 Negroes qualified to vote in Petersburg. The increase in qualified Negro

voters has been due to the activities of the League of Negro
Voters, whose primary objective has been to stimulate interest
in voting among Negroes and to urge them to pay the poll tax.
There has been no opposition to the Negro vote from whites,
and several white candidates for office have encouraged the activity of the League in stimulating Negro political participation.[3]

Some of the states commonly classed as "border" states, such
as Virginia, North Carolina, and Tennessee, have scarcely followed in the border state tradition insofar as liberality toward
Negro enfranchisement is concerned—at least not until very
recent years. In these states the Negro has generally had to
overcome many obstacles before any significant number of
black voters could enter the polling booths. Negro voting is tend-
ing to increase fairly rapidly in all three of these states now,
since the restrictions on the Negro franchise have been softened
by court action and the pressure of Negro organization.

In the urban areas of North Carolina there is no vigorous opposition to Negro voting, generally speaking. In the rural areas,
however, the Negro does encounter difficulty, though it is taken
for granted that in such areas he would be discreet enough not
to try to vote. There have been no recent instances of violence at
the polls because of Negro efforts to vote. In some places the
Negro vote is openly solicited, while in others there is definite
opposition to it. The total Negro vote in this state is probably
somewhere between forty and fifty thousand, and there is a
strong Democratic support among black voters. Perhaps as
much as three-fourths of the Negro vote in recent years has gone
Democratic. In many counties Negroes vote freely in the Democratic primaries. A law to eliminate "haulers and markers" from
the primaries, which was enacted in 1935, significantly decreased the vote in the predominantly Negro precincts of
Raleigh, although the vote in the general election that followed
was large.

Negro political leaders in Durham pride themselves on the
fact that in 1938 the Negro vote under their leadership defeated
the airport bond issue. It is said, in fact, that the responsible
white community holds it against the city's Negroes for what it
considers the blacks' major responsibility for having defeated
the proposition. Negroes felt that, with schools, streets, and
other municipal services very inadequate, such services should

3. James Jackson's interview with Dr. L. P. Jackson, president of the
League of Negro Voters, Petersburg, Virginia, October 1939.

come first. They also assumed that Negroes would not be permitted to use the airport. Many poor whites and other white groups also opposed the bond issue because it would raise the tax rate. The Durham Committee on Negro Affairs took an active part in the campaign to defeat the proposed airport. The Negro churches were canvassed. An editorial in the Negro-owned *Carolina Times* was reprinted, and Negro captains were put to work to obtain a heavy black registration. These captains were paid. Promises were made to Negroes that they would be able to ride in the planes. Threats to oppose school bond issues when they arose were issued, and there were instances of intimidation of Negro workers; but an approximate registration of 2,400 Negroes was secured, and it is commonly accepted in Durham that it was Negro opposition that finally accounted for the defeat of the airport bond issue.[4]

The Negroes of Durham vote in all elections. In some instances, as in the case of the fight over the airport, Negroes have shown an intense interest in voting. Labor organizers, liberal white candidates who merely need the vote, and some of the liberal and interracially minded whites urge Negroes in Durham to vote.

Buck Waller is an old-time Negro political leader in Durham who is still able to "deliver the vote" to the white candidates who are willing to bid for it. According to Waller, when he first came to Durham back in 1911: "Only a few Negroes were voting, but they were not interested in the other fellow voting. I was, so I began working to build up a bloc of voters to give the best candidate." Waller has built up a large following which he estimates to embrace "at least 300 to 400 people." He has not organized these supporters into a political club, but only corrals them near election time with the aid of "some ten or eleven youngsters I'm trying to get interested in politics." Waller insists that, unlike "the big niggers, I love money, but don't bow to it. I still am recognized 'downtown' as the power and the real father of Negro voting in Durham."

The county Democratic executive committee in Durham has about thirty members, and for the last four years has had one Negro member. Since 1932 Negroes in North Carolina have

4. Wilhelmina Jackson's interview with Renchell Harris, Durham, North Carolina, 13 November, 1939. Except where otherwise indicated, the quoted material dealing with North Carolina in this chapter is taken from the notes of interviews conducted by Miss Jackson in late 1939 and early 1940. —Ed.

been attending the state Democratic conventions as official delegates. The Negroes of North Carolina held a Negro Democratic rally during the 1936 presidential campaign.

Negroes in Charlotte vote in all elections and participate actively in the Democratic primaries, though we have no figures on the actual number of Negroes registered and voting in the city. There are the usual number of Negro professional politicians eager to commercialize upon the black vote, and many Negroes take the attitude that "votin' don't git you nowhere, and just a few people put money in their pockets." Only one Negro minister actively encourages Negro political participation and he admits that, due to his church affiliation, there are limitations upon his activity. The Negro voters of Charlotte chiefly support the Democratic party. In national elections—since the advent of Roosevelt—the swing has been away from the Republican to the Democratic party.

In Winston-Salem two powerful corporations—one engaged in tobacco and the other in hosiery—exert strong influence on the political life of the city. It was not possible to obtain an official statement of the number of Negroes registered for voting in Winston-Salem, but several of the leading Negro citizens have estimated that from 750 to 800 Negroes are qualified voters there. The general impression is that the Negro population is not very interested in voting, although those who do vote are able to do so without opposition and in all elections. There is only one minister in the city—and he is a recent addition—who actively urges the Negro population to engage in politics. The general impression is that the corporations which employ most of the Negroes are opposed to their registration on any large scale. As a result, the local registrars sometimes employ devices in order to avoid registering Negroes.

Bill Phol, county Democratic committee secretary, is recognized in the community as the man "in charge" of the Negro vote. He is said to have received an important promotion just recently when the Negro vote, which he controlled, was the deciding factor in the Winston-Salem mayoralty election. In the complete reregistration held in the spring of 1940 Phol was again active in getting Negroes to register, and to register Democratic. Since this registration, Phol has formed an organization of Negro voters, and included among its membership are the leading Negro business and professional men of Winston-Salem. In the country outside of Winston-Salem, few Negroes vote. There is said to be a considerable amount of feeling among the whites against it.[5]

Those Negroes who are registered in Greensboro vote in all elections, including the primaries. The returns indicate a slight interest in the elections on the part of Negroes, and this tends to be confirmed in the opinions of Negro leaders. It appears that Negro ministers are somewhat more active than usual in urging Negroes to vote and in getting out the vote. White candidates and politicians in Greensboro frankly urge Negroes to vote, and the candidates make open bids for their ballots, often coming to the meetings of Negro organizations to make their appeals. Most of the Negroes who vote support the Democratic tickets, though it is said that there are about ten Negroes in the city who vote Republican because "deep down in their hearts Negroes are still Republican." Negro workers in the Cone Mills indicated that there may be some form of mill pressure employed with respect to the control of their vote. One of them said: "At voting time, party come out here and git us. . . . You understand, one who you works for wants you to vote like they want."

High Point has a very significant Republican voting population, and the struggle between Democrats and Republicans is keen. It is a highly industrialized town with not very much labor organization. Of the approximately 10,000 qualified voters in High Point, 650 to 750 are Negroes. Negroes are able to vote in all elections, but they have not given evidence of great interest in voting. In large measure, the Negro voters have maintained allegiance to the Republican party, and the GOP organization has been diligent in its efforts to get Negroes registered. The last campaign for the municipal election on 3 May 1939 was regarded by Republicans as certain to return them to control of city politics. The Democrats, who were the "ins," ordered a new registration and instructed all of their registrars to be mindful of the legal provision that registrants "must read and write to satisfaction of registrars" and to govern themselves accordingly. It seems that Negro voters were turned down wholesale when they came to register. Interviews with eight of those who sought to register give some idea of what happened.

An elementary schoolteacher at the Leonard School who is a

5. George Stoney's observations, Winston-Salem, North Carolina, July 1940.

graduate of the University of Toledo related that when he attempted to "sign up": "The registrar asked me to read a section of the Constitution, which I did, and then asked me to define terms, which I knew was not part of the North Carolina law. I said to him, 'that is not a part of the law, to define terms.' He said, 'You must satisfy me, and don't argue with me.'" He was not registered. A Negro grocery clerk stated: "The registrar asked me if I owned any property and if I paid taxes. I told him, no, that I rented, but that I owned what furniture I had in my house and I didn't pay no property tax. He said then that I wasn't legal to vote. I said, 'Well, you know I don't have to,' and then I walked out." Willie Martin, an embalmer at the Haizlip Funeral Home, related: "The registrar asked me to read what he called the Constitution, but I knew it was part of an amendment to the High Point city charter and told him so. After some dilly-dallying, he let me vote." Arthur Reid, a Negro contractor and plumber who was rejected, states: "The man wanted me to 'mit to memory the Constitution, and I couldn't do it. All them Democrats 'bout near hate us Negroes. I ain't interest in politics no more." Luther Kern, a Negro porter at the High Point *Enterprise* office, testifies as follows:

> I was in the habit, you know, of taking my wife's place at registering her and registration. I'd done it for years. After I'd finished registering last spring, I said to the man, "Can I register my wife?" He said, "No, bring her down to register herself." I brought her down, and she missed two words— "contingency" and "constitutionality"; the man snatched it out of her hand and said "I can't register you. You don't satisfy me." That made my blood boil, so I said, "You'll hear more from this." I went to my boss and told him. He got on the phone, and I went down to the board of elections office where he sent me. The man said, "Boy, what do you want?" I said, "Do I look like a boy to you?" He said, "What are you looking for?" I said, "Mr. Schoch. My boss told me to look for him and the registrar of my precinct." He said, "I'm Mr. Schoch. The registrar will be down to your home at 5:30." When I went home, blood still in my eyes, the man was there registering my wife. I may be a Negro, but the blood in my veins is red.

A Mrs. Saunders, an intelligent and well-educated Negro housewife, recalls: "The registrar gave me an article out of the Constitution to read. It was supplemented with words I couldn't pronounce, so he wouldn't register me. He grabbed the paper out of my hand and said, 'You just don't know and can't pass me, that's all.' " It is notorious in High Point that the registrar in precinct 41 is a habitual drunkard.

There are some three hundred Negro voters in Reidsville, North Carolina, in a total population of 11,067. There has been a significant increase in the Negro vote here during the past three or four years. Just a few years ago there were only fifty Negro voters in Reidsville. The incident that provoked the increase in Negro registration was a bond election held by the city a few years ago in which Negroes desired to have included their demands for improved street surfaces in the Negro quarter. The city council ignored the Negro demands, and consequently the Negroes—led by the Negro Civic Club—got about 230 blacks registered and directed them to stay away from the polls the day the election was held. They did so, and the bond issue was defeated.

In Statesville, a small flour-mill town with a total population of some 11,000, the Negro vote has jumped from 18 before 1935 to between 250 and 300 now. The Negro vote in Statesville was given this impetus because of the Allison case. T. E. Allison, Jr., a Livingston College graduate and a resident of Statesville, applied for registration to vote in a county election in May 1934 and was refused. An aggressive young fellow who had previously attempted to organize an NAACP chapter in Statesville, he decided to fight the case.

Two recent events have directed unusual attention to the Negro's political status in Florida. One, the repeal of the poll tax qualification for voting in 1937, has served to reawaken Negro interest in voting and has led to a gradually increasing Negro political activity. The other, the defiance with which Negroes of Miami met the attempts of the Ku Klux Klan to frighten them from the polls in 1939, has fired Negroes in other Florida communities with new courage and has resulted in a number of vigorous Negro "get-out-and-vote" campaigns. Possibly ten thousand Negroes are able to go to the polls in Florida.

Prior to 1939, Negroes in Miami scarcely participated politically at all. The essential obstacles to their participation were (1) their ignorance of the nonpartisan nature of city elections and (2) the apathy attendant upon years of nonvoting. It seems that for years Otis Mundy, a prominent Miami Negro, had been aware that Negroes could vote in city elections, but despite his insistent agitation among Negroes toward this end, he could not enlist the support of the then most powerful Negro organization, the Negro Civic Club. Only fifty Negroes were registered voters. In 1936 Samuel B. Solomon came to Miami and gave enthusiastic support to Mundy's efforts. Cognizant of the nonpartisan nature of the Miami city government and of the terrible conditions under which Miami Negroes have had to live, these two leaders felt that by the exercise of the ballot Negroes could improve their conditions, if only to a small extent. They decided, as their initial strategy, upon enlistment of the support of the Negro ministers. This they succeeded in doing, and from then on the fight to stimulate interest within the Negro community was much easier.[6]

The upsurge of the Negro voters of Miami at the polls in 1939 was made in the face of odds greater than the mere threats of the Ku Klux Klan. The effort to get out the Negro vote had to overcome an apathy born of years of disfranchisement and disinterest in things political, bad housing, poor schools, social disease, and widespread crime. It had to combat a timidity and an inferiority complex born of the fact that the Negroes were tucked away in "colored town" on the other side of the Seaboard Line railroad tracks. It is not at all certain, moreover, that this valiant effort by Negroes will bring permanent gains. In the first place, the Negroes who were stimulated to register last year must reregister this year, since Florida does not have permanent registration. In the second place, there is a good deal of group and individual factionalism at work in the Negro community. Negro leadership, itself, is split between ordinary personal opportunism and the welfare of the group. Negro voters of Miami are chiefly Republican because they feel that their votes will be thrown out if they register as independents, and the white Democratic party excludes them.

Negroes in Jacksonville consider the school bond election of 1938 to have been the political issue of most recent political significance to their race. Negroes claim that this bond issue was defeated by the black vote, which was overwhelmingly opposed to the issuance of new school bonds. Negro politicians worked strenuously for the defeat of the bond issue. The whites apparently worked equally as strenuously to nullify the attempts of Negroes to defeat the bond proposal.

The Negroes' Civic Improvement League of Jacksonville dis-

6. The discussion of Negro political activities in Florida is based on Wilhemina Jackson's notes of field interviews conducted in 1940. —ED.

tributed a leaflet urging Negro voters to stay away from the polls at the time of the school bond issue election in 1938.

> These bonds will be used to build a better Court House, a bigger Armory, an Auditorium, a Yacht Basin, and other things for the use of the white people, but we will have to pay our share of the taxes for these expenditures.
> Have we had our share of improvements paid for by taxes for sewers and streets in our sections?
> What benefit will we colored people get from a bigger Armory or a Yacht Basin?
> Do you think that the City will let us use the proposed new Auditorium?
> A colored organization has recently been refused permission to use Durkee Field or the Stadium. Therefore, we have had to move to Atlanta to hold our planned celebration.
> The proposed bond elections will not give us our share of the proposed improvements, but we will sure have to bear our share of the increased taxes.

Another leaflet distributed among Negro voters read as follows:

> IF YOU VOTE "NO" AGAINST THE BONDS YOU WILL BE COUNTED IN THE 51 PER-CENT SOUGHT TO CARRY THE ELECTION,
> So DON'T Vote At all.

Negroes who vote in Jacksonville chiefly support the Republican party, although the figures give evidence of a large group of independent votes. There is little political organization among Jacksonville Negroes. The Republican party has committees in all eighteen of the precincts and, in certain of the precincts, Negroes hold party office and exert considerable influence, especially in precinct six. Factionalism is rife among Negro political leaders in Jacksonville. The Negro Republicans are split wide open. There are "old-liners" and the more progressive younger Negro leaders, but neither group can claim complete control over black voters. Thus split, the fight between the leaders becomes so personal that it defeats the possibility of an intelligent alignment of the Republican Negro voters with any enlightened group in the community. Politics is largely a personal and partisan thing, and issues take second place. The general attitude is summed up in: "We hate the Democrats. They don't want us. . . . We got to fight for our rights within the Republican party."

The white primary is the really serious obstacle to full Negro participation in politics in Tampa as elsewhere in Florida. The following experience, which threatened to take the form of court action, is related by B. Z. Williams:

> I went down to register, and when the registrar went to put "R" beside my name, I made objection to it. Then she said I couldn't register as a Democrat. She left my name blank. I waited until the books were turned over to the county clerk and then made protest. They drew a line through my name. The district attorney, whom I called up, told me that I should sue for an injunction against the registrar. I did not, because of funds. I'm just waiting for the organization [the Voters' League] to get sufficient funds, and the case will begin.

In September 1939 an intensive effort was made by the Negro Voters' League in Tampa to get Negroes registered, and this resulted in the casting of 1,330 Negro votes. The activity of the Voters' League was intensive enough to stir up considerable discussion and comment. In September the Tampa *Tribune* reported: "The white municipal party, charging that 'corrupt politicians' are urging Negroes to register in large numbers, had its campaign committee call on white persons in Tampa yesterday to support the party on November 7th." In the same month the *Tribune* informed its readers:

> The campaign committee of the white municipal party passed a resolution saying that scheming politicos had dominated politics in Tampa before, due to the Negro vote and before the white party was formed. The resolution said that in the old days, politicians herded thousands of Negroes together, served them liqueurs and cigars, and marched them to the polls and voted them for candidates as suited the crooked machine. To *end* these conditions, the white party was formed, enabling white persons to nominate officials at a primary in which Negroes could not participate. Then, in the last ten days, 310 Negroes have registered as against 34 whites.

Despite the fact that Tennessee is a great deal more liberal than most Southern states toward extending the franchise to Negroes, especially in such cities as Memphis and Chattanooga, it may be taken for granted that the Negro voting average in the state is considerably below that of whites. Somewhere in the neighborhood of fifty thousand Negro votes are cast in the state. A recent analysis of voting in Tennessee has suggested that "with rather few exceptions those Tennessee counties with an above-average percentage of Negroes have a below-average percentage of voters. To a smaller degree, counties with a below-average percentage of Negroes generally have an above-average voting percentage."[7]

Memphis is the most significant spot in Tennessee for Negro voting. Indeed, Memphis is the great voting oasis for Negroes in the entire South. But Memphis is typical of neither Tennessee nor the South. Next to Memphis, the Negro in Chattanooga has been most active politically. There also, though on a smaller and less spectacular scale, the Negro vote has fallen under machine domination.

Although the Negro votes in Chattanooga in significant numbers, he is considered no threat to white supremacy. George Fort Milton, editor of the late Chattanooga *News*, said in an interview on 30 January 1940: "The Negro's no 'menace' here or threatened 'menace' from the administration point of view. They will follow the machine and their bought political leaders till hell freezes over, I think. Sometimes I wonder if they aren't more a menace to themselves. . . . I don't know. . . . A small group of them are breaking away."

It is rather difficult to discover just what the Negro of Chattanooga gets for his vote other than the immediate dollar or the drink from the ward heeler. The Negro's "place" in Chattanooga is probably considerably larger in the life of the city than it is in most Southern cities. Nevertheless, the Negro is either kept or stays within his "place." This "place" seems to expand only when the whites stake out new boundaries, as in trade unionism and politics, rather than from Negro pressure. The commissioner of fire and police, in discussing the extent of the Negro vote, declares:

> Darkies? We got a world of them. I guess 38 percent of our city's population is black, and out of that about 1,500 or 2,000 vote. Sometimes as many as 2,500 vote. The third, fourth, fifth, sixth, seventh, eighth, and the fourth precinct of the 12th are all black or almost. There's a peppering in the rest. The poll tax has a tendency to keep most of them

7. Paul K. Walp, "Factors Influencing Voting in Tennessee," *The University of Tennessee News Letter,* 18 (December 1939): 2.

from voting. There's no attempt to keep them from voting the way there is in most Southern cities, except in the Democratic primary. In the city elections, by gracious, they go out after the nigra vote. I believe if they were left to themselves, they wouldn't vote at all, or damn few of them would, but I wouldn't know.[8]

As to the independence of the Negro vote, a political reporter for the Chattanooga *Times* told Stoney:

I'd say the average colored voter doesn't vote just to be exercising his democratic privilege, but because there is something in it for him that same day. A big percentage of the whites do it, too, but the number is a good bit smaller than the colored. I'd say we have about 20 percent independent vote here in Chattanooga, and that's a bigger percent than you'll find in most cities in the country, certainly in the South.

Speaking of the Negro vote in Chattanooga, the reporter observes:

The nigras do vote as a whole—anyone, any way you pay them. It's known. Everybody knows it. The Negro leaders themselves will tell you. There's about three bosses, and every damn one of them has a white boss on his neck. Walter Robinson, he used to have a hell of a death grip on them, but they've kind of broken away from him a little now. Until four years ago he was truant officer under the Commissioner of Schools. With his ability to influence the placing of teachers and janitors, he built a black machine all over the city.

They finally got him out of that by voting his boss out of office. Walter was a big issue in that campaign. Now he bosses the fourth ward and puts out his paper.

Sid Byers has a job at city hall as sanitation inspector, or something. He votes first for the Republicans and then for the Democrats, according to who pays him. Of course, in the city election [nonpartisan] he always votes with the mayor. Nominally, he's a Republican. When he was elected to the Republican executive committee one time recently, they refused to seat him, because they said he was a Democrat. The next elec-

8. George Stoney's interview, Chattanooga, Tennessee, 26 January 1940. The material on the Negro in Chattanooga politics in this section is based largely on Stoney's notes of interviews conducted in early 1940. —ED.

tion he carried his ward for the Democrats. He can deliver his precinct for the mayor—something like 300 to 80.

The political reporter for the *Times* explains how Walter Robinson controls the Negro vote:

> He works what they call a "system." Walter rents a house right across from the poll where you drop in to get your registration slip and your poll tax list, and a drink, maybe, and find out what Walter's doing. The first thing in the morning, Walter gets somebody to go in and vote, but just make out like he's dropping his ballot in the box. He brings that bona fide ballot over to Walter to be marked. Then the next fellow that goes into vote carries this marked ballot in his pocket. He gets another genuine ballot, goes into the booth, makes out like he's writing, slips the blank ballot in his pocket, puts the one Walter marked in the box and brings the blank one back over to the house for Walter to give to the next fellow. If he don't bring it back, he don't get nothing for his vote. . . . That's democracy.

In the 1938 Democratic primary in Chattanooga some Negro wards were opened up which had never been permitted participation in a Democratic primary before. They supported the Democratic machine. In the Tennessee Valley Authority election of 1935 the private power interests hired Walter Robinson to corral the Negro vote for them, but on the day of election Negro voters turned against Robinson. When he upbraided them about double-crossing him, he was told: "We want that TVA." That is the one occasion on which Negroes in Chattanooga voted on *issues*.

Another big influence over the Negro vote in Chattanooga is exercised by "Big Bill" Grossman. Grossman is described as a "big racketeer. Runs gambling joints and night clubs over here in the nigra section. He don't hesitate to come out in the papers and say so, too. When some preacher said he had so and so many saloons, Bill told the papers it wasn't so. He had more, and he gave the right number." It is said that "Big Bill" plays the role of the benevolent despot in the third ward, a predominantly Negro ward. Apparently Grossman—a Jew and very rich— scorns any social contact with white people. All of his social relations, it is said, are with Negroes, and, though this is common knowledge in the community, Grossman is never attacked by the white powers, probably because of his political control over the vote in the strategic third ward. In addition to the racketeers who deliver a sizable vote to the candidates of the Chattanooga machine in return for the promise of protection from police interference with their "businesses," the city machine also has the energetic support of several outstanding Negro political bosses or ward heelers who control the majority of the Negro vote and deliver it for a financial consideration plus personal patronage.[9]

In Chattanooga Negroes ordinarily support the Republican party nationally and one or other of the Democratic factions locally. White candidates, though seeking the Negro vote, never make an open play for black voters. They work through bosses and on occasion speak at Negro election gatherings, but they try to avoid publicity on that dangerous issue.

In answer to the question, "What do Negroes get for the vote?" one informant states: "They have a big new Negro swimming pool here, a playground that's fixed up as well as one for white children. . . . That is about all I can think of. Walter Robinson gets most out of it, I suspect. If they get any more, there isn't any outward manifestation of it." The commissioner of fire and police states that there is "a pretty good reason" for not having a Negro on the police force:

> He'd have to work exclusively in the colored section, and you know, yourself, one nigger won't respect another like he would a white man. Then, if a nigra and a white man got in a fight, he'd have to treat them both alike and he'd be at a disadvantage there. . . . I don't think they have them in any city in the South.

Labor union leaders in Chattanooga are attempting to teach Negroes to vote "with labor." The union rules theoretically require members to qualify themselves and exercise their rights as citizens. The business agent for the Hod Carriers and Common Laborers' Union in Chattanooga points out that probably few of his members, either black or white, pay the poll tax and vote, because: "Two dollars is so much food and clothes and rent." He expressed the suspicion that the few of the union members who did vote had their poll tax paid by one or another of the ward heelers, even if they did not vote with him.

Because only "known" Democrats can vote in the Hamilton County primary, few Negroes are "allowed" to vote. In the heavily populated Negro wards, the registration books are "just

---

9. James Jackson's Chattanooga field notes, November 1939.

not open" for this election. The 1938 county primary was the first in which Negroes generally were allowed to vote in the Hamilton County Democratic primary. Roy Reynolds, president of the Pressmen's Union local of Chattanooga and active in local politics, claims that he and his group were largely responsible for persuading the county Democratic committee to allow Negroes to vote in the 1938 primary. The opposition group agreed to it and then beat Reynolds' faction out at the polls. As Reynolds put it:

> We got the intelligent Negro vote, but the machine boys bought out the rest and beat us with the very group we got the vote for. I'm afraid the Negroes in Chattanooga still belong to the white bosses. They are content to follow his leadership or to follow their own bosses who are the hirelings of the white leaders.

Referring to the candidate his group was backing for sheriff in the primary—a Captain Fred Payne, an ex-sheriff, described as "the best of a bad lot" and "a reactionary on the race question"—Reynolds related:

> I got him [Payne] in the room the other day with about ten young Negroes. They backed up Fred and asked him if they supported him, would he give them two uniformed Negro deputies. Fred, he squirmed and he squirmed, and finally he said he'd see what he could do. He would see if he could get permission. Fred is honest. You have to give him credit for that. He's a machine-backed man, all right, and he's conservative as hell, but he's not a member of the rackets or the vice ring the way the present sheriff is. That's about the best you can say. Fred went up to city hall and talked with the boys up there. They said they couldn't back him if he did that. If he gave them [the Negroes] this, then the Negroes would put the heat on them in the city. So, he came back and told them he couldn't do it. I expect they will support him, though. They haven't much choice. At least he believes in treating them like human beings. That guy in there now don't.

Negroes in Chattanooga used to be elected to public office twenty-five or thirty years ago. That is, before the city commission form of government was put through. Since then, however, none has held office, mainly because the councilmen are elected by the voters of the city at large. Occasionally a Negro does run for office and receives a scattering of votes. The Negro vote was steadily Republican in both state and national elections until 1933. In Chattanooga the white candidates negotiate for the Negro vote through the Negro intermediaries. As one political figure puts it: "The general picture is this: pay the Negro preacher twenty-five dollars—not a bribe, understand, something to help fix up his church—they always put it down in a little book. . . . See Walter Robinson, Sid Byers, and Doc Harper, and you have the Negro vote."

The labor leader previously quoted says that he and his faction of "progressives" have worked consistently since 1932 to get the Negro vote, but that he feels quite despondent about Negroes ever "being any good" to the liberal cause. The local Negroes refused to work for constitutional change, and Walter Robinson used his newspaper to campaign against it on the grounds that "they might put over something worse on us." A brighter picture was presented in the power election of 1935, however. President Roosevelt, it is said, has had considerable influence on the number of Negroes "who call themselves Democrats."

Nevertheless, it would seem difficult to deny the validity of the indictment contained in the following statement by a local Republican:

> What we need more than anything else here is some honest negra leadership. For the most part they are in the hands of whatever white man can pay them the most. Walter Robinson is the most outstanding leader, . . . but he's bought up body and soul. He's editor of a negra paper here and boss of the fourth ward. . . . His wards vote heavy—around six to seven hundred. It ought to vote two thousand by the population they've got there. He can't vote any more than he can get money to pay poll taxes for. . . .
>
> Buckner, a colored barber here, is an avowed Democrat. He's run for Democratic precinct chairman several times and tried to vote in the primary lots of times, and I guess he's got a little following. Robinson calls himself a Republican, but I know he votes several times as many for the Democratic ticket than Buckner does.

Knoxville is located in Knox County in eastern Tennessee. In political matters, eastern Tennessee has had little identity with the rest of the state. Until about 1910, Knoxville had Negro magistrates, and as far back as Grover Cleveland's administration some Negroes were voting the Democratic ticket, though most black voters were traditionally Republican. In recent years, however, since the New Deal and the TVA, more Negroes have been shifting their loyalty to the Democratic party. It is now estimated that about 60 percent of the Negroes of Knoxville vote the Democratic ticket in all elections. One informant feels that Negroes in Knoxville have lost political influence,

> not so much from outside pressure, but through internal organizational disintegration brought on by the machinations of corrupted, self-seeking traitorous Negroes who have wormed their way into the leadership, splitting the solidarity of the Negro vote and betraying the confidence of the Negro voters for their own selfish promotional interests.[10]

There are no restrictions on Negro voting in Knoxville except the poll tax, and little effort is put forth to enforce the collection of that. In addition to six Negro policemen, there are several Negro deputies. The vote in Knoxville has not exceeded 13,000 in any local or national election. The Negro vote is now between 800 and 1,000. There is but slight effective political organization among Negro voters. As usual, Negro ward heelers sell out the black vote to white candidates. It is felt that Negroes in Knoxville have a fine opportunity to hold the balance of power in the city's politics if they would only exercise the franchise. It is estimated that about 15 percent of the Negroes of voting age actually vote. White candidates for office in Knoxville give some recognition to the Negro vote, but the black vote is not considered sufficiently significant to modify any candidate's program or platform.[11]

Thomas L. Cummings, who became mayor of Nashville in 1938, was formerly a successful criminal lawyer, and in this position he had established contacts with Negro racketeers and bootleggers. When he became a candidate for office, he relied upon these men to deliver the Negro vote for him. Jack Keefe, Cummings' first opponent, made the main issue of his campaign the fact that "Bill" James, a Negro numbers baron, was investing heavily in Cummings' campaign. This attack on James was interpreted as an attack on the Negro people and drove most Negroes to vote for Cummings. Although Negroes supported Cummings, they voted against his choice for city judge. The incumbent was noted for his courteous attitude toward Negroes

10. James Jackson's interview with C. W. Cansler, Knoxville, Tennessee, November 1939.

11. James Jackson's interviews, Knoxville, Tennessee, November 1939.

in his court. Notwithstanding Cummings' bitter opposition to him, he was reelected with a blanket endorsement of the Negro vote. In the August 1938 Democratic primary for sheriff in Nashville, the mayor's choice for the office—one Ivey Young— was nominated and subsequently elected. Sheriff Young then appointed a number of anti-Negro deputies who were subsequently very brutal in their treatment of Negroes. When election time came again, the mayor conducted a personal campaign in all of the Negro wards in support of the incumbent sheriff, but Negroes went to the polls and defeated Young.

Negroes in Nashville have just begun to participate in the Democratic primary. For years they voted Republican and, therefore, were not influential in local elections. The Republicans never put up a candidate, thus leaving the Negroes virtually inactive politically in city elections. It is only in the last three years that Negroes in Nashville have been an important influence in local politics. President Roosevelt has not been able to carry any of the Negro wards in Davidson County.[12]

Practically all of the Negro voters in Arkansas were Republicans until the GOP adopted its lily-white policy for the South and evicted Negroes from political participation. Of the seventy-five counties in Arkansas, the Negro population is predominant in three of them—Hempstead, Jefferson, and Phillips. Negroes, however, do not hold a single elective office in the state. Arkansas has always been classified among the "bad" states on Negro disfranchisement. It is highly improbable that more than 7,000 or 8,000 Negroes are ever permitted to vote in the state.

Negroes are excluded from the Arkansas Democratic primary. But several years ago they won a temporary injunction against the Pulaski County Democratic party (the county in which Little Rock is located) restraining the Democratic party from denying Negroes the right to vote in the primary. Subsequently, when a permanent injunction was sought, it was denied, and the state supreme court affirmed the ruling of the lower court in denying the petition for a permanent injunction.

A more detailed version of the Arkansas Democratic primary injunction petition is presented by Dr. J. M. Robinson, president of the Negro Democratic Association:

> In 1928 a group of Negroes . . . formed themselves into the Arkansas Negro Democratic Association for the purpose of mobilizing the Negroes of the state for participation in the

12. James Jackson's interviews, Nashville, Tennessee, November 1939.

national election of that year and to use the activity and interest on the part of Negroes in this election to build an organization which could conduct a fight for the removal of present restrictions on the right of franchise.

In the 1928 campaign we had an understanding with the State Democratic Committee and the National Committee to the effect that if we corralled the Negro vote for Senator Robinson and presidential candidate Al Smith, then we would be admitted to the Democratic primary thereafter.

The following spring, Negroes were denied the right to vote in the Democratic primaries still. Our organization thereupon immediately sought an injunction in the Chancery Court to restrain the election officials throughout Arkansas from interfering with the voting privileges of Negroes. Our attorney handling the case was John H. Hibbler. A temporary injunction was granted us, and we struck off a gentlemen's agreement with members of the State Central Committee of the Democratic party . . . acting under the instructions of Senator Joseph T. Robinson and others . . . wherein we would operate continuously under this temporary injunction and, through a process of evolution (allaying the prejudices of the white Democrats), evolve into the party permanently without further litigation. We operated under this agreement and injunction for a period of two years and did vote in the primary. Then, our attorney (whom we suspect saw in a prolonged court struggle an opportunity for personal aggrandizement as well as rich financial returns), decided to go back to the court and ask for a permanent injunction and was denied, and also the temporary injunction was dissolved. The decision was upheld by the Arkansas Supreme Court (1932). Immediately an appeal was taken to the United States Supreme Court on various contentions, but the Chief Justice denied a hearing on "lack of grounds for jurisdiction."

Our petition has again been filed with the Arkansas State Democratic Central Committee, and they will probably approve of our receiving a temporary injunction anew, under the original conditions, with the qualification that we give assurances that we will not push the question in the city, where we are likely to face concerted reaction from white Democrats.[13]

---

13. James Jackson's interview with Dr. J. M. Reynolds, Little Rock, Arkansas, December 1939.

It is said that a few Negroes have always voted in the Democratic primaries in Jefferson and Hempstead counties "out of the charity of an election official." The claim is made that in the 1928 campaign for Senator Robinson and Al Smith a Negro campaign manager was appointed in the state to work with the Negro vote. The state went Democratic by only 30,000 votes, and of this majority 20,000 were cast by Negroes. This is almost certainly a greatly inflated figure. In 1937 a special senatorial election was held in Arkansas to fill the seat of Senator Robinson, who had died. It is claimed that in this election the Negro vote held the balance of power for the first time in the last three decades. In this contest John E. Miller ran as an independent Democrat and opposed the Democratic committee nominee, Governor Carl Bailey. In the general election, about 6,000 Negroes voted, of whom 1,000 were in Little Rock. Miller, in sub rosa fashion, solicited the Negro vote and received it, and won the election. The Negro vote in Arkansas is of some significance in bond issue elections and occasionally in the general elections, in those rare instances when the choice of the Democratic party has an opponent.[14]

Because of the Texas primary cases, a great deal of attention has been attracted to the plight of the Negro voter in that state —perhaps more than any other Southern state. There is no uniformity with regard to the Negro's political status in Texas. Although the basic pattern is one of exclusion from the Democratic primary, the Texas Negro of the urban areas does wield a considerable degree of influence. A good many Texas Negroes even vote in the Democratic primary, despite the exclusion rule of the state committee. In central Texas, especially, the Negro makes his presence felt in local politics. The chief barriers to effective Negro political participation are, of course, the white primary and the poll tax, and the latter also impinges upon the rights of white voters. We have no reliable estimate of the number of Negro voters in Texas. If the computation includes local elections as well as general elections, the total black vote must be considerable, perhaps 50,000. We were able to do only a very limited amount of field work in Texas, and this in great haste.

Negroes have been active in San Antonio politics for a long time. In 1910 John G. Tobin, as county sheriff, deputized Negroes to hunt for a notorious ax-slayer who had killed an entire Negro family and several other individuals. Tobin, who became

14. Ibid.

mayor in 1918, represented the beginning of the San Antonio political machine, and his Negro aide was Charles Bellinger. Tobin died in office during his third term as mayor and was succeeded by "Mac" Chambers. Bellinger also supported the Chambers administration. In Chambers' last administration (1931), he went to the state Democratic convention and sought to have the white primary law repealed. It is said that he appointed more Negro policemen, detectives, sanitary inspectors, and street workers than any other mayor of the city.[15]

Mayor Chambers was succeeded in 1932 by Charles K. Quin. Under Quin the San Antonio machine reached its acme of corruption and control. Quin maintained his power over the Negro through Charles Bellinger and by parading the ghost of John Tobin before them. Bellinger's ascendancy as a Negro political leader came about through his success as a gambler. He came to San Antonio around 1907 from Lockhart, Texas. Under Tobin he operated saloons and made money. Through his wealth, he financed the campaigns of Democratic candidates in the city, plus bearing, personally, the entire expense of Negro campaigns.

The benefits received by Negroes from all of this political activity have been purely incidental. San Antonio whites are said to have been traditionally friendly to Negroes, and this is cited as the basic reason for the paved streets, equal teachers' salaries, and other favorable aspects of municipal services for Negroes in the city. As for Bellinger, he was a menace and a great harm to Negro progress because of his unrepresentative stooges, who got positions of responsibility through his influence in the city hall and the school board. Bellinger of San Antonio, Negro political boss, built up his political influence on money—a typical Tammany Hall politician in bronze. He was king of the lottery, allowed no competitors, and used his lottery kingdom to deliver votes for the candidates who would promise protection to his racket. He was arrested for evasion of income taxes in 1935 and died the following year.

In the Maverick-Quin mayoralty contest of May 1939, Charles Bellinger's son, Valmo, supported the Quin machine and carried the East Side and East End Negroes of San Antonio for Quin. The younger Bellinger has ambitions to wield the influence of his father, but he lacks the ability and the following

15. The material on Texas contained in this chapter is based on James Jackson's field notes, February and March 1940. —ED.

which the elder Bellinger commanded. Valmo Bellinger was arrested by city police in San Antonio on 23 February 1940, in connection with lottery operations there. At the same time, Harold Mann, formerly known as the "first lieutenant" in the various enterprises of the late Charles Bellinger, was also arrested on the same charge; that is, "keeping and exhibiting a policy game."

Although in 1939 a grand total of 5,580 Negroes were registered in San Antonio, only about 50 percent of this number actually voted. About 31 percent of this number voted for Maverick in the May 1939 mayoralty contest.

Out of a Negro population of approximately 90,000, there are about 8,000 Negroes in Houston who have paid poll taxes. Negroes in Houston are not permitted to vote in any city, county, or state election, but can vote on bond issues and in school board elections. A few Negroes have voted in the Democratic primaries. Some election judges are known to have said that they had no objection to Negroes voting in the Democratic primaries.

It is estimated that in Beaumont there were four hundred Negroes who had paid poll taxes and were qualified to vote in 1938. Of this number, it is said that about one-half were eligible to vote by virtue of exemption from tax payment. Negroes under the leadership of the Laboring Man's Protective Association sought admission to the Democratic primary in the city elections of 1934, and many Negroes were permitted to vote in that primary. In 1936, however, when Negroes sought the right to vote in the gubernatorial contest, they were denied participation in the Democratic primary.

Negroes vote in the city elections and the bond issue elections in Dallas. The city elections are nonpartisan, general elections. The Negro is not an issue in the political campaigns, and white candidates often quietly solicit the Negro vote. On 30 December 1938, there were 3,400 Negroes with poll taxes paid and qualified to vote in Dallas, out of the city total of 32,000. In the past four years the Negro vote in Dallas has been used as the balance of power in city elections. It is said to be about 90 percent organized through the efforts of the Progressive Voters' League. As a result of organizational efforts, Negro leaders report, the number of black votes in Dallas has increased from 1,900 in 1936 to 7,000 in 1940, out of a total registration of 39,000. A prominent Negro citizen of Dallas observes:

I believe the only way in which Negroes can advance in politics in Texas is by allying themselves with progressive or politically opportunist forces in the Democratic party; that is, to form a combination with the political majority of whites who are within the Democratic party. The Negro must declare himself a Democrat and thereby seek to win support of white party members for letting down the barriers to Negro participation in the primaries.

Since the municipal elections in Austin are nonpartisan, general elections, Negroes are able to vote in them. Of the 18,000 Negroes in the Austin population, from 1,200 to 1,500 are said to be registered voters with poll taxes paid. As a result of their political activities, Negroes have secured several city jobs, though these are chiefly of a menial character. There are four Negro city policemen in Austin, several garbage men, a proportionate number of trash collectors, and janitors in the city buildings. There is an adequate recreational center for Negroes, embracing 13½ acres, with a swimming pool, a lighted football field, a softball diamond, and a full-time recreational director.

Some border states have never employed severe measures to curtail Negro voting, and in these states the black vote has become a real factor to be reckoned with. While this political privilege has failed to solve the major disabilities of race for this group, it has been something of a leavening influence, and it tends to result in generally better treatment insofar as educational, health, recreational, and other such facilities are concerned, not to mention employment in state and local governments.

Kentucky displays a minimum of Jim-Crowism toward Negro political participation. It is not possible to say just how many Negroes vote in this state, but the figure would certainly be somewhere between 80,000 and 100,000. Negroes participate freely in the Democratic primaries, and in the neighborhood of one-third of the black voters are now supporters of the Democratic party. Kentucky, like West Virginia among the border states, is distinguished by the fact that in modern times a Negro has been elected to its state legislature, and now sits there. The percentage of Negroes in Kentucky is even less than for the nation as a whole. The main center of Negro political activity is to be found in Louisville. Here again, however, the Negro voter is confronted with the twin problems of machine control and venal, self-seeking political leadership.

In 1930 Louisville had a Negro population of 47,354— equivalent to 15.4 percent of the city's inhabitants. It is estimated that there are approximately 30,000 Negro voters in Louisville. Until 1933 the vast majority of these voters were Republicans. The Negro politicians were traditionally preachers, professional opportunists, racketeers, bootleggers, and ex-convicts, and this is largely characteristic of Negro political leadership in Louisville today.[16]

In 1931, however, a Negro attorney named C. Eubank Tucker began to discern the strategic value of a sizable black Democratic vote in a political community in which the Negro vote had always been pledged a priori to the Republican party. The fifty-eighth assembly district in Louisville is 95.5 percent Negro. Numerous efforts had been made to elect a Negro from this district, but the white Republican committee would not yield to the demands for a Negro candidate. In 1931 attorney Tucker walked into the Republican headquarters and insisted that the GOP committee withdraw the white Republican candidate in favor of a Negro. This the committee promised to do but subsequently welshed on its promise. When the next election occurred, in 1933, Tucker himself filed as a Republican candidate. He did not have the support of the Republican machine, however, and was defeated. Tucker then went to the Democratic organization. The Democrats, with nothing to lose, readily withdrew their candidate and made Tucker the Democratic standard-bearer in the fifty-eighth district. Yet in spite of the fact that Tucker—a Negro—ran against a white man in a solid Negro district, he was defeated—indicating the strong Republican sentiment among the Negro voters in the district. This episode had repercussions, however, for the agitation aroused by Tucker's fight deflected enough Negro votes to the Democratic ticket to cinch the victory for the Democrats over the city administration. The new Democratic city administration gave full credit to the Negro vote for giving it the margin of victory.

Since 1933 there has been a considerable shift of the Negro vote to the Democratic party in Louisville. This has been in part the result of the attractiveness of the Roosevelt New Deal program to Negroes and in part a consequence of the fact that

16. This discussion of Negro politics in Louisville is based on James Jackson's notes of interviews conducted in January 1940. —ED.

a Republican candidate for mayor was accused of being a member of the Ku Klux Klan and failed to deny the charge. When the Democrats assumed power in 1933, they shared some of the patronage with Negro supporters. Among these jobs were the following: a deputy in the county clerk's office at $150 a month; a deputy in the county tax assessor's office at $150 a month; a stenographer in the county court at $125 per month; a deputy recorder in the magistrate's court at $125 per month; twelve or more inspectors in various city departments; two foremen in the department of public works; and a deputy in the internal revenue office. A second colored fire company was established in the east end of the city. A probate commissioner in the county court was appointed on a fee basis. The men put in these positions were key men in the Democratic machine structure— precinct leaders, ward leaders, and so forth. For the most part, they have followed the narrow course of self-interest and have entrenched themselves in their positions.

It is thought that there are about 9,000 qualified Negro voters registered as Democrats in Louisville. The Negro electorate is split by factionalism, however, and it is difficult to get the majority of Negro voters to support a black candidate. In November 1938, for example, Dr. Sweeney, a Negro dentist, ran for the school board and could have won by a clear victory had he received a solid Negro vote. Although Louisville Negroes hold the balance of power in local elections, the machines of the victorious party pay off for Negro support not in substantial benefits to the Negro community but "in condoning vice and giving the underworld Negroes certain license," says a Negro minister.

Despite the size of the black vote in Louisville and the political influence of Negroes, there are no Negroes on the county Democratic committee. Although there are Negro Democratic precinct leaders, they are not chosen by the Negroes themselves, but are appointed by the county Democratic committee. According to Barry Bingham of the Louisville *Courier-Journal*, his newspaper "has been most sympathetic to the political aspirations of the Negro people. It has been interested in getting a Negro on the board of aldermen from the seventh ward, also a Negro member of the board of education. We supported Charles W. Anderson's candidacy for representative to the state legislature."

The Negro vote in Oklahoma has been estimated to be as high as 60,000 or more, and it should show a steady increase. A conservative estimate of the total Negro vote in the state today would be about 50,000. Roscoe Dungee, editor of the *Black Dis-*

patch and the outstanding Negro political leader in Oklahoma, in discussing the political status of the Negro, says:

In the last [1938] primary, it was our vote that represented the balance of power in electing Governor Phillips. In areas in which the Negro population is dominant, we have all Negro election officials. We hold Democratic caucuses and elect Negroes to the county and state Democratic conventions, notwithstanding the fact that this 1915 registration law [the law which succeeded the grandfather clause] is still on the books. When J. B. Robertson was governor, we developed a strategy for effecting a practical invalidation of the registration law by supporting nonracial administration measures. For instance, Governor Robertson sought to pass a highway bond issue which was opposed by most of the whites, but I hammered away in my newspaper for the bond. This action, in turn, obligated Robertson's faction to the Negro, and he didn't dare enforce the registration law against the interest of the Negro. Likewise, with each successive administration, we got on the Democratic bandwagon until now they have in fact—if not in law—rescinded the registration discrimination. In the last gubernatorial Democratic primary, Negroes cast over 40,000 votes. . . .

Local office-seekers here in Oklahoma City have always made a strong bid for the Negro vote. Even the most vicious Negro baitor, as for example "Alfalfa Bill" Murray, will get a dozen Negroes and pay them five dollars a day to work among Negroes for his election.

I managed Senator Thomas' campaign in the last election and was provided with an expense account and elaborate headquarters. I also managed Governor Marland's state campaign among Negroes.[17]

Despite the legend concerning Roscoe Dungee's political power and his ability to influence the Negro vote, another prominent Negro, the purchasing agent for Langston University, observes:

The Negro electorate is not disciplined at all. Negroes have political organizations on paper, but I question the contention that any Negro in the state can guarantee the delivery of 100

17. James Jackson's interviews, Oklahoma City, Oklahoma, March 1940. The following material on Oklahoma is taken from Jackson's notes of field interviews conducted in March 1940. —ED.

votes to any designated candidate. The Negro leaders maintain their influence through personal contacts with white politicians and not on a basis of a mass following. Every politician in Oklahoma plays the game for his own self-interest and for what money he can get out of it for himself. No Negro politician, to my knowledge, has ever acted in the interest of the whole people without regard to selfish ambition. The white politicians in the state deliberately and successfully keep the Negro divided and split into impotent factions.

In the April 1938 municipal election in Oklahoma City there was a weak progressive lineup in support of candidate N. Hall for mayor against Robert Hefner. Hall, an attorney, had labor support. Hefner was the candidate of the Associated Industries and the chamber of commerce. Hall lost by 1,000 votes. The first ward—the "silk stocking" district of Oklahoma City—voted solidly for Hefner, while the fourth ward—the working-class district—voted for Hall, who offered a program of jobs, relief, improved health facilities, and schools. In this election, however, Roscoe Dungee supported Hefner, as did the *Daily Oklahoman* and the Oklahoma City *Times*. Thus Dungee played an important role in defeating the progressive bloc.

In Tulsa there are ten exclusively Negro precincts where all election officials are Negroes. The Negro district was predominantly Republican until Roosevelt's administration. Now it is largely Democratic. There is no discrimination against or intimidation of Negroes in politics. Both the Republican and Democratic organizations have Negro representation on their county and state committees and at their conventions. Political affairs in the Negro district of Tulsa—in contrast with the fact that Negroes are completely segregated—are split up among a great many groups and leaders. There is no centralized political leadership. If Negroes would vote in a bloc, they could be a decisive factor in Oklahoma elections. In Tulsa in 1937 the local bus company sought to get a twenty-five-year franchise, and it was the Negro vote which carried this franchise. Negroes supported the company because it employs black drivers. In the same year a vote was held on a civil service proposal, and Negroes defeated the measure because it contained discriminatory clauses.

The editor of the Tulsa *Eagle* informed James Jackson that a group of prominent Negro leaders in Tulsa are attempting

to establish a unified race conscious leadership which will remove the self-appointed political opportunists and ward heelers from their seats of influence, and unify the Negro vote around a community program. Our political task here is to unify the Negro vote and raise its level of political intelligence toward the end of achieving our full 10 percent share of all jobs in city services in opposition to the hand-out practices of the past.

It is said that in Tulsa "Negroes represent 10 percent of the population and also 10 percent of the vote." Great respect is claimed for the Negro vote in Tulsa, notwithstanding the fact that it is poorly disciplined. The white politicians apparently spend a considerable amount of money to attract the black vote.

Missouri, insofar as Negro voting is concerned, is definitely a border state, and probably 130,000 Negroes vote there. No great difficulty to Negro voting now exists, and places like St. Louis and Kansas City are quite similar to Northern cities in the freedom of Negro voting, officeholding, and public employment as a reward for political effort. Negroes vote freely in the Democratic primaries of Missouri, and from 50 to 60 percent of the Negro vote in the state is probably Democratic.

The growth of the Democratic party under Tom Pendergast in Kansas City, Missouri, almost wiped the Republicans out of local politics. This was due in part, it is said, to the pressure of the Pendergast machine, in part to disillusionment among Negroes with Hoover Republicanism, and in part to the appeal of the New Deal. In 1936, 87 percent of the Negro vote in Kansas City was cast for the Democratic presidential nominee. In the 1938 Kansas City municipal election, 72 percent of the Negro vote was Democratic.[18] It is reported that the strategy of the Negro political leadership in Kansas City, apart from callous self-aggrandizement, has been in terms of negative voting. That is, Negroes have been content to vote against issues which did not include them rather than to advance a program of progressive issues. The Negro vote in Kansas City has been variously estimated at from 18,000 to 31,000.

It is claimed that the sole value received by the Negro voters in Kansas City for their support of the Pendergast machine has been the protection given to the Negro operators for their vices and rackets. No Negroes appear to be represented in any super-

18. James Jackson's interview with C. A. Franklin, editor of the Kansas City *Call*, Kansas City, Missouri, March 1940. The following discussion of the Negro in Kansas City politics comes from Jackson's field notes, March 1940. —ED.

visory or administrative capacity in the Pendergast organization. All ward organizations have been headed by whites, mostly
small-time politicians and racketeers who have depended upon
the Negro underworld element to mobilize the black vote. The
election on 19 February 1940 for the amendment of the city
charter offered a fine opportunity for Negroes to improve their
political status by voting for a one-chamber aldermanic form of
government in lieu of the present bureaucratic eight-member
council. This would have given an opportunity for Negroes to
have representation in the city government. The Negro political
leadership in Kansas City was not vigilant, however, and the
charter amendment was defeated, with a very small vote being
cast. Negro politicians in Kansas City, remarks one Republican
ward leader, "place an undue amount of stress on national politics every four years, but are most apathetic and uninformed
on local issues. Also the old-line political leaders are opportunistic and selfish with an abhorrence for collective work."

Out of a population of approximately 23,000 Negroes, there
are perhaps 10,000 Negro voters in Kansas City, Kansas. The
Kansas City *Call* reports the Negro vote as 16,026. In the last
few years, the political loyalty of the Negro voters in Kansas
City, Kansas, has swung sharply from the Republican to the
Democratic camp. Negroes received their first appointments in
the city departments under a Republican administration, but
since the Democrats have been in city hall, they have appointed
even more Negroes to white-collar jobs in the city departments.

West Virginia is an important border state which we were
unable to touch in our field work. It presents a favorable picture
of Negro voting, with few if any restraints and an active Negro
electorate of approximately 60,000. Negroes have held political
office in the state and have been elected to the state legislature.
The absence of a poll tax qualification, the fact that it is not a
one-party state, and the fact that it eschews the "white primary"
are factors favorable to wholesome Negro political participation.
West Virginia is a state in which some fruitful digging into Negro suffrage might be done, especially in view of the fact that
the Negro mine workers have learned the lessons of economic
as well as political democracy through their membership in the
United Mine Workers.

For a decade after 1899, white supremacy was the chief issue
in Maryland politics. Three concrete attempts were made by
the Democratic party to disfranchise the Negro after 1899: in
1903, in 1909, and in 1911. All of these proposals carried the

salient features of the grandfather clause. One amendment also included a constitution-interpretation clause. Many Republicans and Democrats opposed these amendments for fear their passage would make Maryland a one-party state. The law of 1900 requiring individuals coming from other states to declare their intentions in a court to vote and requiring a fee of 50 cents is said to be the chief barrier to Negro voting. There is a gerrymander of Negro voting districts in Baltimore which is effective in local though not in national elections. In 1932 Negroes formed 16 percent of the population of voting age, but were only 12 percent of the voters. Fifty-one percent of the Negro population in Maryland lives in Baltimore.

FOURTEEN

Negro Voting in Selected Southern Cities

We have thought it advisable to segregate a few examples of Negro political involvement in Southern cities in order to emphasize the fact that, even in the face of severe restrictions, there are occasions when the black man and woman exert decisive political influence. Although the Negro may be permitted to vote only in general elections, is confronted with all manner of registration obstacles, and is excluded from the Democratic primaries, he is sometimes able to make his presence felt in municipal elections, bond issue referendums, and special called elections. In some instances, by shrewd bargaining, he has been able to get some valuable rewards in the form of improved facilities in trade for his vote.

In Mobile, Alabama, there are two or three hundred qualified Negro voters. Several times that number of Negroes are registered, but most of them are disqualified because of delinquency in poll tax payments. Prior to 1936 Negroes voted in all Democratic primaries in the city, but in recent years the all-white primary rule has been in effect. Ten or twelve years ago the current mayor of Mobile made a bid for the small black vote in his successful race against a Ku Klux Klan candidate. In the elections for city commissioners, for which there are no primaries, white candidates come into the Negro districts—especially the seventh ward, which is heavily Negro—and hold meetings, bring loud speakers, make speeches, and offer all sorts of promises for the Negro vote. The candidates spend some money in the Negro districts, too. The candidates, however, seldom keep their promises. It is claimed that at times the Negro vote comes close to deciding elections for city commissioner. According to the sheriff, any organized effort by Negroes to become registered in large numbers would create

> an unnatural situation, and we would find the means to deal with it. Frankly, I am opposed to Negroes participating in the vote. Our system is fair. We want to give Negroes more and more of education, but we do not want them ever to become full citizens. The Negroes don't seem to take any interest in voting anyhow. The upper-class Negro looks upon the situation quite as we do, and he has only contempt for the lower-class Negro.[1]

As far back as 1900, Negro loyalty to the Republicans in the Birmingham area was rewarded through limited federal patronage. Ocie Long was the leader of the Republican forces in Birmingham beginning in the early 1920s. The beginning of Negro civic movements came in the same period. The first such movement, under the leadership of P. D. Davis, died quickly. The first civic movements were concerned chiefly with political spoils. From this limited objective, the horizon was broadened to include work to achieve civic improvements. At the beginning of the thirties, the various civic groups came together to form the Negro Non-Partisan League. The objective of the League was to solidify all Negro voters. It was hoped that by having the black vote in a bloc for a specific candidate, it would be possible for Negroes to secure certain benefits by having the particular candidate commit himself to the specific needs of the Negro community. The Non-Partisan League lasted only about two years. The leaders in these early movements were usually professional men or men with good jobs in the major factories. The maximum number of participants was about two hundred people.

The Alabama State Federation of Colored Civic Leagues was organized around 1933 by W. L. McAlpine with the objective of having Negroes enter politics on a much larger scale than formerly. Various leaders within the State Federation gained their influence among white politicians by their promise of being able to deliver "so many" Negro votes. They thus sought to secure financial and other personal favors by themselves. The rivalry between the leaders in their efforts to deliver votes to

---

1. Gunnar Myrdal's interview with Sheriff W. H. Holcombe, Mobile, Alabama, 12 November 1939.

white candidates led to a split within the ranks of the State Federation. Consequently, the Negro Democratic Council was formed by D. L. White, a tailor by trade, and Henry Harris, an errand man for the Southern Railway Company. From the influence of existing civic groups, the South Side Negro Democratic Club was formed by Clint McKinney, a barber, who succeeded in securing a charter from the national Democratic committee. The Negro Democratic Council and the South Side Democratic Club were merged in 1939 into the Jefferson County Negro Democratic Club, under the leadership of H. D. Coke, managing editor of the Birmingham *World.*

The later civic movements arose primarily in answer to specific needs in the Negro community for lights, street pavement, sewage disposal, and so forth. At all times, however, these movements were limited in the number of people who participated. Nor did the early civic leagues conceive as their mission the winning of universal suffrage for the Negro. It was only when the white politicians stopped granting the small requests of the civic leaders that the organizations began seriously to turn their attention to suffrage.

In 1938 the maximum Negro voting strength of six hundred was cast in a Birmingham bond election where matters of new schools, hospitals, a new city hall, and parks were at stake. The Negro vote was cast against the bonds. All efforts to approve the bonds were defeated. Wherever there is a close race in city elections, the limited Negro vote may prove decisive. In the ninth congressional district, the Negro and labor votes have been most important.

Negroes in Birmingham were largely Republican in politics until the Negro Democratic clubs were formed beginning about 1936. But since there is no Republican primary, Negroes who wish to vote participate in the Democratic primary. It is thought that some Negroes vote for the Republican ticket in the general elections. Local political activities among Negroes in Birmingham are mostly scattered efforts and are not based upon adherence to any fixed principles. The Negro Democratic clubs endorse candidates on the basis of "He's a good man" or "He's my friend."

The State Federation of Democratic Clubs (white) is accustomed to admit one representative from the Negro groups to its council. This leader was formerly D. L. White. The position of this representative is that of being used to "bring around" Negro organizations to endorse the candidates selected by the machine and to silence Negro protests against the selected candidates. The 1938 elections presented a case in point. A candidate endorsed by the white Democrats was Jim Simpson, who was running for the state senate. Labor unions supported a rival candidate for the same office. Certain local civic clubs in Negro neighborhoods, known as "Right to Vote" clubs, announced their support for the candidates endorsed by the labor unions. D. L. White was reportedly given the job by the white leaders of getting these "Right to Vote" clubs to affiliate with the regular Negro Democratic organization and to keep the Communists away from the Negroes. Thus, White invited these clubs to join his organization, but without success. Moreover, the senatorial candidate endorsed by state Democratic leaders proved so unpopular that even regular Negro Democratic organizations ultimately refused to support him.[2]

The editor of the *News Journal* of Daytona Beach, Florida, presents a vivid picture of Daytona Beach politics and the role which the Negro has played in it:

> The political ring of Daytona Beach and Volusia County reached maturity under the excellent hands of Bert Fish, now United States Minister to Egypt. He prospered, as Florida prospered, in the boom days of the twenties and gained control of the citrus industry, of banks, and of property. When the big crash came in 1929, the ring was defeated, and a big scandal was attached to the failure of the big ring-controlled bank. . . .
>
> In 1932 again, the ring was defeated in the county for a goodly number of county officials. . . . With the departure from the city of Bert Fish, attorney Francis P. Whitehair and his firm took over control of the ring and have retained control of it ever since. Now, this Whitehair is a bond attorney and has built up quite a big business with bonding companies. As a natural result, he has attracted to himself numerous bright young lawyers in crucial spots around the county who are his mouthpieces. Meanwhile, there grew into power . . . Armstrong, who held his power very largely by control of the Negro vote. To get their vote when he was running for mayor, he promised all kinds of things and actually placed them in good city positions. He would line them up at the polls, feed them soda pop and sandwiches. He incited, by this method, quite a great deal of racial antagonism because unthinking

2. Edward Strong's Birmingham memorandum, May 1940.

whites thought Negroes were to blame. Meanwhile, too, Armstrong played hand in glove with Whitehair. Early in 1938 Armstrong suddenly died. Frank Couch succeeded him as mayor, appointed by the remaining commissioners. This setup proved to be a Whitehair organization for a few months, then there loomed up a quarrel over patronage. Three of the commissioners revolted and explained, or rather, revealed everything. These three and the mayor were indicted for various misfeasances in office.

Meanwhile, there was organized a nonpartisan committee which drew up an excellent plan—rezone the city with seven instead of six zones in such a way as to make it impossible for the Negro vote to control the selection of commissioners; and, among other things, call for an election of new officers. A petition was circulated to which 6,000 names were signed, but the ring jumped in, faked some petitions, and hastily put through the charter which did some of the things—for example, the rezoning portion of the plan—but provided that the governor should appoint city officials from April 1939 to October 1940. The governor was induced to select men named by the ring. There now is in power this group who are surprisingly good officeholders because they want to disprove charges that the ring has been corrupt. Wholesale changes in offices have been made by them.

To briefly go back to Armstrong, the Negroes' friend here: When he was in power, he used to pay poll taxes and pass receipts around at election time; and be used to hire Negroes in droves to cut weeds and vote them just before election time, then fire them. In the fall of 1936, Governor Scholtz removed the Armstrong bunch from office on the grounds that they were stealing money. They stuck in, however, and the state militia was sent down here. The culprits then sued for injunction to restrain the state from employing such tactics. While the case was pending in court, Governor Scholtz went out of office and Lane, then incumbent, reinstated the culprits.

In 1933, a long line of Negroes went to vote at the instigation of Armstrong, and the election officials closed the polls on them. The militia was sent down to force reopenings of the polls, and the Negroes got the right to vote.[3]

3. Wilhelmina Jackson's interview, Daytona Beach, Florida, 8 March 1940.

Some of the Daytona Beach Negroes, however, relate a different story and are much more sympathetic to Edward H. Armstrong. For example, a former meat inspector for Daytona commented:

> Armstrong helped the Negro become powerful in Daytona Beach politics. He really put us on the police force on an equal basis with whites. About 1933, the reaction of the white community against Armstrong became severe. They did not want him reelected because they felt that he was a "Negro lover." White voters, at the time of this election, were arranged in one line and the Negro voters in another. The official killed time for us by asking a lot of nonsensical questions; so much so that the polls were closed before even half of us had voted. We protested and the militia was called out to keep order. There was a great deal of raving, but the polls were reopened and stayed open until eleven o'clock that night and until all of the Negroes had voted. Negroes are now losing jobs that used to be ours when Armstrong was living. For instance: all janitors were Negro; all construction work was done by Negroes; there was one Negro man in the water department; there were Negro sanitary inspectors. These jobs have been cut almost in half since Armstrong died. There are just a few people interested in retaining political power. When Mayor Armstrong was coming up, he asked what we wanted—you see we have a nonpartisan city government— and was told: policemen, freedom on the beach to a reasonable extent, and so on. We got them. To show you how regular he was, the night that the militia was called out to keep us free from harm to vote, Armstrong had three white policemen burning fires in guarding my house.[4]

It is estimated that approximately 4,550 Negroes are registered in Raleigh, North Carolina. Negroes vote in all elections and without opposition. But there is also the unscrupulous white candidate who is willing to buy the Negro vote and the Negro ward heeler who is willing to corral it for a small fee. Concerning the young Negro voter, the black political boss of precinct 16 states: "For a drink, a free shindig at a piccolo center, and a barbecue, they'll vote."[5]

---

4. Wilhelmina Jackson's interview, Daytona Beach, Florida, March 1940.
5. The discussion of Raleigh politics in this chapter is based on Wilhemina Jackson's notes of field interviews conducted in the fall of 1939. —ED.

Serious efforts were made in 1930, 1931, and 1932 to stop Negroes from voting in Raleigh. It seems that during the Bailey-Simmons campaign for United States Senator in 1930, Negro registration increased from some 300 to about 2,500. Josephus Daniels, then editor of the *News and Observer*, took note of this increase in Negro registration, and in a well-known editorial entitled "A Dagger in the Heart," lashed out against it in these terms:

> The report that something like 400 Negroes, 253 in the 16th precinct, have been allowed to register as Democrats in Raleigh calls for investigation and action. There are no Negro Democrats in Raleigh and those who are allowing Negroes to register are placing a dagger at the heart of the Democratic Party. What has happened . . . opens the door to political evils of 1894–1900. . . . Those Negroes [who insist on registering] should be denied the opportunity to kill the vote of white Democrats in their own primary.

Daniels ran a series of editorials on this subject. In one of 14 June 1930 Daniels quotes from a Dr. Wright's letter to the governor chastising certain party members who have said, "What's a few registered Negroes?"

> We've already a taste of what the Negro vote means here in Raleigh. Our present mayor was defeated in the white primary, but elected in the general election by the aid of the Negro vote.

In this period, candidates were freely accused of being Negro-lovers, and a cry went up to challenge and stop the Negro voters at the polls. Hundreds of Negro votes were thrown out. In 1932 in the campaign for state senator one of the candidates declared that he did not want to be elected by bellboys, washwomen, maids, and bootblacks. "I've never registered a Negro in my life. I am a Democrat and a white man, and do not care for their votes." Pamphlets denouncing the Negro vote and its threat as the balance of power in the Democratic primary were distributed by the thousands. The editor of the *Carolina Tribune,* a Negro weekly, replied vigorously to all of these attacks, and threats were made that his newspaper plant would be burned down for his effrontery.

Judge Riley Barnes is still considered by many to be the power behind the throne in Raleigh, though he is no longer on the bench. He has strongly encouraged the Negro vote and uses it as often as he can get it. There are, however, no district or ward political clubs in the Negro districts. The Negro voters are listed, and the machine goes after them on election days, but it maintains no formal precinct or ward organization. Negroes could have controlled the Democratic committee in precinct 16, it is said, except that C. A. Haywood, who is the leader of the Negroes in this precinct, did not desire this because:

> Negroes would not put up the necessary money to defray the expenses in the headquarters. Moreover, it was decided that it would be more tactful for Negroes to assume control of the committee gradually, because the Southern white man must be dealt with differently from the Yankee. When the third Negro is placed on the committee of five, it is anticipated that the two remaining white men will withdraw and the Negroes will then assume control without any unnecessary hard feelings.

The two big political factions in Raleigh are the "Buck" Jones and the Carl Williamson groups. Both of these factions have their Negro representatives in the black precincts. These are selected through some of the more prominent Negroes in town. The candidates for office make a regular bid for the Negro vote, but they avoid promising any more than they must. The chief problem of Negro participation in Raleigh politics is said to arise from the fact that there are a number of Negro ward heelers who can be bought cheaply by white candidates. The machines maintain a number of Negro ward heelers in each ward, and they are paid off at each election. It is reported that the bond issue for the new city auditorium of about five years ago was put across by the Negro vote. The issue won by only thirty-three votes. This new auditorium and all of its facilities are completely available to the Negroes.

One prominent white official of Raleigh echoes the widespread belief that the Negro vote goes to the highest bidder. As he puts it: "It is one thing for the Negro vote to be controlled by unscrupulous whites and another thing for it to be controlled by unscrupulous Negroes—the latter is the situation here." It is said that the average price for the Negro vote in Raleigh is one dollar per vote and cars to carry voters, plus five or six hundred dollars to "the Negro undertaker or doctor whose boss is the white politician with the money bag." The whole process is on a horse-trading level. It is alleged that two of the commissioners now sitting in the city hall would not be there at all except for the Negro vote, and these men are looked upon as cheap and incompetent politicians.

Prior to 1937 the city of Atlanta was divided into thirteen wards, each of which had the right to elect its own councilmanic and aldermanic representatives. In two of these wards Negroes comprised more than 50 percent of the population and thus constituted a potential threat to the white politicians seeking these offices. In 1937 the city was redistricted and the number of wards was reduced to six, in only one of which Negroes made up a majority of the total population. Whether this was a pure and simple case of gerrymandering is difficult to determine, since a search of councilmanic records and newspapers reveals no allusion to the potential domination of the two wards by Negroes. But it is clear that there was no concerted opposition to the redistricting, for the whole matter was submitted to the electorate for approval.[6]

The growth of the Negro population of Atlanta has been of considerable importance in the growth of the city as a whole. During the decade of the 1920s the Negro population of Atlanta expanded by 43.4 percent, as compared with a white increase of 30.8 percent. This rapid growth of the Negro population has occasioned no great increase in the facilities provided for blacks by the city. The failure of the city to provide its Negro citizens with more adequate recreational, cultural, and educational facilities has taken its toll in the high rate of juvenile delinquency, crime, and disease within the Negro community. The city spends $29.77 on the education of each Negro child and $91.27 on that of each white child annually. The city maintains, with some help from Fulton County, a wing at Grady Hospital to take care of the hospital needs of its Negro population. A recent report of the hospital's board of trustees stressed "the overcrowded conditions of both the white and Negro units of the hospital. It is still necessary to postpone treatment of many deserving cases and the waiting list for operations on colored women extends from five to six months ahead." It should be noted that Negro doctors are not permitted to treat patients in Grady Hospital or to intern there.

Of the 54,155 theoretically eligible Negro voters in Atlanta, 2,106 are actually on the registration lists. Of this small number a still smaller number vote, for all of these do not pay their poll taxes. It is impossible to determine the exact number of Negroes

6. The following material on Atlanta is taken from "Negroes in Atlanta," a special report prepared for Dr. Bunche by B. A. Jones, a graduate student at Atlanta University. Bunche incorporated this report, with "minor revisions," into his memorandum (chapter 10, pp. 1073–1111). —Ed.

and whites who pay their poll taxes, since the payments are not recorded on the books by color of payer. The small number of registered Negro voters cannot be taken as an indication of the Negro's lack of any genuine interest in the political life of the community. It is, however, indicative of a general attitude among all Atlantans. Several factors account for the political apathy among Negroes. These are (1) the existence of the one-party system, with its membership exclusion policy; (2) the poll tax, with its cumulative features; (3) the general failure of Negro ministers to launch any concerted and sustained attack upon the status quo; (4) the failure of the Negro intelligentsia to provide the proper leadership for the masses in political matters; and (5) the lack of any well organized and continuously functioning mechanism for the promotion of civic responsibility among Negroes.

That the Negro early recognized the evils of the white primary is illustrated by the following excerpts from an editorial in the Atlanta *Independent* of 5 January 1928:

> The Democratic party has disfranchised, brow-beaten, bull-dozed, intimidated and suppressed the Negro until 75% of them fear wholesale bodily harm if they attempt to use the ballot as a weapon of political or economic defense. . . . Not being able to exclude the Negro entirely from the exercise of his political rights by Constitutional amendment, they have adopted a system of peonage and conspiracy through the abominable and iniquitous white primary infamy. Not a party primary but a race primary. . . . Under this system all the white people without regard for affiliation, are invited to participate in a white man's primary, in which no Negro is permitted or eligible to vote under Democratic rules. So it is clear that the Negro is reduced to a state of peonage and not permitted to use the ballot. . . . On the other hand the white South lives in a state of peonage in the Democratic party. Outside of local government, the South has no voice in the selection of party leaders or party candidates, and is content to have none, so long as their acquiescence in party disfranchisement will enable them to keep white heels on black necks.

Neither Atlanta nor Georgia has any effective opposition party. There is a Republican party in the state, but it is so torn by factional strife that it offers no real opposition to the party in power. Frequently it does not even offer a candidate for office in local elections. At one time the Republican party in Georgia was very strong in national affairs. Under the leadership of Benjamin J. Davis the party was frequently heard in the national convention. With the development of the spirit of "lily whiteism" in Georgia, however, the party came under control of a group of whites who saw in it an opportunity to secure some patronage plums for themselves and their friends. Thus the party, having no local objectives, degenerated into a mere cabal. Consequently, by the end of 1937 the Republican party in Georgia, according to one observer, was as "dead as a doornail."

In the meantime, Ben Davis (as he is affectionately known to Negroes and whites) had overcome his personal difficulties and in the fall of 1937 had begun to organize interested Negroes in a Young Men's Republican Club of Georgia. Operating on the hypothesis that every Negro in Georgia is bound to be a Republican, if for no other reason than that he cannot be a member of the Democratic party, the Young Men's Republican Club immediately launched a state-wide program to increase the number of registered black voters in Georgia. At the same time a vigorous membership drive was begun. In 1938 a women's auxiliary was formed under the leadership of Mrs. C. R. Yates, wife of a prominent Atlanta businessman.

As the 1940 election approached, the somnolent executive committee of the Republican party began to bestir itself and make plans for sending a delegation to the national convention. The first local evidence of these movements was shown when this group issued, through E. L. Collier, local Negro Republican and a bitter foe of Ben Davis, a call for a Republican mass meeting. On the night of the meeting, the room was crowded with Young Republican Club members and staunch followers of Ben Davis. There ensued a brief but acrimonious struggle for control of the meeting through the election of a chairman. Many accusations of bribes received and offered were passed. The one tangible result of the rally was a promise (made by the national committeeman and other whites) to work in cooperation with the Negro group, and especially with the Young Men's Republican Club.

Atlanta is an educational center for Negroes of the South. It has four colleges, one graduate school, and two professional schools. Yet the masses of Negroes are without the intellectual leadership that is necessary to the attainment of their political objectives and they are, consequently, frequently the victims of demagoguery. One hears from all sides the constant complaint that the college teachers and the college-trained citizens offer the masses no assistance in their struggle against greater numbers and superior leadership.

There are three principal types of organizations working among Negroes in Atlanta to raise the group's political status. There are those organizations that are strictly racial in membership and whose program is primarily political; there are those organizations that are biracial in membership and whose program and attack are along political, social, and economic lines; and there are those organizations that are racial in membership and political in purpose, but that seek to work within the existing party alignment, whatever that may be.

In group one are to be found the Atlanta Civic and Political League and the Woman's Civic Club. The former is an organization under the leadership of John Wesley Dobbs, a retired railway postal clerk and leader in fraternal affairs. The league has as its purpose the promotion of civic interest among the Negroes of Atlanta and the creation of a large electorate for the express "purpose of securing, through political action, a status of political equality for Negroes." It claims a membership of 2,500 persons, a claim which, because of the lack of any authentic records, is difficult to verify. The present writer would estimate that the figure is too high by at least 1,500, and that of the remaining 1,000 there is active participation by only a small number. Though nonpartisan in name, the organization, because of the strong "New Dealish" tendencies of its leaders, frequently reflects a Democratic bias. The most notable achievement of this group was the fight against the 1938 bond election, at which time the publishing of pamphlets and other materials describing conditions affecting Atlanta's Negro population was highly effective in persuading Negroes to register and to vote against the issue.

The Woman's Civic Club is a very recent organization of Atlanta's younger women, having been formed on 21 April 1940 by Mrs. Oscar Hall. Mrs. Hall, the president, is a social service worker who was formerly attached to the department of public welfare and is now social investigator for the Atlanta Housing Authority. Mrs. Hall attributes her interest in political affairs to her work among underprivileged Negroes, who are so lacking in the number of facilities accorded to the white group by the city and secured by the more privileged Negro group because of its economic strength. Another leader, Mrs. Carrie Pitman, is an elementary school principal who has "long been interested in political activity among Negroes" but who "became disgusted with the men for doing nothing" and sought to organize the Negro women. The work of this organization during the three weeks of its existence prior to the closing of the registration lists for the November election was commendable.

Among the organizations that are biracial in membership are the Southern Conference for Human Welfare, the Commission for Interracial Cooperation, and the Georgia League of Women Voters (white). These groups attack the problem of political disfranchisement as only one of the factors preventing the spread of democracy in the South. They are concerned with the abridgment of civil rights in any form whatever, regardless of race. Of these three organizations, the most aggressive is the Southern Conference for Human Welfare, whose policy is one of refusing to recognize, in any form, the prejudices of the South. The Georgia League of Women Voters seeks to effect within the white group a sense of political responsibility and "to establish in Georgia and Atlanta a political system worthy of the name." The Interracial Commission is less aggressive than either of the aforementioned organizations and works more quietly. Its program in Atlanta is primarily socio-economic, though there is considerable attention given to political disfranchisement.

Within this group might also be included the local branches of the National Association for the Advancement of Colored People and the National Urban League. Both of these organizations do some work in promoting political activity among Negroes in Atlanta, but since the former has abandoned some of its political aggressiveness in the South, the activities of the local chapter consist mainly of supporting the work of the national office. Furthermore, many persons who might secure aid from the association fail to seek it. The work of the Urban League is felt mainly in the organization of Negroes into labor unions and the struggle to secure a place within the organized labor group for these unions.

In group three, organizations racial in membership and political in purpose but seeking to work within the existing party alignment, are the Young Men's Republican Club and its Women's Auxiliary, the work of which parallels that of the male branch. No mention has been made of the Atlanta Negro Chamber of Commerce, whose object closely parallels that of the white organization of the same name. Although it operates quietly, the chamber exerts its influence in all of the above-mentioned activities.

There are approximately 200 Negro churches in Atlanta which claim a membership upward of 15,000. Thus the Negro minister has access to the largest black following of any single group of persons touching community life—far more than teachers, physicians, or any other single professional group. That more progress has not been made in bettering the social, economic, and political life of the Negro is in a large measure the fault of the ministers, who direct the social thinking of so large a part of the population. Although there have been occasional blasts from the pulpit against the political apathy of the group, there has not yet been launched any really aggressive attack upon the archaic social structure of the South. An examination of the local daily reveals the following subjects, picked at random, as a typical Sunday's offering at some of the leading Negro churches of the city: "Dry Bones," "What Shall I Do to be Saved?" "True Repentance," "Church Loyalty," "Hebrew Children in the Fiery Furnace," "Meet Me in Galilee," "Heaven—a Place of Conditions," "The Lord's Supper," "Amos Pleads for Social Justice."

Despite the many factors operating against them, Negroes in Atlanta do vote. Some few of them vote regularly in general elections, but in order to arouse the group as a whole it is necessary to formulate a grievance. The 1938 bond election is indicative of the kind of action to which Negroes can be aroused when there exists a condition which is intolerable to them. In 1938 the city council decided to float a bond issue of $7,500,000. The money was to be used for the purpose of making improvements in the various city establishments: schools, Grady Hospital, streets, libraries, and so forth. When making plans for the use of the money, the council failed to include a new high school for Negroes or even an addition to the present building. Since overcrowded schools are a feature of Negro life in Atlanta, there has been an almost constant undercurrent of complaint against the city for failing to provide Negroes with additional high school space. Further, many Negroes felt that the group was cheated when the city was permitted to build a Negro high school without either auditorium or cafeteria space. The Atlanta Civic and Political League went into action by calling for a "huge mass meeting." Some eight hundred persons answered the call by attending the meeting. Here it was decided that a committee should be appointed to study the needs of the Negro group. When this committee made its report to the Civic and Political League, it listed a number of school and recreational needs of the group. Using this report as a basis for its requests for a more equitable distribution of the bond money, the league appointed a committee to negotiate with the mayor and city council. When the negotiators failed to reach an agreement, the league formally announced its opposition to the bond issue and began an active campaign to defeat it. When the smoke of battle had cleared, it was evident that the issue had failed to obtain the necessary vote for its passage. Negro voters contributed to the result.

There are two classes of whites in the community who consistently urge Negroes to register and vote. First, there are those who have a very real interest in the spread of democracy and consequently see in the denial of the franchise to Negroes a limitation upon that spread. Second are those who urge Negroes to vote for ulterior motives. Among these are the "lily-white" Republicans who see in a large Negro vote a possible chance for their promotion in the councils of the party. Also in this group are the renegade Democrats. There is open and widespread solicitation (by all parties and persons) of the Negro vote in the case of certain special elections, particularly in bond issues.

Whites make little attempt to obtain white votes by an attack on Negroes during the course of local campaigns. It may be that they do not feel it necessary, or it may be that they feel such an attack would only serve to awaken Negroes to their insignificance in the political plans of the community. But in the campaigns for national and state office the attacks upon Negroes are numerous. Especially is this true when the candidate is addressing himself to rural or semirural audiences. In some such areas it is quite true that a candidate's fitness for office is measured in large part by his hatred for Negroes. Persons who listened to the broadcast speeches of the last senatorial election in which the president sought to "purge" the incumbent, Walter F. George, report that both the New Deal candidate, Lawrence Camp, and Senator George made violent attacks upon Negroes when speaking in rural areas.

Negroes do not exercise any appreciable influence upon the political life of the community. As a consequence, Negro contact with white appointive and elective officials is quite frequently unsatisfactory. Feeling no responsibility to the Negro citizen, these officials generally address a Negro man as "boy," "uncle," or "preacher." When any recognition at all is given, it is usually in the form of "doctor," "professor," or "reverend." Seldom is the word "mister" used. It might be noted here, though, that those officials who call Negroes by their first names in the privacy of their offices generally refer to these same Negroes as "mister" when speaking before a large group of Negroes. Despite the "accommodation attitude" adopted by appointive and elective whites when addressing Negroes, the Atlanta police habitually refer to Negroes as "niggers" and frequently qualify this epithet by the use of the most opprobrious terms. Theirs appears to be the lowest type of police mentality. Among them is a constant and implied threat of the use of violence when accosting a Negro. That they openly insult both Negro men and women can be observed at any time that one watches the flow of downtown traffic and hears a policeman bellow: "All right, girl, move on"; "Come on, boy, what're you waiting for?" In 1936–37 a local radio station was wont to broadcast every afternoon except Saturday the trial of cases in the police court presided over by recorder Fred B. Cone. Frequently during the course of these broadcasts from the courtroom one heard the terms "nigger," "black boy," "nigger wench," and so on, used by the recorder and court attendants alike in referring to or addressing Negro defendants. Atlanta still has on its statute books an archaic curfew law under which any person on the streets after midnight without a reasonable excuse is subject to arrest and fine. Because police court fines are added to the department's pension fund, policemen are often overzealous in enforcing certain city ordinances. This has resulted in the arrest and fining of many Negroes who were on the streets after midnight "without reasonable excuse."

No Negroes are currently employed as policemen or firemen by the city of Atlanta, nor does the state employ Negroes in its equivalent of these agencies. The local branch of the NAACP made an effort to have Negroes taken into the police force, but the attempt failed because of "the lack of full support of the move from Negroes." The Interracial Commission is now working on this problem.

The term "radical" as used in the South is synonymous with the epithet "bad nigger." It is applied to anyone who urges the adoption by Negroes of a vigorous attack upon their problems and upon white reaction generally. Within the Negro group itself there are few persons so dubbed, and those so designated are classified according to their religious, rather than any political or social philosophy. There have been several attempts by radicals, specifically Communists, to work among Negroes in Atlanta. Their activities consisted mainly of the distribution of so-called "subversive literature" and the holding of interracial meetings in which several young white women were present. Such tactics did not gain more than a few adherents, but they served to create a "red scare" promoted by the newspapers—especially the Hearst papers—and by a "red-baiting" chief of police and solicitor general. The activities of the latter culminated in the arrest and conviction of Angelo Herndon under an archaic law governing incitement to insurrection. This action so crippled the party in Atlanta that it has not yet recovered.

There is a cultural pattern within which the Georgia political system operates. Within the framework of this system Negroes in Atlanta are attempting to achieve some degree of status— political, social, and economic. Lacking a cohesive factor (the whites have white supremacy), it is difficult for this group to attain any real unity of action. This hampers the development of organizations which seek to promote civic responsibility among Negroes.

In 1930 Memphis, Tennessee, had a population of 258,340, of whom 156,528 were native white Americans, 96,550 were native Negro Americans, and 5,262 were foreign born. The chamber of commerce estimated in 1939 that the population had increased by 40,000, and gave the total Negro population as 110,000. Because of its strategic location on the boundaries of three states and because of its importance as a railroad center, Memphis has served as a clearing port of Negroes who leave the South for Northern industrial centers. It is important to note that quite a few Negroes who have come into Memphis on their way to Northern cities have cut short their odyssey and settled in the Bluff City.

In 1933 the old police tradition of intimidation of Negroes in Memphis was revived. As Ben Kohn, a prominent white lawyer of Memphis, put it: "The police are very brutal to Negroes here in Memphis. They pick them up without a warrant for their arrest and 'put them on the hook,' that is, charge them with threatened breach of the peace. The boys in the street call this 'putting the breeches on 'em.' " In his report, *People's Rights in Memphis*, Laurent Frantz lists several cases in the Memphis police reign of terror on Negroes during a two-week period, including the following:

On January 3, 1938, Sergeant A. O. Clark of the city police force shot and killed George Brooks, a Negro mail carrier. Police explained that they had set a trap for Brooks because a white woman had complained that he had been annoying her. They let the white woman leave, however, without finding out her name. Sergeant Clark was exonerated by his superiors.

The Memphis *Press-Scimitar* on 23 January 1939 carried two reports of Negro intimidation. According to the first item: "Injuries received while confined in the city jail at Memphis 'contributed' to the death of a Negro insane patient, physicians at Western State Hospital at Bolivar, Tennessee, said today." The second report reads: "Two 26-year old Memphis policemen today faced charges of murdering Philip Hadley, 43, Negro, at 8:45 A.M. yesterday." These young patrolmen had not learned the proper finesse for use in killing Negroes—a method at which older members of the department are expert. This method consists in the police making a report to police officials before the newspapermen, and in claiming that the Negro "resisted arrest."

The Memphis police department is actively engaged in breaking up strikes. City officials ask only one favor from industrialists for their aid in preventing unionization: a cash donation from the industrial plant to the coffers of the local political machine. The real attitude of the Shelby County machine toward organization of workers was shown in the case of the CIO's endeavors to organize the Ford plant in Memphis. The city officers openly sided with company officials in their determination to prevent unionization of the plant's employees. Mayor Watkins Overton led the way when he declared that "imported C.I.O. agitators, Communists, and highly paid professional organizers are not wanted in Memphis. They will not be tolerated." Norman Smith, a CIO organizer, was beaten on the streets of Memphis, and Charles Phillips, a local Ford employee who had been assisting Smith, was also beaten.

It was prophetic that the man who did most to make Beale Street nationally famous deserted Memphis for New York just after the World War. This reference is, of course, to William C. Handy, the author and composer of "The Beale Street Blues." At the time Handy made Beale Street his headquarters it was literally a sea of black faces. There were a few whites doing business on Beale—mostly in hot-dog stands, pawnshops, theaters, and dry good stores. But the main business of Beale Street (gambling joints and red-light houses) was in the hands of Negroes. Things have changed since Handy departed for New York. Beale Street's red-light district is gone (its remains are found on Hernando Street and in scattered innocent-looking houses in the southern part of Memphis). The gambling joints are in the hands of whites who are at the same time precinct captains for Edward H. Crump's political machine. And the few white businesses of old have mushroomed into many white businesses on Beale Street. Negro businesses have shriveled into a few tailoring establishments, barber shops, and district offices of Negro insurance. The Negro banks are gone—those glorious banks that radiated confidence in Negro business enterprise and gave credence to the slogan "Buy Black."

The Negro exposed to the profit economy is also profit-conscious. He, too, is aware of the cash nexus between man and man, and uses race as an added means of selling his product to his black laboring brother. A white attorney of Memphis states:

> In the Negro south Memphis section "Coal Oil" Johnny Laugher, white, controls 3,000 to 5,000 voters, with their poll taxes filed away in his safe. Laugher organizes the underworld in south Memphis to deliver the vote on election day for the machine. For this political activity he receives police protection for his far-flung businesses (rackets). He is also permitted absolute sway over the establishment of commercial enterprises in his territory. . . . It is necessary to get his approval before one can open any kind of small business in "his territory"—the police are at his disposal to enforce his rule over south Memphis; his only obligation being to deliver the vote as ordered by the machine and contribute substantially to the poll-tax-paying slush fund.

Laugher is not an isolated case. There are other whites operating in other Negro neighborhoods in Memphis. The independent black economy of Beale Street has been blacked out by white folks.

In 1919 Robert R. "Bob" Church made a deal with one candidate for mayor whereby the candidate got Church's support in exchange for a promise to appoint six Negroes to the police force. When elected, the candidate did appoint three Negroes to the detective force. One died; the other two were suspended after a run-in with white hoodlums, one of whom was shot in the arm. From that time until now the only connection Negroes have had with the Memphis police force has been Negro heads colliding with nightsticks in the hands of white policemen.

There have never been any Negroes in the Memphis fire department. Only manual labor jobs are open to blacks in the municipal government; Negroes can only be janitors and garbage men. There are some sixteen Negroes employed as public health nurses. And Negro playgrounds give employment to Negro ground-keepers and recreation leaders. The latter are under the general supervision of a white director. Negro teachers enter the Memphis school system at a salary of sixty dollars per month. White teachers begin at one hundred dollars. Soon Negroes will be restricted to laboring jobs so far as federal employment in Memphis is concerned. Well might a prominent Negro businessman wail: "Negroes are not represented here in any of the city or county offices, notwithstanding the fact that we represent 39 percent of the total population, with a potential voting population of some 40,000. . . . The situation here is that you get what Mr. Crump wants you to have, and this holds true for both Negroes and whites."

How do Negroes share in the benefits accruing from taxation? Let us take one example. In the "Budget Expenditures of Memphis Park Commission for Year 1936 and Estimated Expenditures for 1937," we find that the city of Memphis spent a total of $300,752.73 for its parks. Of this amount, $3,272.73 was spent for Negro parks. Negroes are excluded from white parks, except in two cases. Once each year Negroes are allowed the use of the Memphis Fairgrounds for one week for the "Colored Tri-State Fair"; and one day each week (Tuesday) Negroes are allowed to visit the Memphis Zoological Garden between the hours of 10:00 A.M. and 4:00 P.M.

Even the average employed Negro of Memphis is in need of relief. But he does not get it. And the unemployed often whisper about the kickbacks they have to give relief officials for getting relief checks. Many who have been on relief tell bitterly of their experience in having been cut off and sent to do work for some white person at three or four dollars per week. This applies particularly to Negro women. There have been several charges of dishonesty hurled at relief officials in Shelby County, but the Crump political machine has so far withstood successfully all attacks, and none of the charges have been publicly proved even though there have been several dismissals of officials following such charges.

Political power in Memphis rests with the Crump-controlled political machine. Edward H. Crump, or "Mistuh" Crump as he is popularly known, is the boss of all things political in Memphis and Shelby County. Crump allied himself with Beale Street in 1909. This alliance has continued until the present day. When it was first formed, Negro gamblers profited by being given carte blanche to fleece Negroes as they fit. But with the growth of Crump's power he has been able to withdraw this concession. Because of police pressure, Negroes were forced to continue the alliance and to give the gambling privileges to white ward healers. Thus Negroes now give their votes and receive nothing in return. But perhaps it is unfair to say that Negroes receive *nothing* from their political partnership with "Mistuh" Crump. W. P. Adkins, a student of Memphis politics, says:

> The greatest return which the mass of colored voters receive from this position of catspaw in Democratic primary struggles is the comparatively fleeting prestige of participation in the election. More tangible are the rather dubious advantages in connection with the financial outlay for the colored vote (it is generally alleged that Negro votes are purchased for a price ranging from a drink of gin to two dollars), protection for a limited number of police characters, and ephemeral promises of better schools and paved streets.

Only once has Crump's control of Memphis been seriously threatened. That was in the mayoralty election of 1923, when the Ku Klux Klan placed a ticket in the field against Crump's "boy." The Klan attempted to get the Negroes of Memphis to join them in the uprising, but past acts of the Klan were too fresh in the minds of Negro voters to allow them to join the KKK in its fight against Crump. The flaming cross, the hooded night riders, and tar and feathers were seen by Memphis Negroes as worse terrors than police nightsticks and guns. Just as Crump killed the Klan as a political organization in the election of 1923, so has he cracked down on all rival political movements in Memphis which threatened the rule of his political machine.

Like most Southern states, Tennessee requires the payment of poll taxes annually in order for citizens to participate in elections. The Crump machine, by buying up poll tax receipts wholesale, collecting registration receipts, herding Negroes to the polls, and paying for vote-casting at the lowest competitive retail prices—except for those votes which are cast gratis to avoid police brutality—is able to manipulate the Negro vote in the Democratic primary in Shelby County as it sees fit. So long as it continues to do so, its rule is insured. But there is some danger in this method of procedure, as the Loyal Tennesseans League points out in *Edward H. Crump, Public Enemy No. 1:*

But by bringing the vice-controlled and the terrorized section of the Negro group into politics, the Crump machine has
sown dragon's teeth. It is only a matter of time until the Negroes, now comprising almost half of the total registration of
the county, demand representation in the legislature and
county court. Already they are talking such representation at
Orange Mound, a Crump controlled suburb.

But, for the present, "Mistuh" Crump need have no fear of such
a development; the Negro balance of power bows before police
nightsticks, guns, and gin.

Just as Robert R. Church, Sr., was the most important individual developed in the Negro economy, his son, Robert R. "Bob"
Church, Jr., is the most important individual to emerge on the
Negro side of the Memphis political situation. Bob Church was
educated at Oberlin College, and his college training was topped
with "nearly five years as an apprentice in the banking business
on Wall Street." With this background Church entered politics
in 1912, when he successfully campaigned for membership on
the Tennessee Republican delegation to the national convention.
Since 1912 Church has continued as a delegate to national Republican conventions and has steadily grown in political stature,
though his power has waned in recent years.

But Church has had to keep up a running fight to maintain
his position against the attacks of the "lily-white" movement
within the Republican party in Tennessee. That he has been able
to do so is an indication of his political shrewdness. Church is
one of those rare Negro politicians who understands the importance of keeping quiet, remaining outside the limelight, accepting no personal political jobs as pay for political aid, and pulling
political strings from the shadows of the sidelines. This explains
his continued importance in the national councils of the Republican party when men like Ben Davis and Perry Howard have
been disgraced and threatened with political ostracism.

Bob Church has never sought political office. He has been content to remain a representative on the state Republican committee and a delegate to the national Republican convention.
The odd part about the political life of Church is the fact that he
has exercised far more influence on national politics than on
the poltical situation of his home town. This anomaly has been
due to the fact that during the 1920s there was a Republican
national administration, and thus patronage in Tennessee was
placed in the hands of Church, the leader of the GOP forces in

the state. At the same time, Crump's machine was in control of Memphis, and Church—even though he allied himself with Crump—was unable to get more than political crumbs from Crump's political machine. Crump—through his police—has had as much of the Negro vote as he wished to have; thus Church is of little consequence in municipal affairs in Memphis.

There is little to support George W. Lee's contention that "Church's office is the clearing house for the city's distressed. Unfortunate toilers both black and white go there each day to lay their sorrows and disappointments at his feet and implore his help in their fight to rescue themselves from the strangling grip of circumstances."[7] Church may very well have acted as a father confessor. But that has been the limit of his aid. He and his lieutenants, George W. Lee and Dr. J. B. Martin, have been able only to quash traffic tickets and secure a few appointments of Negro teachers, whose tenure is dependent upon the whim of the white superintendent of schools. In 1938 Church opposed in a quiet way Crump's "man" for governor. Church did so because of the increased brutality of Memphis police toward Negroes. As a result, many Negroes stayed away from the polls, and "Mistuh" Crump did not pile up his usual huge majority in Shelby County. But Crump has cracked down on Bob Church. He has had city officials push Church for the payment of overdue taxes on his extensive real estate holdings. Recently Church's real estate was sold to the city for the taxes due— some eighty thousand dollars. Church's last wisp of local political power passed with the sale of his tax-toppled fortune in real estate.

The two men left as leaders in the Republican party in Memphis are Church's lieutenants, Lee and Martin. The latter frankly admits that there is little he can do for Negroes in Memphis, because Crump's machine need do him no favors whatever; it owes him no political debt. It is Lee who perhaps exercises most political power among Negroes in Memphis. He has achieved this position mainly through a glib tongue and the ability to straddle political fences. Lee is a great admirer of Bob Church, yet he has held onto the dubious friendship of Crump even during Crump's political assault on Church. Lee has been able—amidst much fanfare for Lee—to get city officials to build a wooden football stadium for Negroes, to build

7. George W. Lee, *Beale Street: Where the Blues Began* (New York, 1934), pp. 284–85.

two swimming pools for Negroes, and to erect Handy's Park on Beale Street. For all these things he has taken due credit. Yet he recognizes the futility of these small gestures—or else he again illustrates his political wisdom—for in an interview he said:

> For the long-term view, I believe that the Negro problem will be solved by the growth of class consciousness among the Southern white masses. This will remove the necessity of demanding rights on the basis of race or color and will place our struggle on the plane of class interest. The Negro must go out and propagandize the poor whites toward this end.

So far Lee has failed to do any of his proposed propagandizing himself.

It is well to note, too, that Dr. J. B. Martin thinks effective Negro leadership in Memphis will come not from politicians but from progressive labor leaders.

The last of the Negro political leaders in Memphis to be considered is Dr. J. E. Walker, president of the Universal Life Insurance Company and of the National Negro Business League. In 1936 Dr. Walker headed the Negro Shelby County campaign for Roosevelt. He helped to organize the Negro Democratic Club in Memphis and is its chairman. Walker is attempting to gain bargaining power within the local Democratic party (which is, of course, the Crump machine) by organizing the Negroes who vote in the Democratic primary. But Crump already has them organized and has an instrument (the police) to keep them organized and to keep them doing as he pleases. Thus Dr. Walker's efforts are superfluous—which is why Crump allows him to proceed. Walker is far more interested in the development of Negro business than he is in politics. In an interview he stated:

> I believe the development of the race is going to depend much on the Negro's development as a businessman. . . . A race of people who have nothing can't get anything. I think well of Negroes joining the trade unions. Of course, Negroes should vote, and their voting will be most effective when their leaders stop accepting pay for delivering the vote and demand equal justice instead.

Beaten into submission by police nightsticks and guns, the Negroes of Memphis are in a terrible predicament. But they have their religion. In Memphis there are 375 churches, of which 213 are for Negroes. How are these churches aiding Negroes in solving the vexing social, economic, and political problems facing them today? An indication of what the churches have been doing may be found in T. O. Fuller's *The Story of the Church Life Among Negroes in Memphis, Tennessee:*

> Long years ago, the people of the South learned that religion had a quieting and soothing effect upon the mind of the Negro. They discovered in the Negro a deep consciousness as to the existence of a God. Religion seemed to give to the Negro a mysterious idea of the supernatural. The Holy Ghost was to him the invisible presence of God hovering over and around him that was available in times of great distress and need. With this in mind the South encouraged the Negro in his religious activities more than in any other way.

The Negro preachers of Memphis as a whole have avoided social questions. They have preached thunder and lightning, fire and brimstone, and Moses out of the bulrushes, but about the economic and political exploitation of local blacks they have remained silent.

In January 1936 the local secretary of the Workers' Alliance, William A. Mardis, was arrested and held in jail for a day and a half because he committed the offense of "calling niggers 'mister.'" That such a thing should have occurred is indicative either of the total absence of a liberal group in Memphis or of the presence of nonvocal progressives. J. R. Butler, the president of the Southern Tenant Farmers' Union, has declared:

> One could not begin to recite the instances of thuggery imposed upon honest labor leaders by the Crump machine. Smith, the first CIO organizer who came here a couple of years ago to organize Firestone Tires Company, was bloodily and brutally beaten on several occasions—after two weeks they ran him out of town. Franz came here two years ago [that is, in 1937] to make an investigation of civil liberties in Memphis and was beaten and run out of town in short order.

Nebraska Jones, secretary of the Community Welfare League, organized the "Independent Craftsmen Association" after failing to gain admission for Negroes to AFL craft unions. The Independent Craftsmen Association tried to get Negro workers hired on slum clearance projects and PWA construction jobs. Jones was called in by the commissioner of police for questioning on suspicion of being a Communist. Jones says:

"Our organization never became more than a threat and an instrument for the purpose of putting pressure upon the A.F. of L. to take in the Negro mechanics into the respective craft unions. The red scare that was raised against us pretty nearly dispersed our group."

Finally there was the case of Tom Watkins, a Negro organizer for the International Longshoremen's Association. Watkins was able to organize the longshoremen in Memphis and to lead a strike for an increase in pay. At this point Memphis police decided he had become too dangerous. He was arrested by three officers, one of whom was the experienced Negro-beater, A. O. Clark, and taken down to the wharf and severely beaten. Watkins broke away and escaped under gunfire. He left Memphis and went to St. Louis. Miss Marie Waltham, a white newspaperwoman of Memphis, has said: "They tried to kill Tom Watkins. . . . They will kill him if he comes back and tries to organize the poor people to struggle for a life with human dignity. . . . They will kill all the new Tom Watkins. . . . The people must stop this thing." Attorney Booth, the oldest Negro lawyer in Shelby County, told us:

> Race conditions and prejudice here is much worse now for the professional Negro. I think it dates back to Booker T. Washington's speech about not educating the minds but educating the hands. This famous speech tremendously impressed the local whites and established a stereotype of what the Negro should be allowed to do.

James Jackson, Negro field worker for this study, was hauled down to police headquarters in Memphis in December 1939 for his temerity in attempting to interview Joe Kirsky, one of Crump's Beale Street lieutenants. Jackson, fearing a personal experience with Crump's police methods of handling obstreperous Negroes, took advantage of an opportunity to flee and got out of town.

FIFTEEN

Negro Voting in
AAA Cotton Referenda

THOSE who are eligible to vote in the cotton marketing quota referenda include farmers who were engaged in the production of cotton in 1938 as owner-operators, cash tenants, standing-rent or fixed-rent tenants, share-tenants, or sharecroppers. The regulations provide that no cotton farmer—whether an individual, partnership, corporation, firm, association, or other legal entity—shall be entitled to more than one vote in the referendum even though he may have been engaged in 1938 in the production of cotton in two or more communities, counties, or states. Voting by mail, proxy, or agent is not permitted, but a duly authorized officer of a corporation or other legal entity may cast his vote. In case several persons, such as husband, wife, and children, participated in the production of cotton in 1938 under the same rental or cropping agreement or lease, only the person or persons who signed or entered into the agreement or lease shall be eligible to vote. In the event that two or more persons engaged in producing cotton in 1938, not as members of a partnership, but as tenants in common or joint tenants or as owners of community property, each is entitled to vote.

It should be noted that anyone having an interest in the cotton crop is permitted to vote in these elections and that this includes sharecroppers and tenant farmers. For example, in Bolivar County, Mississippi, there are about 11,000 producers, of whom some 9,000 are Negro and 2,000 are white. In that county 9,000 votes were cast in the November 1938 referendum, and only some 20 of these votes were in the negative. I. W. Duggan, the director of the Southern division of the Agricultural Adjustment

Administration, asserts that there has been no significant white opposition to Negro participation in these elections. He adds further that there are no reported instances of any attempt on the part of white owners to coerce Negro tenants or croppers in voting against the quotas, though he is willing to admit that there have probably been some unreported instances. It is his belief that any such effort is quite unlikely on any broad scale since, on the whole, the majority of the owners are in favor of control. Moreover, there is an agency in the AAA for the purpose of prosecuting any irregularity, and the landowners would be taking a great risk. Rather whimsically, Duggan remarked that there would be greater likelihood that the white landowner would try to coerce both Negro and white farmers to vote *for* the control.

There is no evidence of any direct political attack on the cotton control program because of the equal Negro participation in the referenda. It may be significant that Senator "Cotton Ed" Smith of South Carolina did not oppose the program, despite the fact that it permitted Negro participation in the elections. It is said, however, that in Senator Smith's last campaign a printed pamphlet was circulated by a group that opposed him, asking him why he voted for a bill which permitted Negroes to vote on an equal basis with white men. Apparently Smith never made any effort to answer this question and did not raise the issue in his campaign.

The most essential factor in the conduct of the AAA cotton control program is the educational work. The purpose of this work is to sell the idea of crop and market control to the farmer, and an elaborate setup exists for this purpose. In the nine Southern cotton states there are about four hundred Negro county agricultural and home demonstration agents, and it is through them that the educational program is conducted. There are three Negro employees of the Southern division of the AAA: A. L. Holsey, James T. Davis, and Mrs. Robert R. Moton. Davis is the head field worker for the Southern division of the AAA. Holsey and Mrs. Moton are field officers. Holsey is also a publicity agent.

In carrying on the educational work, meetings of the male and female county agents are held in each of the land grant colleges in January and February of each year. These agents are given three days of training in order to acquaint them with the details of the program. Then each county agent goes back to his county, and three or four sectional meetings are called in each state at strategic points. The county agents bring three or four "key" farmers from their districts to these meetings, and one day's training on the benefits of the program is given to them. The agents then return to their districts with these key farmers as aids and hold meetings to explain the program to all of the farmers. The vocational agricultural teachers are also employed in this educational work. Male and female agents receive the same training. The Washington headquarters also sends one or more office representatives to the annual meetings of the Jeanes School supervisors, and the purpose of the program is explained to them.

E. A. Miller, the assistant to the director of the Southern division of the AAA, insists that the problem is being approached from the standpoint of the economic interest of the South and that, while there may be some slight maladjustments and mild injustices, the program is generally carried out without regard to race. He emphasizes that there has been a complete lack of political purpose with regard to the Negro appointments in the division. "We think we understand each other," he observes.[1]

A two-thirds majority of the producers is necessary to confirm a marketing quota. The figures on recent referenda indicate that the quota referenda in the Southern states draw larger proportionate votes than do the political elections. Table 2 indicates the extent of participation by Negro operators in the cotton referendum of December 1938. This table was prepared by James T. Davis and submitted to me on 21 October 1939 from Little Rock, Arkansas.

We are told that the Negro churches and life insurance companies in the South have given excellent support to the cotton control program. Our informants say that the Negro minister still remains the most important influence in the county, and that "we must have him on our side."

The assistant director of the Southern division is the typical paternalistic, kindly, "confidential" type of white Southerner, extremely courteous and friendly, constantly expressing his feelings on the race question, and stating that it is nonsense that Negroes and whites in the South "do not love each other." He tells how he has addressed Negro groups in New York and informed them that he is from Alabama. On such occasions he asks how many in the group are from Alabama or other Southern states. He counts the hands that are raised and then tells

1. Duggan and Miller were interviewed in Washington, D.C., on 21 September 1939. The Bunche memorandum does not identify the interviewer. —ED.

TABLE 2. COTTON CONTROL PROGRAM:
COTTON REFERENDUM OF DECEMBER 1938

State	County	Negro farmers	White farmers	Votes for referendum	Negro illiteracy percentage
Alabama	Baldwin	437	2,261	534	
	Blount	106	4,606	2,649	26.2
	Dallas	6,146	783	3,801	
	Wilcox	3,716	763	3,431	
Arkansas	Baxter	0	1,512	143	16.1
	Boone	0	2,085	22	
	Jefferson	5,925	1,712	3,634	
	St. Francis	4,574	1,784	3,785	
Florida	Jackson	1,156	2,371	949	18.8
	Leon	1,311	356	625	
	Suwannee	482	1,382	267	
	Washington	188	1,016	163	
Georgia	Appling	170	1,224	482	19.9
	Brantley	50	718	17	
	Sumter	1,369	812	860	
	Taliaferro	674	365	512	
Louisiana	Allen Parish	178	1,107	346	23.3
	Caddo	5,552	1,410	2,889	
	DeSoto	3,162	1,352	3,077	
	Lafourche	54	1,142	6	
Mississippi	Bolivar	10,309	1,959	8,179	23.2
	Forrest	229	956	392	
	Harrison	84	1,095	25	
	Leflore	6,942	888	3,231	
Oklahoma	Bryan	249	3,888	884	9.3
	Leflore	288	469	692	
	Okfuskee	1,181	2,339	927	
	Okmulgee	1,330	2,204	796	
South Carolina	Beaufort	2,048	271	1,575	26.9
	Berkeley	2,233	875	1,206	
	Greenville	1,739	5,810	2,421	
	Horry	1,162	5,177	528	
Texas	Harrison	4,757	1,992	3,893	13.4
	Limestone	933	3,630	1,786	
	Live Oak	2	1,148	330	
	Lubbock	25	2,629	1,158	
	Marion	1,027	571	924	

them that while he does not know how long they have been "up North," he knows that they feel that they did not get all that was due them down South. But he declares that things down there are getting better every day, that deep down in their hearts he knows they "still love Dixie," and that he is sure that will some day return to their first love. In his estimation, the trouble in the South results from the fact that there are "two small minority groups"—one in the white and one in the Negro race—which stir up all the trouble, and that if this were not the case, people would get along together down there. He speaks with pride of the large number of Negro schools in the South, contends that a majority of white Southerners are interested in seeing the Negro gets a fair break, and cites the fact that counties in the South advance tax money to aid in support of county agencies, to aid in the support of schools, and so on. He is proud of the fact that men like himself and his chief, Duggan, come from poor classes in the South and that they are approaching the region's problems realistically. There can be no doubt that Miller and Duggan are very much elated at the fine support given their program by the Negro producers in the cotton states and that they will bitterly oppose every effort to disfranchise the Negro in these cotton elections.

No intensive survey of Negro participation in these referenda has been undertaken. But the field workers, especially George Stoney, picked up some more-or-less incidental information concerning such participation in selected counties in certain states, and this is summarized in the following pages. It will be seen that, while Negroes have been permitted to vote without serious opposition in the referenda, they seldom serve as committeemen and often are not permitted to, or for reasons of "tact" do not, vote for committeemen.

Negroes in Bibb County, Alabama, take a great deal of interest in the cotton elections. Of the total number of contract holders (those eligible to vote) in the county, 22 percent are Negro and 78 percent are white. Of the total number of voters, it is estimated that 35 percent are Negro and 65 percent are white. It is further estimated that 85 percent of the Negro contract holders vote. The county agent suggests that Negroes take so much interest in these elections because voting is such a strange and "special" privilege for them. Although some of the communities have a majority of Negro voters, none have black committeemen, and the explanation is that the white farmers would not tolerate it. The percentage of farmers voting in the cotton elections is low "because they know it is going to pass anyway."[2] The results of the elections in Bibb County for the past three years are as follows:

Year	Yes	No	Challenged	Total
1938	1,641	58	6	1,705
1939	1,106	177	0	1,283
1940	1,139	58	2	1,199

2. George Stoney's interview with T. P. Lee, the county agent, Bibb County, Alabama, March 1940. The material that follows comes from Stoney's notes of field interviews conducted in 1940. —ED.

An independent Negro farmer near Notasulga in Macon County, Alabama, states that though Negroes are free to vote in the cotton elections, he does not think this amounts to a great deal. He and one other Negro were appointed by the Negro county agent to assist in holding the last elections at Notasulga. When they got there, they found that the whites had already set things up and ignored them. He and the other man, sensing the situation, voted and left. He commented: "nobody paid no attention and nobody's ever said anything about it."

At the time of the last cotton election in Macon County, the Negro county agent appointed several blacks to serve as officers of election. Few of them got to serve, however, because they were "frozen out." The Negro county agent did serve along with the white agent at the courthouse where the biggest voting took place. There are no community or county committeemen in the program who are Negroes. This is because all nominations are made through the office of the white agent. Nominations can be made from the floor. It would be "awkward," however, and there would be an "open break" which might "cause trouble" if Negro nominations were thus made. Negroes do attend the meetings at which the committeemen are selected, but not a great many of them come, because no general invitation is sent to them. Those who do come vote. There has been no trouble thus far about Negro participation in these cotton elections. This is probably because the landlords know that they must have a majority vote to continue the program which they favor.

The Negro manager of a resettlement project at Tuskegee, Alabama, thinks that the "triple A" elections are serving a very useful purpose for Negroes. In the first place, it is familiarizing Negroes on the plantations with reading and writing and with written contracts. It is bringing them some knowledge of their government and giving them practice in voting.

In Coffee County, Alabama, the cotton elections occasion little interest. There is the feeling that the program will be approved without the need for "one more vote." The larger number of "no" votes recorded in this county than in the black belt counties is said to result from the larger number of whites and independent voters. Negroes who farm vote in the cotton elections, but "they don't say much about it." There seems to be no opposition to their participation, however, though they rarely attend meetings.

In Lee County, Alabama, Negroes take greater interest in the cotton elections than do the whites. Over 60 percent of the Negro contract signers vote, while less than 40 percent of the whites do so. There are no Negro committeemen, however, although they comprise about 72 percent of the contract holders. The county agent explained this by stating: "If we had, it would mean a nigger'd be working on a white man's work sheet and he'd have to sit down with that nigger across the table. People wouldn't stand for that." Incidentally, this agent is reputed to have done more for the welfare of his Negro clients than any other agent in the state. Several dozen of the Negro clients are buying small farms from the Federal Land Bank at less cost than they could rent a shack in Auburn or Opelika.

In connection with the AAA elections in Alabama, every Negro agent is instructed to call meetings of his contract signers and explain to them what the election means. The white agent is supposed to be present, but it is to be the Negro agent's meeting. It has been said that few black agents can get a good turnout unless the letters are sent out over the name of the white agent. On the other hand, experience has proven that few white agents can explain the program so that Negroes can understand it.

The experience of voting and participating in the elections has been of considerable value to Negroes because it has made them aware of the fact that they are "independent farmers," that they are not inevitably tied to one or another landlord. On the other hand, it has made the whites aware of the fact that the Negroes have "a few more rights. . . . It hasn't been so long since a lot of these big farmers in Alabama thought what mattered to a nigger, didn't matter." The supervisor of Negro work at the agricultural experiment station at Auburn states that to his knowledge there has never been any friction between the races at the polls in these elections. A few complaints have been made about the participation of Negroes, but these have come from "a few fanatics who are always scared the nigger is going to get into power politically." All of these complaints, however, have been outside of the farming field.

The percentage of Negro contract signers voting has been consistently higher than that of whites. Also the counties with the heaviest Negro majorities always have the smallest percentages of opposition votes in Alabama. The only county where there are Negro committeemen in the AAA program in Alabama is Hale County. In that county three Negroes serve as committeemen, representing three separate communities. No Negroes are on the main county committee, however. These committeemen work on the contracts of Negroes only. In all of the other counties the agents either do not call the Negroes to meetings where committeemen are elected, or only whites have been nominated.

About Negro participation in the cotton elections in Marengo County, Alabama, an officer of elections says: "Yes, they vote, but they don't know what it's all about, and we take care that they don't. They vote like we say. The niggers are 17 to 1 in this part of the county, so we don't fool with them." The editor of the Greene County *Democrat* is much disturbed about the Negro participation in the cotton elections. He notes that the rules require that Negroes vote and, therefore, the landlords are forced to resort to the old methods to "get by": "I see them riding them into town in trucks and voting them like cattle. They vote as they're told." He admitted that most of these Negroes would probably vote for the program anyway because of the checks.

Out of approximately 4,300 people eligible to vote in the cotton elections in Etowah County, Alabama, 3,060 voted favorably in the March 1938 election; 2,212 in the December 1938 election; and only 1,565 in the December 1939 election. There were, however, only 217 negative votes in March 1938, 404 in December 1938, and 218 in December 1939. The county agent explains that the main reason for the decrease in the vote and the apparent decline in interest in these elections is the fact that "a fellow will go to a helluva lot of trouble to vote agin something, but he won't bother much about voting for it, especially when he knows everybody else will." Interest in the program was great when it was first instituted. The few Negroes who have farms in Etowah County take considerable interest in the elections. The county agent feels that a much larger percentage of black farmers participate in the cotton elections than whites, due to the fact that "it's the only election they get to take part in."

Of the 1,721 farm families in Greene County, Georgia, about 60 percent are Negro and about 50 percent are tenants. There are 1,321 cotton contracts with 1,700 odd signers. Out of this number about 1,300 vote in the cotton elections. At the last cotton election the "no" vote totaled only 89. Negroes vote freely and in large numbers. According to the county agent: "They look forward to it. . . . I don't think half of them know what they're voting about." Some four hundred people attend the community meetings at which committeemen are selected. Since there is a large tenant purchase program and this group also has Farm Security Administration duties, the election is more important here than in many places. Negroes attend these meetings, though they are not invited directly. Nominations are made from the floor, and Negroes vote. In response to the question as to whether there are Negro committeemen, the county agent replied: "You know that would never do in the world in this part of the country." There has been no objection to Negro voting in these elections since the little opposition at the beginning. The county agent explains that this early opposition was quickly quieted when he explained the full program to the whites.

Although there are very few Negro farmers in Hall County, Georgia, these few participate freely in the cotton elections and both attend and vote at the meetings where committeemen are elected. There was considerable opposition to this on the first vote, according to the county agent, but he states that he had to be firm and told the white farmers that the election would not be legal if the black farmers were left out. He also assured them that they had very little to worry about with so few Negro farmers in the county.

According to the county agent of Macon County, Georgia, Negroes take the most interest in the elections "because they don't have any other election to go to." The same thing applies to the elections for committeemen. All of the committeemen in the county are white. They are nominated from the floor. At the Cotton Valley meeting last year there was only one white man present. He was elected the committeeman. The county agent that the Negro farmers present could have nominated a Negro, but he deemed it best that they not do so, because the white people in the county would have become angry, and it would have made it hard for the county agent to get their cooperation.

In Putnam County, Georgia, there are 635 contract work sheets for cotton allotments and about 1,000 individual signers. Of these, only 302 cast votes at the last cotton election, 12 of which were "no." The reason for the small vote is that the people in the county have been discouraged. The allotments were made when the county was at its lowest production level and the farmers have not been able to increase their allotments. Thus, the program has been unfair to this county in this respect. Over two-thirds of the work sheets are filled out by Negroes, and approximately 70 percent of those eligible to vote in these elections are Negro. But there are no Negro committeemen, though the county agent states that there could be, since all committeemen are nominated from the floor. He cites, for instance, a case of a few months ago at one community meeting where everyone present except one person was a Negro. The Negroes nominated this one white man and elected him as committeeman. The county agent believes that Negroes take more interest than whites in the program and in the elections.

In Burke County, Georgia, about 2,400 work sheets have been signed for cotton this past year and perhaps a third more people are eligible to vote in the cotton election. The total vote for these elections in 1938 was 1,654 "yes," 52 "no"; for 1939 it was 1,482 "yes," 17 "no." According to the county agent, Negroes are "anxious" to take part in these elections. They also vote for committeemen. Often, he states, Negroes have made nominations, but no Negro has ever been nominated. All of the committeemen are white. Meetings have always been joint—black and white—with the two races sitting on opposite sides of the courthouse auditorium. The Negro county agents come to the meetings and speak. In several sections of the county where the population is almost 100 percent Negro, the meetings turn out to be all Negro, although this is not prearranged. There has been no protest made about this Negro participation. The reason for this is because no separate start was made.

In Beaufort County, South Carolina, Negroes serve as cotton committeemen. One Negro has been elected as committeeman in the Beaufort district, two alternative committeemen have been elected from another district, and all three of the committeemen from the St. Helena and Lady's Island community are Negroes. But the assistant county agent explained apologetically that "I use them as little as I possibly can," and that this has "happened" because the Negroes were so much in the majority at the meetings and had nominated their own members as well as the whites.

Although the whites in Saluda County, South Carolina, resent any attempt by Negroes to vote in political elections, blacks vote freely in the cotton elections. There were some complaints from the whites at first, but according to one prominent Negro in the community: "When they found out Daddy Sam say do that, they didn't try any mess up." While the cotton elections in Saluda County are thought to have had little or no effect on the white political vote, the feeling is that it has caused Negroes to begin "getting restless." As the clerk of court for the county puts it: "Sure. They all vote in that. They think it's big. Nine out of ten don't know what the hell they're voting for."

No attempt is made here to appraise the cotton control program itself in terms of Negro or white interest. Suffice it to say that Negro cotton producers, either independently, by the "educational" propaganda carried on by government agents, or by direction from white landowners, overwhelmingly support the program in the referenda. This is significant in many ways. Not the least significant is the experience in voting practice obtained by Negroes in these elections and the fact that whites are not horrified into repressive action at the sight of large numbers of Negroes casting ballots at the referenda polling booths. Moreover, the Negro who participates in these elections must inevitably develop a new perspective—he finds himself for the first time cast in an active role as a citizen in a democracy; he is permitted, even urged, to express his will on a matter of important government policy, with the knowledge that his vote will influence public policy as it relates to his own interest.

There is, of course, one other aspect of this process that cannot be ignored. The landowner is undoubtedly often able to direct the tractable Negro to vote in accordance with the wishes of the landlord. The protective machinery of the AAA is not effective enough to prevent this. But more important still, perhaps, is the fact that the government bureaucracy is able to employ this same tractable Negro vote to assure acceptance of its program. I suspect, however, that virtually the same situation prevails with regard to the poor and often illiterate white cotton farmer.

SIXTEEN

Some Notes on Republican Politics in the South

IN 1938 former Republican chairman John D. M. Hamilton made a strong bid for the anti–New Deal Democratic vote in the South. In a speech before the Alabama state Republican convention in Birmingham, he characterized the Republican party as the "only organized champion of Jeffersonian philosophy," and he proposed a union of "rural Democrats" and Republicans. Hamilton's arrival in Birmingham marked the first time a Republican national chairman had ever come to Alabama to drum up votes. There was, asserted Hamilton, "no insurmountable barrier between the real Democrats of the South and the Republican party," for "today we are speaking a common language with many Southerners."[1] Hamilton's visit, which admittedly was made to pep up and help revitalize the Republican party in Alabama, was hailed by Southern Republican leaders as the first step in a new drive to end the South's solid support of the Democratic party.

It is not without significance that the Willkie campaign is now beating drums all through the South. The chief forces now in evidence in support of the Willkie campaign are the Georgia and Alabama Power companies (subsidiaries of Commonwealth and Southern), the Duke Power Company (North and South Carolina), and various Northern concerns with offices in the South. In Alabama the combine has employed its old lobbyist and political handywoman, Mabel Jones West, to head up the campaign. This lady politico and ex-Klan member formed the League for White Supremacy in Alabama in 1928 to defeat the Republicans. She is now leading Willkie's fight. On 24 July 1940

1. Washington *Evening Star,* 25 June 1940.

Mrs. West took to the air for an hour on a seven-station hookup to get the Willkie campaign in Alabama off with a bang. Two of her lieutenants made appropriate speeches for Willkie; and a number of the women members of her Alabama Women's Democratic Clubs, Incorporated, and her Alabama Women's League for White Supremacy had their say about third terms. Her organization has pledged itself to support Willkie as a *Democrat* against Roosevelt, who is labeled a socialistic, third-term dictator. With Mrs. West at the head, the campaign will, of course, be strictly lily-white. Undoubtedly, with the lily whites in control in Georgia, Alabama, North Carolina, South Carolina, and Virginia, the Republican campaign throughout the South will be a lily-white campaign.

The Republican party liquidated itself as a serious factor in Virginia politics in 1920, when it did away with the Republican primary in the state and instituted the convention system, refusing to seat its Negro delegates to the convention. By thus adopting a policy of lily-whiteism, the Republican party abandoned its main source of strength. This action of the Virginia Republicans was led by Colonel Henry W. Anderson. In the 1921 gubernatorial campaign in Virginia, Anderson declared that the Republican party despised the Negro and did not want his vote. When the Republicans refused to seat Negro delegates to the district convention in 1920, the Negroes walked out and held a rump convention at which they selected a full slate. In this campaign, under the banner of the Republican party, with Lincoln's picture at the masthead, Negroes polled some 15,000 votes for governor of Virginia—12,000 more than did the white Republicans. This was the final significant effort of Virginia Negroes under the Republican banner in state and local politics.

Thus the elections of 1921 signaled the end of the two-party system in Virginia. The political liberties of Virginia Negroes would henceforth be in eclipse until they could participate as Democrats. They had been repudiated by "their own" party, and the doors of the Democratic party were also closed to them, since Negroes were excluded from the Democratic primary. It became imperative for Negroes to win the right to vote in the Democratic primary if they were to entertain the hope of casting an effective vote. This was achieved only after a long court fight. Following this victory in 1930, Negro political activity in Virginia was focused upon support of "good" Democrats. The Negro thus began a policy of "boring from within" the Democratic party.

The Republican party in North Carolina pursued a similar course. It is alleged that the North Carolina mountain counties, though traditionally Republican in politics, are yet more intolerant toward Negroes than the Democrats in South Carolina or people elsewhere in North Carolina.

Republican politics in South Carolina are divided between two continually contesting factions—the Tolbert forces and the anti-Tolbert or Hambright faction established in 1930. The Hambright group has been labeled the "lily-white" faction. At the national Republican convention in 1932, however, the Hambright faction, including a number of Negro alternate delegates, was seated, since it was sponsored by President Hoover and other leading Republicans. In 1936 the Tolbert group was recognized because Northern Negroes were convinced that J. C. Hambright was a lily white despite the window dressing of alternate Negro delegates. Since 1936, both factions have been busy organizing for the 1940 convention.

"Tieless" Joe Tolbert is often referred to as "a carpetbagger Republican" in South Carolina. He assumed control of the Republican organization in South Carolina in the 1890s. Because he has been content to work chiefly with Negroes, the Republican party in the state has always been known as the "Negro party." It is charged that Tolbert never really tried to build up a Republican party in South Carolina and that before each convention he would organize a delegation, take it to the national convention, and "sell it to the highest bidder."[2] One Republican leader, Mrs. Messervy, stated with elation, after referring to the vastly exaggerated news accounts which asserted that 30,000 South Carolina Negroes had voted in 1936 for Roosevelt: "The Democratic party is the Negro party, now." Admitting that the members of her (Hambright) faction could never get seated at the Republican convention if they were clearly established as "lily-whites," she gave her "private opinion" of Negro political participation in the state as follows: "Negroes are going to be citizens. They are here. We can't get rid of them. They are getting education. They have got to be taken into one party or the other or they are going to be a fertile field for the Communists. . . . No, I don't try to keep the Negroes from voting."

Mrs. Messervy had a petition which she claimed had been

2. George Stoney's interview with Mrs. Messervy, a member of the Hambright faction, Charleston, South Carolina, June 1940. The interviews in this chapter, unless otherwise noted, were conducted by Stoney in 1940. —Ed.

brought to her by thirty Negro preachers and signed by 1,500 Negro laymen, petitioning the national Republican convention to seat her faction. They are "ashamed of Tolbert," claiming that they want to belong to some political party, but that they cannot conscientiously belong to the Democratic party. Yet Mrs. Messervy admitted that she "would try to organize a lily-white party if I could, because this is the biggest handicap we have to overcome. But we have got to overcome this prejudice. What we really need is two white parties in this state." These two parties, as she visualizes them, would be composed of the New Dealers on the one hand and the Republicans and anti–New Deal Democrats on the other. It should be noted that the anti–Tolbert faction, with which Mrs. Messervy is identified, triumphed over the Tolbert forces at the recent Republican convention in Philadelphia and was seated. It should be noted also that the Hambright delegation included Negroes.

A white Republican leader of Sumter contended that neither he nor the Hambright faction is lily-white. The week before the Republican convention in Philadelphia, he was able to aver that:

> Right now, we have four niggers in Philadelphia. In 1932 we had such a good bunch of niggers up there, they took up with the ones from Pennsylvania and Ohio, who helped us get recognized. . . . Herbert Hoover and Taft sponsored our delegation mostly on account of them. . . . I tell you what we did. We went out here to the college and got the best-educated one we could find. . . . We got the best-known nigger preacher in the state. . . . etc.

These Negroes were quite probably alternate delegates. This Republican went on to point out that in 1936 his group went to the convention again with Negro delegates and that they were not recognized because their leader "got on the wrong bandwagon." He anticipated, however, that in 1940 they had a good chance to get seated because they had an even more impressive Negro delegation. This turned out to be correct. Continuing, he observed:

> We never have been lily-white. We treat niggers like Southerners ought to, that's all. We give them everything they are entitled to under the franchise, but we don't play up to them like Tolbert does. Hell! He goes around kissing their feet. All he does is work up a delegation so he can take it to the convention and sell it. I don't know how the national committee has stood him as they have.

A Missourian, this gentleman was "shocked" at the conditions prevailing in the general elections of South Carolina. There is no secret ballot, he complains: "We have to print our ballots. They have to be exactly legal size. . . . We have to physically take them around to every polling place and put them on the tables so they don't get out. . . . And then we have to put somebody there to watch them or we'll find them in the trash can the next minute." In contrast, he added, the Democratic tickets are sent out in the boxes. In this man's estimation, however, the worst feature of the South Carolina situation—from the Republican standpoint—is the "coercion." He told about how people are humiliated when they ask for a Republican ticket. Businessmen, he said, are

> ashamed to go in and pick one up. They know they'll get kidded all around town. . . . I'm not a Socialist, understand. I'm against everything they stand for, but, just the same, I think they ought to get a fair chance, too. A girl here in town —it was in 1932, I think—she voted the Socialist ticket. In an hour, it was all up and down the street. People wouldn't let her get away from that for years.

He thinks that if there was a secret ballot in South Carolina the Republicans could put a "big dent" in the Democratic majority. Support for this, he believes, would come chiefly from the anti–New Deal businessmen. This man denied that one is able to split his ticket in elections in Sumter, unless he gets a blank piece of paper just the legal size of the ballot and writes out the full ticket, spelling all names correctly, and so forth. Otherwise the ballot will be thrown out, he says.

Only twice in the past eleven years have Republicans served as election officials at Sumter, and on each of these occasions they were appointed by a friend as a "personal favor" rather than as a recognition of their right. The above informant claimed that Republicans in South Carolina do try to get Negroes to register. In former times, he said, they would have trouble with the registration board, that is, "back before 1936 when the Democrats started getting them to vote for Roosevelt." He stated that the Democrats voted five hundred Negroes for Roosevelt in the town of Sumter and that now Negroes have no trouble registering there. The main support for the anti–Tolbert Republicans in Sumter does not come from Negroes, but from the business people who have moved in from out of the state. The state is getting more and more of these people, many of whom are "solid Republicans." This man pointed out that with all of these old-time

Republicans and "the amount of foreign capital they bring in," the Republicans in South Carolina could "go places." He feels that the two obstacles to the progress of the Republican party in South Carolina are Joe Tolbert and the lack of a secret ballot. He contends that none of the "real" Sumter Republicans vote in the Democratic primary for county and state offices, though they do so in the city primary because "that isn't really a primary. It's just a white man's election." Several Republicans are, in fact, active in the organization.

There are two small but lively rival Republican factions in Sumter, but there seems to be no local feeling against the white Republicans insofar as city politics is concerned. One of their leaders was elected to the city council in the Democratic primary. This was because "everybody liked him" and his party affiliation made no difference to the voting population.

Ordinarily, Charleston Negroes support the Republican party, but with the Hoover "purist movement" of 1932 a good many of the habitual Negro Republican voters became alienated from the party and the Roosevelt reforms attracted a large number of them over to the Democratic camp. An elderly Negro Republican has related his experience in 1928 when the Hambright faction was first asserting its lily-white policy:

> Hambright had a meeting here in Hibernian Hall. Although I wuzn't invited, being as I was a Republican, I picked up and went. When I got there, the group said, "We don't want no nigger in this meeting." And I said, "Let me go and sit on that stove yonder and burn and die, for I've been a Republican all my life—never voted for no other party. En'n you don' want me, let me die. Let me get on that stove and die."[3]

This man believes that if the anti–Tolbert forces, who have employed a few Negroes to cover up the fact that they are lily-white, were to be recognized by the Republican convention in Philadelphia—as they were—then "the 'nigger' is a gone baby in South Carolina politics. In 1876 Wade Hampton put red shirts on niggers and said just help us get rid of carpetbaggers this once—after that he and they didn't need the nigger no mo'!"

The rank and file of Republicans in Charleston County— that is, the white Republicans—vote in the Democratic county and state primaries, and they have continued to do this despite

3. Wilhelmina Jackson's interview with Peter Bennett, Charleston, South Carolina, 11 April 1940.

rule 32 of the Democratic party, which bound participants in any South Carolina Democratic primary to support the nominees of the party for local, state, and national offices. Commenting on the 1932 presidential election returns in Charleston, the editor of the Charleston *News and Courier* wrote in that newspaper on 9 November 1932:

> The Republican vote, in the opinion of local political observers, represented a negro protest against the reorganization of the Republican Party which, until two years ago, had been almost entirely negro "controlled by 'tieless' Joe Tolbert". . . . Majority of negroes in Charleston County who are registered stayed away from the polls and of the few who did go, the majority voted the Democratic ticket. This, they did in the open, . . . going to the polls and requesting the Democratic ticket.

Some local observers believe that, if they could obtain unity, Charleston Republicans might become a powerful factor in South Carolina politics. At present they could capitalize on the strong anti–New Deal feeling among an influential group of South Carolinians. The Tolbert faction cannot get very far because of the disgraceful character of its leadership, while the anti–Tolbert faction cannot establish itself because it does not command Negro support.

The recent modification of rule 32 of the Democratic party of South Carolina is regarded by many as a factor which will be helpful to the development of a strong Republican organization in the state. Many old-line Democrats in South Carolina feel that the fight to get rule 32 changed was all a part of a Republican plot. One old-timer in Pickens declared that, as a delegate to the state Democratic convention, he watched George Norwood, who is now a Republican leader but was formerly a state Democratic convention delegate, work around to get rule 32 changed. He states that Norwood did it so that Republicans could vote in the Democratic primary, where they have no business, and, in his estimation, Norwood is no better than Tolbert.

> He's up there in Philadelphia right now with a tribe of niggers. It says right here in the papers that he's got enough to lend Tolbert a few. . . . He's up there selling those niggers like Tolbert has done since 1892. You know he's got to pay those niggers' way up there, and he's not going to come home empty-handed.

In Beaufort, it is said, there are no "real Republicans" among the white population, although a few Northern white people have come down and preserved their Republican leanings. These, however, have not been expressed at the polls, because the Republican party has always been "the nigger party" in Beaufort County. In 1928, recalls the city manager, one of the town's most influential Democrats who did not like the idea of "having a Catholic for President" began a Republican movement. Later he joined the lily-white Republican group and, according to this informant: "We didn't get mad at him. We dropped him quietly. He never talks with us about politics now." There are no avowed Republicans except Negroes in Beaufort County, and fewer and fewer Negroes are voting there. The enrollment committeeman at Sheldon, when asked if he knew a Republican, thought hard and then replied: "Naw. Wait a minute. There used to be a man over on Ladies' Island. . . . But he's dead now. You've asked me something I can't hardly answer, brother."

It is said that in Saluda County, South Carolina, about eight years ago some white Republicans "did come out openly and admit their party affiliation. Since then, none have dared to do so." Republicans have never asked for representation among the poll holders for the general elections in the county. The secretary of the Saluda County Democratic committee states flatly that the Republicans would not get such representation even if they did request it; not unless there were some white Republicans. He receives through the mail, as secretary of the general election commission, Republican ballots which he places in the boxes that go to the polls. He admits that few, if any, of these tickets are put on the tables at the polling places. The Negroes who vote Republican bring their own tickets and he presumes that "Joe Tolbert mailed them one." Very few Republicans bother to vote in the general election even in presidential years. In 1936, 549 voted. The reason, of course, is that there are no party contests in Saluda. Many more than this register, however, in order that they may be called for jury service.

The Pickens County *Sentinel* of 6 November 1930 carried the following announcement of the organization of a new "white" Republican faction in South Carolina:

Fourteen Republicans from Pickens County attended the organizational meeting of a new white Republican Party in South Carolina held at Columbia, October 28. Total attend-

ance was 700 to 800 and every county in the state was represented except Dorchester. No Negroes were allowed as
delegates.

... J. C. Hambright, business man of Rock Hill, was named
State Chairman of the new party. . . .

In speaking of the meeting, Mr. A. M. Morris states that
the new party has the best wishes and confidence of the
Hoover administration and in his opinion has bright pros-
pects for developing considerable strength in the state during
the coming years.

A former general election commissioner in Pickens County
states that he instructed his election managers and clerks to ask
for poll tax receipts and certificates of the voters in the general
election. He says that he saw that this was done at his home
town, but he doubts that it was required at other places. The
Republicans sent him tickets through the mail, and he gave
them out to the election managers who called for the boxes:
"Some of them had the tickets torn up before they got to the
door. . . . The only way anybody can vote the Republican ticket
in this county is to carry his ticket or to write it out there." That,
he added with a bitter smile, "is how pure democracy is in this
state."

Negroes in Orangeburg County, South Carolina, have a Republican organization. John Williams, the black proprietor of
the Williams Shoe Repair Shop, is president of the Orangeburg
Republican committee. In a private interview he informed us
that 150 members of the Republican party comprise the Orangeburg setup, and that of these 150, only 10 are white. The main
concern of the local party members is getting delegates to the
national convention. A majority of Negroes have always made
up the delegations to these conventions. When asked about local politics, Williams said: "Usually five members of the club
call a meeting under some assumed name for purposes of registering and voting in local elections."[4]

The Pickens *Sentinel* of 11 August 1932 ran an article
entitled "Many Negroes get Voting Certificates," which
announced:

Many negroes at Easley and Pickens have obtained registration certificates entitling them to vote in the general elec-

4. Wilhelmina Jackson's interview, Orangeburg, South Carolina, 1
February 1940.

tion, according to members of the County Registration Board. It has come to the attention of the *Sentinel* that negroes throughout the county are being urged by members of the Hambright Republican faction to obtain registration certificates in order that a larger Republican vote than usual may be cast in the county next November.

A large number of certificates are also being issued to white persons, of course. There is no way to tell whether an applicant intends to vote a Republican ticket unless he makes his intentions known voluntarily; but according to one member of the registration board, the negroes make no bones about saying they haven't been doing what they should about voting heretofore and they intend to make a better showing this year.

In 1939 the state Republican committee of Georgia had forty-seven white members and three Negroes. Negroes had controlled this committee until 1928, when Herbert Hoover began to build a white Republican party in the South. Benjamin Davis was secretary of the Georgia committee for fifteen years. He was the last Negro secretary, a position in the state party organization that had been held by Negroes for fifty-six years. In the pre-Hoover days there would be a considerable number of black district and county chairmen, while now there are no Negro district chairmen and only about thirty-five Negro county chairmen out of 159 counties. The Republican vote in the state has decreased about 60 percent since 1928. The last Republican candidate for governor was in 1928. According to Ben Davis, in an interview on 4 November 1939, "the Republican party in Georgia now is just a few poor whites who meet every four years for the purpose of controlling patronage." There remain several counties in the state which are normally Republican, but they are in the mountain areas and have an overwhelmingly white population. The state legislature in 1939 had two Republican members—one senator and one representative.

Republican political activity in Putnam County, Georgia, revolves about one man who, some years ago, started organizing a Republican group by working first with the small group of Negroes who were voting and subsequently with the dozen or so whites who would vote with him as Republicans. This white group entered the Democratic primary en bloc, and its members feel now that they have made their presence felt in local politics. The chairman of the county Republican committee adds: "When Republicans first set up here, the Democrats started hollerin' 'niggah.' Do that 'cause they want to keep out competition. We're going to break that down." He is encouraging the Negro vote here and is sure that no Negroes now have any trouble registering and that some few do vote, though they get cheated out of their voting rights by the white primary and thus cannot help him in his efforts to form an opposition bloc in local politics. Although he favors Negro voting, he thinks Republicans in the South will have a hard time until many Negroes vote Democratic. He does not believe that the Negro vote could be "driven" any longer and would first like to see some way of permitting intelligent Negroes to vote. While this man is chairman of the county Republican committee, he has voted in the Democratic county primary for years, and his vote has never been challenged.

In Hall County, Georgia, the Republicans also vote in the Democratic primary. In Gainesville it is said that so few of them show themselves that this is considered safe, but "they've got to be *white* Republicans." The chief activities of the Hall County Republicans are attending state and district meetings, selecting state and national delegates, and playing in local Democratic politics. It is claimed that in several counties of the ninth district, Republicans who vote freely and as an organized faction in the Democratic primary are really in control of politics. One county, Fannin, has all Republican county officers. In Georgia it is said that the Republican counties have always been the white counties. Thus the Republican party has always been the white man's party, and the chairman of the Hall County Republican committee thinks that it should be kept this way: "It's getting more that way all the time. The niggers are voting for Roosevelt." While stating flatly that if the Republican party is to get anywhere in Georgia it must be a white party, he added: "All over the country it's the trend to give the nigger the vote. I don't see how they can keep it out of Georgia long. It does look like they ought to get a vote somewhere, but I don't know what the black counties will do when that day comes." No Negroes have participated in the Hall County Republican convention since 1930, though Negro Republicans still attend the Fulton County conventions and are active in Savannah.

In Chatham County, Georgia, the Republicans vote freely in the county and state Democratic primaries. While they do not form any sizable bloc, their leaders will work and they generally form a part of the opposition. In 1936 the Republicans backed Eugene Talmadge, and it is thought that they will support him again in the 1940 election. In Savannah, as throughout the state, the lily whites have taken over control of the Republican party. The big split came in 1932 when Negroes charged that the white Republicans had packed the convention with Democrats in order to swing it. In the words of a Republican member of the board of registrars, "They said that every white man was a Democrat and every nigger a Republican." When the Negroes were voted out, they formed a rump group, elected their own delegates, and went to Atlanta, where they failed to be seated. The fight was carried to the national committee and they lost there. The Savannah Republicans are now combined, with the Negroes accepting a silent minority status. Only three of the twelve members of the Republican committee are Negro, and the Republicans do not make any effort to increase the registration of blacks.

The Republicans in Chatham County, declares the clerk of the county commissioners, are

> a bunch of niggers and two or three white men looking for jobs. We had so few white people in the party, they had them holding two jobs at once. One time they couldn't find a white Republican to make collector of the customs and they put a nigger in there. I mean, but he was a really good nigger, what you call a "white man's nigger!" The white people that worked for him got along just fine. He never tried to step out of his place, and when he wanted anything, he knew coming to a white man right here in town was the place to get it.

It is estimated that "about 1,000" Negroes vote in Chatham County.

Mrs. George Williams, former Negro Republican committeewoman from Georgia, is very resentful toward the Republican party for condoning a lily-white policy in Georgia. She discusses her grudge in the following terms:

> In 1924 I was elected in my own right a committeewoman from Georgia; was reelected in 1928 and served until 1932. I was the first Republican committeewoman from the state of Georgia and the first Negro committeewomen in the country. Now, I am a Republican from principle—I have always voted the Republican ticket. In 1932 Walter Brown and Herbert Hoover lily-whited the party in Georgia, but they were so busy lily-whiting the party that they didn't know they were permanently kicking themselves out in this country. I have

stumped this entire state for the Republican party, but I wouldn't do it now. I have urged young Negro women to register, vote, and pay their poll taxes regularly, but I wouldn't do so now. It makes me boil when I recall that Ben Davis, a Negro, first sold us out—for a mess of pottage, he sold his birthright; but I didn't go quietly, I'll tell you that now.[5]

The chairman of the Burke County, Georgia, Republican committee is an elderly Negro who states that he has "lost faith" in his people. He has been the Republican leader in the county for thirty years or more, and he regrets that "mighty few" Negroes have ever voted in Burke County, and there are "getting to be fewer." In the 1920s he had from fifty to seventy-five Negroes in his Republican bloc, but now he has fewer than two dozen. He feels that the New Deal has something to do with the decline of Republican interest among Negroes in the county, because his people tell him that they are satisfied with the present administration. But even more responsible is the lily-white movement that began in 1928 and succeeded in 1932 in "stealing" control of the first district in the county. He himself has had no trouble with the lily whites. In 1932, when there was some threat of this, leading white men came to him and made this offer:

> We will protect you. We will lend you cars to go around the county and gather up your registered Negroes for the county convention. We will go to the courthouse and warn every white man who comes in that he must choose his party. If he enters the courthouse for the Republican convention, then he will be batted from any participation in the primaries.

This word was passed out, and there was not a white man at the 1932 county conventions. This man explains: "I always have had mighty fine cooperation from the white folks here." No white man has been active with the local Republicans in a long time. Lately, however, the chairman reports, many businessmen are telling him that they may vote Republican because of their feeling against the New Deal.

In Statesboro, Georgia, there are a few white Republicans. They are trying to usurp the whole local organization and put the Negroes out. They exclude Negroes from the committees of the group. At local meetings there will be about a dozen whites and two dozen Negroes, but the chairman is always a

5. Wilhelmina Jackson's interview, Savannah, Georgia, 15 February 1940.

Negro. Although the Negro members can always outvote the whites, the whites hang on in the hope of getting patronage that Negroes cannot hold in the South, such as small town postmaster's jobs, which go to white middle class folk.

In Ware County, Georgia, the Republicans are at a disadvantage because there is no one-ballot system in the general elections, that is, a large ballot with all tickets printed on it. In Ware County a voter must vote either a straight Republican or a straight Democratic ticket. Few people in the county care to vote a straight Republican ticket. There are many voters, however, especially businessmen in Waycross, who would like to vote against Roosevelt, but hesitate to vote Republican either locally or in state races. Negroes do not have much influence in the Republican party setup in Ware County, although there are two Negro county officers. County delegates to the state Republican convention are elected from wards, and it is reported that Negroes are not informed when the elections are to be held. According to one prominent Negro Republican: "The lily-white movement has deeply affected our Republican party movement here in Ware County."[6]

At one time there were as many as sixty or seventy Negro voters in Johnson County, Georgia, under Negro Republican leadership. In 1932, however, the Negro Republicans ran into difficulty with the lily whites. The Negro Republicans—about 50 of them—went to the courthouse to hold a convention but found the place filled with about 250 whites, many of whom were from the worst element in the county. None of these whites had previously shown any interest in the Republican party. They proceeded, however, to vote out all of the Negro members and to replace them with whites. The new white chairman was a prominent sawmill and turpentine operator who had his crews there to work for him. After the Roosevelt victory in 1932, all but one or two of these whites fell away from the Republican group. At the last county Republican convention there were only six members present, all of whom were Negroes, and now the Negroes have control of all offices again.

The white Republicans in Dougherty County, Georgia, are for the most part people who have moved in from the North. The pecan and peanut industries brought down several families from the North thirty years ago. The meat packing plant

6. Wilhelmina Jackson's interview with Tom Williams, Waycross, Georgia, 14 February 1940.

brought others in the late 1920s, and before that a couple of families of "carpetbaggers settled in . . . and made a lot of money." Some of the lumbermen in Dougherty County are also Republicans. Many of these are not active Republicans, however, and most of them vote in the Democratic county and state primaries, as the chairman of the Republican county committee himself does.

The chairman of the committee states that:

> We used to have a lot of niggers here. We don't fool with them now. . . . We've taken the party away from the niggers in this county—and all over the district about. There was one nigger from this district up at Atlanta last Saturday at the state convention.

The Republicans chose four Negro delegates out of a total of fourteen, and as the chairman added:

> There were enough whites there till we could have kicked out all the niggers if we'd wanted to, but there were some there wanted to temporize. The national committeeman said we got to be careful about the niggers in the North. Hell! They don't have nigger delegates up there. Why do they expect us to have them down here? . . . Some people wanted to make it five blacks. We said, hell, no!

The chairman observed that Ben Davis is still one of the delegates, but that he carries little weight. Continuing, he declared:

> The niggers in the North are going Democratic. These boys around here better not start yelling "nigger" at me. I might get mad, cause if there ever was an administration that was friendly to the nigger, it's been this one.

This Georgia Republican is as good a Southerner as he is a Republican. He contended that the South is the only place where people ever treat the Negro well, commenting:

> I've seen what they get up there. They don't like the nigger noway. We like him down here for what he can do for us. I've worked as high as 50 of them at a time, and I've always treated them the best a body could. That's only common sense. If you got a good horse and he gets sick, you get the best veterinary you can get for him, don't you? Well, if any of my niggers get sick, I have my family doctor look him over. I can't afford to lose a good man after I've trained him in. . . .

Sure, a nigger's got to come to the back door down here with his hat in his hand, but he gets decent treatment when he does.

The chairman believes that Georgia Republicans are so firmly set in lily-whiteism that when the GOP starts giving out patronage again, the recipients will be "equal" in color and ability with the Democrats—or better.

The Republican party has lost favor among the Negro voters of Tampa, Florida, as a result of a recent episode. In March of 1940 the state Republican convention was held in Orlando. This convention was split over the Negro question. Among the questions before the convention was that of whether it would continue to elect national committeemen in the convention or hold primaries for that purpose. The reason for not holding the primaries was clearly put before the convention by Tom Swanson, a senatorial aspirant. The reason, he contended, was fear that, if primaries were held, a larger number of Negro Republicans in the state might result in a predominantly black group of national committeemen and consequently a redistribution of patronage. Swanson alleged that he, for one, was tired of it. A group in the convention agreed with him, but the motion to hold the primary was defeated by a four to one ratio. The dissenting Republicans now turned "radical," got up and walked out of the meeting, and asked all in favor of the motion to make it known by adjourning with them to another room in the Hotel San Juan—the swankiest in Orlando.

Before all this occurred, however, a resounding indictment of the instability of modern Negro political leadership was delivered. It appears that one J. L. Lewis, a Jacksonville lawyer, had been given $1,500 by the Republican party to aid in the organization of Florida Negroes. These funds were dispensed mainly in Lewis's own county of Duval. It was revealed that the funds were intended to promote the Jim Crow principle in the Republican party, as separate Negro Republican clubs were to be the organizational aim of Lewis, according to the terms of the agreement. At the convention, after the decision not to hold primaries, Lewis and Sam Solomon of Miami were "selected" along with ten whites as the lawful delegates to the Philadelphia convention. This was pointed to by Tom Swanson as an act of "dirty poltics" where, for $1,500, a man sold the birthright of his people in the Republican party. Lewis attempted to make denials, but affidavits of witnesses to his acceptance of the money were produced. Lewis refused to follow the "radical" faction of the convention which had adjourned to an upper floor in the hotel in its attempt to make retribution for the sins of lily-white Republicans against Florida Negroes.[7]

There are full Republican organizations in about half of the counties of Alabama. In twelve or fifteen of these, however, the Republican organization is weak. In all but ten counties in Alabama there is at least a party secretary. The Republican organization of the state generally runs a complete state ticket. In Montgomery County, however, no county Republican ticket has been presented for over thirty years, and this tends to be true of all of the black counties of Alabama.

In Huntsville the city attorney, the city treasurer, and the city clerk are all Republicans. City elections are held on a nonpartisan basis. There is a Republican organization in Huntsville, but it does not amount to much as far as a party organization goes because there has been little to keep one together there since the post office patronage was lost in 1932. There are relatively few Republicans in Huntsville and Madison County. As an organized minority, they have taken little part in things for the past ten years. They have put up no local candidates for an even longer period. The county Republican vote in national elections runs from 350 to a top of 500 for presidential elections. A large number of Republicans vote in the Democratic primary.This is a well-accepted practice. As one prominent Republican in the county puts it: "They vote Democratic locally because of necessity. They vote Republican nationally because of conviction." Apparently no efforts are ever made to bar Republicans from the Democratic primary. There is a county Republican committee with an executive body of twenty-two whose main activity is to keep the organization together and select delegates to the district and state meetings. Now and then they will endorse a man running for state office on the Republican ticket, but there has been no county Republican ticket for thirty-five years.

There are three or four counties in Alabama which are "normally" Republican. Three or four of the probate judges now serving in the state are Republicans. Winston County, known as "the free state of Winston," small, hilly, and backward, is overwhelmingly Republican and has always been so. When Alabama seceded from the Union, "Winston seceded from Ala-

7. Wilhelmina Jackson's Tampa, Florida, field notes, March 1940.

bama." Cullman County occasionally has Republican adminis-
trations, as does DeKalb County. Since the constitution of 1901,
Republicans in Alabama have accepted the rule of the Demo-
crats that Negroes shall not take part in politics. In Madison
County and in Huntsville, according to one local Republican, the
Republican organization has "never tried to register them or en-
courage them to register, emphatically not! And, off the record,
I might say that they never will."

In the twenty-five years that he has been in politics in Madison County, Alabama, one circuit judge can recall only one instance in which the Republicans offered any threat. That was
in 1928 in the Hoover-Smith campaign, when Hoover carried
Madison County by a small number of votes. The judge believes
that Hoover actually carried Alabama, but that he was "counted
out" to the tune of about 8,000 votes. Although in Madison
County the election fights are always within the Democratic primary and "among friends," it is customary to have many candidates. The county has not had a closely-knit political organization for some time. Often three or four men will run together
on an unofficial "slate," but this slate is always publicly denied.
The city of Huntsville has no primary system and its elections
are nonpartisan. Thus, it has happened that for a good many
years "Republicans have dominated city politics." The mayor
has frequently been a Republican, though the present mayor is
a Democrat.

In Cullman County, Alabama, the probate judge is the only
Republican holding office. In 1928, at the time of the Hoover-
Smith campaign, a virtually complete slate of Republicans was
swept into the courthouse in this county, but by 1934 only one
of these survived. The Republicans hold no primary in Cullman
County. They are entitled to one under the laws of Alabama, but
according to the most prominent Republican in the county: "We
don't want one. It breaks up the harmony in the party." The Republicans have always put up a full slate of county officers.
These are selected in conventions. First, committeemen are
selected from each beat in meetings at or near the polls on the
same day the Democrats have their primary. There are 3 of
these committeemen for each beat, or a total of 126 members.
About half a dozen Republicans attend each of the beat meetings. This same informant states that the Republicans come
from no one section of Cullman County, since every box in the
county is "split wide open." He feels that this two-party division
makes for a healthier political situation: "We have plenty of

crookedness around elections here, but very little in office."
This, he thinks, is due to the check resulting from two parties.
He contends that there are only a few Republicans who do not
vote in the Democratic primary at least occasionally.

There are only three Republicans in Bibb County—one of
whom is a Negro. One is the former postmaster, and one "never
did care what people think."

The Republicans of Birmingham have little or no power. Although no effort is made to keep them out, not very many of
them vote in the Democratic primary. If they imitated the Republicans in northern Alabama and entered the Birmingham
primaries in an organized bloc, they could be a real power. In
Chilton, the Republicans joined the Democratic party and proceeded to run it.

It is estimated that there are from five to eight Republicans in
Greene County, Alabama. That is the number who vote a
straight Republican ticket in general elections. Yet most of
these vote in the Democratic primary without any objection
from anyone.

In Etowah County, as representative of northern Alabama,
the basis of Republican party strength has for years been the
old die-hard Republicans in the hills and mines, the leadership
and money of a few local businessmen, periodic interest in the
presidential races, occasional bits of patronage from the Republican national administration, and, more recently, the addition of Northern people who have come into towns such as
Gadsden with the new big industries. The Republican vote in
Etowah County is said to be much larger than is shown by the
results, due to the fact that "Republicans have been tricked by
the Democrats into voting in their primary." Since a good many
Republicans vote only once every four years, they feel the poll
tax burden greatly.

There are no filing fees for candidates on the Republican
ticket. They are all chosen at county conventions. The only
incentive for a person to be a candidate is "service to the party."
All expenses of campaigns are paid by the committee, and these
are collected from constituents "and usually come in small fees."
Many of the large officials of local manufacturing companies
contribute, and help is also extended by the national committee.
It is admitted that hundreds of Republicans—perhaps a majority of them—vote in the Democratic primary in Etowah County.
Then, they "turn right around and vote Republican" in the general election, at least for national offices. The chairman of the

county Democratic committee told George Stoney: "Everybody knows they do, but you can't do anything about it unless you stop and challenge every single person. Why, we've had officers in Democratic primaries that came out with Landon pins on the next day." The small Republican party in Etowah County does not act as a check on election evils, asserts the Gadsden postmaster, because it has always worked "in cahoots with" the Democrats.

Republicans have not tried to register Negroes in Alabama since 1920. The whole Alabama Republican party is "lily-white." In Dallas County about twenty-five people vote Republican regularly in general elections. Most of these vote in the county Democratic primaries because there is no Republican action then. It is almost impossible, in a place like Dallas County, to talk with people about voting Republican. There is no county organization.

In Tuscaloosa County some twenty-five years ago, there was a fairly liberal white Republican group with which the Negro voters worked. Relationships were broken off, however, when the Negroes outvoted the white Republicans in a county convention about fifteen years ago. The whites thereupon moved their convention to a hall where Negroes were not allowed. Since that time there has been no cooperation between the two groups. The Republicans do not want the Negro vote and do not help Negroes to register.

The Republicans in Macon County have never tried to do anything with the Negro voters. There used to be a great deal of work done from Republican headquarters in trying to get support from Tuskegee for Republican candidates. Twenty years ago there was a real county organization of Republicans, and a few Negro voters were members. In the Harding campaign of 1920, the Republicans polled their last big vote, but it was not bona fide Republican. One Macon County Republican, a former postmaster at Tuskegee, averred that "the Republicans in Alabama want to keep their party small so when it comes time to divide up the jobs, they'll have enough to go around."

The following is the story of how Perry Howard and Dr. S. D. Redmond came into power in the Republican party in Mississippi, as told to James Jackson, our field worker, by Dr. Redmond, Negro chairman of the Republican state central committee. It should be kept in mind that Perry Howard is now the last and only Negro national Republican committeeman. Although still "representing" Mississippi, Howard has long been resident in Washington, D.C. In the words of Dr. Redmond:

During Reconstruction days, Negroes controlled the Republican party in the state of Mississippi, but they divided the offices among the whites very liberally. Subsequently, this was a factor in their losing control of the Mississippi Republican party. Negroes still constitute the bulk of the Republican party membership in Mississippi, but have had many hard struggles with the lily whites to retain leadership of the party.

James Hill and John R. Lynch, Negroes, were the recognized leaders of the party from Emancipation until about 1904. About this time, Major John R. Lynch took a post in the regular army and retired from politics, leaving the state for good and locating in Chicago. James Hill died about the same time—1904. After Hill's death and with Lynch removed from the scene, a white man by the name of L. T. Mosley was elected national committeeman and became the titular head of the Republican party in Mississippi, though persistently opposed by S. D. Redmond, Perry W. Howard, and M. E. Mollison. During the great exodus, attorney Mollison left the state in 1915 and located in Chicago, thus leaving the political leadership of Republican affairs in the hands of Howard and Redmond. Mosley was titular head of the party until his death in 1918. Mosley was not anti-Negro. He was more liberal than the present lily whites and accepted collaboration with Negroes. He had a considerable Negro following.

Mosley was succeeded by M. J. Muldihill, a white Republican from Vicksburg—being elected by the state committee upon the death of Mosley. Mr. Muldihill was, therefore, elected at a special meeting of the state committee and not by the state delegation to the national convention which customarily elects the national committee. Perry Howard was a candidate for national committeeman at the same state committee meeting that elected Muldihill and contested Muldihill's election before the national committee which met in St. Louis in 1919. But the national committee ruled in favor of Muldihill nonetheless.

The next year marked the historic 1920 national convention, when Governor Frank Lowden and General Leonard

Wood tied for the nomination before the Republican national convention in Chicago and stalemated the convention for three days, until the tie was broken by the nomination of the dark horse, Warren G. Harding. During the preconvention campaign, Mr. Howard had been a very prominent advocate and spokesman for General Wood through Mr. Proctor—The P & G soap man. To this 1920 convention there went two contesting delegations from Mississippi. One was represented by Perry W. Howard, S. D. Redmond, *et al.*, and the other by Muldihill and his followers. The Howard-Redmond faction supported General Wood and the Muldihill group supported Lowden. The delegations had not been in Chicago long, however, when it was discovered and reported to the Lowden people that the Muldihill people were not keeping faith in their pledge to support Lowden's candidacy for nomination. Redmond had received a certified copy of a hotel register from one of the Wood delegation which listed pro-Lowden delegates staying and eating in the Wood Hotel. This discovery later on was used against Muldihill and led to his subsequent downfall as Republican leader of Mississippi and the return of Negro leadership to the Mississippi Republican party.

The two contesting delegations at this convention were both seated on a half vote each, but Muldihill was appointed as national committeeman by the convention.

Later, when President Harding was inaugurated on March 4, 1921, Redmond had not forgotten the Muldihill episode and lost no time in corralling the Lowden influence—which was more responsible for the nomination of Harding than the Wood people were, and reminded them of Muldihill's bad faith in Chicago. With this cudgel in his hands and the powerful backing of the Lowden forces who wanted to get even with Mr. Muldihill, Redmond was able to get President Harding to agree to give the Howard-Redmond faction of Mississippi one-third of all Mississippi patronage, one-third of all municipal, county, and state committee membership, and the chairmanship of all committees. This agreement was quite unusual and unique in its provision for the handling of Republican patronage because, as a rule, the national committee and state chairman of the victorious faction is given full control of patronage dispensation for the respective states. S. D. Redmond had a full leadership in bringing this matter about as Mr. Howard was then a candidate for appointment as Assistant Attorney General for the United States and did not desire to risk engendering further enmity which might militate against his being appointed. Perry Howard, though not active in bringing about this compromise, yet did not think much of it. He did not see how we could cope with Muldihill, who had two-thirds of the patronage when we only had one-third. Redmond, however, reasoned that sufficient disaffection would develop within the Muldihill camp through a scramble for patronage jobs so that Muldihill's allotment for patronage would be inadequate to go around for the appeasement of the malcontents. This actually happened, for in 1924 the Muldihill state committee and the Howard-Redmond state committee were called to meet together, and at this meeting of the Mississippi Republican state central committee six of the members of the Muldihill committee deserted and voted with the Howard-Redmond faction, giving them a majority. At that point, the Muldihill faction thereby became a minority faction, withdrew to one corner of the convention hall, and issued a call for a state convention. The Howard-Redmond majority also issued a call for a state convention and, at these respective conventions, each faction elected delegates to the Cleveland convention. At the Cleveland convention in 1924, Calvin Coolidge was nominated for President, Perry W. Howard was elected national committeeman, defeating Muldihill, and Mrs. Booze was elected national committeewoman. Redmond was elected chairman in Mississippi.

Perry Howard is national committeeman from Mississippi at the present time, and I remain chairman of the state central committee, and the leadership of the Republican party in Mississippi remains in our hands.[8]

The chairman of the Warren County, Mississippi, Republican committee presents a very frank appraisal of the ends of that committee, in the following terms:

There are no whites who are members of the Warren County committee. There are between 250 and 300 Negroes qualified to vote in national elections, special elections, bond issues, or general elections. During the presidential campaigns, our committee performs its only cause for being. We proselytize these few score Negroes to vote for Hoover or whoever the Republican standard-bearer may be and, after

8. James Jackson's interview, Jackson, Mississippi, January 1940.

pocketing the handouts from the party slush fund—and this is the only real purpose of our organization—we put our committee back in moth balls to await another presidential election. Hell, naw! We got no local program. We are doctors and preachers and barbers. We make enough money to buy enough liquor to wash the inconveniences of being a nigger out of our brain.[9]

The leadership of the Louisiana Republican organization, that is, the state central committee, is controlled by whites. The national committeeman and the secretary of the state committee are both white. But there are four Negro members on the state committee. John E. Jackson, the present national committeeman, was made committeeman in 1936 at the behest of Herbert Hoover, pursuant to his policy of making the party acceptable to Southern whites. Jackson was recognized as national committeeman despite the fact that his lily-white faction in Louisiana was a distinct minority. Only in New Orleans and Baton Rouge were there enough Negro Republicans registered to hold Republican election primaries in 1940. Thus, unless the two Republican factions in the state can get together on some basis, it will not be possible to poll the required 5 percent of the vote necessary by Louisiana law to keep the Republican party on the ballot. According to a Negro Republican leader in Baton Rouge: "The turning over of the leadership of the Republican party to the lily whites by Hoover hurt the strength of the party very much. It discouraged and alienated the Negroes, and did not attract the anticipated numbers of whites."[10]

In December 1936 there were 750 Negroes and 17 whites in Baton Rouge Parish who were registered as Republicans. In New Orleans there was a total Republican registration of 500 in the same year. As of 16 December 1939 the total number of registered Republicans in Baton Rouge was 130 Negroes and 17 whites. Only 95 Negroes cast votes in the Baton Rouge Republican primary on 16 January 1940. Our interviewer was told that the only reason Louisiana white Republicans accept Negroes in the state organization is because they are needed to make it possible for the Republicans to meet the 5 percent vote requirement for the establishment of a legal party. One promi-

9. James Jackson's interview with the county chairman, a Negro physician, Vicksburg, Mississippi, February 1940.
10. James Jackson's interview with Dr. Baranco, a Negro dentist and leader of young black Republicans, Baton Rouge, Louisiana, February 1940.

nent Negro doctor in New Orleans admits that, despite his firm and traditional Republicanism, he considers the Negro in the South to be 100 percent better off since Franklin D. Roosevelt. Yet he says that if Roosevelt should run again, he would vote for his Republican opponent because he could not keep his "self-respect" by voting for a Democrat in the general election when he and other Negroes are not permitted to vote in that party's primary.

A former Republican member of the board of elections of Hamilton County, Tennessee, points out the difficulties encountered by the Republicans as a minority party in a Southern county. He explains:

> The fate of a minority party in this county depends upon the honesty, the diplomacy, and the effort of its representative on the county board of elections. If he wants to work hard for his party, then he can appoint real Republicans to supervise the elections as I did . . . and get fired from the place right soon, or he can do as this fellow now is doing. . . .
>
> On the three-man board, since the Democrats have two, naturally the chairman and the secretary are both Democrats. In this county these three men select one officer of election, two clerks, two registrars, three judges, and one assistant registrar. The minority member generally gets to select one clerk, one judge, and one registrar. The assistant isn't in the law, but it's customary to have one in this county. That means each member of the commission has three appointees (for each precinct).
>
> The officer of election really controls the conduct of elections. Of course, he's a Democrat. The assistant registrar is important, too. She (it's usually a lady) is usually the vice-chairman in the precinct for the party. She is supposed to keep up with who has voted and how many of their folks haven't voted yet and direct the people who are running the cars.
>
> . . . Two Democrats on the board can overrule anything the Republican member might want to do. Lots of Republicans in Tennessee, and especially here in Chattanooga, are Republicans nationally, but Democrats locally. The law just says the third member of the board has to be a member of the minority party, and so they take one of these halfway Republicans and say it's all right. The Republican county committee has nothing to say about who shall be their represent-

atives on the commission. The state board of two Democrats and one Republican is appointed by the governor, with the consent of the legislature. They appoint the county commission. The commission designates the places where elections are held—that's one big power they've got. They employ men to go out and find these places. They put up the money to erect booths, and so on, and have the ballots printed. All this helps pay political debts.

In this city they try to pick places that will be advantageous to the Democrats. They use the city fire hall for elections—I don't believe that would be legal in a court of law. All the firemen and policemen get their jobs by political appointment, and they're just the biggest political workers you ever saw. Every single one of them are out working on election day or hanging around the house intimidating voters. I bet the Baptist church could catch on fire and burn to the ground if it was election day, and they wouldn't leave the polls to piss on it.

In the country it's mostly stores. If it's a Democratic store, they can pay as high as $25.00 rent for what brings the man in extra trade. If they can't find anything but a Republican store, they can pay as low as $2.50.

Continuing, this sturdy Hamilton County Republican said:

I served only one term on the commission, four years ago. . . . The county court appropriated a certain amount to the election commission to be distributed among the three members as they saw fit. Time has been when the chairman got $900.00, the secretary $500.00, and the third member got nothing. That's just one of the ways they have to whip you into line.

When I was on the commission, I jolted them by saying I thought I ought to be chairman, since it was the minority party that needed the protection. They didn't agree. Then I told them the same thing about the secretary's place. They compromised by splitting the money three ways. I got $500.00.

. . . The first list of people I sent in as recommendations for the precinct officer, I sent in three or four days ahead of the time they went to press. Well, when the list was published, I found that a lot of my active Republicans had been left out on me. They didn't do that but once. After that, I hung off and hung off until the last minute. Then I'd have my secretary copy off my list and I'd have the reporter come down for a copy, and then send a copy to the other two members of the board, too late for them to change them. They soon got rid of me, though. They were anxious to get somebody who'd play ball with them and they sure got one now.

The Republicans, he observes, have tough sledding in Hamilton County because

the Democrats have paid organization in this county. Each precinct, or all but three or four, have a chairman and a vice-chairman. That's 72 times 2. Every Democratic candidate who qualifies has to put up a fee. That helps pay for part of it. These two officers are paid according to the increase in the vote of their precinct over the last time. If they don't have an increase, then they get paid the minimum.

Under such conditions:

The Republican organization has degenerated to one for patronage only. It's been that way in this county for the past ten years. It used to be that the Republicans swung federal patronage to the Democrats for state and county favors. They'd come after you only for the national election. The postmasters were in control of the county and city organizations, and all patronage flowed through them. There are two factions in Republican politics here now. One is the old patronage bunch. The other faction is made up of those who are Republicans by inheritance or choice and who are in politics for a chance to serve the party.

The commissioner of fire and police in Chattanooga sees the threat of a dangerous tie-up between Republicans and the Negro vote if the poll tax is repealed. He warns:

I believe if they repeal the poll tax it would give the Republicans control. You see we've got this helluva big, ignorant darky vote and, without the poll tax, the Republicans could haul around 10,000 of them to the polls. They'd be the balance of power. The Republicans are all for it. I guess if I was a Republican, I'd be for it too—but I'm not!

In Knoxville, Tennessee, it is reported, the Democrats tend to be more liberal toward Negroes than are the Republicans. A Negro doctor in Knoxville recalls "a Republican Landon rally in November 1935 which was held in a Gay Street theater. Negroes were roped off. Even the speakers' platform was divided by a rope. The Democrats have never gone to such ludicrous extremes to enforce the Jim Crow ordinance and offend Negroes."[11]

The Lincoln Independent Party was organized in Louisville, Kentucky, in 1929 as a reaction on the part of Negro Republicans to the rule of the lily whites who had assumed power in that city in 1917. This Negro group put up a full Negro ticket and conducted a heated campaign that year. According to a prominent Negro member of the Lincoln Independent Party: "We were met with violence on the part of Negro Republicans and at the hands of white police—tools of the lily-white Republican city administration. My printing press was smashed. I was beaten up along with several others."[12]

11. James Jackson's interview with Dr. O. B. Taylor, Knoxville, Tennessee, November 1939.

12. James Jackson's interview with William Warley, editor of the *Fall City News*, Louisville, Kentucky, January 1940.

SEVENTEEN

Southern Negroes and the Rewards of Politics

IN areas where Negroes are nonparticipants in the local political life, they can point to almost nothing in the way of representation, either in the form of elective offices or municipal jobs. Even more deplorable is the lack of equitable schooling and the absence of recreational facilities, sewage systems, and most of the other essential services. The sole effective political activity by Negroes in Southern municipalities is in the nonpartisan city-wide elections, bond issue and tax rate referenda, and occasional special elections. While the participation of Negroes in politics in Southern communities is neither widespread nor of an intensive nature, there have been instances in which blacks sought to take advantage of existing opportunities. Naturally, Negroes are more politically active in the border states, where the white primary is not established; in this region they have made numerous efforts to elect members of their race to local, state, and even national offices.

Excerpts from the notes of the field workers are presented in this chapter. The material falls into three classifications: (1) Negro political participation and attempts to return elective officials; (2) Negroes as appointive officials and holders of ordinary municipal jobs; and (3) Negroes as political beneficiaries as far as urban services are concerned.

Although Negroes hold no political offices in county or state government in Charleston, South Carolina, one Negro has run for office there in recent years. Dr. J. E. Beard, A.M.E. minister, ran for Congress in 1924 or 1926—he does not remember which year. He states that a few whites voted for him and that he had to contest the election due to the fact that the ballot containing his name was issued only upon request for it by a voter. Feeling that this was ground for a contest, Dr. Beard observed:

> On the day that I went up to contest the election, I was told that my friends could not go with me. I went alone, therefore. I had to go up a long flight of stairs, which itself was an intimidation because, as I wound my way up, I felt that if anything happened upstairs in the room, with the board of election officials, that I never would be able to get out of the place. Anyway, I went up and the group of men stared at me as if I were the criminal up for judgment instead of a few of them. Even after I told the story of how certain precinct officials had hidden my name, and even after I pointed out one man in the room and called several names of guilty ones, I received no satisfaction. The election count remained as before I contested.

Beard states that a few white Republicans voted for him, and he remarked that "some Negroes didn't vote for me because they thought I had personal aspirations in running."[1]

An examination of many of the ill-fated attempts to elect Negro representatives reveals that the Southern politician is Machiavellian, to say the least. When the end is to defeat a Negro candidate, any means is employed. For example, an old election trick was perpetrated on a Negro candidate for office in one of Tennessee's larger cities. Negroes in Nashville have often run for office. In recent years one Negro doctor has been a constant candidate for city council, offering for election from the fourteenth ward, which has a Negro majority. On one occasion he was declared elected, but before the vote was audited the ballot box was stolen. When he ran for council in 1938, the city council passed a law to install voting booths in all wards but the fourteenth. A stormy protest was raised and the fourteenth ward was subsequently included. According to this candidate:

> In the election of March 1934, I was a candidate from the fourteenth ward for the office of city councilman. My opponents—all white—were Rilie, Barfield, and Tom King. In this election, I polled 602 out of 1,230 votes cast. Before

1. Wilhelmina Jackson's interview with Dr. J. E. Beard, Charleston, South Carolina, 13 April 1940. Except where otherwise noted, all of the quoted material dealing with Virginia, North Carolina, South Carolina, Georgia, and Florida in this chapter is taken from Miss Jackson's notes on interviews conducted in 1939 and 1940. —ED.

the vote was officially added and audited, the ballot box was stolen. Another election was called for. In this election my only opponent was George Lowery—the others had been persuaded to lessen my chances of victory. There was fighting and rioting at the polls. A Negro man, Charles Gooch, was killed. The ballot box was stuffed and I lost by 150 votes.

I ran again in May of 1937, against Charlie Rilie. Rilie won by a vote of 450 to my 350. This was another notorious deal. A group of white women repeatedly voted. The watchers were completely intimidated and subdued. In this election, the teachers and the lawyers and the preachers sold out to the white man, saying it was "inopportune for a Negro to be on the council." Along with them, Mark Hughes and Sam Bostic (Negro bootleggers) worked for Rilie's election; Rilie, himself, being a big shot bootlegger.

In the election of this year, May 11, 1939, I was again an opponent of Charlie Rilie and others. In this race, I polled 165 votes out of about 700 cast.

The only issue in these elections was Negro representation in the city government.

The Negro vote has increased five times since I first offered as a candidate—attesting to the interest that can be stimulated in politics when there is a Negro candidate in the field. In Tennessee and Kentucky the Negro has a real political opportunity if he would but use it.

I am a Republican in all national elections, but locally I vote and run on the Democratic ticket in the Democratic primary.[2]

There are some whites in Nashville who think that Negroes should be represented on the city council. According to one of them:

> There are three Negro-dominated wards. I would like to see them send a Negro representative to the council. I think it would be a qualitative improvement over the types that now clutter up the chamber. Certainly a Negro could do no worse. Negroes have run for office from these wards before. On one such occasion, a couple of years ago, they stole the ballot

2. James Jackson's interview with Dr. H. H. Walker, Nashville, Tennessee, November 1939. Except where otherwise noted, the material on Tennessee, Kentucky, Mississippi, Louisiana, Texas, Oklahoma, Arkansas, Missouri, and Kansas in this chapter is based on James Jackson's field notes in 1939 and 1940. —ED.

box for fear of him being elected. I don't think the people at large would resent violently the presence of a Negro on the city council. It's only the politicians who are opposed to any threat to their power who foment the disorders at the polls.

The following episode from Durham, North Carolina, as told to Wilhelmina Jackson, gives another sample of Southern ingenuity in offsetting the political bids of Negroes.

The Negro who filed for the board of education race in 1938 found that his candidacy had not been confirmed by the state legislature, as it must be in North Carolina for the board of education. This same candidate proposes to run again for the same position and to demand reason for the failure to confirm his candidacy if this occurs again.

In most instances, particularly in the Southern states, Negro candidates run as independents, without the backing of a party machine. The most serious handicap here is a lack of financial support, as is often attested to by the candidates. An unsuccessful Negro candidate in Charlotte, North Carolina, recently complained of this handicap.

No elective offices are held by Negroes in Charlotte. One Negro is employed as a truant officer—an appointive position. In 1935 the first Negro ran for public office in Charlotte since Reconstruction days. Bishop Dale, a local Negro politician, ran for the office of city councilman. He was backed by American Legion members (Negro). He was surprisingly well supported and received votes in practically all wards in the primary. In the general election, he claims that a white candidate spent five thousand dollars to defeat him and bought off the Negroes who had supported him. He vows that he will never run again. The Charlotte *Observer's* comment of 19 April 1935 on Dale's candidacy is interesting: "The heavy vote for Bishop Dale [in the primary] was not surprising in view of the fact that the registration of Negroes in wards had been unusually heavy and numerous cases of voters single-balloting Dale only occurred—for instance, in Ward 11, there were votes for Dale only, 399 of them." After the general election, in which Dale was decisively defeated, the *Observer* remarked, on 8 May 1935:

Although he gained more than 200 votes over the number he received in the primary, Bishop Dale, Negro insurance man and a leader in affairs of Colonel Charles Young, Negro Post of American Legion, fell far behind in the race and dropped from eleventh place to 119th with but two candidates receiving less votes.

In 1937 other Negroes ran for office in Charlotte: a man for council and a woman for the board of education. Without any sustained campaign, the two made a fair showing. In each case Negroes apparently received white votes.

In several instances Negro candidates have entered political contests knowing that their chances for victory were very slim. These candidates do not even wage serious campaigns, but contend that they run for the sole purpose of stimulating the Negro vote. Three North Carolina cities have had such candidates in recent years.

Negroes hold no elective offices in Greensboro. There is a Negro truant officer and there are Negro employees of the Unemployment Compensation Commission. But in some instances Negroes have run for public office in Greensboro. For example, the Reverend Mr. Thorpe, a Negro undertaker-preacher, has run for the city council three times. When he first ran in 1935, he explains, it was merely to get Negroes interested enough to vote. His last candidacy was sponsored by the Greensboro Men's Club. He made but one appeal for votes, yet he received a total vote of 740. There are both whites and Negroes in Greensboro who feel that he actually had a good chance of election had he made a campaign, and that he would have received a wholesome number of white votes. The Negro candidate dismissed the episode by stating, "I'm not and never will be a politician."

No Negroes hold public office in Winston-Salem, but they have run for city office. Dr. Bruce, who was defeated for alderman in the last election—receiving about a third of the vote— proposes to run for the same office again in the 1941 city election. At the last election he received something over 250 votes without waging a very intensive campaign.

About twenty-five years ago, three Negroes ran for public office in Raleigh. As one of the three, George Lightner, tells it:

I ran for commissioner of public welfare, my friend Dr. Polk for mayor, and Mr. Cheek for commissioner of public safety. They are dead now. At that time political interest in this town was dead, too, and we ran as a stimulant to the Negroes, because I know I would have been afraid to hold the office if I'd won. I almost did, too. I ran third in the first primary and five men were running for that office. We held a mass meeting, succeeded in getting about 350 on the books.

You see, then it was a nonpartisan government. . . . The papers commented on what a run we made with no money. It was a mystery to the white folks who spent so much to win. Most of ours was gotten out over the grapevine.

On several occasions Negroes have manifested a political shrewdness worthy of any politician. This is evidenced by instances in which legal technicalities have been taken advantage of in cases involving minor political offices.

There were two Negro justices of the peace in Durham. In North Carolina there is a law that for every one thousand citizens there shall be a justice of the peace. It seems that the first of these Negro justices was elected in 1935 by a ruse. The Durham County quota for justices of the peace was not filled in that year so Louis Austin, a Negro, waited until the last two minutes before filing his candidacy. The whites were upset about it, but it was too late. Austin "won" and in so doing established a precedent. Negroes in Raleigh also hold one justice of the peace office —an elective position obtained in a manner similar to that in which Louis Austin was elected.

A Negro attorney in Norfolk, Virginia, is a member of the city Democratic committee, a position he has held since 1937. According to this Negro member:

> I looked over the record for city Democratic committeemen and saw where one was elected from each of Norfolk's thirty-two precincts. From my precinct, the twenty-first, which is popularly entitled "the barometer" of the Negro vote and the vast majority of whose people are colored, I noticed that no one had ever run. I filed my petition in 1937 and ran. I knew even if I got only one vote, that I'd win. You see, in former years at the first meeting of the committee, a committeeman would be appointed for those precincts which had no representation. So for years committeemen from the twenty-first precinct had been one or the other white man. Well, I ran knowing I'd get one vote; no campaign. I received two hundred votes. I never miss a meeting. The members are very polite to me. . . . I'm always on time. They always shake my hand. I ran again in 1939 and won again.

The field notes cite numerous instances of Negroes having run for elective offices in which, though not victorious, they polled most of the black vote and an appreciable number of white ballots. These instances are cited in order to substantiate the contention that frequently the only serious white opposition is from the politicians and not the electorate.

In 1939 in Houston, Texas, a Negro, J. B. Grigsby, ran for the school board and received about 900 votes, many of which are said to have been cast by white voters.

In Raleigh, North Carolina, Negroes have run for mayor and for the three commissioner offices, and have polled almost the entire Negro vote and perhaps a few white votes.

A Negro attorney in Durham ran for county commissioner in 1936 and received about 1,500 votes—and this without a vigorous campaign. This candidate was supported by the Durham Committee on Negro Affairs, and it is reported that some white votes were cast for him.

In 1938 another Negro lawyer in Durham, M. Hugh Thompson, ran for county commissioner, and another Negro attempted to run for the board of education. Thompson's campaign bogged down seriously, however, when he was informed that as county commissioner his salary would be only $380.00 a year and it would be illegal for him to practice law while in office. He promptly lost interest in the position but still polled some 3,000 votes. In connection with Thompson's candidacy, a white woman states that when she approached the polls one of the hangers-on around the polling place walked up to her and whispered: "That man's a Negro," pointing to Thompson's name on the ballot. This white informant says that she waited around the polls for a spell and that every white voter was so informed.

Negroes have periodically offered themselves as candidates for public office in Oklahoma City, though unsuccessfully. Only recently a Negro ran for the city council from the second ward.

There are no Negroes among the twelve aldermen in Louisville, Kentucky, but in the election of 1939 there were two unsuccessful Negro candidates for the aldermanic position. Both of them were Republicans and represented the seventh ward, which has a heavy Negro population though not a majority.

Negroes have run for office in Knoxville, Tennessee, on several occasions. In the 1917 state and municipal elections, a Negro doctor was a candidate at large for the city council and a Negro attorney was a candidate for the state legislature. Both of them ran as independents, but neither waged a vigorous campaign and neither was able to make any significant showing in the race. Yet some white voters balloted for them. A Negro minister has also run for membership on the school board.

Negroes hold no elective offices in Newport News, Virginia.

A Negro woman has been appointed by the judge of the domestic relations court as assistant juvenile officer. Negroes have not run for office in Newport News in recent years. In 1920 a Negro attorney did run for the city council. He was a highly respected man in the community and was lauded for his efforts by both Negroes and responsible whites. He was put up for office by the Newport News Negro Republican League during the first year of the nonpartisan council. The Negro candidate lost, and it was the general consensus of opinion that the small Negro vote was the cause. It is said that the names of nine white men were listed on the petition filed by the Negro candidate.

In 1934 and 1936 a Newport News Negro ran for the house of representatives on the Communist party ticket. He claims to have been supported by the International Labor Defense, the Workers' Alliance, and the Communist party—groups claiming a combined voting strength of about 500. But the Negro candidate received only 130 votes in 1934 and only 142 votes in 1936. He was severely criticized by both white and Negro groups for making the campaign. Many people in Newport News feel that his candidacy was advanced merely to gain prestige for himself and the Communist party.

Negroes in modern times have run for office in Arkansas. In 1924 Dr. J. M. Robinson ran for governor as an independent Democrat and polled a significant number of votes. In this election John H. Blunt of Forrest City ran for governor as a Republican candidate. From Reconstruction times until about 1906, Negroes held several important elective and appointive offices in the city administration of Little Rock and the state government of Arkansas. M. M. Murray and Joe Brooks were members of the state legislature from Lafayette County. John Connor was the tax collector in Fayetteville. M. W. Gibbs was the municipal judge of Little Rock just prior to the turn of the century. In 1906 J. E. Bush held the office of receiver of lands and land claims. Another representative to the state assembly was Fred Haywood from Pine Bluff.

No Negroes have been elected to the Maryland legislature, though three have been nominated. From 1890 to 1903, Negroes in Baltimore had continuous representation in the city council. Two Negroes were on the city council from 1927 to 1931, though none has sat since, probably as a result of the gerrymander and the lack of experienced candidates and political leadership. The highest appointment held by Negroes in

Baltimore is that of assistant solicitor of the city from 1927 to 1931, an appointment made by the mayor.

Negroes have frequently been candidates for the state legislature from the fifty-eighth district of Kentucky since 1919. But only one has been successful in his campaign. Attorney Charles W. Anderson won reelection for his third term as state representative from this Louisville district in the November 1939 election. Anderson was elected on the Republican ticket. While the Democratic party carried the state in electing the governor by more than a 10,000 majority, Anderson was successful in surviving the Democratic landslide.

William Towers, a Negro lawyer, was elected to the legislature of Kansas in 1936, winning out over a field of six candidates in the Republican primary. Three of the candidates were Negroes. Towers won in the general election with a majority of 414 votes over his nearest opponent—a white candidate. Towers succeeded Dr. W. M. Blount, a Negro who had held office in the legislature from 1928 to 1934. Prior to Blount's election, there had not been a Negro representative in the Kansas legislature since the Reverend Fairfax represented the Kansas City district fifty years ago. In the 1936 election, Towers received about 2,800 white votes, and his white opponent received about 2,000 Negro votes. Although Negroes do not represent an overwhelming majority of the voters in this district, in 1938 both parties nominated Negroes. Towers was the nominee of the Republican party for the second time and another Negro, David D. Wilhite, was the Democratic standard-bearer.

Towers states that he is treated very cordially in Topeka and that really he is "the pet of the House." He is chairman of one committee and a member of four others. He asserts that he has never lost a bill on the floor of the house. He has introduced bills for the equalization of teachers' salaries, for teachers' pensions, to secure tenure of office for teachers, and so forth. He also introduced a bill calling for an appropriation of $900,000 for the erection of the new Sumner High School in Kansas City, and this bill was carried. He introduced a labor bill drawn to forbid the state from letting contracts to manufacturers or unions that refuse to employ a proportionate number of Negro workers.

A woman resident of Birmingham, Alabama, says: "In public offices, Negro prisoners work in the courthouse as janitors. There are also some paid janitors. In the city hall there is an exceptional situation—it hires a couple of Negro maids and a janitor who is a relief elevator boy."[3] Another citizen of the same city states:

> The only jobs Negroes hold in connection with the government are those in the post office. There was once a large number of postmen in the Birmingham post office, but they are gradually dwindling down until now only a comparatively few are working. You find a few Negroes as street sweepers, and on the garbage trucks they go along as helpers with the white truck driver whose duty it is to drive and drive only. There are no [Negro] policemen. But you do find Negroes acting as stool pigeons for the police. They tell on other Negroes and in some cases are allowed to carry pistols. Last spring a Negro youth was fighting with another youth; one of the police informers told him to stop, and he did not heed and was shot down on the streets. The murderer was not even arrested.

In Montgomery there are Negro helpers on the trash wagons and on the garbage trucks. There are some four hundred white employees on the capital payroll, but Negro convict labor is used for the Negro jobs.

In Mobile only one or two Negroes are now employed by the city. There are no Negroes in the water service or as street sweepers, garbage truck helpers, and so on. There is, however, a Negro fire company, the number one station, called the "Creole" Station and staffed by Creoles. These firemen get the same pay as the white firemen. They have a Creole captain and about ten firemen on the staff. All of these men are married to Negro women and, socially, they are completely assimilated into the Negro community.

It is claimed that Mayor Bright of Richmond, Virginia, in his four terms of office has never had a Negro on the payroll of the city except for schoolteachers, who are appointed by the school board. The only public jobs now held by Negroes in Richmond are a few maids at the capitol, a Negro branch librarian, and a few part-time jobs at the Negro swimming pool.

Norfolk Negroes are not employed in the city government as police, firemen, or road builders and repairmen, nor even as waiters in the government restaurants. A fight is now being

3. Edward Strong's interview with Marion E. Jackson, Birmingham, Alabama, May 1940. The quoted passages that concern Alabama in this chapter are taken from Strong's field notes. —ED.

waged to obtain the appointment of Negro policemen. Police jobs are civil service jobs.

Negroes hold no political office in the city government of Miami, Florida. A strong move has recently been initiated by Negro leaders there, backed by a petition with six hundred names attached, to get Negro policemen on the city force and a social worker employed to work in the black sections of the city. The committee sponsoring this movement has had several appearances before the city commissioners. A few Negro janitors are employed in the city buildings, but there are no Negro elevator operators. There are no Negro messengers, policemen, or firemen. There are Negro teachers and principals, and a few Negroes are employed as street sweepers.

In Tampa Negroes are employed as teachers, principals, road workers, and janitors, but not as ashmen, street cleaners, or garbage men, nor are there Negro policemen or firemen.

The garbage department of the department of public works of Beaumont, Texas, is operated almost exclusively by Negroes. This does not result from any pressure on the part of Negroes —it has always been so. There is one Negro uniformed policeman in Beaumont, but he is not permitted to arrest white people. He has been on the force for twenty-five years.

During the last thirty years in Dallas Negroes have held no political offices—not even as justices of the peace—nor have they served as policemen, as mail carriers, or on petty or grand juries.

No Negroes hold any city jobs in Baton Rouge, Louisiana. Until the 1940 gubernatorial contest, Negroes were employed as janitors, maids, and firemen at the state capitol building. In an effort to appeal to the poor white vote, Governor Earl K. Long —brother of Huey—discharged all of the Negro employees and invited whites to come and get the jobs. No Negroes are employed in the street cleaning or garbage collection departments in Baton Rouge. There are four Negro mail carriers in the city.

There are but two Negro janitors and one Negro charwoman employed in the city buildings of Macon, Georgia. Three or four Negro men drive dump carts. Some of the older Negro schools have no janitor service at all.

Negroes hold no offices in Augusta, and there have been no Negro candidates running for office in recent years. They do hold some appointive positions, however. There is a Negro juvenile officer whose appointment was obtained by virtue of the fact that for a number of years the Rosenwald Fund had paid the salary of the woman who got the job. There are very few Negro janitors in the city buildings and hardly any Negro scrubwomen. There are no black messengers, watchmen, street cleaners, ashmen, garbagemen, policemen, or firemen. There are Negro teachers and principals in the Negro schools, and Negroes are also employed in road building and repairs.

No Negro holds elective office in High Point, North Carolina, and none has ever run for office, but a Negro Democrat holds the appointive position of boys' commissioner. One of the offices of the unemployment compensation for colored in High Point is manned by an all-Negro staff. Negroes are employed as janitors, scrubwomen, teachers, and principals. Until 1931, when the Democrats gained control of the city government, Negroes had been employed as street cleaners. Today none is so employed.

The last Negro officeholders or city employees in Jackson, Mississippi, were two policemen who served over forty years ago. Today some Negroes in the city work as laborers on the street cleaning gangs and as garbage removal helpers.

In the citations made so far, it is obvious that the Negro's share of the city payrolls in the areas mentioned is pitifully small. Several communities are reported as having no Negro city employees, and those that do hire Negroes have so few— and these in the very lowest income brackets, doing the most menial work—that they have been characterized as "negligible." It should be pointed out here that Negroes are repeatedly mentioned as schoolteachers and principals. Inasmuch as all these communities have separate school facilities for the races, and Negroes are universally employed where such systems are operative, I think that for our purposes in this chapter such positions may be fairly eliminated as an important result of Negro participation in local politics, or the lack thereof.

The next group of cases includes those cities which carry a little more than a negligible number of Negroes on their payrolls, but at the same time fall far short of what might be termed an equitable proportion.

Despite the relatively large Negro vote in Raleigh, North Carolina, about the only real gains obtained through Negro political activity are the Negro manager and clerks in the state alcoholic beverage control store in the black section. Negroes do have the same privileges as whites in the city auditorium. Negroes hold only laborer's jobs in the city government, though one Negro woman was appointed as a maid at the city auditorium at a wage of fifteen dollars per week in 1938. There are white drivers and Negro helpers on the city's garbage trucks. In the city buildings the janitors are Negro. There are two Negro case-workers and one Negro truant officer. All policemen and firemen are white.

Negroes in Charlotte are employed by the city government as janitors, a few as messengers and scrubwomen, as watchmen on the roads, and as teachers and principals. There are no Ne-gro policemen or firemen, nor are there Negro street cleaners or ashmen.

Negroes find general employment in the city government of Greensboro, with the exception of white collar jobs, policemen, and firemen.

In Durham's whole history there have been only two Negro post office employees. In municipal employment there are white truck drivers and Negro helpers, Negro school janitors, and black courthouse elevator operators and janitors. In the city hall, however, all janitors are white. There are no Negro policemen, but there is the usual charge of police brutality against Negroes. At one time, about a quarter of a century ago, there were Negro firemen in Durham, but there have been none since.

In Newport News, Virginia, Negroes are employed in the city government as janitors, scrubwomen, messengers, watchmen, street cleaners, ashmen, garbagemen, road builders and repair-men, teachers, and principals. There are no Negro police or firemen.

Negroes in Portsmouth occupy only a small portion of the municipal employment, including such jobs as janitors and messengers. Due to the segregated school system, there are, of course, Negro teachers and principals. But the "all Negro" areas such as Brighton, Truxton, and Mount Herman are inadequately lighted, the roads are not paved, there is but one playground (in the Mount Herman section), and there are few schools. The police of Portsmouth are generally thought by members of the Negro community to be rude, insulting, threatening, and occa-sionally brutal.

There are a few Negroes employed by the city of Chattanooga as street cleaners and on garbage trucks as helpers. Several are employed as janitors and maids in the city offices and buildings. There are no Negroes on the Chattanooga Housing Authority, though there is a special Negro advisory committee. There are no Negro doctors and health experts on the staff of the city clinics and hospitals where Negroes are served.

There are six Negro policemen in Knoxville. Three of these drive patrol wagons, and the other three are privates who walk beats. Two of the three patrol drivers have a much higher seniority rating than many white police who have subsequently been promoted. No Negro policemen are on the patrol cruisers. The Negro officers receive the same salary as the whites, but do not receive promotions. Knoxville has two Negro USHA projects, while there is only one for whites.

There is one Negro policeman—a plainsclothesman—still active on the St. Augustine, Florida, police force, which in earlier years employed a number of black policemen. In the St. Augustine city hall the elevator boys and the janitor are Negro, and the same situation prevails in the county courthouse. There are a few Negro foremen of street work, but there are no Negro street cleaners, the last Negroes to work in this capacity having been replaced five or six years ago.

Negroes are not employed in the county or state governments in Charleston as street cleaners, policemen, or as waiters in government restaurants. There is an all-Negro fire station in Charleston—a hangover from the old days. Negroes are employed as janitors, ashmen, scrubwomen, road workers, and helpers on garbage trucks. There are, of course, Negro teachers and principals, though for a year white teachers taught in Negro schools.

Negroes in Columbia are employed in the local and state government as janitors, messengers, road builders and repairmen, teachers, and principals.

Finally, we have the much smaller but refreshing classification that includes those communities which have Negroes as city employees in a fairly equitable proportion.

Among the benefits enjoyed by Negroes in Louisville, largely as a result of the Negro's political influence, are the following: one stenographer in the second magistral court; two workers in the state old-age employment setup; twelve workers in the re-employment bureau; one full-time recreational director; one health center manned by Negro personnel under the direction of a Negro doctor; two Negro city physicians; two Negro school physicians; two Negro fire companies—the Negro firemen receiving the same salary as whites; two Negro detectives; ten Negro policemen who receive the same salary as white policemen; one head librarian; eight librarians; a Negro member of the housing commission; 350 Negro schoolteachers; seventeen Negro schools; two Negro junior high schools; one Negro senior high school; and one Negro municipal college. Approximately 350 Negroes are employed in the department of public works of Louisville as street cleaners, garbage collectors, and so forth. Eight Negro truck drivers have been given city contracts for hauling. A Negro woman was made matron of the city jail. Two black deputy jailers were appointed and also one Negro woman matron in the police court.

Among the jobs that Negroes hold in the city departments of Oklahoma City are the following: a proportionate share of street cleaners, garbagemen, and janitors; six Negro policemen; a school dentist and physician; city nurses and city physicians.

With respect to the possibility of returns from Negro political participation and support, a prominent Negro editor in Tulsa observed:

> I supported this administration, which has been in office about six years, and we were able to get from the administration the appointment of a Negro policewoman at a salary of $150.00 a month; a Negro health inspector at $145.00 a month; a Negro water meter reader at a salary of $125.00 per month; and have been promised a proportionate number of electric and gas meter readers. These things have been done through the efforts of our paper. Not only have we raised political issues, but we have carried on a campaign for the employment of Negroes in industry. . . .
>
> A unified Negro vote would be of greater significance than the small percentage of the Negro population would indicate, because such a large number of candidates offer in the primaries. The general election is held two weeks after the primaries.
>
> The coming election presents a contest [19 March 1940, city primary]. At this time mayor and commissioners will be elected. The main issue to Negroes will center around the election of a police commissioner, because in this department Negroes have eight white collar jobs; also around the election of a commissioner of water utilities. We are seeking more white-collar jobs in this department since there is only one Negro employed there at the present time.

Negroes have the following city positions in Tulsa: one Negro policewoman; six Negro policemen who receive the same wages as the white police; one health inspector; one Negro

janitor at the police station; and a large number of street laborers. In the county, there is a Negro deputy sheriff and two Negro
janitors. The county also operates the municipal hospital for
Negroes. This is a well-equipped hospital and is entirely staffed
by Negroes, including a Negro superintendent.

According to one active supporter of Mayor Maury Maverick
in San Antonio, Texas, sixteen Negro men were added to the
garbage collection force by the Maverick administration. It
made a promise of more Negro policemen—there are now three
Negro policemen in San Antonio, but they are permitted to arrest only in emergencies. There are also sixty Negro janitors
and maids in the city buildings and a Negro health inspector.
According to James Jackson's survey, there were thirty-one Negroes on San Antonio's payroll before Maverick's administration,
while now there are ninety-one. However, the wages received by
these Negro employees are lower than formerly, and there are
fewer white-collar jobs, such as inspectors, librarians, and so
forth.

The following account of the benefits derived from political
participation is given by a Negro racketeer and leader of the
opposition to the incumbent administration. Although these
two versions of the situation in San Antonio are primarily concerned with the fruits of Negro political activity, they also go a
long way toward revealing an exceptional political liveliness
among Negroes in a deep Southern town where the city elections
are nonpartisan in character.

According to Valmo Bellinger, who inherited his father's allegiance to the Quin machine and who marshaled the Negro
vote against Maury Maverick in the May 1939 mayoralty election, Negroes get less now under Maverick in San Antonio
than they ever received before. Maverick, he said, is determined
not to see a Negro in any leading capacity. He declares that before Maverick took office, there were three Negro women health
inspectors receiving $110.00 a month, one Negro male health
inspector receiving $125.00 a month, and three Negro city
nurses at $100.00 a month. Now, he says, there is only one Ne-
gro health inspector who receives $80.00 a month and one Ne-
gro nurse. He admits that sixteen garbage men were added, but
these, he states, receive only $9.00 per week now, though they
were started out at $15.00. He charges that Mayor Maverick
stripped the Negro policemen of their authority to arrest and
transferred them to night patrol beats in the business section of
town to serve as door watchers. There have been three police

cadet schools held since Maverick came into office, and Bel-
linger claims that not a one of them has had any Negro pupils.
The cadets receive $60.00 a month while in training. To quote
Bellinger:

> Maverick has made brave and courageous speeches in the
> South and over the country for civil rights and for economic
> justice to the Negro, but here in San Antonio he hasn't done a
> goddam thing for Negroes that they didn't receive and to a
> much greater extent under Quin or Tobin. As a matter of
> fact, he has done proportionately much less than these two
> did. They built the fine schools, the playgrounds, the library
> auditorium, and established the precedent of Negro in-
> spectors and assistants in the department of health—not
> Maverick.

The Communist party in San Antonio, which had supported
Maverick and the fusion party in the 1939 election, has recently
come out with a proclamation of "grave misgivings as to whether
progressive support can continue to be given Maverick and the
fusion party." The declaration gives Maverick credit for a somewhat improved health department, a vigorous stand for civil
rights, the right of workers to picket, and more efficient operation of the various departments of the city government. On the
other hand, it points out critically that Maverick has done nothing to establish unemployment relief for San Antonio's thousands of impoverished masses, that civic improvements such as
streets and recreation facilities are still missing from the chief
working class neighborhoods, and that adequate neighborhood
venereal, maternal, and tuberculosis health centers are still
only in the blueprint stage.

Negroes hold several city jobs in Kansas City, Kansas. There
are schoolteachers, but it is to be noted that this is the only city
in the state of Kansas where there is a separate school system.
On the whole, it is said that race relations in Kansas City, Kansas, are friendly. There is no Jim Crow on the streetcars, as there
is none in Kansas City, Missouri.

Kansas City, Missouri, Negroes traditionally have had some
representation in the city departments. There are now eighteen
Negro policemen, and there have been as many as fifty. There
are eighteen Negro firemen. The wages of Negro policemen and
firemen are the same as for whites. There is one Negro woman
in the city welfare department, one turnkey in the county jail,
one county juvenile officer, one county juvenile investigator,

and one county deputy coroner. The Negro branch of the city hospital is entirely staffed by Negroes. Garbage disposal is let out to private contractors, and only a few Negroes are employed in this work. There are a few Negro foremen and a proportionate number of Negro street cleaning gangs in the department of public works. The NAACP local has made a strong appeal to the political parties for Negro inclusion in the administrative personnel of the municipality. This appeal indicates to some extent the political consciousness and technique of the Negroes in an important city of a border state.

Equally, or probably more, important to the general Negro communities is the matter of municipal services, the adequacy or inadequacy of which has a direct bearing upon the health, morals, and safety of a city's inhabitants. For example, in Opelousas, St. Landry Parish, Louisiana, there are no library, park, or other recreational facilities provided for Negroes. Baton Rouge, Louisiana, makes no provision for Negro recreational or park facilities. Negroes live in widely-scattered sections of the city, and consequently the streets, as a whole, are generally well paved and well lighted in the black residential sections. There are no playground or park facilities for Negroes in Jackson, Mississippi. There is no delinquent home for Negro youth. Streets, sidewalks, and lights in the Negro neighborhoods are totally inadequate.

According to S. D. Redmond, prominent Negro Republican in Jackson:

Negroes are closed out of all government benefits in Mississippi. The WPA and the New Deal agencies haven't meant a goddamned thing to the Negroes of Mississippi. Last year they cut out the only Negro sewing project we had in the city, and, at the same time, they added to the white project. WPA projects have to be sponsored by the county, state, or municipality, and the Mississippi politicians refuse to put up a dollar for work relief for Negroes in cooperation with the government. I went to Washington to take this matter up with Colonel Harrington and offered to furnish a building, heat, and light for the sewing project, but Harrington insisted that cloth also had to be furnished by the city before the project could be approved and funds let. The city refused to contribute the necessary $31.00 a week to give 100 Negro women work on this project. Fifty thousand dollars is spent for WPA sewing projects in Jackson alone, but Negroes do not receive one cent of it. One hundred forty-six thousand dollars of WPA money is spent every month in Jackson, yet there is not a single Negro white collar worker. Negroes in Mississippi are not getting any direct relief at all. A meager amount of surplus food commodity groceries is doled out, however. No Negro has been appointed as custodian or clerk in the post office since Hoover went into office. Less than one-half of the mail carriers are Negroes, and no new Negro appointments to the carrier service have occurred in several years.

Negro teachers get 40 cents a month more than they received forty-five years ago. The average salary for Negro county schoolteachers is $31.00 a month. In the city schools, the salary ranges from $35.00 to $50.00 a month; that is, if you have a college degree and have served satisfactorily for five or ten years, you might be included in the higher brackets and receive the breathtaking sum of $50.00 a month.

There was no high school here until 1925. [This school was built after many years of agitation and struggle on the part of Negroes of the community under the leadership of Redmond.] It now has about 900 pupils.

Alcorn College receives only $25,000 per year from the state, though it is a land grant college. It receives an additional $25,000 from the United States government.

There are no library facilities or parks for Negroes in Natchez, Mississippi. The first Negro high school in Natchez was built in 1926 at a cost of $80,000. This school also has elementary grades. It employs twenty-one teachers and has about a thousand pupils. The appropriation for this school came as a result of a special bond issue election and in spite of the fact that no Negroes were allowed to vote in the election. According to the Natchez superintendent of schools, this is thought to be

> indicative of the good feeling of the white people toward their Negro friends and servants. The relation here between the races is cordial. That is, the white people do not hesitate to give Negroes anything they want in reason, but they will not tolerate any noisy demands on the part of Negroes from their own initiative.

Negroes do not have adequate clinical and library facilities, garbage and trash removal, lighting, or playgrounds.

In Charleston, South Carolina, Negroes cannot ride through the city's Hampton Park without being stopped by police and told, "Niggers aren't allowed here." But the city authorities disclaim responsibility for this, stating that it is a mistake. Negroes are not permitted to visit the aviary, the zoo, or the botanical gardens. The Kiwanis Club of the city donated benches for Colonial Lake Park, but the benches are designated "for white only." The city authorities claim that they have no responsibility for these benches. It is a common saying among Negroes in Charleston that Negroes cannot sit on these benches unless they are holding a white child.

South Carolina law prohibits Negroes from using any public buildings available to whites. Fire protection is said to be good, due to the fact that most of the houses in Negro sections are owned by whites. In the Negro sections, however, paving, roads, lights, and street marking are not good. But Negroes do live all over Charleston. School facilities for Negroes are very poor—inadequate and terribly crowded—so much so in fact that they run on shifts. There are no playgrounds for Negroes, and blacks do not have access to the white parks. There is a library for Negroes, but land on which it is built was donated to the city by a Negro woman.

There is no park in Macon, Georgia, for Negroes, and there is no black swimming pool. Negroes can only walk through the white parks and can sit down only when carrying white children.

There is no four-year accredited high school for Negroes in Augusta, Georgia. There are some private Negro church high schools which charge tuition. There are no playgrounds for Negroes except the school areas, which recreation leaders on WPA employ to develop their programs. Street lights are bad.

In Gainesville, Georgia, although the Negro citizens pay full city taxes, there is no sewage service in the Negro section of town. Surface privies are used by all Negroes. The houses are jammed so close together that there is neither light, ventilation, nor privacy. Negroes have been almost completely displaced in the street work by whites. There has been virtually no police protection, and in the 1920s when the Klan was active, many Negroes were threatened, beaten, and run out of town without police interference.

There is one Negro park in Beaumont, Texas, and Negroes gave the land for it. It is equipped with a swimming pool. In the South Park district, there is a very fine Negro high school which stands on land given by Negroes. The hospital accommodations for Negroes in Beaumont are quite inadequate, and the Negro physicians cannot practice in the city hospitals. When it rains, the streets in the Negro quarter are virtually impassable. There are blocks and blocks of the Negro quarters without street lights.

Quite generally the streets in the Negro neighborhoods of Houston, Texas, are abominable. They are unpaved and without sidewalks. This is true only to a slightly less extent in the Mexican quarter.

Negro schools, playgrounds, paving, lights, libraries, and clinics are woefully inadequate in Charlotte, North Carolina.

In Little Rock, Arkansas, Negroes have for their use only about seventy hospital beds in the entire city. They are given basement accommodations in the city hospital, but no Negro physician can treat his patients in that hospital. In the public school system the average salary for Negro teachers is about one-half that of the average for white teachers doing the same work, notwithstanding the fact that the average white teacher's salary in Little Rock is greatly below that of the country as a whole. There are no Negro policemen or firemen in Little Rock.

In some communities where Negroes live in Birmingham, trash and ashes are never taken up by the city. They just have to pile the stuff—ashes and tin cans and old bottles—up in the yard. In most Negro neighborhoods that are paved, private owners have taken the cost upon themselves. The real estate men never pave a Negro street. Street lights appear in Negro neighborhoods mostly where there is a business corner. As for street signs, there have been plenty of those since the WPA started putting them up on Negro corners. In 1915 Enon Ridge could boast of only one paved street. It was a through street which led to the highway and to the Jewish cemetery. Although Enon Ridge was and remains a residential district with a large percentage of home owners, street pavement, lights, and sewage facilities were relatively unknown until recently. Prior to the WPA there were only five streets in this area with any pavement, and only one or two blocks on each street were paved. With the help of the WPA an additional four streets have been partially paved on the ridge within the last two years. The limited success in securing lights, pavement, sewage disposal, and the collection of garbage has come through the personal relationships which Negro residents had with leading white people, through the petitions signed by the citizens and addressed to the authorities, and through the few votes which the Negroes on the ridge have exercised under the direction of their civic league.

"Policemen," said one resident of Birmingham, "generally speak to Negroes like they are speaking to an animal." This, he added, is to keep Negroes frightened into acceptable behavior. Tax collectors are always very sharp to Negroes. Small peddlers are very much troubled with getting licenses and with being forced to stop business when they cannot obtain the license. "We have a lot of police stool pigeons," this man said. Individuals in practically every Negro neighborhood can be found who inform the police of every move in their community. Often these stool pigeons are bootleggers who are given permission to carry on illegal sale of liquor without police interference in return for the information they give on Negroes in the neighborhood. The stool pigeon reports petty crimes of all types.

Some instances of communities in which living conditions for Negroes are somewhat better, though not good, follow. In general in these Negro sections fire protection, water supply, and garbage and trash removal are fairly adequate. Yet the Negro sections are often neglected with regard to sidewalks, road and street paving, street lights, school facilities, playgrounds, and libraries. There are frequently to be found in the Negro quarters the almost impassable roads, the ramshackle houses, the dark, narrow streets, and the flagrant lack of playgrounds.

Despite extensive Negro political activity in Chattanooga, Tennessee, the Negro population is in need of better recreational facilities and better housing. The streets in the Negro section are inadequately marked and lighted, and they are kept in ill repair.

There are no playgrounds for Negroes in Norfolk. It is said, however, that fire protection is good because, as one Negro puts it, "all the property is owned by white realtors." Police protection is negligible in Negro residential areas. Sidewalks, roads, and street paving in Negro sections are bad. Garbage and trash removal is regular. Street lights and street signs are inadequate. Schools are frequently firetraps. Library facilities are poor. Clinics are few. The one public clinic for Negroes was run for years —since 1932, in fact—by Dr. Byrd, a prominent Negro physician who ran it on a private basis. There is no library for Negroes, but the schools are thought to be good. There are three playgrounds. Police protection, fire protection, street lighting, water supply, and paving are fairly adequate in the Negro sections. Just recently, $1,125,000 was set aside for an all-Negro slum clearance project—after several months of argument in the city council.

Municipal services for Negroes are fair in Winston-Salem, North Carolina. Most of the streets in the Negro sections are paved—at least with tar and rock. There are relatively good schools and street markings, though the playground facilities are inadequate. There is a branch library for Negroes and a new modernistic hospital—the "Kate Bittings Memorial Hospital"—in which there are Negro interns but no Negro resident physicians. The work force of this hospital—switchboard operators, information desk, and so on—is all white.

On the whole, Negroes receive a totally inadequate share of the municipal services in Miami, Florida. Housing is deplorable. Police protection comes only from police cruisers which travel through "colored town" about once a day. There are two new sidewalks in the Negro section obtained since the voting of last year. Otherwise, the sidewalks and roads in the Negro sections are rocky and rough. Garbage removal is poor but is said to have improved some since the Negro voting of last year. There is only one park for Negroes, and it contains no seats and has poor recreational equipment. The schools are crowded and poorly constructed. One Negro grammar school consists of twelve portables. There is as yet no Negro library in Miami, but one has been promised. The branch Negro library has been authorized through the kindness of a black realtor in Miami who donated the land for the building. Negroes of Miami have organized a library club which has as its sole objective a library for the Negro children of the city. Hospital facilities are deplorable.

The streets in the Negro sections of Jacksonville, Florida, are bad. Few of them are paved. There are few street lights, and police protection is virtually nonexistent in Negro sections. There are only two playgrounds for Negroes in the city. There is only one high school for Negroes. There is a branch library for Negroes. Older residents of the city recall that about fifteen years ago Negroes were permitted to use the city public library, and at one time a Negro was employed as a librarian in the city library.

In San Antonio, Texas, Negro teachers' salaries are the same as those of white teachers, and the schools are relatively good. There are three Negro parks, and Negroes are not excluded from the other city parks.

Although Greensboro, North Carolina, Negroes are inclined to think that they do not fare too badly with regard to municipal services, the fact is that their two-story hospital with sixty beds and their $150,000 YMCA are benevolences from white philanthropists and not from the city government. On the "other side of the railroad tracks," the visitor to Greensboro is confronted with the usual picture of a Negro "residential area" in the South, with its typical squalor.

When the third and "better" group of cities is considered, it is found that largely the same situation exists as was pointed out in the case of elective officials and appointive jobs. That is to say, the cities in the border states offer most to the Negro. St. Louis and both Kansas Cities have complaints of poor sewage, garbage removal, and unsanitary drinking water. The schools, though separate, come closer to being equal to the white setups than in any other communities under consideration here. There are library facilities in these cities, and although there are not enough, there are recreational centers, institutions for delinquents, and the like. While the Negro sections of these communities are far from being perfectly serviced, there are paved streets with sidewalks and lights and reasonable transportation facilities. All things taken into consideration, conditions are better.

The view has been expressed that Negroes receive representation, municipal services, and jobs in direct relation to the effectiveness or potential effectiveness of their participation in the political life of their respective communties. A rough attempt has been made to give some picture, though admittedly sketchy and incomplete, of the comparative situations in cities where Negroes vote or do not vote. Although the difference is apparent, the conclusion should not be drawn that Negroes have derived local benefits on a pro rata basis as a result of this participation in any city, either North or South. More logical is the deduction that, with or without the political participation, Negroes receive only that amount of dividend which is necessary, not to satisfy their equitable claims, but merely to soften their demands for their "just deserts." To this perhaps we should add the statement that in cases where the Negro voter might be used by the politicians he is given just enough to produce a sort of expectancy or anticipation for better things if his political behavior is satisfactory.

Now that they have the vote, large sections of Negroes in Nashville and Chattanooga are demanding small concessions in return for their party obedience. They receive representation on the police force, better streets, and more equal treatment as regards sanitation and health facilities than formerly. As George Stoney has put it:

Even in those places where the Negro vote has been brought about purely for machine purposes, however, some direct benefits in the form of streets, garbage collection, and so on, have resulted. The Miami vote is especially significant here. Despite the fact that it was an independent movement (or more properly *because* of it) direct improvements in garbage collection and other city services were seen almost immediately. Encouraged by this, similar Negro-inspired movements to register are going on in Winston-Salem, Greensboro, New Orleans, Little Rock, and—most successfully of all—in Birmingham, Alabama.

EIGHTEEN

Negro Political Activity in the North

PRIOR to World War I, the Negro population in Northern urban centers was small and scattered; so much so that as a political factor in these areas it was negligible. The bulk of the Negro population in the United States was still centered in the South, engaged for the most part in agricultural pursuits. The great migration of Southern blacks during the last quarter-century has changed this situation. It is not difficult to understand that the great majority of this new Negro population in the North was ignorant and in many cases illiterate, economically poor, and entirely unacquainted with the intense political life that flourished in the Northern cities. Yet, despite the fact that his educational background was meager and that he was a political novice, the transplanted Negro soon became a political factor of importance to the politicians. A few cities with sizable "black belts" have been selected for discussion in this memorandum in an effort to give a clear picture of the Negro's participation in the political life of the North.

Prior to 1910 Negroes constituted about 2 percent of the population of Chicago. This relatively small segment of the citizenry was naturally insignificant in politics.[1] The influx of migrants during the war and regularly thereafter expanded the Negro community to such an extent that by 1930 a densely

1. The following discussion of Negro politics in Chicago is based largely upon Harold F. Gosnell, *Negro Politicians: The Rise of Negro Politics in Chicago* (Chicago, 1935), and Elmer W. Henderson, "A Study of the Basic Factors Involved in the Change in the Party Alignment of Negroes in Chicago, 1932–1938" (M.A. thesis, University of Chicago, 1939). —ED.

populated Negro area stretched about seven miles long and a mile and a half wide, starting from the Loop (Chicago's downtown district) and running southward. Packed within the confines of this area were 191,001 Negroes, or 80 percent of all the city's Negroes. This is Chicago's famed "Black Belt." Most of the Negroes who came to Chicago were adults and consequently of voting age.

The political activity of the Negro in Chicago began very soon after he was enfranchised in Illinois in 1869. Despite the fact that the Negro electorate was small during this period, John Jones, a Negro businessman, was elected a commissioner of Cook County in 1871. Five years later a Negro was returned to the state legislature. By the 1880s Chicago politicians, including such Democrats as Mayor Carter Harrison, were catering to the small Negro vote. As early as 1897 the *Broad Ax*, a Negro newspaper, became the official organ of the Democratic party among Negroes in Chicago and operated for about thirty years thereafter. One of the earliest issues of this paper endorsed the Democratic party and urged Negroes to split their vote.

The large majority of the newcomers from the South could not think of the Republican party without thinking at the same time of Lincoln, emancipation, rights as American citizens, philanthropy, and Frederick Douglass. They had implicit faith in Douglass' warning that "the Republican party is the ship—all else the sea." On the other hand, mention of the Democratic party was the stimulus that gave rise to such abhorrent thoughts as slavery, oppression, lynching, the Ku Klux Klan, and disfranchisement. Most of the early Negro political leaders were from the South and were dyed-in-the-wool Republicans with no inclination to shift party allegiance. Democratic party leaders in the North realized this hostility on the part of the large Negro addition to the electorate and attempted to gird the party by subjecting the European immigrants (particularly the Irish) to intense propaganda against the Negro. Many of these Europeans became staunch Democrats because they saw in the migrant Negro a potential competitor for the unskilled and low-paid jobs in which they were told they had a vested interest. These circumstances probably account for the fact that no strong Negro Democratic leaders appeared on the American political scene before the 1920s.

The Negroes in Chicago began their very active political participation in 1915, when William Hale "Big Bill" Thompson was elected mayor. The fact that Thompson's success was due almost entirely to the heavy Negro vote cast for him in the first and second wards indicates the extent to which black voters were active. Thompson was not one to overlook this fact, and during the three terms he served as mayor, he took great pains to maintain the goodwill of the Negro citizenry. Thompson did his job well, for he established a control over the Negro vote which seemed impossible to break. This faithful devotion of the Negro electorate to the Republican party did not receive a serious jolt until the economic crisis of the early 1930s. As the New Deal program swung into action, the Democratic machine in Chicago became more powerful and the small minority of Negro Democrats soon became a majority. By 1939 there were indications that the Democratic party had taken over the Negro vote almost as completely and strongly as the Republicans had under Thompson.

Notwithstanding this shift in local party loyalty and the distasteful policies of Herbert Hoover, Chicago Negroes gave the Republicans 76.6 percent of their votes in 1932. Experts believe that one of the most important reasons for the heavy Republican vote among Negroes in 1932 was the fact that John Nance Garner, a Southerner from one of Texas' worst towns so far as they were concerned, was Roosevelt's running mate. Not until 1934, two years after the New Deal had been initiated, did Chicago's Negroes show any signs of deserting the Republican ranks. The intensity of the depression and the assumption of relief activities by the government were probably the most important factors in this switching of party loyalty. Other factors which contributed to this realignment of political allegiance were: (1) the friendly attitude of the Democrats as reflected in the appointment of a Negro ward committeeman in 1932, and the support given to a Negro congressional candidate in 1934; and (2) Roosevelt's increasing popularity.

Since Negroes first won places as aldermen from the second and third wards (1915 and 1921 respectively), they had been consistent Republicans in this area up to 1939. In that year the Negro Republicans were replaced by Negro Democrats. Except in the sixth ward, Democratic aldermen were elected in all the wards in which Negroes were numerous enough to be a definite political factor.

It is the contention of several prominent Democrats in Chicago that Mayor Edward J. Kelly hired more Negroes than received city government jobs under Mayor Thompson. Of course, the Negroes received these jobs because the black electorate was an important cog in the Democratic party machine, and the most effective method of building up and maintaining a worthwhile machine is to make patronage available to the party workers. According to Edward Sneed, the only Negro Democratic committeeman in Chicago, some forty-five precinct captains in the third ward alone were city employees. Although most of these jobs are of the minor variety, they serve as an index to the degree of recognition the Democrats are now according the Negro voters. Under Kelly, Negroes were also appointed to many upper-bracket positions. The chief elective offices to which Negroes were returned through Democratic backing were: United States congressman, from the first district (Arthur W. Mitchell); state senator, from the third district; county commissioner; and alderman, from the first and third wards.

In addition to the ordinary methods which are employed by politicians to build up an effective political machine—getting jobs for voters, doing small favors, securing bonds, or reducing sentences—the Democrats had an unusual advantage over the Republicans which has enabled them to keep many of their Negro supporters in line. The Negroes of the city felt the worst pangs of the depression and, as a result, swelled the ranks of the unemployed and indigent. When the government took over the administration of relief, the Democrats were in a position to manipulate the relief and the WPA. Still another factor which has had its effect upon the recent political activity of Chicago's Negro electorate is the wave of trade unionism which swept the city. Chicago is one of the leading union cities as far as Negroes are concerned, and the CIO is the Negro's choice in the majority of instances, since the AFL has been traditionally discriminatory in its policies. Not only were the employed Negroes unionized to a large extent, but even the unemployed were recruited by organizations of the unemployed, the most important of which was the Workers' Alliance of America. It is claimed that over half of the membership of the Cook County local of the Alliance is Negro.

In Chicago, as in most other cities, the Negro church occupies a most important position in politics. In all of the Northern communities the influx of Negroes during the period of migration greatly increased the number and membership of Negro churches. Professor Gosnell estimates, on the basis of the 1930 census, that more than half of Chicago's Negro voters were church members and that about a fourth of them attended regular Sunday services. Any politician would look upon this as a source of votes worth tapping. The problem of utilizing the Negro church is simplified to some extent because the preachers have rather strong motives for playing the great American game. A large number of the churches are mortgaged to the hilt, and not infrequently the congregations are poor. In most instances, the purchase or erection of a building presents a serious problem to the minister. Seeing a chance to ingratiate themselves and, at the same time, obligate the church, the politicians have been very liberal with loans and even gifts. During a political campaign it is not hard to find a white or Negro candidate sharing the church platform with the clergyman during Sunday morning services.

Being obligated by loans or gifts is not the only reason for many ministers entering politics. Sometimes enterprising members of the cloth rent their pulpits to politicians, that is, charge a fee for opening the pulpit on Sunday to candidates. Then, too, there are those men of God who solicit campaign funds in return for the delivery of a certain number of votes. A Chicago preacher of the Father Divine type is described as the liaison man between the politicians and gangsters on the one hand and the Negro masses on the other. The employers pay this minister very well. At election time he is kept very busy, since he is one of the instruments in keeping the Negro masses "in line." Finally, there is that small group of ministers who sincerely believe that though the game is "dirty" it presents the only opportunity for really making some gains for their people. If this is possible, they are willing to "soil their hands."

In their efforts to capture the Negro electorate, politicians have used, and now utilize, any media which reach this special group. Next to the church, the Negro press is probably most important in this connection. Generally speaking, Negro newspapers are weeklies, with circulations which are too small to be attractive to big advertisers. In addition to this, it is no easy matter to interest a businessman in advertising through a medium which reaches, for the most part, that segment of the population comprising the lower economic level. This is a serious financial handicap. The result is that the Negro press is made particularly susceptible to the proposals of politicians and others who are interested in having a say in the matter of "running the town." In Chicago only the *Defender* and the *Bee* have stood the test of time since 1919, when seven weeklies were published.

Almost without exception, when one hears the term "political machine," he immediately thinks of "corrupt politics." Chicago, which made international headlines for years on account of its underworld activities, has its share of this sort of thing. And the Negro underworld comes in for its share of notoriety. The vice lords and their cohorts occupy a rather privileged position and are subjected to what might be termed protective custody. The racketeers and small-time criminals insure their freedom of action by making themselves as useful as possible to the politicians. A sizable portion of the so-called "protection payoff" is devoted to campaign contributions, and the "big shots" exert all their efforts to deliver as many votes as possible to a "winner." It should be reported that one of Chicago's most famous policy barons and a few lesser lights in the underworld furnished the funds to keep a WPA project running for Negroes.[2]

A graphic picture of the connection of Chicago's politics with the underworld is given as follows. There are three units: A, "down town," headed by the mayor; B, "the ward committeemen"; and C, "precinct captains." The racketeers of various kinds are usually in class C. Jobs and protection go from A to B to C. The protection money or the "payoff" goes from C to B to A. Much goes on in the Negro underworld that needs protection. The ward committeemen usually have well-paid jobs in the city administration. The precinct captains are the vice lords.

As in most cities of any size, the Negroes of Chicago have been made very much aware of the existence of the Communist party. To anyone who is even casually familiar with the effect of the depression on the Negro, it is easy to understand why the Communists considered the time ripe to appeal to American Negroes. The Communists took full advantage of the depression crisis and put their very best tactics into operation in Chicago. Yet, in spite of the high pressure tactics of the Communists, only some five hundred Negroes are estimated to have become party members. In the first place, the Negro church and religion possessed too strong a hold on the underprivileged masses who happened to be doing most of the suffering. The ministers took a militant stand against the "Red Menace" and did their best to counteract the propaganda. Secondly, the industrial squad of the police department, commonly referred to as the "Red Squad," had no reputation for gentleness. Demonstrations were

2. Gunnar Myrdal's interview with Horace Cayton, Chicago, 2 January 1940.

forbidden, meetings raided, leaflets confiscated, and, more often than not, leaders and speakers beaten up and incarcerated. Finally, the coming of Roosevelt and the launching of the New Deal relief, labor, and social legislation knocked much of the wind out of the Communists' sails from the point of view of propaganda.

The participation of the Negro in politics has secured for him a number of desirable jobs. The chief source of employment in this group is the postal service. Of the municipal departments, the public library, the health department, and the water bureau have been most liberal. Negroes have also secured more positions on the city's police force than in any other American community and have attained the rank of lieutenant and sergeant. There are also several high school teachers and principals in the city's school system. All of these employment opportunities are attributed to the Chicago Negro's general participation in the city's politics. The Negro voter in Chicago has traded on political loyalty. He has exercised his political privilege within the shadow of machine politics, and he has reaped gains in the form of jobs, municipal services, and some voice in city affairs. But he has not shared in the most lucrative kinds of graft that have been typical of Chicago and all machine-ridden communities. There have been no large Negro contracting firms to bargain for city contracts, no Negro banks, Negro realtors, or Negroes in those administrative posts which provide the best opportunity for harvesting the "spoils." The Negro spoils have been chiefly petty—police "protection," court "fixing," and so forth. The important jobs obtained as political rewards by Negroes in Chicago have, in addition to their economic significance, a prestige value for the group. They afford a new tone, a psychological "lift" for the entire Negro community. Another result of Negro political activity in Chicago has been the stimulation of race-consciousness among white voters and those of other minority groups.

The first Negro to hold an elective office in Cleveland was John P. Green, an attorney, who was elected as justice of the peace in 1873.[3] Although this was a minor political office, it was regarded as very significant that a Negro should hold it in those days. Green served in this capacity for nine years and then was elected for two terms to the lower house of Ohio's general assem-

3. The following discussion of Negro politics in Cleveland is based upon "The Cleveland Negro in Politics," a memorandum prepared by Harry E. Davis, a Cleveland attorney and politician, in March 1940. —ED.

bly. He wound up his political career by serving a term in the state senate. Since the time of Green, whenever the Republicans have carried the county, a Negro has represented the district in the state legislature. Beginning in the late 1890s, there was a heavy influx of Negroes in Cleveland which soon augmented the black population to the point that it was a substantial voting bloc. This sudden increase resulted in the nomination and election of a Negro, Thomas W. Fleming, as a councilman at large in 1910. Fleming was the first Negro to hold an elective office in Cleveland's municipal government.

During the wartime migration of Negroes from the South to Northern communities, Cleveland's black population swelled to about four times its normal size and reached the 80,000 mark. Naturally this increase had its political effect. Four wards became predominantly Negro, and three wards had a Negro vote which was the balance of power. With the coming of such large numbers of Negroes and their participation in the political life of the community, the Negro councilmen increased to three and this number has been consistently maintained. In 1934 Harry E. Davis was elected as one of the fifteen members of the first county charter commission. This latter election was on a county-wide basis. Naturally this impressive Negro voting strength was considered when public offices were distributed under the patronage system. Davis was chosen as a civil service commissioner by the city council in 1928 for a term of six years and was succeeded by Claybourne George, another Negro, who was appointed by the mayor. George is still in the position. Harvey B. Atkins was elected as an assistant city clerk and has been promoted to first assistant. L. L. Yancy, another Negro, was appointed as secretary of the city planning commission. Charles Smith advanced from the rank of patrolman in the police department to that of secretary of public safety, drawing a police captain's salary. At the present time, the Negro voters are set upon electing a municipal judge. An attempt has also been made in recent years to arrange for a "Negro" congressional district, that is, a district so patterned that a Negro congressman might be elected by the black electorate.

The widespread political activity of Negroes in Cleveland, according to Harry E. Davis, has also had its effect upon Negroes holding nonpartisan positions. In this connection the board of education has received particular attention. Efforts to have Negroes promoted to principalships and appointed in the city's high schools got very few results until very recently. In

1929 Mary B. Martin, a former teacher in the city, was elected as the first Negro member of the board of education. She served two terms and came back in 1939 for a third term. Political pressure exerted by Negroes also forced the city hospital, which had been a "closed" institution to Negro doctors and nurses for years, to adopt a more liberal policy. This hospital is managed by the medical school of Western Reserve University under contract with the city. Because "it never has been done," Negro interns and student nurses were not used. Davis says that continuous pressure exerted by Negro leaders opened both of these positions and secured one staff appointment.

Although most of this political recognition has occurred under favor of Republican allegiance, Negroes have recognized the value and merit of independent voting. Except in local nonpartisan judiciary elections, however, there are few contests in which independent voting could be effectively practiced. According to Davis's memorandum, the same conditions which made for Republican allegiance on the part of Negroes in other communities had similar effects in Cleveland. In an effort to defeat Warren G. Harding in 1920, the Democratic party openly appealed to race prejudice by intimating that Harding had Negro blood in his veins. In the beginning these efforts were in the form of a whispering campaign, but toward the end of the campaign period, a circular was distributed throughout the country. This appeal to race prejudice caused the defeat of two of the three Negro candidates for the Ohio legislature, but it infuriated the black voters and further postponed the tendency to vote a split ticket.

Negroes had begun to show their resentment against Republican indifference and neglect even as early as 1900. But it took Franklin D. Roosevelt to wean the Negroes from Lincoln's party. This was in 1936. In Cleveland every Negro ward went Democratic and local Republican leaders were unable to stem the tide. Davis points out that this complete reversal in party allegiance was due chiefly to Roosevelt's relief policies and that Negroes admittedly voted for "bread and butter" in preference to outworn party allegiances. Davis substantiates his contention by pointing to the fact that in the 1937 local elections the Negro wards returned to the Republican column and are still there and that even in the 1936 Democratic landslide several "home-owning" precincts in one densely-populated Negro ward voted the Republican ticket. The local Democratic party realized the possibility and desirability of capturing the Negro vote. In order to accomplish this the Democrats very openly used the tremendous amount of patronage at their disposal. Negroes were appointed as ward leaders, ward organizations were set up, appointments to public office were given rather generously, and "relief" was used to further their ends.

Arthur L. Taylor explains the numerous appointments of Negroes to public office by pointing to the support given to Governor Martin Davey by Negroes in 1935. During the Davey campaign a state-wide Negro Democratic organization was formed under the name of the Ohio State Negro Democratic League, with Thomas Davis as its head. This organization still functions and publishes the *Ohio Democrat*. The Workers' Federation of Ohio came into being early in 1936, apparently as an organization to protect Negro workers in the WPA, but it was very active in Cleveland during the presidential campaign. The Glenville Civic and Progressive League is an example of one of the first Democratic organizations established during the administration of Mayor Ray T. Miller (Democrat). It has been active but not very influential in local, state, and national campaigns. A similar organization is the Young People's Civic and Progressive League under the leadership of Dr. L. L. Rodgers. The personal leadership of several Negroes holds the various Democratic organizations together rather loosely, but internal strife and the lack of capable leadership have prevented the formation of any well-organized Democratic Negro organization which would compare favorably with those of the Republicans.

Harry E. Davis characterizes the Negro leadership in Cleveland as "good on the whole, though not exceptional or brilliant," and states that it has generally been able to unite on candidates and issues. He readily admits that these leaders have not been idealists; but they have been "practical" men and have followed the political pattern woven by the dominant group. Under the spoils system, the Negroes have played the political game along the prescribed lines and have demanded their share of patronage. In Cleveland Negro leaders, "by diligent effort," have acquired a new dignity in the inner circles of both party councils. Negroes no longer stand by meekly and take orders, but their advice is sought and respected, and they are not timid in expressing themselves. Davis puts the finishing touches on his picture of Negro political leadership with the following:

> Moreover, Negro leadership in Cleveland has always insisted upon social justice, and social freedom for the colored

group. Leaders have uniformly demanded that colored people be not subjected to social insult, ignomy, humiliation and discrimination. In the past twenty-five or thirty years there has been a persistent and unsuccessful effort to obtain public recreational facilities, libraries, schools, adequate transportation and well paved, well lighted and clean streets in colored residential districts. Further, the areas of tolerance have been explored and expanded by tactful and unobtrusive effort.

Davis attributes the ability of the Negro voters in Cleveland to cast an effective ballot to the regular schooling in marking ballots given by the leaders. Although this procedure lends itself to machine voting, it has some wholesome values. When the proportional representation system of voting was effective in Cleveland, a checkup showed that there were fewer ineffective and void ballots in the Negro precincts than in the so-called "intelligent" wards. Negroes were quick to accept instruction about anything that pertained to the franchise.

Davis's account mentions the fact that the foreign groups brought some left-wing radicalism to Cleveland which has affected the "political complacency" of the American tradition. The various radical movements, however, have gained only negligible adherence from Negro voters, and what little exists is attributable to the "radical assertion of complete racial equality." The Negro voter is naturally conservative, and is only moved from his conservative attitude by economic stress or racial persecution. In commenting on Davis's account of "radicalism" among the Negroes in Cleveland, Arthur L. Taylor of the Neighborhood Association of Cleveland says:

> Actually, membership in either party (Communist or Socialist) has never been widespread among Negroes in Cleveland. The Socialist Party probably numbered a few prior to "depression" years and these, for the most part, were of higher intellectual level than the larger numbers who became active with the Communist Party and its inspired organizations during the early years of widespread economic depression. Participation on the part of Negroes in the activities of the Communist Party, although at no time very considerable in view of the total Negro population, was more in the nature of an economic necessity. The council of the unemployed, for instance, appealed to them as one agency for bringing attention to their economic plight. Mass demonstrations constituted a new technique of protest for them and unity with

whites encouraged them, but the element of social equality had little or nothing to do with the large majority.

With the advent of more permanent relief administration, through federal, state and local agencies, these demonstrations became less necessary and Negro membership in the Communist Party and its inspired organizations reduced correspondingly. At the present time there are probably not more than 100 Negro members in the Communist Party in Cleveland.

In addition to the various organizations prevously mentioned, there are several youth councils, religious and civic, which attract the interest of the young people of the city. Davis claims that all of these activities have contributed to the "increased respect which is accorded the Cleveland Negro." Frequently the city council has adopted resolutions denouncing the subversive activities of such organizations as the Ku Klux Klan and has endorsed antilynching bills. Recently a site on two main thoroughfares was set aside for a monument to the late Colonel Charles Young, a Negro military hero, and the city authorities gave their approval to a proposed Negro cultural garden. Davis, in commenting on the city's press in its relationship to Negroes, says: "Newspapers report colored activities fairly and with reasonably adequate space; the word 'Negro' is capitalized as a part of newspaper policy; reference to race or color in crime 'news' is carefully deleted." Practically every civic movement invites Negro representatives and "scrupulous care is taken not to offend the sensibilities of a group who admittedly are sometimes oversensitive." Davis regards the ballot as the most potent weapon in securing for the Negro in Cleveland his political and social advancement.

Negroes came to Detroit in very large numbers during World War I. According to the 1920 census, the Negro population, which had been about 6,000 in 1910, had reached the 40,000 mark, and the next census (1930) indicated that this figure had grown to over 120,000. During the early twenties, jobs were so plentiful that there was very little competition for employment. But the efforts of the new arrivals to find living space and decent quarters did give rise to clashes between the races.[4]

The city is divided into twenty-two wards. The political importance of these is negligible, since the constables are the only

4. The following discussion of Negro politics in Detroit rests heavily upon T. R. Solomon, "Participation of Negroes in Detroit Elections" (Ph.D. dissertation, University of Michigan, 1939). —ED.

officials chosen on a ward basis. Two of these officers are elected from each ward on a nonpartisan basis in odd-numbered years and serve as execution and process servers. Although this office is looked upon as rather unimportant, Negroes have been elected ward constables for many years. Within the city of Detroit are three state senatorial districts and portions of four others. Except for the third senatorial district, the Negro population is a decided minority. In the third district there are about 69,000 potential voters, and of this number approximately 32,000 are Negroes. In 1926 and 1928 a Pole was elected from the third district. In 1930 a Negro was elected to the state senate for the first time, and at every election since that time one has been a candidate from the third ward. Evidently this third ward has a large number of Poles, because the office of state senator from this district seems to alternate between Poles and Negroes. The former won the seat in 1932 and 1934, while the Negroes took over in 1936 and 1938.

The population of four congressional districts is largely centered in Detroit. Of these four, three have large Negro populations. For some unaccountable reason, no Negroes attempted to secure an elective office from the first district—the most populous black one—and neither did they exert any telling influence on the choosing of congressmen until 1932. This political awakening came too late, for there was a reapportionment in 1931 which rendered this heavy concentration of Negro population ineffective as a political factor. The fifteenth district, which was created by the redistricting process, took in the 15,000 Negroes who were originally in the thirteenth. This reduced the potential Negro vote in the first district to 46,196. After eliminating the unnaturalized foreign-born in the first district, the Negro voters are outnumbered three to one. Despite this fact, however, a Negro has won the Republican nomination for Congress ever since the district was established; but just as regularly as he has been nominated, he has been defeated in the regular elections by the Polish Democrats.

Detroit's politics are on a nonpartisan basis, and all of the city's elective offices are on a city-wide scale, except for the relatively unimportant office of ward constable. This tends to eliminate racial and minority group representation. Obviously the successful candidates for elective offices must enjoy city-wide popularity and support. The Detroit setup also frustrates the building-up of a political machine comparable to those in many other cities.

Up to the coming of Roosevelt in 1932 Michigan was a Republican state, and nomination in the Republican primary was usually equivalent to election. Until recent years the Negro in Michigan was a Republican of long standing. In outlining the Negro's political achievements in the state, the Michigan Freedmen's Progress Commission stated in 1915 that Negroes "have held positions all the way from delegates to the national convention down to committeemen in the Republican organization and from member of the legislature to ward constables in elective offices and not a few appointive positions." When the direct primary law was adopted in 1905, the practice of party bosses' nominating Negroes to office ceased. This cut a sizable slice out of Negro political participation, and no Negro held an elective office in Detroit, except for ward constables, until 1930, when Charles A. Roxborough was elected to the state senate as a Republican. Roxborough was in the legislature because he was a representative of a Detroit district which was largely inhabited by Negroes, rather than because his presence pleased the party bosses.

The Republican county committee and county convention have had Negro members. But until 1928 there were very few Negroes at the county conventions. Prior to that time the convention was a caucus, with very informal rules as to its composition, time and place of meetings, and so on. Since 1928, however, the delegates have been selected by the party voters in their precincts. Naturally, those who wished to gain control of the conventions tried to secure delegates from the Negro precincts. Consequently, Negro delegates have increased in number. Usually there are between 130 and 160 such delegates present. At the 1938 convention there were 142 Negroes. Negroes have also gained membership on the Republican state central committee.

Detroit Negroes officially became a part of the Democratic organization in April 1932, as a result of the efforts of Harold Bledsoe, Charles Diggs, and Joseph Craigen. Since 1932 Negroes have held several high offices in the Democratic party setup in Detroit. They have been elected as delegates to the county convention, as division chairmen, and as congressional district vice-chairmen. Chairmen of congressional district delegations to state conventions and members of the state central committee are other Democratic offices which have been held by Negroes during their brief period of participation in the party. In 1936 Bledsoe was chosen as a presidential elector with a larger vote than that received by Frank Murphy (now Associate Justice of United States Supreme Court). Negro sentiment has shifted markedly to the Democratic party in recent years.

When Negroes became numerous enough to be a political factor in Detroit, white politicians sought all practical methods of getting themselves before the Negro electorate. Because of the necessity of building up a large personal following throughout the city in order to be successful, no groups could be ignored. Soon it became apparent that the most effective method of contacting Negroes was through the churches and the ministers. The usual procedure here was to have the minister present the political aspirants to his congregation at the Sunday morning services.

Several Negro ministers enjoy the privilege of sending members of their congregations to the Ford plant with letters of recommendation which are honored by the company, and their churches have taken on the character of employment agencies for that concern. The fact is that the possibility of getting a job at the Ford Motor Company has been the incentive in many instances for Negroes' joining church. Naturally a minister encounters least difficulty in running his church when the bulk of his congregation is gainfully employed. It follows that the minister will cater to the positions taken by the company which employs large numbers of his flock. The control gained over these churches by the Ford Company has its vicious aspects. The position of the plant on political matters is easily determined, and when such position is made clear, the ministers whose recommendations are honored by Ford lend their influence to support that position. The stranglehold on the churches by Ford is clearly illustrated by the fact that in 1936 and 1937 several Negro ministers closed the doors of their churches to members of the race who were regarded by Ford officials as radical. Any advocate of trade unionism is placed in this category by plant officials.

Another evidence of the tremendous political influence exerted by the Ford Motor Company is the Wayne County Voters Districts Association, which is the largest Negro Republican club in the city. This organization is sponsored chiefly by Willis Ward and Donald Marshall, Negroes employed by Ford in the plant's employment office. Ward, a former University of Michigan athlete of note, is one of the personnel officers. Ward's real job is organizing political clubs among Negroes, in an effort to throw the Negro vote to the Republican party. Ward has said that no one sent to him by the Democrats need expect to get a job at Ford as long as he is a personnel director. Since the main incentive for joining this Republican organization is the hope of a job, the members are not necessarily loyal Republicans. In fact, many people believe that some of the members go through the motions of being Republican, but actually vote Democratic when they enter the polls.

In Detroit, as in other cities, the daily papers constitute one of the most important agencies in influencing elections. The Negro weekly papers, however, do not enjoy such an important position. The Negro weeklies are very unstable and in most cases appear only for the duration of the election period. The fact that none of the papers which appeared in 1932 are now in circulation is evidence of the sporadic nature of the Negro papers. The number of Negro papers at any particular time varies in direct proportion to the intensity of election campaigns. The owners, publishers, and editors of the Negro weeklies, however, look forward to election campaigns since they mean brief periods of prosperity for their publications. The candidates for the various offices purchase all available advertising space in these papers, hoping to present themselves successfully to the Negro public.

The white politicians in Detroit soon found out that in order to marshal the Negro vote it was necessary to have Negroes working in their interests within the black communities. Usually the Negro chosen by the candidate is made the director of a small group which engages actively in the campaign. Soon this nucleus branches out and becomes a political club, and the original director becomes a Negro "political leader." The various sections of the Negro community have their individual clubs which are also politically active.

The Negro Democratic and Republican leaders are active in the city campaigns, but they do not follow party lines. The leaders of both parties often support the same candidates, and it frequently occurs that Negro Republicans and Democrats are found in both political camps during the final campaigns. There is practically no organized political activity so far as the election of councilmen is concerned, and no Negro councilmen have ever been elected. If all of Detroit's Negro voting population formed a solid bloc, it would still be incapable of electing a councilman without the aid of a sizable portion of the white electorate.

Recently there have been only two political issues in which local Negroes have been interested as a group. The first is the opposition to police brutality during Mayor Reading's administration. This was probably the principal reason for Reading's weakness among Negro voters in his campaign for reelection in 1939. The other issue has been the small, unorganized campaign for an increase in the number of Negro appointive and elective positions in the municipal, county, and state governments. Since most of the municipal jobs are under civil service, the demand for more positions has been concentrated upon the Detroit board of education and the county and state departments. This fight has been led by Snow F. Grigsby and his Detroit Civic Rights Committee. His method has been to bring to the attention of the Negro population the scarcity of Negro job holders in the various departments. Although surveys made by the Detroit Bureau of Governmental Research reveal that a smaller percentage of Negroes of voting age vote than do whites, Negroes hold the balance of power in close elections. Realizing this, both parties vie for the Negro's support and are giving him more representation.

In recent years the election laws of Michigan have undergone several major changes. Chief among these is the provision for a system of permanent registration. Before this provision went into effect in 1932, electors were compelled to reregister every four years. During the period from 1928 to 1932 the registered voters were designated according to race, "C" being used for Negroes and "W" for whites. This was the only period during which such a distinction was made, and Detroit was probably the only large Northern city where such a record has ever been kept. When the system of permanent registration was put into effect, the practice of designating the race of the electors was abandoned. Michigan's election laws are very liberal and have no such restrictions as poll taxes, property ownership, or educational requirements. Clerks in the local election commissioner's office believe that most of the Negro men who register have employment references uppermost in their minds, rather than the privilege of voting. It is the majority opinion in this commissioner's office that job references and relief are the chief motives of most of the Negro registrants from the lower east side wards.

There is a rather long period between the time of registration and election day, and although Negroes show much enthusiasm about registering, they seem to take much less interest in actually voting. The chief factor contributing to this lack of participation in elections is indifference. For instance, on 1 April

1929, although there was an incentive for a heavy turnout of the electorate, the vote was very light. The incentives for Negroes to vote were (1) Frank Murphy, an avowed friend to the Negro, was up for reelection; (2) Cecil Rowlett, a Negro, was a candidate for judge; and (3) a charter amendment to increase the numbers of members of the common council from eight to fourteen on a system of ward representation was an issue. Negroes had the opportunity to elect one of their number to the city court, but there were only 26,850 registered and of this number only 8,356 actually voted. The Negro candidate finished fifteenth with only 14,661 votes and Murphy was second with 80,756 votes.

Although Detroit has been Democratic in gubernatorial elections since 1930, the city's Negro districts remained Republican until 1936. In 1932 and 1934 small gains within the Negro electorate were made by the Democrats, but it was not until 1936 that Negroes shifted parties to a great extent. In the 1936 and 1938 gubernatorial elections there was a close vote in some of the precincts and huge Democratic majorities in others. The Negro precincts which had the heaviest Republican vote were on the fringes of the Negro section or in the outlying black areas. The Democratic poll, on the other hand, was strongest in the heart of the Negro district (east side). The east side wards are an extension of the old black belt, including the slum areas in the city.

It is believed that Negroes are habitually straight ticket voters, and if the majority favors the head of the party ticket there will be a majority of straight party ballots. Other possible explanations for the Negro's tendency to vote the straight ticket are: (1) unfamiliarity with voting; (2) lack of effective party organization; (3) limited education; and (4) fear of spoiling the ballot. If one of the candidates for an elective office is considered a friend of the Negroes, they can be depended upon to respond with a heavy poll.

During the period from 1928 to 1932, a Negro was chosen for the first time in thirty years as a member of the state legislature. During this same period, a Negro was a candidate for judge of the recorder's court but was defeated in the election. Up to the present time, no Negro has ever received enough votes to become a member of the city council. Any move to change the representation on the council from a city-wide basis to a single-member district basis and to increase the number of representatives would be supported by Negroes, inasmuch as it would probably pave the way for them to get a representative on that body.

In 1937, when the CIO entered Detroit's political arena with a candidate, Negro support was lacking in both the primary and the regular election. This lack of support for a labor candidate was equally noticeable in the slum areas and the better Negro neighborhoods. The Negro traditionally votes for the Republican party or for his friend. In a partisan election it is usually for the former, and in a nonpartisan contest it is for the man regarded as most friendly to the race. Then, too, there is almost as much anti–labor union tradition among Negroes as there is anti-Democratic tradition. Finally, when the CIO selected its candidate, it did not trouble itself to choose a man who enjoyed a reputation as the Negro's friend.

St. Louis, which probably should be designated as a border city rather than a Northern community, has a total population of 850,000 people, of which 105,000 are Negroes.[5] The bulk of the Negro population in St. Louis comes from the Deep South, and most of this is from the rural sections. As is the case in most of the other cities, the Negro population in St. Louis is concentrated in a so-called Negro section, with a few middle-class Negroes in the outlying districts. Most of the Negroes are concentrated in such heavy industries as steel and packing. Some 58 percent of the men are in the industries, 26 percent in domestic service, and the remaining 16 percent are scattered in the various occupations. Less than 5 percent of the Negro women are in industry, but 78 percent are in domestic service.

When Negroes came to St. Louis in large numbers in 1917, the Republicans were in the saddle, and their machine was well-oiled and working very smoothly. It was not long before the Negroes were drawn into the political machine under leaders appointed by the whites to control their votes. St. Louis was under continuous Republican administration from 1909 to 1933, and during this period the average GOP victory was slightly less than 7,000 votes, with the majorities ranging from 2,800 to 30,000. Although registrations by race are not available for this entire twenty-four-year period, it is considered a safe assumption that at no time were there less than 7,000 Negro registrants, of whom probably not more than 5 percent supported the Democratic party.

5. The following treatment of Negro politics in St. Louis is based on a special memorandum prepared by David M. Grant and Sidney Williams. —ED.

In return for this support, which on more than one occasion has been the margin of victory, the Republicans gave the Negroes only three upper-bracket jobs, which came to be traditional "Negro jobs." These were an assistant circuit attorney whose salary was $4,200; an assistant city counselor who drew $2,500 annually; and a chief custodian at a salary of $1,800. But just prior to the first Democratic city administration in twenty-four years, the Republicans were hiring 672 Negroes in the city government. In 1932, when the American voters had a change of political heart, St. Louis was one of the many cities that switched its party allegiance. The Negroes of the city played a feature role in effectuating the change in St. Louis, and in return for this support they unquestionably realized some benefits. In the first place, the Democrats opened certain heretofore "closed" positions to Negroes.

Between 1920 and 1932 five Negroes were elected to the state legislature, and at one time two Negroes were in office at once. But since the Democrats won Missouri in 1932, no Negro has been elected. This is a direct result of the gerrymandering of the old twelfth congressional district under the 1933 redistricting act. This act placed most of the Negroes who were packed into the twelfth district into the newly-created eleventh, which, with its 300,000 people, is one of the largest in the state. Negro leaders realize the effect of this gerrymander, and they are planning to exert all possible pressure, when the 1941 assembly starts, to redistrict on the basis of the 1940 census. This promises to be an important issue in the state elections next November.

Another issue which greatly affects both political parties in St. Louis—and particularly the Negroes—is the manner in which the aldermen are elected. At the present time they are nominated and elected on a city-wide basis. In 1932 this question became a campaign issue, with the Democrats making solemn pledges to see the necessary legislation through if they were returned to power. In 1933, a Democratic legislature did pass an enabling act, but that is as far as things have progressed toward eliminating the city-wide vote. Negro leaders have made rather half-hearted efforts to force the board of aldermen on this issue through the initiative and referendum, which are in effect in the state.

Generally the Negro preacher's interest in procuring the vote for his congregation varies in direct proportion to his own pecuniary interests. Democratic political campaigns have recently placed great emphasis on the exploitation of the smaller churches of the store-front variety. After being denied hearings in the larger churches, these politicians have played upon the petty jealousies of the smaller preachers. In addition, the preachers of these smaller churches are given cash considerations for allowing political propagandists to address their congregations. David M. Grant states that the Negroes in St. Louis are definitely the balance of power and are recognized as such by both parties. He maintains, however, that the tendency of each party is to do less and less for them, the longer its term in office continues. According to Sidney Williams, industrial relations secretary of the local Urban League, the Negro ministers are backward and conservative as a rule. Until recently, they were even against trade unions. The Republican machine had been running the Negro preachers, along with everything else in the town, and had on occasion paid fifty or sixty dollars for their help.

As is the case in most large cities, the NAACP has a local chapter with a membership of from 1,200 to 1,500 people, most of whom are Negroes. The primary interest of the NAACP is defending civil liberties in St. Louis. This branch was instrumental in the fight for Missouri's sharecroppers, and it very frequently collaborates with the St. Louis branch of the National Urban League. The NAACP has the reputation of being nothing more than a part of the Republican machine.

There is an organized group of militant Negroes in St. Louis called the "Colored Clerks Circle," which is carrying on pressure activities in order to get Negroes employed in the shops which cater to Negro customers.

It is not clearly explained whether the Negro underworld and its various rackets have much political influence, but Sidney Williams did mention to Dr. Myrdal that "gambling and vice are pretty powerful." Some indication of the type of vice which exists in the city is given by a Dr. Gray. He says that the prostitutes, and especially the houses where they are kept, had to pay off to the police. He also contends that the city's program against venereal diseases has actually increased the possibility for the police racketeers to collect money from prostitutes, and that the health department is a means of exploitation in the hands of the police.

Evidently the importance of the Negro vote is fully recognized in St. Louis, because the Democrats, having broken into the winning column largely as a result of it, have taken steps to keep the Negro in their political camp. As evidence of their fair and square attitude toward the Negro citizens of St. Louis, the Democrats point with pride to the Homer G. Phillips Hospital, which was built at a cost of over three million dollars. Second only to the Phillips Hospital are the community centers which have been built since the Democrats have taken over. A bond issue was passed for this purpose and the recommended sum allotted, which sum was augmented by $128,000 from the federal government's PWA. Two centers have been built and a third is on its way.

Missouri has no civil rights law. An attempt was made to put through such a statute, but opponents of the legislation brought up a number of Negro witnesses before the legislative committee who testified that they were satisfied and that Negroes were enjoying all the rights and privileges which they thought they were entitled to. These Negroes further testified that the Missouri Negro was not concerned about being excluded from certain places of public accommodation.

When machine politics are being considered, Philadelphia immediately crops up along with most of the other large metropolitan areas in the United States.[6] During the past few years this machine control has alternated between Republicans and Democrats. In maintaining themselves in power, the machines employ the traditional elements of control—vote buying, graft, office placing, and so forth. In order to give a clear idea of what actually happens, Wilhelmina Jackson relates the following:

> While I was in Philadelphia, the primaries for the 1940 election were on, and the race between Guffey (D) and Jones (Republican-supported Democrat) for nomination as U. S. Senator was very exciting. Vote buying was at its height. Into a neighborhood store in one of the wards walked a white woman worker. "Reserve me chops, beans, tomatoes, etc.," she said, "and as soon as I go and vote and get my $2.00, I'll be back. Gee, it'll be swell eating like this again."

Miss Jackson continues: "I was given to understand by several persons I interviewed that such incidents occurred a thousand times or more during the primaries." The local political leadership in Philadelphia falls into the usual patterns of machine-controlled personalities who hold various public offices and, ac-

6. The discussion of Philadelphia politics in this chapter is based on Wilhelmina Jackson's field notes, April 1940. —ED.

cording to Miss Jackson, "pay lip service to ideals and actual service to money bags."

The ranks of the Negro population in Philadelphia swelled during the mass exodus of Negroes from the South during and after the First World War. In March 1939 the city's Negro population was estimated at 264,000. Naturally this large segment of the city's population produced its Negro political leaders. One of the best-known leaders among the Negroes is the Reverend Shepard, a dynamic Baptist minister. Notwithstanding the fact that he has to "play the game" in order to keep in power with the financial controls, Shepard does interest himself in some aspects of community problems. He has taken a very active interest in the activities of the Philadelphia chapter of the National Negro Congress and the local branch of the National Association for the Advancement of Colored People. The minister is employed in the office of the city treasurer, and while he is described as very personable, he has numerous enemies who are quite dubious about his selection of individuals for certain jobs.

Mrs. Duckett, a Negro woman, has made a place for herself among the present-day leaders in the city, and is doing pretty well. In describing this lady, Miss Jackson says: "Mrs. Duckett is the Democratic ward leader in the 34th ward, is energetic and ardently pro-New Deal. Mrs. Duckett has a rather large following and believes that the Democratic rule in Pennsylvania is always more beneficial to the Negro voter than the Republican." She is an active member of the Philadelphia chapter of the National Negro Congress, and believes that the Congress' efforts to draw organized labor into community activity will result in healthier politics in the city.

Miss Jackson describes a man who probably would not measure up to the Negro "leadership" standard, but who is really quite influential in Philadelphia's Negro political activity. This man—Reading is the name—is a printer and operates a shop of his own. Miss Jackson characterizes Reading as "an erstwhile Democrat (now a Republican) and a behind-the-scenes artist." Reading is a capable, quick thinking man who wields a powerful influence through the publication of numerous leaflets of a political nature. Reading's main publication is a daily one-cent sheet entitled *The Political Digest,* which has the following subcaption: "A Daily Digest of News of the Political World of Particular Interest to Colored Americans." Reading justifies his political switch on the basis of the wretched treatment of Negroes in the South, which is wholly Democratic. Miss Jackson describes Reading as very socialistic, and one who is not unaware of the "dirty deals" of the Republicans but feels more like a race fighter with them than with the Democrats.

A postal employee, Mr. Jason, heads the Philadelphia Council of the National Negro Congress and has the same views on the spread of the organization as those of Mrs. Duckett. Others who might be classified as Negro leaders in Philadelphia are Arthur Fauset, school principal; E. Wright, employed in the recorder of deeds office; J. Norris, member of board of revision of taxes; and Eugene Rhodes, editor of the Philadelphia *Tribune*. Miss Jackson observes that if the positions held by these persons are any indication, one may virtually conclude the character of their leadership—that is, to get the vote out!

The two dominant parties have such political control that it is not very likely that any group without their approval will seriously affect an election. But there are certain hopefuls, particularly among the National Negro Congress members and a Mr. Ames, who is organizer of the cafeteria workers, who believe that, although at the present time labor is not organized in Philadelphia, the gradual spread of organization will change the political scene within a reasonable future. The locals of the various unions, many of which are affiliates of the National Negro Congress, are active in elections; but the pressure of the established poltical organizations with their money and promises almost nullifies the influence of the labor groups in the campaigns. Consequently, at the present time Labor's Non-Partisan League is nearly impotent politically.

The Philadelphia press is definitely under party control. The *Record* is pro-Roosevelt and backed by John Kelly and the Democratic organization. The *Tribune* is a Republican sheet and practically under the thumb of Joe Pew. During campaign periods their editorial policies reflect the views of those who support them.

Out of the total Philadelphia registration of 1,018,490, the Negroes have 130,675. Negroes hold many jobs in the local government of Philadelphia and in the state government which may be attributed directly to their participation in politics. According to the director of the Bureau of Negro Research and Planning, Negroes "have tripled their vote and have made gains so far as political offices are concerned." Reading the printer says:

Although Negroes participated in politics here long before 1865, it was not until 1910 that we had our first Negro state legislator. In the 1921 election we got our first Negro judicial officer in a minor court of no record, and this position has since been filled by Negroes. In the same year we got our second Negro legislator. Mind you, Negroes were elected ad interim to fill out unexpired common council terms until 1935, when the first Negro was selected to fill a council seat (we have twenty-one councilmen). In 1938 the first Negro woman was elected to the state legislature. In 1934 the first Democratic governor in forty years appointed more Negroes to white collar jobs than his Republican predecessors had in the previous forty years. He was defeated in 1938, and his Republican successor removed all of them, with the exception of about fifty. It is said that the Republican governor was looking at the Negroes coming from work once—1,500 of them—and said, "My God, what is this—Uncle Tom's Cabin?" Soon after this reductions in personnel took place.

This Negro vote, which is said to be responsible for the number of jobs held by Negroes, is divided between the two dominant parties on about a fifty-fifty basis. It is the opinion of some of the Negro politicos that the potency of the Negro vote lies in its incalculability, that is, neither party can count its Negro votes ahead of time, so they make efforts to line them up. There are some leaders, however, who claim that this fairly even split of black votes tends to neutralize their importance as a decisive factor.

To what extent is the Negro vote in Philadelphia a "balance of power"? Arthur H. Fauset claims that Negroes determined the outcome of the mayoralty race in 1935 and the gubernatorial contest of 1938. Probably the best illustration of the Negro vote as the balance of power occurred in the magisterial election of 1938, when a Negro named Scott was "cut" from the Republican ticket by the party organization on the afternoon of election day. The Negroes in turn "cut" the Republican ticket and rallied behind the "reform" candidate in sufficient numbers to put him across. Mrs. Duckett claims that in a congressional election of 1938, the Negro vote gave victory to a white "New Dealer" over his Negro Republican opponent.

Up to 1928 the Negro vote was overwhelmingly Republican, and those Negroes who were early Democrats tell stories of being stoned and ridiculed by their race brothers for being "Nigger Democrats" when they paraded in party demonstrations through South Philadelphia as early as 1919. By 1932, however, the division among the Negro voters had become much more evident, and the ranks of the Negro Democrats had swelled to rather large proportions. The Negro vote was no longer "solidly Republican." By 1936 increased registration, more jobs, and the various union leaders' activities had brought about the present split of about fifty-fifty.

Negroes in both parties are hard-working ward people who really go to bat for their organizations, but there are shifts among the voters. As one Philadelphian puts it, "the most notable thing about the Negro vote is that it is opportunistic." Although sensitive to the power of the Negro vote, the major political parties do not appear to have a very high regard for it. According to the secretary of the Philadelphia Urban League, although the migration in the period from 1930 to 1940 was much less than during the twenties, the reaction to it was sharp in political circles. Both of the major parties claimed that Negroes were being brought up from the South to vote; and in the state legislature it was said that the increase in the period of residence for eligibility for relief status from one to two years was made to decrease the Southern Negro migration to Philadelphia.

Nevertheless, the Negro vote is still tied to one or the other of the parties, and the reasons are fairly obvious. In the first place, the poor economic status of the Negro makes him susceptible to the machinations of the parties simply because of the various promises of jobs or money. Secondly, and probably as important as the economic status, is the costly lack of effective organization among Philadelphia's black voters. It is said that all of Philadelphia is poorly organized, particularly Negroes. True, there are such groups as the NAACP, the National Negro Congress, the Ethiopian World Federation, several civic clubs in the various wards, and a few independent unions described by Miss Jackson as "none too dynamic"; but collaboration among the several organizations on lines of mutual interest seldom occurs. It seems that interest in the voting franchise is a short-lived phenomenon in Philadelphia, and the attitude of the rank and file toward the long-term value of the vote is one of utter indifference. On the days of the primary and regular elections, getting the "organization man" in office and receiving the usual two-dollar reward for "the right ballot" are the extent of the odrinary voter's interest. The ward heelers and bosses carry on from day to day because the success of their organizations depends upon their daily grind, and in turn, their daily bread depends upon the success of their organization.

Thus, the political outlook for the Negro in Philadelphia is not particularly encouraging. The one hopeful sign is that the unionization of labor is apparently making some rapid strides, and the organizers have hopes of launching a really effective unit of Labor's Non-Partisan League. It is believed that such an organization will stimulate the thought and interest of the voting populace. One Philadelphian has aptly stated the case in these words: "The vast majority, white and colored, are content in this dead city to complacently attend their own wake."

Like other Northern urban communities, New York had its heavy influx of Negroes during World War I and in the twenties.[7] Although the black population of half a million does not constitute a very large percentage of the city's entire population of seven million, it does make its impression on the political life of New York. Harlem became "political-minded" when these Southern Negroes migrated. This is accounted for in large measure by the Protestant churches, inasmuch as Baptist, Methodist, and "store-front" preachers have been politicians of one kind or another since Negro churches appeared on the American scene. In fact, if a "political machine" is defined as a "deliverable vote," the church is the only effective, disciplined machine that Negroes have developed. These politico-clerics were almost entirely Republican, and up to the present time generally maintain their allegiance to Abraham Lincoln's party.

When New York's Negroes were found on the lower west side, the political lineup was Republican preachers versus "sporting world" Democrats. With the migration to Harlem came socialist Negroes (mainly from the West Indies) who lined up with Jewish socialist groups in many sections, particularly in the area which is now the twentieth and twenty-second congressional districts. The Socialists in Harlem, like the Communists, never got out any appreciable portion of the vote. Free Thanksgiving and Christmas baskets was very practical socialism as far as Negroes were concerned, and they were won over to this bread-and-meat program of New York's political machine.

During the early days in New York, as in all other places, the so-called better element and intelligentsia among Negroes were Republicans—hence the statement that the first political activity of Negroes in New York found the Republican preachers (leaders of the better element) lined up against "sporting house"

7. The following discussion of Negro politics in New York depends heavily on a special memorandum prepared by George Streator. —ED.

Democrats. The latter included saloon keepers, hotel proprietors, and the like. In an interview with one of the survivors of this group, the manner in which the Tammany machine worked is clearly outlined. John A. Nail entered the saloon business in 1882 on lower 6th Avenue. He is now eighty-four years old, still active and clear-headed. Like all businessmen who "had any sense," Nail bought real estate. The business and much of the property was located around 6th Avenue and 23rd Street, in what was known as the "Tenderloin" district. Richard Croker was the "Boss" in 1886 when Nail was summoned to the local Tammany club by John Scannell, Croker's Tenderloin man. According to Nail, the following conversation took place:

"I'm glad to meet you, Mr. Nail. Sit down and have a drink."

"I don't drink, never did," said Mr. Nail.

"You and Ned have quite a business, I understand. We want you to head up Tammany among the colored people. You are not to bother with the white people, just the colored. We teach you, you teach them."

Nail says: "Now what was I to do? I had been Republican. But there were too many ways these fellows could make it hard for you, like licenses, taxes, assessments, and so on."

Nail rented a store and started a club. Scannell paid the rent and stood for the "refreshments" used at the initial meeting. "Contributions" were collected from other businessmen in the neighborhood, and the club was furnished. This club was established for the purpose of furnishing a home for Negro voters who would turn to the Democratic party. There were about 1,500 voters in this Negro section, and Tammany wanted them. The first step toward this end was to get many of the wrongdoers out of jail, and since the area included one of the worst slums in the city, there were plenty to get out. The first patronage for the district consisted of two cart drivers and two street sweepers. Nail found difficulty in getting his "club members" to take these jobs. They wanted to be superintendents or nothing. Tammany dispensed its relief in the form of fuel and food. Big packing houses gave meat and the dealers gave wood, coal, and food. The district leaders called on the merchants and forced them to "chip in." In other words, the political forces "shook down" contributions for their political club members. According to Nail, the line used to reach "around the block." The Negro preachers became alarmed by this sort of thing because they had been distributing Republican patronage in this form. Little by little Tammany broke into Republican control. The whites began to kick, and on more than one occasion Nail was warned that he was giving Negroes too much. When Nail gave up his job as district leader, he dictated his successor, who carried on the work. George Streator states that the Negroes in early Tammany were hampered by the fact that the educated Negroes remained Republicans.

Many persons claim that the entrance of women into Democratic politics raised the tone of Negro Democrats. The first work done to build up the Democratic party among Negro women was undertaken by Mrs. Bessye Bearden, and though several others attempted the task, she was by far the most skillful politician of them all. In January 1925 the Colored Women's Democratic League, affiliated with Ferdinand Q. Morton's United Colored Democracy, is reported to have donated five hundred baskets to needy children. Several of the Negroes who have secured upper-bracket jobs in the city's Democratic government obtained them largely as a result of the political activity of their wives.

Observing the apparent success of the Republican tactics in controlling the Negro vote, Tammany sought to duplicate the GOP procedure. Under President Grover Cleveland a Negro was appointed minister to Haiti. "Boss" Charles F. Murphy, the Tammany leader after Croker, sought to build up in New York a Negro leadership that would match the quality of Republican leadership in the "silk stocking" district. This created an opportunity for Ferdinand Q. Morton, who had spent some time at Harvard University. There is little doubt that Morton advanced Tammany leadership considerably. Members of Harlem's Democratic clubs say today that Morton was selfish. When a group of women started agitating for a Negro judgeship for Harlem twenty years ago, Morton held back his support until the drive gathered momentum. Then he nominated himself for the position! Something of a compromise was struck, and Morton was given personal recognition; and his present position as civil service commissioner is the result of the bargain. It must be said, however, that he has lent dignity to the position, making it one of increasing merit. Considering the time in which he came along, Morton's advance in Tammany circles was spectacular.

After the war, the returning Negro soldiers seemed to be Republican, but there were events that shifted them toward the

Democrats. For example, during James J. "Jimmy" Walker's regime as mayor, the administration building of the 369th Infantry was constructed. It seems that every politician and would-be politician claims credit for this building, including Fred R. Moore, the Negro Republican leader who "played ball" with Tammany and secured the construction of this building, together with a new police station on West 135th Street. The significance of the National Guard in politics is that almost every officer of the 369th regiment seems to be employed in a federal, state, or city position.

The latest census returns reveal that Negroes now dominate the seventeenth, nineteenth, and twenty-first assembly districts of Manhattan, with an appreciable vote in the twenty-second district. The Negro majorities in the nineteenth and twenty-first are overwhelming, while being slightly over half in the seventeenth. A Negro state senator might go through this year, as well as another assemblyman.

In 1929 new judicial districts were set up, and it was agreed that the Republicans would have a chance to elect two judges of the city court in Harlem, since Francis E. Rivers, a Republican, was the author of the bill creating the tenth judicial district. Fate, however, in the form of the West Indian vote, decreed otherwise. Watson and Toney, both Democrats, won. On election morning, 4 November 1930, posters were displayed all over Harlem which declared that Rivers' skin was too light for him to understand Negro problems, and besides, his father had a "pink toe" church in Washington, D.C. Watson is West Indian, and that segment of the Negro vote went solidly for the Democrats. But Watson and Toney were put over by the loyal *white* Democrats; for even with the loss of the West Indian vote, Rivers led in the Negro districts.

Mayor Fiorello La Guardia has done much to offset these two Tammanyites with two young appointees. Jane Bolin, a young Negro woman, was appointed to the domestic relations court; and Myles Paige, after two years as a magistrate, was appointed to the court of general sessions.

Any treatment of the Negro in party politics in New York must necessarily consider Marcus Garvey's role in the swing of the Negro votes to the Democratic party. Garvey is credited with teaching the Negro masses to vote against the Republican ticket. According to George Streator, there is no way of determining whether the Democrats did anything for Garvey, but it is known that Garvey was a Democrat. In 1928 Garvey counseled his "four million followers" to vote for Al Smith. Garvey enlisted the West Indian vote for the Democratic party. The West Indian vote is reputedly clannish. In recent campaigns, some American Negro candidates have emphasized that they were "born in America" or "Virginia" or even "Mississippi." An attempt is made to make this appeal to prejudice subtle, but it is quite obvious.

In the eyes of New Yorkers who desire clean government, the board of aldermen is the core of the rotten political apple. Negroes have served on the board of aldermen on several occasions, but with little or no distinction. It seems that Fred R. Moore, the Republican leader, was the most astute politician to serve on the board. Moore deserves much credit for having wheedled out of a Democratic mayor more than the Negro Democrats themselves. More than likely this was due to Moore's prestige and his ownership of a newspaper. He is characterized as one of the really independent Negro politicians—one who had about as much to give as he got out of the political bag. Except for the period from 1922 to 1925, a Negro served as alderman from either the nineteenth or twentieth assembly district or from both from 1920 until 1938, when the old assembly district was abolished as a basis for city representation. The board was replaced by the city council, selected on a city-wide basis by a system of proportional representation. Not until 1930 did a Negro Democrat win a seat. Negro Democrats represented the nineteenth assembly district from 1930 until the abolition of the system in 1938.

Even though there are about 75,000 Negroes in Brooklyn, their political organization does not offer much promise. The Bedford-Stuyvesant section, however, has potentialities, since it is the first large segregated area in Brooklyn. The Brooklyn Democratic party leadership is archaic and distasteful to a growing number of voters, but very little in new leadership is being created. The old Brooklyn Negro was and still is Republican. There is no real "Negro area" among the old residents, and it seems that they were more assimilated in white life than were Negroes in Manhattan. In the old days, Negroes obtained a bit of economic security, then moved out to Brooklyn where life resembled that in the small rural areas. Brooklyn is rapidly changing, however, and the Negro sections are facing overcrowding. This bids fair to change the political side of the picture.

It is estimated that about 15,000 Negroes live in the borough of the Bronx. This section is rapidly growing, mainly in Irish

and Jewish population. Right now it is predominantly Democratic, with a heavy labor vote also. The Negro vote is of little
consequence, except to decide small affairs in three or four
densely populated areas.

Most of the Negroes in the borough of Queens live in Jamaica,
Long Island. It is said that the Negro population (about 25,000)
creates enough of a problem to call for the erection of a federal
housing project. Negro doctors have been rather conspicuous
in getting appointments to the public hospitals, and since it is a
part of the city of New York, most of the section's "leading
Negroes" are city jobholders and postal employees. In the past,
the Negroes in Queens were Republicans, and those who are not
today are largely fusionists.

The most important underworld influence upon the participation of Negroes in the political life of New York has been the
"numbers" racket. Besides adding money to Negro political ambitions, the "numbers" racket has been the means of developing
a force of Negro campaign workers. There is no doubt that
support of Negro political leadership has come from the "numbers" barons. They have needed police protection, and a friendly
political organization is necessary to their operations. Although
there might be those who argue that Negro politics have been
"clean," it is apparent that there would have been no political
success for Negroes, coming as rapidly as it did, without the
"numbers" game as a financial background. When Thomas E.
Dewey exposed the private life of "Dutch" Schultz and the intri-
cacies and effects of the "numbers" on Harlem politics, it was
felt by many that this was political, Republican, anti-Democratic, and a blow to the Negro's financial and political power. It
was all this and more.

One fact concerning the local branches of the Negro's most
prominent national organizations has repeatedly made itself
evident and should be mentioned as an introduction to the next
few paragraphs. Despite the fact that almost without exception
these locals have professed their absolute nonpartisan character, more than a few interviews have disclosed the local branch
of this or that national Negro organization as part and parcel of
one or the other political machine. William E. B. Du Bois and
James Weldon Johnson catered to the white university people
and their wealth, but the present NAACP officers play up to the
political leaders and behave accordingly. It is a matter of con-
jecture whether the present era of the NAACP shows as much
vigor as the old. The setting is different, of course. Not that the

trade in votes is in itself a crime, but it is a question of the ability to help an oppressed group by making its best-known organization for defense an organization specializing in horse trading.

While the NAACP has been getting its political bearings, the Urban League has been more or less keeping in step, too. It is no secret that this organization has entered the field of organized politics. In 1924 and 1925 the literary prizes bestowed by the League on those in the literary circle were provided from cash donated by many political leaders and even by racketeers. Not only that, but the League has developed some of the most astute politicians Negroes have ever had in the New York area. Most of its officials have tasted political plums of varying degrees of sweetness and are still plucking for more fruit.

Among New York's Negro population, the election of James J. Walker to the mayor's office in 1926 is fondly spoken of as the "second coming of Christ." Walker was the most popular man Negroes had ever met in New York politics. The "wet" issue was important at the time, but Harlem still looked Republican, so Walker set out to corral the Negro vote for Tammany. Most of the gains which Negroes have made in the city's politics came during Walker's regime. The number of Negroes put on government payrolls under "Jimmy" Walker jumped from 247 to 2,275. Instead of Harlem's intellectuals turning to communism, they turned to Tammany. The policy of Walker and James A. Farley of distributing good jobs to deserving Negro Democrats was the attracting force. Walker's popularity is clearly reflected in the election figures of 1929, when he ran against La Guardia. Despite the fact that Herbert Hoover ran away with the 1928 presidential contest and La Guardia was extremely popular among Negroes, the great "Jimmy" took every one of the Negro assembly districts.

Here a word may be said about Joseph A. Gavagan's twenty-first congressional district. This congressional district is an overwhelmingly Democratic stronghold. The Negro vote has been estimated at between 60,000 and 70,000, but the white vote is nearly double this amount. Therefore, says Streator, it must be concluded that Gavagan, while outside the reach of Negro control, is within the reach of Negro vengeance. That Gavagan sponsored antilynching legislation year after year, and particularly during election years, suggests his realization of this fact.

Negroes have no possibility of electing a congressman or a state senator depending strictly on a Negro vote as long as their votes are in the minority.

New York politics, discussed from any angle, must include Fiorello La Guardia, master showman and the city's present mayor. La Guardia is a good leader and a popular politician, to whom party lines evidently do not mean much. La Guardia is a candidate frequently photographed with Negroes. He carried his cook's son to the White House and has been seen holding Negro children in his arms. Under an understanding with the Pullman Porters' Brotherhood, La Guardia fought to have railroad porters and waiters accepted as qualified persons for jobs on the city's subways. Under the present mayor, Negroes have gotten jobs through the civil service and are employed all through the relief service. La Guardia has been criticized for appointing "big Negroes" to office.

Even in New York, however, it seems that Negroes are confused about political appointments. The bigger things drawn from political power are not grasped by black political leadership. Granted that there are four judges, two legislators, some firemen, policemen, and other city, county, state, and a few national jobholders, there are still many things well within reach which are overlooked by Negro political leaders. No attempt is made here to defend the great American game of politics, but mention should be made of the fact that Negroes do not play the game according to established rules. For example, there are the big department stores which are always angling for tax favors and are willing to act accordingly. Evidently Negro tax commissioners are unaware of this. Then, there is the National Guard regiment. Who makes the uniforms? Who repairs them? Who cleans them? Who handles the construction contracts? What about deals made on local real estate? Negroes have held jobs which call for evaluating property, and so on, but have seemed unaware of their powers. The utility corporations in the past made many deals for franchise privileges, tax free grants, and the like, and in each case politics has played an all-important role. But Negroes in positions to influence such things forget that these corporations hire thousands of employees. Negro politicians are still in the kindergarten class in the matter of patronage. Most of them can see little beyond the range of their personal friends and relatives; and because of this shortsightedness, patronage granting small favors to large numbers is neglected for large favors to small numbers.

NINETEEN

Negroes and the New Deal Agencies

IN the campaign of 1932 a Negro division of the national Democratic committee was formed.[1] Franklin D. Roosevelt was elected on a platform that promised to help the "forgotten man" and to bring a "New Deal" to the American people. To meet the exigencies of the depression, Roosevelt developed emergency agencies like the National Recovery Administration, the Agricultural Adjustment Administration, the Civil Works Administration, the Federal Emergency Relief Administration, and the Civilian Conservation Corps. The NRA was designed to stabilize wages and hours, but it did not appreciably help the Negro worker, mainly because of three factors: (1) the codes did not cover the domestic and personal services or the agricultural field, where Negro labor is concentrated; (2) they recognized a differential wage that penalized the South, where the great majority of black workers live; and (3) they did not guard against the prejudicial firing that came with the necessity of paying higher wages to Negro workers.

These factors were recognized by many people who were anxious for the Negro to share in the emergency assistance. In 1934 Trevor Bowen wrote in *Divine White Right:*

> There is generally a differential of 10 to 20 percent against southern workers, on the ground that the cost of living is less

1. What follows is the largest and most significant part of Bunche's chapter 16, "The Negro Officeholder in the Federal Government." The historical sections of the original chapter (pp. 1359–84), which dealt with Negro officeholders prior to 1933, have been omitted. —ED.

in the South. However, the economic Mason and Dixon line shifts widely between codes, and curiously enough these shifts correspond closely to the proportion of Negroes in the industry.

The effect of the administration of the AAA program was especially disastrous on Negro tenants and sharecroppers. The AAA recognized the necessity of government aid to agriculture, but the aid was in the form of payments for the reduction of surplus crops. In 1934 the Annual Tuskegee Negro Conference claimed that the AAA was causing the displacement of Negro tenants because of its "plow under" program: "The most widespread reason . . . for the dislocation of tenants is attributed to the acreage reduction program. Thousands of tenants thus displaced have been set adrift." Another grievance was the bad administration of the programs, which prevented the sharecroppers and tenant farmers from getting adequate compensation for their work. There was also evidence of collusion between county agents and owners to the detriment of tenants.

Thus, these emergency agencies were helpful in ameliorating the perilous condition of the population as a whole, but because Negroes were affected by the factor of race as well as class there were many instances in which they failed to profit from early New Deal legislation. John G. Van Deusen, writing on the eve of the 1936 election, remarked:

> The depression bore with especial hardship on the Negro, and the "New Deal" N.R.A. codes and Agricultural Adjustment contracts did not operate equally regardless of racial lines. Whatever measures of relief they may have afforded white workers and white farmers, they failed conspicuously to relieve the distress of colored workers and colored farmers. There have been numerous complaints of discrimination against colored persons on government constructed projects. These facts may send some of the voters back to Republicanism if a suitable candidate can be found.[2]

But the Negro vote went more heavily for Roosevelt in his second campaign than in 1932, and it was not primarily because a suitable candidate was not found. It was because of the transformation of the New Deal, the growth of the labor movement around the CIO, and the corresponding growth in progressive

2. Van Deusen, "The Negro in Politics," *Journal of Negro History,* 21 (July 1936): 273–74.

movements and vocal pressure groups among the Negro masses.

There were many Negro leaders who were not willing to fall back on the policy of political opportunism; they sympathized with the broad objectives of the New Deal, yet they vigorously fought so that the Negro might share equitably in those objectives. The group which formed around the Joint Committee on National Recovery pursued this policy in its highest form. John P. Davis, later the executive secretary of the National Negro Congress, was one of the leaders in this movement, together with several others such as Robert C. Weaver and John W. Whitten. In an article in the December 1933 *Crisis* entitled "What Price National Recovery?" Davis severely criticized the discrimination which existed under the NRA codes. He also mentioned the formation of the Negro Industrial League, which was the only organization to testify in behalf of the Negro at the first public hearings on the codes. Through it sixteen other national organizations formed the Joint Committee on National Recovery. Its purpose was to achieve unity of organizations seeking betterment of the Negro and agreement on a policy, to make recommendations to those officers of the government who had authority to act, and to seek "federal appointment of qualified colored men and women to positions of usefulness to the race." In 1934 Davis continued to blast away at the contradictions of the New Deal with an article in the October *Crisis* headed "The NRA Codifies Wage Slavery." Finally in May 1935, writing in the same magazine on "A Black Inventory of the New Deal," Davis criticized the unemployment and tenant evictions occasioned by the crop-reduction policies of the AAA. He pointed out that a national conference on the economic status of Negroes under the New Deal would be held at Howard University under the sponsorship of the social science division of the University and the Joint Committee on National Recovery.

This conference was held on May 18, 19, and 20, 1935. It emphasized the development of pressure tactics in order to gain for the Negro his just share; from it the call went out to "build a National Negro Congress" to direct the efforts of the many and diverse organizations interested in the problems of the Negro and to develop a common program in behalf of Negro welfare. The call for the NNC was issued in late 1935, and it first met in Chicago, 14–16 February 1936. It became a pro-New Deal force in the 1936 elections.

The integration of the Negro into the New Deal through departmental appointments was not primarily predicated upon political consideration. It was a recognition of the disastrous effects which the early legislation had upon the Negro because of special racial factors; and in many cases it was a precautionary measure necessitated by the vigorous insistence of Negro organizations upon an equitable application of New Deal measures. Harold L. Ickes, one of the foremost exponents of the New Deal democracy, wrote in the August 1936 issue of *Crisis:* ". . . under our new conception of democracy, the Negro will be given the chance to which he is entitled—not because he will be singled out for special consideration, but because he pre-eminently belongs to the class that the new democracy is designed to especially aid." Speaking of appointments, he declared: ". . . you are probably aware of the fact that no previous administration has provided employment in the various departments and agencies for so many Negroes as this one. This employment ranges from ordinary jobs to executive positions."

In the pages that follow, some consideration will be given to the various federal agencies, after which a critical evaluation of their administrative positions and the effect of their positions on the masses of Negroes will be presented.

THE FERA AND THE WPA

From May 1933 to March 1939 the federal government spent about ten billion dollars for relief and work relief. It was inevitable that a large number of Negroes would be benefited by this program since they formed a highly disproportionate part of the unemployed because of their precarious and subordinate position in the national economy. Concerning the application of the Federal Emergency Relief Administration to the Negro, John P. Murchison, at one time associate adviser on Negro affairs in the Department of the Interior, has said:

> In October 1933 there were approximately 13,600,000 persons or 3,450,000 cases on relief, of which 16.7 percent were Negroes. Negroes on relief constitute about 17.8 percent of the entire Negro population. For 1934 the Research Statistics and Finance Section of the Federal Emergency Relief Administration estimated that there were 857,000 Negro cases on relief rolls in May 1934.

Because of the foresight of its administrators and the pressure of progressive white and Negro organizations, the FERA recognized that problems of discrimination and equal partici-

pation would arise, and it took early precautions to integrate
the Negro proportionately into its program. In February 1934
Forrester B. Washington, director of the Atlanta School of Social Work, was appointed director of Negro work. But Washington only served seven months before returning to his academic
duties. Since that time, until just recently, Afred E. Smith, as
administrative assistant, has directed the staff of workers engaged in the adjustment of racial problems. A release from
Smith's office states: ". . . this office is charged with administer-
ing race relations matters throughout the W.P.A. program. In
effect, it is Federal Unemployment Relief's recognition of Race
Relations as an integral part of modern applied social science."
The release, dated 7 July 1938, describes the personnel of the
office.

The work of the office is distributed among two assistants,
a secretary and four clerical aides. A Junior Race Relations
Officer supervises the handling of the bulk of correspondence;
advises on the preparation and submission of proposed
projects; and supervises matters generally during the Administrative Assistant's absence from the office on field trips.
A Special Assistant in the Information Service maintains public relations through the release of news articles, photographs
and matrices; prepares exhibits; and prepares replies to requests for various types of information.

John W. Whitten held the position of junior race relations officer
until he was recently furloughed; Dutton Ferguson, former district manager of the Pittsburgh *Courier*, succeeded Edward
Lawson, Jr., as special assistant in the information service.

The major activities of the race relations office center around
the receiving and answering of correspondence, investigation
of complaints, and issuing of material relevant to the Negro
and the Works Progress Administration. The office is considerably occupied with the handling of correspondence, and an
average of 7,000 letters are cleared yearly. A majority of these
letters are referred to the WPA by the White House, and they are
sometimes answered individually because of Mrs. Roosevelt's
desire that White House mail receive more than routine handling. Describing this varied correspondence, the release states:

Balanced against letters of complaint anent the Administration of the program, were a like number of requests for

jobs in preference to a dole. Other requests for aid ran the gamut from cash donations to piteous pleas for artificial limbs, and from farms and livestock to false teeth. Requests for information covered the relief field and every related subject.

According to the release:

> The time of the Administrative Assistant is largely taken up by conferences; he is conferred with by the Deputy Administrator and the Division heads concerning the establishment of projects which include Negro workers. His attendance is required at conferences called by the Administrator and he often hears charges and petitions presented by visiting delegations; he also does considerable work in the field. . . . During 1937, the Administrative Assistant made field trips to 15 States, totaling 12,000 miles. He made 30 public addresses and attended 12 national conventions of Negro organizations interested in the welfare of Negroes.

Those in this office are not the only ones who are especially concerned with the problems of the Negro in the Works Progress Administration. James Atkins has served in the Adult Education Division as a specialist in education among Negroes; Sterling Brown is editor of Negro material in the Federal Writers' Project; and T. Arnold Hill served for seven months as a consultant on white collar workers. The curtailments required by the Emergency Relief Appropriation Act of 1939, against which President Roosevelt protested vigorously, have caused some changes in the race relations office.

The administrative assistant also makes an annual report. His 1939 report, entitled "The Works Progress Administration and the American Negro," makes the following statement concerning 1938 participation of Negroes in the program:

> A total of more than 400,000 Negro workers are engaged on projects of the Works Projects Administration throughout the country. Upon these W.P.A. workers are dependent some 1,935,000 Negro citizens who make up the average worker's family of 4.3 persons. . . . In Region III during the week ending September 17, there was a total of 137,331 Negro workers on projects of the W.P.A. This Region embraces the densely Negro-populated States of Alabama, Arkansas, Florida, Georgia, Louisiana, Mississippi, North Carolina, South Carolina, Tennessee, Texas and Virginia.

THE CCC

From the beginning of the Civilian Conservation Corps, colored youths have shared in the program. At the peak strength of the CCC, reached in August 1935, there were 506,000 young men and war veterans enrolled. Of this number, approximately 50,000 were colored. By January 1939 some 200,000 Negro youths had served in the CCC, and an average of $700,000 a month was sent home to colored parents and dependents during the year 1938. Recently, Negro college graduates have been assigned to CCC camps as educational advisers; in 1939, 147 were serving in this capacity.

A lone Negro, Edgar G. Brown, serves in the national office in an administrative position; he was formerly occupied chiefly with publicity work as director of public relations publicity for the Negro press. His position is now that of adviser on Negro affairs, and although a great deal of his work still involves publicity, he also visits camps, addresses national conventions, and is consulted by the director on problems affecting the Negro. The office employs one secretary and is located in the publicity section of the CCC. Of the various offices visited, Brown's was the smallest and most ill-equipped; it was formed by a panel placed across a space at the end of a corridor.

THE FSA

The New Deal's farm relief program was bound to affect Negroes, who occupy a perilous position in agriculture as a heritage of slavery and the plantation system. The exploitation attendant upon this system was already greatly intensified by the crisis which fell upon agriculture in the 1920s, so that the effect of the great depression was well-nigh disastrous. A Public Affairs Committee study, *Farmers without Land,* reads:

> Behind this fact is the loss of tenant farms and the transformation of the Negro tenant into a wage laborer. . . . In the cotton areas the breakdown of credit during the depression, the reduction of acreage, and the payment of relief all played a part in lessening the number of tenants or in reducing many to the position of wage hands.

The integration of the many poverty-stricken Negro farm families into the Farm Security Administration was aided through the work of Joseph H. B. Evans, race relations specialist. He was first employed as a research specialist in the FERA, and then, from October 1934 to 15 June 1935, he served as executive assistant to the general manager of the Federal Subsistence Homestead Division. On 16 June 1935 he became an executive assistant and special adviser to the director of Rural Resettlement, and when this agency was succeeded by the FSA, he continued his duties as an administrative assistant, specializing in race relations. In his personal history sheet Evans states:

> My duties have included: Advising with and making recommendations to the Director of the various divisions on matters pertaining to and affecting Negroes in the Resettlement program, handling matters dealing with Public Relations or touching the colored population, explaining to individuals, in group conferences, and at public meetings the work of the Resettlement Administration. . . .
>
> Reviewing and answering correspondence dealing with the Resettlement program as it affects colored people.
>
> Making such suggestions and recommendations as will insure to colored people a fair and equitable participation in the benefits of the program and in the personnel necessary to carry on this work.
>
> Dealing with complaints of discrimination coming from appointive personnel and from Negro labor on projects.
>
> Conferring with the Administrator's Office on matters of policy, and advising of the progress made on inclusion of Negroes in the program; making necessary contacts and confidential investigations in the various regions.
>
> Reviewing all plans for projects having Negro participation and making such comments and recommendations as may be necessary.
>
> Advising with Division Directors and Regional officers on selection of Negro personnel and interviewing applicants where such interviews seem advisable.

As a result of these efforts, and with the cooperation of the administrator, Evans points to the following achievements: (1) the participation of Negroes in the tenant purchase program under the Bankhead Act; (2) the employment of Negroes at Washington and in the field; (3) the setting up of twenty-three community projects in which Negroes participate, fifteen of which are biracial; and (4) the participation of more than 50,000 Negro farm families who have received rehabilitation loans and grants with supervision of farm practices and programs. Evans administered his office with one secretary. In addition there is one specialist in the Information Division, and recently a farm management specialist has been transferred from the fourth region to the Washington office. Evans is no longer with the FSA, however, and is now employed by the National Youth Administration. His position in FSA has not been filled.

THE FCA

Along with the problems of insecurity of tenants, croppers, and wage hands on the land, there is also that of thousands of farm owners who stand to lose their farms because of debt. This situation has been aggravated by the scarcity of local credit which has made for high rates of interest. In order to meet this situation, an independent agency, the Farm Credit Administration, was created by executive order on 27 May 1933 for the purpose of providing an adequate credit system for agriculture by making long- and short-term credit available to farmers and cooperative business organizations. It is administered by a governor appointed by the president.

A Negro relations section, created on 8 November 1933, six months after the establishment of the FCA, was placed under the direction of the late Henry A. Hunt, founder of the Fort Valley Normal and Industrial School at Fort Valley, Georgia, who functioned as assistant to the governor. He was succeeded by Cornelius King of Louisiana, who directs this office with a secretary and a junior clerk-typist. A specially prepared memorandum for the writer states the "Purpose of the Negro Relations Section of the Farm Credit Administration":

> To publicize the work and service of the Farm Credit Administration among Negro farmers in the United States, and to answer letters of inquiry from Negro farmers on all phases of Farm Credit Administration service, explaining to them the procedure involved in applying for credit through the various lending agencies operating under the supervision of the Farm Credit Administration.
>
> Also to act as an organizing agent for the Credit Union Section by meeting eligible groups of Negroes, explaining to them the aims and methods of the Federal Credit Union Act, and assisting in the preliminary steps for establishing credit unions.

Many Negro farmers are excluded because of certain qualifications which must be met. King explains that the chief causes of failure have been lack of collateral or insufficient collateral and lack of clear title to property or failure to cancel previous mortgages. King has devoted a good deal of time to the establishment of credit unions among Negro organizations. There are cooperative thrift and loan organizations supervised by the federal government for the purpose of encouraging regular savings, making useful loans to members at reasonable rates of interest, sharing earnings among members exclusively, and affording a training course in business management and the handling of money.

A statement prepared by the race relations section shows that as of 30 September 1938 the Negro membership in federal credit unions was 3,511, while the total number of shares held was 35,852. When these statements are kept in mind, while observing the great difficulty Negro farmers have in securing loans because of business-like qualifications, it is possible to visualize the narrow limits within which Negroes generally can partcipate in such a program as that of the FCA. Many farmers who could not qualify had to secure assistance from the Farm Security Administration.

THE PWA AND USHA

The office of the adviser on Negro affairs to the Secretary of the Interior and the office of racial relations in the United States Housing Authority are considered together because of the close administrative relations which have existed between them, and because Dr. Robert C. Weaver has been a guiding force in each. Secretary of the Interior Ickes was the first important official to recognize the problem of assuring the Negro proper participation in and benefit from the various agencies under his direction. A few months after the advent of the New Deal, he established in his department the office of adviser on the economic status of Negroes and called in Clark Foreman, a liberal white Southerner, to administer it. Foreman's first report to the secretary stated:

> In accordance with the orders of the Secretary, the Adviser has sought to integrate Negroes into the work of the Department and also to bring to his attention instances of discrimination. The adviser has been called on by other parts of the Government for help and counsel. At the suggestion of the Secretary he called together an interdepartmental group to

discuss special problems of Negroes which exceed the scope of any one department.

Robert C. Weaver, who came into the office during this period as an associate to the adviser, was elevated to the position of adviser in November 1934. At various times John P. Murchison and Dewey R. Jones were connected with the office as associate advisers. In January 1938 Weaver was appointed special assistant to the administrator of the United States Housing Authority, and in August 1938 his place was filled by William J. Trent, Jr.

The duties of the office are varied, as are the functions of the Department of the Interior itself. The adjustment of personnel problems constitutes a major portion of the work of the office. The office has cooperated with the National Park Service, in its program of organized camping for the underprivileged, to see that these camps are made available to Negroes. Through the interest of the office, employment has been secured for Negroes in the construction of Grand Coulee Dam by the Bureau of Reclamation. In that phase of its activities concerned with the program of the Public Works Administration, the office of the adviser, in addition to personnel work, has given advice to groups which wished to secure aid from local governmental authorities, and when grants were made, further advice was given toward securing full participation of Negro labor on these projects. This office also conducted a survey of the training and employment of Negro white-collar and skilled workers. Volume 1 of this study, entitled "The Urban Negro Worker in the United States 1925–1936," was released in June 1939.

The growth of responsible Negro personnel in the Department of the Interior has also been stressed. Speaking in February 1936, Dr. Weaver, then adviser, said:

> Almost concurrent with the creation of the office of adviser on the Economic Status of Negroes, Secretary Ickes appointed a young, colored lawyer, William Hastie, to the position of assistant solicitor. Today, Mr. Hastie functions as an integral part of the Solicitor's office. Up to now, 243 Negroes have been added to the Government payrolls by emergency agencies under the administration of Secretary Ickes. While most of this number are employed in traditional occupations, there is a new high in the number of colored persons in responsible positions. In the Department of the Interior and the

Public Works Administration, 22 Negroes have been appointed to supervisory, technical, and administrative positions during the last three years.

Finally, we must note the most recent changes which have occurred in this office as a result of the President's Reorganization Plan that went into effect on 1 July 1939. It was found necessary to sever the office from that of the Secretary of the Interior, and so all functions concerned with this department have now ceased, and the office is now strictly an administrative division of the Public Works Administration under the Federal Works Agency. The title of the office is that of adviser on Negro affairs to the Public Works Administration, and the adviser is directly responsible to the PWA administrator. The personnel of the office consists of five persons.

At the dedication of the Howard University Library in May 1939, Secretary Ickes, then PWA administrator, had the following to say concerning the participation of Negroes in the PWA program:

> . . . in 24 of the 48 States and in the District of Columbia, PWA constructed school buildings for Negroes at a total cost of more than $34,000,000. These funds have provided for the construction and alteration of, as well as addition to, 828 different buildings, including a considerable number of libraries. On the whole, 2,885 classrooms have been added, and improved facilities and equipment for about 117,000 students have been provided for. These figures . . . do not include direct PWA grants of $3,502,678 allotted to Howard University, a sum which made possible the construction of six new buildings.

He predicated these statements by saying: "I wish that they had shared more largely because their need has been greater, but it should be borne in mind that PWA cannot initiate projects, but acts upon application from states and local communities."

Before the creation of the United States Housing Authority, all low-rent federal housing was administered under the PWA. Dr. Weaver, who became special assistant to the administrator of the USHA in January 1938, had already become acquainted with the problem of integrating Negroes in a housing program through his activities in the PWA housing program. In his 1937 report to the Secretary of the Interior, he stated:

Since June of 1936 either the Adviser on Negro Affairs or the Associate Adviser on Negro Affairs has visited at least forty of the fifty housing projects now in process of construction. These visits had to do with matters of labor, which include meetings with union officials, labor groups of both races, leaders in communities, and sometimes with city and district governmental officials. In all cases there was but one motive in view, and that was to secure the participation of Negroes in the programs of construction as well as the program of tenancy with as little friction as possible.

Weaver's experience in this program was very valuable to him, and the PWA was the laboratory in which he developed most of the techniques of racial relations to be employed in the USHA position. The office of racial relations employs, besides the special assistant who heads it, an assistant consultant on racial relations, Frank S. Horne; an assistant for Negro labor, Clarence R. Johnson; an assistant for Negro press relations, Henry Lee Moon; and five clerical, stenographic, and secretarial workers. In July 1940 Weaver was transferred to the office of the Defense Committee under Sidney Hillman, where he is to advise on the integration of the Negro in the national defense program.

An official statement of the office of racial relations concerning its activities reads:

> Within the scope of the U.S.H.A. activities, it is the function of the Office of Racial Relations to make available to the Administrator, and the various divisions of the U.S.H.A. and to the local housing authorities factual data and advice concerning racial policy in regard to project planning, employment of labor in the construction of housing projects, management policies, and public relations.

The scrutiny of applications is one of the healthy features of the racial policy of the office. In the matter of site selection, for example, one application stated that a certain site was being selected for the purpose of "pushing out" Negroes. The special assistant easily nipped this discriminatory plan in the bud by pointing out in his recommendation to the administrator that this was not in accordance with USHA policy; thus, the application was rejected and a nasty situation averted.

The same preventative policy is also applied in the field of labor relations. In his early experience in the PWA housing program, Weaver found that it was much better to prevent discrimination against Negro labor in the very first instance than to step in to make adjustments after a dispute had arisen, for the former made for integration, the latter for prolonged friction. But in preventing discrimination it was necessary to work out some objective measure as to what constituted discrimination. Such a measure was worked out for the PWA programs. Favorable results were obtained from the use of this objective measure, and in most instances the payroll percentage of Negro labor was higher than the percentage which it constituted in the fifteenth census. The assistant for Negro labor works with the USHA Labor Relations Division in order to assure the support of organized labor for this clause.

In the field of publicity the office of racial relations seeks to interpret the program of the USHA as it relates to Negroes. The office prepares pamphlets, magazine articles, and newspaper releases concerning the participation of Negroes in the program and the share of the Negro in public housing.

Dr. Weaver also brought with him the personnel policies developed in the Interior Department. Each month his office received a report on Negro personnel in the USHA, and definite efforts are made to increase appointments in the clerical and higher positions. As a result of this activity, the Washington office contains several Negroes who work outside the office of racial relations in technical, professional, and administrative positions.

Concerning the benefits which the black population has received from the USHA program, an official statement claims: "By the end of July 1939, the U.S.H.A. had entered into contracts totalling $472,745,000 for the construction of 267 projects in 129 communities. These projects will rehouse 101,961 low-income families of which number it is estimated that a third will be Negro." Many of the problems which prevent the effective integration of Negroes into the housing program will have to be solved locally because of the decentralized policy of the USHA. One of the most serious of these problems is the inability of the program to accommodate WPA people. Likewise, under the act the USHA can make loans only to public housing authorities, and these must be set up through state laws. The office of racial relations states that: "In 21 cities, Negroes serve as members of local housing authorities, and in two states there are Negro members on State Housing Boards. Negro Advisory

Committees have been appointed to work with the local housing authorities in a number of other cities."

THE NYA

On 26 June 1935 the president, by Executive Order No. 7086, established the National Youth Administration within the framework of the WPA. The NYA from the beginning took frank recognition of the special problems which beset Negro youth, and it called in competent Negro leaders for advice. Frank Horne, a former assistant to Mary McLeod Bethune, wrote in October 1937:

> From the very inception of the N.Y.A., Negroes have been integrated into every phase of its program. Negro educators and other leaders took part in the initial conferences for the setting up of the program. Dr. Mordecai Johnson of Howard University, and Mary McLeod Bethune were appointed members of the National Advisory Committee. To promote the integration and participation of Negro youth in the programs, the Division of Negro Affairs was created as an integral part of the National Administrative office at Washington with Mary McLeod Bethune as its Director with an assistant and two office aids.

The Division of Negro Affairs in the NYA also has a favorable administrative position, since it is one of the seven official divisions which comprise the Washington Office. The director is responsible directly to the NYA administrator, and the salary schedule of the division is similar to that of the other six divisions. There is a close relationship between the division and the Negro personnel distributed throughout the various states. This relationship is very important since there are some twenty-three state supervisors of Negro work, the majority of whom are working in Southern states. Although these supervisors are appointed by and are responsible to the state directors, the Division of Negro Affairs plays an important advisory role in their appointment. In addition the division receives monthly reports covering fully the activities of the supervisors. This relation is also furthered by periodic field trips by members of the division.

The application of the so-called quota rule is significant when it is noted that it operates in a sphere in which Negroes have been notoriously discriminated against. Speaking of this national educational blemish, Mrs. Bethune declared in 1938:

Some 230 counties in these states have no high school facilities whatsoever for Negroes, and the great expense of adequate vocational training has kept the Negro masses out of the channel of even this most practical form of education. As a result of the operation of all these factors, together with the fact that being generally deprived of the vote, the Negro is denied a voice in the expenditure of public funds, most Negro schools for the masses have inferior buildings and equipment, shorter school-terms, over-crowded classes, ill-prepared and poorly paid teachers and highly retarded students.

Another special problem of Negro youth is met by the establishment of a special Negro college and graduate aid fund over and above the regular quota of Negroes.

The favorable administrative position and efficiency of the Division of Negro Affairs are due in large part to the dynamic role of its director, Mrs. Bethune, a recognized national and racial leader. Speaking of her activities in 1937, Mrs. Bethune said:

> As director of the Division of Negro Affairs in the National Youth Administration, I travelled over 40,000 miles last year, visited over 70 centers in 21 states from Texas to the Carolinas and from New York to Florida, preaching the gospel of interracial cooperation, the recognition of Negro needs and the efficacy of trained Negro leadership.

As a result of sympathetic and effective administration, the NYA probably has been more successful than any other governmental agency in promoting full integration and participation of minority groups in all phases of its program.

THE DEPARTMENT OF COMMERCE

The Bureau of the Census had shown an interest in Negro statistics by the publication of two bulletins on "Negroes in the United States," one in 1904, the other in 1915. In 1918 the Bureau published an 844-page report entitled *Negro Population in the United States, 1790–1915.* Three Negro clerks, one of whom was Charles E. Hall, prepared the data for this report. With the advent of the New Deal, it was Hall who took the initiative toward getting the office of specialist in Negro statistics established in 1934. Hall was made the specialist in Negro statistics, and he immediately began work on the volume *Negroes in the United States 1920–32,* which was published in 1935.

The Division of Negro Affairs which was established in the Bureau of Foreign and Domestic Commerce in 1933 is closely related to the office of specialist in Negro statistics, since it was merged with the latter office in 1937. James A. Jackson first had charge of the division; he was succeeded by Eugene Kinckle Jones, executive secretary of the National Urban League, who enjoyed only a brief tenure. Since his departure the office has not been continued.

In his 1935 and 1936 annual reports, Secretary Daniel C. Roper made mention of the work of the Division of Negro Affairs. The secretary mentioned that for the fiscal year ending 30 June 1935, more than 2,000 Negroes had been employed in various temporary white-collar positions in the department in connection with enumeration and tabulation of census data and other activities. In April 1937 the Secretary of Commerce announced that the work of the division had been merged with that of the specialist in Negro statistics, with Charles E. Hall in charge of the combined work.

Hall retired in 1938, and Joseph R. Houchins, former business specialist in the Division of Negro Affairs, was appointed acting specialist in Negro statistics. This office renders service to individuals, organizations, and government units seeking statistical data concerning Negroes or information about organizations composed of Negroes. The office is now chiefly concerned with preparing material on the Negro church.

THE DEPARTMENT OF LABOR

Several positions in the Department of Labor have centered around Lieutenant Lawrence A. Oxley, former director of Negro welfare for the North Carolina State Board of Welfare. On 14 March 1934 he was appointed commissioner of conciliation in the United States Department of Labor. The Conciliation Service is maintained for the purpose of finding a mutually acceptable basis of negotiation in cases of industrial disputes. After serving in this position for eighteen months, Oxley was appointed chief of a newly created Division of Negro Labor in the Bureau of Labor Statistics. In an address in 1936 he described some of the research work being carried on in the Department of Labor, mentioning an inquiry being made on the problem of Negro labor.

The department hopes to obtain an accurate picture of the occupational status and employment opportunities of

Negroes to determine whether Negroes are in general employed in declining occupations and in those occupations that have suffered most during the depression; to secure definite statistical information upon which a redistribution of Negro labor may eventually be made; and finally to collect, analyze, and publish data which will supply public and private agencies with a body of information valuable in planning and fostering their programs.

On 1 July 1937 Lieutenant Oxley was appointed field representative for the United States Employment Service. This service operates under the Wagner-Peyser Act, enacted 6 June 1933 and amended 10 May 1935, which provided for the establishment and maintenance of a national system of public employment offices. Recent reports show that approximately 450 Negroes are employed on the staffs of the public employment service in twenty-four states (this number includes clerical and custodial workers). With this increase of personnel the Employment Service is developing interest in the special problems of Negro applicants. It has developed an educational program for its entire personnel which recognizes that the Negro applicant has problems over and above those of the ordinary applicant.

Under the President's Reorganization Order No. 1, the United States Employment Service has recently been transferred to the Social Security Board as part of the newly-created Federal Security Agency. Under this new setup Lieutenant Oxley has received an appointment as chief of the Negro placement service, Division of Special Services. This position, according to a news release, "places upon Lieutenant Oxley direct responsibility for interpreting the placement program and objectives of the U.S. Employment Service to Negroes throughout the nation."

THE OFFICE OF EDUCATION

The Office of Education, from its inception as an independent agency in 1867 on through its inclusion in the Department of the Interior, has shown a healthy interest in Negro education. Each commissioner has devoted space in his annual reports to some discussion of Negro schools and Negro education. A special division of Negro education was established in 1914. This first division was under the direction of Thomas Jesse Jones. In 1930 impetus was given to this work and a new section of Negro education was established in the Division of Special Prob-

NEGROES AND THE NEW DEAL AGENCIES

lems. The new service differs from the earlier division in that it is an integral part of the regular work of the office, it is supported entirely by federal funds, and its personnel is appointed and works under the civil service.

The education of the Negro still receives attention through the regular channels of the office, but the special educational problems created by the abnormal socio-economic position of Negroes are treated in the Division of Special Problems, primarily through the specialist who has an opportunity to use the other specialist in the course of his work. Dr. Ambrose Caliver, the present specialist, has been very active in his position, and since his appointment there has been a noticeable pickup in the general service of the Office of Education. He has arranged many programs and conferences. In addition, Dr. Caliver has produced twelve publications, three bibliographies on Negro education, and has himself written a number of articles.

THE UNITED STATES PUBLIC HEALTH SERVICE

The United States Public Health Service has a long history and traces its origin to the Marine Hospital Service established in 1798 for the relief of ailing seamen. The present office of Dr. Roscoe Brown, health education specialist, was established as a result of the cooperation of the Public Health Service in promoting National Negro Health Week and in developing a year-round plan for the improvement of the health of the Negro population.

National Negro Health Week was organized around the health philosophy of Booker T. Washington, and, originating in Virginia in 1913, it was soon nationalized by him through the medium of the National Negro Business League. As a memorial to his efforts, the Health Week was set as the eight-day period, Sunday to Sunday, that includes April 5, the date of his birthday. As a result of a request for cooperation in 1921 from Robert R. Moton, Washington's successor, the Public Health Service sent Dr. Roscoe C. Brown, one of its lecturers and special consultants, to the next annual Tuskegee conference. The conference requested assistance in promoting the Health Week and guidance in forming a year-round program. By 1930 a year-round organization, the National Negro Health Movement, had been organized, with the Rosenwald Fund providing financial assistance and Howard University the headquarters.

In July 1932 the Public Health Service began providing quarters and operating facilities for Negro health work. In July

1934 Dr. Brown was appointed director of this office with the title of health education specialist; the office personnel also includes a clerical and stenographic assistant. The Public Health Service also cooperates in Negro health work by publishing a quarterly, *National Negro Health News*, and various studies, the most comprehensive of which is "Mortality Among Southern Negroes since 1920" (1937). During the past two years two Negro physicians, Dr. Harold H. Whitted, acting assistant surgeon, and Dr. William Sperry, special consultant, have been employed for venereal disease work in various states.

TRADITIONAL POSITIONS UNDER THE NEW DEAL

Presidential appointments have continued under the New Deal, although to a somewhat lesser degree than under the previous administration. The positions in the Internal Revenue and Customs services seem to have disappeared, but, a larger plum, a federal judgeship, has been added. The last important traditional position which remains is that of the recorder of deeds for the District of Columbia. The present incumbent is William Thompkins, a former Kansas City, Missouri, politician and member of the so-called "Big Four," a group of Negro Democrats who were active nationally in the 1936 election. Thompkins directs a racially mixed staff of 69 regular employees; he has also set up a WPA white-collar project which at one time employed as many as 250 workers.

Dramatic proof was given recently of the close attachment of politicians and others to the position of recorder of deeds as a "Negro position," when Representative Ambrose J. Kennedy of Maryland introduced a reorganization bill for the District of Columbia which would have drastically changed the office by transferring it to a proposed District Department of Revenue. Representatives of several Negro organizations attended the hearings on the bill and vigorously protested its provisions. The protest was so great that no change was made in the position, and the organizations are prepared to fight against any changes proposed during the next session of Congress.

In the consular service two previous appointees, James G. Carter and Clifford R. Wharton, still serve. In the diplomatic service, Lester A. Walton is minister resident and consul general at Monrovia, Liberia.

Two Roosevelt departmental appointees may also be mentioned, because their positions are in departments in which Negroes were appointed early and because both resemble the traditional appointee in that they have been active in national politics. Robert L. Vann, who was appointed special assistant to the Attorney General, can be classified as a professional politician. He did publicity work in the Harding, Coolidge, and Hoover campaigns. In 1932 he and William Thompkins were members of the newly formed Negro division of the national Democratic committee, and in 1936 he was a delegate at large from Pennsylvania to the Democratic convention. He was also considered a member of the Democratic Big Four, which included, besides Vann and Thompkins, Julian Rainey of Massachusetts and Dr. Joseph L. Johnson of Ohio. Vann soon resigned the position and returned to his duties as editor of the Pittsburgh *Courier;* he has since jumped back on the Republican bandwagon. His position was subsequently held by Bertram Hamilton, who also resigned. The present appointee is William L. Houston, president of the Washington Bar Association, who has been assigned to the antitrust division.

Ralph E. Mizelle received an appointment in the Post Office Department as assistant attorney, office of the solicitor. Mizelle, a New Yorker, has been connected with Tammany Hall.

The appointees in the judicial sphere under President Roosevelt have been Armond W. Scott, who succeeded James A. Cobb as judge in the District Municipal Court, and William H. Hastie, who was appointed a federal judge in the Virgin Islands. The latter position bids fair to become traditional, since upon Hastie's resignation such a clamor was set up that another Negro was appointed as his successor.

A study of the general background of the New Deal departmental appointees serves to throw some light on their experience and qualification for the positions which they now hold.[3] A cursory examination reveals that most of them have a strong educational background, received college training, and served as teachers or instructors. Most of them had no specific training for the position in which they are serving but received their experience in service. There should be no surprise at the absence of professional politicians among all except the traditional appointees, since these men were brought in to aid in solving racial problems and not as political patronage appointees. Even where political affiliation prior to the New Deal is found, as in the case of Mrs. Bethune, Forrester B. Washington, Eugene K.

3. Brief biographical sketches of eleven Negro appointees (p. 1444–48 of the Bunche memorandum) have been omitted. —ED.

Jones, and Charles E. Hall, the affiliation was Republican rather than Democratic.

In national prestige and in personal connection with high New Deal officials, Mary McLeod Bethune stands head and shoulders above the rest of the appointees. As a result she has become the guiding spirit of the higher Negro government officials and has been able to reconcile their petty contradictions and weld them into an informal unit, the Federal Council, popularly called the "black cabinet." The common concern of the appointees about the problems of the Negro brought them together, and the organization exists merely for the purpose of discussing that problem generally, and for the interchange of information. Mrs. Bethune is chairman, Dr. Robert C. Weaver is vice-chairman, and Dutton Ferguson is secretary. Meetings are monthly. The organization is quite informal and has no letterheads. It is not confined to those interested in policies and contains men concerned with the information service and with research.

The appointees have been able to affect public sentiment through their various public relations, the most important revolving around the first and second National Conferences on the Problems of the Negro and Negro Youth. Again Mrs. Bethune took the leadership in the organizational work. The conferences were sponsored by the Division of Negro Affairs of the NYA, and Mrs. Bethune was the general chairman of both conferences. The major subjects of the first conference were increased opportunity for employment and economic security; adequate educational and recreational facilities; improved health and housing conditions; and security of life and equal protection under the law. The second conference was devoted basically to the same problems and had as an additional objective that of determining the progress made since the first. The conferences were addressed by Mrs. Roosevelt and several high government officials. Negro officials functioned as consultants to the various conference committees, and also presented the programs of their respective agencies as related to the Negro. Negro leaders from all walks of life were invited to the conferences in order to express their opinions in organized form and to draw up recommendations. The criticisms centered around the discrimination, inequality, and neglect attendant upon the application of certain government programs. The general failure to include adequate Negro personnel in administrative and supervisory positions throughout the government was noted.

But the conferences recognized the New Deal as being a great step forward in social progress, urging that these evils be removed in order that such progress not be retarded.[4]

Both conferences sponsored by the Division of Negro Affairs of the NYA have viewed with alarm the decentralization policy which the Roosevelt administration is being forced to adopt because of Republican cries of "bureaucracy," "dictatorship," and "states' rights." The first conference stated:

> The Conference favors Federal as against State control of Federal projects and recommends that where projects are turned over to State Committees for management, definite clauses against racial discrimination be written into the plans for such projects before they become the property of State authorities.

4. For two recent studies of the Negro and the New Deal, see Raymond Wolters, *Negroes and the Great Depression: The Problem of Economic Recovery* (Westport, Conn., 1970), and Allen Francis Kifer, "The Negro under the New Deal, 1933–1941" (Ph.D. dissertation, University of Wisconsin, 1961).

Bibliography

In 1939 and 1940, when Ralph Bunche and his assistants were energetically searching for information for "The Political Status of the Negro," they could find almost no scholarly works in print on the role of the black man in politics, aside from several historical monographs. What, the reader of this book may ask, would they find if they were preparing a similar memorandum today? The answer would depend in part on the chronological focus of their study, but whether they were concerned with the 1930s or with the 1970s, they could begin with an impressive array of books on the Negro and race relations in the United States. This bibliography is intended to place Bunche's memorandum on Negro politics in historical prespective by referring to a part of this extensive body of literature.

The bibliography is divided into two parts. Part One is a brief essay on some of the secondary works that deal with the Negro's place in the modern American political system or with related aspects of the political culture in the United States. Many of these writings illuminate the questions and concerns that found expression in Bunche's long report. Part Two is a classified listing of books and articles designed to serve as a handy reference tool for readers who desire to go beyond the Bunche memorandum. The editor hopes that students, in particular, will find this book a useful place to begin original inquiries into the black experience in American political life, and that many of Bunche's themes can be pursued in the relevant works cited below.

It should be noted that this bibliography is far from exhaustive. It includes little on slavery, for example, and its coverage of Southern history is limited. It concentrates on works that treat the Negro as a participant and as an issue in American politics since the Civil War. The careful student will profit from consulting one or more of the following bibliographies: James M. McPherson et al., *Blacks in America: Bibliographical Essays* (Garden City, 1971); Elizabeth W. Miller and Mary L. Fisher, comps., *The Negro in America: A Bibliography*, 2d ed. rev. (Cambridge, Mass., 1970); Dorothy B. Porter, comp., *A Working Bibliography on the Negro in the United States* (n.p., 1961); Erwin A. Salk, comp. and ed., *A Layman's Guide to Negro History*, new ed. (New York, 1967); Erwin K. Welsch, ed., *The Negro in the United States: A Research Guide* (Bloomington, Ind., 1965); and James D. Graham, ed., "Negro Protests in America, 1900–1955: A Bibliographical Guide," *South Atlantic Quarterly*, 62 (Winter 1968): 94–107.

PART ONE: BIBLIOGRAPHICAL ESSAY

In preparing "The Political Status of the Negro," Ralph Bunche relied heavily upon two secondary sources, which he considered to be the best existing studies of recent Negro politics. One of these was Paul Lewinson's *Race, Class and Party: A History of Negro Suffrage and White Politics in the South* (New York, 1932), a good survey of the Negro's experience as a voter and as a factor in Southern politics between the Civil War and 1930. The author made use of miscellaneous sources, including the responses to a suffrage questionnaire sent to a sample of Negro Southerners. The analyses of the effects of the disfranchisement amendments at the turn of the century, of the nature of the restricted Negro participation in politics since that time, and of the circumstances under which blacks could vote in a Southern community are still instructive. Bunche confirmed many of Lewinson's generalizations. During the next few years, several other studies supplemented Lewinson's work, including two books by William Alexander Mabry—*Studies in the Disfranchisement of the Negro in the South* (Durham, N. C., 1938) and *The Negro in North Carolina Politics Since Reconstruction* (Durham, N. C., 1940). Rayford W. Logan, *The Attitude of the Southern White Press toward Negro Suffrage, 1932–1940* (Washington, D. C., 1940), is a convenient source of Southern newspaper opinion on the Negro's political participation, the Democratic primary, and other aspects of the election process in the South.

The other secondary work that proved especially useful to Bunche was Harold F. Gosnell's *Negro Politicians: The Rise of Negro Politics in Chicago* (Chicago, 1935). Gosnell's book was a pioneering study of the rise of Negro politics in a great Northern city. It illuminates Chicago's "Black Belt," machine politics, the role of organized vice, and much else. For another early investigation of Negro politics in Northern cities, see Edward H. Litchfield, *Political Behavior in a Metropolitan Community* (Ann Arbor, Mich., 1941).

Several books dealing with the Negro's participation in politics appeared in the 1940s and early 1950s. The increasing political strength of black Americans in the thirties and forties was the theme of *Balance of Power: The Negro Vote* (Garden City, N. Y., 1948), by Henry Lee Moon. The Negro vote, Moon maintained, was "an important and sometimes decisive factor" in a dozen Northern states and in at least seventy-five congressional districts, making it more decisive in presidential elections than the Solid South! The powerful lily-white trend in the Republican party and the Negro's steady shift toward the Democrats were scrutinized in Elbert Lee Tatum's *The Changed Political Thought of the Negro, 1915–1940* (New York, 1951), while the Communist party's generally unsuccessful efforts to exploit the "Negro problem" in the United States were examined in a well-researched book by Wilson Record, *The Negro and the Communist Party* (Chapel Hill, N. C., 1951).

Meanwhile, a major study of the Southern political process had been launched, culminating in the publication of *Southern Politics in State and Nation* (New York, 1949) by V. O. Key, Jr. In some respects Key's work represents the kind of analysis Bunche had wanted to undertake in 1940. The volume contains a state-by-state account of one-party politics; a discussion of the South's political leadership on the national scene; an examination of the mechanisms and procedures of the one-party system; an analysis of the size and composition of the Southern electorate; and a consideration of the various restrictions on voting in the region. Although Key was not much concerned with the Negro as a participant in Southern politics, he emphasized the black man's historical and contemporary significance in the political affairs of the South, showing how race and the position of the Negro dominated Southern politics and suppressed meaningful political divisions among Southerners. After more than twenty years, Key remains the starting point for any serious student of modern Southern politics.

One of Key's assistants, Alexander Heard, made his own contribution in *A Two-Party South?* (Chapel Hill, N. C., 1952). Heard's sprightly volume deals with several subjects not fully treated in *Southern Politics*, including Southern Republicanism, the region's incipient political realignment, and the activities and political role of the Negro. A section devoted to "the new Negro politics" contains chapters on the NAACP, the Progressive Voters' Leagues, and bloc voting. Another of Key's staff members was Frederic D. Ogden, whose monograph *The Poll Tax in the South* (University, Ala., 1958) is a thorough analysis of the origins, operation, and movement for the repeal of a notorious disfranchising device. Ogden shows that while the ostensible purpose of the poll tax was the disfranchisement of Negroes, its practical effect was to deprive a host of white men of the ballot. Negroes were effectively disfranchised by other means, formal and informal, including the white primary. "The Negro Voter in the South," *Journal of Negro Education* 26 (Summer 1957): 213–431, is a useful historical survey and an analysis of current conditions in each of the eleven ex-Confederate states. Much light is shed on Southern politics in the 1950s by Numan V. Bartley, *The Rise of Massive Resistance: Race and Politics in the South during the 1950's* (Baton Rouge, La., 1969), and Neil R. McMillen, *The Citizens' Council: Organized Resistance to the Second Reconstruction* (Urbana, Ill., 1971). Among broad regional studies, mention should be made of William C. Havard, ed., *The Changing Politics of the South* (Baton Rouge, La., 1972), a collaborative effort to bring Key's *Southern Politics* up to date.

Some investigations of Negro politics concentrated on individual Southern states. Using a large amount of Negro registration and voting participation data, Hugh D. Price sought, in *The Negro and Southern Politics: A Chapter of Florida History* (New York, 1957), to describe the Negro's role as a voter and to measure the impact of black voting on Florida politics, with emphasis on the decade following the invalidation of the white primary in 1944. The Negro's political status from disfranchisement to the breakthrough in the 1960s is traced in Andrew Buni's *The Negro in Virginia Politics, 1902–1965* (Charlottesville, Va., 1967).

By far the most comprehensive and exhaustive treatment of the Negro's political involvement in the recent South is provided in *Negroes and the New Southern Politics* (New York, 1966) by Donald R. Matthews and James W. Prothro. These political scientists attempt to describe the political activities of the South's ten million adult Negroes, to explain why some Negroes participate in Southern political life and others do not, to predict the future of Negro politics in the region, and to explore the probable consequences of these current and future activities for the South and its racial problems. The work is based on what its authors say is "perhaps the largest collection of systematic data on Negro political behavior ever compiled." Some two thousand inhabitants of the eleven former Confederate states were interviewed, while a large body of social, economic, and political data was collected on more than a thousand counties in the region. Four widely differing communities—Crayfish, Bright Leaf, Camellia, and Piedmont counties—were studied in detail. Among the findings were these: that the social and economic attributes of individual blacks are strongly related to the extent of their participation in civic life; that community as well as personal characteristics have a powerful influence on political participation (especially the percentage of Negroes in the population); that the varying political and legal climates among the Southern states are extremely important, as well as such factors as formal voter requirements, state factional systems, and the amount and kind of community racial organizations. In contrast to Bunche and Myrdal, Matthews and Prothro view the Negro church—an almost totally segregated institution—as the most likely "nonpolitical" agency to organize and direct Negro political activity in the South. They conclude that Negroes and whites are dangerously divided on the major issues of Southern politics, that is, racial segregation. In the past this division was not a serious threat to democratic politics in the region, since Negroes had almost no political power. But now that Negroes are becoming politically active and powerful in the South, the system is coming under great strain.

Harry Holloway is the author of another regional study of black politics, *The Politics of the Southern Negro: From Exclusion to Big City Organization* (New York, 1969). Holloway presents a series of case studies to illustrate variations that occur in the emergence of Negro political participation within a society that was once strongly traditional but is now changing rapidly. In tracing the evolution of Negro political life between World War II and the mid-1960s, he examines a number of specific localities—in some cases the same communities described in the Bunche memorandum. Macon County, Alabama, is one such community. See Bernard Taper, *Gomillion versus Lightfoot: The Tuskegee Gerrymander Case* (New York, 1962), for an account of a notorious instance of political discrimination against Macon County Negroes in the late 1950s. Another volume, *Climbing Jacob's Ladder: The Arrival of Negroes in Southern Politics* (New York, 1967), by Pat Watters and Reese Cleghorn, is primarily about the Southern Regional Council's Voter Education Project and the registration campaigns of the 1960s. In one fascinating chapter the authors include excerpts from the field reports of voter registration workers in the VEP campaigns. These reports are especially interesting when compared with the interviews quoted in the Bunche memorandum. By using Durham, North Carolina, and Tuskegee, Alabama, as case studies, William R. Keech has explored the question whether equal voting rights bring equal social and economic opportunities for blacks. The concrete benefits, he concludes in *The Impact of Negro Voting: The Role of the Vote in the Quest for Equality* (Chicago, 1968), are not altogether favorable. The franchise brings some successes, but in some areas of the public and private sectors it seems to have no discernible effect.

Several field studies of community life by sociologists and political scientists have focused on Negro leaders and organizations in the South. One of the earliest and most influential of these was Floyd Hunter's *Community Power Structure: A Study of Decision Makers* (Chapel Hill, N. C., 1953), which contains a chapter on the power structure of the Negro subcommunity and its interaction with the larger community. An investigation of power and decision-making in Durham is reported in M. Elaine Burgess's *Negro Leadership in a Southern City* (Chapel Hill, N. C., 1962). Burgess is interested in the nature, function, and effectiveness of Negro leadership and its relation to the white leadership of the community as revealed in the movement toward the desegregation of schools and other public facilities in the late fifties. Still another community study, Daniel C. Thompson's *The Negro Leadership Class* (Englewood Cliffs, N. J., 1963), focuses on New Orleans in the 1940s and 1950s. It deals with the origins of Negro leaders, changing patterns of leadership, and the functions of black leaders within and outside of the subcommunity. Lewis M. Killian and Charles M. Grigg have written a book with a broader setting which they call *Racial Crisis in America: Leadership in Conflict* (Englewood Cliffs, N. J., 1964). They discuss the personalities and principles in the black politics of Southern cities.

Perhaps the most impressive attempt to demonstrate the utility of the community as a context within which to analyze the location, structure, and function of political leadership is Everett Carll Ladd, Jr., *Negro Political Leadership in the South* (Ithaca, N. Y., 1966). This volume is based on intensive research, including field work, in two cities: Greenville, South Carolina, and Winston-Salem, North Carolina. Ladd describes the collapse of the old structure of accommodating leadership and the emergence of a new type of Negro leader. He analyzes the factors in these two communities that retard or facilitate the exercise of Negro political leadership, discusses the recruitment of Negro leaders and the styles of race leadership, and considers a variety of voting organizations.

Even as Ralph Bunche and his assistants were making their investigation, the South was being illuminated by other regional studies. Some of the most notable of these studies were concerned with particular communities, sometimes the same localities investigated by Bunche's interviewers. Thus in *Shadow of the Plantation* (Chicago, 1934), Charles S. Johnson reported the results of an intensive survey of Negro life in Macon County, Alabama. The candid comments of the people studied—some six hundred families—gave this work an extraordinarily human quality. Johnson's *Growing up in the Black Belt: Negro Youth in the Rural South* (Washington, D. C., 1941) presents an intimate picture of personality development, race relations, and social attitudes through the eyes of Negro youths in eight Southern counties. Greene County, Georgia, and Macon and Madison counties, Alabama—familiar names in the Bunche memorandum—are included in the study. Another sociologist, Arthur F. Raper, made a comparative study of Greene and Macon counties, Georgia, which he described in *Preface to Peasantry: A Tale of Two Black Belt Counties* (Chapel Hill, N. C., 1936). On the basis of interviews, questionnaires, and extended visits, Raper examined every aspect of life in these two counties. In *Tenants of the Almighty* (New York, 1943), he extended his account of Greene County into the early 1940s. Together, these two books constitute one of the best case studies ever made of rural life in the South. A different kind of study, but one that throws light on the rural South in the 1930s and earlier, is Horace Mann Bond, *Negro Education in Alabama: A Study in Cotton and Steel* (Washington, D. C., 1939). In analyzing conditions in the Alabama black belt, Bond showed the methods of white domination, the Negro's loss of power, and his subsequent political decline.

The South during the 1930s provided the setting for still other community studies by social scientists. Two of these were independent investigations of the same Mississippi town: Indianola. The first to be published was John Dollard's *Caste and Class in a Southern Town* (New Haven, 1937). Dollard, a Yale social psychologist, analyzed race relations in terms of the "gains" and "losses" which both Negroes and whites sustained at different levels in the caste-class structure of the Southern community. A more adequate and well-rounded picture of Negro life in Indianola was drawn by Hortense Powdermaker in *After Freedom: A Cultural Study of the Deep South* (New York, 1939). A participant observer in this Delta town for a year during the early thirties, Powdermaker, a cultural anthropologist, wrote a vivid and searching account of Negro life and attitudes in "Cottonville." An examination of social class among both whites and Negroes in Natchez and Adams County, Mississippi, is described by Allison Davis, Burleigh B. Gardner, and Mary R. Gardner in *Deep South: A Social Anthropological Study of Caste and Class* (Chicago, 1941). Davis and his associates employed a conceptual scheme for analyzing race relations in the South which viewed Negro-white dealings as organized by a color-caste system that shaped economic and political relations as well as family and kinship structures, and was itself reinforced by the legal system. It is interesting to compare these studies with David L. Cohn's *Where I Was Born and Raised* (Boston, 1948), a nostalgic commentary on life and labor in the Mississippi Delta written from the perspective of Southern white paternalism.

Soon after World War II a series of empirical community studies was carried out under the direction of Professor John Gillin of the University of North Carolina. Using the approach of social anthropology, these Field Studies in the Modern Culture of the South cast considerable light on racial practices and attitudes in the region at midcentury. In *Plantation County* (Chapel Hill, N. C., 1951), Morton Rubin describes the social structure and cultural values of a black-belt community in Alabama. In portraying the major patterns of behavior, organization, thought, and feeling of one type of Southern community, Rubin suggests how they are related together to form one variety of Southern culture. *Blackways of Kent* (Chapel Hill, N. C., 1955), by Hylan Lewis, is a report on Negro life in a small South Carolina mill town "from the inside." In a companion study entitled *Millways of Kent* (Chapel Hill, N. C., 1958), John Kenneth Morland concentrates on the white textile workers in the same Piedmont community. For a different project, see Wilmoth Annette Carter, *The Urban Negro in the South* (New York, 1961), a sociological study of Negro Main Street in Raleigh, North Carolina.

The community studies were significant in part because of what they revealed about Southern attitudes and values. A diverse lot of other books is also noteworthy in this regard. The best beginning place is C. Vann Woodward's splendid historical interpretation, *The Strange Career of Jim Crow*, 2d rev. ed. (New York, 1966), a work that goes beyond the tracing of segregation practices. An analysis by a social scientist is Melvin M. Tumin's *Desegregation: Resistance and Readiness* (Princeton, 1958). On the basis of intensive interviews conducted in Guilford County, North Carolina, in the fall of 1956, Tumin makes a systematic analysis of white attitudes toward Negroes and desegregation. Howard H. Quint, *Profile in Black and White: A Frank Portrayal of South Carolina* (Washington, 1958), explores the attitudes, ideas, and plans that maintained "a caste system of society" in one Southern state. Another analysis of racial attitudes is presented by Hugh Davis Graham in *Crisis in Print: Desegregation and the Press in Tennessee* (Nashville, 1967), an imaginative study of editorial opinion in a border state during the crucial decade following the Brown decision of 1954. Still another state is analyzed in James W. Silver's *Mississippi: The Closed Society* (New York, 1964), a devastating treatment of the forces that created and perpetuated the nation's most impervious racial orthodoxy, and in Frederick M. Wirt's *Politics of Southern Equality: Law and Social Change in a Mississippi County* (Chicago, 1970), an examination of the impact of civil rights legislation on one county. Finally, from among the numerous travel accounts that report on race relations in the South, one should not overlook the books by two perceptive Negro writers: Jay Saunders Redding's *No Day of Triumph* (New York, 1942) and Carl Thomas Rowan's *South of Freedom* (New York, 1952).

There is as yet no counterpart to Matthews and Prothro's *Negroes and the New Southern Politics* for other parts of the country. James Q. Wilson's *Negro Politics: The Search for Leadership* (Glencoe, Ill., 1960) is the most important work on the Negro in Northern politics to be published since Gosnell's *Negro Politicians*. Concentrating on Chicago, but in the context of several large Northern cities, Wilson explores the state of Negro civic and political leadership, assesses its strength and effectiveness, and attempts to account for its weaknesses and conflicts. He argues that the structure and style of Negro politics in the metropolitian areas can best be understood as a response to the larger, white-dominated political system of which they are a part. At the same time, he notes the consequences of the division and diversity within the black community itself. In classifying Negro leadership styles ("militant" versus "moderate") and goals ("status" versus "welfare"), Wilson developed some useful analytic concepts. Other volumes dealing with Negro politics include Louis E. Lomax, *The Negro Revolt* (New York, 1962); Benjamin Muse, *The American Negro Revolution: From Nonviolence to Black Power* (Bloomington, Ind., 1968); and Harry A. Bailey, Jr., ed., *Negro Politics in America* (Columbus, Ohio, 1967). The first two deal with events and tendencies in the late fifties and the sixties. The third is an excellent collection of essays on the recent period designed to meet the need for an empirical and systematic explanation of Negro politics in the United States.

The mounting interest in Afro-American history is evident in the recent publication of several books on the Negro and the modern metropolis. Historians have begun to reconstruct the growth and development of Negro communities in the North since the Civil War. On New York City, for example, there are several complementary studies: Seth M. Scheiner, *Negro Mecca: A History of the Negro in New York City, 1865–1920* (New York, 1965); Gilbert Osofsky, *Harlem, The Making of a Ghetto: Negro New York, 1890–1930* (New York, 1966); and Oscar Handlin, *The Newcomers: Negroes and Puerto Ricans in a Changing Metropolis* (Cambridge, Mass., 1959). Allan H. Spear's *Black Chicago: The Making of a Negro Ghetto, 1890–1920* (Chicago, 1967) is an outstanding history with an excellent description of the growth of urban black institutions. For a good study of one significant episode in the experience of black Chicagoans, see William M. Tuttle, Jr., *Race Riot: Chicago in the Red Summer of 1919* (New York, 1970). Constance McLaughlin Green's *The Secret City: A History of Race Relations in the Nation's Capital* (Princeton, 1967), while narrowly conceived, is informative on the situation in Washington. The manners, customs, and social position of Negroes in a small Northern city are discussed in Robert Austin Warner, *New Haven Negroes: A Social History* (New Haven, 1940).

In commenting on scholarly investigations of American Negroes and the metropolis, the contributions of sociologists should not be overlooked. The pioneering sociological study was William E. B. Du Bois' *The Philadelphia Negro: A Social Study* (Philadelphia, 1899). (Du Bois devoted one chapter to "Negro Suffrage.") But the classic study of urban Negro life is St. Clair Drake and Horace R. Cayton's *Black Metropolis: A Study of Negro Life in a Northern*

City, 2 vols., rev. ed. (New York, 1962), which combined the research approaches of sociology and social anthropology. This brilliant and exhaustive survey of Chicago's Negro community in the late 1930s reveals the increasingly rigid pattern of discrimination and segregation faced by black Chicagoans in the twentieth century. Nathan Glazer and Daniel Patrick Moynihan undertook a different kind of ethnic study in *Beyond the Melting Pot: The Negroes, Puerto Ricans, Jews, Italians, and Irish of New York City* (Cambridge, Mass., 1963). Glazer and Moynihan examine the differing levels of achievement of the city's major ethnic groups in education, business, and politics.

PART TWO: CLASSIFIED LIST OF ADDITIONAL SOURCES

Black History and the Meaning of Race: General Works

Aptheker, Herbert. *A Documentary History of the Negro People in the United States*. New York, 1951.

Bennett, Lerone, Jr. *Before the Mayflower: A History of the Negro in America, 1619–1964*. Rev. ed. Chicago, 1964.

Berry, Mary Frances. *Black Resistance/White Law: A History of Constitutional Racism in America*. New York, 1971.

Blaustein, Albert P., and Zangrando, Robert L., eds. *Civil Rights and the American Negro: A Documentary History*. New York, 1968.

Board of Education, City of New York. *The Negro in American History*. New York, 1964.

Boulware, Marcus H. *The Oratory of Negro Leaders: 1900–1968*. Westport, Conn., 1969.

Brisbane, Robert H. *The Black Vanguard: Origins of the Negro Social Revolution, 1900–1960*. Valley Forge, Pa., 1970.

Brotz, Howard, ed. *Negro Social and Political Thought, 1850–1920: Representative Texts*. New York, 1966.

Butcher, Margaret Just. *The Negro in American Culture*. New York, 1956.

Cruse, Harold. *The Crisis of the Negro Intellectual*. New York, 1967.

Curtis, James C., and Gould, Lewis L., eds. *The Black Experience in America: Essays*. Austin, Tex., 1970.

Degler, Carl N. *Neither Black Nor White: Slavery and Race Relations in Brazil and the United States*. New York, 1971.

Dowd, Jerome. *The Negro in American Life*. New York, 1926.

Drimmer, Melvin, ed. *Black History: A Reappraisal*. Garden City, N. Y., 1968.

Du Bois, William E. B. *The Souls of Black Folk: Essays and Sketches*. Chicago, 1903.

———. *Black Folk, Then and Now: An Essay in the History and Sociology of the Negro Race*. New York, 1939.

Embree, Edwin Rogers. *Brown America: The Story of a New Race*. New York, 1931.

Eppse, Merl R. *The Negro, Too, in American History*. Nashville, 1938.

Foner, Eric, ed. *America's Black Past: A Reader in Afro-American History*. New York, 1970.

Frazier, E. Franklin. *The Negro in the United States*. 2nd ed. New York, 1957.

Franklin, John Hope, ed. *Color and Race*. Boston, 1968.

———. *From Slavery to Freedom: A History of Negro Americans*. 3rd ed. New York, 1967.

Fullinwider, S. P. *The Mind and Mood of Black America: 20th Century Thought*. Homewood, Ill., 1969.

Gossett, Thomas F. *Race: The History of an Idea in America*. Dallas, 1963.

Grimes, Alan P. *Equality in America: Religion, Race, and the Urban Majority*. New York, 1964.

Grimshaw, Allen D., ed. *Racial Violence in the United States*. Chicago, 1969.

Herskovits, Melville J. *Myth of the Negro Past*. New York, 1941.

Isaacs, Harold R. *The New World of Negro Americans*. New York, 1963.

Johnson, Charles S. *The Negro in American Civilization*. New York, 1930.

Katz, William Loren, comp. *Eyewitness: The Negro in American History*. New York, 1967.

Konvitz, Milton R. *A Century of Civil Rights*. With a study of state law against discrimination by Theodore Leskes. New York, 1961.

Locke, Alain L., ed. *The New Negro: An Interpretation*. New York, 1925.

Meier, August. *Negro Thought in America, 1880–1915: Racial Ideologies in the Age of Booker T. Washington*. Ann Arbor, Mich., 1963.

Meier, August, and Rudwick, Elliott M. *From Plantation to Ghetto: An Interpretive History of American Negroes*. New York, 1966.

Miller, Kelly. *Radicals and Conservatives and Other Essays on the Negro in America*. New York, 1968.

Myrdal, Gunnar, with the assistance of Richard Sterner and Arnold Rose. *An American Dilemma: The Negro Problem and Modern Democracy*. 2 vols. New York, 1944.

Nash, Gary B., and Weiss, Richard, eds. *The Great Fear: Race in the Mind of America*. New York, 1970.

Osofsky, Gilbert, ed. *The Burden of Race: A Documentary History of Negro-White Relations in America*. New York, 1967.

Parsons, Talcott, and Clark, Kenneth B., eds. *The Negro American*. Boston, 1966.

Pettigrew, Thomas F. *A Profile of the Negro American.* Princeton, 1964.

Quarles, Benjamin. *The Negro in the Making of America.* New York, 1964.

Redding, J. Saunders. *On Being Negro in America.* Indianapolis, 1951.

Resh, Richard. *Black America: Accommodation and Confrontation in the Twentieth Century.* Lexington, Mass., 1969.

Roady, Elston E. *The Negro's Role in American Society.* Tallahassee, 1958.

Rose, Arnold M. *The Negro in America: The Condensed Version of Gunnar Myrdal's* "An American Dilemma." New York, 1964.

Shade, William G., and Herrenkohl, Roy C., eds. *Seven on Black: Reflections on the Negro Experience in America.* Philadelphia, 1969.

Simpson, George Eaton, and Yinger, John Milton. *Racial and Cultural Minorities: An Analysis of Prejudice and Discrimination.* New York, 1958.

Tannenbaum, Frank. *Slave and Citizen: The Negro in the Americas.* New York, 1947.

Thorpe, Earl E. *The Central Theme of Black History.* Durham, N. C., 1969.

———. *The Mind of the Negro: An Intellectual History of Afro-Americans.* Baton Rouge, La., 1961.

Warner, W. Lloyd, et al. *Color and Human Nature.* Washington, D.C., 1941.

Weatherford, Willis D. *The Negro from Africa to America.* New York, 1924.

Woodson, Carter G., and Wesley, Charles H. *The Negro in Our History.* 10th ed. Washington, D.C., 1962.

Woodward, C. Vann. *American Counterpoint: Slavery and Racism in the North-South Dialogue.* Boston, 1971.

After Slavery: Negroes in Southern Life And Politics

Bentley, George R. *A History of the Freedmen's Bureau.* Philadelphia, 1955.

Bleser, Carol R. *The Promised Land: The History of the South Carolina Land Commission, 1869–1890.* Columbia, S.C., 1969.

Brewer, J. Mason. *Negro Legislators of Texas.* Dallas, Tex., 1935.

Brittain, Joseph M. "Some Reflections on Negro Suffrage and Politics in Alabama—Past and Present," *Journal of Negro History* 47 (April 1962): 127–38.

Bruce, Philip A. *The Plantation Negro as a Freedman.* New York, 1889.

Bryant, Lawrence C., ed. *Negro Lawmakers in the South Carolina Legislature, 1868–1902.* Orangeburg, S.C., 1968.

Carleton, Mark T. *Politics and Punishment: The History of the Louisiana State Penal System.* Baton Rouge, La., 1971.

Casdorph, Paul. *A History of the Republican Party in Texas, 1865–1965.* Austin, Tex., 1965.

Cheek, William F. "A Negro Runs for Congress: John Mercer Langston and the Virginia Campaign of 1888," *Journal of Negro History* 52 (January 1967): 14–34.

Coulter, E. Merton. *Negro Legislators in Georgia during the Reconstruction Period.* Athens, Ga., 1968.

Cox, La Wanda, and John H. "Negro Suffrage and Republican Politics: The Problem of Motivation in Reconstruction Historiography," *Journal of Southern History* 33 (August 1967): 303–30.

Daniel, Pete. "Black Power in the 1920s: The Case of Tuskegee Veterans Hospital," *Journal of Southern History* 36 (August 1970): 368–88.

———. *The Shadow of Slavery: Peonage in the South, 1901–1969.* Urbana, Ill., 1972.

De Santis, Vincent P. *Republicans Face the Southern Question: The New Departure Years, 1877–1897.* Baltimore, 1959.

Donald, Henderson H. *The Negro Freedman: Life Conditions of the American Negro in the Early Years after Emancipation.* New York, 1952.

Du Bois, William E. B. *Black Reconstruction: An Essay toward a History of the Part Which Black Folk Played in the Attempt to Reconstruct Democracy, 1860–1888.* New York, 1935.

Durden, Robert Franklin. *James Shepherd Pike: Republicanism and the American Negro, 1850–1882.* Durham, N.C., 1957.

Dyer, Brainerd. "One Hundred Years of Negro Suffrage," *Pacific Historical Review* 37 (February 1968): 1–20.

Edmonds, Helen G. *The Negro and Fusion Politics in North Carolina, 1894–1901.* Chapel Hill, N.C., 1951.

Evans, W. McKee. *Ballots and Fence Rails: Reconstruction on the Lower Cape Fear.* Chapel Hill, N. C., 1966.

Fortune, T. Thomas. *Black and White: Land, Labor, and Politics in the South.* New York, 1884.

———. *The Negro in Politics.* New York, 1886.

Franklin, John Hope. *Reconstruction: After the Civil War.* Chicago, 1961.

Gatewood, Willard B., Jr. *"Smoked Yankees" and the Struggle for Empire: Letters from Negro Soldiers, 1898–1902.* Urbana, Ill., 1971.

———. *Theodore Roosevelt and the Art of Controversy: Episodes of the White House Years.* Baton Rouge, La., 1970.

———. "William D. Crum: A Negro in Politics," *Journal of Negro History* 53 (October 1968): 301–20.

Gillette, William. *The Right to Vote: Politics and the Passage of the Fifteenth Amendment.* Baltimore, 1965.

Gordon, Asa H. *Sketches of Negro Life and History in South Carolina*. Hammond, Ind., 1929.

Harris, Robert J. *The Quest for Equality: The Constitution, Congress, and the Supreme Court*. Baton Rouge, La., 1960.

Hirshson, Stanley P. *Farewell to the Bloody Shirt: Northern Republicans and the Southern Negro, 1877–1893*. Bloomington, Ind., 1962.

Jackson, Luther Porter. *Negro Officeholders in Virginia, 1865–1895*. Norfolk, 1945.

Kolchin, Peter. *First Freedom: The Responses of Alabama's Blacks to Emancipation and Reconstruction*. Westport, Conn., 1972.

Langhorne, Orra. *Southern Sketches from Virginia, 1881–1901*. Ed. Charles E. Wynes. Charlottesville, Va., 1964.

Lewis, Elsie M. "The Political Mind of the Negro, 1865–1900," *Journal of Southern History* 21 (May 1955): 189–202.

Logan, Frenise A. *The Negro in North Carolina, 1876–1894*. Chapel Hill, N.C., 1964.

Logan, Rayford W. *The Betrayal of the Negro: From Rutherford B. Hayes to Woodrow Wilson*. New York, 1965.

———. *The Negro in American Life and Thought: The Nadir, 1877–1901*. New York, 1951.

McFeely, William S. *Yankee Stepfather: General O. Howard and the Freedmen*. New Haven, 1968.

McPherson, James M. *The Struggle for Equality: Abolitionists and the Negro in the Civil War and Reconstruction*. Princeton, 1964.

Morton, Richard Lee. *The Negro in Virginia Politics, 1865–1902*. Charlottesville, Va., 1919.

Murray, Pauli. *Proud Shoes: The Story of an American Family*. New York, 1956.

Olsen, Otto H. *Carpetbagger's Crusade: The Life of Albion Winegar Tourgée*. Baltimore, 1965.

Pereyra, Lillian A. *James Lusk Alcorn, Presistent Whig*. Baton Rouge, La., 1966.

Reimers, David M., ed. *The Black Man in America since Reconstruction*. New York, 1970.

Rice, Lawrence D. *The Negro in Texas, 1874–1900*. Baton Rouge, La., 1971.

Richardson, Joe M. *The Negro in the Reconstruction of Florida, 1865–1877*. Tallahassee, 1965.

Rose, Willie Lee. *Rehearsal for Reconstruction: The Port Royal Experiment*. Indianapolis, 1964.

Roussève, Charles Barthelmy. *The Negro in Louisiana: Aspects of His History and Literature*. New Orleans, 1937.

Saunders, Robert. "Southern Populists and the Negro, 1893–1905," *Journal of Negro History* 54 (July 1969): 240–61.

Shadgett, Olive H. *The Republican Party in Georgia from Reconstruction through 1900*. Athens, Ga., 1964.

Simkins, Francis B., and Woody, Robert H. *South Carolina during Reconstruction*. Chapel Hill, N.C., 1932.

Singletary, Otis A. *Negro Militia and Reconstruction*. Austin, Tex., 1957.

Smith, Samuel D. *The Negro in Congress*. Chapel Hill, N.C., 1940.

Stampp, Kenneth M. *The Era of Reconstruction, 1865–1877*. New York, 1965.

Taylor, Alrutheus A. *The Negro in the Reconstruction of Virginia*. Washington, D.C., 1926.

———. *The Negro in South Carolina during the Reconstruction*. Washington, D.C., 1924.

———. *The Negro in Tennessee, 1865–1880*. Washington, D.C., 1941.

Tindall, George B. *South Carolina Negroes, 1877–1900*. Columbia, S.C., 1952.

Urofsky, Melvin I. "Blanche K. Bruce: U.S. Senator, 1875–1881," *Journal of Mississippi History* 29 (May 1967): 118–41.

Wharton, Vernon L. *The Negro in Mississippi, 1865–1890*. Chapel Hill, N.C., 1947.

White, Howard Ashley. *The Freedmen's Bureau in Louisiana*. Baton Rouge, La., 1970.

Williamson, Joel. *After Slavery: The Negro in South Carolina during Reconstruction*. Chapel Hill, N.C., 1965.

Writers' Project of the WPA. *The Negro in Virginia*. New York, 1940.

———. *These Are Our Lives*. Chapel Hill, N.C., 1939.

Wynes, Charles E., ed. *The Negro in the South Since 1865: Selected Essays in American Negro History*. University, Ala., 1965.

———. *Race Relations in Virginia, 1870–1902*. Charlottesville, Va., 1961.

Southern Politics and Society

Bailey, Hugh C. *Edgar Gardner Murphy: Gentle Progressive*. Coral Gables, Fla., 1968.

———. *Liberalism in the New South: Southern Social Reformers and the Progressive Movement*. Coral Gables, Fla., 1969.

Bartley, Numan V. *From Thurmond to Wallace: Political Tendencies in Georgia, 1948–1968*. Baltimore, 1970.

Bertelson, David. *The Lazy South*. New York, 1967.

Cash, Wilbur J. *The Mind of the South*. New York, 1941.

Clark, Thomas D. *The Emerging South*. 2nd ed. New York, 1968.

Cooper, William J., Jr. *The Conservative Regime: South Carolina, 1877–1890*. Baltimore, 1968.

Couch, William T., ed. *Culture in the South*. Chapel Hill, N.C., 1934.

Dabbs, James M. *The Southern Heritage*. New York, 1958.

Furniss, Norman F. *The Fundamentalist Controversy, 1918–1931.* New Haven, 1954.

Gaston, Paul M. *The New South Creed: A Study in Southern Mythmaking.* New York, 1970.

Gatewood, Willard B., Jr. *Preachers, Pedagogues, and Politicians: The Evolution Controversy in North Carolina, 1920–1927.* Chapel Hill, N.C., 1966.

Going, Allen J. *Bourbon Democracy in Alabama, 1874–1890.* University, Ala., 1951.

Grantham, Dewey W. *The Democratic South.* Athens, Ga., 1963.

———. *Hoke Smith and the Politics of the New South.* Baton Rouge, La., 1958.

Green, A. Wigfall. *The Man Bilbo.* Baton Rouge, La., 1963.

Green, Fletcher Melvin, ed. *Essays in Southern History* . . . Chapel Hill, N.C., 1949.

Hackney, Sheldon. *Populism to Progressivism in Alabama.* Princeton, 1969.

———. "Southern Violence," *American Historical Review* 74 (February 1969): 906–25.

Hair, William I. *Bourbonism and Agrarian Protest: Louisiana Politics, 1877–1900.* Baton Rouge, La., 1969.

Havard, William C., and Beth, Loren P. *The Politics of Mis-Representation: Rural-Urban Conflict in the Florida Legislature.* Baton Rouge, La., 1962.

Heard, Alexander, and Strong, Donald S. *Southern Primaries and Elections, 1920–1949.* University, Ala., 1950.

Hero, Alfred O., Jr. *The Southerner and World Affairs.* Baton Rouge, La., 1963.

Highsaw, Robert B., ed. *The Deep South in Transformation: A Symposium.* University, Ala., 1964.

Holmes, William F. *The White Chief: James Kimble Vardaman.* Baton Rouge, La., 1970.

Howard, Perry H. *Political Tendencies in Louisiana.* Rev. ed. Baton Rouge, La., 1971.

Jarrell, Hampton M. *Wade Hampton and the Negro: The Road Not Taken.* Columbia, S.C., 1949.

Jones, Lewis Wade. *Cold Rebellion: The South's Oligarchy in Revolt.* London, 1962.

Kirby, Jack Temple. *Darkness at the Dawning: Race and Reform in the Progressive South.* Philadelphia, 1972.

Kirwan, Albert D. *Revolt of the Rednecks: Mississippi Politics, 1876–1925.* Lexington, Ky., 1951.

Larsen, William E. *Montague of Virginia: The Making of a Southern Progressive.* Baton Rouge, La., 1965.

Lerche, Charles O., Jr. *The Uncertain South: Its Changing Patterns in Foreign Policy.* Chicago, 1964.

McIlwaine, Shields. *The Southern Poor-White: From Lubberland to Tobacco Road.* Norman, Okla., 1939.

McKean, Keith F. *Cross Currents in the South.* Denver, 1960.

McKinney, John C., and Thompson, Edgar T. eds. *The South in Continuity and Change.* Durham, N.C., 1965.

Maclachlan, John M., and Floyd, Joe S., Jr. *This Changing South.* Gainesville, Fla., 1956.

Marshall, F. Ray. *Labor in the South.* Cambridge, Mass., 1967.

Michie, Allan A., and Rhylick, Frank. *Dixie Demagogues.* New York, 1939.

Miller, William D. *Mr. Crump of Memphis.* Baton Rouge, La., 1964.

Moger, Allen W. *Virginia: Bourbonism to Byrd, 1870–1925.* Charlottesville, Va., 1968.

Morris, Willie, ed. *The South Today: 100 Years after Appomattox.* New York, 1965.

Morrison, Joseph L. *Josephus Daniels Says . . . : An Editor's Political Odyssey from Bryan to Wilson and F.D.R.* Chapel Hill, N.C., 1962.

Nicholls, William H. *Southern Tradition and Regional Progress.* Chapel Hill, N.C., 1960.

Odum, Howard W. *Southern Regions of the United States.* Chapel Hill, N.C., 1936.

Orr, Oliver H., Jr. *Charles Brantley Aycock.* Chapel Hill, N.C., 1961.

Peters, William. *The Southern Temper.* Garden City, N.Y., 1959.

Pope, Liston. *Mill Hands and Preachers: A Study of Gastonia.* New Haven, 1942.

Potter, David M. *The South and the Sectional Conflict.* Baton Rouge, La., 1968.

Proctor, Samuel. *Napoleon Bonaparte Broward: Florida's Fighting Democrat.* Gainesville, Fla., 1950.

Pulley, Raymond H. *Old Virginia Restored: An Interpretation of the Progressive Impulse, 1870–1930.* Charlottesville, Va., 1968.

Reed, John Shelton. *The Enduring South: Subcultural Presistence in Mass Society.* Lexington, Mass., 1972.

Rogers, William Warren. *The One-Gallused Rebellion: Agrarianism in Alabama, 1865–1896.* Baton Rouge, La, 1970.

Savage, Henry, Jr. *Seeds of Time: Background of Southern Thinking.* New York, 1959.

Scott, Anne Firor. *The Southern Lady: From Pedestal to Politics, 1830–1930.* Chicago, 1970.

Sellers, Charles G., Jr., ed. *The Southerner as American.* Chapel Hill, N.C., 1960.

Sherrill, Robert. *Gothic Politics in the Deep South: Stars of the New Confederacy.* New York, 1968.

Simkins, Francis B. *Pitchfork Ben Tillman: South Carolinian.* Baton Rouge, La., 1944.

————, and Roland, Charles Pierce. *A History of the South*. 4th ed. New York, 1972.

Sindler, Allan P., ed. *Change in the Contemporary South*. Durham. N.C., 1963.

————. *Huey Long's Louisiana: State Politics, 1920–1952*. Baltimore, 1956.

Smith, Frank. *Congressman from Mississippi*. New York, 1964.

————. *Look Away from Dixie*. Baton Rouge, La., 1965.

Tannenbaum, Frank. *Darker Phases of the South*. New York, 1924.

Tindall, George Brown. *The Disruption of the Solid South*. Athens, Ga., 1972.

————. *The Emergence of the New South, 1913–1945*. Baton Rouge, La., 1967.

Vance, Rupert B. *Human Factors in Cotton Culture: A Study in the Social Geography of the American South*. Chapel Hill, N.C., 1929.

————. *Human Geography of the South: A Study in Regional Resources and Human Adequacy*. Chapel Hill, N.C., 1932.

————, with Danilevsky, Nadia. *All These People: The Nation's Human Resources in the South*. Chapel Hill, N.C., 1945.

————, and Demerath, Nicholas J., eds. *The Urban South*. Chapel Hill, N.C., 1954.

Vandiver, Frank E., ed. *The Idea of the South: Pursuit of a Central Theme*. Chicago, 1964.

Wilkinson, J. Harvie III. *Harry Byrd and the Changing Face of Virginia Politics*. Charlottesville, Va., 1968.

Williams, T. Harry. *Huey Long: A Biography*. New York 1969.

————. *Romance and Realism in Southern Politics*. Athens, Ga., 1961.

Woodward, C. Vann. *The Burden of Southern History*. Rev. ed. Baton Rouge, La., 1968.

————. *Origins of the New South, 1877–1913*. Baton Rouge, La., 1951.

————. *Reunion and Reaction: The Compromise of 1877 and the End of Reconstruction*. Boston, 1951.

————. *Tom Watson: Agrarian Rebel*. New York, 1938.

Zinn, Howard. *The Southern Mystique*. New York, 1964.

Restrictions On Negro Voting

Adams, Mildred. *The Right to Be People*. Philadelphia, 1967.

Alilunas, Leo. "Legal Restrictions on the Negro in Politics," *Journal of Negro History* 25 (April 1940): 152–202.

Baker, Riley E. "Negro Voter Registration in Louisiana, 1879–1964," *Louisiana Studies* 4 (1965): 332–50.

Berier, G. Galin. "The Negro Suffrage Issue in Iowa, 1865–1898," *Annals of Iowa* 39 (Spring 1968): 241–61.

Beth, Loren P. "The White Primary and the Judicial Function in the United States," *Political Quarterly* 29 (October-December 1958): 366–77.

Bernd, Joseph L., and Holland, Lynood M. "Recent Restrictions upon Negro Suffrage: The Case of Georgia," *Journal of Politics* 21 (August 1959): 487–513.

Claude, Richard. "Constitutional Voting Rights and Early U.S. Supreme Court Doctrine," *Journal of Negro History* 51 (April 1966): 114–24.

Ewing, Cortez A. M. *Primary Elections in the South: A Study in Uniparty Politics.* Norman, Okla., 1953.

Farris, Charles D. "The Re-Enfranchisement of Negroes in Florida," *Journal of Negro History* 39 (October 1954): 259–83.

Fenton, John H., and Vines, Kenneth N. "Negro Registration in Louisiana," *American Political Science Review* 51 (September 1957): 704–13.

Fishel, Leslie H., Jr. "Northern Prejudice and Negro Suffrage, 1865–1870," *Journal of Negro History* 39 (January 1954): 8–26.

Graves, John W. "Negro Disfranchisement in Arkansas," *Arkansas Historical Quarterly* 26 (Autumn 1967): 199–225.

Hiller, Amy M. "The Disfranchisement of Delaware Negroes in the Late Nineteenth Century," *Delaware History* 13 (October 1968): 124–53.

Holland, Lynwood M. *The Direct Primary in Georgia.* Urbana, Ill., 1949.

Jones, Lewis, and Smith, Stanley. *Voting Rights and Economic Pressure.* New York, 1958.

Lichtman, Allan. "The Federal Assault against Voting Discrimination in the Deep South, 1957–1967," *Journal of Negro History* 54 (October 1969): 346–67.

Mabry, William Alexander. *Studies in the Disfranchisement of the Negro in the South.* Durham, N.C., 1938.

McMillan, Malcolm Cook. *Constitutional Development in Alabama, 1798–1901: A Study in Politics, the Negro, and Sectionalism.* Chapel Hill, N.C., 1955.

Martin, Robert E. *Negro Disfranchisement in Virginia.* Washington, D.C., 1938.

Price, Margaret. *The Negro and the Ballot in the South.* Atlanta, 1959.

———. *The Negro Voter in the South.* Atlanta, 1957.

Strong, Donald S. *Registration of Voters in Alabama.* University, Ala., 1956.

Wardlaw, Ralph Wilkinson. *Negro Suffrage in Georgia, 1867–1930.* Athens, Ga., 1932.

Weeks, O. Douglas. "The Texas Direct Primary System," *Southwestern Social Science Quarterly* 13 (September 1932): 95–120.

Weeks, Stephen B. "History of Negro Suffrage," *Political Science Quarterly* 9 (December 1894): 671–703.

Werdegar, Kathryn Mickle. "The Constitutionality of Federal Legislation to Abolish Literacy Tests," *George Washington Law Review* 30 (April 1962): 723–43.

Williams, Frank B., Jr. "The Poll Tax as a Suffrage Requirement in the South, 1870–1901." Ph.D. diss., Vanderbilt University, 1950.

Negro Politics in the North and West

Allswang, John M. "The Chicago Negro Voter and the Democratic Consensus: A Case Study, 1918–1936," *Journal of the Illinois Historical Society* 60 (Summer 1967): 145–75.

Andrews, Norman. "The Negro in Politics," *Journal of Negro History* 5 (October 1920): 435–36.

Blair, John L. "A Time for Parting: The Negro during the Coolidge Years," *Journal of American Studies* 3 (December 1969): 177–99.

Callcott, Margaret Law. *The Negro in Maryland Politics, 1870–1912*. Baltimore, 1969.

Chafe, William H. "The Negro and Populism: A Kansas Case Study," *Journal of Southern History* 34 (August 1968): 402–19.

Chicago Commission on Race Relations. *The Negro in Chicago: A Study of Race Relations and a Race Riot*. Chicago, 1922.

Cuban, Larry. "Strategy for Racial Peace: Negro Leadership in Cleveland, 1900–1919," *Phylon* 28 (Fall 1967): 299–311.

Daniels, John. *In Freedom's Birthplace*. Boston, 1914.

Dykstra, Robert R., and Hahn, Harlan. "Northern Voters and Negro Suffrage: The Case of Iowa, 1868," *Public Opinion Quarterly* 32 (Summer 1968): 202–15.

Fishel, Leslie H., Jr. "The Negro in Northern Politics, 1870–1900," *Mississippi Valley Historical Review* 42 (December 1955): 466–89.

Fleming, G. James. *An All-Negro Ticket in Baltimore*. New York, 1960.

Glantz, Oscar. "The Negro Voter in Northern Industrial Cities," *Western Political Quarterly* 13 (December 1960): 999–1010.

Gosnell, Harold F., and Martin, R. E. "The Negro as Voter and Office Holder," *Journal of Negro Education* 32 (Fall 1963): 415–25.

Grantham, Dewey W. "The Progressive Movement and the Negro," *South Atlantic Quarterly* 54 (October 1955): 461–77.

Katzman, David M. *Before the Ghetto: Black Detroit in the Nineteenth Century*. Urbana, Ill., 1972.

Lane, Ann J. *The Brownsville Affair: National Crisis and Black Reaction*. Port Washington, N.Y., 1971.

Litchfield, Edward H. "A Case Study of Negro Political Behavior in Detroit," *Public Opinion Quarterly* 5 (June 1941): 267–74.

Livesay, Harold C. "Delaware Negroes, 1865–1915," *Delaware History* 13 (October 1968); 87–123.

Lubell, Samuel. *The Future of American Politics.* New York, 1952.

McKay, Claude. *Harlem: Negro Metropolis.* New York, 1940.

Miller, J. Erroll. "The Negro in Present Day Politics with Special Reference to Philadelphia," *Journal of Negro History* 33 (July 1948): 303–43.

Nowlin, William Felbert. *The Negro in American National Politics.* Boston, 1931.

Quillin, Frank U. *The Color Line in Ohio.* Ann Arbor, Mich., 1913.

Sherman, Richard B. "The Harding Administration and the Negro: An Opportunity Lost," *Journal of Negro History* 49 (July 1964): 151–68.

————. "Republicans and Negroes: The Lessons of Normalcy," *Phylon* 27 (Spring 1966): 63–79.

Thornbrough, Emma Lou. "The Brownsville Episode and the Negro Vote," *Mississippi Valley Historical Review* 44 (December 1957): 469–83.

Walton, Hanes, Jr. *The Negro in Third Party Politics.* Philadelphia, 1969.

Weaver, John D. *The Brownsville Raid.* New York, 1970.

Wolgemuth, Kathleen L. "Woodrow Wilson's Appointment Policy and the Negro," *Journal of Southern History* 24 (November 1958): 457–71.

Wright, R. R., Jr. *The Negro in Pennsylvania.* Philadelphia (1909?).

Black Leaders and Organizations

Bardolph, Richard. *The Negro Vanguard.* New York, 1959.

Brawley, Benjamin G. *Negro Builders and Heroes.* Chapel Hill, N.C., 1937.

Broderick, Francis L. *W. E. B. Du Bois: Negro Leader in a Time of Crisis.* Stanford, Calif., 1959.

Chesnutt, Helen G. *Charles Waddell Chesnutt: Pioneer of the Color Line.* Chapel Hill, N.C., 1952.

Coleman, Lucretia H. *Poor Ben: A Story of Real Life [Benjamin Arnett].* Nashville, 1890.

Du Bois, William E. B. *The Autobiography of W. E. B. Du Bois: A Soliloquy on Viewing My Life from the Last Decade of Its First Century.* New York, 1968.

————. *Dusk of Dawn: An Essay toward the Autobiography of a Race Concept.* New York, 1940.

Elliott, Lawrence. *George Washington Carver: The Man Who Overcame.* Englewood Cliffs, N.J., 1966.

Embree, Edwin Rogers. *13 Against the Odds*. New York, 1944.

Farrison, William E. *William Wells Brown, Author and Reformer*. Chicago, 1969.

Foner, Philip S. *Frederick Douglass*. New York, 1964.

Fox, Stephen R. *The Guardian of Boston: William Monroe Trotter*. New York, 1970.

Green, Ely. *Ely: Too Black, Too White*. Amherst, Mass., 1970.

Handy, William C. *Father of the Blues: An Autobiography*. New York, 1941.

Harlan, Louis R. *Booker T. Washington: The Making of a Black Leader, 1865–1901*. New York, 1972.

Hawkins, Hugh, ed. *Booker T. Washington and His Critics*. Boston, 1962.

Holley, Joseph W. *You Can't Build a Chimney from the Top: The South through the Life of a Negro Educator*. New York, 1948.

Hughes, Langston. *The Big Sea*. New York, 1940.

————. *Fight for Freedom: The Story of the NAACP*. New York, 1962.

Hunton, Addie. *William A. Hunton*. New York, 1938.

Jack, Robert L. *History of the NAACP*. Boston, 1943.

Kellogg, Charles F. *NAACP: A History of the National Association for the Advancement of Colored People*. Vol 1: *1909–1920*. Baltimore, 1967.

Langston, J. Mercer. *From the Virginia Plantation to the National Capitol*. Hartford, Conn., 1894.

Mathews, Basil J. *Booker T. Washington: Educator and Interracial Interpreter*. Cambridge, Mass., 1948.

Mathews, Marcia M. *Henry Ossawa Tanner: American Artist*. Chicago, 1969.

Mays, Benjamin E. *Born to Rebel: An Autobiography*. New York, 1971.

Ovington, Mary W. *The Walls Came Tumbling Down*. New York, 1947.

Parker, Robert Allerton. *The Incredible Messiah: The Deification of Father Divine*. Boston, 1937.

Peare, Catherine O. *Mary McLeod Bethune*. New York, 1951.

Quarles, Benjamin. *Frederick Douglass*. Washington, D.C., 1948.

Record, Wilson. *Race and Radicalism: The NAACP and the Communist Party in Conflict*. Ithaca, N.Y., 1964.

Rudwick, Elliott M. *W.E.B. Du Bois: A Study in Minority Group Leadership*. Philadelphia, 1960.

Savage, Horace C. *Life and Times of Bishop Isaac Lane*. Nashville, 1958.

Scott, Emmett J., and Stowe, Lyman B. *Booker T. Washington: Builder of a Civilization*. New York, 1916.

Spencer, Samuel R. *Booker T. Washington and the Negro's Place in American Life*. Boston, 1955.

Sterne, Emma Gelders. *Mary McLeod Bethune.* New York, 1947.

Sterling, Dorothy. *Captain of the Planter: The Story of Robert Smalls.* Garden City, N.Y., 1948.

Strickland, Arvarh E. *History of the Chicago Urban League.* Urbana, Ill., 1966.

Terrell, Mary Church. *A Colored Woman in a White World.* Washington, D.C., 1940.

Thornbrough, Emma Lou. *T. Thomas Fortune: Militant Journalist.* Chicago, 1972.

Torrence, Frederic Ridgely. *The Story of John Hope.* New York, 1948.

Troup, Cornelius V. *Distinguished Negro Georgians.* Dallas, Tex., 1962.

Tucker, David M. *Lieutenant Lee of Beale Street.* Nashville, 1971.

Walls, William J. *Joseph Charles Price.* Boston, 1943.

Washington, Booker T. *My Larger Education.* New York, 1911.

———. *Up From Slavery: An Autobiography.* Garden City, N.Y., 1901.

Wells, Ida B. *Crusade for Justice: The Autobiography of Ida B. Wells.* Ed. Alfreda M. Duster. Chicago, 1970.

White, Walter F. *How Far the Promised Land?* New York, 1955.

———. *A Man Called White: The Autobiography of Walter White.* New York, 1948.

Wittner, Lawrence S. "The National Negro Congress: A Reassessment," *American Quarterly* 22 (Winter 1970): 883–901.

Wright, Richard. *Black Boy.* New York, 1945.

Race Relations and Racial Attitudes

Alexander, Charles C. *The Ku Klux Klan in the Southwest.* Lexington, Ky., 1965.

Archer, William. *Through Afro-America: An English Reading of the Race Problem.* London, 1910.

Bailey, Kenneth K. *Southern White Protestantism in the Twentieth Century.* New York, 1964.

Bailey, Thomas P. *Race Orthodoxy in the South.* New York, 1914.

Baker, Paul E. *Negro-White Adjustment: An Investigation and Analysis of Methods in the Interracial Movement in the United States.* New York, 1934.

Baker, Ray Stannard. *Following the Color Line: American Negro Citizenship in the Progressive Era.* New York, 1964. First pub. in 1908.

Blair, Lewis H. *A Southern Prophecy: The Prosperity of the South Dependent upon the Elevation of the Negro (1889).* Ed. C. Vann Woodward. Boston, 1964.

Buck, Paul H. *The Road to Reunion, 1865–1900.* Boston, 1937.

Burrows, Edward F. "The Commission on Interracial Cooperation in the South." Ph.D. dissertation, University of Wisconsin, 1955.

Cable, George W. *The Silent South*. New York, 1885.

Carmer, Carl Lamson. *Stars Fell on Alabama*. New York, 1934.

Carter, Dan T. *Scottsboro: A Tragedy of the American South*. Baton Rouge, La., 1969.

Chadbourn, James H. *Lynching and the Law*. Chapel Hill, N.C., 1933.

Chalmers, David M. *Hooded Americanism: The First Century of the Ku Klux Klan, 1865–1965*. Garden City, N.Y., 1965.

Clayton, Bruce. *The Savage Ideal: Intolerance and Intellectual Leadership in the South, 1890–1914*. Baltimore, 1972.

Culver, Dwight W. *Negro Segregation in the Methodist Church*. New Haven, 1953.

Current, Richard N., ed. *Reconstruction in Retrospect: Views from the Turn of the Century*. Baton Rouge, La., 1969.

Cutler, James Elbert. *Lynch-Law: An Investigation into the History of Lynching in the United States*. New York, 1905.

Davenport, F. Garvin, Jr. *The Myth of Southern History: Historical Consciousness in Twentieth-Century Southern Literature*. Nashville, 1970.

Doyle, Bertram W. *The Etiquette of Race Relations in the South: A Study in Social Control*. Chicago, 1937.

Dykeman, Wilma. *Prophet of Plenty: The First Ninety Years of W. D. Weatherford*. Knoxville, Tenn., 1966.

————, and Stokely, James. *Neither Black Nor White*. New York, 1957.

————, and Stokely, James. *Seeds of Southern Change: The Life of Will Alexander*. Chicago, 1962.

Edwards, G. Franklin, ed. *E. Franklin Frazier on Race Relations*. Chicago, 1968.

Evans, Maurice Smethurst. *Black and White in the Southern States: A Study of the Race Problem in the United States from a South African Point of View*. London and New York, 1915.

Friedman, Lawrence J. *The White Savage: Racial Fantasies in the Postbellum South*. Englewood Cliffs, N.J., 1970.

Graham, Howard J. *Everyman's Constitution: Historical Essays on the Fourteenth Amendment, the "Conspiracy Theory," and American Constitutionalism*. Madison, Wis., 1968.

Greenberg, Jack. *Race Relations and the American Law*. New York, 1959.

Guild, June Purcell. *Black Laws of Virginia: A Summary of the Legislative Acts of Virginia Concerning Negroes from Earliest Times to the Present*. Richmond, Va., 1936.

Haller, John S., Jr. *Outcasts from Evolution: Scientific Attitudes of Racial Inferiority, 1859–1900*. Urbana, Ill., 1971.

Harkey, Ira B., Jr. *The Smell of Burning Crosses: An Autobiography of a Mississippi Newspaperman.* Jacksonville, Ill., 1967.

Harlan, Louis R. *Separate but Unequal: Public School Campaigns and Racism in the Southeastern Seaboard States, 1901–1915.* Chapel Hill, N.C., 1958.

Hart, Albert B. *The Southern South.* New York, 1910.

Jackson, Kenneth T. *The Ku Klux Klan in the City, 1915–1930.* New York, 1967.

Johnson, Charles S. *Patterns of Negro Segregation.* New York, 1943.

———, and associates. *Into the Main Stream: A Survey of Best Practices in Race Relations in the South.* Chapel Hill, N.C., 1947.

Johnston, Sir Harry Hamilton. *The Negro in the New World.* London, 1910.

Kerlin, Robert T. *The Voice of the Negro, 1919.* New York, 1920.

Linder, Suzanne C. *William Louis Poteat: Prophet of Progress.* Chapel Hill, N.C., 1966.

McCulloch, James E., ed. *The Human Way: Addresses on Race Problems.* Atlanta, 1913.

McEntire, Davis C. *Residence and Race.* Berkeley, Calif., 1960.

Mangum, Charles S., Jr. *The Legal Status of the Negro.* Chapel Hill, N.C., 1940.

Mann, Harold W. *Atticus Greene Haygood: Methodist Bishop, Editor, and Educator.* Athens, Ga., 1965.

Marx, Gary T. *Protest and Prejudice: A Study of Belief in the Black Community.* New York, 1967.

Miller, Kelly. *Out of the House of Bondage.* New York, 1914.

———. *Race Adjustment.* 3rd ed. New York, 1910.

Mims, Edwin. *The Advancing South: Stories of Progress and Reaction.* Garden City, N.Y., 1926.

Moton, Robert R. *What the Negro Thinks.* Garden City, N.Y., 1929.

Murphy, Edgar Gardner. *The Basis of Ascendancy.* New York, 1909.

———. *Problems of the Present South.* New York, 1904.

Murray, Andrew E. *Presbyterians and the Negro: A History.* Philadelphia, 1966.

Murray, Pauli, ed. *States' Laws on Race and Color . . . .* Cincinnati, 1951.

Nelson, Bernard Hamilton. *The Fourteenth Amendment and the Negro Since 1920.* Washington, D.C., 1946.

Newby, I. A. *Challenge to the Court: Social Scientists and the Defense of Segregation, 1954–1966.* Baton Rouge, La., 1967.

———, ed. *The Development of Segregationist Thought.* Homewood, Ill., 1968.

———. *Jim Crow's Defense: Anti-Negro Thought in America, 1900–1930.* Baton Rouge, La., 1965.

Nolen, Claude H. *The Negro's Image in the South: The Anatomy of White Supremacy.* Lexington, Ky., 1967.

Odum, Howard W. *Race and Rumors of Race: Challenge to American Crisis*. Chapel Hill, N.C., 1943.

——. *Social and Mental Traits of the Negro*. New York, 1910.

Osborne, William A. *The Segregated Covenant: Race Relations and American Catholics*. New York, 1967.

Page, Thomas Nelson. *The Negro: The Southerner's Problem*. New York, 1904.

Randel, William P. *The Ku Klux Klan: A Century of Infamy*. Philadelphia, 1965.

Raper, Arthur F. *The Tragedy of Lynching*. Chapel Hill, N.C., 1933.

Reimers, David M. *White Protestantism and the Negro*. New York, 1965.

Reuter, Edward B. *The American Race Problem*. New York, 1927.

Rudwick, Elliott M. *Race Riot at East St. Louis, July 2, 1917*. Carbondale, Ill., 1964.

Seabrook, Isaac DuBose. *Before and After: Or, the Relations of the Races at the South*. Ed. John Hammond Moore. Baton Rouge, La., 1967.

Shapiro, Herbert. "The Muckrakers and Negroes," *Phylon* 31 (Spring 1970): 76–88.

Siegfried, André. *America Comes of Age: A French Analysis*. New York, 1927.

Smith, Bob. *They Closed Their Schools: Prince Edward County, Virginia, 1951–1964*. Chapel Hill, N.C., 1965.

Southern, David W. *The Malignant Heritage: Yankee Progressives and the Negro Question, 1901–1914*. Chicago, 1968,

Spain, Rufus B. *At Ease in Zion: A Social History of Southern Baptists, 1865–1900*. Nashville, 1967.

Steiner, Jesse F., and Brown, Roy M. *The North Carolina Chain Gang*. Chapel Hill, N.C., 1927.

Stephenson, Gilbert T. *Race Distinctions in American Law*. New York, 1910.

Stone, Alfred H. *Studies in the American Race Problem*. New York, 1908.

Styles, Fitzhugh Lee. *Negroes and the Law*. Boston, 1937.

Synnestvedt, Sig. *The White Response to Black Emancipation: Second-Class Citizenship in the United States since Reconstruction*. New York, 1972.

Taeuber, Alma F. *Negroes in Cities: Residential Segregation and Residential Change*. Chicago, 1965.

Toll, William. "The Crisis of Freedom: Toward an Interpretation of Negro Life," *Journal of American Studies* 3 (December 1969): 265–79.

Trelease, Allen W. *White Terror: The Ku Klux Klan Conspiracy and Southern Reconstruction*. New York, 1971.

Turner, Arlin. *George W. Cable: A Biography*. New York, 1962.

Vose, Clement E. *Caucasians Only: The Supreme Court, the*

NAACP and the Restrictive Covenant Cases. Berkeley, Calif., 1959.

Warren, Robert Penn. *Segregation: The Inner Conflict in the South*. New York, 1956.

————. *Who Speaks for the Negro?* New York, 1965.

Waskow, Arthur I. *From Race Riot to Sit-In, 1919 and the 1960s: A Study in the Connections between Conflict and Violence*. Garden City, N.Y., 1966.

Waynick, Capus M., ed. *North Carolina and the Negro*. Raleigh, N.C., 1964.

Weatherford, Willis D., and Johnson, Charles S. *Race Relations: Adjustment of Whites and Negroes in the United States*. Boston, 1934.

Weisbord, Robert G., and Stein, Arthur. *The Afro-American and the American Jew*. Westport, Conn., 1970.

Weston, Rubin Francis. *Racism in U.S. Imperialism: The Influence of Racial Assumptions on American Foreign Policy, 1893–1946*. Columbia, S.C., 1972.

White, Walter F. *Rope & Faggot: A Biography of Judge Lynch*. New York, 1929.

Wood, Forrest G. *Black Scare: The Racist Response to Emancipation and Reconstruction*. Berkeley, Calif., 1968.

Woofter, Thomas J., Jr. *The Basis of Racial Adjustment*. Boston, 1925.

————. *Southern Race Progress: The Wavering Color Line*. Washington, D.C., 1957.

Workman, William D., Jr. *The Case for the South*. New York, 1960.

Social Institutions and Status

Bernard, Jessie. *Marriage and Family Among Negroes*. Englewood Cliffs, N.J., 1966.

Bond, Horace Mann. *The Education of the Negro in the American Social Order*. New York, 1934.

Bone, Robert A. *The Negro Novel in America*. New Haven, 1958.

Bullock, Henry Allen. *A History of Negro Education in the South from 1619 to the Present*. Cambridge, Mass., 1967.

Clark, Kenneth B. *Dark Ghetto: Dilemmas of Social Power*. New York, 1965.

Claspy, Everett. *The Negro in Southwestern Michigan: Negroes in the North in a Rural Environment*. Dowagiac, Mich., 1967.

Courlander, Harold. *Negro Folk Music, U.S.A.* New York, 1963.

Curry, Jabez L. M. *Education of the Negro Since 1866*. New York, 1894.

Davis, Allison, and Dollard, John. *Children of Bondage*. Washington, D.C., 1940.

Du Bois, William E. B. *The Negro Common School*. Atlanta, 1901.

Edwards, G. Franklin. *The Negro Professional Class*. Glencoe, Ill., 1959.

Fauset, Arthur Huff. *Black Gods of the Metropolis: Negro Religious Cults of the Urban North*. Philadelphia, 1944.

Frazier, E. Franklin. *Black Bourgeoisie: The Rise of a New Middle Class in the United States*. Glencoe, Ill., 1957.

———. *The Negro Church in America*. New York, 1963.

———. *The Negro Family in the United States*. Chicago, 1939.

———. *Negro Youth at the Crossways*. Washington, D.C., 1940.

Gallagher, Buell G. *American Caste and the Negro College*. New York, 1933.

Hare, Maud Cuney. *Negro Musicians and Their Music*. New York, 1936.

Huggins, Nathan Irvin. *Harlem Renaissance*. New York, 1971.

Johnson, James Weldon. *Black Manhattan*. New York, 1930.

Leavell, Ullin Whitney. *Philanthropy in Negro Education*. Nashville, 1930.

Lee, George W. *Beale Street: Where the Blues Began*. New York, 1934.

Mays, Benjamin E., and Nicholson, Joseph W. *The Negro's Church*. New York, 1933.

Office of Policy Planning and Research, U.S. Department of Labor. *The Negro Family: The Case for National Action*. Washington, D.C., 1965. [The so-called Moynihan Report.]

Ovington, Mary White. *Half a Man: The Status of the Negro in New York*. New York, 1911.

Range, Willard. *The Rise and Progress of Negro Colleges in Georgia, 1865–1949*. Athens, Ga., 1951.

Rohrer, John H., et al. *The Eighth Generation Grows up: Cultures and Personalities of New Orleans Negroes*. New York, 1960.

Scott, Emmett J. *The American Negro in the World War*. Washington, D.C., 1919.

Smith, Samuel L. *Builders of Goodwill: The Story of the State Agents of Negro Education in the South, 1910 to 1950*. Nashville, 1950.

Washington, Joseph R. *Black Religion: The Negro and Christianity in the United States*. Boston, 1964.

Weaver, Robert C. *The Negro Ghetto*. New York, 1948.

Wesley, Charles H. *History of the Improved Benevolent and Protective Order of Elks of the World, 1898–1954*. Washington, D.C., 1955.

Wirth, Louis. *The Ghetto*. Chicago, 1928.

Woodson, Carter G. *Mis-Education of the Negro*. Washington, D.C., 1933.

———. *The Negro Professional Man and the Community, with Special Emphasis on the Physician and Lawyer*. Washington, D.C., 1934.

Woofter, Thomas J., Jr. *Negro Problems in Cities*. Garden City, N.Y., 1928.

Wright, Marion Thompson. *The Education of Negroes in New Jersey*. New York, 1941.

Economic Conditions

Alexander, Donald Crichton. *The Arkansas Plantation, 1920–1942*. New Haven, 1943.

Allen, James S. *The Negro Question in the United States*. New York, 1936.

Bell, Carolyn Shaw. *The Economics of the Ghetto*. New York, 1970.

Bloch, Herman D. *The Circle of Discrimination: An Economic and Social Study of the Black Man in New York*. New York, 1969.

Bontemps, Arna, and Conroy, Jack. *Anyplace but Here*. New York, 1966.

———. *They Seek a City*. Garden City, N.Y., 1945.

Brandfon, Robert L. *Cotton Kingdom of the New South: A History of the Yazoo Mississippi Delta from Reconstruction to the Twentieth Century*. Cambridge, Mass., 1967.

Brazeal, Brailsford R. *The Brotherhood of Sleeping Car Porters: Its Origin and Development*. New York, 1946.

Cayton, Horace R., and Mitchell, George S. *Black Workers and the New Unions*. Chapel Hill, N.C., 1939.

Donald, Henderson H. *The Negro Migration of 1916–1918*. Washington, D.C., 1921.

Du Bois, William E. B. *The Negro Artisan*. Atlanta, 1902.

Franklin, Charles L. *The Negro Labor Unionist of New York*. New York, 1936.

Fulmer, John L. *Agriculture Progress in the Cotton Belt since 1920*. Chapel Hill, N.C., 1950.

Greene, Lorenzo J., and Woodson, Carter G. *The Negro Wage Earner*. Washington, D.C., 1930.

Harris, Abram L. *The Negro as Capitalist: A Study of Banking and Business among American Negroes*. Philadelphia, 1936.

Haynes, George E. *The Negro at Work in New York City*. New York, 1912.

Holley, William C., and others. *The Plantation South, 1934–1937*. Washington, D.C., 1940.

Jacobson, Julius, ed. *The Negro and the American Labor Movement*. Garden City, N.Y., 1968.

Johnson, Charles S. *The Economic Status of Negroes*. Nashville, 1933.

———, et al. *The Collapse of Cotton Tenancy: A Summary of Field Studies and Statistical Surveys, 1933–35*. Chapel Hill, N.C., 1935.

Kelsey, Carl. *The Negro Farmer*. Chicago, 1903.

Kennedy, Louise Venable. *The Negro Peasant Turns Cityward*. New York, 1930.

Kiser, Clyde Vernon. *Sea Island to City*. New York, 1932.

Light, Ivan H. *Ethnic Enterprise in America: Business and Welfare among Chinese, Japanese, and Blacks*. Berkeley, Calif., 1972.

Marshall, F. Ray. *The Negro and Organized Labor*. New York, 1965.

Northrup, Herbert Roof. *Organized Labor and the Negro*. New York, 1944.

Oak, Vishnu V. The Negro Entrepreneur. Vol. 2: *The Negro's Adventure in General Business*. Yellow Springs, Ohio, 1949.

Pinchbeck, Raymond B. *The Virginia Negro Artisan and Tradesman*. Richmond, 1926.

Raper, Arthur F., and Reid, Ira DeA. *Sharecroppers All*. Chapel Hill, N.C., 1941.

Ross, Arthur M., and Hill, Herbert, eds. *Employment, Race, and Poverty*. New York, 1967.

Scott, Emmett J. *Negro Migration during the War*. New York, 1920.

Spero, Sterling D., and Harris, Abram L. *The Black Worker: The Negro and the Labor Movement*. New York, 1931.

Street, James H. *The New Revolution in the Cotton Economy: Mechanization and Its Consequences*. Chapel Hill, N.C., 1957.

Weare, Walter B. *Black Business in the New South: A Social History of the North Carolina Mutual Life Insurance Company*. Urbana, Ill., 1973.

Weaver, Robert C. *Negro Labor: A National Problem*. New York, 1946.

Wesley, Charles H. *Negro Labor in the United States, 1850–1925*. New York, 1927.

Woofter, Thomas J., Jr. *Landlord and Tenant on the Cotton Plantation*. Washington, D.C., 1936.

The New Deal and the Roosevelt Years

Agee, James, and Evans, Walker. *Let Us Now Praise Famous Men*. Boston, 1941.

Baldwin, Sidney. *Poverty and Politics: The Rise and Decline of the Farm Security Administration*. Chapel Hill, N.C., 1968.

Bunche, Ralph J. "A Critical Analysis of the Tactics and Programs of Minority Groups," *Journal of Negro Education* 4 (July 1935): 308–20.

———. "A Critique of New Deal Social Planning as It Affects Negroes," *Journal of Negro Education* 5 (January 1936): 59–65.

———. "The Negro in the Political Life of the United States," *Journal of Negro Education* 10 (July 1941): 567–84.

———. "The Programs of Organizations Devoted to the Improvement of the Status of the American Negro," *Journal of Negro Education* 8 (July 1939): 539–50.

————. *A World View of Race.* Washington, 1936.

Caldwell, Erskine, and Bourke-White, Margaret. *You Have Seen Their Faces.* New York, 1937.

Dalfiume, Richard M. "The Forgotten Years of the Negro Revolution," *Journal of American History* 55 (June 1968): 90–106.

Fishel, Leslie H., Jr. "The Negro in the New Deal," *Wisconsin Magazine of History* 48 (Winter 1964–65): 111–26.

Freidel, Frank. *F. D. R. and the South.* Baton Rouge, La., 1965.

Garfinkel, Herbert. *When Negroes March: The March on Washington Movement in the Organizational Politics for FEPC.* Glencoe, Ill., 1950.

Gordon, Rita Werner. "The Change in the Political Alignment of Chicago's Negro during the New Deal," *Journal of American History* 56 (December 1969): 584–603.

Harrell, James A. "Negro Leadership in the Election Year 1936," *Journal of Southern History* 34 (November 1968): 546–64.

Hayes, Laurence J. W. *The Negro Federal Government Worker.* Washington, D.C., 1941.

Hill, T. Arnold. *The Negro and Economic Reconstruction.* Washington, D.C., 1937.

Johnson, James Weldon. *Along This Way.* New York, 1933.

————. *Negro Americans, What Now?* New York, 1934.

Kesselman, Louis Coleridge. *The Social Politics of FEPC: A Study in Reform Pressure Movements.* Chapel Hill, N.C., 1948.

Krueger, Thomas A. *And Promises to Keep: The Southern Conference for Human Welfare.* Nashville, 1967.

Lawrence, Charles Radford. "Negro Organizations in Crisis: Depression, New Deal, World War II." Ph.D. diss., Columbia University, 1952.

Lee, Alfred McClung, and Humphrey, Norman D. *Race Riot.* New York, 1943.

Lee, Ulysses G. *The Employment of Negro Troops in World War II.* Washington, D.C., 1966.

Logan, Rayford W., ed. *What the Negro Wants.* Chapel Hill, N.C., 1944.

McKay, Claude. *Harlem: Negro Metropolis.* New York, 1940.

Martin, Robert E. "Negro-White Participation in the A.A.A. Cotton and Tobacco Referendums in North and South Carolina: A Study in Differential Voting and Attitudes in Selected Areas." Ph.D. diss., University of Chicago, 1948.

Nolan, William A. *Communism Versus the Negro.* Chicago, 1951.

Orlansky, Harold. *The Harlem Riot: A Study in Mass Frustration.* New York, 1943.

Ottley, Roi. *New World A-Coming.* Boston, 1943.

Ross, Malcolm. *All Manner of Men.* New York, 1948.

Ruchames, Louis. *Race, Jobs and Politics: The Story of the FEPC.* New York, 1953.

Salmond, John A. "The Civilian Conservation Corps and the Negro," *Journal of American History* 52 (June 1965): 75–88.

Shogan, Robert, and Craig, Tom. *The Detroit Race Riot: A Study in Violence*. Philadelphia, 1964.

Silvera, John D. *The Negro in World War II*. N.p., 1946.

Sterner, Richard. *The Negro's Share*. New York, 1943.

Sternsher, Bernard, ed. *The Negro in Depression and War: Prelude to Revolution, 1930–1945*. Chicago, 1969.

Sullivan, Lawrence "The Negro Vote," *Atlantic Monthly* 166 (October 1940): 477–84.

Van Deusen, John G. *Black Man in White America*. Washington, D.C., 1944.

Van Zanten, John W. "Communist Theory and the Negro Question," *Review of Politics* 29 (October 1967): 435–56.

Wolters, Raymond. *Negroes and the Great Depression: The Problem of Economic Recovery*. Westport, Conn., 1970.

Zangrando, Robert L. "The NAACP and a Federal Antilynching Bill, 1934–1940," *Journal of Negro History* 50 (April 1965): 106–17.

Civil Rights and the Second Reconstruction

Aikin, Charles, ed. *The Negro Votes*. San Francisco, 1962.

Anderson, J. W. *Eisenhower, Brownell, and the Congress: The Tangled Origins of the Civil Rights Bill of 1956–1957*. University, Ala., 1964.

Ashmore, Harry S. *Epitaph for Dixie*. New York, 1957.

Baldwin, James. *The Fire Next Time*. New York, 1963.

Bainfield, Edward C., and Wilson, James Q. *City Politics*. Cambridge, Mass., 1963.

Bennett, Lerone, Jr. *What Manner of Man: A Biography of Martin Luther King, Jr.* Chicago, 1964.

Berger, Monroe. *Equality by Statute: The Revolution in Civil Rights*. Rev. ed. Garden City, N.Y., 1967.

Berman, William C. *The Politics of Civil Rights in the Truman Administration*. Columbus, Ohio, 1970.

Bickel, Alexander M. *The Supreme Court and the Idea of Progress*. New York, 1970.

Blaustein, Albert P., and Ferguson, Clarence C., Jr. *Desegregation and the Law: The Meaning and Effect of the School Segregation Cases*. New Brunswick, N.J., 1957.

Bond, Julian. *Black Candidates: Southern Campaign Experiences*. Atlanta, 1969.

Brink, William J., and Harris, Louis. *The Negro Revolution in America: What Negroes Want, Why and How They Are Fighting, Whom They Support, What Whites Think of Them and Their Demands*. New York, 1964.

Carter, Hodding III. *The South Strikes Back.* Garden City, N.Y., 1959.

Carter, Robert L., et al. *Equality.* New York, 1965.

Chapin, F. Stuart, and Weiss, Shirley F., eds. *Urban Growth Dynamics.* New York, 1962.

Clayton, Edward T. *The Negro Politician: His Success and Failure.* Chicago, 1964.

Coles, Robert. *Children of Crisis: A Study of Courage and Fear.* Boston, 1967.

Conway, M. Margaret. "The White Backlash Re-examined: Wallace and the 1964 Primaries," *Social Science Quarterly* 40 (December 1968): 710–19.

Cook, James Graham. *The Segregationists.* New York, 1962.

Cosman, Bernard. *Five States for Goldwater: Continuity and Change in Southern Presidential Voting Patterns.* University, Ala., 1966.

Dabbs, James McBride. *Who Speaks for the South?* New York, 1964.

Dalfiume, Richard M. *Desegregation of the U.S. Armed Forces: Fighting on Two Fronts, 1939–1953.* Columbia, Mo., 1969.

Davidson, Chandler. *Biracial Politics: Conflict and Coalition in the Metropolitan South.* Baton Rouge, La., 1972.

Dionisopoulos, P. Allan. *Rebellion, Racism, and Representation: The Adam Clayton Powell Case and its Antecedents.* De Kalb, Ill., 1970.

Dorman, Michael. *We Shall Overcome.* New York, 1965.

Dulles, Foster Rhea. *The Civil Rights Commission: 1957–1965.* East Lansing, Mich., 1968.

Friedman, Leon, ed. *Southern Justice.* New York, 1965.

Gates, Robbins L. *The Making of Massive Resistance: Virginia's Politics of Public School Desegregation, 1954–1956.* Chapel Hill, N.C., 1964.

Ginzberg, Eli, and Eichner, Alfred S. *The Troublesome Presence: Democracy and the Negro.* Glencoe, Ill., 1964.

Golden, Harry. *Mr. Kennedy and the Negroes.* Cleveland, 1964.

Hamilton, Charles V. *Minority Politics in Black Belt Alabama.* New Brunswick, N.J., 1960.

Handlin, Oscar. *Fire-Bell in the Night: The Crisis in Civil Rights.* Boston, 1964.

Hays, Brooks. *A Southern Moderate Speaks.* Chapel Hill, N.C., 1959.

Hentoff, Nat. *The New Equality.* New York, 1964.

Inger, Morton. *Politics and Reality in an American City: The New Orleans School Crisis of 1960.* New York, 1969.

Ippolito, Dennis S. "Political Orientations among Negroes and Whites," *Social Science Quarterly* 49 (December 1968): 548–62.

Johnson, Haynes. *Dusk at the Mountain.* Garden City, N.Y., 1963.

King, Martin Luther, Jr. *Stride Toward Freedom.* New York, 1958.

———. *Why We Can't Wait.* New York, 1964.

Kramer, John, and Walter, Ingo. "Politics in an All-Negro City," *Urban Affairs Quarterly* 4 (September 1968): 65–87.

Kurland, Philip B. *Politics, the Constitution, and the Warren Court.* Chicago, 1970.

Lane, Robert E. *Political Life.* Glencoe, Ill., 1959.

Leiserson, Avery, ed. *The American South in the 1960's.* New York, 1964.

Lewis, Anthony, and the *New York Times. Portrait of a Decade: The Second American Revolution.* New York, 1964.

Lewis, David L. *King: A Critical Biography.* New York, 1970.

Liebow, Elliot. *Tally's Corner: A Study of Negro Streetcorner Men.* Boston, 1967.

Lubell, Samuel. *White and Black: Test of a Nation.* New York, 1964.

Mack, Raymond W., ed. *Our Children's Burden: Studies of Desegregation in Nine American Communities.* New York, 1968.

McConaughy, John B., and Gauntlett, John H. "The Influence of the S Factor upon the Voting Behavior of South Carolina Urban Negroes," *Western Political Quarterly* 16 (December 1963): 973–84.

McGill, Ralph. *The South and the Southerner.* Boston, 1963.

Martin, John Bartlow. *The Deep South Says "Never."* New York, 1957.

Mendelsohn, Jack. *The Martyrs: Sixteen Who Gave Their Lives for Racial Justice.* New York, 1966.

Meredith, James. *Three Years in Mississippi.* Bloomington, Ind., 1966.

Miller, Loren. *The Petitioners: The Story of the Supreme Court of the United States and the Negro.* New York, 1966.

Miller, William R. *Martin Luther King, Jr.: His Life, Martyrdom, and Meaning for the World.* New York, 1968.

Morgan, Ruth P. *The President and Civil Rights: Policymaking by Executive Order.* New York, 1970.

Muse, Benjamin. *Ten Years of Prelude: The Story of Integration since the Supreme Court's 1954 Decision.* New York, 1964.

———. *Virginia's Massive Resistance.* Bloomington, Ind., 1961.

Orum, Anthony M., "A Reappraisal of the Social and Political Participation of Negroes," *American Journal of Sociology* 72 (July 1966): 32–46.

Patterson, Beeman C. "Political Action of Negroes in Los Angeles: A Case Study in the Attainment of Councilmanic Representation," *Phylon* 30 (Summer 1969): 170–83.

Peck, James. *Freedom Ride.* New York, 1962.

Peltason, Jack W. *Fifty-Eight Lonely Men: Southern Federal Judges and School Desegregation.* Rev. ed. Urbana, Ill., 1971.

Record, Wilson and Jane. *Little Rock, U.S.A.: Materials for Analysis.* San Francisco, 1960.

Reddick, Lawrence D. *Crusader Without Violence: A Biography of Martin Luther King, Jr.* New York, 1959.

Roche, John P. *The Quest for the Dream: The Development of Civil Rights and Human Relations in Modern America.* New York, 1963.

Rustin, Bayard. "From Protest to Politics: The Future of the Civil Rights Movement," *Commentary* 39 (February 1965): 25–31.

Sarratt, Reed. *The Ordeal of Desegregation: The First Decade.* New York, 1966.

Silberman, Charles E. *Crisis in Black and White.* New York, 1964.

Sindler, Allan P. "Negroes, Ethnic Groups and American Politics," *Current History* 55 (October 1968): 207–12.

Southern Regional Council. *The Effects of Federal Examiners and Organized Registration Campaigns on Negro Voter Registration.* Atlanta, 1966.

Strong, Donald S. *Negroes, Ballots, and Judges: National Voting Rights Legislation in the Federal Courts.* University, Ala., 1968.

———. "The Rise of Negro Voting in Texas," *American Political Science Review* 42 (June 1948): 510–22.

Sutherland, Elizabeth, ed. *Letters From Mississippi.* New York, 1965.

United States Commission on Civil Rights. *Freedom to the Free, 1863–1963: A Report to the President.* Washington, D.C., 1963.

Vander Zanden, James W. *Race Relations in Transition: The Segregation Crisis in the South.* New York, 1965.

Wakefield, Dan. *Revolt in the South.* New York, 1960.

Walker, Jack L. "Negro Voting in Atlanta: 1953–1961," *Phylon* 24 (Winter 1963): 379–87.

———. *Sit-Ins in Atlanta: A Study in the Negro Revolt.* New Brunswick, N.J., 1964.

Walton, Hanes, Jr. *The Political Philosophy of Martin Luther King, Jr.* Westport, Conn., 1971.

Watters, Pat. *The South and the Nation.* New York, 1969.

Weinberg, Kenneth G. *Black Victory: Carl Stokes and the Winning of Cleveland.* Chicago, 1968.

Weltner, Charles L. *Southerner.* Philadelphia, 1966.

Westin, Alan F., ed. *Freedom Now! The Civil Rights Struggle in America.* New York, 1964.

Wilson, James Q. *The Amateur Democrat.* Chicago, 1962.

Young, Richard. "The Impact of Protest Leadership on Negro Politicians in San Francisco," *Western Political Quarterly* 22 (March 1969): 94–111.

Young, Whitney M., Jr. *To Be Equal.* New York, 1964.

Zinn, Howard. *SNCC: The New Abolitionists.* Boston, 1965.

Black Nationalism and Black Power

Barbour, Floyd B., ed. *The Black Power Revolt: A Collection of Essays.* Boston, 1968.

Bennett, Lerone, Jr. *Black Power U.S.A.: The Human Side of Reconstruction, 1867–1877*. Chicago, 1967.

Boggs, James. *The American Revolution*. New York, 1964.

Bracey, John H., Jr., et al. *Black Nationalism in America*. Indianapolis, 1970.

Carmichael, Stokely, and Hamilton, Charles V. *Black Power: The Politics of Liberation in America*. New York, 1967.

Cleaver, Eldridge. *Soul on Ice*. New York, 1968.

Conot, Robert. *Rivers of Blood, Years of Darkness*. New York, 1967.

Cronon, Edmund David. *Black Moses: The Story of Marcus Garvey and the Universal Negro Improvement Association*. Madison, Wis., 1955.

Draper, Theodore. *The Rediscovery of Black Nationalism*. New York, 1970.

Essien-Udom, E. U. *Black Nationalism: A Search for an Identity in America*. Chicago, 1962.

Garvey, Marcus. *Philosophy and Opinions of Marcus Garvey*. Ed. Amy Jacques-Garvey, 1923. New York, 1969. A reissue.

Grier, William H., and Cobbs, Price M. *Black Rage*. New York, 1968.

Hill, Roy L. *Rhetoric of Racial Revolt*. Denver, 1964.

Killian, Lewis M. *The Impossible Revolution? Black Power and the American Dream*. New York, 1968.

Lincoln, C. Eric. *The Black Muslims in America*. Boston, 1961.

————. *The Negro Pilgrimage in America: The Coming of Age of the Black-Americans*. Rev. ed. New York, 1969.

Little, Malcolm, with the assistance of Alex Haley. *The Autobiography of Malcolm X*. New York, 1965.

Lynch, Hollis R. *Edward Wilmot Blyden: Pan Negro Patriot, 1832–1912*. New York, 1967.

Meier, August, et al., eds. *Black Protest Thought in the Twentieth Century*. 2nd ed. Indianapolis, 1971.

Mphahlele, Ezekiel. *The African Image*. New York, 1962.

Redkey, Edwin S. *Black Exodus: Black Nationalist and Back-to-Africa Movements, 1890–1910*. New Haven, 1969.

Ross, James Robert, ed. *The War Within: Violence or Nonviolence in the Black Revolution*. New York, 1971.

Rubenstein, Richard E. *Rebels in Eden: Mass Political Violence in the United States*. Boston, 1970.

Stone, Chuck. *Black Political Power in America*. Indianapolis, 1968.

Ulman, Victor. *Martin R. Delany: The Beginnings of Black Nationalism*. Boston, 1971.

Wagstaff, Thomas. *Black Power: The Radical Response to White America*. Beverly Hills, Calif., 1969.

Williams, Robert F. *Negroes With Guns*. New York, 1962.

Wright, Nathan. *Black Power and Urban Unrest: Creative Possibilities*. New York, 1967.

Index

DEWEY W. GRANTHAM, professor of history at Vanderbilt University and a former president of the Southern Historical Association, is a specialist in twentieth-century United States history. He is the author of *Hoke Smith and the Politics of the New South, The Democratic South,* and *The United States since 1945.* He is the editor of three historical studies, including Ray Stannard Baker's classic *Following the Color Line.* [1973]